INTRODUCTION TO
CONFLICT
STUDIES | EMPIRICAL, THEORETICAL, *and* ETHICAL DIMENSIONS

JEAN-FRANÇOIS RIOUX | VERN NEUFELD REDEKOP

OXFORD
UNIVERSITY PRESS

OXFORD
UNIVERSITY PRESS

Oxford University Press is a department of the University of Oxford.
It furthers the University's objective of excellence in research, scholarship,
and education by publishing worldwide. Oxford is a registered trade mark of
Oxford University Press in the UK and in certain other countries.

Published in Canada by
Oxford University Press
8 Sampson Mews, Suite 204,
Don Mills, Ontario M3C 0H5 Canada

www.oupcanada.com

Library and Archives Canada Cataloguing in Publication

Rioux, Jean-François, 1958–
Introduction to conflict studies : empirical, theoretical, and ethical dimensions /
Jean-François Rioux & Vern Neufeld Redekop.

Includes bibliographical references and index.

ISBN 978-0-19-544654-8

1. Social conflict—Textbooks. 2. Interpersonal conflict—Textbooks.
3. Conflict management—Textbooks. 4. Conflict management—Moral and ethical aspects—Textbooks.
5. Peace. I. Redekop, Vernon Neufeld, 1949– II. Title.

HM1121.R56 2012 303.6 C2012-903503-3

Cover image: Paul Taylor/Stone +/Getty Images

This book is printed on permanent (acid-free) paper ∞.

Printed and bound in the United States of America

1 2 3 4 — 16 15 14 13

CONTENTS

PREFACE

With the inception of an Honours BA in Conflict Studies at Saint Paul University in 2006, Jean-François Rioux suggested writing a textbook that would serve the needs of students and instructors. Vern Neufeld Redekop offered to co-author the textbook, a move that surprised some colleagues because the two were perceived as being quite different in personality, style, and expertise. That was the point. In welcoming Redekop's offer, Rioux perceived that a balanced and comprehensive textbook required two authors with different perspectives.

The emerging field of conflict studies includes many voices and theories. Rioux comes to the subject as a political scientist with a background in diplomacy, international arms control, and peace operations. He taught in several political science departments before joining Saint Paul University, where he has taught graduate courses in the history of conflict resolution, theories of conflict, and peacebuilding. As a social scientist, he values empirical truth emanating from positivist approaches. Besides his university work, he has experience as an analyst in governmental and non-governmental organizations.

Redekop completed his doctoral work in theological ethics. He was preoccupied with how people interpreted their experiences so as to justify committing atrocities. In his hermeneutic approach, he emphasizes the internal life of individuals and groups, investigating the use of memory to justify actions, the interplay between emotion and thought, and the use of reconciliation to conquer antagonistic feelings. He has practical experience with community conflict resolution in Rwanda, Bosnia and Herzegovina, Aboriginal communities, and third-party neutral training with people from around the world.

These respective strengths meant that we each brought expertise in a number of subfields to the project. As we developed the initial outline, we both contributed ideas of what should be included and divided the chapters based on these assets. However, neither our academic training nor experiences were in tight silos; we both had a great deal to say about each other's chapters and contributed subsections.

Our differences translated into contrasting perspectives on how material was to be presented and nuanced. We both went through the painful experience of having sections of our writing either deleted or significantly revised. We were each other's most trenchant peer reviewers. We entered the project with our own values and priorities, and these were expressed in many ways. In the end, we both learned and grew from the process, often conceding that the other really did have a good point. The result is a book that is certainly different, and much better, than what either of us would have produced individually.

One matter that was particularly controversial was the role of normative approaches associated with peace and justice in such a text. Within many of the social sciences, the objective of value-free methodologies is important. Normative principles drive the intellectual passions of people in peace research and peace education, even though they might use empirical methodologies. How were we to deal with the issue? Our solution was to give the normative material its own section at the end of the book. This way, instructors who are not inclined to emphasize this approach can choose not to cover this aspect of the field, while those for whom it is a priority can use the section at whatever point they wish. (In fact, the entire book was constructed with such flexibility in mind.)

Besides the significant amount we learned from each other, the research we did for this book led to many new insights. As we lived with the challenge of producing a relatively comprehensive textbook, a new world opened to us, some of which has influenced our other research projects.

In the end, our mutual respect for one another grew, as did our respect for the field itself and the many pioneering academics who opened up new lines of inquiry. It is out of our historical panoramic view of the field that we have been committed to paying tribute to those who introduced new ideas that stimulated the development of new disciplines, schools, and approaches. In fact, we think that an introductory textbook such as this one must give precedence to the development of the field and to the main schools of thought that have influenced it. Naysayers might argue that some of these ideas are now dated, but that is to ignore how indebted we are to them for what we know and understand today.

ACKNOWLEDGEMENTS

Saint Paul University's Conflict Studies Program, nestled within the Faculty of Human Sciences, provided a critical intellectual community that supported and enabled us to complete this textbook. We are grateful to all our colleagues, particularly Christian Belhumeur, Ken Bush, Christina Clark-Kazak, Cheshmak Farhoumand-Sims, Jean-Guy Goulet, and Hélène Tessier, who contributed encouragement and ideas. Deans Karljin Demasure and Gilles Fortin and Conflict Studies Coordinator Paul Rigby were completely behind us as we proceeded through each step of this project.

Among professional colleagues in the wider field, many of whom gave words of support and anticipation, we must pay tribute to Richard McGuigan, a scholar/mediation practitioner who offered significant input about ethical issues facing practitioners, provided a mediation case study, and validated material on levels of consciousness. Our former student Oscar Gasana provided us with a great deal of relevant information about the Rwandan genocide and the post-genocide situation.

Some graduate students were also involved in this project. We strongly commend Alison Marshal for her top-notch work on several sections. Jennifer Jones-Patulli assisted us with the conflict resolution section with great competence. Aycha Fleury and Francis Sales were an immense help with bibliographies and data gathering.

At Oxford University Press, we thank Katherine Skene, acquisitions editor, who graciously received our proposal and advocated for its publication. Lisa Peterson, our developmental editor, contributed perceptive comments and shepherded the manuscript through a peer review. Finally, Janna Green, copyeditor, delved deeply into the intricate details of the text to polish the final version.

In addition to those who provided anonymous feedback, we join the publisher in thanking the following reviewers, whose thoughtful comments and suggestions helped shape this text: N.C. Doubleday, McMaster University; Felicia Eghan, Mount Saint Vincent University; Nathan Funk, University of Waterloo; Paul Gecelovsky, University of Western Ontario; Rosanna Langer, Laurentian University; Logan Masilamani, Simon Fraser University; and Andrew Pirie, University of Victoria.

Over the last few years, we have devoted long hours to this project, which meant that we were sometimes not available to our families on evenings and weekends. Large segments of time during summers and sabbaticals were also devoted to working on the text. We are grateful to our respective lifelong partners, Josie Marino and Gloria Neufeld Redekop, who have supported this project in untold ways.

Jean-François Rioux
Vern Neufeld Redekop

INTRODUCTION

WHAT THIS BOOK IS ABOUT

Although human conflict appears simple and is something that everyone experiences, it is nevertheless extremely complex. *Introduction to Conflict Studies* is about the study of the causes and processes of human conflict, the ways that people try to use conflict to their advantage or try to minimize its occurrence, the severity of conflict, and the various ways that people deal with conflict. Conflict studies—also referred to as peace studies, conflict analysis, conflict resolution, or conflict transformation—is a rapidly growing academic field, with new diploma, undergraduate, and graduate programs emerging in scores of universities worldwide.[1] This field is part of the increased interest in the understanding and resolution of conflict. To cite just a few examples of this phenomenon, large organizations such as government departments are establishing conflict resolution teams; non-profit organizations are providing conflict resolution training in communities; consultants are briefing executives in conflict management; Indigenous peoples are framing traditional teachings and processes in relation to conflict resolution; law firms are developing mediation expertise and retired judges are finding new work as arbitrators; former politicians are offering their mediation services to help resolve violent conflicts in the world; conflict resolution processes are being tailored for religious groups; and people are learning to use the win–win approach in their conflicts with co-workers, family members, and neighbours.

The development of conflict studies as a field of inquiry transforms the study of social processes and institutions into what can now be seen as contributing to the management and resolution of conflict. The democratic evolution of the world; the empowerment of poor people, women, and minorities through recognition of their human rights; the emergence of the rule of law and judicial systems; and the desire to avoid violent confrontation and costly legal proceedings are only some of the factors that will sustain the development of the field in the foreseeable future. At the international level, we see international law, the United Nations, the evolution of various forms of peacekeeping, and the emerging normative concepts of human security and the responsibility to protect as signalling similar trends.

While there are many contemporary reasons to be interested in this field, it is clear that conflicts have been at the heart of human intellectual, artistic, and religious endeavours for as far back as we have written records. Without conflict, novels, plays, and movies would be devoid of interest.[2] Disciplines such as sociology, political science, social psychology, and ethics have emerged in large part out of an interest in different aspects of conflict. The challenge is to draw from the rich, diverse resources available to shape a coherent field.

Just as academic inquiry into the nature of conflict can be discerned over the centuries, so too can an interest in peace. Many of the realizations regarding the nature of conflict have come from peace studies scholars, who study conflict for the sake of making peace. Peace research, peace education, the culture of peace, and peace movements have become part of the international landscape. These perspectives also fall under the purview of scholars of conflict. We have devoted Chapter 16 to the topic of peace, placing it within the context of normative approaches to conflict. There are also numerous points throughout this textbook where insights derived from different approaches have implications for an understanding of peace. We note, however, that there is some controversy between those who weigh in on the side of peace and those who look at conflict through different lenses. Our intention is to offer a book that is broad enough in scope to engage the student of conflict in an open-ended quest for understanding.

DEFINING CONFLICT STUDIES

The main challenges in writing a book such as this one are defining the field of conflict studies, identifying the main sources and disciplines of the field, and selecting the topics that should be included. To start with defining the field, it is important to discuss the level of analysis and intervention with which conflict studies is concerned. The strong divergences of views that we call conflicts can occur between nations, large or small groups, or individuals, as well as within the minds of people. We concur with scholars who see conflict studies as focusing on conflict among people and as being concerned primarily with inter- and intragroup dynamics and secondarily with the impact on individuals. Conflict studies should be mainly concerned with social conflict, which is conflict among groups of people.[3] However, because the various levels of conflict are interconnected, we cannot put aside the conflicts between individuals because they can sometimes help to understand what happens at a group level.

Another important aspect to defining conflict studies is recognizing that it does not mean the same thing as conflict resolution. Conflating the two terms implies that any conflict can be resolved and that harmonious solutions are always at hand. Furthermore, it fails to consider that some conflicts are unavoidable and can even be beneficial, as long as their more negative effects can be mitigated. For example, the long-standing class conflicts between workers and employers in Europe have led countries such as Great Britain, Germany, and France to develop social legislation, democratize the political system, and strengthen human rights. However, had these conflicts led to civil wars and revolutions, their outcomes might have been less favourable. Though conflict studies cannot be equated with conflict resolution, there are some important links. The management and resolution of conflicts depend in large part on the analysis of the causes and dynamics of conflict. This analysis is an important part of conflict studies and is necessary in developing truly effective efforts in the abatement of conflicts.

Several people in conflict studies believe this field to be one of applied studies and practical interventions, meaning that research should always have direct consequences for guiding actions related to conflict resolution. In other words, this practical orientation is what distinguishes conflict studies from traditional university disciplines that are concerned with conflict, such as political science or sociology. However, we maintain that the field can also accommodate scholars and students who are interested in theoretical, philosophical, or historical issues. The specificity of the field is not its practical aspect, as important as that might be, but its perspective that focuses on conflict and uses the tools offered by a number of disciplines. As with most branches of academic study, there are pure and applied orientations to research.

There is also the argument that conflict studies should be defined by ideals. For example, some analysts believe that the real rationale for the field is the desire to help humankind reach a higher stage of development. Others claim that non-violence is the ideal and that the discipline should promote the values associated with pacifism or non-violent activism. Several theorists contend that conflict studies is about attaining positive peace, which is a state of justice, emancipation, and fulfillment. Still others prefer to talk about social justice, a generous ideal of equality and equity often favoured by socialists and Christian thinkers alike. However, there are several problems with defining a discipline by the ideal that it serves. The first is whether a field of study should reflect a particular human preference. If it is to be self-referential, the field should apply its own insights to itself. In this case, preferences and ideals can be the object of conflict; therefore, the different options should be scrutinized. Second is the question of how one validates any claims of truth. The dominant response, which has been inspired by the scientific model and has been accepted by all major governments and higher education institutions in the Western world, is that a discipline should be defined by its object of inquiry and by the methods that it uses to verify its conclusions. The third problem is that there is no agreement about what ideals are to be served by conflict studies. Non-violence, positive peace, and social justice are worthy and inclusive principles to which many people subscribe; however, they are not without controversy. For instance, not all experts in conflict studies are pacifists. Most of them share the opinion that the use of force is sometimes necessary in social life. Many people proclaim to be in favour of social justice, but they may diverge on the exact meaning of the term. Some see social justice as being equivalent to complete economic equality, while others think that it means only the provision of a minimal social safety net. As one can imagine, there are also many possible positions between these two viewpoints. Furthermore, the normative definition of conflict studies becomes even more debatable when we consider that some people might believe that this field of study should be about promoting controversial ideals, such as communism or a type of religious fundamentalism.

Although it is preferable not to define conflict studies by the higher goals that it may serve, the personal motivations of its analysts and practitioners are a strong incentive in the field's development. All areas of study are connected to the real world and have implications for human beings. Practitioners of conflict resolution, for example, face issues of justice, fairness, and efficiency that sometimes clash with one another and cannot be resolved scientifically. For instance, should the peaceful but unjust resolution of a conflict be preferred to the status quo? This type of concern explains why this textbook deals with the moral and ethical issues related to the study of conflict.

Having considered all these factors, we define the field of conflict studies by the unique outlook that it offers on conflict:

> Conflict studies is a multidisciplinary field of study that is devoted to the understanding and analysis of a) the causes, contributing factors, and dynamics of conflict; b) the methods and institutions used to manage conflict; c) the approaches and processes to resolve and transform conflict; and d) related concepts such as violence, non-violence, peace, genocide, reconciliation, and healing.

Note that this definition refers to the analysis of causes, contributing factors, and dynamics. The study of the elements creating conflict cannot be limited to the well-known "root causes" that many believe to be the only relevant subject in conflict analysis. The fact is that there are several types and levels of causes. Furthermore, analysts may disagree on the root cause of a particular conflict. It must also be remembered that, without a favourable context and precipitant factors, many conflicts do not evolve into a full-fledged form, even though they are fed by root causes. In this book, we will use the classification of long-term (structural) causes, medium-term (contextual) causes, and short-term (conjectural) causes of conflict. The analyst must understand how they interact with one other to create actual conflicts and how conflict dynamics often take on a life of their own. For instance, escalations and crises can transform a dispute into a harsh conflict, even when people are not actively seeking this result.

The second part of our definition involves methods to steer and manage conflict. More specifically, we mean the efforts to channel conflict into peaceful and productive challenges rather than fruitless or destructive confrontations. These endeavours are what liberal democracy is about, but similar efforts at channelling conflict are at work at all levels of society, such as in the family and the workplace. These methods also include ways to moderate the expression of conflict so as to minimize the possibilities of violence and anger among participants. How to direct conflict and when and how it is possible to attempt actual conflict resolution are other facets of the field, which brings us to the third part of our definition.

For many people in conflict studies, the crux of the matter is the resolution and transformation of conflict. We will discuss this crucial topic in more details later, notably in Part III. For the moment, it is more important to define the prevalent term *conflict transformation*. This term signifies the use of conflict as a means to change the relations among people and the social and institutional context in which they live in order to establish lasting peaceful relations. However, insisting too much on transformation may detract practitioners from more pragmatic objectives, such as conflict management and violence prevention. It may also negatively affect the prospects of intervention and employment of conflict studies graduates because some of them will work in fields where conflict transformation is impossible. For instance, marital counsellors specialized in divorce usually try to manage and minimize conflict for the benefit of the spouses and their children rather than transform the relationship and reunite the couple. Commercial arbitrators do not aim at conflict transformation among rival companies but attempt to avoid costly legal battles and commercial wars. To focus only on conflict transformation in the definition of the field would limit graduates to work only in subfields such as community relations and personnel relations. Transformation is a valuable ideal; however, as we mentioned, a field of study should not be defined by its ideals but by its object of study. In this case, the purpose is the analysis, management, resolution, and transformation of conflict.

Finally, it is important to recognize that conflict studies draws into its purview other important concepts that are the focus of significant multidisciplinary studies in their own right. Violence is one such concept. What is there about violence that qualitatively changes a conflict? What exactly is violence? What is non-violence and how does it relate to differing styles of conflict? Peace is another key concept that is broken down into categories, including negative and positive. Genocide, which often represents the most destructive aspects of conflict, is a significant field of study that overlaps significantly with conflict studies. Likewise, the questions of coexistence and reconciliation in the wake of atrocities are important to the field, as is the challenge of healing when conflict has significantly traumatized a population.

PERSPECTIVE OF THIS BOOK

Along with defining conflict studies, it is also important to determine what kinds of conflict belong to the field and what other disciplines are involved. On the first point, the concept of conflict applies to processes that range from serious differences between siblings or spouses to enormous and extremely violent clashes between alliances of nations, such as world wars. There are a myriad of conflicts between these two extremes, including those between associations of people and local governments over development projects, between the workers and the owners of industrial plants over unionization, between two religious or linguistic groups over constitutional reform, and among political parties over crucial economic policy decisions. Sources of conflict can also vary in different parts of the world. For example, although the issue might be unfamiliar to Western audiences, a role play written by participants of conflict resolution training in Sudan involved a conflict over who would get the head of a dead hippopotamus. All these conflicts legitimately belong to our field of study.

Conflict studies is based on the idea that there are basic causes, structures, dynamics, and processes common to most conflicts. Even if some aspects of family conflicts (e.g. issues of care and affection) differ from the characteristics of large-scale political and military conflict and should be studied in themselves, several mechanisms of conflict that are at work in a sibling rivalry, such as envy and mistrust, can be found at higher levels. Similarly, diplomacy, intelligence, and the military balance may not be of much interest to the student of family differences, but the study of decision-making and crisis behaviour in foreign policy can generate insight into family matters. This commonality and the fact that conflict is such a widespread phenomenon means that it is studied in countless disciplines. Along with those previously mentioned, history, geography, philosophy, theology, management studies, criminology, religious studies, international affairs, women's studies, urban studies, and Aboriginal studies all include the study of conflict. Ethology, neurobiology, sociobiology, and mathematics have also contributed important insights into conflict.

The number of books and articles that have been published about conflicts is simply astonishing. Covering even a tiny fraction of this literature is an impossible task. In this textbook, we focus on what is considered the classic and standard literature about conflict. Our goal is to provide an accurate and balanced vision of the main schools of thought about conflict analysis and resolution. We have incorporated an implicit historical approach, showing how key schools of thought have evolved and signalling some of the most significant figures who have contributed to the evolution of the various disciplines and subfields. We have also included cutting-edge research that illustrates future issues and insights.

Another broad area that demands attention is the Western domination of many areas of culture and power relations. This matter is currently in great flux, as we will see in sections addressing globalization. The implication for conflict studies, and for those who wish to address conflict in any number of roles, is that one must always be attentive to cultural biases. In different parts of the world, indigenous traditions create distinct values, methods of arriving at truth, and historical authorities. It is also clear that there is resonance among indigenous cultures in many parts of the world. These very phenomena impact the study of conflict within different disciplines. Those interested in political power relations, for example, look at colonialism and post-colonialism as factors in some conflicts. Anthropologists examine the symbols and root metaphors that express core identities and values. Conflict resolution practitioners learn from traditional processes, some of which are described in Chapter 11.

The emphasis on drawing on different disciplines and cultures necessitates a warning about the limits of multidisciplinarity and cultural inclusiveness. No one is fully multidisciplinary and inclusive. We all have our preferences and our limits, and we simply cannot equally appreciate and understand all the aforementioned disciplines and approaches that are concerned with conflict. The integration of knowledge promised by conflict studies is sometimes more an ideal than a reality. However, what really counts is being exposed to different methods. We may all have our strengths and fancies, but the outlook generated by the confrontation of several academic disciplines or cultural approaches offers remarkable perspectives. We can personally testify to the changes in our understanding of conflict after expanding our quest for knowledge beyond the boundaries of our initial academic field or culture of origin. This pursuit also included relying on the professional expertise of several colleagues to verify and complement this textbook, especially on topics that are at the margins of our official academic expertise.

The other significant limit of multidisciplinarity and cultural inclusivity is in the realm of practice. Conflict resolution is often the province of specialized professional orders and associations. In particular, conflicts between individuals are often handled by psychologists, lawyers, pastoral counsellors, and social workers. For example, in many jurisdictions, a graduate of conflict studies wanting to practise in marital conflict must have specialized qualifications and an accreditation by a professional association, which may require a university degree or prescribed training program other than conflict studies. (In North America, the ability to practise may depend on federal, state/provincial, or even local regulations). Likewise, it may be important in international or multicultural environments to construct teams of people with roots in different cultures to address conflicts within specific cultures or between cultural groups.

This being said, there are some professional associations in commercial arbitration, labour relations, family mediation, and other areas that are open to graduates of conflict studies. Students may take training in leadership skills—including mediation, facilitation, and conflict resolution systems design—before, during, or after their formal training in conflict studies. Expertise about conflicts is also valued in the fields of international and community development, where conflict plays a significant role. Whichever aspect of the field one chooses, dealing with conflict well requires the following qualities: process skills; good interpersonal relations; analytical skills enhanced by an immersion in the field of conflict studies; a capacity for reflection and personal growth; creativity and ingenuity; observation skills; and a combination of humility in the face of the complexity of conflict and courage to try to do something about it anyway. All this is to say that conflict studies is a necessary but not sufficient condition for someone to become a practitioner in the field of intervention.

ORGANIZATION OF THIS BOOK

We have organized this book into five parts, with each section addressing one of the following questions:

1.   What is conflict?
2.   How is conflict currently experienced at different levels in the world?
3.   What are the causes and dynamics of conflict from different perspectives?
4.   How can we and how do we deal with conflict?

5.   What ethical issues emerge from the study of conflict and from interventions in conflicts?

In Part I, we discuss what conflict is and how it relates to disputes, contests, and violence, and we provide a discursive field of terms to employ in our analyses of conflict. Part II explores the phenomenon of conflict as it is experienced at different levels. Using historical, comparative, descriptive, and statistical data, we demonstrate the increase in the occurrence of conflicts as well as their rising complexity and the relative decrease of violence as a response to conflict. Chapter 2 looks at small group and interpersonal conflicts; Chapter 3 covers large-scale intranational conflicts; and Chapter 4 discusses the international and global scene.

Part III provides an overview of how conflict is understood from the perspective of different disciplines and fields. Drawing on game theory and economics in particular, Chapter 5 examines conflict as a rational dimension of human experience. Chapter 6 shows how conflict can be understood in terms of biology, sociobiology, and neurobiology. Chapter 7 focuses on psychological approaches to understanding conflict. Chapter 8 looks at conflict as a social phenomenon, drawing on disciplines such as sociology and political science. Here, we address power, social class, modernization, culture, religion, and gender as sources of conflict. Chapter 9 draws on the work of some recent philosophers who have tackled the issue of the meaning of conflict and its significance in understanding humanity. Each of these chapters introduces key thinkers whose seminal works have shaped the emergence of the field.

In Part IV, our attention shifts to the question of what we do when there is conflict. Chapter 10 is concerned with the different behavioural styles and orientations of people in conflict. This chapter also includes a section on communication as a factor in conflict dynamics. Chapter 11 provides an overview of conflict resolving/transforming processes, including negotiation, conciliation, mediation, arbitration, and traditional cultural processes. Chapter 12 shows how diplomacy, international mediation, treaties, and international organizations have shaped the manner in which international conflict is dealt with. Included are intervention strategies such as peacemaking, peacekeeping, and peacebuilding. Chapter 13 explores how to respond to conflict that results in profound animosity and trauma and how truth, reconciliation, and forgiveness can help alleviate the consequences of the harshest conflicts, including instances of genocide and other atrocities.

Part V takes a step out of the experience of conflict to reflect on what conflict means for humans as moral creatures. Chapter 14 introduces key ethical concepts, showing how they can be used to examine conflict from the perspective of human action. Just war theory is studied as an example of an influential moral perspective on conflict. In Chapter 15, the concepts of justice and injustice, central in most conflicts, are examined. Chapter 16 studies peace in its relation to conflict and discusses pacifism and non-violence. Chapter 17 is devoted to ethical and deontological issues facing people engaged in conflict as well as those who are practitioners in some form of intervention.

Each chapter also features a summary and discussion questions for further consideration. Where appropriate, we have also included boxes covering specific aspects of conflict studies and case studies of actual conflicts. A conclusion revisits the objectives of this text, while a glossary defines key terms used in the discipline and in this textbook. Together, the components of *Introduction to Conflict Studies* provide a comprehensive analysis of how conflict is described, understood, and resolved.

NOTES

1. In this textbook, the term conflict studies will be preferred because it is comprehensive and relatively free of bias in relation to how conflict is viewed or handled.

2. This book does not deal with literary or cinematic conflict, however.

3. This position is taken by Schellenberg (1996, p. 8), among others.

PART I | BACKGROUND

1 | WHAT IS CONFLICT?

CHAPTER OBJECTIVES

This chapter will help you develop an understanding of the

- nature of conflict;
- objects of conflict;
- positional, underlying, and intractable aspects of conflict;
- differences between disputes and conflicts;
- negative and positive aspects of conflict; and
- relationship between violence and conflict.

INTRODUCTION

The purpose of this chapter is to define **conflict** and situate it within a field of related concepts, particularly **dispute** and **violence**. The multi-faceted nature of conflict will be addressed through a discussion of the different aspects of conflict—**interests**, **needs**, **identity**, **desires**, **values**, and **rights**—as well as reference to the levels of conflict, from interpersonal to international. We also examine the role of conflict in relationships and society, particularly in regard to the following questions: When is conflict destructive and when does it stimulate creativity and constructive change? Does conflict have a special function within society?

THE DEFINITION OF CONFLICT

The notion of conflict seems to be clear to most of us, but when we try to define it we realize that there are different meanings of the word and different opinions as to what should be included in the concept. Conflict evokes clashes of views, personal antagonisms, feuds among ethnic groups, and bitter disagreements among political parties. It applies to the rivalry of two children wanting to play with the same toy and to major wars among **states**. At first glance, we could state that conflict is any difference of opinion among people. However, this definition does not allow us to readily differentiate between a genuine conflict and other forms of divergence.

The word *conflict* comes from two Latin words, *con* ("together") and *fligere* ("to strike"). Hence, the root concept involves a striking together, or a violent clash. This description coincides with the popular view that conflicts are violent and that the word is synonymous with war. Indeed, some conflicts involve violence, and most imply the threat of violence. However, violence is not a necessary component of conflict. We will see that humankind has learned to rely on processes other than force and intimidation to settle differences. In this book, we define conflict as *an antagonistic relationship between two or more parties over intractable divergences regarding what is mutually significant to the parties involved.*

Let us briefly review the elements of this definition. Conflict is a relationship—it takes at least two parties to create a conflict. The idea of relationship does not imply a positive situation, as in a sentimental relationship. It is a descriptive term signifying that the parties interact and that they influence each other. In a conflict, this relationship is antagonistic, meaning that there are elements of hostility, sometimes even hate, among the parties. In a simple dispute, **contest**, or rivalry, the antagonistic character is not usually present among most participants. We must acknowledge that the word *conflict* is commonly used in situations where the degree of antagonism is not as great as is suggested here. Our point is that there is a qualitative difference between straightforward clashes of positions or interests and those that involve a complex array of factors that stir up antagonistic feelings, behaviours, and orientations.

A conflict implies intractable divergences, an important concept for conflict analysts. Intractable divergences cannot be resolved through a simple **compromise** arrived at after some **bargaining** and negotiation. In other words, conflicts do not lend themselves to compromise solutions. The most classic case is two men wanting to marry the same woman. In most **cultures**, there is no compromise to this situation. The rivalry becomes a conflict if the two suitors persevere and develop hostility towards each other. Another example is a couple that constantly argues and rarely or never compromises. In this relationship, there may be a more profound conflict between the two in terms of their expectations of one another. Maybe they differ fundamentally over what values should be promoted regarding the education of their children or what kind of parenting style should be preferred. In this case, their relationship might be said to be conflict-ridden. Classic examples of conflicts on the world stage are the Israeli–Arab clash over the existence of Israel and the Indian–Pakistani antagonism over the future of Kashmir. In sum, the parties in a conflict cannot just divide the marbles amongst themselves and go their separate ways. The situation is much more complicated, important, and emotional to be terminated by a compromise. Compromises on certain points can be important components of a conflict's resolution, but they do not unilaterally solve the conflict.

An intractable conflict also cannot be resolved by a third party. While a third party can impose a temporary solution and calm the conflict for a period of time, the parties may still harbour resentment and animosity, causing the conflict to continue. This situation has occurred in several ethnoreligious rivalries of the Cold War that were muffled by communist states but re-emerged in the 1990s, such as those in Yugoslavia, Central Asia, and Ukraine. In Canada, the conflict between Aboriginal people and other Canadians over territorial claims has been silenced by the federal government for a long time but has never been extinguished. Since the 1980s, First Nations have been very active on the political and legal scenes—some groups even endorsing violence—in order to defend their land rights. In other circumstances, however, the parties in a conflict refuse the involvement of an intermediary. This is sometimes the case in international affairs. For example, India and Pakistan both reject any external **facilitation**, **mediation**, or **arbitration** in the conflict over Kashmir.

Conflict can occur at different levels that range from intrapersonal to interpersonal, intragroup, inter-group, intranational, interstate, international, and global. Conflict can be caused by real positions that each party understands or by miscommunication and misunderstanding. Parties might be close in their ideas but perceive each other to be starkly at odds. Friends may develop serious conflicts that jeopardize their relationship.

In other instances, people are enemies from the outset and do everything they can to defeat one another.

Conflicts can also vary significantly in intensity, length, and presentation. Some conflicts start almost instantaneously, triggered by an emotional response to an event or action. Other conflicts are a matter of deliberation as one party might strategize how to get ahead at the expense of another. Conflicts can last a long time, even decades or centuries. They may go through phases of being overt, with people actively fighting one another, and being latent, in which case the animosity is beneath the surface and is manifest in attitudes and subtle behaviours.

THE OBJECTS OF CONFLICT

Conflict involves differences of views over many things, including interests, needs, identity, desires, values, and rights. We will discuss each of these elements in turn. Because they frequently represent the causes of conflict, we will also encounter these terms throughout the text.

Interests

We use the term *interests* in the widest sense, as the goals that people set for themselves in order to ameliorate their lives and the lives of others. Groups of people, such as associations, political parties, or nations, also have interests. Usually, interests are said to correspond to the desire for **power**, money, and glory. However, contrary to this perception (which is sometimes found even in the conflict literature), interests are not simply equivalent to those egoistical passions. Interests represent all that an individual or group deems important. Interests may comprise power and greed objectives, but they may also include those that enhance relationships, help others, or contribute to a more fulfilling life.

Analyzing the interests of the parties in a conflict is the most widely used method of understanding the reasons for conflicts and the ways in which they can be settled. When looking at a conflict, most analysts try to identify the divergences of interests among adversaries. Some schools of thought, such as **rational choice**, **realism**, and **Marxism**, focus on the interests of the parties. They may consider other factors at times but always as secondary influences on the behaviour of people. Other analysts look at the role of values, needs, and identities as basic underlying factors of conflicts but cannot ignore that conflicts are triggered by and structured around interests.

Needs

The notion of needs is of great importance, as some theorists believe that it plays a role in all conflicts where deep passions are involved. Psychologist Abraham Maslow (1948) established a hierarchy of needs, starting with those required for survival (food, shelter, and clothing; see Chapter 7). He also included non-material needs such as **security**, affection,

(AP Photo/Lefteris Pitarakis)

Workers in conflict often express their main interest in clear and simple terms. During a national teachers' strike in England in April 2008, the teachers' interest was plainly stated on their banners and placards.

recognition, identity, belonging, and relationships for meaning and self-actualization. His work stimulated a whole body of literature about needs.

We can distinguish between the popular use of the word *need*, meaning a lack of something deemed important or essential and **identity need**, which is wired into our emotional makeup. Identity needs and interests are similar, but they differ on the basis of the emotional attachment and drive attached to identity need satisfiers. What might be a need satisfier for one person might be an interest for another. For example, when a person is close to starvation and willing to sacrifice virtually anything for something to eat, food is a need satisfier. This situation is different from a well-fed person having an interest in, say, eating a shrimp cocktail.

The link between needs theory and conflict was made by famous Australian academic John W. Burton (1915–2010). He recognized that identity needs are non-negotiable (Burton, 1990a). That is, people are not prepared to compromise something that is linked to the core of their identity but will fight vigorously if the satisfiers to these needs are threatened. This concept has led many scholars to emphasize the study of the root causes of conflict found in the biological, psychological, and identity needs of the protagonists.

Identity

The concept of identity became a major tool for analyzing conflicts in the 1990s, after the fall of the Soviet bloc. While **ideology** diminished as a central factor in armed conflict, membership in ethnonationalist groups, referred to more generically as identity groups, became increasingly significant. For example, the populations of the Balkans returned to their pre-communist historic ethnic and religious identities when Yugoslavia was experiencing major problems with the decline of communism. The increasing diversity of Western populations following massive immigration is another reason for the current interest in identity.

Conflicts often occur when a person's identity is repressed or downgraded by another group. Identity is an important factor in a person's balance, self-esteem, and **empowerment**. People define themselves as members of an ethnic, religious, or linguistic group and may also find their identity in their profession, hobbies, political associations, gender, or sexual orientation. Indian economist and Nobel Prize winner Amartya Sen (b. 1933) argues for the concept of complex identity, recognizing that we can appreciate multiple sets of values and identity markers simultaneously. In some conflict situations, complex identities are compressed into one defining identity that becomes a matter of life and death (2006). Such was the case during the Rwandan **genocide** of 1994, when people were killed for being Tutsi.

Related to identity are memories of being victimized. These memories can be carried for many years and passed to subsequent generations. Some conflicts are based on stories that become what Vamik Volkan (1998) describes as chosen traumas. Through these stories, other groups are framed as "bad guys" who are depersonalized and demonized (see Chapter 7). Memories are linked in narratives, pointing to the fact that the latter are important in establishing identity, values, and meaning. They can be significant contributors to both conflict and **conflict resolution** (see the discussion of narrative mediation in Chapter 11). Likewise, imagination can play a role in conflict. People might imagine that following a certain course will bring dire consequences. If, for instance, there are high levels of distrust, people might believe that they will be taken advantage of if they compromise; as a result, they become entrenched in their positions.

Desires

Desires are things that people want, even if they appear to an outside observer as being of little value or of little improvement to one's life. Consider a child who desires a certain expensive brand of clothing. He or she could be properly clothed much more cheaply, but he or she desires the more costly brand because his or her friends have it. At the international level, countries have fought wars over barren islands that had no real commercial value partly because they both desired the same thing. The most obvious types of desires involved in conflicts are those for power, money, status, and glory. Several of the theories reviewed in Chapter 8 stress desire as the fundamental source of strife: political realists emphasize power, while Marxists and other economic analysts emphasize greed and status. In the view of philosopher René Girard (1978, 1987b), any desire can, through a process of jealousy and imitation, lead to conflict. We explore this notion of desire more fully in Chapter 9.

Values

Values are what one believes should be upheld in society so that people can have happier and more meaningful lives. **Justice**, **equality**, liberty, order, religious belief, honour, and tradition are examples of values that are at the core of many conflicts. These values may be linked to the desires, needs, and interests of people. For instance, a leader who wants to increase his personal power may justify the value of power by stating that authoritarian rule is the only way to establish stability.

Values are grounded in tradition, culture, religion, and ideology. In many encounters with colonizers and explorers, non-Western societies sought to defend the values carried by traditions, language, and customs and to maintain their community orientation to social life, their ideals about the rights and duties of people, and their religious beliefs, symbols, and rituals. Religions carry very strong sets of values that extend to domains such as personal conduct, family life, social relations, and political institutions. People make great sacrifices to follow and defend their religious ideals. In many parts of the world, wars are fought over religion. In many countries, religiously motivated dissidents have risked their lives for democratic values—Buddhist monks demonstrating in Myanmar is just one example. There are also cases of religious extremists using violence to fight for their particular values, sometimes framing their actions as being directed by God (Juergensmeyer, 2003). Ideologies, the sets of social and political ideas developed to provide people with a view of the world and their roles within it, are a more recent invention. **Liberalism**, socialism, communism, fascism, and anarchism are some of the best-known ideologies. During the Cold War, the ideological clash between liberalism and communism was intense at the world level between the West and the East and was also played out in numerous countries and in local and personal settings.

Some people believe that values are always the expression of personal interests or material needs. However, most analysts of conflict do not want to restrict themselves to deterministic or one-dimensional explanations of human behaviour. In reality, people sometimes uphold values simply because they believe them to be worthwhile. Religious beliefs, artistic tastes, or ideological preferences are not always related to the power or material interests of the beholder. In some cases, people will even support values that are not in their own interests. For example, it is often argued that manual workers should vote for socialist parties because those organizations are in favour of redistributing revenues, which could improve the workers' lot. For several reasons, however, many poor workers vote for conservative and liberal parties, even though doing so may go against their economic interests. This is a classic illustration of the differences between interests and values.

A further distinction between values and interests is that the former can include an element of **altruism**, the concern for the well-being of other people. Our capacity for empathy and reasoning has given us the ability to do good things, even at the cost of our own advancement. For example, people who spend time and effort promoting high ideals such as peace, justice, and liberty do so because they believe that they will help their society or the whole of humankind. They are ready to accept personal losses in terms of salary, social opportunity, and leisure time in their pursuits. The concept of values, in the context of ethics, is developed further in Chapter 14.

Rights

Many conflicts seem to be about rights—the right to do this or that, to live in peace, or to be recognized and celebrated. Rights are the expression of a conception of justice. When people strongly demand that their rights be protected, it is because they believe that those rights have been or risk being denied. They experience a sense of injustice, which is one of the strongest drivers of conflict. Injustices can be thought of as existing on a continuum of severity, with distributive injustices (who gets how much) at one end and injustices caused by human atrocities such as rape, mass murder, and genocide at the other. The more significant the injustice, the more challenging it is to deal with a conflict in which it plays a role. When both sides feel severely victimized by injustices, the conflict becomes extremely intractable.

There are different ways to talk about rights. One school of thought claims that people have fundamental rights that exist independently of the society in which they live. These "natural rights," such as the right to (in the words of the US Constitution) "life, liberty and the pursuit of happiness," are given to people by God or by nature and must be upheld by the political system, be it a **democracy**, a monarchy, or a tyranny. Otherwise, people will rebel. In this view, all conflicts can be said to be caused by an offence to the natural rights of a group of people. The concept of natural rights is related to that of **natural law**, which is based on the observation of patterns across cultures and results in universal claims of legitimacy (see Chapter 14).

Another perspective states that rights are what people agree to declare as rights. This positivistic conception of rights was born in sixteenth-century Europe in order to create the basis for diplomatic treaties among Protestant and Catholic monarchs, who did not share the same values. **Positive law** has been a major influence on constitutional law in most Western countries as it specifies a number of civic and political rights to citizens, rights that can be modified with the passage of time. In this view, conflicts about rights involve differences over the granting of rights and their application in a given society.

The existence of conflicts about rights differs among various types of societies. Such conflicts are vigorously pursued in societies where the **rule of law** predominates. In most countries, the evolution towards the affirmation of rights is manifest in the inclusion of a charter of rights in most contemporary constitutions. However, conflicts over rights also exist in non-democratic societies, when, for example, a group believes that the state or another group is infringing on traditional political arrangements and customary law. There are also conflicts over rights when a group advocates the predominance of the rule of law over the power of the political authorities.

THE STRUCTURE OF CONFLICT

All conflicts display a multi-layered **structure**. It is important to understand that the outward expressions of a conflict do not always correspond to the basic objects of contention among the parties involved. For instance, people may claim that a conflict is about rights when they are actually fighting about who should predominate in the relationship. In a conflict over resources, parties may not be able to reach a straightforward compromise on sharing equitably because there are long-standing deep-rooted feelings of animosity between them. As Figure 1.1 shows, we can generally observe three types

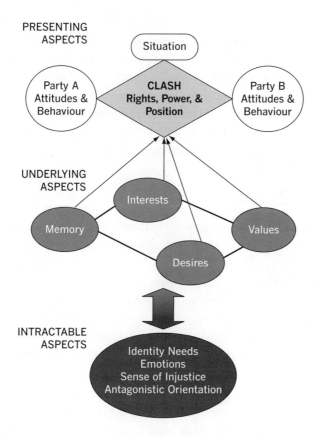

FIGURE 1.1 | ASPECTS OF CONFLICT

(Note that Chris Mitchell [1981] introduces conflict as a function of attitudes, behaviour, and the situation.)

of aspects within a conflict: positional, underlying, and intractable. Recognizing these aspects demonstrates how even what appears to be a simple conflict may actually be very complex.

Positional Aspects

When there is a clash between parties, each takes a position in opposition to the other. They demand something, accuse the other party, and present a favourable view of themselves. The positions are often how the conflict presents itself—at the outset, it seems to be only about the clash of positions. These positions constitute the outward image of the conflict but do not always reflect the exact nature of the situation. For instance, some people in conflict—for instance, politicians in democratic countries—present themselves in a moderate and pleasant manner. Underneath these placid appearances, there may be strong divergences about interests and values. In other cases, such as labour negotiations, parties present themselves as aggressive and uncompromising, sometimes as a tactic devised to impress the other party.

In certain conflicts, the positions are diametrically opposed. The parties may even be in a **zero-sum game**, meaning that one party's gains correspond exactly to the losses of the other(s). Many conflicts about land, resources, and political power are or appear to be zero-sum (although creative solutions can sometimes be found to change the situation). At other times, the positions of the parties have some areas of compatibility; the parties may be in agreement over broad goals but clash over the details. Non-zero-sum items, such as recognition, ideas, and validation, are intangible. In conflict resolution, a great deal of effort is put into transforming situations in which the positions of the parties are incompatible into situations of mutual gains. These efforts will be studied in detail in Chapter 11.

Underlying Aspects

As the name suggests, underlying aspects are those beneath the external appearance of conflict. One well-known underlying aspect of conflict is constituted by the full interests of the parties. In effect, interests are not always clearly expressed, either because parties do not want to reveal their position completely or because they are unsure about the true content and extent of their interests. In the context of conflict negotiation, many analysts insist that it is necessary to discover parties' interests by asking why people chose certain positions (Fisher & Ury, 1981). These interests can be diverse and preclude a negotiated solution. However, in other cases, common ground can be identified between the interests, offering the possibility of a compromise or creative solution.

Other underlying factors to conflicts include values, desires, memories, and imagined future outcomes. These can intensify a conflict, but they can also provide the key to resolution when they are shared by the other party. Memories, for example, can function as both underlying and intractable aspects, depending on the degree to which they lead to identity differentiation, dehumanization, and stereotypes. Where a clash of memories represents misperceptions about what happened, direct and open communication between parties can clear up misunderstandings about intentions and the reasons for certain actions.

Intractable Aspects

At another level, there are the truly difficult aspects of conflict—the intractable, non-negotiable, and antagonistic aspects. These elements include the identity needs, memories, **traumas**, and sense of injustice that are deeply felt by the participants in conflict. Many conflict specialists believe that these intractable aspects are the essence of conflict. Without them, there is not really a conflict but a dispute.

According to theorists such as Julien Freund (1983), another aspect of conflict that distinguishes it from disputes is its antagonistic aspect, meaning that people in conflict want to defeat and hurt their adversary. There is often an element of hatred and **aggression** in conflict that is usually not found in disputes. A key challenge for conflict specialists is to identify the reasons for intense antagonism.

DISPUTES, CONTESTS, AND CONFLICTS

Should different terms be used for clashes of varying degrees of intensity, duration, and stakes? While some might argue that such divisions are pedantic, basic distinctions within the field are significant to our understanding. They allow us to realize the kinds of challenges that are involved and the kinds of processes that can be used for different types of situations.

Disputes

As previously mentioned, there are several differences between disputes and conflicts, even though the words are often used as synonyms. The word *dispute* comes from the Latin *dis* and *putare* and means "to calculate apart from one another," suggesting that parties have different ways of making meaning or strategizing about a situation. Although the parties do not see eye to eye, they are not necessarily estranged or hostile toward each other, as in real conflict. Disputes are differences of view that can usually be resolved by compromise among the parties or by the intervention of a third party. An example of a dispute is a husband and wife arguing over how much money to spend on a new car. This issue can be resolved when each spouse agrees to move toward a compromise. Similarly, a disagreement between a seller and a buyer over the price of a good or service can be resolved by their agreeing on a mid-point figure. These negotiated settlements happen constantly in markets around the world. If a negotiation fails in a formal situation, an arbiter can impose a solution to the parties. Even if the case goes to a court of law, it still constitutes a dispute because both the buyer and the seller agree to the legitimacy of settling their differences legally by a mutually acceptable third party.

Beyond the questions of hostility and intractability, there are also differences of time and salience in disputes and conflicts. Two children can be in a dispute over a toy, but the issue will disappear as soon as a parent offers cookies or turns on the television. Conflicts last for an extended period of time. In many cases, they take precedence over most matters in the thoughts and actions of the parties involved. Some conflicts are so ingrained that they seem to define one or both protagonists. For example, the Israelis and Palestinians often seem to be defined by the conflict that exists between them.

Contests

Some rivalries are non-antagonistic but can be harsh and intense. Competing firms or sports teams want to dominate their domain, and compromise is impossible—there cannot be two Super Bowl champions. Yet we cannot realistically call their relationship a conflict. After all, they both recognize that they are in a competitive milieu and accept the rules of the game and the risk that they may lose. This situation is **competition**, not conflict. The parties enjoy the stimulation that comes with good competition. To suggest that they need a mediator would be ridiculous.

Some people go so far as to say that highly institutionalized competitions are not conflicts. Therefore, political life in liberal democracies would be more of a contest than a conflict and should be put on the same level as sports events (Kriesberg, 2003, p. 17). This position is faulty in the sense that it confuses form and substance. Even if a difference is ritualized and civilized, it may still be a conflict. In political life, we can see conflict over rights, interests, identity need satisfiers, and deeply held values. The reality is that democratic politics is often about conflict, as it is also about disputes and mere popularity contests. The major gift of representative democracy has been to allow people to wage their disputes and conflicts peacefully. The task of the conflict analyst is to discover when political contests involve serious social conflicts.

Should Conflict Studies Deal with Disputes?

Including disputes in **conflict studies** not only creates an enormous field of study, but it also raises the issue of whether the discipline should consider fairly trivial differences alongside serious issues or concentrate on the latter. Burton (1990a, 1996) suggests that we differentiate between conflicts and mere disputes and focus on the former. The distinction between conflict and dispute is a well-known attempt to better define conflict and has inspired many researchers and practitioners. However, it is not without problems. Given that the differences between disputes and conflicts are not always obvious and that disputes may lead to conflicts, we contend that the study of serious disputes must be included in the field of conflict studies.

It is not always easy to draw the line between dispute and conflict. Are the couple that argues most of the time experiencing a series of disputes or fighting a marital conflict? Their disputes could be manifestations of a conflict. A typical conflict analyst may say: "Treat the conflict and the disputes will be resolved." But what if there is no conflict? A practitioner may be trying to resolve a problem in ways that will have no impact on the dispute. In some cases, he or she may want to find a conflict in every dispute in order to justify his or her intervention, thereby creating a conflict where there was none. Furthermore, if a divergence cannot be settled by compromise, is it in fact a conflict or simply a case where the parties are currently unwilling to compromise? Perhaps the antagonism remains only because mediation efforts have been insufficient and/or poorly conducted.

Another issue is that some disputes can be as serious or even more serious than some conflicts. For example, conflicts among siblings may have less effect on their self-esteem than the angry disputes that they may have with their parents. While conflicts can have positive aspects (when they are conducted within the bounds of humanity and decency), disputes can be poisonous to the conduct of life. Why should conflict resolution have a superior status to dispute settlement? Are disputes that risk degenerating into violence less important than conflicts that are played out peacefully? Note that the Charter of the United Nations, concerned with preventing grave armed conflicts, speaks of the "pacific settlement of disputes," which can be interpreted as meaning that any dispute among states matters because it can lead to crisis and war.

Finally, a crucial point is that the distinction between dispute and conflict is not completely objective but often depends on the perspective of the analyst. For example, a failed **collective agreement** negotiation that leads to a strike may be interpreted by someone with liberal ideas as a regrettable dispute over wages, while a Marxist observer may consider it a class conflict.[1] A commercial disagreement between two states may be perceived by a liberal economist as a dispute between trading partners, while someone sharing the power politics perspective may conceive of it as a conflict between national interests.

Some theorists agree to the distinction between conflict and dispute but will not exclude dispute from the field of conflict analysis and resolution. Alan C. Tidwell (1998, pp. 8–10) believes that conflicts and disputes should be understood as belonging to a continuum between grave disputes and conflicts per se. This view supports our claim that the field of conflict studies is mostly concerned about the divergences among people that cannot be resolved through compromise but also includes the serious disputes that may degenerate into conflicts.

IS CONFLICT ALWAYS DESTRUCTIVE?

Common-Sense Perceptions

If you polled people on the street, you would probably find a majority that would agree to such statements as "Conflicts among people are destructive"; "Most human conflict is bad"; or "We should try to abolish social conflict, as it is quite harmful." One reason for this opinion is that conflicts have been associated with violence, war, murder, and destruction for thousands of years. However, conflict is mostly perceived negatively because it seems to be against the ideals of human concord that most of us hope to benefit from and to teach our children about. In fact, most traditional philosophies of life emphasize order and peace. For instance, Confucianism is based on the idea of a natural harmony that has to be maintained, notably by shunning disputes and the expression of conflict. In the next chapter, we will see how it is only since the advent of **liberal democracy** in the eighteenth century that humankind has gradually started to change its conception of conflict.

Although most people consider conflict in negative terms, they also tend to be fascinated by it. Most of what we encounter on the news is about conflict. A good story, whether on the news, in a novel, or as part of office, family, or neighbourhood gossip, is one characterized by conflict. Stories are often embellished to intensify the conflict, thus increasing their value and interest level.

The Roles and Functions of Conflict

The belief that conflict is generally to be avoided has influenced not only popular beliefs but also the study of society itself. Alongside thinkers who emphasized the role of conflict in human societies, there have always been social observers who have been more interested in the integration of and order within societies. Between the 1950s and 1970s, the main social science theory in the United States was structural functionalism, which was mostly concerned with the harmonious development of societies. In the 1950s, American sociologist Lewis Coser (1913–2003), who had studied in Germany, became fascinated by the conflict insights made by German sociologist Georg Simmel (1858–1918; see Simmel, 1972). Coser (1964) wrote *The Functions of Social Conflict*, in which he tried to reconcile the existence of conflict with the dominant sociological tradition. Following Simmel, Coser argued that conflict is a natural human behaviour that fulfills important social functions. For instance, conflict is a means to express and articulate grievances; it gives an identity and a purpose to human groups; and it reinforces group integration. Coser's work was an indirect criticism of those sociologists who embraced integration and downplayed conflict. However, Coser did not support the Marxist notion of violent class conflict as the motor of history. His view of conflict was still functionalist in the sense that conflict was seen as a necessary condition of gradual human progress. In other words, conflict is not necessarily destructive or nefarious.

Today, many social scientists have taken issue with Coser's functional approach. The main criticism is that his work amounts to a teleological view of conflict, that he implied that conflicts happened for reasons of social integration and progress. Most social scientists prefer not to attribute a meaning and a function to conflict, especially in the direction of progress, which has become a suspect concept. However, since the publication of Coser's seminal book, the study of conflict has been very high on the agenda of most contemporary sociological schools of thought.

Conflict and Change

Conflicts can lead to positive and constructive change. This change may be the result of a process designed to deal with the conflict or it may happen without conscious direction.

(The Granger Collection, New York)

Soldiers of the South Carolina Volunteer Regiment (African Descent) celebrate the emancipation of the slaves on 1 January 1863. The long-term conflict regarding the abolition of slavery in Europe and the Americas ended peacefully in England, France, and Canada but led to civil war in the United States.

Political, institutional, and legal innovations result from conflicts. The evolution of social institutions such as democracy occurred as a result of conflict. Bitter conflicts have also forged new insights. Roger Martin (2007) argues that, when presented with two opposed ideas, the most effective leaders will choose neither but will create something new that incorporates elements of both alternatives. Some conflicts bring changes in norms, behaviours, and mentalities. Scholar–practitioners such as John Paul Lederach (1995) have argued for using conflict to create a new reality that can transform many aspects of the situation. Whatever the process, it is clear that out of conflict comes change. For example, in the 1920s, Nellie McClung and four other women took strong issue with the systemic exclusion of women in key aspects of society. Despite derision from many quarters, they initiated and won the Persons Case, resulting in women being officially recognized as persons under the British North America Act and gaining political rights. As women gained the right to vote, the Canadian political landscape was transformed.

CONFLICT, AGGRESSION, AND VIOLENCE

Behind most conflicts lurks the possibility of the use of force, either because the parties may resort to violence to affect the resolution of the conflict in their favour or because a third party, such as the government, steps in to impose a solution by force. Conflict-related violence can be minimal. For instance, a protest by striking union workers may include minor acts of vandalism. In this case, the idea is to impress upon the media that the problems facing the workers are very grave and upon the bosses that the workers may have recourse to more severe forms of violence if things are not settled to their liking. In cases where ethnic or religious groups want to intimidate their opponents and generate fear in the population, violence may involve assassinations, ambushes, and terrorist bombings. This type of violence may lead to a wide insurrection and even to a full-fledged war. In order to prevent an increase in violence, a foreign country or another third party may use violence to enforce a solution or to weaken the participants to the point that they will desist. These phenomena are well known and constitute the stuff of television news.

Violence destroys lives, property, and the natural world, as well as values such as trust, empathy, love, and hope. It also leaves profound psychological marks on the protagonists and sometimes on observers of and third parties to conflict. There is a range of responses to the existence of violence, from those who are passionately committed to its reduction and eradication to those who are convinced that it is a necessary part of human existence and must be an option to limit greater violence. Some pacifists refuse to use violence themselves but recognize that its disappearance is unlikely. Those committed to non-violent action are convinced that strong measures that do not replicate violence are needed to fight injustice.

Many people working in conflict resolution were attracted to the field by their desire to see violence disappear from human relations. Some are influenced by religious beliefs and others by humanistic secular ideas in their embrace of **non-violence**. However, others hold that violence or the threat of violence may have a role to play in the management and resolution of some conflicts, for instance, when the state can stop a conflict from degenerating into armed struggle. Conflict studies specialists often disagree on the usefulness of force in settling disputes. Some are involved in conflict studies to abolish violence and war, while others are mostly interested in reducing the use of force in human affairs. This difference indicates that ethical values play a role in how people engage in conflict and how they approach intervention (see Part V).

As we pointed out earlier, conflict and violence are intimately related in the minds of many people. In reality, many conflicts are played out peacefully. For example, many countries hitherto characterized by constant conflict between their authoritarian governments and their populations (e.g. the Philippines, Brazil, Argentina, Russia, and Poland) evolved toward democracy in an orderly fashion in the 1980s and 1990s. In particular, the end of apartheid in South Africa in 1990–1 was remarkably peaceful despite the previous two decades of guerrilla warfare and urban riots.

The other error in the equation between conflict and violence is the idea that the former is usually the cause of the latter. Violence is a result of aggression, a process that is not only conflict-related. Aggression is a hostile behaviour directed against others or oneself. It may be caused by fear, mental illness, desire, and/or perceptions of a threat. A criminal who kills a security guard in a botched robbery does not do so because of a conflict but because he is terrified, extra aggressive, or determined to eliminate a witness.

We should also add that not all political violence stems from conflicts. Some political violence occurs when a state or a group of people want to intimidate, weaken, or exterminate another group of people with whom they may not even have a true quarrel. In this case, violence serves to gain power or is inspired by some malicious ideology that advocates the use of force against specific groups. For example, the Jewish minority in 1930s Germany was not in conflict with the rest of German society. Many tried hard to assimilate into the mainstream, while others kept their traditions alive but strictly abided by the country's secular rules. Furthermore, most of the German people did not consider themselves to be in conflict with the Jews. However, the Nazis convinced a part of the population to support the expulsion, repression, and even physical elimination of Jews. The genocide that followed was an act of pure hatred, not a consequence of a historical conflict. As in this case, political violence often stems not from an overt conflict but from the desire of one party to punish or eliminate another.

Despite these examples, it remains that violence or the possibility of violence exists in many conflicts. As a result, aggression, violence, and conflict are frequently studied together. We will often allude to these links in the course of this book. However, it is important to keep in mind that not all conflicts are violent and that political violence has other causes.

CONCLUSION

We have defined conflict as a relationship characterized by intractable divergences over any number of issues, including interests, needs, identity, desires, values, and rights. On the surface, conflict appears as a clash among positions. However, conflict also contains underlying aspects such as interests, values, desires, and imagined future outcomes, as well as the intractable aspects of hatred, memory of past conflicts, painful traumas, unfulfilled identity needs, and a deep sense of injustice.

Conflict can be differentiated from disputes in that the latter tend to involve issues that are subject to negotiation and compromise. However, because it is not always easy to distinguish disputes from conflicts and because some disputes may lead to conflict, we argue that conflict studies should deal with serious disputes as well as obvious conflicts. Conflict can be hurtful and destructive, but it can also be the means for social cohesion and collective identities. Moreover, conflict leads to change, creativity, and transformation. Parties to a conflict may be violent or threatening to one another, but violence is not necessarily the result of conflict, and many conflicts are played out peacefully.

DISCUSSION QUESTIONS

1. Think of some of the national political issues of the day. Which ones are genuine conflicts and which are serious disputes, personal rivalries, or popularity contests?

2. Choose a current conflict that you feel informed about. What is the level of conflict? What is the cause of the conflict: interests, needs, identity, desires, values, or rights?

3. Analyze a current conflict to distinguish its presenting aspects, underlying aspects, and intractable aspects.

4. Choose a particular interpersonal relationship. List the conflicts that have occurred through the life of this relationship and identify how the relationship has changed as a result of these conflicts.

NOTE

1. We use the original meaning of the term *liberal* to denote a partisan of free markets and personal liberties.

PART II | CONFLICT AND CONFLICT RESOLUTION IN THE CONTEMPORARY WORLD

The following chapters provide an analysis of the state of conflict in today's world. Using key facts and indicators, we discuss the degree of conflict in various levels of society, the most prominent types of conflicts, and how these conflicts are managed or resolved. While each chapter is devoted to one level of conflict—small group and interpersonal, large-scale societal, and international—the characteristics and issues relevant to the three types are often similar. Throughout the section, we hypothesize that

1. the variety and the frequency of conflicts are increasing;
2. conflicts tend to become more complex, by which we mean that they are interconnected and involve many participants;
3. violence is a slowly decreasing answer to conflicts; and
4. the repertory of conflict management and resolution processes is growing.

2 | SMALL GROUP AND INTERPERSONAL CONFLICT

CHAPTER OBJECTIVES

This chapter will help you develop an understanding of the

- trends in conflicts within families, businesses, and communities;
- prevalence and interconnectedness of conflict in modern society;
- decreasing level of violence in small-scale conflict; and
- methods of managing and resolving small-scale conflict.

INTRODUCTION

Within the category of small group and interpersonal conflicts, we include conflicts that occur at the smallest scale in society, such as marital and family conflicts, feuds among neighbours, clashes within corporations, and local political battles. We understand that the large-scale conflicts of society are also experienced at the individual level (where they affect many people in their daily lives) and that local and personal disputes are often the tangible expression of larger conflicts. However, this chapter focuses on conflicts that are not directly related to the larger conflicts of society, meaning that they have not been ordered by a larger organization and are not always articulated in political terms by the protagonists.

We begin by examining the rise in small group and interpersonal conflicts within the family, workplace, and political environments. As these conflicts become more complex, they become part of the social fabric and often involve many secondary players. We also consider the role of violence in this type of conflict, which appears to be decreasing in the Western world. Finally, we discuss methods used to manage and resolve small-scale conflict, from the political system to mediation.

TRENDS IN SMALL-SCALE CONFLICT

Measuring the level of small-scale conflict in modern societies is a challenging task, primarily because of the lack of significant indicators that gauge conflict in both the past and present. For example, it is difficult to know how many marital conflicts there were in North America before the 1960s because people tended to hide such matters in those days. It is also difficult to assess what proportion of these conflicts were settled and in what manner. Furthermore, non-democratic regimes and poor countries usually do not collect or authorize much reliable data regarding these matters.

The indicators that are available suggest that small group and interpersonal conflict has been increasing over the centuries, particularly since World War II. We will provide four types of evidence for this trend in the Western world: lawsuits, divorce rates, labour grievances, and local opposition to economic development projects. In each type, people are becoming more aware of their own rights, interests, and needs and are framing their experiences in terms of some form of victimization. They are also attentive to issues of fairness and, out of a perception of injustice, can become vindictive.

Lawsuits

Democracies, although they tend to be peaceful, are also confrontational and litigious. Small- and medium-scale conflicts abound in these liberal societies: workers contest decisions made by their employers; citizens demand to be consulted about changes in their environment; and consumers sue companies over corporate abuse and professionals over malpractice. Such lawsuits allow many people to protect their interests and are often beneficial to society, such as when they create precedents that will protect other people from abuse and exploitation or force the government to change legislation in this regard. There are even class-action suits, which are filed on behalf of large numbers of people and sometimes result in major reparations.

However, there is a negative side to all this litigation. Families are divided and couples separate over peccadilloes. Citizens oppose the construction of anything that can be seen from their backyards. Fake or marginal victims of corporate or professional abuse claim substantial compensation. These circumstances are certainly due to the opportunities offered by freedom, but that is not the only cause. After all, liberal democracies vary in their

(AP Photo/Evan Vucci)

On 21 June 2011, demonstrators protested the US Supreme Court's refusal to hear a sex discrimination class-action lawsuit against Wal-Mart Stores, Inc. The litigants have decided to pursue the case through other lawsuits.

degree of litigiousness. For instance, while Americans are generally fond of court orders and lawsuits, the Japanese try to avoid litigation as much as possible. The main source of this propensity for small conflicts seems to be the individualism that has developed following the liberal democratic revolution and the urbanization and **secularization** of European-based societies. In this perspective, it is unlikely that, barring a return to traditional life patterns, the tendency for interpersonal and inter-group conflicts will ever disappear in the West. The trend of litigation might decrease, however, if exaggerated quarrelsome attitudes drop out of fashion and if the tools of conflict resolution are used in more cases.

While lawsuits indicate an increase in conflict, it is important to note that a great deal are settled out of court. It is estimated that the great majority of lawsuits in the United States are resolved in this manner. This percentage has been rising since the 1970s, when litigants and lawyers realized that lawsuits were extremely prolonged and expensive and that the courts were overburdened by small claims cases. Most out-of-court settlements emerge from a negotiation between the lawyers of the two parties, but a third party is sometimes involved as a mediator or an arbiter. In the 1970s, Supreme Court Chief Justice Warren Burger became the champion of **alternative dispute resolution** (ADR) in the United States (Barrett, 2004). Over the years, law schools began to teach mediation and arbitration courses and lawyers started to master new techniques and approaches to help their clients reach negotiated out-of-court settlements. Professionals other than lawyers became more involved in many marital and commercial conflicts. However, the increase in out-of-court settlements is not indicative of an alleviation of conflict in modern society. On the contrary, the judicial system has had to adapt and favour more flexible ways to deal with lawsuits because conflicts and disputes are so prevalent.

Divorce Rates

There are currently more open conflicts between spouses in Western societies than in the past. Our indicator for this trend is divorce rates. Divorces are not the only aspect of marital and family conflict, but they are representative of other similar conflicts (such as separation without divorce between both married and unmarried couples) and are relatively easy to define and count. There has been an explosion of divorces all over the Western world, starting in the 1960s. The rates of divorce per 1,000 inhabitants from 2003 to 2005 are reported to be 3.60 in the United States, 2.80 in Great Britain, 2.24 in Canada, and 2.09 in France. However, rates are very low in Catholic countries such as Spain (0.75) and Italy (0.73). In the East, the divorce rate in Russia is 4.42 per 1,000 inhabitants. The officially published rates for China and India (1.28 and 1.10, respectively) are much lower than those in North America, despite the fact that these two countries also have permissive divorce laws (United Nations, 2007). The US Census Bureau (2004) estimates that approximately 40 per cent of American men and women born between 1945 and 1954 were divorced by 2004.

Most divorces are synonymous with marital conflict and also entail a number of potential family conflicts involving children, siblings, and grandparents. Additionally, divorce is often accompanied by conflicts over custody, visiting rights, alimony, separation of assets, etc. In order to lessen the impact of divorce and to avoid clogging the courts with lengthy divorce proceedings, many countries have instituted no-fault divorce procedures, in which the plaintiff is not required to prove wrongdoing (e.g. adultery or abuse) to dissolve his or her marriage.[1] Canada recognized this form of divorce in the Divorce Act of 1968, while the United States first implemented it in California in 1970. The introduction of no-fault has stimulated the rise in divorces. A study of 18 European countries revealed that no-fault has resulted in a 20 per cent increase in the divorce rate between 1960 and 2002 (González and Viitanen, 2009).

Another common practice in divorce settlements is negotiation between the parties and their lawyers, which is usually mediated by a professional third party. Such proceedings are settled without a trial and are typically less destructive and traumatizing than those involving costly and aggressive court hearings. All people involved, especially children, gain from separations and divorces not being fought in the tribunals.

The increase in the divorce rate does not mean that there were no marital conflicts in the past but only that they have become more prevalent. This change is understandable, given that religion is no longer the major disciplining factor that it once was, that strict gender role differentiations have given way to an egalitarian redefinition of responsibilities, and that people are generally more oriented towards their personal needs and freedoms. It should also be added that an increasing part of the population in affluent countries chooses common-law unions rather than marriage. Common-law unions are increasingly recognized and regulated but may be more fragile than marriages. Therefore, the figures about divorce could be seen as an indicator of the tenuous state of couples in society.

Labour Grievances

Another symptom of conflict is the rise in workplace grievances and claims, which employees may submit if they feel that they have been wronged and other conflict resolution processes have been unavailable or ineffective. Not all work environments offer extensive possibilities for workplace grievances. For instance, unionized shops are more likely than non-unionized ones to harbour a formal grievance process. Some jurisdictions are also more prone to force employers to adopt grievance procedures than others.

According to Statistics Canada (2003), 49 per cent of the workers studied in the 1999–2000 Workplace and Employee Survey reported having access to a grievance system. It was estimated that 11 per cent of workers had filed a grievance during the period of the survey: 46 per cent of these claims were informally addressed at the level of managers, 16 per cent through a management committee, 22 per cent through a labour–management committee, and 9 per cent by an outside arbitrator. In 20 per cent of cases, other methods (which could include ombudspersons, mediation offices, industrial psychologists, and chaplains) were used alongside the usual channels. With the decline of unionization in North America and the resulting lack of resources available to non-unionized employees, it is possible that the number of work grievances will decrease over time. However, non-unionized environments change too, affected by worker demands for more responsiveness and fairness.

Local Opposition Movements

In local politics, conflicts involving citizens, associations, political parties, developers, corporations, and governments are growing. These divergences concern environmental protection, land use, urban planning, and infrastructure development. While large-scale development projects generally did not arouse many controversies prior to the 1970s, millions of people affected by controversial plans have since used their political weight and legal rights to force changes in their favour. They organized into political movements, started lobbying campaigns, and effected public demonstrations. An expression has even been coined to express the most extreme forms of citizens' opposition: "Not in my backyard" (NIMBY). However, most local opposition movements are not frivolous. They are based on strong evidence and are defended by informed people. Government and industry often spend large sums of money fighting their opponents, but they do not always succeed in stopping the controversies.

Opposition to the nuclear industry is a case in point. Citizens' opposition became so intense worldwide that nuclear plant development in the United States stopped completely by the mid-1970s. No nuclear power generation projects have been started since. Eventually, these protest movements successfully blocked the growth of nuclear power in several countries, such as Canada, Sweden, Germany, and other European states.[2]

(AP Photo/dapd, Thomas Lohnes)

An anti-nuclear protest in Germany in 2011. After decades of massive anti-nuclear actions by several groups and parties, the German government decided to withdraw from nuclear energy altogether.

The nuclear issue was followed by countless opposition movements over the years. In the United States, these political and legal challenges soon cost money and votes, to the point that federal, state, and local administrations had to create and implement measures to prevent and manage these conflicts. The planning of large-scale projects now requires public consultations to ensure that the welfare of citizens and the natural environment will be protected. Many US states and cities have created environmental mediation agencies to attempt mediations in environmental conflicts, in the hope of saving costly and prolonged lawsuits. **Non-governmental organizations (NGOs)** such as Resolve (created in 1978) were established in the United States to provide mediation services to disputants in wildlife and environmental quarrels.

ENTANGLED CONFLICTS

Just like international and national conflicts, small group and interpersonal divergences tend to become more complex over time. They also become part of the social fabric and interconnected with one another. If we return to marital conflicts for an example, we can observe that they are now a "normal" feature of Western society—people are no longer shocked by separation or divorce. Many people think that it is better to split up than to submit to a life of unhappiness. This view is widely held in Western culture, be it in literature, cinema, theatre, television, or music. Thus, we can say that marital conflicts are woven into the fabric of society. This statement can also be applied to certain labour conflicts. For example, the use of grievance procedures has become an unavoidable aspect of life in unionized and highly protected work environments, such as the civil service or school boards.

These conflicts affect many aspects of people's lives, such as their work, family situation, leisure, investment and property, and personal development. As a result, conflicts are intertwined with other social and personal conflicts and involve several people—supporters, opponents, third parties, witnesses, and victims. Again, marital conflicts provide an excellent example because this type of conflict can affect the development of children, raise women's rights issues, unearth deep psychological anxieties, and disrupt social links. Family conflicts also involve a growing number of participants and third parties, including parents, grandparents, children, social workers, psychologists, lawyers, judges, police officers, civil servants, religious officials, and professional mediators.

As these examples suggest, the number of participants in small-scale conflicts appears to be increasing. On the one hand, the involvement of several people does not seem to be a new concept. After all, the collective life of traditional communities included all members in resolving issues, even family and property conflicts. It is also true that many conflicts in contemporary individualistic societies are conducted privately, involving, for example, a lone individual battling a municipality over a property issue. However, today's citizens are more empowered, better educated and informed, and rely on more means of communication and influence than their ancestors, all of which makes them more capable of knowing and fighting for their rights. This is certainly the case with women, who regularly fight for equality and participate fully in all major social controversies, but it also extends to poor people, people with disabilities, and members of visible minority groups. In sum, there has been a growth in small-scale conflicts concerning labour relations, community tensions, local politics, business dealings, consumer complaints, malpractice issues, etc. These conflicts have become a significant aspect of our society, confronting more and more people at various times in their lives.

VIOLENCE IN SMALL GROUP AND INTERPERSONAL CONFLICT

Many people believe that interpersonal violence is increasing because there seem to be more occurrences of violence in the world. For instance, criminal violence, such as murder, assault, and armed robbery, is rising in several developing states where urbanization and the uneven creation of wealth create tensions. This phenomenon is well known in countries as diverse as Brazil, the Philippines, and Nigeria. There are also claims that rape and domestic assault cases have increased in recent years. For instance, world reported rapes have more than doubled since 1977 (Human Security Centre, 2005, p. 82).[3] Political violence seems to be growing everywhere, as recent events in Iraq, Afghanistan, Lebanon, and Sudan illustrate.

Despite these disturbing examples, the general trend in interpersonal relationships and local politics shows a gradual decrease in the use of violence. While violent crime rates have risen in some emerging countries, they have decreased in many lands. If we take murder as an example, the world homicide rate has been relatively stable since 1959. The rate in industrialized countries rose between 1975 and 1995 but has been decreasing ever since (Human Security Centre, 2005, pp. 81–82).[4] Although there has recently been a slight increase in murder rates in some large American cities, the overall trend is that human relations are becoming less violent. In Canada, both the frequency and severity of criminal offences have declined, as shown in Figure 2.1.

Although incidents of violence in interpersonal conflict have decreased, there are still areas of concern. For example, violence against women remains a very serious issue. The Human Security Centre (2005, p. 83) notes that the United States, Canada, Australia, and New Zealand have the highest rape rates in the world, over 10 times those of Asian countries. However, this difference reflects the fact that more incidents are being reported and investigated in some countries. Other statistics paint a more realistic picture of the situation. In the United States, the FBI and the Bureau of Justice Statistics report a strong decrease in rape and a significant decrease in homicide cases between 1970 and 2010 (see Figure 2.2).

The use of violence in labour relations is also decreasing in the West. Since the beginning of the Industrial Revolution, work conflicts have often been characterized by violent behaviour, including the repression of strikes by police or private armed forces, the use of strike breakers, assaults on and assassinations of union leaders, large-scale industrial sabotage by employees, illegal work stoppages and strikes, and violent worker uprisings. Although these actions still occur in developing countries, they have become rare in

2006 = 100

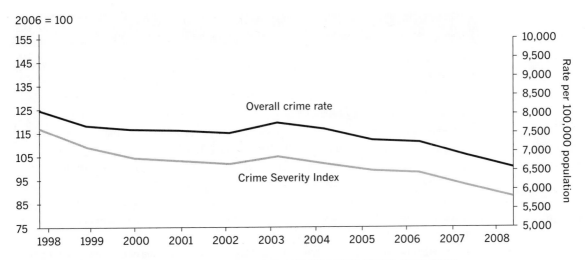

FIGURE 2.1 | POLICE-REPORTED CRIME RATE AND CRIME SEVERITY INDEX, 1998–2008

Source: Statistics Canada, Canada Year Book, 11-402-XWE 2011000, September 2011; www.statcan.gc.ca/bsolc/olc-cel/olc-cel?catno= 11-402-x&lang=eng.

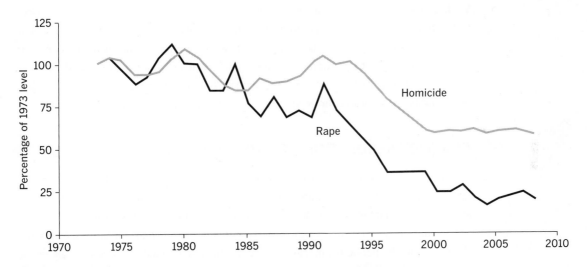

FIGURE 2.2 | RAPE AND HOMICIDE RATES IN THE UNITED STATES, 1973–2008

Source: Pinker, S. (2011). *The better angels of our nature: Why violence has declined.* New York, NY: Viking, p. 402. Used by permission of Viking Penguin, a division of Penguin Group (USA) Inc.

industrialized societies. Workers in these areas are generally better protected by laws; corporations and governments have become less prone to use intimidation and repressive measures; the workforce is now fragmented into different trades and specializations that do not always act in a united and decisive manner against employers; the white-collar workers who compose the majority of the workforce are relatively well remunerated and well treated; and many instruments of conflict resolution are available to disputing parties.

BOX 2.1 | THE HISTORICAL DECLINE IN MURDER RATES

An example of the decline in murder rates is provided by French historian Robert Muchembled (2008, pp. 33–34), who studied the rates in Artois County, an area that was part of the Holy Roman Empire for centuries and is now part of Belgium. Muchembled found that the rate of murder was 100 for every 100,000 persons in the thirteenth century and 10 per 100,000 in the mid-seventeenth. The murder rate in this area fell to 1 per 100,000 by the mid-twentieth century and has diminished by almost half in the last 50 years. The difference in these statistics is even greater when we consider that infanticides and certain assassinations (especially those committed by nobles) were not reported in medieval times. This example indicates that the current murder rate is much lower than it was in the Middle Ages, a change that can be attributed to the increased repression of violence by the state, an improved justice system, better living conditions, and the decline of the culture of violence. The result is clear: in Western societies, violence is no longer the answer to personal feuds and is not the main means of deciding who gets what and when.

With **globalization** creating a freer movement of goods and the possibility for services to be offered online, large corporations have the capacity to relocate, thus making labour disruptions at home a less attractive option for workers. On the other hand, corporations facing the potential of bankruptcy and shutdowns have been helped by negotiated contracts that reduce labour costs. Labour relations are still eminently marked by conflict and have become more complicated; however, they are also less violent.

CONFLICT RESOLUTION AT GROUND LEVEL

The main forums for addressing conflict at ground level are the political system, the legal system, traditional structures, and modern structures. New forms of conflict resolution, such as professional mediation, have also become common in the Western world.

The political system is often a catalyst of conflict, as people fight for their interests and their ideas in the public realm. However, as we have seen, politics is not only about the expression of conflict but also about its management. Some conflicts are expressed in political battles and electoral contests. These exist at all levels of society, including the local level, where interpersonal conflicts occur. For instance, small groups of people divided by a municipal issue, such as a divergence over the construction of a road, may decide to bring their feud to the electoral level by supporting candidates and parties that share their views and by letting the voters decide who will predominate on the matter at hand. Although electoral contests are an expedient way to manage some conflicts, they do not necessarily end them. The citizens in our example who lose the election may still conclude that the voters did not really reject their cause and may continue their fight using a variety of non-electoral means.

There is another important limit to resolving small group and interpersonal conflict through the political system. Politics is about public issues (the *res publica* of the ancient Romans), and in liberal democracies there is a demarcation between the public and the private. Politicians are not supposed to interfere in private affairs. It is unlikely that fighting couples or feuding neighbours would call their mayor to help resolve their problems. If they did, the mayor would rightly claim that the matter is private and not part of his or her mandate. Mediating every interpersonal quarrel in the city would leave no time for him or her to attend to municipal issues.[5] It is also very unlikely that these private litigants would transpose their fight to an electoral contest. They would soon find out that party organizers and militants would have no patience for their problems!

The legal system is another place where private disputes and conflicts can be expressed and resolved. Many divorces, inheritance issues, work conflicts, consumer battles, feuds among neighbours, and local controversies are settled in the courts. The expansion of a neutral and competent justice system is generally considered to be favourable to the mass of the population because it offers the poor, not-so-rich, minorities, and women the possibility to sue, individually or collectively, people who are richer and more powerful than them. Where there are no programs that offer financial assistance to those lacking resources (e.g. legal aid), access to the courts is ruled out for many on economic grounds. Although judicial systems may be crowded, slow, and expensive, they offer possibilities to settle disputes in a fair and consistent manner. This is why access to the legal system is a priority in democratizing countries and still a notable public policy issue in established liberal democracies. However, the justice system will never be the solution to all conflicts. It leaves many quarrels intact and even plays a role in worsening some situations. For example, the justice system has been historically important in protecting women and children in divorce cases. However, divorce cases that are brought before the courts are usually the most acrimonious ones, and their outcomes may lead to interpersonal reprisals and manifestations of anger.

A different form of conflict resolution is found in the traditional mechanisms of tribal societies. To resolve marital conflicts, family feuds, or rivalries with neighbouring villages, these societies relied on long consensus-seeking discussions, symbolic **reconciliation** ceremonies with magical or mystical overtones, and appeasement through the exchange of gifts and prayers. They used mediation or arbitration by village elders, religious leaders, aristocrats and warriors, or heads of families or clans. As anthropologists have observed, these methods were usually helpful in resolving most quarrels in traditional societies. In traditional societies, these mechanisms are regularly supplemented with political negotiation and/or the use of force and legal appeals. They are also instrumental in keeping most private conflict out of the state's domain.

The fragmentation of modern Western societies along socioeconomic, religious, racial, and regional lines has rendered traditional conflict resolution methods obsolete. After all, how could the mediation of a priest and reconciliation Mass be influential in conflict resolution when the parties practise different religions or no religion at all? While elders and

(AP Photo/Eric Risberg)

Legal proceedings are often crucial in the settlement of conflicts and the transformation of society. In some cases, judgments can even invalidate political decisions. On 4 August 2010, demonstrators celebrated the federal court decision to overturn the results of a referendum that would have banned same-sex marriages in California.

clan leaders no longer have sway over Western populations, rich notables, celebrities, and intellectuals are sometimes called upon to help settle conflicts, even though they usually do not have the same aura of legitimacy or impartiality and may not master the art of conflict resolution.

However, many modern institutions and characters play innovative conflict prevention and resolution roles. For instance, as previously mentioned, consulting the local population before launching large-scale work projects is now commonplace and is encouraged by governments and interest groups alike. These discussions often result in a compromise regarding the desirability of the project and the conditions in which it should be realized. Therefore, consultation has a conflict prevention and resolution potential that is valuable in the complex and litigious societies of today.

Conflict resolution methods are also expanding beyond those found in the political and legal systems. These new approaches often attempt to replace adversarial procedures with more co-operative and creative ones and rely on neutral third parties to help those in conflict reach an agreement through negotiation. When looking at the situation in developed countries, what strikes the most is the expansion of conflict resolution mechanisms, as we will see in Chapter 11. Those instruments are often used in place of adversarial procedures in conflict. These approaches to conflict resolution are characterized by their reliance on neutral third parties to help the parties come to an agreement.

What is certain is that people in advanced democracies negotiate more than ever. In some ways, social and personal life in modern societies has become a constant negotiation. Employees negotiate their work conditions, salaries, and job descriptions. Family members negotiate their roles in the household, share of the family income, leisure time and expenses, and say in the acquisition of valuable property. Because modern liberal democracy is based on innumerable contracts among free individuals, one can say that negotiation is at the core of this form of social organization (Thuderoz, 2000). Everybody negotiates throughout the stages of their lives and in various environments, including the family, workplace, and civic interactions.

One form of conflict resolution that uses negotiation is mediation. This method is commonly found in marital conflicts and divorce cases. In fact, many jurisdictions impose mediation before any such case goes to court in order to lighten the burden on the legal system and to avoid harsh proceedings on the disputants and their relatives. As we have already discussed, most small suits are settled out of court. Children are even socialized into learning mediation. Many NGOs, school boards, and education departments now support initiatives to teach simple ADR techniques in primary and secondary schools. Many large organizations organize conflict resolution seminars in which employees are introduced to neutral third-party roles such as mediation. We will discuss these roles further in Chapter 11.

The penetration of conflict resolution ideas in the general population has been remarkable in recent years. Consider, for example, the popularity of the vocabulary related to conflict resolution. **Win–win solutions** are now advocated by politicians, business executives, union leaders, and the proverbial person on the street. Many people have heard of ADR, **interest-based negotiation**, neutral third parties, and **integrative negotiations** (see Chapter 11). Even though some people might not always know exactly what such concepts entail or practise what they mean, a more benevolent and creative approach to conflicts is gradually taking root in the West, where political and legal solutions to conflicts had been preferred for centuries. In the non-Western world, many countries are careful to maintain or reform their traditional institutions of conflict resolution, such as village councils, in order to avoid relying too much on the courts for the settlement of small conflicts and disputes.[6] In this approach, the local champions of conflict resolution are sometimes assisted by technical and financial support from foreign donors.

Another interesting development is the widespread interest in interpersonal and group communication as a major factor in the prevention, management, and resolution of conflict (see Chapter 10). Communication is one of the key themes of psychology, with most psychologists believing that an improvement in communications does marvels for personal well-being and for relations among people. This idea has been disseminated by the popular media and by countless self-help best-sellers. **Dialogue**, listening, and conversations are advocated for the couple in conflict. Exchanges of ideas, discussions, and airing of differences are popular in community relations. Governments and corporations demand consultations, focus groups, town hall meetings, and opinion polls to hear what the public thinks. Again, it is difficult to judge the impact of this fascination for communicating on the state of conflict in the Western world. On the one hand, an emphasis on expression of **frustrations** and demands may increase the level of conflict. On the other hand, communicating is crucial in managing conflict and moderating the most negative aspects of the divergences among people.

CONCLUSION

People in the West have more conflicts because societies are more complex, there are fewer preventive norms against conflict, and people enjoy more individual rights. Many conflicts and disputes are direct consequences of the modernization and liberalization of societies. People who are free are able to fight for their interests. Conversely, people who have no political rights cannot contest the decisions of the political authorities. Where private property does not exist or is very limited, lawsuits over commercial contracts or land boundaries make no sense. In societies where individualism is unknown or proscribed, people do not file complaints against their employers for wrongdoings. In societies dominated by ancient beliefs, women do not ask for divorce, custody, alimony, or division of assets.

In short, people are in conflict in the modern world because they have won the right to fight for their interests. They are in conflict because they see other people in conflict and believe that they should also fight for their rights. This trend is unlikely to diminish in the developing world, as countries experience democratization and liberalization. As for the developed world, it is difficult to see at this point whether and when conflicting behaviour will start to decrease.

This argument does not mean that conflict does not exist in traditional societies. However, members of these societies fight over a limited range of issues. They do not fight over wages and benefits, religious discrimination, polluting emissions, infrastructure construction, technical regulations, or divorce settlements. Today's citizens are in conflict because there are more opportunities for conflict. All the complexities of modern life are found in the innumerable conflicts that affect them in their numerous roles as parents, workers, employers, neighbours, consumers, investors, etc. Fortunately, this increasing level of conflict is not accompanied by a rise in interpersonal violence. The decrease in this type of violence suggests that the use of force is becoming less acceptable in the management of social relations and conflict. Instead, conflict is managed and resolved through other means, including the political system and mediation.

DISCUSSION QUESTIONS

1. How do the trends in small group and interpersonal conflict discussed in this chapter mesh with your experience and with what you observe in your community and circle of friends?

2. What kinds of conflict are most apparent in the media you are exposed to (e.g. television, movies, and newspapers)? What evidence suggests that these conflicts are inherent in society?

3. Discuss the ways in which people deal with interconnected and self-standing interpersonal conflicts. Include the involvement of third parties in your analysis.

NOTES

1. Divorces still have to be declared by a court of law, but there is no need for long court debates in a no-fault system, where the agreement is negotiated by the parties.

2. There are other reasons to explain the lack of nuclear development, such as cost overruns, safety issues, nuclear weapons proliferation, and the availability of alternative and cheaper energy resources. However, it is undeniable that citizen opposition was an important element in countries deciding to forgo nuclear development.

3. When considering such statistics, it is important to remember that many incidents of rape go unreported; many countries do not report rapes; and the definition of rape varies from country to country.

4. This report shows two peaks in homicide rates between 1959 and 2001, which are attributable to countries such as Nigeria, Peru, and Rwanda classifying victims of political violence as homicides. Otherwise, the figure is flat.

5. The distinction between the public and the private does not exist in primitive societies and in totalitarian regimes where the public is everything. In such societies, political authority figures such as a village chief or a Communist Party official would not find it objectionable to interfere in marital conflicts, as they would be considered part of community life. In kingdoms and other pre-industrial complex traditional societies, there is usually some form of separation between the public and the private, but the exact boundaries and the possibilities for political intrusions in the latter sphere vary enormously from one case to another.

6. Local mechanisms of dealing with conflict are vulnerable to being disrupted by violence and the widespread availability of small arms. In Sudan in 2003, for instance, it was reported that the power of some village elders was usurped by young people with arms, who threatened violence if people did not follow their directives. In some urban neighborhoods in Canada and United States, gangs can play a highly disruptive role in community life.

3 | LARGE-SCALE SOCIETAL CONFLICT

CHAPTER OBJECTIVES

This chapter will help you develop an understanding of the

- major sources of contention in societies and how they have evolved in Western countries and developing states;
- impact of modernization and globalization on groups within society, such as the intergenerational clashes of basic values;
- roles of modernization, democratization, and globalization in the growing complexity of conflicts within states;
- changing nature of armed conflict, particularly regarding the involvement of non-state actors;
- slow decrease in state-induced violence;
- historic trends in the transition from authoritarian regimes to democracy; and
- non-violent factors in large-scale social change.

INTRODUCTION

In this chapter, we examine the causes and complexities of large-scale conflicts, the conflicts that occur on a national level. Resource distribution, class struggles, globalization, and **modernization** within a particular state are the main contributing factors of this type of conflict, which is becoming more complex as societies become more modern and democratic. We also discuss the use of violence in large-scale conflict, particularly in terms of one-sided violence and armed conflict. Finally, we consider how the rise of democracy in the world influences large-scale conflict and its peaceful resolution.

DISCORDANT SOCIETIES

As is the case with interpersonal relations, conflicts within societies are caused by several immutable factors, such as the fight for resources and power, idealistic and ideological motives, and disputes over many new stakes. Societies evolve rapidly in the context of modernization and globalization, which also has an impact on conflict.

"Who Gets What, When, and How"

In the 1930s, British political scientist Harold D. Lasswell (1902–78) wrote that politics is essentially about "who gets what, when, and how," a phrase that was also used as the subtitle for one of his books (1950). Lasswell argued that politics is about the distribution of resources among people and that those with the most legitimate power to rule in society (i.e. the most **authority**) decide who gets what, when, and how.[1] Consequently, the powerful often get more than their share, while the people with little political influence get few resources. Canadian political scientist David Easton (b. 1917) was more precise when he later wrote that politics is about the authoritative allocation of values (1965). In other words, things that are valued in societies are often distributed among people through authority relationships. A power that is badly justified or unjustified is a weak power that is always subject to criticism and subversion. Because the distribution of valuable things in societies is bound to create serious feuds, especially when the survival and welfare of people are at stake, we can also say that politics is about conflict. Therefore, by large-scale societal conflict we mean conflicts regarding who gets what, when, and how in a given nation. Authority is a fundamental element in this distribution of wealth and status.

In a way, one can say that all national politics is about who gets the most food, the best clothes, and the biggest houses. Some societies display egalitarian distribution, meaning that these valuable objects are distributed relatively evenly among people. This is the case with archaic societies and communist regimes.[2] In other societies, including many ancient civilizations and modern poor countries, the majority of the population lives in squalor while a few extended families enjoy a luxurious lifestyle. Both ancient and modern Egypt are examples of this type of uneven distribution. Other countries, such as most modern-day Western democracies, favour a mixed distribution of revenues so that social unrest is kept to a minimum but people still have incentives to try to get rich.

These kinds of distributive arrangements are influenced by many variables: economic organization, the state of technology, culture, religion, history, etc. However, politics is also an important factor because political and constitutional provisions stipulate how many people have access to power and how much influence they each can expect to have. In a pure monarchical regime, such as Egypt under the pharaohs, only the ruler and a few important aristocrats had any say in the government of the kingdom. Most conflicts were kept under the table, and the most troublesome opposition leaders were probably eliminated before they could weaken the pharaoh's power.

In such relatively simple societies, the sharing of wealth was straightforward. Matters started to become complex as sources of wealth diversified, surpluses became more common and abundant, and new social categories began to claim their share. For example, when new sources of wealth enriched many families in the ancient Mediterranean world, it became necessary to extend social privileges in several kingdoms. Aristocratic monarchies, in which the aristocrats had significant power in their own right and did not depend solely on the rulers' good will, emerged. Some societies became truly aristocratic, with power and wealth equitably shared among several influential families or clans. Such was the case with most Greek city states, Rome, and the Germanic kingdoms that replaced Roman rule over most of Europe. Some societies, such as classical Athens, even experimented with forms of democracy (in which participation was restricted to free males born in the land).

In the Middle Ages, societies gained wealth primarily from agriculture but also from mining, forestry, crafts, trade, and plunder. Along with nobles and peasants, artisans, merchants, professionals, and clerks gradually emerged as contenders for resources. Furthermore, political systems were hopelessly mixed up as kings, emperors, feudal lords, the pope, and free cities all wanted to dominate the population. The kingdoms and estate of what is now Germany were particularly confusing because the authority of the German emperor often clashed with that of the pope, local kings and princes, and other kingdoms of Europe, such as Spain and France. The era was a long period of semi-anarchy, from which some forms of monarchical order gradually emerged.

The absolutist states that took shape in Western Europe in the sixteenth and seventeenth centuries (e.g. France, Great Britain, and Spain) were fraught with dissension between the monarch, aristocrats, bourgeois notables, and peasantry. However, by concentrating legal coercion in the hands of the state and stifling the private use of force, the establishment of these societies led to an impressive decline in violence. Later, representative democracy also had a positive effect on the pacification of Western societies.

The Industrializing State

Despite a decrease in violence, the modern state has been the locus of many serious conflicts. The most salient ones concern the inequalities among groups of individuals. For instance, conflicts between **social classes** (segments of the population divided by economic position) were very deep and often brutal in the nineteenth century. In such a class system, the lower classes tend to perform manual and subordinate tasks; the middle class is composed of supervisors, professionals, and self-employed businesspeople; and the upper class is made up of the owners and high executives of companies, as well as those with inherited wealth. The tensions between the classes were at their peak during this time, when the poor and exploited working class attempted—against the will of the other classes—to improve its living conditions. Several people thought that only a violent revolution could change things, while others preferred to use persuasion and influence to bring about change. This acute conflict between the classes can still be observed in many emerging economies and drives many social controversies.

In Western Europe, a number of social reforms were eventually implemented, especially at the turn of the century, in order to alleviate the problems of the working class. The contemporary **welfare state**, which offers basic educational and social services to all citizens, has been the most widespread answer to the contradictory demands of the social classes. Modern capitalist states have also been characterized by the spread of unionization in the twentieth century. Labour contracts have sometimes been bitterly negotiated, with employee strikes and other work stoppages being opposed by employers through strikebreaking and lockouts. However, unionization and strikes have been on the decline in many countries since the 1970s. Figure 3.1 illustrates that union membership and work stoppages in the United States have declined by approximately 65 per cent since World War II. In Canada, the number of hours lost to labour disputes has also strongly decreased since the 1970s (see Figure 3.2), a trend that can be found in all major developed states. The decline of union membership and industrial production, along with the rise of service jobs, are some of the factors that have led to fewer major workplace conflicts. However, it does not mean that all labour disputes and conflicts have disappeared.

Conflict between social classes in developed countries may not have the dramatic consequences that it had in the past, but it still occurs on innumerable planes: collective bargaining, labour unrest, divergences within organizations, grievances and appeals, differences over urban planning, demands for more and better social services, etc. The more employment categories that exist, the more sources of complaint and resentment there are to be found in society. Governments are constantly pressed to give more to one group so that their working conditions equal those of another. A greater cause for concern is that there are still many people who feel that they do not get their fair share and are excluded from the rest of society. Poor and sick people, immigrants, inhabitants of remote

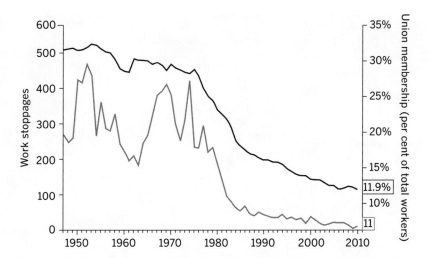

FIGURE 3.1 | UNION MEMBERSHIP AND WORK STOPPAGES IN THE UNITED STATES, 1947–2010

Source: Perry, M. J. (2011, 12 Feb.). The waning power of private unions in the U.S. *Carpe Diem.* Retrieved from www.benzinga.com/11/02/855664/the-waning-power-of-private-unions-in-the-u-s?quicktabs_1=2.

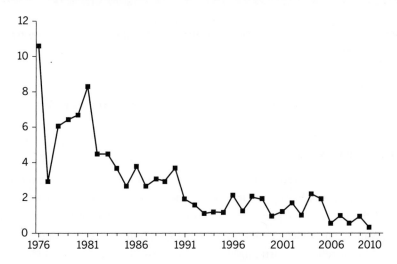

FIGURE 3.2 | ANNUAL AVERAGE HOURS LOST TO LABOUR DISPUTES PER EMPLOYED WORKER, CANADA, 1976–2010

Source: (2011) Indicators of Well-being in Canada, Work - Strikes and Lockouts, www4.hrsdc.gc.ca/.3ndic.1t.4r@-eng.jsp?iid=14. Human Resources and Skills Development Canada. Reproduced with the permission of the Minister of Public Works and Government Services Canada, 2012.

(Jean-François Rioux)

In October 2010 in France, massive crowds protested the government's plan to alter the retirement and pension funds system. Class conflicts still erupt in affluent countries, but they tend to be relatively peaceful.

regions, minority groups, and many women all have reasons to complain that the modern state does not fulfill all their needs.

Post-Industrial Demands

In the 1970s, American social scientist Ronald Inglehart (b. 1934) began studying the opinions and world views of Europeans and North Americans. He wanted to know if the social turmoil of the late 1960s—characterized by student revolts, demonstrations against the Vietnam War, and new ideological causes—was a symptom of a deeper transformation in the outlook of citizens of industrialized democracies (see Inglehart, 1990). Inglehart (1995) polled thousands of people in several rounds and observed that the attitudes of those born after World War II were significantly different from those of the previous generation. In general, the older citizens favoured traditional values such as economic development, hard work, national security, and family life, which Inglehart termed materialist values. However, the youths were more interested in individual rights, **social justice**, peace and disarmament, the emancipation of women, affirmation of minority groups, and the preservation of the natural environment. Inglehart referred to these values as post-materialist because they were not directly related to survival or the accumulation of wealth. The switch from one set of values to another was, according to him, a very profound historical change that helped to explain contemporary conflicts in liberal societies. He attributed this change in values to the fact that the older generation, having been raised in the uncertainty of the Great Depression and World War II, favoured more materialist values that protect jobs, income, and public safety. The younger generation, raised in an unprecedented period of steady growth and increasing liberty, preferred values that had more to do with personal growth and emancipation than materialist security, which they took for granted. Inglehart concluded that even the two oil shocks of 1974 and 1979 and the recessions of 1981–2 and the early 1990s did not affect this transformation.

Two other famous analysts of modern societies came to similar conclusions. Since the late 1960s, French sociologist Alain Touraine (b. 1925) has studied what is now called new social movements. First interested by the student movement, he turned his attention to pacifist, anti-nuclear, and women's groups, trying to prove that these organizations were profoundly changing the way political action was conducted in the West (Touraine, 1971, 1981). The new social movements offered direct participation in many new ways, some spontaneous and some more strategic to social categories that were previously excluded from politics. Well-known British sociologist Anthony Giddens (b. 1938) has also been interested in finding out how society is being reshaped by the actions of previously uninvolved groups of people and by new social categories (1984).

The work of Inglehart, Touraine, Giddens, and countless other theorists has been important in opening our eyes to the changes brought about by the baby boom generation, which altered public policy in many ways. From the emancipation of women and homosexual people to environmental movements and from animal rights to peace movements, there has been a profusion of new causes that reflect many fundamental transformations of our complex societies and bring more conflicts to life. Post-materialist values are rapidly spreading the world over, even in countries that have not reached the industrial and democratic stage. For example, the struggle for women's emancipation is now a quasi-universal movement.

While materialist values diminished in favour of those of the baby boomers, it has been observed since the 1980s that they have not disappeared in the West. The return of ideological conservatism may be an indication that post-materialistic ideas and behaviours are far from universally shared. Economic difficulties in affluent countries and the threat of terrorism are two major factors behind the perpetuation of materialistic values. Actually, some of the more romantic analyses of the 1960s look dated today. Politics has definitely changed; however, it would be far-fetched to state that all social movements are inevitably remaking politics in a socialist and revolutionary sense. We should not forget that social movements also include more right-wing issues, such as movements for the rights of firearms owners and the teaching of creationism. Furthermore, the followers of the baby boomers, the so-called Generation X and Generation Y cohorts, do not have the same values as their predecessors and may be more moderate.

When reflecting on new social movements, it is important to realize that political participation is slightly declining. The most obvious illustration of this trend is voter turnout, which has decreased slowly but steadily in most established democracies (except those where voting is compulsory, obviously) since the 1970s. The reasons for this change are hotly debated among political scientists and sociologists, with some blaming the lack of ideological options, others attributing it to voters' indifference or contentment, and still others pointing to the public's disappointment and cynicism. Since the 1990s, many social scientists have also lamented that participation in political parties, associations, and interest groups is also declining (Putnam, 2000).

One issue that has come on the horizon more recently is that Western societies must now integrate millions of immigrants and refugees who are not from the Western Christian tradition. Controversies about dress codes, freedom of speech, and access to public facilities abound. Some countries, such as Great Britain, have adopted a liberal, multi-ethnic approach to this question, while others, such as France, have preferred a republican integrative (or assimilationist) model. The results of both approaches have been mixed. Both countries have been affected by discrimination lawsuits, ethnic riots, mass peaceful protests, and bitter controversies. The integration of newcomers is a major conflict issue in Western societies, and its management and resolution require the input of interreligious dialogue and conflict resolution specialists.

Globalization, Modernization, and Westernization

The developing world is currently experiencing all the feuds related to modernization that Europe went through during the twentieth century: class conflicts, rapid urbanization, feuds between country and city, and rivalries among ethnic groups. At the same time, it faces post-industrial issues, such as the status of women, environmental protection, and the integration of minorities.

The problems of developing countries are compounded by the fact that their development and modernization were largely instigated and even enforced by other nations, largely through their colonization by European powers. Development was often influenced by the needs of the mother country rather than the needs of the developing country's own population. The difficulties of colonization and forced modernization translated into chaotic and violent political processes after independence. For example, the countries of Latin America were emancipated in the 1820s and 1830s, but they did not begin to see a truly peaceful democratic evolution until the 1980s. Asian countries gained their independence between the 1940s and the 1960s, while African nations did so in the late 1950s and early 1960s. The post-independence era in these two continents has been challenging because constitutional and economic arrangements had to be created and implemented and much of the population lived a precarious existence.

In many cases in the developing world, strongmen, military officers, or ideologues leading mass parties took power by force and imposed a model over the society. Barely legitimate governments ruling by repression, such as those in the Philippines and Indonesia, became the norm in the non-Western world. However, this situation was not limited to former Western colonies. Post-independence troubles were also observed in countries that were not colonized by a Western European power, such as those emerging from the Ottoman and Russian empires. Even countries that never knew direct foreign rule (e.g. Ethiopia, Thailand, and China) also encountered severe growing pains.

In recent years, many developing countries have democratized, or at least liberalized, to a certain extent. However, contemporary developing countries still exhibit many of the wrenching and violent conflicts about who gets what, when, and how that plagued European societies until recently. The worst off are usually called **failed states** (also referred to as failing or collapsed states) and have been much studied in the 1990s and 2000s to explain the major security problems of the post-Cold War world.[3] Failed states cannot maintain public order, extract sufficient fiscal resources, or provide adequate public services. They cannot protect their own citizens from violence nor can they enforce laws. They lack legitimacy, are plagued by political unrest and insurrections, and are constantly threatened by civil war. In Figure 3.3, the countries designated as being in critical condition are failed states.

THE INCREASING COMPLEXITY OF MAJOR SOCIETAL CONFLICTS

Like small-scale conflicts, major societal conflicts are also linked with one another in many ways, involve an ever-increasing number of participants, and, accordingly, have become

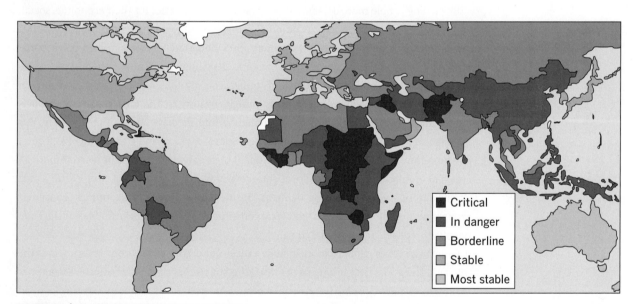

FIGURE 3.3 | UNSTABLE AND FAILED STATES
The journal *Foreign Policy*, in co-operation with The Fund for Peace, publishes an annual survey of state stability in the world. The index is based on a dozen indicators and ranks the countries according to their degree of stability.

Source: The Failed States Index 2011. (2011). *Foreign Policy*. Retrieved from www.foreignpolicy.com/articles/2011/06/17/2011_failed_states_index_interactive_map_and_rankings.

extremely complex. Again, the example of the environment comes to mind. The preservation of nature is an issue with many variables: economic development, technological innovation, business interest, political rights and freedoms, the common good, and social justice. One cannot try to resolve ecological problems without addressing these factors, such as the jobs that would be cut and created, the technology that should be developed (and paid for), the interest of firms, the rights of citizens to be consulted, and the interest of society at large. All these matters are interrelated. Modernization also creates an increasing number of conflict participants, as it constantly adds new social and economic categories of people in society. New industrial and commercial firms are created all the time, and new categories of workers and managers emerge.

Democratization also adds an element of complexity in the sense that it increases the interactions among issues and the number of participants that are involved. Political democracy is a much more complex system of government than monarchy or autocracy, regimes in which leaders have more opportunities to hide problems from the public, compartmentalize issues, and make decisions with limited consultation. Democracy sometimes looks like a never-ending rollercoaster ride of consultation, contestation, and negotiation. From the perspective of any one interest group, the process sometimes tends to inflate issues of "minor importance." The most obvious example is in urban planning, where decisions on development are sometimes postponed for decades because of opposition from local residents or from those advocating for the protection of the natural environment.

By making people more dependent on those in other societies for their economic, social, and cultural development, globalization also makes conflicts more complicated. In short, it links local and national issues with international ones and involves foreign participants in debates over national questions. Economic development is now largely attributable to decisions made in the boardrooms of foreign corporations, the parliaments of foreign capitals, and the households of countless foreign consumers. The intricacy of trade issues, for instance, is legendary and is compounded by intermediary levels of government. For instance, trade relations between the United States, Mexico, and Canada involve federal governments, state and provincial authorities, a regional organization (the North American Free Trade Agreement), and a global intergovernmental organization (the World Trade Organization). Add the lobbying by firms, business associations, trade unions, consumer groups, environmental activists, and local constituencies and you have an idea of the complexity of modern international trade.

Other aspects of globalization include culture and communication. Mass media, the Internet, and social networking have erased the boundaries of popular culture. Sometimes the wave of new cultural trends runs counter to traditional cultures, creating conflict between generations. However, when seeds of change are planted within a country, they can be nurtured and spread quickly through social media, making spontaneous demonstrations possible. These protests, in turn, are made available first-hand as cell phone videos are posted on YouTube or shared through distribution links. Therefore, the immediate dissemination of information also allows more people to become involved in conflicts.

The number of significant actors in modern societies has grown significantly in the twentieth century. This growth is primarily found in democracies because they generate major organized forces such as political parties, interest groups, trade unions, and mass media. The set of free associations that allow citizens to assemble in order to defend their interests and ideals is often called civil society. Civil society flourishes in modern democracy but is crushed by repressive regimes. However, many authoritarian regimes now tolerate a small civil society and some free media, a development that shows how the ideals of autonomy and expression are spreading in the world.

VIOLENT AND PEACEFUL TRANSFORMATIONS

In our discussion of political violence, we will focus on the two categories used by the Human Security Report Project (2011): one-sided violence and armed conflict. One-sided political violence occurs when a state or powerful insurgent group uses force to intimidate and punish potential opponents who are not organized as a fighting force. Therefore, most one-sided violence targets unarmed civilians. This type of violence includes police and military abuse, arbitrary control of dissent, massive imprisonment of opponents, ethnic cleansing, and massacres.

According to the Human Security Centre's *Human Security Brief 2006*, there was a slight increase in incidents of one-sided violence from 1989 to 2005. This increase has two causes. First, there is better reporting of abuse against citizens the world over. Second, there seem to have been more cases of one-sided violence perpetrated by non-state armed groups. This has been witnessed in the wars of the Democratic Republic of the Congo (DRC) and Sudan, where insurgent groups, militias, and other groups have been involved in countless massacres of unarmed people.

Despite the horrors associated with non-state one-sided violence, the violence engineered by governments is much more deadly due to the greater means of the state. Extreme manifestations of government violence were common in most parts of the world until recently. For example, the Roman, Mongol, and Ottoman empires routinely used massacres and other unspeakable cruelties to repress opposition to their rule. Political mass murder started to decrease in Europe in the eighteenth and nineteenth centuries but rose again in the twentieth, with the emergence of totalitarian regimes.[4] Political scientist Rudolph Rummel (1997) has estimated that there have been 170 million victims of genocides (mass murders of ethnic or religious groups), **politicides** (mass murders targeting people for their class position and/or political affiliation), and other **democides** (general term used for any mass murder) organized by states between 1900 and 1987 (see also Figure 3.4). With the end of the Cold War, there was a short increase in this type of violence, including the genocide in Rwanda and the massacres in Bosnia, Chechnya, Somalia, and Sudan.[5] Nevertheless, the general trend since the mid-2000s is a decrease in one-sided violence (see Figure 3.5).

Analysts usually divide armed conflict into three categories. **Low-intensity armed conflict** is defined as conflict that results in less than 1,000 deaths during the entire period of fighting.

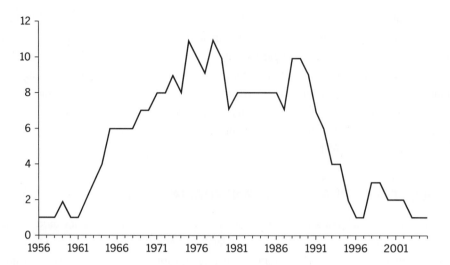

FIGURE 3.4 | NUMBER OF GENOCIDES AND POLITICIDES, 1956–2005
The number of genocides and politicides plummeted following the end of the Cold War, a trend similar to that of high-intensity civil conflicts.

Source: Human Security Brief 2006.

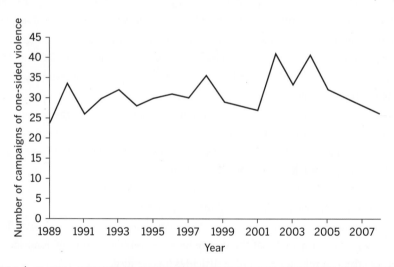

FIGURE 3.5 | GLOBAL TRENDS IN CAMPAIGNS OF ONE-SIDED VIOLENCE, 1989–2008

Source: Uppsala Conflict Data Program, Uppsala University, Sweden/Human Security Report Project, School for International Studies, Simon Fraser University, Vancouver, Canada.

Assassinations, acts of terrorism, coups d'état, riots, and feuds are usually assigned to this category. **Medium-intensity armed conflict** results in more than 1,000 casualties in total. This type usually includes revolts, insurrections, and large-scale terrorist acts. **High-intensity armed conflict**, also called warfare, results in more than 1,000 deaths per year of conflict. **Interstate** (or international) **war** and **intrastate** (or civil) **war** are high-intensity conflicts.

The total number of armed conflicts has increased since the late 1950s, following the decolonization movement in Africa and Asia, and remained high during the Cold War and its aftermath. According to the *Human Security Report*, all forms of armed conflicts declined for several years after 1992 but have increased slightly since the mid-2000s due to several conflicts in Muslim countries, many of which resulted from the "war on terror" orchestrated by the United States.[6] Armed conflicts have, however, become less deadly. The average number of people killed per conflict per year was 38,000 in 1950 and 600 in 2002, a decrease of 98 per cent (Human Security Centre, 2005, p. 2). These numbers include only deaths reported by political authorities. They do not include unreported or indirect casualties of war, the latter being suspected to be in the millions in a country such as the DRC.[7]

Most people think that political violence occurs primarily between authoritarian or imperialistic governments and resistance movements. Conflict studies tends to concentrate on state-related political violence because information on this type is more readily available and because this knowledge can help change the way certain countries are governed. However, there are many non-state armed conflicts waged between non-governmental groups. These conflicts can also be called community violence or communal conflict. Although some incidents of community violence, such as those occurring in remote areas of India or the DRC, are never reported, a true assessment of the reality of violent conflict must acknowledge the existence of this type of violence.

According to the Uppsala Project, over half of all armed conflicts in 2002 and 2003 were non-state (Human Security Centre, 2005, p. 70). Examples include interreligious clashes in India, Indonesia, Iraq, and Nigeria. Inter-ethnic violence in the DRC, Sudan, Myanmar, and India is very frequent. Many of these local community violent clashes are not widely reported in the media because they occur in remote areas and do not involve resources or other factors that would influence the interests of larger political bodies. Intercaste violence in India is another case in point. It has been argued that this community violence is largely a result of the state doing nothing to prevent it or fuelling it by tolerating and even aiding militia and vigilante groups. While it is true that some state violence is hidden and some community violence is state-induced, the existence of communal conflicts in a country does not automatically prove collusion between the state and one of the parties. It may be that the state is simply too weak to do anything about the conflict. The only positive aspects of this kind of violence are that 81 per cent of it lasts for less than a year and that it is usually responsible for a small proportion of battle deaths in larger conflicts (Human Security Report Project, 2011, pp. 175–176).

Although there have been increases in particular forms of political violence in the twentieth century, the total number of violent conflicts within nations has decreased. One reason for this change is the improvement in the welfare of states, which has had dramatic effects on conflict. In the Institute for Economics and Peace's *Global Peace Index 2011*, the Institute of Economics and Peace correlated the gross domestic product (GDP) per capita of various countries with the global peace index (GPI), which measures national peacefulness. As Figure 3.6 shows, the countries with the highest GDP have the lowest GPI; in other words, they are the most peaceful. The report also compares mean years of schooling, life expectancy, and infant mortality with the GPI. The data for these measures of welfare support the conclusion that the more developed a country is, the more peaceful it tends to be.

The links between welfare and peacefulness are numerous. One way to express them is to state that people are less likely to take up arms to improve their lot when their basic needs are assured. Also, people with even minimal wealth and property are bound to realize that using violence entails significant risks to their welfare. To most people, violence is not an attractive proposition. Most tend to prefer holding a modest job in a stable and peaceful society over gambling on possible gains from looting and conquest. In relatively wealthy soci-

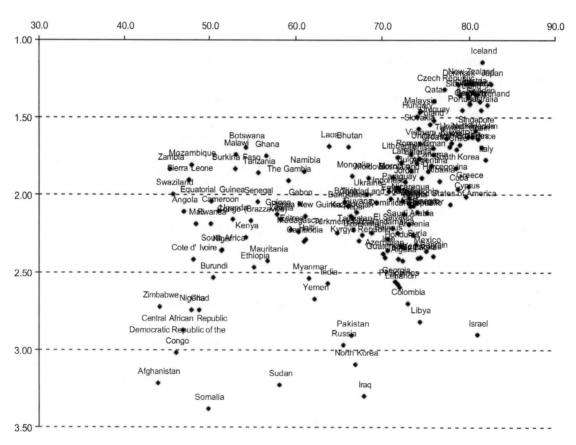

FIGURE 3.6 | LOG GDP PER CAPITA AGAINST OVERALL GPI SCORE

Source: Global Peace Index 2011 by The Institute for Economics & Peace.

eties, people believe that they can improve their lot by work and investment and that their children have a real chance to live even better lives than they do. People in such societies develop work skills and life habits that distance them from the rough life of the soldier. They are also more educated than people in developing societies, and many have more options for coping with an economic downturn. With education and economic security comes a tendency to have fewer children (which impacts the perception of the value of life), develop more sophisticated tastes and activities, and see violence as a poor alternative to enjoyment.

CONFLICT RESOLUTION AT THE NATIONAL LEVEL

Along with improvements in social welfare, the increase in conflict resolution processes has also contributed to the reduction of violence in large-scale conflicts. The main cause of this increase is the spread of democracy. In the 1960s and 1970s, the vast majority of countries were led by exclusionary autocratic or oligarchic regimes (see Figure 3.7). But things began to evolve in 1974–5, when Portugal, Spain, and Greece (the last three authoritarian regimes in Western Europe) shed their old ruling classes, organized free elections, and wrote new constitutions. The example was not lost on Latin America, and

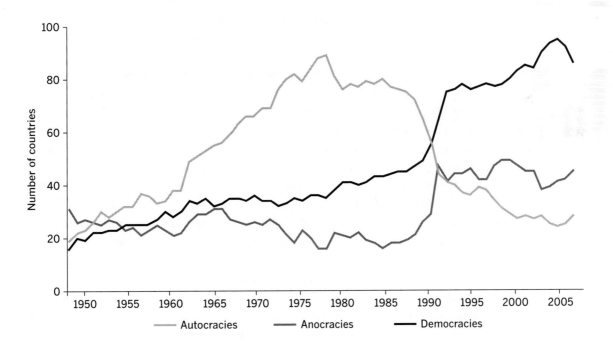

FIGURE 3.7 | GLOBAL REGIMES BY TYPE, 1945–2007

Source: Pate, A. (2010). Trends in democratization: A focus on minority rights. In J. Joseph Hewitt, J. Wikenfeld, and T. R. Gurr (Eds.), *Peace and conflict 2010: Executive summary*. College Park, MD: Center for International Development and Conflict Management, University of Maryland, p. 20.

progress in this region was surprisingly rapid and peaceful in the 1980s. In the span of one decade, almost all Latin American regimes moved from dictatorship to democracy (several were not completely free, but they at least allowed some free media, interest groups, and political parties). In effect, both the elites and the masses realized that authoritarianism, even under the form of "enlightened dictatorships," was not working. What has been called the third wave of democratization (Huntington, 1991) continued in the 1980s and 1990s with other spectacular cases such as the Philippines, Indonesia, Taiwan, Senegal, Ghana, Mali, and South Africa. In the early 1990s, the fall of the Communist bloc and the dismantlement of the Soviet Union added some new democracies to the world's total (Diamond, 2009).

The rise of democracy is evident in estimates made by the NGO Freedom House (Puddington, 2011, p. 35), which uses the categories of free, partly free, and not free to classify the countries of the world. A free country exhibits open political competition, respect for civil liberties, and independent media. A partly free country has limited respect for political rights and civil liberties and, as a result, often features corruption and ethnic and religious strife. Finally, a country that is not free lacks basic political rights and denies fundamental civil liberties. According to these definitions, Freedom House calculates that only 25 per cent of the world's countries were free in 1975, while over 40 per cent were not free and the rest partly free. In 2011, 45 per cent of the world's countries, accounting for nearly 43 per cent of the global population, are considered completely free. Only 24 per cent are not free, while 31 per cent are classified as partly free. The map in Figure 3.8 shows which countries are included in each category. While Freedom House warns that small setbacks for liberty have been observed for five consecutive years, recent events in Tunisia, Egypt, Yemen, Libya, and Syria may be the start of another wave of democratization. However, it is too early to tell.

The increase in the number of free countries raises the question of whether democracies resolve or create conflicts. Liberal democracy in itself usually does not resolve all the major conflicts of society. For instance, conflicts among small farmers, agricultural workers, and big landowners (which are fundamental realities of Latin America) have not been resolved magically with the introduction of universal suffrage. In developed countries, these conflicts have weakened mostly because industrialization has marginalized the rural world. However, democracy does allow for the peaceful expression of these conflicts and offers ways to alleviate and manage them, even if they have been hidden for a long time. For example, the grievances of Indigenous peoples in Latin American countries were muffled by generations of politicians until civic rights and free elections recently allowed them to express their demands and elect their representatives. New requests also surface with democratization. For instance, new demands from white-collar workers and the emerging middle classes are increasingly heard around the world. The link between democracy and peace is quite obvious in Figure 3.9, which shows that the most democratic countries are also the most peaceful. However, there are a few exceptions: some established democracies (India, Colombia, and Israel) are plagued by violence, while some authoritarian regimes (Qatar, the United Arab Emirates, and Kuwait) are peaceful.

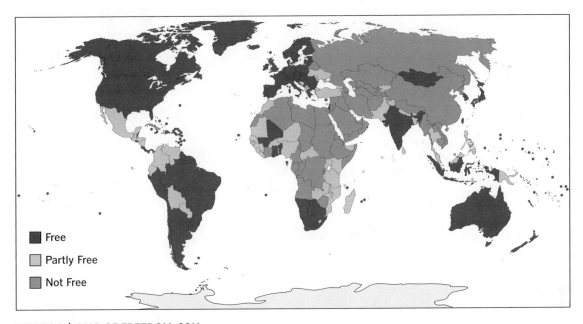

FIGURE 3.8 | MAP OF FREEDOM, 2011

Source: "Freedom in the World 2011," www.freedomhouse.org.

That said, democratization remains an uneven and shaky process for three reasons. First, democracies are still often dominated by affluent, urban, and educated men. Therefore, women, minorities, youths, the poor, and the elderly may have problems accessing the political system and having their demands taken into consideration. Second, some countries experience fallback in their evolution. Russia, for example, developed rapidly as a parliamentary democracy in the early 1990s but reverted to a form of authoritarianism under the leadership of Vladimir Putin in the 2000s. Many countries see some gains of democratization being threatened and more may be to come, especially if unrest persists and governments respond by curtailing liberties or if opportunistic leaders surfing on popular dissatisfaction create autocratic regimes. However, for the moment, the course of the current democratic counterwave is still relatively slow and is not a massive trend. Third, in instances where there are strong historical ethnic or religious groups, democracy can be completely subverted if the most powerful group is assured victory. This was the case in the early 1990s in Yugoslavia, where violent conflict occurred in the wake of nationalistic governments pushing an exclusionary agenda.

Along with democratization comes the extension of the rule of law around the world. As authoritarian regimes are toppled, people write constitutions, vote for new laws, and upgrade their judicial systems. In many countries, individuals and groups are now free to undertake legal action to protect their rights. However, it must be said that access to the legal system is difficult. The costs of litigation are very high in all parts of the world,

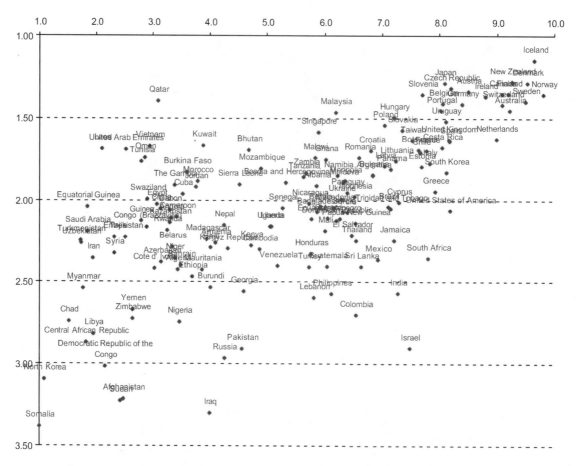

FIGURE 3.9 | POLITICAL DEMOCRACY INDEX AGAINST OVERALL GPI SCORE

Source: Global Peace Index 2011 by The Institute for Economics & Peace.

and the courts often experience a large backlog of cases. Furthermore, in poor countries, lawyers and judges frequently do not have required competencies and are sometimes corrupt. Although litigants may be helped by third parties such as national and foreign NGOs, the matter of accessing the legal system will persist for a long time.

The democratization of societies has also led to evolution in labour relations. Parties have endorsed some of the demands of the working classes, and several countries have enacted legislation that protects workers' rights. Trade unions have adopted pro-negotiation positions in their dealings with the government and firms and have started to explore new areas of contention. For instance, workers in Latin America now add demands about working hours, maternity leave, and health and safety regulations to the more traditional petitions about better wages. However, a lot remains to be done in the new industrialized countries, where the working class is still subjected to harsh conditions.

Besides the institutionalized contests of modern democracies, the modern world has witnessed the creation of new non-violent tactics and instruments (see Chapter 16). The opposition of Mahatma Gandhi (1869–1948) to segregation and British rule in South Africa and India has been celebrated the world over as a milestone in the development of peaceful protest. The famous leader is credited with many innovative actions, such as protest marches and demonstrations, petitions and letter-writing, non-collaboration, boycotts, fasts, and sit-ins, that made colonial life difficult for the British and instilled hope and courage among Indians.[8] Following the example of Gandhi and beginning in the 1960s, non-violent forms of protest became very significant in Western democracies. For instance, desegregation in the southern United States and the civil rights movement were mostly peaceful, despite many violent incidents. Although a part of the movement advocated the use of force and several spontaneous uprisings took place in 1966–7, most African Americans, led by religious figures such as Reverend Martin Luther King, Jr (1929–68), were convinced that political participation and non-violent protest could achieve their objective rapidly and peacefully. During the same period, the opposition to the Vietnam War was

(AP Photo/Reportagebild)

On 26 August 1980, union leader Lech Walesa shows his fellow workers the contract that he had just negotiated with the Polish government. This event was not lost on other Eastern Europeans, who understood that communist rule could be weakened by peaceful mass protests.

also mostly non-violent. Many draftees chose to fight political and legal battles regarding their conscription or to leave the country rather than serve in the war. Concerned citizens and disillusioned veterans staged protest marches, sit-ins, and rock concerts in order to advocate the US withdrawal. They petitioned politicians and became more active, usually in the Democratic Party. Eventually, the opposition to the war became strong enough to convince the politicians to bring the troops back home.

Although non-violent protest is facilitated in the context of lawful societies, such actions have also been conducted in the world's authoritarian regimes. For example, the peaceful strikes and protests spearheaded by union leader Lech Walesa (b. 1943) considerably weakened the legitimacy of the Polish communist government and contributed to its downfall. When institutionalized political contests are impossible and violence is not favoured, non-violent protest becomes a vital alternative. The past half century has been characterized by the peaceful expression and resolution of many major conflicts in the world.

In the case of pre-democratic violent insurrections, it should be noted that many of these conflicts are now dealt with through conflict resolution processes that can involve players from outside the country—the United Nations, other international organizations, NGOs, or the **good offices** of global leaders (see Chapter 12). Negotiation and mediation are particularly important in moving from violent conflict to ceasefire and the establishment or improvement of democratic institutions.

CONCLUSION

The general verdict about large-scale societal conflict is that it seems to be growing as countries are confronted with the important and irreversible changes caused by modernization and globalization. However, violent political and social domestic conflict has been decreasing in most of its manifestations for a long time. The most remarkable thing about the contemporary world is that many historic and fundamental changes, such as **democratic transitions**, political and economic liberalization, the marginalization of traditional elites and institutions, and the affirmation of many groups and classes, have occurred in a relatively peaceful manner. Obviously, there are exceptions to this trend, as some countries still experience more than their share of riots, insurrections, and civil wars. To state that violent conflict is decreasing historically should not lead us to minimize the suffering endured by people in these regrettable situations but help us to assess the real-world situation and the possibility of better things to come.

In terms of large-scale conflict resolution, the rise in democracy has played a major role in the growth of adjudication; the use of elections, referendums, and parliamentary battles; and the development of new third-party mechanisms (arbitration, mediation, and facilitation). The pace of innovation is slow and uneven, but the emergence of peaceful conflict management and resolution mechanisms is a significant global trend.

DISCUSSION QUESTIONS

1. What are the major differences between social conflicts in older democracies and those in newer democracies?

2. Describe Inglehart's two types of values. Which type do you think is prevalent in the world today? Give reasons to support your answer.

3. Is it likely that the size and duration of violent conflicts will continue to diminish? Why or why not?

4. Which institutions are best suited to deal with social conflict in a constructive and creative way? How could they be improved?

NOTES

1. By legitimacy, we mean the justification for power that accepts that some people make decisions in the name of others. German sociologist Max Weber (1997) identified three types of legitimacy: traditional legitimacy is based on history, legends, and religion; charismatic legitimacy is a rare form based on the impressive personality of the leader; and rational-legal legitimacy is based on reason and law. According to Weber, the third type is the modern form of legitimacy.

2. By archaic societies, we mean the hunter-gatherer, nomadic, or semi-nomadic types of societies that are now fairly rare in the world.

3. Scholars such as I. William Zartman (1995b) have used the term *collapsed states* as a synonym of failed states, while others see it as an extreme form of failed states (see Rotberg, 2003). We prefer the latter usage in this book.

4. In a totalitarian regime, the state and/or the governing party imposes total control over society. Free associations of people are banned and crushed, and individual rights are non-existent. Examples are Hitler's Germany, Stalin's Russia, and Mao Tse Tung's China.

5. There has been much controversy about whether the Sudanese case is a genocide.

6. The Stockholm International Peace Research Institute (SIPRI) also confirms that the sum of major armed conflicts has not declined significantly in the 2000s. Since 2001, the number has been between 14 and 18 per year. See www.sipri.org/yearbook/2011/02/02A.

7. Data regarding indirect casualties—primarily derived from rough estimates of pre-war populations and fertility and mortality rates—are notoriously unreliable. Basically, analysts take the population numbers before the war in question and try to evaluate the replacement rate (births minus deaths). Then, they calculate how many people should be in the country at a certain time if there had been no war and subtract the number of actual people remaining after the war. The difference represents the number of indirect casualties. A major problem with this formula is that, in a case such as the DRC, nobody knows the exact population of the country before or after the war. Fertility rates before and during conflicts are also hard to evaluate.

8. Although India has since been at war with Pakistan and violence is a daily part of Indian life, the heritage of Gandhi still exists. India is an extremely complex society of many languages, religions, cultures, castes, classes, regions, and ideologies. The remarkable fact is that this enormous country, through a combination of electoral contests, political arrangements, and peaceful protests, has been able to manage and settle many major disputes and conflicts without major political repression.

4 | INTERNATIONAL CONFLICT

CHAPTER OBJECTIVES

This chapter will help you develop an understanding of the

- traditional sources of conflict among societies, such as the quests for territory, resources, and power;

- new sources of conflict created by many economic, technological, and social developments;

- effect of globalization on the increase of international conflicts;

- role of connections among various interests and players on the complexity of international conflicts;

- many different actors exercising influence in the world today;

- gradual decrease of armed conflict in the context of international relations;

- factors that contribute to the decrease in violence; and

- use of processes other than violence to resolve many international conflicts.

INTRODUCTION

International conflict refers to conflicts involving two or more states (known as interstate conflict), as well as conflicts involving organizations located in different countries (known as **transnational conflicts**). In this chapter, we discuss the former first but devote much attention to the latter, which are growing under globalization. While international conflicts have been and continue to be caused by traditional rivalries and desires for territory, resources, and power, modern developments have created new sources. We examine both groups of causes, as well as the impact of globalization on this type of conflict. We also continue our discussion of trends within the different levels of conflict and find that, as with small group, interpersonal, and large-scale conflict, international conflict has become more complex and interconnected and involves more participants. The decline in violence is also found in the various forms of international conflict, as is an expanding supply of conflict resolution processes.

A WORLD OF CONFLICTS

The Struggle for Resources and Power

Currently, there is great variety in international conflict. Some of these conflicts, such as those over territory, resources, and power, are caused by national rivalries. Countries are still competing with each other (sometimes violently) in order to become more prosperous, more powerful, and more prestigious. It is commonly assumed that great power rivalry is the essence of world politics and that large countries will continue to compete against each other, leading to conflicts and wars. While there are reasons to think that nations could manage their conflicts more peacefully in the future, it is impossible to deny that rivalries among states remain an important source of conflict in the international system.

Traditionally, states have often fought for territory, which can take many forms. It can be the acquisition of an economically valuable region or a piece of land that has military value. The establishment of borders among states has often been combative in the past, especially when there were no natural barriers and when populations were sparse. Access to waterways and to the sea has also been contentious. In many cases, governments have quarrelled over distant colonies and client states. Today, most borders are set, but there are still major territorial controversies, such as the Kashmir issue between India and Pakistan, the border between Eritrea and Ethiopia, and the question of the borders of Israel and Palestine.

Resources are another object of controversy among states. In history, human societies have coveted rich agricultural land, mineral deposits, fishing banks, and petroleum reserves. Many times, the resource issue translates as a territorial dispute among rival neighbours. In other cases, states compete over the control of resources located in other regions of the world. Such has been the situation with gold, diamonds, oil, copper, uranium, and rare strategic minerals, the supply of which is always coveted by foreign firms and governments.

(AP Photo/K.M. Chaudary)

India and Pakistan have been in conflict over many issues since the partition of 1947. Their rivalry for territory, influence, and honour is symbolized in the ritualistic parading of Pakistani (left) and Indian border guards at a border post near Lahore.

In order to acquire what they need and to ensure their own survival against rivals, states try to influence the decisions of other states, notably their neighbours. In some cases, they try to dominate the international system. According to their capabilities, states may become great powers, regional powers, or local powers. The struggle for power is an important part of international rivalries, although it may not have the importance that "realists" accord it (see Chapter 8).

While trying to obtain riches and territories, states usually also instill fear in other states. Fear in itself is a cause of armed conflict when states conclude that they have no other option than to use force to resist conquest or subjugation. According to many analysts, states are constantly in a **security dilemma** (Herz, 1951): they do not want to appear too weak in the eyes of potential rivals, but they worry that high defence preparedness may lead other states to increase their own military resources in turn. This process has often lead to costly and dangerous arms races, which may add an ingredient of instability in international crises.[1]

Rivalries over power and other goals tend to pit coalitions of states against each other. During the Cold War, the United States formed a large coalition against the Soviet Union and its allies (see Figure 4.1). This conflict ended in the early 1990s, but large coalitions still

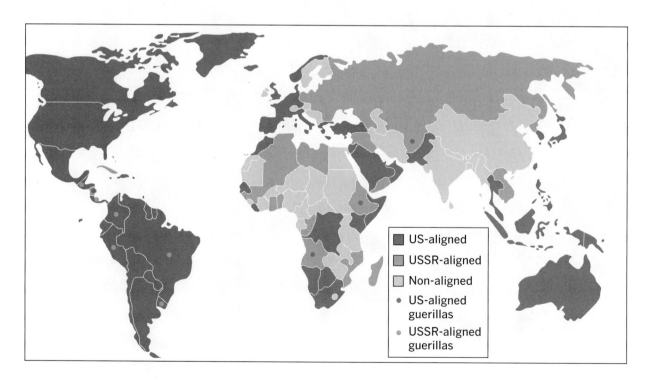

FIGURE 4.1 | COLD WAR ALIGNMENTS, c. 1980

Source: www.essentialhumanities.net/his5.php.

BOX 4.1 | REPRESENTING THE ECONOMIC DIFFERENCES IN THE WORLD

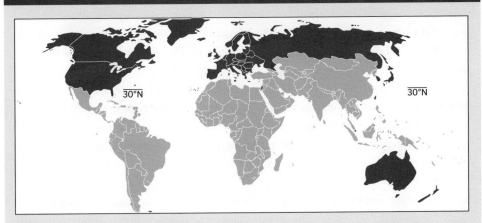

FIGURE A | NORTH–SOUTH DIVIDE

Source: World Poverty and Human Rights: wphr.org/2010/tessa-regis/government-accountability-in-developing-nations/.

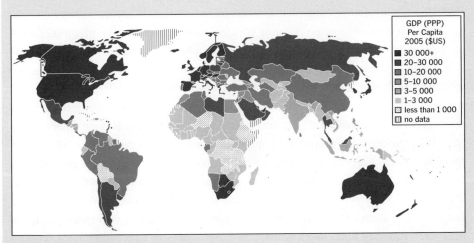

FIGURE B | GDP PER CAPITA, 2005

Source: mapsof.net.

These maps provide two methods of presenting the economic differences among countries. Figure A illustrates the North–South divide. Because most of the world's rich countries are located in the north and most of the poor ones are in the south, this distinction is frequently used. However, it obscures the vast differences of wealth among developing countries and suggests that there is no "middle class" in the international system. By representing each country's GDP per capita, Figure B shows a more nuanced picture of the international system.

exist on many other topics, including economic issues related to development, trade, and monetary management. For example, within the United Nations (UN), developing countries tend to vote together on issues of trade and development and on some political subjects, such as the Israeli–Palestinian conflict. The Western democratic powers tend to collectively defend their interests through the North Atlantic Treaty Organization (NATO) and the Organisation for Economic Co-operation and Development (OECD).

International rivalries are also caused by other interests and desires of leaders and populations. Questions of honour and reputation and the quest for fame and glory have often pitted societies against each other. These ideals may sound trivial compared to power and resources, but they are nonetheless important. For instance, the intense emotions that pull people into wars often find their source and justification in the "tarnished honour" of the nation, the humiliations endured at the hands of despised rivals, the need to measure up to ancestors, and the eternal recognition and admiration that warriors enjoy for their feats. Although the language of honour and glory may have somewhat diminished in the West, political leaders are still interested in leaving an honourable legacy and citizens still consider the consequences of their actions on their self-esteem and in light of the judgment of others.

Ideologies add another dimension to international conflict. While the current international system is heterogeneous in terms of values, some systems of the past were homogeneous. In other words, the main participants competed against each other but did not disagree on how the game should be played. This was the case with the Greek city states of the fifth century BCE and the European monarchies of the eighteenth century. However, fundamental disagreements appeared at the time of the American and French revolutions, creating doubts about colonial rule, imperialism, and monarchism (among other things). Since then, the world has been divided by ideologies such as **nationalism**, liberalism, communism, and fascism, which have each proclaimed their superiority as the guiding principle that should rule international affairs. For instance, the Cold War was not only an illustration of power politics but also an example of the clash of values on the international level. In the contemporary world, communism and fascism may have receded in importance (even though China, North Korea, and Cuba remind us that communism is still a factor), but anti-imperialist and Islamist doctrines are important ideas that influence many societies. Given the overwhelming power of European nations and empires through the colonial era and the dominating economic and political power of the United States, there are currently strong anti-Western ideologies at play, leading to some deep-rooted conflict.

Religion is also a factor in international conflict. Since the treaties of Westphalia in 1648, church and state have become gradually separated, meaning that the latter should not be controlled by any particular religion and that people should be allowed to practise their faith without state interference. However, religion is now playing a bigger role in state affairs, with some arguing that states in which a particular religion is in the majority should be subject to certain laws, principles, and customs of that faith. Some of these advocates use violence to support what they believe to be a higher calling.

The Emergence of New Contentious Issues

International relations have never been as extensive as they are in the early twenty-first century. The world is currently a complex system of interactions among a growing number of participants, ranging from diplomatic meetings to personal links for business, tourism, or education. This globalization is often presented as a new phenomenon; however, exchanges among nations have been expanding since the Middle Ages. In the nineteenth century, the Industrial Revolution, colonialism, communications, and transportation further increased world interdependence. From 1914 to 1950, the two world wars, economic recession, and totalitarianism stopped the trend, but it resumed in the 1950s and has continued ever since. Although globalization has been a continuing and growing presence in international relations, the term is controversial. For some, it represents a greater sense of connection and is therefore positive. Others feel that globalization signifies the Americanization of the globe, the dominance of multinational corporations, and the homogenization of culture. Whichever way you look at globalization, the increased interaction between nations has created conflict.

As we saw earlier, international conflicts can be divided into two categories: interstate conflicts and transnational conflicts. The former concern conflicts between sovereign states, while the latter include those involving non-state groups of people located in different countries. For example, a quarrel between two states over a borderline is an interstate conflict, while a disagreement between two industrial firms in different countries over patent rights is a transnational conflict. However, some conflicts have both components. For example, the 2006 war in Lebanon involved the states of Israel, Lebanon, and the Israeli-occupied territories and non-state entities such as Hezbollah and the Palestinian Authority. Another example is a large-scale commercial conflict such as that between Canada and the United States in the early 2000s over softwood lumber tariffs, which involved the two federal governments, lumber and construction industries, and state and provincial politicians.

In today's world, the sources of international conflict are not limited to the traditional issues that we have discussed. Issues such as the environment, human rights, democracy, and the emancipation of women take more and more space on the international agenda. Every activity undertaken by contemporary democratic governments involves regular international exchanges to improve the performance of the activity and to reconcile diverging points of view among countries. Table 4.1 lists several sources of conflict among nations. While the evolution of the world has created new causes for strife, the old causes of disputes have not necessarily disappeared.

In this increasingly interdependent world, it is not surprising that opportunities for conflict are more numerous. Three things deserve to be mentioned, however. First, international relations are not only composed of what political scientists used to call high politics, or contests about power and security. High politics account for a small part of international relations, albeit still a crucial and sensitive one. Most intergovernmental disputes are about issues of trade liberalization, foreign investment, environmental protection, development

TABLE 4.1 | SOURCES OF CONFLICT

Age-Old Sources of Conflict	Modern Sources of Conflict (sixteenth century, extending to the twentieth)	Recent Sources of Conflict (emerging in the twentieth century and extending to the twenty-first)
• Power and domination	• Ideology	• Women's rights
• Resources	• Human rights	• Environmental protection
• Territory and population	• Trade	• Humanitarian aid
• Religion	• Technical regulations	• Development assistance
• Honour	• Technological innovation and diffusion	• Mass migrations and immigratiion
• Glory and fame		• Democratic governance
	• Arms control and arms transfers	• Polar, space, and underwater exploration

aid, and human rights. Second, conflicts among governments constitute a diminishing part of international relations as the private exchanges between firms, associations, and individuals increase. Thus, when we say that international conflicts are more numerous, we refer to the large number of differences of views that do not threaten international peace and security. Finally, the overwhelming majority of relations at the international level are peaceful, ordered, and legal. Despite the association that many people make between international affairs and violence (such as in war, terrorism, military interventions, etc.) and the fact that international violence and chaos receive a great deal of media coverage, most international relations do not involve violence or even the threat of it. Instead, they are conducted according to norms prescribed by international treaties and institutions. Many international relations are performed by bureaucracies following national and international law and custom, using routine procedures. Of course, not all foreign relations are co-operative and cordial. Many interactions are characterized by power rivalries, domination, exploitation, and conflict. Resentment, envy, and hatred are widespread. However, the use of force is relatively rare in world affairs and, as we discuss later in this chapter, is slowly decreasing.

THE GROWING COMPLEXITY OF INTERNATIONAL CONFLICTS

A Worldwide Web of Interdependent Issues

Along with the number of international issues, the connections between them are also growing. Problems that confront nations and people can rarely be separated from an array of other difficulties. Regional problems have repercussions on global issues. Initiatives from states and groups of people have consequences that are difficult to foresee. In this section, we focus on two significant examples—global warming and population migration—to illustrate the complexity of intertwined concerns and interests involved in modern international conflicts.[2]

For decades, scientists have warned that the earth's climate is rapidly getting warmer. Although the exact role of humankind in this trend is difficult to evaluate precisely, there is a great deal of evidence that carbon dioxide emissions from industrial activities are responsible for a large part of this change. However, many industries that emit carbon dioxide resist a curtailment of their activities, as do a portion of workers in the automobile and petroleum industries. Public opinion seems more and more interested in fighting climate change, but there are doubts that the affluent consumers in rich countries are really ready to sacrifice their material comfort for a possible slowdown of temperature increase. The issue of climate change is intimately related to the prosperity of the industrialized world, but it also affects developing nations. In international meetings about the greenhouse effect, the latter usually oppose measures to restrict carbon dioxide emissions so as not to hinder their economic development. They believe that the main emitters of carbon dioxide (i.e. developed nations; see Table 4.2) should reduce their fossil fuel consumption, spend more money on pollution control systems and new energy sources, and make this technology available to the developing world.

The issue of climate change has been an important source of conflict between rich and poor countries since the 1980s. Basically, the question is how to foster economic development without damaging the environment and depleting resources. Finding an answer is a complex undertaking that requires considering several connected topics, such as industry, labour, democracy, social welfare, human rights, species preservation, lifestyle, and transportation.

Other complex and interdependent issues are involved in population migrations. Migrations have always existed, but in the modern world they occur constantly and on a large scale. The purpose of population migrations is to seek a better life. They can happen suddenly and put thousands of people on migratory paths, such as in the cases of wars, natural disasters, and famines (which often involve both drought and conflict).

Migrations are often the results of conflicts, but they are also the cause of several conflicts in themselves. For instance, conflicts can occur between refugees in camps, between migrants and local authorities, and between populations that had never been in contact with one another before. Migrations raise issues of criminality and terrorism, multiple citizenships and divided loyalties, economic development, employability, disease transmission, and so on. Together with the migrants themselves, massive migrations to developed countries such as the United States and Canada involve national and local governments, international organizations such as the United Nations High Commissioner for Refugees (UNHCR) and the World Health Organization (WHO), humanitarian organizations such as CARE and OXFAM, diaspora groups, business firms, trade unions, religious organizations, the media, and the general public. Each party has a specific perspective on migrations—especially the fundamental issue of how to protect the migrants and offer them new opportunities without harming the host population—which is influenced by a mixture of self-interest, ideology, and compassion. Conflicts also arise when migrations flow in reverse. When people return to homes that are occupied by others or find their positions in society taken by others, they demand restoration out of a **sense of justice**. Some who fled for safety in war and are denied the right to return live in limbo as refugees. One of the most intractable examples of the latter is Palestinians who left Israel in 1948 and wish to go back. The implications for all parties are enormous.

TABLE 4.2 | TRENDS IN CARBON DIOXIDE EMISSIONS IN SELECT DEVELOPED AND DEVELOPING COUNTRIES, 1990–2010[1]

	1990	1995	2000	2005	2010
Developed Countries					
Australia	0.27	0.30	0.36	0.41	0.40
Canada	0.45	0.48	0.55	0.57	0.54
France	0.39	0.39	0.41	0.41	0.37
Germany	1.02	0.92	0.87	0.85	0.83
Great Britain	0.59	0.55	0.54	0.55	0.50
Italy	0.42	0.44	0.46	0.48	0.41
Japan	1.16	1.25	1.27	1.31	1.16
Netherlands	0.16	0.17	0.17	0.18	0.18
Poland	0.31	0.32	0.29	0.31	0.32
Russian Federation	2.44	1.75	1.66	1.72	1.75
Spain	0.23	0.25	0.31	0.36	0.29
Ukraine	0.77	0.45	0.35	0.34	0.31
United States	4.99	5.26	5.87	5.93	5.25
Developing Countries					
Brazil	0.22	0.27	0.34	0.36	0.43
China	2.51	3.52	3.56	5.85	8.94
India	0.66	0.87	1.06	1.29	1.84
Indonesia	0.16	0.21	0.29	0.36	0.46
Iran	0.20	0.28	0.34	0.45	0.40
Mexico	0.31	0.33	0.38	0.42	0.43
Saudi Arabia	0.16	0.21	0.26	0.32	0.43
South Africa	0.27	0.29	0.31	0.36	0.38
South Korea	0.25	0.40	0.45	0.50	0.59
Taiwan	0.13	0.17	0.23	0.27	0.27
Thailand	0.09	0.16	0.17	0.23	0.24

1. Unit: billion metric tonnes of carbon dioxide.

Source: Olivier, J. G. J., Janssens-Maenhout, G., Peters, J. A. H. W, & Wilson, J. (2011). *Long-term trend in global CO2 emissions: 2011 report*. The Hague, Netherlands: PBL Netherlands Environmental Assessment Agency, p. 33. Retrieved from http://edgar.jrc.ec.europa.eu/news_docs/CO2%20Mondiaal_%20webdef_19sept.pdf.

The Crowded World Stage

There has been spectacular growth in the involvement of new and different actors in world conflicts. To return to one of our previous examples, the issue of climate change involves many significant actors who have a stake in the matter. As mentioned in the last section, both developed and developing countries play an important role. International organizations of states are also interested parties, as are large industrial firms, trade unions, and the governments that represent regions where carbon dioxide is produced. Interest groups, the media, scientific associations, and concerned citizens also want a say in the decision-making. The political leaders, industrialists, and interests groups of the developing world as well as their young populations that aspire to a better future are significant actors as well.

This example shows how many international actors there are in the system today. Table 4.3 also illustrates the diverse groups that can, to varying degrees, be involved in international conflicts. States form the first of these groups. For many people, states are less interesting and significant than some of the new actors, such as the electronic media. However, many things have changed about states. For one thing, there are more independent states now than at any other time in history.[3] Since World War II and especially following the fall of the British, French, and Russian empires, the number of states has more than doubled. In 2011, there were 204 states in the international system, each with rights and prerogatives guaranteed by international law and usages. For instance, a state can have diplomatic representation in as many foreign states and international organizations as it wants. This position allows a state to express its recriminations, hopes, and demands, alone or in coalitions. Other states are bound by law and tradition to listen to and acknowledge these assertions, and they may have to negotiate agreements devoted to resolving contentious issues. These international debates are reported and sometimes amplified by the media, which means that conflict among states can be high on the agenda of policy-makers and citizens.

TABLE 4.3 | THE EXTENDED FIELD OF INTERNATIONAL ACTORS IN THE
TWENTY-FIRST CENTURY

Actors	Examples
• States	• United States, China, Canada
• Sub-national governments (federated states, regions, large cities	• Quebec, Catalonia, New York City
• Large sub-national institutions	• US Congress, US Federal Reserve
• Intergovernmental organizations (IGOs)	• United Nations, European Union, NATO
• International non-governmental organizations (INGOs)	• Greenpeace, Amnesty International, International Committee of the Red Cross
• Transnational organizations	• Exxon, the Catholic Church, al-Qaeda
• Public figures	• Bono, George Soros, the Dalai Lama, Al Gore
• Individual citizens	• You and me

(AP Photo/Karsten Thielker)

In May 1994, the Benaco refugee camp in Tanzania became the largest refugee camp in the world, housing more than 300,000 Rwandans escaping the genocide in their country. Refugee movements in the modern world result in a great deal of sufferance and conflicts, but they also save countless lives.

Another modern reality is that regional and local governmental entities want to play a role in foreign affairs. The cases of Catalonia in Spain, Quebec in Canada, and the regions of Belgium represent attempts by culturally different areas and federated states to assert their right to be heard in matters that directly concern their cultural and educational development. A related trend is the increasing involvement of major cities in foreign relations. Other subnational governmental actors that are not controlled by the executive can also be influential in world affairs. Such groups are mostly found in the most powerful countries. The US Congress, for example, is often an international actor in its own right, especially when it opposes the president on issues of foreign policy, defence appropriations, or trade liberalization. Central banks, which are independent from the executive in most capitalist states, are also very influential in world affairs because they determine interest rates and expand or limit the money supply.

To states and governments, we must add the growing number of **intergovernmental organizations (IGOs)**, such as the UN and its family of agencies. IGOs are associations of states based on a treaty and managed by plenary meetings, an executive, and a bureaucracy. The first IGO was created in the 1820s; there are currently hundreds of them (see Figure 4.2). Some IGOs have a global membership (e.g. the UN; see Table 4.4), while others have a regional outlook (e.g. the European Union) or a sub-regional or even bilateral membership (e.g. the International Joint Commission between the United States and Canada). Although the public is more familiar with the large multi-purpose institutions, such as the UN or the EU, most IGOs are specialized and many are single-issue outfits. They provide nations with negotiation chambers for such issues as trade, industrial development, natural resources management, and technical and scientific co-operation.

Since these associations of states are often dominated by the most powerful, they might not qualify as a true international actor but simply as an instrument for states. However, because states are usually divided over most issues, IGOs occasionally take on a life of their own and create initiatives to help remedy the problems that confront states. For example, the UN, through the conflict resolution efforts of its secretary-general, is sometimes seen as an international actor. The importance of IGOs in international politics is best exemplified by the EU, which (in effect) governs the trade, monetary relations, agricultural policies, norms and standards, and large aspects of the economic policies of its member states.

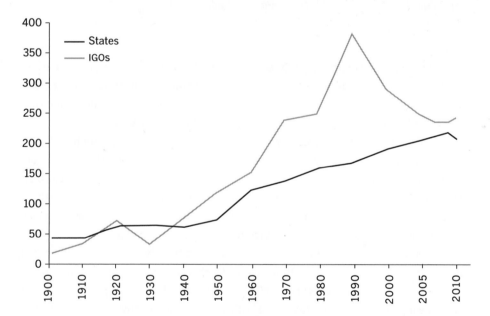

FIGURE 4.2 | NUMBER OF STATES AND IGOS IN THE INTERNATIONAL SYSTEM SINCE 1900

Since 1900, the number of independent states has increased dramatically, and that growth accelerated especially after World War II, when the decolonization movement began. But note that the number of intergovernmental organizations has grown even more rapidly in this period, declining only since the late 1980s, when a number of formerly independent IGOs began to merge with one another.

Source: The Yearbook of International Organizations, edited by Union of International Associations.

TABLE 4.4 | INCREASE IN THE NUMBER OF MEMBER STATES OF THE UNITED NATIONS

Year	Number of Member States
1945	51
1950	60
1955	76
1960	99
1965	117
1970	127
1975	144
1980	154
1985	159
1990	159
1995	185
2000	189
2005	192
2010	192

Source: Based on information from www.un.org/en/members/growth.shtml.

The international system is also characterized by the growing involvement of associations of people, or **international non-governmental organizations (INGOs)**. These private organizations are created mostly to serve the interests of their members, but they are also involved in the promotion of altruistic global objectives. Well-known examples of this type of organization are Greenpeace, the Sierra Club, Amnesty International, Human Rights Watch, the International Committee of the Red Cross (ICRC),[4] and Doctors Without Borders. But there are thousands of INGOs (see Figure 4.3), including large global ones that undertake several activities (such as international trade unions), more specialized global organizations (such as scientific associations), and regional associations (such as those existing in Europe). INGOs provide unique services that states do not perform in the international system. The ICRC, for example, is primarily known as a provider of humanitarian assistance to the victims of war, be they sick and wounded combatants, prisoners of war, or destitute civilians, refugees, or displaced persons. Most INGOs do not receive media coverage because they are usually not involved directly in the resolution of conflict. They mostly connect people with similar interests and values and give them the means to learn from each other and influence policy in their favour.

The next group of international actors are private groups but are not of the associative type that people join by buying a membership card. Transnational organizations, as we will call them, are business, religious, and underworld structures that deploy their activities in many countries. Therefore, this category is very diverse, comprising firms such as IBM, Exxon, and Toyota; religious denominations such as Catholicism and Anglicanism;

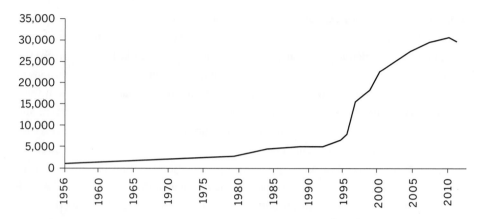

FIGURE 4.3 | INCREASE IN THE NUMBER OF INGOS SINCE 1956

Source: The Yearbook of International Organizations, edited by Union of International Associations.

terrorist organizations such as al-Qaeda; and criminal syndicates such as Mafia families. Major media outlets that can influence decision-makers and public opinion, such as CNN and Al Jazeera, can also be included here.

In this category, some attention must be accorded to multinational corporations (MNCs), the financial, industrial, and commercial firms that have long been the key players in matters of trade, money, and investment. MNCs also have enormous political influence, as they often try to bend foreign policy to their profit objectives. For example, in order to secure oil supply, coffee imports, or cheap labour, they sometimes favour the development of commercial links with authoritarian foreign states, despite the reticence of the government and the public. There is considerable controversy over the role of multinational corporations, which are accused of being involved in every crisis, conflict, and war in the international system. On the one hand, multinational corporations have contributed jobs, technology, and wealth to many economies. On the other, their narrow concern for the bottom line often results in their running roughshod over cultural sensitivities and issues of social justice. In any case, it can be acknowledged that MNCs are significant actors in international relations and that they are party to several labour, environmental, and community conflicts in modern societies.

Individuals are also participants in many international conflicts. Obviously, the major decision-makers in governments, such as presidents and prime ministers, have enormous impact in these conflicts and can influence the course of international affairs with their personalities and values. But what about other people? A person from one country can, for example, be in a dispute about a commercial transaction with someone from another country. Such small-scale differences are more numerous with globalization. Furthermore, in modern democratic societies, people have many channels of influence and are sometimes mobilized by major international causes, such as peace, development, human rights, or the environment. They express their views by voting, talking to their politicians, answering opinion polls, and attending demonstrations. Public opinion can sometimes change foreign policies. As mentioned in Chapter 3, the American public's lack of support for the Vietnam War was instrumental in the administration's decision to withdraw the troops in 1973. Finally, a few well-known public figures can be minor international actors in their own right. For example, Bono has been an indefatigable proponent of humanitarian and foreign aid for Africa, AIDS campaigns, and the cancellation of foreign debt. Billionaire George Soros is perhaps the only man who can be called an international actor on three different levels: as a high-end currency speculator who can affect the value of currencies with his business decisions; as an influential political activist and author, notably in the American Democratic Party; and as a major philanthropic figure whose foundation has invested millions of dollars in democratization, economic development, and humanitarianism.

THE RELATIVE DECLINE OF INTERNATIONAL VIOLENCE

The best-known form of international violence is war among countries, or interstate war. This type of armed conflict has been predominant since the Middle Ages and has culminated with the two world wars. However, it seems that the level of violence in interstate relations is slowly declining.

In 1942, American political scientist Quincy Wright (1890–1970) wrote *A Study of War*, in which he attempted the first scientific survey of this human activity. Wright (1964, p. 45) concluded that the preparation for war and wars themselves were becoming more costly in life and resources over time. He pointed out that the proportion of men under arms in 1937 Europe was three times that of the Roman Empire under Augustus (Wright, 1964, p. 55). He also argued that modern wars, although on average shorter than wars of the past, involved more combatants, battles, destruction, and loss of life.

However, Wright (1964) observed that the frequency of wars had been diminishing for some time: "In the sixteenth and seventeenth century the major European states were formally at war about 65 per cent of the time. In the three succeeding centuries, the comparable figures were 38 per cent, 28 per cent, and 18 per cent, respectively" (p. 55). In the early 1960s, British historian F.H. Hinsley concluded from his analysis of 278 wars since 1550 that the occurrence of wars among great powers was slightly decreasing. He even attacked the common-sense view that the first half of the twentieth century was "the age of violence." Hinsley (1963) stated that, despite the enormous calamities of both world wars, there were "fewer wars in the first half of the twentieth century than in any previous period of the same duration in modern times, and, except for the interval of the nineteenth century, fewer major wars involving major Powers" (pp. 277–278). Recent research has also suggested that war and the use of force are steadily diminishing in the international system (Holsti, 1991, 1996). Some theorists (e.g. Mueller, 1989; Fukuyama, 1992) have even claimed that we have entered a new era of history where wars among great powers are destined to disappear.

Since 2005, the Human Security Research Project has published the *Human Security Report (HSR)*. Using data originating mostly from the famous research group led by Peter Wallensteen in Uppsala, Sweden, the *HSR* proposes a concise and precise picture of modern warfare and political violence. The 2009/2010 report finds that interstate war now accounts for less than 5 per cent of all armed conflicts, supporting the conclusion that interstate war is less frequent. The HSR also states that the period since the end of World War II is the longest interval without wars between the major powers in hundreds of years (see Figure 4.4). Furthermore, this relative pacification of international affairs was associated with a worldwide decline in arms transfers, military spending, and troop numbers.[5]

Other forms of international violence include border clashes, armed interventions, transnational wars, transnational terrorism, and special operations. These types of international violence have known different evolutions.[6] Border clashes are light engagements designed to intimidate another state or to enforce **sovereignty** claims. Most border clashes are now a result of the movement of refugees and insurgents in regions where grave forms of violence, such as civil wars, occur. Many of these clashes are short and involve limited violence. However, some are of great importance for international peace and security, the most conspicuous being the Indian–Pakistani exchanges of fire in Kashmir that periodically re-emerge.

In an armed intervention, a state or group of states invade another in order to transform a political situation rather than to conquer the country as a whole or to declare war. Intervention is still regularly practised by states and by coalitions of nations under IGO

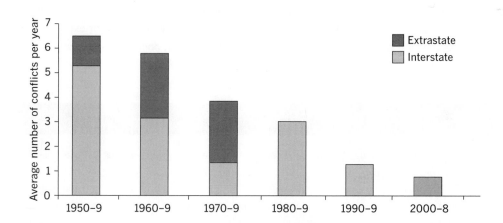

FIGURE 4.4 | THE DECLINE OF INTERNATIONAL CONFLICTS

There has been a steady decline in the number of international conflicts—defined here to include interstate and extrastate conflicts—around the world. Extrastate, or colonial conflicts, ended in the 1970s.

Source: Human Security Report Project. (2011). *Human security report 2009/2010: The causes of peace and the shrinking costs of war.* New York: Oxford University Press.

mandates, such as the NATO interventions in Bosnia and Herzegovina in 1994, Kosovo in 1999, and Libya in 2011. The United States is the main perpetrator of this kind of violence, sometimes for typical national security reasons and sometimes for a mixture of power and idealistic motives. Of the 22 interventions that occurred between 1990 and 2005, the United States was involved in 14 (63.6 per cent). During the Cold War, the country participated in 9 of 36 interventions (25 per cent) (Rioux, 2007, pp. 11, 263–266). There has been an overall augmentation of this type of violence in absolute numbers since the Cold War; however, there is no real proportional increase because the number of countries in the world is also higher. Furthermore, as shown in the *HSR* data, the level of violence employed in all conflicts, including foreign interventions, has been decreasing steadily over time.

Transnational wars are armed conflicts fought in whole or in parts by non-state actors beyond borders. They include civil wars where foreign countries send troops, money, and arms to the affected areas, where neighbouring countries offer safe havens to insurgents, and where non-state actors of all kinds (mercenaries, militias, bandits, vigilantes, etc.) proliferate. This type of conflict is characteristic of the post–Cold War era, mostly in African failed states such as the Democratic Republic of the Congo (DRC), Sierra Leone, and Liberia. Transnational wars have increased in the second half of the twentieth century, with the end of colonialism and with the "wars by proxy" of the Cold War. However, contrary to popular opinion, they have declined, as have all civil wars, since the mid-1990s.

The *HSR 2009/2010* also compiles the numbers of all wars in the international system, including international wars and civil wars, since the end of World War II. As we can see from Figure 4.5, the total number of wars was highest at the end of the Cold War and in the early 1990s. The number of people killed directly in war operations has also decreased significantly over time, as shown in Figure 4.6. These numbers do not include the indirect deaths of armed conflicts—deaths caused by starvation, disease, accidents, or exposure—because they are notoriously difficult to evaluate, especially in poor countries ravaged by

BOX 4.2 | THE KANTIAN HYPOTHESIS

Another explanation for the gradual pacification of international affairs is what political scientists call the Kantian hypothesis, after German philosopher Immanuel Kant (1724–1804). Kant believed that republics would be more peaceful than monarchies and dictatorships and that they would one day create a universal federation in order to abolish war. Several analysts have studied the link between democracy and wars, and the great majority of them have concluded that democracies fight each other extremely rarely, if at all (although they often wage wars against non-democracies). By this rationale, any increase in the number of democracies in the system would translate into fewer interstate wars. There is an enormous amount of literature on this topic: among the classic writings are Russett and Maoz (1992), Russett (1993), and Doyle (1983a, 1983b).

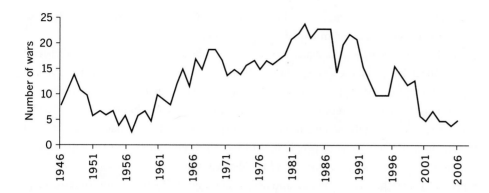

FIGURE 4.5 | TRENDS IN THE NUMBER OF WARS IN THE INTERNATIONAL SYSTEM, 1946–2008

The decline in the number of wars—defined as armed conflicts that cause 1,000 or more battle deaths per year—is more pronounced than the decline in overall conflict numbers.

Source: Human Security Report Project. (2011). *Human security report 2009/2010: The causes of peace and the shrinking costs of war.* New York: Oxford University Press.

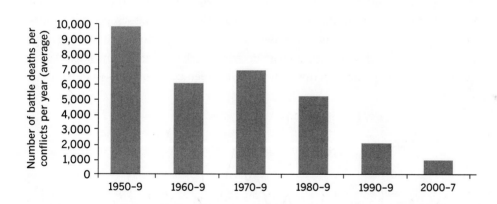

FIGURE 4.6 | AVERAGE NUMBER OF BATTLE DEATHS PER CONFLICT PER YEAR, BY DECADE, 1950–2007

There has been a clear, though far from consistent, decline in the deadliness of armed conflict since the end of the Korean War. In the 1950s, the average armed conflict killed nearly 10,000 people a year; by the new millennium, the average had fallen to just over 1,000.

Source: Human Security Report Project. (2011). *Human security report 2009/2010: The causes of peace and the shrinking costs of war.* New York: Oxford University Press.

civil wars. For instance, in the case of the wars in the DRC during the 1990s and early 2000s, estimates of casualties range from 900,000 to 6 million.

The decline in the frequency and the severity of warfare can be attributed to several factors. Sovereignty and the strengthening of nation-states have marginalized some causes of war among the states of Europe, such as border disputes, religious quarrels, dynastic pretensions, honour, and reputation. The strengthening of states in other regions of the world is slowly having the same effects (Holsti, 1996). The capitalist economy has diverted the energies and ambitions of people toward more peaceful purposes than waging war. The culture has changed over time, and the old glorification of violence and war has been replaced by more humane, tolerant, and democratic values (Mueller, 1989). To these long-term factors of peace, two other trends have appeared since 1945: the increase in the peaceful settlement of disputes (notably with the UN) and the existence of nuclear weapons, which deters great powers from going to war against one another.

Transnational terrorism is violence against the general population conducted across borders by specialized militant units for the purpose of intimidating governments and gaining publicity for their own cause. Figure 4.7 includes all acts of terrorism (both national and transnational). What can be observed is that terrorism grew in the 1970s and 1980s when groups such as the Palestine Liberation Organization (PLO) endorsed its use. The frequency of terrorist attacks diminished dramatically in the 1990s after the PLO changed its strategy and because the end of the Soviet Union meant that it no longer supported terrorist groups. While terrorist incidents have risen again sharply since 2004, this increase is not due to transnational al-Qaeda type groups but strictly to the insurgency and interreligious conflict in Iraq. Hence, most terrorist incidents between 2004 and 2010 were not trans-

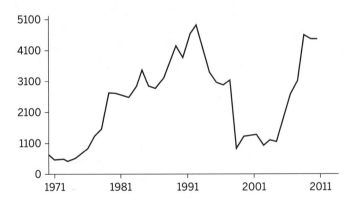

FIGURE 4.7 | TERRORIST INCIDENTS IN THE WORLD PER YEAR, 1971–2011

The number of terrorist incidents has decreased over time, but the case of Iraq has led to a temporary increase during the 2000s.

Source: National Consortium for the Study of Terrorism and Responses to Terrorism (START). (2011). Global Terrorism Database [Data file]. Retrieved from www.start.umd.edu/gtd.

national in nature but related to only one country. The frequency of terrorist attacks in Iraq has strongly declined since the national elections and the American withdrawal. Overall, terrorism is not on the rise. Furthermore, despite its spectacular nature, it kills far fewer people than insurgencies, wars, or state repression. The real danger of terrorism lies in the possibility that its perpetrators might one day use weapons of mass destruction (WMDs) to inflict maximum terror and destruction.[7]

AN INCREASING INTERNATIONAL REPERTORY OF CONFLICT RESOLUTION PROCESSES

The international system is now characterized by a large number of conflict resolution processes. While many of those processes are relatively recent in human history, the age-old methods of intimidation and war have not disappeared. Much conflict resolution in foreign relations is done through power, which means that the larger states impose their order onto the weaker ones. The classic case of this practice is the Cold War, where the United States and the Soviet Union imposed their will onto the members of their respective ideological blocs. Many conflicts were then suppressed or repressed, some of which came back to haunt the world after the war.

The demise of the blocs has not meant that power is no longer the main conflict resolution mechanism but that it is primarily in the hands of the United States, the planetary **hegemon**.[8] The United States still has impressive assets, such as its armed forces, intelligence capabilities, enormous domestic market, and industry and technology. It can use these power resources to put pressure on other states on many issues. Some analysts, such as Joseph S. Nye (1991) have asserted that we live in an era of *Pax Americana*, a period where the rest of the world has submitted to America's mostly benevolent authority. Perhaps the decline in the use of force worldwide is due to the order that Washington can impose on the world. However, it is easy to succumb to a schematic realism in which absolute power translates into absolute domination. This "American moment" will probably be short-lived and will most likely be followed by the rivalry of China for the governance of world affairs.[9]

In any case, the reality is that the United States cannot stop all conflicts or make everyone submit. For example, the Israeli–Arab conflict continues despite the avowed preference of the United States for a definitive solution. Furthermore, the problems encountered by the American interventions and military support in Iraq and Afghanistan show that preponderant political and military power does not necessarily translate into local acquiescence and deference when it is projected in foreign lands. Similarly, the United States cannot impose its views on international trade or the value of currencies in the world community.

In the absence of a complete hegemon, negotiation among states is necessary in order to manage and resolve conflicts. International **diplomacy** (the attempts of professional governmental negotiators to find agreement between sovereign states) as an instrument of conflict resolution in the world has been on the rise for centuries. As we will see in Chapter 12, diplomacy has evolved since the Renaissance to become increasingly professional, secure, and broad-minded. As a result, an increasing proportion of conflicts are resolved through negotiated agreements or ceasefires as compared to military victory, and those settlements last increasingly longer (Human Security Centre, 2006).

International conflict resolution is also increasingly influenced by non-governmental movements. One of the early non-governmental movements to have crucially affected a major issue was the anti-slavery movement that led, 200 years ago, to the ban on slavery in the British Empire. In more recent times, the most notable movements have been in the fields of human rights, women's emancipation, nuclear disarmament, environmental protection, and humanitarian care. The names Greenpeace, Amnesty International, Doctors without Borders, and others are forever associated with successful opinion campaigns. Modern electronic media, including the Internet and social media, have been extremely important in the promotion of the new causes and policy proposals of such organizations.

The participation of private citizens is not only noticeable at the highest level but also in the myriads of low- and medium-level initiatives established to improve communications among adversaries and explore avenues for conflict resolution. There are many variations in the theory and practise of these groupings, which are often called track II or track III diplomacy (see Chapter 12) and are often encouraged by governments, IGOs, and INGOs. Public opinion and NGOs have also been influential in promoting important policies that favour concord among states, including trade liberalization, harmonization of technical norms, student and scientific exchanges, tourism, and free and fair election processes. The implementation of international agreements depends heavily on the participation of major non-governmental actors, such as trade unions, business groupings, professional associations, and religious congregations. Third parties also play a role in international conflict resolution, particularly in international tribunals, arbitration panels, mediation attempts, **fact-finding missions**, and **peacekeeping** forces.

International conflict resolution, like international conflict, has become a very complex business. There are many issues left unanswered, and new controversies emerge all the time. However, today's world can count on an unprecedented array of official and non-official means to address these international conflicts.

CONCLUSION

Our review of international conflict has highlighted the rise of new conflicts and disputes following modernization and globalization. The ongoing inclusion of all the countries of the world into the globalized capitalist economy means that the trend will continue for the foreseeable future. Furthermore, these conflicts are often intimately joined to one another and involve a growing number of participants. The complexity of international conflicts is not likely to decrease anytime soon. Contrary to public perceptions, however, violence in international relations is decreasing. Interstate violence is infrequent, and transnational violence does not seem to be growing significantly. This trend is by no means definitive, as levels of violence may rise again in the future; however, many factors, including the existence of nuclear weapons, the costs of war, the benefits of peace, and the changes in attitudes and beliefs, have made interstate war a diminishing presence since World War II.

Another element in the current pacification of international relations is the growth of conflict resolution. Modern formalized diplomacy has been an important ingredient in this respect, especially since the advent of permanent international institutions that facilitate and regularize negotiations among states. Furthermore, the development of mechanisms based on the presence of third parties since the nineteenth century has been a major historical factor of change in international affairs.

DISCUSSION QUESTIONS

1. Why are there more opportunities for international disputes and conflicts now than in the past?

2. What are the most important reasons for the decline in international war?

3. Do you think that the rate of international violence will increase in the coming years? What could cause a surge in international armed conflicts?

4. List five emerging sources of conflict in the international system that could become important in the future.

5. What strategies, actions, and institutions could help to reduce the amount of violence experienced globally?

NOTES

1. Reciprocal, or mimetic, dynamics are examined in Chapter 9.

2. For more information on international issues, actors, and processes, see Kegley (2009) and Goldstein & Pevehouse (2010), two of the best introductory textbooks on international relations.

3. In addition, many ethnonational groups are seeking statehood.

4. The ICRC is unique in that much of its funding comes directly from states. As a result, it takes great pains to be neutral in relation to conflict.

5. According to the Stockholm International Peace Research Institute (SIPRI), there has been no major interstate conflict in the last seven years and only 2 of the 29 major conflicts in the 2000s have been interstate wars. See Appendix 2A of the *SIPRI Yearbook 2011*, available at www.sipri.org/yearbook/2011/02/02A.

6. Special operations, which include sabotage, assassination, and kidnapping conducted secretly by the operatives of governments, will not be discussed here because there are no reliable data for this type of violence.

7. WMDs include those weapons with the potential to kill a great number of individuals in one strike. They include nuclear weapons (explosives using the fission of heavy atoms

or the fusion of light atoms), chemical weapons (artificial poisons), biological weapons (a category including naturally occurring poisons and natural or artificial diseases), and radiological weapons (devices intended to spread radioactive substances in order to poison people).

8. The word *hegemon* has been borrowed directly from the Greek by political scientists to describe a state that is a true centre of power, which means that it controls political, military, economic, technological, and cultural resources that enable it to impose its power onto other states. In international relations, the theory of hegemonic stability indicates that the stability of the international system is more likely to be achieved if it is dominated by one strong state (Keohane, 1984).

9. Most authors, from the political left to the political right, believe that the American domination will be a short episode. See Kennedy (1987), Chomsky (2003), and Kagan (2008).

PART III | THE CAUSES OF CONFLICT

INTRODUCTION

For millennia, people have attempted to explain why and how people engage in conflict. Ancient philosophers and religious leaders have speculated on the subject, expressing their reflections in myths and stories, laws and teachings, and discourses about human nature. Over the last few centuries, a number of disciplines have also focused on conflict and offered various ideas regarding its causes. Each chapter in this part examines conflict through a different lens—rational choice theory, biology, psychology, social sciences, and philosophy—and reveals various dynamics within conflict situations. Embedded within each discipline are theories that enable us to see different aspects of a conflict that we might otherwise overlook. These concepts are based on the epistemologies and methodologies of the particular discipline.

Theories are sets of propositions aimed at explaining something. They typically start from a few axioms. From these postulates, a number of hypotheses can be deduced and empirically tested. The results of verification tend to either confirm or reject a theory. In conflict studies, for example, evolutionary theorists start from the postulate that human beings are a species and that their behaviour is largely determined by their genetic background. From this assumption, one can deduce propositions regarding the role of aggression and conflict in the survival and reproduction of individuals. Specific hypotheses related to human behaviour in conflict can then be formulated and verified. Any particular theory helps to explain the dynamics of a conflict and find meaning within it. As we deal with different theories in this section, we will identify both their strengths and weaknesses.

Epistemology is concerned with how we know something to be true. Each approach to conflict has rules that determine how data and the interpretation of that data should be validated. Within some disciplines, such as those in the social sciences, the dominant epistemologies are empirical, meaning that they are based on observation, experimentation, and proof. Those that focus on the observation of patterns are inductive epistemologies, while those based on experiments and proof are deductive. In other disciplines, such as philosophy, the dominant epistemologies are based on interpretation and reflection.

Methodology is concerned with the kinds of questions we ask and the manner in which we get answers. Each approach to conflict asks different questions based on certain presuppositions. For example, Chapter 5 examines rational choice theory, which assumes that people are basically rational creatures whose behaviour is based on their personal interests. This theory, then, asks the following question: Is conflict based on rational choices that people make? One presupposition of the biological approach (discussed in Chapter 6) is the theory of evolution. In terms of conflict, the accompanying question is, How is conflict a function of survival of the fittest?

Inductive and deductive epistemologies translate into inductive and deductive methodologies. In other words, our explanation of conflict can be based on the observation of patterns or the logical deduction of the implications of verified theories and data. American logician Charles Sanders Peirce (1839–1914) also identified the abductive methodology, a combination of the two types (1998). John W. Burton (1987) adapted Peirce's system to conflict studies as follows: because conflict is extremely complex, it is best to start with a theoretical framework and examine conflicts in an open way. As our observations provide new information and show weaknesses in this framework, we continue to adjust it accordingly.

A group of theories, epistemologies, and methodologies can sometimes unite to form a paradigm, an entirely new way of perceiving reality and determining what is true. Following the ideas of American philosopher Thomas S. Kuhn (1962), this process can be described as the replacement of outdated paradigms by ones that are better suited to resolve certain anomalies. One of the best examples of a paradigm shift is society's accepting the fact that the earth is not the centre of the universe but one of a number of planets that revolve around the sun. In the social sciences and humanities, the concept of paradigm shift is contested. Because these disciplines deal with complexities of human existence that are not subject to definitive proof in the same way as mathematics and physics are, there is a great deal of latitude for discrepant events. In this environment, there may be many competing paradigms and few shifts. However, certain theories and insights in these fields have a profound influence on how we see ourselves. For instance, in conflict studies we could mention that Burton (1987) concluded that conflict is a clash of non-negotiable identity needs after he discovered the psychological literature on human needs. Another example is the almost simultaneous discovery by scholars such as Morton Deutsch (1960), Thomas Schelling (1960), and Anatol Rapoport (1960) of the importance of game theory, especially the Prisoners' Dilemma, in the explanation of conflict situations and outcomes.

INTRODUCTION

As one of the main approaches to understanding human behaviour, rational choice theory will be the starting point in our analysis of conflict. Our examination from this perspective involves looking at how and on what basis people determine a course of action and the degree to which they are committed to their decisions. In other words, if a particular choice involves engaging in a conflict and there is a risk that the person might lose, are there enough potential benefits to proceed? This chapter traces the history of the rational choice approach and its implications for different levels of conflict. We also discuss game theory as a means of examining how rational decisions are influenced by those of another party.

WHAT IS RATIONAL BEHAVIOUR?

Most human behaviour is rational. In other words, our conduct is usually guided by reason, the capacity to use logic to think, understand, and make decisions. Conflict behaviour may be rational as well, which means that it is chosen by people in order to achieve particular objectives. The main concept here is that of choice. While some perspectives claim that people are pushed into conflict in certain circumstances, the rational choice approach emphasizes the options and the decisions of people in conflict.

Utility and Cost–Benefit Analysis

Rational behaviour is purposive. The central tenet of rational choice theory is that people set personal goals that reflect their preferences. Sometimes people make decisions on the basis of something other than utilitarian interests (e.g. emotional memories or reacting to injustice); hence they would be non-rational or irrational. (This kind of behaviour will be addressed later in the book, notably in Chapters 7 and 8.) As an example, consider a student deciding on a program of study. The rational student will make his or her choice based on what program brings the most benefits, be they intellectual, material, or status-related. In economics, this level of benefits is known as utility, but we can also equate it with the less precise term *interest*. The utility of different fields will have different values. Areas in which the student has no interest will have a very low utility value.

One way to look at such a choice is to calculate utility from several dimensions. For instance, some programs may provide better

5 | IS CONFLICT BEHAVIOUR RATIONAL?

CHAPTER OBJECTIVES

This chapter will help you develop an understanding of the

- concept of rational behaviour and how people make rational decisions;

- origins of rational choice theory, how it differs from the sociological theories, and how it is applied by economists and political scientists to explain political and conflict decisions;

- applications of the rational approach, particularly in nuclear deterrence and conflicts over natural resources;

- concept of game theory, including the examples of the Stag Hunt, the Prisoners' Dilemma, and the Game of Chicken;

- experimental use of game theory in the study of conflict and conflict resolution; and

- major criticisms of the rational choice model.

TABLE 5.1 | UTILITY ANALYSIS

	Enjoyment	Prospects	Friends	Total
Program A	1	3	2	6
Program B	2	2	3	7
Program C	3	1	1	5

employment prospects but be less enlightening than others. Let us say that a student evaluates the utility of three programs on the basis of three equally important criteria: personal enjoyment of the topic, prospects for employment, and number of friends in the program. His or her optimal choice would be the program that offers the highest aggregate score. Table 5.1 shows one possible outcome of this ranking system. According to the table, the student would choose Program B because it has the highest utility.

People also use cost–benefit analysis to make decisions. Economists have formalized this type of decision-making with complex formulas and theorems, but at its source is a simple notion. Basically, people evaluate the positive and negative results of a course of action. The greater the benefits, the more utility the decision has. This process is presumably what each of us does when confronted with a decision.

While utility is an important aspect of decision-making, analysts differ about the source of utility. In most of the liberal economics literature, it is assumed that all decisions are self-interested, that actors strive to fulfill their personal utility only. In this utilitarian position, people are interested in the needs of others only if it helps them accrue their personal advantage. However, some theorists, such as famed French sociologist Raymond Boudon (1981, 2001) claim that this is a restrictive assumption. One can perform rationalist analysis of behaviour without claiming that all behaviour is selfish. After all, an altruistic person can be as rational as a self-serving individual, and his or her behaviour can be studied with exactly the same instruments. In this book, we tend to side with this approach simply because we believe that the narrow utilitarian postulate is not necessary to understanding rational behaviour.

Some Ancestors of the Rational Approach

During most of human existence, rational behaviour has been somewhat neglected as an explanation of human actions. Other factors, such as magic, destiny, the will of God or the gods, and the natural order, held a more important place in the understanding of behaviour. Utility-seeking behaviour was often associated with sins such as greed, luxury, or pride, a view that is still held by many people. To counter the calculating tendencies of human beings, philosophers and theologians have preferred to stress more elevated and altruistic notions of sacrifice, devotion, and solidarity.

During the Renaissance, some thinkers began to reject Christian idealism and its emphasis on unselfish notions for what they considered to be a more realistic portrayal of human life. The main initiator of this change was Italian statesman and writer Niccolò Machiavelli (1469–1527), who is best known for claiming that personal power is the only goal of politics (see Chapter 8). Although this claim has been strongly criticized by many over time, Machiavelli (2003) can be considered an early exponent of the purposive decision-making perspective in that he contended that people in politics are motivated by self-interest and that they will use rational—if not moral—means to attain their goals.

Another early application of the rational approach is the diverse manifestations of contract theory. Contract theories are conceptions of society as a contract among rational individuals. The first clear enunciation of contract theory was made by English philosopher Thomas Hobbes (1588–1669). Hobbes (1651/2008) thought that the state was an arrangement created by people in order to remove themselves from the misery and brutality of primitive life. His contract theory, which we discuss further in Chapter 8, gave a rational explanation for political organization that seriously challenged the traditional explanation of the divine will and became immensely influential.

Differences with the Standard Sociological Approach

Rational choice theory focuses on individual decisions and not on the deep structural and cultural forces that, according to most social scientists, are supposed to determine behaviour. In the rational approach, institutions, cultural norms, and economic opportunities are seen as factors that lead to particular situations requiring decisions and that also constrain decision-making by limiting the number and the expected **payoffs** of different options. Seen through this lens, conflict is the result of a social choice. People decide to enter into an argumentative and even conflicting relationship when they decide that doing so will help them improve their welfare, keep their autonomy, increase their social standing, or achieve whatever other goal they set for themselves. The availability of options and the strategies played by their opponents are as important as the root causes of a conflict because they determine the calculations that they have to make about a course of action.

For example, a typical sociological explanation of a rural rebellion would state that farmers facing a decrease in crop prices and a degradation of their income have no recourse but to enter into violent conflict with the authorities. The equation is simple: *depressed prices → heightened conflict*. While this formula is a familiar explanatory pattern to many social analyses, incidents of such behaviour are far outnumbered by non-violent responses. The rational perspective, however, would explore the choices facing every individual in the group. Let us say that the farmers could leave for the city, start a co-operative venture to sell their products elsewhere, or rebel against the authorities. Each of these choices would incur costs and promise some benefits. Each would have a utility for each farmer.

Because people's decisions are heavily influenced by the probable attitude of other players, the farmers must also consider the actions of other groups and individuals. In this case, the government could do nothing, offer some financial compensation, or use preventive violence in order to deter rebellion. Other farmers may be unwilling to devote their time and efforts to create a new co-operative or to start a violent rebellion. In this situation, leaving the region may be the option with the most utility. Either way, estimating what the government and other farmers will likely decide is crucial in selecting a course of action. Conflict may or may not occur, depending on the calculations that the farmers make.

LIBERAL ECONOMICS AND CONFLICT

The Rise of *Homo Economicus*

Developed in large part by economists, rational choice theory guides the overwhelming majority of economic research in the Western world. Considered the father of modern economics, Scottish philosopher Adam Smith (1723–90) is best known for his theory that an economic actor—*Homo economicus*—is what is known today as a rational utility maximizer. For Smith, utility included a complex assortment of factors leading to a good life, such as adequate living standards, freedom of choice, and a fulfilling job that uses one's gifts and abilities. According to Smith (1776/2003), the major economic instrument is the free market, which is guided by supply and demand. He argued that this market is the most effective mechanism to allocate resources and develop production.

In the free market, payoffs are allocated automatically. Consumers ultimately decide what products and what companies will succeed. Society, however, is a very different institution, characterized by serious differences between resolute political actors. In social and political life, conflicts must be settled by negotiation, the intervention of a third party, or force.

While this text is not the place for a history of economics, suffice it to say that most specialists have elected to follow in the footsteps of Adam Smith and have stressed the rational choice model as the fundamental tool of inquiry in economic behaviour. Liberal economics is one of the most impressive intellectual edifices of the social sciences, but it may not have always paid enough attention to conflict. Philosophically, for conflict analysts, one major insight from Smith is that economic competition brings benefits for all. This notion is in line with the changes brought by the Enlightenment to our conception of society: we do not have to repress and hide contests and rivalries but should acknowledge their benefits.

Public Choice

When economists have considered politics and conflict, the result has been public choice theory. Starting in the 1950s, analysts such as Kenneth Arrow (1951), Anthony Downs (1957), Mancur Olson (1971), and Raymond Boudon (1981) used economics to investigate how people make rational decisions about issues such as voting, political participation, public policy, and conflict. Their work shows that, in a sense, many political processes resemble the market. For instance, in elections, the political consumers (the public) decide what policies and what leaders they want. The result is a generally peaceful and satisfactory political process, at least in affluent countries. However, public choice has highlighted some classic problems of political life, such as the difficulties of translating individual choices into a coherent political platform. Public choice theorists are particularly sensitive to the

coordination problem, which states that an outcome favourable to all can be achieved only with a high degree of co-operation. If we return to the example of the farmers, we could say that those who want to organize a co-operative face a coordination problem. Many farmers might pull out of the project (i.e. defect) or take advantage of the work of others (i.e. take a free ride). Therefore, achieving a high level of support may be difficult. Finding ways out of coordination problems is one of the central challenges of social life, according to rational theorists. Cultural norms, institutions, coercion, and persuasion are instruments that can be used to convince people to work together.

The coordination problem is especially acute in the provision of **public goods**. These goods are non-rivalled and non-excludable, meaning that their consumption does not reduce their availability. Public goods can also be described as things that are of value for everyone but do not need the co-operation of everyone to be produced. National defence, police, tribunals, a democratic political system, and a clean environment are classic examples of public goods.

For example, a clean neighbourhood is a public good because it benefits all its inhabitants. However, many people litter and do not take care of their surroundings. How can this problem be fixed? The market can be used for the provision of public goods, but is often limited because it cannot always mobilize **free riders**, in this case the people who litter because they know that someone will pick up after them. This situation is called a market failure. Because the market cannot always provide public goods, other ways (e.g. government regulations, educational changes, and cultural transformation) to convince people not to litter have to be found.

In the real world, many social and political conflicts are actually about the provision of public goods such as basic education, public health, security, environmental protection, and democratic rights. Such conflicts are often caused by questions of who will supply and pay for public goods. How will they be supplied? By local authorities, the national government, the private sector, mixed entities? Who will pay for them: the rich, the middle class, or all users?

TWO EXAMPLES OF THE RATIONAL CHOICE THEORY IN CONFLICT STUDIES

Our two examples of a rational choice approach to conflict studies—nuclear **deterrence** and natural resources—occur at the international and intranational level, respectively. In both cases, this approach guided policy: it steered the actual development of nuclear weapons and had an impact on foreign aid policies. Besides this practical side, the examples also show the potential and the limits of this approach at whatever level it might be used.

Nuclear Deterrence Theory

The rational choice approach to politics and conflict has found its most dramatic expression in the nuclear deterrence model that governed American–Soviet relations during most of the Cold War. After the first atomic bomb was launched in Hiroshima in 1945, it became clear that this weapon was here to stay and that the task of politicians and experts was to keep it from being used again, except as a last resort.

In order to save the world from nuclear war, the understanding of decision-making, especially in times of international crises, needed to be improved. However, nuclear powers did not want to unilaterally disarm. They wanted to use nuclear weapons as a deterrent against threatening actions and as a means to exert more influence in the international system. Experts became famous for analyzing the most central aspects and the most exotic possibilities of confrontation among nuclear powers.[1] Essentially, they used cost–benefit analysis to study the conditions in which it would be reasonable to use nuclear weapons. The result was the concept of mutually assured destruction (MAD), in which both adversaries risk total obliteration by launching a nuclear attack. Because it is not in the nuclear powers' interests to use such a course of action, the possibility of nuclear war is lessened. Instead, these nations tend to base the tenor of their responses to the actions of their opponents and use communication to limit misperceptions.

The main danger in this situation is that one of the parties could be convinced that it has a definite advantage over the other and could launch an attack that would destroy its adversary. Over the years, the policies of nuclear states have been geared specifically toward eliminating this dangerous possibility through two basic responses: the second strike capability and the absence of defence. Second strike capability involves the acquisition of numerous well-protected weapons that would survive any sneak attack and could be used to destroy the aggressor. The attainment and the maintenance of a second strike capability is the most important goal of nuclear policies and now governs the decisions made by new nuclear powers such as India and Pakistan. However, this policy is quite expensive and potentially dangerous (in the sense that the more weapons one has, the more possibilities of diversion and unauthorized use there are). To reduce this risk, the United States and Soviet Union agreed to limit their number of nuclear weapons by signing major diplomatic agreements, such as the SALT and START treaties of the 1970s.

While the absence of defence seems paradoxical to national security, it is understandable in deterrence theory. If a state thought that it was protected against a nuclear attack, it might be willing to inflict a first strike on its adversary, calculating that the weakened second strike could be countered. Because such reasoning could seriously endanger stability, the superpowers signed the Anti-Ballistic Missile (ABM) Treaty in 1973, prohibiting the deployment of defensive nuclear weapons. This threat is also why defensive projects such as President Reagan's Strategic Defence Initiative (SDI) and other counter-missile plans under presidents Clinton and George W. Bush have often been criticized.

Deterrence theory has frequently been seen to neglect the risk that irrational behaviour could be involved in nuclear confrontations. Analysts such as Robert Jervis (1976), Jack Snyder (1978), and Irving L. Janis (1982) have pointed to faulty perceptions, high levels of stress, and the groupthink mode as potentially catastrophic influences on crisis behaviour. Other factors need to be considered as well. Technical errors such as false radar alerts could be a

President John F. Kennedy signs the declaration of quarantine against Cuba on 29 October 1962. Kennedy had excluded several options, including attack scenarios, before settling on this decision. It was nevertheless a bold move that could have gone wrong if the Soviets had not acted rationally and agreed to back down.

danger. Internal undue pressures from politicians, bureaucrats, military leaders, pressure groups, and public opinion could also push decision-makers into disastrous confrontations. Finally, one can never exclude the possibility that a troubled political leader may prefer mutual nuclear destruction to military defeat and conquest.

In his analysis of the 1962 Cuban Missile Crisis, political scientist Graham Allison (1969, 1971) showed that the peaceful resolution of this conflict was due to astute decisions. In the period leading up to this crisis, the Soviet Union had secretly begun to install nuclear missiles in Cuba. When this activity was discovered, the American people and its leaders were outraged. Many argued for offensive military actions. If narrow political interests had prevailed, the US administration might have undertaken dangerous actions, such as aerial strikes against Cuba or attacks on Russian navy vessels. However, President Kennedy decided to blockade Cuba—calling it a quarantine so as not to make it an act of war—until the Soviets renounced their project. High-level diplomacy between the Kremlin and the White House followed, and the crisis was finally resolved.

The safety of the world in relation to nuclear weapons is largely based on the rationalist assumption that decision-makers will not launch a nuclear attack because doing so would be detrimental to their interests. Deterrence theory is therefore one of the most influential applications of the rationalist approach to conflict.

Natural Resources

An empirical application of the rational choice approach to armed conflicts has recently drawn much attention. In the late 1990s, World Bank economist Paul Collier (2000) began to analyze the cause of civil wars in the contemporary world. He was struck by the fact that many countries well endowed with natural resources were caught in terrible conflicts. The cases of Angola (oil), Sierra Leone (oil and diamonds), Nigeria (oil), Congo (several minerals, including precious stones) come to mind. Collier demonstrated that countries that earn most of their gross national product (GNP) from natural resources have a definite chance of becoming involved in civil wars. His findings are an example of the **resource curse hypothesis**, a phenomenon whereby countries with abundant natural resources tend to have less growth, democracy, and peace.

For Collier, political leaders in non-democratic regimes can be assimilated to **rent-seekers**, which means that they try to gain a monoloply of a particular activity and prosper from the revenues. In other words, they use force to gain control of a prized commodity and push the competition away. For a number of reasons, this behaviour is not possible in a mature pluralist democracy with an industrial or post-industrial economy. The complexity and interdependence of production processes in modern economies, the existence of a lawful state with a plurality of political actors, and the unwillingness of the overwhelming majority of citizens to take up arms to earn a living protect against any descent into **anarchy**.

In less privileged contexts, however, rent-seekers will use force when they have the re-sources to do so (Collier & Hoeffler, 2005). In some cases, their control of natural resources or public revenues enables them to convert cash into soldiers, weapons, and supplies. However, if the resources can be extracted by relatively small groups, as gold and dia-monds can be, rebel groups can use their own militias to protect them as they harvest the resources and use part of the profits to pay for this protection. According to Collier, young men will join these groups because their lack of education and job prospects limits their own choices. These young men decide that earning a living is worth taking the risks and enduring the hardships of military life. To summarize Collier's theory, countries endowed with lootable natural resources, a large cohort of uneducated young men, and serious eco-nomic difficulties are the most likely candidates for violent insurrections.

Furthermore, the use of violence and intimidation by the warlord and his troops helps to resolve some of the coordination problems associated with political life. The main method of coordinating people against their will is to use coercion. In a way, governments are the ultimate response to coordination problems in modern societies because they can threaten intimidation. In terms of the predatory wars that Collier studies, the use of force by warlords and governments alike helps bring all those young, unemployed men together for joint action and reduces defections to a minimum.

For Collier, then, the participants in armed conflicts—be they warlords or foot soldiers—are primarily motivated by greed. They are rational actors looking after their economic well-being and choosing to use force to make money. In other words, they are bandits. Collier claims that, contrary to the usual explanations of conflict, neither the grievances nor the ideals of participants have much importance in their decisions to wage war.[2] In several publications, Collier and his co-authors have tried to devise development policies, notably in employment, education, and investment, that could counter the aggressive rent-

---

BOX 5.1 | RENT-SEEKING WARLORDS: FODAY SANKOH AND CHARLES TAYLOR

(AP Photo/Brenna Linsley)

(AP Photo/Ben Curtis)

Sierra Leone's Foday Sankoh (left) and Liberia's Charles Taylor were among the most famous warlords of the 1990s. They started insurrection movements in their respective countries in the 1980s and used extreme violence, including mass execution, torture, rape, and amputation, to attain their goals. They financed their military campaigns with the sale and export of Sierra Leone's diamonds (the so-called blood diamonds) through Liberia. Along with briefly serving as Sierra Leone's vice-president, Sankoh was chief of the infamous Revolutionary United Front (RUF), the country's main opposition movement. He was condemned as a war criminal and sentenced to death but died of a heart attack in 2003. Taylor took power in Liberia following a coup d'état in 1990 and ruled the country with an iron grip. He has been brought before the Special Court for Sierra Leone and accused of crimes against humanity. His lengthy trial ended in the spring of 2011; with a guilty verdict delivered in 2012.

seeking and recruitment behaviour in resource-rich countries (Collier et al., 2003; Bannon & Collier, 2003).

Collier's work has attracted a great deal of criticism. A well-known qualifier to Collier's thesis is that it is the presence of non-renewable resources, not all resources, that is conducive to predatory rent-seeking behaviour. In countries where renewable resources are found, grievance factors are more important (Kahl, 2006, p. 15). Furthermore, Collier's data may have been biased by the weight of the numerous predatory wars in Africa during the 1990s and early 2000s. However, not all civil wars exhibit traits of greed and opportunism. For example, the Central American conflicts of the 1970s and 1980s (in Nicaragua, El Salvador, Honduras, and Guatemala) had important ideological and grievance-related causes. More fundamentally, critics such as Christopher Cramer (2002) claim that Collier's rationalist framework ignored the explanatory variables traditionally preferred by social scientists, such as colonialism, imperialism, injustice, and repression, in the explanation of the observed facts.

Whatever the limitations of his model and empirical verification, Collier offers one of the most sophisticated and influential public choice models for the study of violent conflict. His work also highlights the local causes of many conflicts. While many social sciences analyses routinely attribute armed conflicts to the actions of external actors only, Collier emphasizes the internal dynamics of contention. As a result, the possibility of interested, rent-seeking behaviour can no longer be excluded in the analysis of violent conflict.

GAME THEORY

Despite its name, **game theory** is not the study of board and computer games but is a generic term used to describe the formalized study of rational decision-making. Begun in the 1940s by American mathematician John von Neumann and economist Oskar Morgenstern, game theory has generated much research in disciplines such as mathematics, logic, computer sciences, biology, psychology, economics, and political science.[3] In this section, we review the most common applications of game theory in the study of conflict: the Stag Hunt, the **Prisoners' Dilemma**, and the Game of Chicken.

The Stag Hunt

Old versions of game theory can be found in the writings of contract theorists. The most famous is the stag hunt metaphor presented in 1754 by Jean-Jacques Rousseau (1712–78). His allusion to the stag hunt is only a short footnote in his *Discourse on the Origin and Basis of Inequality among Men* (Rousseau, 1755/2003), but we will expand upon it here. In this game, two men from the same village are hunting in the forest and go off in different directions. The hunters are constantly in a dilemma. On the one hand, they can try to kill a stag by acting together, which would provide them with a good meal and plenty of food for their families. On the other hand, each hunter can decide to go after a hare, which brings them a small meal. The problem is that one hunter is never sure whether the other will co-operate

TABLE 5.2 | THE STAG HUNT

		Hunter B	
		Stag hunting	Hare chasing
Hunter A	Stag hunting	I Both hunters enjoy a big meal and have plenty of food to spare	II Hunter A eats nothing while Hunter B has a small meal.
	Hare chasing	III Hunter B eats nothing while Hunter A has a small meal.	IV Both hunters eat a small meal.

with him in the stag hunt. The worst outcome for each hunter is to keep looking for the stag alone while his companion goes for a hare. In this case, the stag-hunting man will get no meal at all. Therefore, the natural tendency of both hunters is not to co-operate in the pursuit of a stag in case the other hunter goes after a hare. Table 5.2 presents the choices and outcomes (i.e. payoffs) of the Stag Hunt. As the table shows, the payoffs can be positive or negative.

Rousseau's metaphor demonstrates how people are torn between short-term self-interest and long-term joint interest. While both hunters should prefer the stag hunt, they are strongly tempted by the lone pursuit of easier rewards because they do not know if the other will defect and leave them alone, without a meal. The situation is a classic coordination problem. In effect, the two hunters must find a way to ensure that they both behave as stag hunters if they want to enjoy the best outcome for themselves and their families. The Stag Hunt in all its variations is the basis for the analysis of the many social situations characterized by the clash between interests. It is also a two-person **non-zero-sum game**. This type of game features variable payoff combinations that result in joint gains, joint losses, or mixed outcomes for the players. Conflict situations are fundamentally non-zero-sum games, as are most complex social situations. The opposite type of game is zero-sum, in which the gains of some players are always matched by the losses of other players (see Chapter 1). Casino games and lotteries are examples of zero-sum games.

The Prisoners' Dilemma

The most famous non-zero-sum game is the Prisoners' Dilemma (PD), named after a tale elaborated by A.W. Tucker (see Davis 1997, p. 109). This game strongly resembles the Stag Hunt in that it is a non-zero-sum game involving two players and the temptation of non-collaboration is strong. In PD, two men are arrested one night and found to be carrying weapons. They are detained separately. The police officers tell them that they are suspected of a robbery in the neighbourhood and that they should confess if they want a lighter sentence. However, the prisoners also know that the officers have no proof of their guilt. The suspects could conceivably be released if neither confesses.

TABLE 5.3 | THE PRISONERS' DILEMMA

		Suspect B	
		Confess	Not Confess
Suspect A	Confess	I -5/-5	II -10/-2
	Not Confess	III -2/-10	IV 1/1

Table 5.3 shows the possible outcomes of the situation. Ideally, the prisoners should prefer the payoff in quadrant IV: to get away scot-free (attributed the values 1 and 1). This is their minimax, the best outcome of the game for both players. However, attaining it requires perfect co-operation between them. The danger for each man is that, if he stays silent while his partner confesses, he risks a heavy jail term for armed robbery (represented as -10 in the table), while the other would receive only a light sentence (-2).

Therefore, the logical choice for the prisoners is to avoid the major penalty by admitting their guilt. This outcome is shown in Quadrant I of the table, with each man receiving a medium-term sentence (a -5 payoff). This outcome is quite mediocre and should not be preferred by the prisoners.[4] Quadrant I represents what is known as the Nash equilibrium. Named after mathematician John Nash (b.1928), who found and proved this concept in 1950, a Nash equilibrium is the set of strategies (one per player) that affects players the least, whatever the other player decides to do. In PD, each player will rationally confess because he understands that this option has the least risk. By confessing, both players have come to a decision that they cannot regret later. The problem here is that the Nash equilibrium is not the optimal strategy. The players would do better if neither confessed, but they are afraid of the consequences of the other player's betrayal.

The PD may lead us conclude that co-operation among people is illusory and that double-crossing and defection bring more benefits than coordination. There is evidence to support this conclusion. Starting in the 1950s, psychologists have conducted experiments where people play PD-type games against other people or a computer. It is now known that approximately 80 per cent of people tested in a neutral environment play the non-collaborative move in a single, one-shot PD game. This finding conforms to the hypothesis that most rational people understand that the uncooperative move is the logical one. However, it raises the question of why one-fifth of the people tested would play the co-operative move. This group seems to be a mixed bag of people who did not understand the game, thought that they were being tricked, or were strongly convinced that the other player would co-operate.

Experimenters hypothesized that, in a long series of games, people would eventually learn that mutual co-operation is preferable to conflict. The logic is that, when playing a single game (or a short series of games), people are motivated by the desire not to be betrayed by the other and thus tend not to co-operate. However, when the PD game is iterated, the situation is different. The players know that their joint non-collaborative stand is not the optimal solution to their dilemma. They calculate that they can try to obtain the optimal result once in a while, even often, and that their total payoff will be better than if they are constantly uncooperative. Therefore, they become interested in trying collaboration.

In the late 1950s, noted psychologist Morton Deutsch (b. 1920) had subjects play several rounds of a PD experiment. To his surprise, he observed that subjects were less co-operative as the games series progressed (Deutsch, 1960). Because the subjects knew how many games they would be playing, they started to play uncooperatively towards the end so that they would not be exploited by the other party and lose late in the game. In other experiments where the subjects did not know how long they would play, co-operation rates tended to be higher. Deutsch did other experiments using undisclosed numbers of games, instructing subjects about co-operation, and increasing monetary rewards. The rate of co-operation in these tests was as high as 96.9 per cent.

Some researchers also affirm that, in all cultures and milieus, iterated PD games lend to general co-operation only after a few rounds. Well-known conflict resolution specialist William Ury (2000) states that he has conducted dozens of PD exercises around the world and that people invariably understand the benefits of co-operation. However, it should be kept in mind that these exercises were strongly oriented to produce this result and cannot be considered controlled experiments.

Different results have been found in other PD experiments. A review of 37 studies from several disciplines and using various conditions found that the average co-operation rate was 47.4 per cent (Sally, 1995). Many explanations for why people are often uncooperative in PD simulations have been proposed: the players did not understand the game; they were bored; the rewards were too low; or they could not communicate. In tests where these variables were modified, the results were different but still showed the tendency of some not to co-operate. Researchers have also tried to control for factors such as intelligence, experience, and gender but found no major differences in the results. Maybe some people are just very competitive in games and do not mind taking risks if it means that they can beat an opponent. Maybe they are also a bit mischievous with others and with the experimenters.

One famous experiment about the possibility of co-operation was conducted by American political scientist Robert Axelrod (b.1943), who was interested in how co-operation can emerge from PD situations. Axelrod (1984) thought that people would choose collaboration in the long run when they realize that it pays more than defection. He was particularly interested in the strategies that people can use to win when playing iterated PD games with other people. His theory was that co-operative strategies were better than uncooperative ones.

To prove this hypothesis, Axelrod used computer simulations. He invited famous experts in the field to each submit a strategy that would be tested against others (and against itself) in a long series of PD games. In this experiment, a strategy is simply a set of instructions telling the computer how to play against other players. A pure co-operative strategy, for example, would be "the sucker" (i.e. co-operate all the time). Such a strategy would do well in conjunction with other co-operative strategies but would be weak against unco-operative strategies, which would exploit it and consistently amass full payoffs. Conversely, a pure non-collaborative strategy, which could be called "the crab," involves a player who never co-operates. This strategy would reap only the mediocre rewards shown in Quadrant IV of Table 5.3. In between those two extremes, hundreds of strategies are possible. Some are more co-operative, meaning that the player tries to collaborate as much as possible, does not retaliate too strongly against uncooperative moves, and forgets the bad hits against him or her. The more aggressive strategies involve some co-operation at times, but the player will often or occasionally defect in order to take advantage of the co-operation of others.

The winning strategy in Axelrod's experiment was submitted by psychologist Anatol Rapoport (1911–2007), a famous specialist of game theory. Called Tit-For-Tat, Rapoport's strategy was very simple: it started with a co-operative move and then simply repeated the latest move of the other player. With opponents that consistently co-operated, Tit-For-Tat led to important payoffs. With uncooperative adversaries, the strategy led to mediocre payoffs, but it could not be fully exploited by the other side because it did not play co-operatively against a negative opponent. Later, another tournament was organized by Axelrod. There were many more entries, and the strategies were more sophisticated. Nevertheless, Rapoport's uncomplicated co-operative game plan won again.[5] In fact, collaborative strategies predominated over non-collaborative ones in both tournaments. In the first tournament, the eight highest scores belonged to "nice" strategies, meaning strategies that were never the first to defect (Axelrod, 1984, p. 33). In the second tournament, 14 of the 15 top strategies were nice, and the bottom 15 were not nice (Axelrod, 1984, p. 44).

Axelrod's experiments were a sensation at the time. They were celebrated for their originality, sophistication, and impact on research. The main conclusion that many people drew from this important work was that co-operation in iterated PD games is rational and pays off. Therefore, the PD is not a calamity upon humanity. Collaboration is possible, even among adversaries in a situation of uncertainty and limited communication. Later experiments have toned down Axelrod's results, and we now know that uncooperative strategies can be more effective than previously thought (Axelrod, 1997). However, Axelrod's conclusions are generally still very pertinent today.

In real life, it seems that people also use co-operative strategies in the PD games that they play in business, politics, and the home. People constantly find themselves in situations of the PD in the workplace, in community relations, even in love and friendship. While they know that the game will be repeated several times, they do not know when it will end. In this case, their interest is to develop co-operation so as to avoid constantly repeating the mediocre results of joint non-collaboration. Otherwise, it would be difficult to lead a normal life. There are also other ways to elude the PD. Co-operation among people is facilitated by cultural norms, family ties, and political institutions.[6] In terms of game theory, we could state that all our laws, institutions, social norms, and taboos have one general function: to make co-operation possible in PD-type situations.

The Game of Chicken

Another game that often appears in the literature about conflict is that of Chicken. Originating in the 1950s, this game was named after a high-risk contest in which participants (typically teenagers) would drive toward another car, obstacle, or cliff; the one who swerved or jumped first was declared the "chicken."[7] Let us say, then, that two teens are speeding their cars towards each other on a narrow road. They have the choice of either swerving their car or staying the course. The payoffs of this game are shown in Table 5.4.

If a player swerves to let the other pass, he or she loses (quadrants II and III). If both players turn to avoid collision, it is a draw; they are both safe but do not win (Quadrant I). However, if they keep going, both expecting the other one to get out of the way, disaster happens (Quadrant IV). In the game, participants tend to play it safe because of the huge penalty of not collaborating. This situation often occurs when people know that the consequences of non-collaboration are potentially disastrous to both parties and completely overwhelm the cost–benefit calculations. For instance, a strike in a struggling company may threaten the workers as much as the owners, and both groups have an interest in co-operating to avoid bankruptcy. Many negotiations are conducted with the warning that disagreeing means disaster.[8]

The best-known example of Chicken is found in crises among superpowers where the worst outcome would be nuclear annihilation. For example, during the Cuban Missile Crisis and the 1999 India–Pakistan confrontation over the Kargil glacier, none of the parties risked bold moves that might have led to tragedy. If nuclear confrontations are all Chicken games played by rational persons in possession of adequate information, nuclear equilibrium may indeed persist. As previously discussed, this notion is a tenet of nuclear deterrence theory. However, the world does not always correspond to the postulates of game theory, and this reality can fuel major concerns about nuclear deterrence.

TABLE 5.4 | THE GAME OF CHICKEN

		Teen B	
		Swerve	Not Swerve
Teen A	Swerve	I 0/0	II -1/2
	Not swerve	III 2/-1	IV -10/-10

Games and Co-Operative Behaviour

Over the years, researchers have used game theory to investigate whether altruistic behaviour is possible. For example, Joyce Berg, John Dickhaut, and Kevin McCabe (1995) used a game to study trust and reciprocity. In this game, Player 1 receives $10 and is offered the choice to keep it or to send a certain amount to Player 2. If Player 1 shares the money, Player 2 receives three times that amount and is given the choice to return money to Player

1. Ideally, a trusting player would give all the money to the other player and make $15 (if the $30 payoff was shared equally by Player 2). However, this decision requires a great deal of trust on the part of Player 1. Untrusting players would keep the money for themselves. However, players often try to co-operate. On average, Player 1 sends $5.16 and Player 2 returns $4.66. Player 1, therefore, makes about $9.50.

In other words, Player 1 tends to make slightly less money by sharing than he or she would have made by keeping the entire $10. Even though Player 1 tries to co-operate, the fact is that Player 2 does not always reciprocate. After all, nothing but a sense of obligation forces him or her to return any of the money. It must be noted that, in repeated experiments, players 1 and 2 learn to increase the amounts that they send to the other party, augmenting the mutual payoffs of the game and allowing Player 1 to make more money than if he or she kept the original $10. There are many more games like this one, and this area of game theory has become quite popular in economics in the last decade.

Other experiments study the physiological reactions of people playing games in order to verify whether co-operation could bring more rewards than treason. For instance, researchers such as Rilling and colleagues (2002) have had people's brains scanned as they played PD games versus a computer or other human beings. They found that the striatum zone of the brain, which is involved in satisfaction, was more stimulated when co-operation was established with the other player. Furthermore, stimulation was significantly higher when the other player was a real person.

As the discussion of the Stag Hunt, Prisoners' Dilemma, and Chicken show, game theory is not only about self-interested cads trying to beat other egoistical monsters. It is perfectly capable of investigating co-operation, obligation, empathy, altruism, and a sense of justice. Game theory also supports our previous suggestion that the postulate of egoistical behaviour is not necessary to the rational choice approach to conflict.

CRITIQUES OF THE RATIONAL CHOICE APPROACH

Many other perspectives do not agree with the version of reality offered by rational choice theory. Some analysts insist that people are driven into conflict and violence out of cultural norms, learning and conditioning, misperceptions and delusions, structural constraints, and simple penury. In this line of thinking, rational decisions may not even occur at all in many acts of conflict behaviour. In other cases, rational decisions occur but are simply the result of the more important processes that are the root causes of behaviour.

In the philosophy of science, rational decision-making analysis belongs to methodological individualism, a term for all approaches that consider that individual decisions and actions explain behaviour better than large-scale structural and cultural causes. In the social sciences, methodological individualism now guides most of the research in economics and psychology. However, sociologists, anthropologists, and political scientists are divided about individualist assumptions, as most of them still prefer to explain social phenomena only by reference to social causes. This attitude is especially pronounced among followers of sociologists such as Karl Marx, Émile Durkheim, and Talcott Parsons, who consider methodological individualism to be irremediably flawed as an explanation of social behaviour. In relation to rational choice, we can summarize this criticism in four main points.

The first critique is that rational approach overemphasizes the importance of decisions in behaviour. In fact, most human behaviour is not conscious but is determined by such factors as history, culture, and social structures. This approach is very common—if rarely stated outright—among social scientists and historians. Some even support a strict structuralist position in which individuals and their decisions simply do not matter. Although this latter view is far from universal, most social analysts would state that the context and circumstances in which people act are so constraining that the idea of rational choice is of little importance. In short, people usually have very limited and unbalanced options and often do not have real choices in life.

Another criticism is that the factors influencing social life are different than those governing individual existence, and self-interested behaviour is often detrimental to common goals. Much of the research is done in a synchronous environment, meaning that it does not account for long-term diachronic considerations. Sometimes what appears rational in the short-term is irrational if, for instance, it damages long-term relationships that might pay dividends in the future. For example, reckless actions—such as cheating on tax returns or driving gas-guzzling automobiles—may increase utility for the individual but are detrimental to society. A variation of this idea is found in the tragedy of the commons, a popular theory in current environmental writings. The concept, imagined by Garrett Hardin (1968), refers to the unregulated behaviour of farmers who let their cattle graze on the communal land in a village, which risks depleting that resource and endangering the livelihood of the entire community. The villagers could erect fences to protect the grass, but that would result in accrued social inequality. According to this thesis, there is a fundamental antinomy between self-interested and social behaviour. Consequently, the role of culture and politics is to make people behave in the interest of the community.

The third argument against rational choice is that rational decision-making is a Western concept that is not universally shared. According to some feminist authors, even people of different genders may exhibit a different kind of rationality. Furthermore, people from other cultures and eras may have had different expectations and definitions of utility. This accusation of **ethnocentrism** has been widespread in postmodern and anthropological literatures and is debated today. Many experiments are being conducted to verify whether people of different cultures and genders share the rational decision-making ability described by theorists.

Rational decision analysis is also criticized as an ideological device concocted to make people believe that they have more power than they really have and to minimize the importance of the oppressive social and cultural forces that actually shape their lives. This latter criticism is especially present in Marxism and critical theory.

To these arguments, rationalists answer that, philosophically, the rational approach stresses the autonomy of the individual. In this perspective, life is a series of decisions.

People do not just go through life like automatons or fatalistic victims but as reasonable individuals trying to make as much as possible from their circumstances.

Finally, another line of criticism comes from psychology. Psychologists share the individualistic **methodology** of economists and are very interested in game theory. In fact, much game theory research is conducted by psychologists. However, psychologists contend that rational choice cannot explain a significant part of human behaviour. A lot of human action is pre-programmed or influenced by genetic factors, life experience, environment, and altered perceptions. As the experiments on the Prisoners' Dilemma have shown, our thought processes are not abundantly clear. Psychologists consider game theory to be an interesting tool of study that informs us about the normal mode of thought, the "default" mode of human behaviour. However, most of us depart at least occasionally from that rational model, which is where psychology comes in.

CONCLUSION

Rational choice theory is an important component in understanding the decisions made by people in the difficult situations that confront them. This theory has inspired a great deal of research, notably in economics, and has led to many applications in the real world. It has always been a central model of conflict studies, especially in the development of game theory. However, as a model for explaining human behaviour, it is also contested by many people of the sociological and philosophical traditions and therefore cannot aspire to dominate the study of conflict the same way as it does economics research. Nevertheless, rational choice theory offers an excellent perspective on the situations in which individuals operate. Because the model does not specify the main influences and constraints on people (it only postulates that people are rational), it can be mixed with several theories emphasizing different explanations of behaviour.

DISCUSSION QUESTIONS

1. Choose a conflict in which you were involved. Identify the decisions you made in the course of the conflict. What were the reasons for those decisions? How did they advance your interests? Would you claim that they were rational? Analyze your opponent's decisions in the same way.

2. Do you think that deterrence theory is a good instrument in the safe and secure management of nuclear weapons? Why or why not?

3. Discuss whether the perspective developed by Paul Collier implies that all politicians, rebels, and revolutionaries involved in conflicts in the developing world are gangsters and bandits.

4. Does a reasonable course of action mean the same to all people? Is it the same for men and for women? What about for people from different social classes, education backgrounds, or cultures? Give reasons to support your answers.

5. If you were to use rational choice theory to analyze a situation, what questions would you ask the parties involved?

NOTES

1. See Brodie (1946), Kaplan (1958), Schelling (1960, 1966), and Kahn (1960).

2. One of the offshoots of Collier's writings is the use of a rhymed vocabulary to distinguish approaches that stress creed (ideologies, religion), need (penury, injustice), and greed (power, money) in the explanation of conflict (Arnson & Zartman, 2005).

3. Von Neumann and Morgenstern (1946) is the foundational text of game theory. Another classic is Rapoport (1960). For an accessible introduction to game theory, see Davis (1997). Complete reviews of game theory, including mathematical proofs, can be found in Myerson (1997) and Gintis (2009). One of the most famous journals in conflict studies, the *Journal of Conflict Resolution*, has published articles on game theory since its inception.

4. This outcome reveals a difference between the PD and the Stag Hunt. In the latter, the two hunters are not doing so badly if they decide to go after the hare.

5. It is interesting to note that Tit-For-Tat never wins any sequence of play against another strategy because it never defects unexpectedly in order to take advantage of the other player's co-operation. Tit-For-Tat wins because it gains more in co-operation over time than it loses by being exploited.

6. For example, if the two prisoners were members of the Mafia, they would automatically have applied omertà, a code of silence that requires them to never say anything to the police. They would also know that they could be executed by the mob if they spoke.

7. A famous example of this game is in *Rebel Without a Cause* (1955), directed by Nicholas Ray and starring James Dean.

8. Obviously, this warning is not always true. Parties often use it to obtain concessions from the other side.

6 | ARE CONFLICTS DRIVEN BY BIOLOGICAL NEEDS?

CHAPTER OBJECTIVES

This chapter will help you develop an understanding of the

- biological approach to human behaviour and how it applies to conflict;

- influence of evolution and social Darwinism on understanding human behaviour;

- role of sociobiology in rejuvenating the study of aggression, survival, and reproduction in conflicts;

- link between resource depletion, overpopulation, and conflict;

- neurobiological sources of emotions, including anger and empathy; and

- new field of systems biology, especially in terms of complex adaptive systems and emergent creativity.

INTRODUCTION

While the humanities and social sciences claim that humans are essentially rational creatures limited by our senses and thought processes and strongly influenced by social structures, biology argues that we are first and foremost a type of animal. As such, we compete with members of our own species and with other species to acquire the resources that enable us to survive, reproduce, and enjoy a better life. Focusing on four specific areas, this chapter examines the biological approach to human behaviour and its applications regarding conflict, particularly in terms of human aggression. Charles Darwin's theory of evolution provides the starting point for our investigation of whether conflicts have biological roots. The concepts of Robert Thomas Malthus and contemporary scholars regarding demographics and resource levels are also important in the biological approach to conflict. Another factor is human emotions, particularly how they are produced and how they contribute to conflicts. Finally, complex adaptive systems and emergent creativity have new implications in both biology and conflict studies.

BIOLOGICAL ROOTS OF HUMAN CONFLICT

Using factors at the species level to explain human behaviour is a modern notion. Although some negative comparisons between human beings and animals were made in ancient times—for instance, the Romans used to say *homo homini lupus* (humans are wolves for other humans)[1]—the cornerstone of all Western philosophy is the belief that humankind is created in the image of God (or the gods). It was considered heretical in monotheistic religions to compare people to beasts because it also indirectly implied a comparison between the latter and God. In the Western tradition, animals were considered inferior and not worthy of much investigation; therefore, the study of animals was underdeveloped. Ethology, the systematic and comparative study of animal behaviour, came into its own only in the scientific age. In the nineteenth century, the fundamental contribution of Charles Darwin (1809–82) caused a true scientific revolution in biology. Darwin's evolutionary theory allowed scientists to view humankind as a species and to comprehend behaviour as largely influenced by natural selection principles.

Evolution and Conflict

In *The Origin of Species*, Darwin (1859/2008) explained the development and behaviour of all species with one crucial biological notion: the law of natural selection. This law states that, in any species, the individuals with adaptive attributes tend to survive and reproduce more than the less adaptable ones, thereby slowly contributing to the favourable evolution of the entire species and the morphing into new species. Darwin's theory implied that all species—even humans—descended from less sophisticated ancestors that had evolved over eons. After Darwin, the perceived difference between human beings and animals narrowed considerably, stimulating a great deal of religious animosity towards his theories. However, Darwin himself was a religious man and was reluctant to speculate openly about the application of evolutionary hypotheses to human behaviour.

Nevertheless, some scholars began to apply categories used in the study of animals to the human species. For example, Herbert Spencer (1820–1903), a philosopher, psychologist, and sociologist who was a good friend of Darwin and who coined the expression "survival of the fittest," applied the principle of evolution to all human matters in *The Study of Sociology* (1873/2006). This practice led to the development of social Darwinism, which is based on the assumption that the laws of nature apply to the human species and other animal species equally. According to this theory, human beings are ruled by evolutionary factors, such as the need for survival and the need to procreate, and most of their behaviour is inherited genetically. For example, people choose partners, have children, stay close to their families, are suspicious of strangers, and fight against other groups because millions of years of evolution have programmed them to do so in order to survive. Most human institutions, be it conflict, war, co-operation, law, government, etc., exist to indirectly fulfill the biological needs of people. In biological terms, most of the learned part of behaviour (culture) supports the most basic instincts. The Darwinist view strongly influenced other eminent sociologists of the late nineteenth century, such as Ludwig Gumplowicz and Gaetano Mosca (1960).

More problematically, social Darwinists contended that the most gifted individuals tend to do better than others and that they naturally dominate societies. This crude version of the survival of the fittest law was often used by nineteenth-century aristocrats and imperialists to justify rigid class hierarchies, the submission of the lower classes, the acquisition of colonies, and international wars. It was an essential element in the doctrines of "scientific racism" spread by, for example, Count Arthur de Gobineau and Houston Stewart Chamberlain.[2] These theories enjoyed a great deal of support in the Western middle and upper classes until World War I and influenced the development of Nazism.

Social Darwinism drew much opposition. As previously mentioned, Christians disliked the link between humans and animals and the possibility that natural laws could explain behaviour without reference to God. Many Christians also opposed the idea of eugenics, an extreme application of social Darwinism that encourages controlled breeding to improve the human species.[3] Socialists disagreed with some of the consequences of natural selection, such as the idea that capitalism represents the best system for the rise of society's natural elite and should not be restrained by equalitarian laws.[4]

If the biological approach to conflict is so contested today, it is largely in reference to the hypotheses of social Darwinism. For many people, Darwinism applied to human beings continues to raise the spectres of a justification of racial and class inequality, savage un-restricted capitalism, elimination of the weakest individuals and races, and wars among great powers. However, as we will see later, these fears may have been exaggerated.

Despite such criticisms, evolutionary theory changed how humans view themselves. As we will see throughout this chapter, it also had a profound impact on research methodology, prompting scientists to ask new questions and propose new hypotheses. In relation to conflict, the following questions were raised: Why are we, as animals, prone to conflict? Are we programmed to fight? What is the survival advantage to aggression? What do animal studies teach us about our humanity? The lines of questioning revealed by evolutionary theory were to have implications for methodologies in psychology, political science, sociology, neuroscience, systems theory, and even theology.

The Aggressive Instinct

Among zoologists, the question of aggression has long been a scientific puzzle. What are the origins of aggression? Is violence its inevitable outcome? Is conflict a consequence of aggression? For many Darwinists, the struggle for survival and natural selection automatically implied that aggression was a biological necessity, as functional to life as breathing, feeding, and breeding. Austrian biologist Konrad Lorenz (1903–89) was a pioneer in demonstrating that most behaviour is genetically programmed. Lorenz (1982) is also famous for his studies on imprinting, the identification of animals to the first living being that they encounter. (He imprinted many geese that docilely followed him wherever he went.) For Lorenz, imprinting proved that behaviour, in this case the "following" behaviour, was innate and not learned. He also showed how some birds often exhibit pre-programmed behaviour, such as insect chasing even when there are no insects around.

Lorenz (2002) believed that human behaviour was determined by primary and secondary instincts. Primary instincts include aggression and sexual drive and are first acquired through evolution. Secondary instincts, such as altruism and love, are acquired later. In this perspective, the origins of conflict are primary instincts, with the secondary instincts affecting (and in some ways restricting) the way conflict is conducted. Given his emphasis on primary instincts, it seemed to Lorenz that an authoritarian government was a reasonable way to manage people's gregarious and aggressive nature. In his youth, Lorenz was a member of the Nazi Party and fought with the Germans in World War II. After the war, he apologized for his Nazi past. He had come to realize that secondary instincts can mitigate the negative primary urges in individuals, and he became an advocate of education and culture that could allow people to become more civilized.[5]

The existence of an aggressive instinct has been a very contentious issue in biology and the human sciences. As we will see in Chapter 7, Sigmund Freud believed in the aggressive nature of humans. However, with Ivan Pavlov's work on conditioned reflexes in the late nineteenth and early twentieth centuries, psychology rapidly evolved towards the study of learned behaviour. Under the influence of Franz Boas (1928/1987), the American school of anthropology focused on the cultural determinants of behaviour. Most anthropologists, including Ashley Montagu (1976), have since insisted that human beings are different from other animals in the sense that they have not inherited any instincts and that there is no aggressive predisposition. As the social sciences began emphasizing the concept of nurture in the twentieth century, the aggressive instinct became an obsolete point—and even a dangerous one, as it was associated with Lorenz's Nazi past.

The issue of innate aggression reappeared in the 1970s, leading to a vigorous reaction from the mainstream social scientists. In 1986, several scientists from Western, communist, and neutral countries signed the Seville Statement on Violence, which condemns the view that violence is in our genes and that our species is inherently predisposed toward aggression.[6] This initiative was in line with the United Nations Educational, Scientific and Cultural Organization (UNESCO)'s concern for international peace and inspired its efforts to create and nurture a "culture of peace." This episode confirms that the biological approaches to human behaviour remain controversial. Currently, however, most biologists concur that the nature–nurture debate cannot be settled definitively one way or another. The behaviour of life forms, from single-cell to complex organisms, is a complicated interaction between internal and external factors, and human culture is an important part of the explanation of violent conflicts (Niehoff, 1999).

Sociobiology

Evolution and Human Behaviour

The signing of the Seville Statement on Violence was largely a response to sociobiology, the study of the biological aspects of social behaviour in animals and humans. In 1975, Edward O. Wilson (b. 1929), an American biologist specializing in insects, wrote *Sociobiology: The New Synthesis*, a book that was to have a profound impact on research in the field. Wilson thought that the lessons drawn from evolutionary biology could also account for fundamental human actions. Basically, he argues that most human behaviour is inherited, functional, and adaptive. Because the raison d'être of behaviour is to reproduce and thereby reinforce the species, the competition to breed creates conflict among individuals. For instance, males have historically tried to attract the most beautiful and healthy females in the hope of producing many children. To achieve this goal, males have used all means, from self-improvement to the acquisition of property to open violence against contenders. In this perspective, the acquisitive objectives of men are served by an aggressive behaviour that expresses itself in conflicts over the wooing of prospective mates. The most successful individuals tend to have more children, thereby reinforcing the species.

While the human and social sciences tend to see aggression as an extreme behaviour caused by pathologies or unusual pressures on individuals, sociobiology views it as a fundamental pattern of human survival and procreation. Wilson (1975) believes that humans are naturally aggressive. Developed in the long evolution of species, aggression is a behaviour that manifests itself in many forms: some are non-violent; some involve intimidation and harm; and some are murderous. However, Wilson warns that we should not see human beings as the most aggressive species on earth. While many people (including Lorenz)

BOX 6.1 | PRIMATES: AGGRESSIVE AND EMPATHETIC

(Masterfile Royalty Free)

(Masterfile Royalty Free)

Primates such as the chimpanzee are routinely used to personify different biological conceptions. They are shown either as aggressive beasts or as caring parents, indirectly reflecting the
two faces of humankind. Two trends have become apparent in the past few decades. First, it has
been demonstrated that primates are capable of murder, making them more violent than was
previously thought. Second, scientists have begun to study the capacity for empathy and altruism in primates and other mammals, as we will see in Box 6.2.

claim that only human beings kill other individuals of their own species, Wilson argues
that hyenas and lions, for example, have higher rates of infanticide, murder, and war than
do human beings. Furthermore, our close cousins the chimpanzees are also involved in of
murder and wars.

Sociobiology is concerned not only with individualistic aggressive behaviour but also
with altruistic behaviour. In some species, females will feed another's offspring, even if it
means that they and their own children may be weakened as a consequence. Socbiologists
usually claim that co-operation among animals and human beings is undertaken to make
the altruistic individual more attractive to other individuals, thereby improving his or her
chances of surviving and mating. A problem for sociobiology is that some human behaviour is radically altruistic and does not seem to fit this model. Why does a young woman
become a nun, eschewing marriage, progeny, and riches, to devote her life to sick and
dying people? Why would a soldier jump on an enemy grenade to protect his comrades
rather than run away from the explosion? These people would certainly have made dif-

ferent choices if they were motivated by only survival and procreation. These are extreme cases, but they serve to illustrate the difference between animals and people and represent a sociobiological puzzle.

There are two ways to deal with the altruism problem. The first assumes that the reproduction of the species or another type of group (kin, family, race, nation, etc.) is the paramount objective to which individuals instinctively subscribe. Therefore, people and animals sacrifice themselves for the survival of the group. According to this idea, the behaviour of, for instance, Mother Teresa is explained by the belief that we should take care of all people of our kin. Soldiers are influenced by the idea that they are all faced with the risk of sacrificing their lives to protect others. Howard Bloom (1997), a popular exponent of sociobiology, thinks that most human ideas work for the reproduction of society. To him, society is a "superorganism."

The superorganism thesis does not satisfy most contemporary evolutionists. They believe that attributing altruism to a natural submission of the individual for the benefit of the masses is an anthropomorphic error that extrapolates human conceptions of altruism onto animal species. Mainstream sociobiology prefers to believe that individuals act in order to protect only their own chances of survival and reproduction. For famous British biologist Richard Dawkins (b.1941), human beings are "survival machines" in the service of their immortal genes. Dawkins (1976) contends that risky behaviours also exist in animals, such as dominance fights between males or individual birds patrolling for predators. However, he does not try to explain these actions through the group survival model. To him, altruism serves only the individual's need to reproduce. Over time, an animal creates **evolutionary stable strategies (ESS)** that maximize its chances to procreate. Dawkins uses the language of game theory to explain how an ESS emerges as the best possible response to a particular survival problem. For example, flocks of birds that adopt the lone patrol ESS would tend to predominate over flocks that do not. Having several individuals take a risk at different times accrues each individual's chances of reproduction. As for the example of the dominance fight, it may be a risky gamble as to who will inherit the harem and liberally procreate for years to come.

However, most sociobiologists admit that extreme human altruism is primarily a result of culture. Many behavioural habits are learned within a culture and transmitted through teaching and example. Wilson argues that most human behaviour is cultural in origin. Dawkins is usually credited with creating the term **meme** to label a cultural pattern or norm that is passed on to future generations and that reproduces in the minds of people.[7] Many memes are functional in reproduction, but some fulfill religious or political needs that have nothing to do with evolutionary biology. For example, celibacy in human society must be explained by memes that support or even require such behaviour, such as those for priests of the Catholic Church. While Wilson and Dawkins believe that most behaviour can be understood as being guided by innate reproductive instincts, they allow that other types of behaviours—some even contrary to genetic interests—can prevail and thrive in the human species. This point of view is also espoused by social scientists and psychologists who are interested in complementing their own understanding of society with the study of evolutionary instincts.

Social Applications of Evolutionary Science

The sociobiological approach tells us that people will display behaviours that allow them to fulfill their fundamental biological needs, such as eating, keeping warm, and, most important, breeding. Other needs, such as the need to dominate, the need for affection, and the need for recognition, are simply indirect means to fulfill our basic biological requirements.

Evolutionary hypotheses have been used to study various forms of conflict. Since the late 1960s, American anthropologist Napoleon Chagnon (b.1938) has studied the Yanomamö people of Brazil. In his book *Yanomamö: The Fierce People*, Chagnon (1983) suggested that the violent ways of the people illustrate some basic biological principles. He found that 30 per cent of Yanomamö males are killed in combat or in assassinations and that 40 per cent were complicit in the murder of another Yanomamö man in their lifetime. He also observed that the men who killed had more status in society. Many captured women in neighbouring villages, and some mated with the widows of the men whom they had killed. As a whole, the men who killed the most also procreated the most. These findings were intended to show that killing is a way to eliminate rivals, acquire more sexual partners, and engender more offspring. Chagnon's research and conclusions have been criticized by mainstream anthropologists (see Borofsky et al., 2005). However, many other anthro-pologists have abandoned the cultural **paradigm** dominant in the discipline and have used biological theories to explain several phenomena, such as aspects of family, governance, aggression, and war.

The biological approach has also made inroads in psychology, sociology and criminology, where scholars have attempted to demonstrate that behaviours such as child neglect and abuse, rape, crime, and violence have biological and social roots. The new discipline of evolutionary psychology has attracted a lot of attention in using genetic hypotheses in place of learning models to explain human behaviour (Dunbar, Barrett, & Lycett, 2007; Pinker, 2002). For instance, Martin Daly and Margo Wilson (1998) have found that, in line with sociobiological hypotheses, the rates of child neglect and violence are much higher against non-kin children in reconstituted families than in households led by the two natural parents, even when one controls for socioeconomic status.[8] In their controversial *A Natural History of Rape*, Randy Thornhill and Craig T. Palmer (2000) argue that rape is not caused by the will to dominate women, as claimed in standard feminist and sociological literature, but is an ugly manifestation of ancient urges to procreate. Their primary evidence is that rape victims tend to be of a particular type, namely young, attractive females.

The study of primitive warfare, in particular, has received a great deal of attention from evolutionary sociologists and psychologists, who claimed—with some reason—that the field had been neglected by cultural anthropologists.[9] Steven Pinker (2002) claims that this derives from a modern Western tendency to deny the biological roots of human nature. Sociobiologists are quick to point out that the most advanced primates are usually bellicose and that there are strong similarities between chimpanzee warfare, Yanomamö warfare, the Crusades, and the US intervention in Iraq, in that these are all instances of gene machine coalitions fighting each other in an effort to generate the most offspring.

As we can conclude from this discussion, the level of generality in sociobiological hypotheses is very high and may not lead to precise explanations. For example, Bradley A. Thayer (2004) offers a complete Darwinist theory of international relations by using sociobiology to confirm "realist" hypotheses on war and peace. This extreme generality is also found in Joseph Lopreato and Penny A. Green's (1990) study of political revolutions. In their view, revolutions are displacements of alpha males by beta males (who eventually become the new alphas), a situation that also occurs in chimpanzee colonies.

Critiques of Sociobiology

Sociobiology has elicited substantial criticism since the 1970s and has acquired a kind of diabolical reputation. Some of the harshest critiques of the approach come from other eminent biologists who refuse to apply evolutionary theses about the animal world to human beings (see Gould, 1978; Lewontin, Rose, & Kamin, 1984). Although the modern-day variants of Darwinist theory found in sociobiology are much more refined and circumspect than the late-nineteenth-century imperialist theories, they still raise issues of social Darwinism and scientific racism.

Sociobiologists' answer to these accusations is that elitism and racism are not derived from biology but are normative positions. To say that nature amounts to a harsh struggle among egoistic individuals does not mean that one endorses it. Actually, many sociobiologists contend that the point of their approach is to develop more humane behaviours. Such was the task that Lorenz set for himself after his repudiation of Nazism. Nevertheless, suspicions that sociobiology can be used by elitists and racists bent on the weakening of democracy, human rights, and the welfare state linger and will likely continue to affect many people's perception of biological approaches.

If we look beyond the moral and political issues of sociobiology, we can observe that the approach suffers from its failure to explain important points of human behaviour. We have already alluded to the puzzle of altruistic behaviour, which remains a constant sore point in sociobiology. In particular, the inability to solve this problem leads many people to conclude that sociobiologists neglect the psychology of people and the importance of culture and ideologies in human society. Other nagging puzzles include the existence of several self-defeating behaviours (e.g. depression, alcoholism, drug use, suicide) in the human population. In a well-regulated species endowed with adequate ESS, such behaviours should be extremely rare, if not absent. After all, they go against the individual reproductive imperative.

Another puzzle is the question of **demographic transitions**, which occur when the birth and death rates in a population decrease. When population growth slows down (or stops), demographic decline sometimes follows, as is currently the case in some European countries. The demographic transition began in eighteenth-century Europe and is now spreading across the world. This phenomenon raises the question of why people voluntarily reduce the number of their descendants. If the purpose of human behaviour is to further the species, we should be having as many children as possible. However, large families are now rare, and this change is probably better explained by economic, social, and

---

BOX 6.2 | VARIATIONS IN THE STUDY OF EMPATHY

In response to the criticisms levelled at sociobiology, some scientists claim that aggression may have been overstated as a natural instinct and that empathy (the ability to understand another's feelings) and sympathy (the impulse to do something about the suffering of others) should be given more attention. For example, biologist Mary Clark (1990) observes that the human capacity to develop language and culture derives from a capacity to connect with one another and develop significant relationships. She points to the long period of time during which a child is dependent on its mother, making it necessary to have a supportive community within early stages of human development. She also suggests that the field of biology has been skewed by far more research that focuses on aggression rather than caring relationships.

Empathy research dates back to 1959, when Russell Church (as cited in de Waal, 2009, p. 70) published a scientific paper documenting experiments in which rats chose to deprive themselves of food in order to alleviate the pain of fellow rats. Since Church's paper, the field of empathy studies within biology has taken on a life of its own. As the hypotheses regarding aggression are tempered through a supposition that much of the biological world functions on the basis of empathy, care, and connection, the problem of altruism diminishes. Empathy studies also offers new ways of understanding the dynamics of reconciliation (see Chapter 13).

In 1980, eminent ethologist Frans de Waal (b. 1948) experienced a significant change of view regarding empathy when he assisted a veterinary surgeon with a chimpanzee that had suffered massive injuries at the hands of two fellow chimps. The shock of being beside the vet in that "bloody operating room" prompted him to shift his focus to "what holds societies together" (de Waal, 2009, p. 44). In the three decades since, de Waal has conducted numerous experiments, made countless observations of animals, and assembled formidable documentation regarding the dynamics of empathy. For example, he observed chimpanzees in the Ivory Coast's Taï National Park caring for other chimpanzees who had been attacked by leopards—licking their wounds, chasing away flies, and protecting them (de Waal, 2009, p.7). In experiments where capuchin monkeys had to choose between a token that would give the subject food and one that would also give food to a monkey in a neighbouring cage, different monkeys showed a strong inclination towards choosing the latter token (de Waal, 2009, pp. 112–113).

De Waal also warns us about the naturalistic fallacy, which connects what is to what ought to be. For instance, because there are examples of a harsh struggle for survival among animal species, the naturalistic fallacy implies that this is how things should be among humans. Biology has the capacity to shape our attitudes toward conflict and the arguments we make for certain contentious policies. It is also the focus of social conflict. However, it does not lead to clear-cut conclusions about the human species. Whether we value an aggressive approach to life or a more convivial approach may be shaped by how evolution is presented to us.

cultural factors than by biological ones. Nevertheless, biological explanations of conflict and violence are more influential now than ever before, as neo-Darwinian hypotheses and methods have found their way into mainstream social sciences and psychology (especially evolutionary psychology). Plainly put, it is impossible to ignore the sociobiological explanations of conflict.

POPULATION, RESOURCES, AND CONFLICT

Malthusianism

The interplay between population pressures and resource scarcity has been suggested as a possible explanation for conflict for a long time. In short, the hypothesis states that the higher the discrepancy between available food (and other resources) and the number of people to feed, the higher the chances that conflict and violence will occur. One of the major proponents of this relationship was Robert Thomas Malthus (1766–1834), an economist and Anglican clergyman. His anonymously published *An Essay on the Principle of Population* (1798/2008) posited that population growth followed a geometric curve (2, 4, 8, etc.), while food production increased arithmetically (1, 2, 3, etc.). As a result, population grows much faster than food supplies. In order to provide enough for the population (the subsistence level), the number of people must be restricted. Some social mechanisms, such as abstinence, contraception, abortion, infanticide, emigration, political repression, and war, limit population growth. The most striking modern example of this type of population control is China's one-child policy. However, these methods are far from sufficient to limit growth. For Malthus, the natural phenomena of famines and epidemics were the most important factors in population control. Therefore, unchecked population growth is likely to result in calamities such as starvation, pestilence, massacres, and wars. The point for conflict studies is that, in what Malthus called the struggle for existence, human beings are regularly in conflict with each other if they fail to increase the food supply or reduce the population.

Malthus's theories were quite influential. For example, the careless attitude of the British government towards famines in India and Ireland in the nineteenth century has been attributed to the internalization by many Britons of the notion that such penuries were natural population control mechanisms. However, Malthus's ideas were also severely criticized, notably by socialists such as Karl Marx and Friedrich Engels, who believed that overpopulation and famines were caused by capitalism. Liberal writers disliked Malthus's lack of faith in humanity's capacity to improve its lot through social and technological advancements. Moralists objected to his harsh views about the problems that confront humankind. Over time, his influence diminished. The main empirical problem with his theory was that Europe did not experience the ecological catastrophes that he had envisioned. To the contrary, the population decreased without large-scale tragedies; the production of foodstuffs increased significantly; and the general lot of Western Europeans improved dramatically in the second half of the nineteenth century. The demographic transition had occurred, and Malthus was generally considered to be wrong.

Interest in Malthus's hypotheses was renewed in the 1970s, when the high birth rate in Third World countries, the overexploitation of resources, and the deterioration of the natural environment created alarmist descriptions of a catastrophic future. Economist Paul Erlich (1968) foresaw an incoming overpopulation crisis accompanied by epidemics, famines, decrease in life expectancy, and political violence. The 1972 report by The Club of Rome analysts predicted the exhaustion of many resources, an agricultural crisis, and an environmental disaster. These conclusions have not been realized, discrediting Malthusian thought once again.

Contemporary Research on Resources and Conflict

In the 1980s, the discovery of the hole in the ozone layer and the first evidence of global warming aroused another generation of scientists preoccupied with the dangers of environmental degradation, such as water scarcity (see Figure 6.1). Although most have been careful not to prophesy catastrophic scenarios for the near future, they have nevertheless hypothesized that, in the medium- to long-term, the effects of human-made environmental destruction could increase the number and severity of human conflicts and incidents of violence. One example of this reasoning is the work of Canadian academic Thomas Homer-Dixon (b. 1956). In the 1990s, Homer-Dixon (1991, 1993, 1994) wanted to verify that "environmental scarcities" caused by resource depletion, population growth, and inequitable resource distribution result in increased animosity among groups of people over the control of the remaining resources. His team of researchers studied a number of cases, often concentrating on the issue of water (e.g. in the Senegal River basin, the Ganges and Jamuna rivers in South Asia, and the Euphrates River in Western Asia) but also dealing with overpopulation (e.g. in Rwanda) and deforestation (e.g. in Chiapas). Their conclusions were tentative. While there was support for the idea that environmental issues played a role in conflicts in these parts of the world, it was not proven definitively because the research design did not permit the elimination of economical, cultural, or political factors in the development of conflicts.

Other research has refuted Homer-Dixon's claims. Sponsored by the American government to study the conditions leading to the implosion of societies, the State Failure Task Force (SFTF, 1999)—later renamed the Political Instability Task Force—concluded that environmental stress resulting from deforestation and water scarcity is such a minor factor as compared to economic and political determinants of conflict that its influence is unnoticeable. The Environmental Change and Security Program (ECSP) at Woodrow Wilson University has regularly observed in its reports that the sharing of water resources is mostly an opportunity for co-operation, not conflict.[10] Some empirical studies have also confirmed that, with the partial exception of extremely dry basins, the sharing of a water resource led to more co-operative outcomes than violent ones (see Wolf, Stahl, & Macomber, 2003).

Emphasizing environmental factors has always struck some theorists as an overly complex model of conflict analysis. According to Nils Peter Gleditsch (1998), Homer-Dixon's model attempts to include economic and political variables but is too complex for the

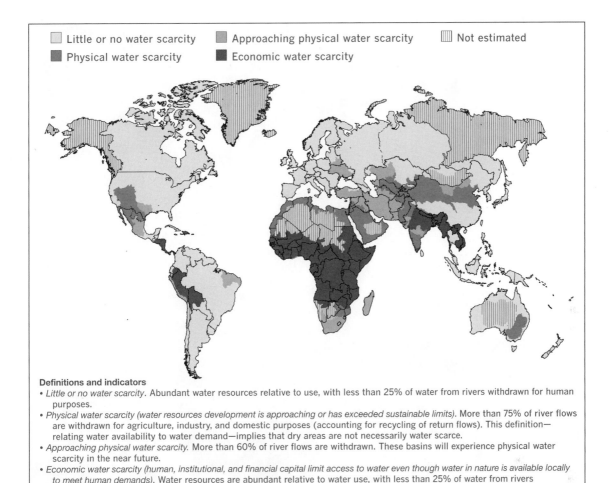

Definitions and indicators
- *Little or no water scarcity*. Abundant water resources relative to use, with less than 25% of water from rivers withdrawn for human purposes.
- *Physical water scarcity (water resources development is approaching or has exceeded sustainable limits)*. More than 75% of river flows are withdrawn for agriculture, industry, and domestic purposes (accounting for recycling of return flows). This definition—relating water availability to water demand—implies that dry areas are not necessarily water scarce.
- *Approaching physical water scarcity*. More than 60% of river flows are withdrawn. These basins will experience physical water scarcity in the near future.
- *Economic water scarcity (human, institutional, and financial capital limit access to water even though water in nature is available locally to meet human demands)*. Water resources are abundant relative to water use, with less than 25% of water from rivers withdrawn for human purposes, but malnutrition exists.

FIGURE 6.1 | AREAS OF PHYSICAL AND ECONOMIC WATER SCARCITY

The high population in many regions, combined with poverty and limited water resources, worsens life conditions and may lead to conflicts.

Source: Reprinted with permission of the International Water Management Institute.

verification of causal relationships between environmental scarcities and conflict. Furthermore, Gleditsch notes that students of environmental causes of conflict tend to select cases where political contention is present and neglect the many cases where environmental stress is not accompanied by strife. Homer-Dixon is no longer involved in researching the environmental sources of armed conflict, but other theorists such as Colin H. Kahl (2006) have picked up the issue and have tried to improve on his model.

The environmental conflict hypothesis has been represented in the general public primarily by American scientist Jared Diamond (b. 1937), who has written two best-selling

(AP Photo/Alexander Zemlianichenko)

Due to agricultural overexploitation, the Aral Sea in Uzbekistan has lost most of its water, turning boats into desert wrecks. Will similar disasters threaten other water bodies? Will this threat lead to violent conflicts? For the moment, answers to these questions are uncertain, but we cannot ignore the potential for conflict within environmental degradation.

books—*Guns, Germs, and Steel* (1997) and *Collapse* (2005)—about the effects of the environment and resources on human societies, including human conflict and war. In *Collapse*, Diamond argues that the methods and policies that human groups use to address their environmental problems make the difference between success and failure, survival and extinction—a thesis that has obvious applications in debates about our planet. He points to successful cases of resources husbandry, such as the Edo period and Meji restoration in Japan (1603–1868). However, his book abounds with examples of complete failures, such as Viking Greenland, Easter Island, the Maya civilization, and modern-day Haiti. The almost complete destruction of the tree cover on Easter Island, caused by centuries-long deforestation and resulting in famine, disease, massacres, and war, is a particularly dramatic instance of human disaster. Diamond writes convincingly and provides impressive evidence for his case studies, including the most recent archaeological, bio-archaeological, genetic, and climatological data. However, one cannot leave the book without the impression that he has summoned the most extreme cases in the service of his thesis. Surely, most civilizations (including our own, we hope) have been more successful in managing their ecological balance.

Even if we put aside the extreme cases described by Diamond, there remains the possibility that environmental degradation—be it air or water pollution, soil exhaustion, desertification, biodiversity reduction, industrial contamination, or the decline in mineral resources—leads to serious conflicts and even wars among human groups. The cases identified by Homer-Dixon and Diamond may not have all led to catastrophic outcomes, but they are troubling because they could have caused violent feuds.

A BIOLOGICAL APPROACH TO EMOTIONS

Another way to study the link between biology and conflict is to look at the influence of biochemical, neurological, and endocrinal factors on the propensity of people to engage in conflict and aggression. In this section, we shift the focus to one aspect of this effect. We will see how neurobiology helps explain some of the processes implicated in the emotions that fuel violent conflict and how the brain can override involuntary emotional effects in order to resist violent impulses.

The Evolution of Emotions

Within the mammalian brain, emotions are controlled by the limbic system, a set of structures located on the inner edge of the cortex. While larger in size, the mammalian cort is identical in structure to that of reptiles, one of the oldest and most primitive animals. However, reptiles do not have a limbic system and therefore no emotions—for example, a crocodile can eat its young without feeling a thing (Lewis, Amini, & Lannon, 2000). The capacity for emotions reaps several benefits for mammals. First, emotions make bonding possible. Mammals often live in herds, where the members look out for one another. Elephants, for example, have been known to go back to where one of their "friends" died in order to mourn the death six months after the fact. Second, emotions allow mammals to care for their young, facilitating both the safety of the offspring and the passing on of vital skills. Everyone knows not to get between a mother bear and her cub lest she get angry and attack. Third, emotions empower animals to respond quickly to threats—either to flee or to fight (Lorenz, 2002). Finally, emotions enable the communication of information and feelings, making it possible to have complex, multi-party responses. This communication works on the basis of sounds, gestures, and information fields. For instance, biologist Rupert Sheldrake (2003) is researching such phenomena as the ability of pets to visibly demonstrate that they anticipate their owners' arrival, even though there are no sensory stimuli indicating their return.

As humans evolved, we not only maintained and built upon the emotional capacity of other mammals but also developed an aptitude for reason and the use of symbol systems, including language. We will return to the relationship between these cognitive functions and emotions later. For now, we will examine how emotions are conveyed and activated.

The Role of Neurotransmitters

Neurotransmitters are protein molecules that move from cell to cell in order to convey information, including thoughts and emotions (Pert, 1997). There are over 20 different neurotransmitters, each of which carries different information and has a unique effect. Some cells give off neurotransmitters and others receive them. Each cell has receptor molecules on its surface, which are specialized to receive only one particular neurotransmitter. Put another way, receptor molecules are like keyholes and neurotransmitters are the keys. For example, if the body is flooded with the neurotransmitter associated with anger, it knows what to do: various glands produce hormones that carry more specific information; various blood vessels dilate so that more blood flows to muscles that could be used for fighting; the stomach and intestines stop working to conserve energy; and adrenalin is released, which stimulates the heart to beat faster.

Blockers are like neurotransmitters in that they are also keys to receptor molecules. However, they do not convey the same information. Their function is to fill receptor molecules in order to obstruct the neurotransmitters. As soon as the body releases a large number of neurotransmitters associated with a given emotion, some blockers are immediately discharged to balance the effects (Pert, 1997). Otherwise, in our anger example, the heart would beat faster and faster, eventually causing heart failure. If, however, a person has a chemical imbalance, he or she is unable to properly control his or her emotions. In such cases, he or she can be prescribed drugs that artificially infuse the body with certain neurotransmitters and blockers, thereby providing an emotional effect similar to what the mind and body would produce naturally.

Any person can become addicted to having a flood of neurotransmitters associated with a certain emotion. The addiction can be based on using artificial neurotransmitters or on having the kind of experience that produces the neurotransmitters naturally. Consider the following quote by chemist and Holocaust survivor Primo Levi (1988):

> Power is like a drug: the need for either is unknown to anyone who has not tried them, but after the initiation, which . . . can be fortuitous, the dependency and need for ever larger doses is born, as are the denial of reality and the return to childish dreams of omnipotence . . . : a distorted view of the world, dogmatic arrogance, the need for adulation, convulsive clinging to the levers of command, and contempt for the law. (p. 67)

This statement suggests that, if certain goals have an emotional tie, the vigour with which we pursue them may be out of proportion to their overall importance when examined critically.

How an Emotion Is Triggered

We constantly take in information through our senses. These stimuli travel along neurological pathways to the brain, where they are filtered by the amygdala, an almond-shaped structure that is part of the limbic system (Niehoff, 1999). If a particular sense perception involves ongoing emotional concerns, the amygdala sends it to other parts of the limbic system for processing. If it requires thought, it is sent to the cortex for processing. However, if it is linked to a powerful emotion that demands no processing, the amygdala acts unilaterally and releases neurotransmitters that initiate an immediate response. For example, when we touch something extremely hot, we feel a burning sensation and withdraw our hand immediately. The amygdala recognizes the signal of burning as urgent and sends a signal to the hand to immediately withdraw. For some people, certain sights or sounds instantly trigger anger or fear. New research has also linked the amygdala to our immediate responses to injustices, which we discuss in Chapter 15 (Gospic, et al., 2011).

We learn a whole repertoire of emotions early on in life. As children, the feeling of comfort and security that we felt when on our mother's breast produced a positive emotion. The fear when we are alone and unable to connect with our parents is another. The face is hardwired to our emotional system, and the facial expressions associated with different emotions are universal (Goleman, 2003). From early on, we learn to read emotions on the faces of others, which contributes to an emotional repertoire.

Just as external stimuli trigger emotions, so do our memories of the deep and profound feelings that we have experienced in the past. Some of these memories are stored at the cellular level and are pervasive within the body. We may not always be conscious of the fact that we have this pile of emotional memories. However, if a situation similar to the one that initially produced the emotion occurs, it can recall that emotion, often as powerfully as the first experience. The trigger simply sets in motion the release of the appropriate neurotransmitters, which flood the body and produce the emotional effects.

Emotional memories also have a strong impact because the emotional part of the brain has no comprehension of time. When a given emotion is triggered, something that happened, say, 20 years ago is experienced as though it is happening in the present. If a negative emotional memory is initiated in the course of a conflict, it can intensify the reaction and lead to conflict escalation. Chemical imbalances and physical conditions that impede the healthy function of the neurological system can also have grave consequences. For example, the autopsy of a man who shot a number of people revealed a large growth on his amygdala (Noll, 2003). This is an exceptional case, but it supports our argument that emotions play a huge role in conflict, that they are often difficult to control, and that the field of conflict studies benefits from understanding how they are produced.

A Systems Approach to Emotions

It is now clear to neurobiologists that what we experience as emotions is the result of a complex inter-related system. While we have identified the limbic system of the brain as the central player, researchers such as Paul Pearsall (1998) have suggested that the heart and other organs may play a more substantial role than was previously thought. Based on this argument, it makes sense to think of the relationship between reason and emotions as one that occurs within a complex system in which each component has an impact on the other elements (Noll, 2003).

Thinking about emotions in the biological mode affects our understanding of how conflicts start, how they play out, and how they instigate other conflicts. As previously mentioned, emotional memories can influence conflicts. Even something as simple as a smell that was present during a past event can cause an involuntary return of emotions. If another party responds defensively to these emotions, the conflict may become more severe. Once there is a flood of neurotransmitters, the whole body is engaged in an emotional response. The more parts of the body that get involved, the harder it is for the cognitive aspect of our minds to override the emotional impulses. Furthermore, new emotional memories are created, which can return at another time.

In a situation where a whole population has had a common experience resulting in an emotional response, there is a collective emotional memory. Political leaders can seize on symbols related to these memories and use them to stir feelings within the population that can be directed against a target of the leader's choosing.[11] One reason for Hitler's success was his ability to draw on the German people's shame and anger at having been defeated in World War I and subjected to heavy penalties. In 1989, Serbian President Slobodan Milošević used the remains of Lazar, the vanquished hero of the 1389 Battle of Kosovo, to rouse nationalist emotions during the anniversary of the event (Volkan, 1998).

Emotions play a powerful role in our lives and sometimes take control of our reactions, which can create or intensify conflicts. However, there may be a way to avoid this situation. Medical scientists such as David Servan-Schreiber (2005) have discovered that the left frontal lobe of the brain has the power to override the promptings of the amygdala. This means that we can train our minds to recognize when our bodies are subject to a given emotional reaction and control it. Because emotional reactions can be immediate, sometimes simply taking time to make a decision can diminish the degree to which they determine behaviour. As a result, some conflicts could be less severe or even avoided.

When we see people in conflict, we inevitably see people expressing strong emotions. In some cases, it is impossible to figure out the dynamics of the conflict without understanding the emotions involved. Looking at emotions from a biological perspective helps us realize that they are a significant part of our makeup. However, human behaviour is not completely determined by chemical reactions and neurotransmitters. In the next chapter, we will continue to examine the relationship between emotions and conflict.

COMPLEX ADAPTIVE SYSTEMS

Darwin's theory of evolution offers many insights into the dynamics of how some species survive and others become extinct. However, it offers little in the understanding of how new species come into existence and how existing species adapt to new environments. The new field of systems biology addresses these questions. Systems biologist Stuart Kauffman (b. 1940) is one of the pioneers of the concept of complex adaptive systems. These systems, which can be as tiny as a cell or as large as an ecosystem, contain such a multitude of variables that it is impossible to control what occurs within them (Kauffman, 1995, 2008). Any community is an example of a complex adaptive system. There are so many possible relationships, dynamics, and individual variations that it would be impossible to account for everything that happens with a single explanation. Change can sometimes be brought about by one small event that ends up cascading as individuals influence one another in unforeseen ways. Complex adaptive systems are self-creating in that they emerge from the interplay of a number of factors.

Kauffman (2008) also advances the concept of emergent creativity to describe how new entities come into being. When there are enough different elements present and enough possible combinations of connecting them, conditions are right for something new to emerge. However, this result cannot be pre-determined. Consider the following two scenarios. A number of individuals in the same geographical area cannot or will not communicate with one another. In this case, a community will not emerge because there are no possibilities for connections. In another area, a number of different people are brought together and are forced to communicate by a catastrophe. As they work together, they make connections. Eventually, a sense of community emerges among them. In the second scenario, both conditions are met—diverse elements and possibilities for connections to be made. More abstractly, through the interaction of the complex elements in a given context (called a platform), a new combination of elements produces something that is qualitatively different and cannot be deduced from its parts (Kauffman, 2008). Kauffman uses the term *criticality* to refer to that state when the number of elements and the possible combinations is optimum. Too much of either can lead to chaos and too few to stasis.

The first and most dramatic example of emergent creativity was the development of life from inorganic matter. Kauffman traces how the principle of emergent creativity is evident in the evolutionary progression to new life forms. One of the implications of this evolution is that, as new forms are created, there is a built-in tendency to diversity. Each new emergent entity introduces adjacent possibilities—new uses for what was produced or new possibilities for other things to develop. Kauffman provides many biological examples, but a case that relates to contemporary reality is that the emergence of the Internet has offered the adjacent possibility of such applications as Facebook. Kauffman (2008) goes on to show how the legal and economic systems exemplify principles of emergent creativity.

Another manifestation of emergent creativity in complex adaptive systems is their ability to self-organize. The implications of this quality in terms of conflict studies is that, in instances of conflict within a complex situation, there is a realization that the factors cannot be controlled. Furthermore, the dynamics among the factors do not work in a linear fashion but interact in a way that cannot be controlled by any one variable. In complex systems at the edge of chaos (i.e. point of criticality), a small alteration can be the catalyst for massive changes. For example, the end of the Cold War and the complete breakdown of the Soviet system occurred in a manner that no one was able to foresee. In this case, a few factors came together. First, the Soviet economy was overextended, in large measure because of the arms race. Second, President Reagan started a program of space-based missile defence. Matching this program would have pushed the Soviet economy over the edge. Third, Soviet leader Mikhail Gorbachev introduced policies of glasnost and perestroika, leading to more openness on the part of government. Finally, he introduced the rule of law, with a commitment to not suppress dissent violently. These events meant that new combinations of elements became possible. The massive system of state control fell apart; a new form of government was introduced; a market economy came into being; the various republics within the Soviet system achieved independence; and the antagonistic Cold War came to an end. A chain reaction then led to similar transformations in various countries of the Warsaw Pact. For example, the dismantling of the Berlin Wall became a powerful symbol for the changes in East Germany.

Many conflicts are complex, as are the processes of reconciliation. Hence, the application of complexity theory within this field is rich with new possibilities. One example is the work of Deborah Sword (2003), who used complexity theory to understand the dynamics of protest crowds. Cases of reconciliation (see Chapter 13) bear a striking resemblance to emergent creativity.

CONCLUSION

The study of conflicts, aggression, and violence through biological lenses has led to interesting discoveries and theories but has fluctuated over time. Darwinism was quite popular in the late nineteenth century, receded after World War I, and was revived in modified forms in the late 1970s. The link between resources, the environment, and conflicts peaked in the early 1800s, the 1970s, and the 1990s but was long forgotten for most of the twentieth century. Despite these variations, the biological research applied to human behaviour and to societies has made significant progress in the last 40 years. Sociobiological studies are theoretically refined and based on a large number of observations. The links between human activity and the degradation of the natural environment are better documented. Neurobiology has given us a new awareness about the dynamics of emotions and how emotions play a role in conflict. These insights, in turn, can be used to increase our own understanding of ourselves, leading to increased emotional intelligence. The concept of complex adaptive systems provides a new analytical tool for examining conflict, where many variables come into play.

There will always be normative and scientific objections to using biology to explain human behaviour. However, understanding biological processes can provide a more complete explanation of human strife and aggression, thereby contributing to the analysis of conflict. Biologists are aware of the false conclusions that almost killed the career of Konrad Lorenz and others. Their research is heavily peer reviewed and also monitored and commented upon by ethics specialists, social scientists, and psychologists. The faint perspective of the return of social Darwinism should not stop us from drawing on biology for a more complete explanation of human strife, aggression, and co-operation.

DISCUSSION QUESTIONS

1. How can the theory of evolution help us understand ourselves and the conflicts that we wage?

2. Is aggression part of human nature or a learned behaviour? Give reasons to support your answer.

3. What environmental factors might naturally induce or intensify conflict among groups of people?

4. Will we develop a "cure" for aggression and conflicts? How would such a remedy work? Would that be a good thing?

NOTES

1. This statement was also used by Thomas Hobbes (see Chapter 8). Frans de Waal (2009) calls the comparison "a questionable statement about our own species based on false assumptions about another species" (p. 4).

2. It should be remembered that Gobineau published his major treatise between 1853 and 1855, before *The Origin of Species*, and that most of the authors of the scientific racism school were unacquainted with modern biology.

3. A major proponent of eugenics was Francis Galton, Darwin's cousin. Eugenics remained a fashionable idea until the 1930s.

4. For example, Spencer (1884/1969) was considered a libertarian, meaning that he was hostile to the state playing a role in the economy.

5. Lorenz shared the 1973 Nobel Prize in Medicine with Otto Frisch and Nikolaas Tinbergen, who had reached the same conclusions in their separate observations of different animal species.

6. For the full text of the statement, see http://portal.unesco.org/education/en/ev.php-URL_ID=3247&URL_DO=DO_TOPIC&URL_SECTION=201.html

7. To Dawkins, memes are the "new replicators" (as opposed to genes, the "old replicators") that survive or fail according to Darwinian law. For example, a political ideology will emerge and prosper only if it replicates in enough individuals over time.

8. Daly and Wilson (1988) have also contributed a study of homicide using evolutionary hypotheses.

9. We will return to these debates in Chapter 8.

10. For ECSP annual reports and publications, see www.wilsoncenter.org/index.cfm?topic_id=1413&fuseaction=topics.publications

11. This theme is echoed in the literature on emotional intelligence (see Goleman, 1997).

INTRODUCTION

The psychology of conflict is a varied and complex field of study that includes behaviourism, personality theory, and social psychology. Following an introduction of Freudian psychoanalysis, this chapter focuses on these three areas in relation to conflict. We discuss various psychological approaches, from humanism to needs theory and conformity, and review both classic and contemporary research within the field.

PSYCHOANALYSIS

Psychoanalysis addresses struggles, relational dysfunctions, and personal problems through an exploration of an inner psychic world that is largely shaped through childhood experiences. We begin with Freud's contribution to an understanding of psychology, examine how his theories were developed by his disciples, and highlight major critiques of his work.

The Study of Neuroses

No introduction to the psychological aspects of conflict can ignore the seminal contribution of Sigmund Freud (1856–1939), who revolutionized the study of the human mind. By treating patients with mental afflictions such as hysteria and other neuroses, Freud concluded that these problems were not related to physical health, sex (hysteria was often diagnosed as a woman's ailment), or immorality (as was often claimed by religious authorities).[1] Noting patterns among his patients, he realized that they had all suffered from some kind of childhood trauma (a physically and/or psychologically painful wound or shock). Some were exposed to indecent sexual behaviour; others were poorly groomed by their parents; and still others had been excessively punished. Because these traumas could not be overcome, patients developed anxious or obsessive thoughts and behaviours. For example, those who were abused by their parents might develop an obsessive behaviour about health, food, or dress in later life, thus hiding the painful memories of their childhood.

Freud believed that the key to curing such afflictions was discovering the trauma that caused the neurosis. He did not believe that physical treatments, medications, and persuasion could deliver the victims of their ills. He thought that the key to their cure was to discover what traumas had caused the neurosis in the first place. This process, which became known as the psychoanalytical cure, involves a long and

CHAPTER OBJECTIVES

This chapter will help you develop an understanding of the

- background and key concepts of psychoanalytic thought;
- role and limits of behaviourist psychology in relation to conflict studies;
- psychological approaches to studying personality and how they help to understand conflict;
- key social psychological explanations of conflict;
- potential of human needs theory to understand conflict dynamics; and
- function of prejudice and conformity in conflict, particularly in violent behaviour.

systematic dialogue between the patient and his or her therapist, who analyzes the patient's thoughts, remembrances, and dreams. Freud developed this approach, wrote extensively about it, and taught it to several students and colleagues. In treating his patients, Freud developed a theory that the mind has both conscious and unconscious parts. While the former includes everything in our awareness, the latter contains the feelings, thoughts, and memories of which we are unaware. Freud became convinced that the unconscious, fed by childhood experiences and the internalization of social norms, was the source of most of our ideas and behavioural patterns.

The Human Psyche

Freud mapped the unconscious and conscious regions of the human psyche, labelling the three main parts the ego, id, and superego. In Freudian terms, the ego is the central part of the human psyche; however, it is not the rational thinking self of Descartes or simply a cybernetic data processor. The ego is not always conscious but relies on mental mechanisms (such as transfer, avoidance, and projection) of which people are unaware. Constructed from the two other components of the psyche, the ego acts as a sort of manager while also taking charge of the interactions with the outside world. In fact, the ego is continually torn between various objectives, such as fulfilling basic impulses, obeying social norms, affirming personal needs and values, and responding to external demands.

Freud also hypothesized the existence of two fundamental biological drives—Eros and Thanatos—that constitute the id. Eros is the instinct of life, which is necessary in human reproduction and is also the source of many human emotions, including love, friendship, spirituality, aesthetics, and hope. Thanatos, the death instinct, is responsible for our tendencies toward aggression and the infliction of pain, despair, and melancholy. (As mentioned in Chapter 6, Freud believed that human beings were naturally aggressive.) This part of our mental makeup is always unconscious. However, the life and death instincts are at work in the numerous conflicts that exist within ourselves, and we can indirectly observe their effects in our behaviours.

Obviously, human beings are not guided exclusively by their erotic and murderous impulses; otherwise social life would be completely anarchical and precarious. It would truly be a war of all against all. Freud posited the existence of another region of the psyche called the superego, which is largely subconscious. The superego, stores the multiple norms of behaviour acquired from society. The superego acts as a brake against the expression of the fundamental impulses of the id; however, it is far from being an infallible shield. It is clear that, when they want to satisfy their desires, people are often conflicted about whether to follow or ignore the prohibitions and imperatives of society.

The Future of Civilization

Freud also wrote about collective psychology, now known as social psychology. One of his main subjects of inquiry was human crowds, both natural (e.g. bands) and artificial (e.g. religious or political groups). In his investigation of why people behave like sheep in crowds, he pointed to the importance of several factors: the presence of a more or less evident father figure behind all crowds (e.g. the illustrious ancestors or current leaders of movements), the emotional Eros-driven need to relate to and love others, the negative instincts that push people to fight enemies, and the internalized norms of identity and conformity spread by the dominant culture. According to Freud, the need to congregate around a common cause is so strong that people will use and accentuate the slightest differences with their neighbours to justify regrouping against them. This practice, called the narcissism of small differences, has been used to explain puzzling cases of group competition and repression, including Nazism in the 1930s. In recent years, the concept has been revived to explain contemporary ethnic conflicts in Northern Ireland and Rwanda. For instance, Canadian philosopher and former Liberal leader Michael Ignatieff (1995) has used the concept in his well-known essay on the Yugoslav conflict. We return to the subject of crowds later in this chapter.

Freud's research greatly influenced his view on the future of society. On one hand, he thought that human beings were perfectible to an extent. For example, he thought that the development of non-violent social norms ensured a more peaceful and predictable life for most people in advanced societies. On the other hand, his witnessing of such events as World War I, Soviet totalitarianism, and Nazi fanaticism reminded him that there remains a powerful death instinct in each of us. Under some circumstances of mindless crowd behaviour and skilful mental manipulation, modern people can still perform awful acts.

Applications of Freudian Thought

Freud inspired the development of a psychological approach that deals with most aspects of human behaviour, including conflict, aggression, and violence. In this section, we survey three popular offshoots of Freudian theory: personality studies, the process of civilization, and projection.

Personality and Conflict

In the 1920s, a group of German-Jewish intellectuals, several of whom were practising psychoanalysts, combined the contributions of Freud with the analyses of Karl Marx to develop an original perspective on human behaviour.[2] The Frankfurt School, as this group was called, was concerned with how capitalism negatively influenced individual development and how freedom from the constraints of tradition and the market could be achieved. In the 1930s, the rise of Nazism stimulated their thinking about personalities, how some people are predestined to become leaders and followers of the most extreme movements. In particular, Erich Fromm (1900–80) and Theodor Adorno (1903–69) created the concept of the authoritarian personality to explain the mental makeup of Adolf Hitler and his supporters. Adorno believed that fascist attitudes were derived from personality and later devised the F-scale to measure fascist tendencies in people (see Adorno, Frenkel-Brunswik, Levinson, & Sanford, 1950). The Frankfurt School members also studied how the development of society trumps the personal development of people toward a fully free and fruitful existence. Along with Wilhelm Reich (1933/1980), a student of Freud, Fromm (1994) posited that the submission to authority and the market instilled a "fear of freedom" in people, limiting their aspirations for a better life and reinforcing the power of social elites.

These studies were not systematic, however. Fromm's books were mostly based on philosophical and Marxist analysis, with some individual and anecdotal evidence. Adorno's authoritarian personality studies were more structured, but they were methodologically and theoretically flawed and were superseded by decades of scientific research on personality. Nevertheless, these works inspired the scientific study of personality and its influence on conflicting and violent behaviours.

The Process of Civilization

In a very different approach, German sociologist Norbert Elias (1897–1990) used Freudian thought to study the emergence of modern Western civilization. Instead of looking toward Karl Marx for guidance, Elias took some of his inspiration from sociologist Max Weber (1864–1920). Elias was interested in explaining how lawful and democratic societies had begun to emerge in eighteenth-century Europe and North America. Weber attributed this development to several factors, including monarchical unification, the codification of law, Protestantism, and capitalism. Elias (1940/2000) did not oppose these ideas but believed that Weber had not properly understood the mental and cultural aspects of modernity, about which psychoanalysis could offer interesting insights. Elias believed that there was a "civilizing process" at work, in which the crude and violent ways of medieval society had been gradually replaced by more refined and placid manners. This transformation occurred when the noble class was tamed by absolutist monarchs and the process of civilization continued under bourgeois societies. In sum, Elias thought that historical changes in the Western superego are one of the reasons why the number of violent conflicts has diminished over time.

Projection and Conflicts

The best-known contemporary Freudian analyst of conflict is probably Vamik Volkan (b. 1932), who has led and assisted with conflict resolution processes all over the world. A practising psychoanalyst, Volkan states (1990) that feelings of prejudice in society are rooted in people's attempts to resolve their basic psychic problems. In order to help their egos cope with old traumas and disturbing impulses, people tend to transfer these uncomfortable thoughts to objects or other people.

The three main psychic defence mechanisms identified by psychoanalysis are externalization, projection, and displacement. Externalization is the process of discharging the negative feelings that we harbour about ourselves to an outside person, group, or object. For instance, one could attribute negative qualities to another ethnic group in order to feel better about oneself. Projection is the attribution of our undesirable thoughts and impulses to others. For example, a person who feels violent urges may accuse another group of being brutes to justify his or her own behavioural problems. Finally, displacement is the process of transferring the dislike that one feels for another person onto an object, person, or group. For example, the Oedipal hatred of the father may be transformed into the dislike of any authority figure.

Analysis linking debatable attitudes to neurotic tendencies has been propagated for some time, ever since the Fromm and Adorno studies. In this view, the sources of prejudice are to be found in the human mind. People often express racist, sexist, and xenophobic attitudes because they have not dealt with their inner problems. Although Volkan does not explicitly make this statement, it can be derived from his analysis that prejudiced people are likely to be neurotic and helpless, while well-adjusted individuals are generally free of prejudice and tend to embrace inclusive and progressive agendas. These conclusions, however, are questioned by behavioural and cognitive psychologists, as well as other social scientists.

Criticisms of the Psychoanalytical Approach

While the Freudian approach is universally known, it does not enjoy universal support. Freud has maintained many followers on the European continent; however, in North America he is seen as a respectable ancestor at best and, at worst, as a quack. In the non-Western world, Freudian theories are considered foreign and do not receive much attention. There are several critiques of his work, of which we will mention only four.

Freud's notion that all inner and most outer conflicts originate in childhood trauma, specifically sexual experiences, is strongly contested today.[3] Psychologists and biologists who emphasize other behavioural influences, such as genetics, medical conditions, personality, perceptions, learning, needs, and groupthink, claim that the importance of trauma has been overstated. (We will return to some of these aspects in the next sections of this chapter). The Freudian approach is also often criticized for being ethnocentric and sexist. Many of the traumas identified by Freud, notably the Oedipal complex (a boy's sexual attachment to his mother and rivalry with his father), are said to have been extrapolated from a few cases in nineteenth-century Vienna. Critics contend that those traumas, if they exist at all, are not universal but culturally bound. Women, especially since the feminist movement, have criticized Freud's sometimes condescending approach to their sex and dismissed such concepts as penis envy.[4]

Another criticism of psychoanalysis is that it limits its investigation to inner psychic phenomena, ignoring the social context in which the individual lives. The members of the Frankfurt School, who attributed most psychic problems to the nefarious influences of capitalism and authoritarianism, attempted to avoid this oversight by complementing Freud with Marx. Although most modern scholars have rejected the school's view of mental problems, they do stress the influence of social, political, economic, and cultural factors on the individual. For social scientists in particular, strict Freudian analysts are guilty of trying to explain social phenomena solely by individual traumas and transfer mechanisms.

Finally, the Freudian approach is attacked for its lack of scientific rigour. For example, most scientists consider the id to be a metaphysical construct, an entity that cannot be explained rationally or observed scientifically.[5] Most central Freudian concepts, including transfer processes, are currently seen this way—as speculative notions that cannot be observed or verified in individual cases and even less so in collective action situations.

In spite of its shortcomings, Freudian thought has made an important contribution to the understanding of conflict. Freud understood that conflict was inherent in both the conscious and unconscious aspects of behaviour. To him, conflict was not an aberrant behaviour but a central reality of psychic life. He insisted that most of our behaviour, including that associated with discrimination and aggression, stems from unrecognized inner conflicts. For example, it has become common to attribute a person's aggressive behaviour to his or her unresolved personal issues. Freud would even suggest that this phenomenon may explain collective behaviour, a conclusion that is, however, more difficult to prove.

Freud knew that conflict cannot always be repressed or cured. It can sometimes be sublimated in higher pursuits, be they in work, humanitarianism, science, or the arts. But, in many cases the most we can expect is that inner conflicts be managed by the individual. To achieve this outcome, we need analytical tools to identify the sources of conflict and a method to alleviate its negative effects. The understanding of conflict that we extrapolate from the works of Freud is very close to the modern conception of conflict as an inherent, often productive, and partly manageable aspect of human behaviour.

BEHAVIOURISM

Behaviourism stresses conditioned reflexes and learned behaviour, reinforced by rewards and punishment.

A contemporary of Sigmund Freud, Russian physiologist Ivan Pavlov (1849–1936) became famous for his experiments on how animals learn. Pavlov's best-known experiments involved dogs trained to associate the ringing of a bell with the supply of food. Pavlov predicted that, after a short period of training the dogs, the mere ringing of the bell would trigger the salivation usually associated with the introduction of food. Pavlov had created a conditioned response in which a natural behaviour (salivation) is stimulated by a spurious stimulus (the bell). These experiments and several others by Pavlov became the basis of the behavioural school of psychology, which purports to comprehend thoughts and behaviours as the results of learned reflexes. The core of this approach is that we learn and develop by associations.

Original behaviourist thought posits that all our ideas and actions, including conflict and violence, are instilled in us through learning. One of the most famous early behaviourists, John B. Watson (1878–1958) even claimed that, given total control of the experiment and regardless of the subject's abilities, he could train any child to become anything in life—doctor, artist, thief, or beggar—by conditioning him or her to specific stimuli (Watson, 1930). While these exaggerated claims and similar ones by the other major figure of behaviourism, B.F. Skinner (1904–90), have been dismissed[6], behaviourism offers a method of understanding certain thought processes and an approach to behaviour modification that has been crucial in the development of psychology.

Learning and Conflict

In terms of conflict, two main conclusions of behaviourism are relevant: people display certain behaviours (e.g. conflict-prone and violent tendencies) because they have learned them at some point in their lives, often in childhood; and people can be trained to change their behaviour through learning. According to behaviourism, most human behaviour has been transmitted by personal example (primarily by one's parents) and is not innate or biological. Therefore, it can be changed. For instance, a therapist could try different methods to reduce the adversarial and violent tendencies of a given patient. He or she could use an aversive therapy, in which the patient learns to associate violence with a negative stimulus (e.g. a loud noise or electric shocks). Another approach is positive re-inforcement, in which adversarial patients are rewarded immediately and consistently for their positive behaviours (e.g. monetary or performance rewards). Behaviourists contend that people can become better individuals and that the general human condition can improve by applying scientific research to behaviour, or what Skinner called cultural engineering (Skinner, 1971).

(AP Photo/Musa Sadulayev)

Two Chechen boys play with homemade toy guns. Are they simply playing or are they being conditioned to fight in another war?

In conflict studies, the implications of behaviourism are clear: people adopt conflicting and violent behaviour because they have learned it. If people were subjected to more benign and more positive stimuli, they would use more accommodating postures when dealing with their peers. But for behaviourists, behaviour modification in conflict-prone or violent people is just another application of essentially Pavlovian principles. Use some punishment and a lot of reward, and people behave better. This view has been important within progressive circles in America for most of the twentieth century and inspired Skinner's *Walden Two* (1948/2005), a best-selling novel about a utopian community using behavioural principles to raise their children in an exemplary manner. It has also contributed to the "carrot-and-stick" approach to international mediation (see Chapter 12).

Limitations of Behaviourism

Over time, many scientists have had reservations about the behaviourist perspective, particularly regarding biological principles; the role of variables such as personality, perceptions, and emotions; and the importance of free will and imagination. For example, researchers have long noticed that animals do not learn in the same way. While rats quickly learn to press a bar to receive food, cats learn this behaviour only after much conditioning, even though they are more intelligent than rats. These results suggest that animals (and people) are hardwired to learn different things at different paces.

Human beings do not all respond identically to a given stimulus, even when their biologies and personal histories are similar. For example, when faced with an angry challenge from a stranger, individual members of a family may respond with anger, puzzlement, passivity, reasoned argumentation, or panic. People, after all, have different personalities. Psychoanalysis, humanist psychology, and biology have various ways to explain personality, but they agree that responses to external stimuli are strongly influenced by the mental makeup of the individuals.

Another line of criticism is that behaviourism cannot actually explain how people learn. Behaviourists consider people blank sheets over which experience gradually leaves its complex marks. However, students of human physiology have long been trying to go beyond this theory. Their studies on factors such as brain functions, neurotransmitters, and physical traumas have illuminated the processes that facilitate or hinder learning. They have insisted that human beings do not simply accumulate knowledge but process information in their own way according to their genetic potential, personal history, and contextual situation.

Finally, behaviourism fails to explain how people form ideas beyond their own experiences. How, for example, have artists and scientists imagined fantastic new concepts and ideas that go beyond present reality? History is full of people who have behaved atypically, departing from their family, class, or religious upbringings. Even ordinary people can exercise their free will and behave differently than the conditioned responses that they have learned. Some have become political protesters, conscientious objectors, sceptics, or social reformers, while others have been impeachers, **spoilers**, bandits, or terrorists.

Therefore, human proclivities for conflict, co-operation, peace, and aggression are more complicated than what has been advocated by the behavioural school.

PERSONALITY AND CONFLICT

Since Freud, the perspective on personality has changed, as have the methods used to help people overcome their problems and live a more rewarding life. In relation to conflict, personality theory raises two important questions: Is conflict, especially violent conflict, caused by certain personality types? To what extent can conflicts be attributed to personality clashes?

Confrontational Personalities

There is some evidence that, at the small group and interpersonal levels, conflict occurs whenever conflict-prone people meet. Everyone has witnessed situations where the presence of conflict-prone individuals led to disturbances in a group. Certain individuals like the challenge of conflict and seem to create controversies that satisfy their craving for fighting. Some people are also quick to use intimidation and violence in interpersonal relations. Many political and business leaders, such as former French President Nicolas Sarkozy, former Italian prime minister Silvio Berlusconi, and American mogul Donald Trump, seem to have a fiery personality and a taste for confrontation. The personalities and behaviour of some leaders—for example, former Libyan dictator Muammar Gaddafi, former Yugoslav president Slobodan Milošević, and Zimbabwe's President Robert Mugabe— have had dire consequences.

As we have seen earlier, some Freudian psychologists unsuccessfully tried to link conflict behaviour with personality types (e.g. the authoritarian personality). The study of personality has progressed, and most specialists do not identify such behaviour as an indication of an authoritarian or conflicting personality. Rather, certain elements of personality can be linked to a stronger propensity to enter into debate with others. Beginning in the 1940s, British psychologist Hans J. Eysenk (1916–97) developed a model comprising the four personality types identified by Roman doctor Galen in the second century CE: phlegmatic, melancholic, sanguine, and choleric. Although the typology of Eysenk (1997) inspired many followers, it has been superseded by more complex conceptions based on the aggregation of a number of crucial traits.

It is not clear which dimensions of personality should be considered in terms of conflict behaviour. The main dimensions of personality, as portrayed in contemporary research, are extraversion/introversion, emotional stability/instability, openness/closedness to experience, agreeableness/disagreeableness, and conscientiousness/expediency (Hunt, 2007, pp. 397–400). There is no single element in these dichotomies that would help us predict whether people exhibit conflicting behaviour or to what degree. Furthermore, one cannot attribute social conflicts and aggression solely to the personality attributes of participants. This would mean that all or most individuals in a serious dispute would have a certain

BOX 7.1 | SLOBODAN MILOŠEVIĆ

(AP Photo/Srdjan Ilic)

Slobodan Milošević addresses Serbia's Socialist Party after being elected its president in 1992.

Slobodan Milošević was a quiet and introverted civil servant and industrial manager who meta-morphosed into a fiery orator and ruthless operator. In the 1980s, he gradually rose into politics by starting a campaign to keep Yugoslavia united by force. He became president of Serbia in 1989 and served as president of Yugoslavia from 1997 to 2000. During this time, a bloody civil war (1991), a NATO intervention (1995), and another war in Kosovo (1999) occurred. In 2001, Milošević was brought before the International Criminal Tribunal for the former Yugoslavia and charged with war crimes and crimes against humanity—his trial ended when he died of heart failure in 2006.

personality type. However, differences in personality can lead to conflicts in small groups such as families, offices, or neighbourhoods. These clashes may result in separation and/or divorce and be factors in business disputes and workplace feuds.

Despite widespread references in popular culture, the concept of personality clashes has some drawbacks. For one thing, it is of limited use in analyzing most conflicts above the small group scale. There are instances in international relations where personal chemistry or personality clashes influence the dealings between countries. For example, the relationship between President Ronald Reagan and Prime Minister Brian Mulroney exemplifies the former, while that of President Kennedy and Prime Minister Diefenbaker illustrates the latter. However, when a serious labour unrest or a war among nations develops, it is not because of personality clashes (although they may aggravate the situation later on). Second, it is not exactly clear how or under what conditions clashes among personalities occur. Few researchers agree on a universal classification of personalities, and most cannot reliably predict what personalities will clash, what they will disagree about, or with what severity. Finally, the concept of personality clashes can be contested on the basis that it provides an oversimplified explanation for conflicts.

Psychological Disorders

A psychological disorder is a condition that produces dysfunctional and/or distressful behaviour in an individual. Specific types of this disorder cover a broad range, from mild depression to severe hallucinatory schizophrenia. Since Freud, the study of psychological disorders (formerly known as abnormal psychology) has flourished. As a result, there is a better understanding of the biological, psychological, and social causes of mental problems.

At first glance, one might think that there is no relationship between psychological disorders and conflict. After all, most anxiety disorders (e.g. phobias and obsessive-compulsive behaviours) and mood disorders (e.g. depression, bipolar disorders, and most types of schizophrenia) do not have much of a connection to conflict. Only a handful of rare psychological disorders are directly related to the propensity to engage in conflict and violence. People with antisocial personality disorders lack the ability to feel guilt. Therefore, they lose the natural inhibition to harm people and are capable of doing anything to serve their impulses. People with paranoid schizophrenia experience delusions and hallucinations of threats and persecutions against them. The link between such disorders and conflict reveals new areas of research, including an examination of brain activity to determine whether there is a lack of connection between the cortex and the limbic system.

Although troubled individuals have been involved in conflict, this does not mean that all conflicts can be attributed to this factor. For one thing, conflicts among groups are related to tangible issues such as money, power, and security and to abstract qualities such as justice, honour, and identity. It is possible that some people are predisposed to starting and entertaining conflicts, but most do not suffer from a psychological disorder. In many cases, their actions can be beneficial, as seen in some labour negotiations and social movements. Nevertheless, the presence of conflict-prone personalities is certainly a factor in the aggravation of several conflicts.

Current Perspectives on Personality

The study of personality is now divided into several schools, each with its own view of what constitutes personality, what factors contribute to its evolution, and what methods help in its development and change. In this section, we will look at two such schools: humanism and the social-cognitive approach.

Humanism

In the 1960s, Abraham Maslow (1908–70) took personality studies beyond the bounds of psychoanalytical and behavioural approaches. In particular, Maslow (1999) thought that research had focused too much on weaknesses and disorders of the mind, and he sought to emphasize what makes many people well adjusted and happy. He went on to study famous successful people to understand the keys to their achievement and happiness. He also identified self-actualization, the process whereby individuals fulfill their potential at different times of their lives. This optimistic and empathic view of personality development was called humanism and was also developed by another famous psychologist, Carl Rogers (1902–87; see Rogers, 1961). The perspective has been very successful, inspiring countless scientific and popular psychology writings and influencing governmental policies in education, health care, and social services.

Humanism is well adapted to helping people adjust and develop. However, it does not tell us much about conflict other than generalizing that genuine and positive people will conduct their disputes with respect and tolerance and will eschew the recourse to force. Its main influence on conflict is probably in the attitude changes that it effects in modern societies. Humanism reinforces the desire for autonomy and critical thought in individuals, therefore weakening the control of political and social elites over them. Educators have also been inspired by humanism, in that they emphasize the contributions of peaceful individuals such as Gandhi and King instead of military and revolutionary heroes. Similarly, the values of dialogue, empathy, and co-operation are often preferred over honour, courage, and competition.

Social-Cognitive Approach

In the social-cognitive perspective—which is not entirely opposed to humanism—personality is the result of the interaction of individual traits with the circumstances of life. Canadian psychologist Albert Bandura (b. 1925) has been the leader in this field. Bandura (1976) believes that our behaviour is partly learned but that we also develop our own ways of coping with what happens to us. In this perspective, the individual has more control over his or her destiny than acknowledged by other schools of thought. In fact, an individual's achievements and happiness are largely factors of his or her sense of control over his or her existence. The main role of psychologists and other interveners is to persuade people to adopt a more cheerful attitude and to learn methods to develop their potential. Bandura (1973) has also studied aggression and the means to avoid this kind of behaviour.

Social-cognitive approaches have influenced psychological practice and governmental policy. For instance, the peaceful resolution of differences is now presented as an important goal in schools, and students are trained to use negotiation and mediation in their relationships. The purpose of these efforts is to replace the age-old habits of responding to challenges with defiance and force with new attitudes favouring habits of collaboration and non-violence. Violent political and criminal activity has diminished among young people in the West. However, it is hard to verify whether teaching methods or other factors (such as demographic decline, socioeconomic improvements, and urban spread) are responsible for this change. In the end, behavioural learning about peace and conflict resolution may have had a secondary but significant role to play.

Conclusions on Personality and Conflict

It is possible to link the onset of several low-level conflicts with the personalities or personality clashes of the participants. However, one must keep in mind that there is not much empirical evidence for predicting what kind of people are bound to initiate conflict or in what circumstances they would do so. Furthermore, most social psychologists and sociologists concur that, to understand a conflict, one has to look at more than its individual participants. Interpersonal and social situations are characterized by dynamics that are above and beyond the will of each player. For example, social conflicts are generated by important social differences that exist independently of the actors involved. As we have previously mentioned, conflict-prone personalities might not create particular conflicts but merely be attracted to existing ones.

Psychologists often warn about the attribution fallacy, the tendency to attribute behaviour to the personality of the individuals involved rather than to the circumstances of their actions. For example, when engaged in a bitter dispute, people often blame the situation on the bad character and low morality of their opponents rather than accepting that their rivals are, like themselves, motivated by their own interests. Therefore, in most cases of conflict, it could be that our negative perceptions of our opponents are more important than personalities.

SOCIAL PSYCHOLOGY AND CONFLICT

Social psychology is devoted to the study of diverse phenomena such as family ties, social behaviour, economic choices, and political attitudes. By investigating how people relate to, interact with, and are influenced by other people, this sub-discipline bridges the gap between mainstream individual psychology and other social sciences. In this section, we focus on some of the most important themes of social psychology and conflict.

Frustration–Aggression Theory

In 1939, John Dollard (1900–80) and colleagues hypothesized that the source of aggression is the frustration experienced by an individual. This hypothesis is not foreign to common sense, as when, for example, people attribute a hockey fight to the frustration experienced by the players involved. Dollard defined frustration as interference in reaching a goal. It was the era of behaviourism, and psychologists liked simple and testable hypotheses such as that frustration leads to aggression, a hypothesis that can be expressed under the form F → A.

In the following decades, many experiments were conducted to test the F → A hypothesis. In some, subjects were interrupted from performing certain tasks that they had been given (e.g. puzzles or memorization). The intent was to verify whether subjects disturbed in their tasks were more likely to display aggressive behaviour than those who were not. The results often confirmed the hypothesis but were largely influenced by the experiment. Furthermore, a number of subjects did not react aggressively to the frustrating circumstances, leading many psychologists to doubt the grandiose claim that all aggression is the result of frustration.

From the 1940s to the 1960s, the F → A hypothesis was also used in sociology to explain phenomena such as violent criminality, urban riots, and political violence. It fit well with the idealism of the time, when social scientists were convinced that violence was the by-product of injustice and poverty and that progressive social policies could resolve this problem once and for all. For instance, Carl I. Hovland and Robert R. Sears (1940) were able to correlate the number of lynchings of African Americans in the American South with indicators of economic downturn, such as the fall in cotton prices. However, David O. Sears and John B. McConahay (1973) have observed that attitudes favouring race rioting were higher among African Americans from the middle class than from poor neighbourhoods, a finding that contradicts pure frustration–aggression theory.

One of the main problems with this theory is in assessing when an individual's (and groups') frustration is strong enough to make him or her use violence to remedy the situation. In other words, what makes people angry? What is the benchmark that will make an individual conclude "My patience has been exceeded; I am going to hurt somebody"? The research has not been able to answer these questions convincingly. The hypothesis also fails to explain why some people never become aggressive. Furthermore, it does not indicate what type of aggressive response is to be chosen. As applied by social scientists, the theory assumes that people will direct their aggressions toward the source of their frustrations, which is often the state or a dominant social class. However, they could also perpetrate violent crimes, fight in soccer stadiums, persecute a harmless minority group, or abuse their spouses and children. Finally, the concept cannot explain why some people direct their anger at themselves and display depressive, self-defeating, or suicidal behaviours. The approach was gradually replaced by relative deprivation theory but has re-emerged since the 1970s under the guise of needs theory.

Relative Deprivation

Realizing that the frustration–aggression theory could not explain all behaviour, psychologists and social scientists felt that frustration had to be defined in a more sophisticated manner. After all, many instances of aggression are not linked to a sudden drop in income or the experience of a rash political repression. Aggression often develops over time and seems associated more with the frustration of not achieving expectations than with having current activities impeded. Researchers soon adopted the view that frustration results mostly from a comparison of one's situation with a more desirable state of affairs. In other words, **relative deprivation** is the cause of conflicts, crime, and aggression (Box, 1983). This theory signifies that the people most likely to engage in conflict and violence are not the most destitute but those who feel that they cannot achieve what they consider their "just rewards."

There are different methods of measuring relative deprivation. One way involves a person's comparing his or her condition with that of other persons or groups. For instance, people who are exposed to more affluent groups could develop aggressive tendencies toward those groups. Another way is for a person to consider the difference between his or her actual situation and his or her aspirations. In other words, the more people sense that their lives are below their expectations, the more aggressive they might feel.

In sociological studies, this latter thesis was applied to historical revolutions by James C. Davies (1962), the originator of the famed "J-curve" representing the relationship between unmet rising expectations and growing unrest. The relative deprivation hypothesis was also applied to a number of societies by Ivo Feierabend and Rosalind Feierabend (1966), who partially confirmed the hypothesis. They hoped to demonstrate that relative deprivation is higher in developing countries than in stagnating or developed nations. Therefore, the

BOX 7.2 | CURVILINEAR AND LINEAR RELATIONSHIPS

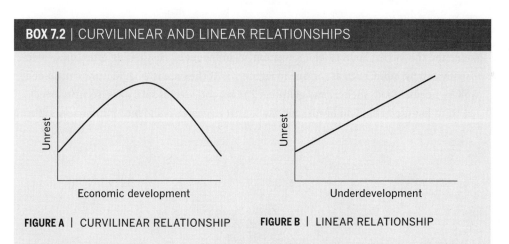

FIGURE A | CURVILINEAR RELATIONSHIP   FIGURE B | LINEAR RELATIONSHIP

Many early analysts of conflicts, such as James C. Davies (1962), believe in a curvilinear relationship between violent political conflict and development (Figure A). In other words, poor societies, where expectations are low, and rich countries, where satisfaction is high, would be less prone to social unrest than developing nations and those that have experienced serious economic setbacks. Other analysts conclude that unrest evolves directly from underdevelopment, producing a linear relationship (Figure B). Usually, such scholars point to the fact that the large majority of civil insurrections and wars occur in the poorest countries, which cannot answer the needs of their populations.

correlation between level of development and violence should be curvilinear, meaning that low-level and high-level societies should be more stable than medium-level societies. However, they could not prove this idea. In fact, it seems that stability augments with income in a linear relationship.

One of the best-known applications of the theory is that of sociologist Ted Robert Gurr (b. 1936), who defined relative deprivation as the difference between value expectations and value capabilities. Gurr (2000) applied his framework to a wide sample of cases of political violence around the globe and devised his research design carefully, trying to use meaningful and accurate measurements of frustration and violence. He found some confirmation of his hypothesis, but factors unrelated to relative deprivation (such as history of violence and type of government) were as important, if not more so, in his results.

The relative deprivation theory has led to many studies and has had some success explaining social and political violence in many contexts. However, it suffers from the same limitations as the frustration–aggression model. It cannot explain how frustration is translated into conflict behaviour at the societal level or how certain types of actions are preferred over others. Another way to understand the links between relative deprivation and conflict is through René Girard's theory of **mimetic desire**, discussed in Chapter 9.

Needs Theory

The Hierarchy of Needs

As mentioned in Chapter 1, Maslow (1943, 1948) developed a hierarchy of needs to account for the varied sources of motivation in individuals. His idea is often expressed visually as a pyramid, such as the one in Figure 7.1. At the base is what Maslow considered welfare needs—food, shelter, and clothing. The second level is safety and security needs, the third love and affection needs, and the fourth self-esteem and recognition needs. The

FIGURE 7.1 | MASLOW'S HIERARCHY OF NEEDS

summit of the pyramid is made up of self-actualization needs, or the needs to fulfill one's potential.

Maslow's pyramid has become a central psychological concept, but other theorists soon saw that he had overlooked certain important human motives. For one thing, Maslow had neglected needs related to control, autonomy, and freedom. In the 1970s, a number of social scientists continued work on Maslow's theory, eventually identifying over 20 need categories. For example, Paul Sites (1973) argued that control of physical and social environments is also a basic need. He pointed out how people became frustrated if they lacked control over their lives. Like the frustration–aggression hypothesis, needs theory was expanded upon and tested by numerous sociologists and political scientists.

Among many needs theorists, it became apparent that these needs did not always function according to Maslow's pyramid structure. For instance, people fighting for a cause related to identity and language could risk their need for security for the sake of their own group. This realization led to need categories being presented as interrelated, without the rigid hierarchy. One such scheme is the idea of deep-rooted conflict, developed by John W. Burton (1993).

In the 1970s, Burton was already recognized as a leader in the field of conflict resolution. He discovered needs theory through the work of Sites and began to see that the theory filled a gap in understanding the dynamics of conflict. According to Burton, deep-rooted conflict is a threat to non-negotiable identity need satisfiers (see Figure 7.2). In other words, people will put their lives on the line to maintain what is closely linked to the core of their identities. These could take the form of values, certain freedoms, kinship ties, recognition of language, sense of justice, religious beliefs, or ethnic tradition.

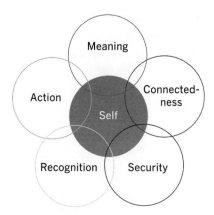

FIGURE 7.2 | IDENTITY NEEDS IMPLICATED IN DEEP-ROOTED CONFLICT

Identity Needs and Emotions

Paul Sites (1990) was the first to argue that particular identity needs could be analogically mapped onto emotions (see, as an example, Table 7.1). This connection between identity needs and emotions has been used by thousands of people to aid in determining the dynamics of conflict. For example, Burton (1993) suggested that, when there is a threat to core values associated with identity, there is an emotional reaction. People may not always act immediately on this reaction, but the fact that it is present indicates that something to do with needs is occurring.

While emotions play an important role in needs theory, they are not the only factor. Each need category is associated with a number of elements, some of which can be discovered empirically and others upon reflection. For example, connectedness is associated with belonging, mutual understanding, empathy, and support. Recognition can be overt and visible or implied. It may be obvious that certain people are effective in taking action, but it may be only through reflection and interaction that it becomes clear that those actions are truly meaningful to them.

Need Satisfiers

Scholars acknowledge that, while need categories are universal, the types of satisfiers that are important to people are a function of culture, values, experience, and interpretation (see Clark, 1990; Fisher, 1990; Gillwald, 1990; Nudler, 1990). Consequently, even members of the same family might have different need satisfiers because they experience life differently. Whether something is an identity need satisfier depends on the degree to which someone is attached to something. The same thing may be in the realm of interests to one person and at the level of identity need satisfier to another. Money and power, for example, may function in different ways for people: as a need for security, the means to take action, basic values and primary satisfiers, or recognition.

Need satisfiers can be acquired tacitly through experience. For instance, a child growing up in a given household will pick up on certain values, which can be internalized. Some children might eventually rebel and establish reverse satisfiers, doing anything they can to distance themselves from the teachings of their youth. Need satisfiers can also be acquired through effort. If someone spends years studying something and developing a certain per-

TABLE 7.1 | LINKS BETWEEN NEEDS AND EMOTIONS

Need Category	Emotion when Threatened	Emotion when Satisfied
Meaning	Anger	Self-Recognizance
Connectedness	Sadness	Self-Respect
Action	Depression	Self-Esteem
Security	Fear	Self-Confidence
Recognition	Shame	Self-Actualization

spective, that perspective might become associated with identity, prompting a profound reaction if it is threatened. Need satisfiers link the cognitive and emotional in that they are matters of interpretation that have an emotional pull. Take, for example, the need for connectedness. At one level, there can be an emotional attachment to a friend that comes with spending time together, but the significance of this attachment is enhanced when people verbally affirm their friendship, interpreting their time together as something of significance.

It is sometimes useful to distinguish between need satisfiers that are obtained within the self and those that depend on other people. Connectedness and recognition as categories are particularly sensitive to the responses and actions of others. Another factor to consider is time. In this regard, it becomes important for people to have a sense of being that is historically rooted—their stories become an essential part of their identities. It is also important for them to envisage a hopeful future so that a sense of continuity, growth, and an imagination for newness become possible.

Asking what need satisfiers are being threatened in a conflict can help to understand its dynamics and stakes. Some need satisfiers are zero-sum; if one person has a given item, the other cannot have it. If the same zero-sum object is a need satisfier for two parties, the challenge to transformation is immense. For example, the city of Jerusalem is key to the identity of both Israeli Jews and Palestinian Muslims and Christians. To resolve this conflict, one side wins and the other loses; the groups share the city; or one or both parties makes an identity change, which is not an easy task.

Advantages and Limitations of the Needs Approach

The relationship between human needs theory and conflict was made in response to the challenge of understanding why, in some circumstances, people fight so strongly for a cause even though the material stakes and payoff would be negligible. The observation that there was something related to identity in these instances became a recurring link. Human needs theory helped to make sense of this link and also helped people in conflict to make sense of their own experience, including their emotions and motivations.

Human needs theory works in conjunction with other theories to better understand certain phenomena. For instance, when used in conjunction with an analysis of domination structures, it reveals that, for those who become aware of having been dominated, the struggle for equality is linked to their identity and becomes a profound motivator. Members of separatist movements who have felt that their identity groups have been unfairly dominated will work for years for the sake of recognition of their ethnonational groups. When used together with the theory of mimetic desire—"I want what you want" (see Chapter 9)—it helps to explain how rivalries can become bitter when each party forms a set of identity need satisfiers in relation to the other. When used with developmental psychology, it becomes clear that, as people's levels of consciousness become more complex, their identities and identity need satisfiers can also become more complex (see Chapter 10). As a result, they might not react as strongly if there is a threat to one aspect of their identity. Furthermore, in an open society where people develop complex identities, individuals react very differently in the same situations. Other aspects of their identities, such as profession or political involvement, might be more important. It is in situations where belonging to an identity group is crucial that there is a greater tendency for people to adopt a similar response to events. Such was the case during the war between Bosnia and Herzegovina in the 1990s, where one could be killed on the basis of ethnic identity.

The needs approach is currently one of the most popular perspectives regarding conflict. It inspires a great deal of research and advocacy related to conflict situations. Nevertheless, there remain a number of unanswered questions related to needs theory. The connection between needs and emotions requires more attention and research. If there is an emotional expression, human needs theory can be used to better understand the roots of the emotion. But how is needs theory to be used in situations where emotions are repressed or masked? Though there are many links between identity, emotion, and passion, identity need satisfiers are not only about emotions. They also entail commitments, beliefs, values, desires, and insights. Emotions themselves can be understood internally—how we feel when having an emotional reaction—and by their external manifestation. However, some passions, which are a mix of emotion and ideas, are manifest over a long period of time. Those plotting a political assassination, for instance, are highly motivated by a passion derived from what they interpret as an injustice—a threat to meaning and recognition. Their plans involve careful planning, using their rational capabilities to plan and execute the attack. There might not be an immediate display of emotion, but the high level of motivation points to a threat to identity need satisfiers. It is easy to show in retrospect how need satisfiers have been threatened in a given conflict. The challenge is to use the theory to anticipate potential conflicts and take preventative measures. While the needs approach is a useful model that is applicable to most conflict situations and offers many propositions and hypotheses for verification, more research is needed on how conflict and violence emerge from unmet needs.

Ignorance and Prejudice

Stereotyping

Many conflicts have been fuelled by the stereotypes that people or groups have about each other. The ancient Greeks believed that every non-Greek was a "barbarian." This conception has been echoed in many ancient non-Western civilizations as well, notably among the Chinese and the Japanese. The Romans were less restrictive and believed that some people, such as the Greeks, were as advanced as themselves. They also thought that some nations of their empire, after enjoying a long period of Roman peace and education, could become civilized. However, preconceived negative ideas about other people have been the norm in history. Although the great monotheist religions such as Christianity and Islam stress the equality of human beings and believe that religious conversion is the road to civilization, people have remained biased against other nations, ethnicities, and religious groups. Many conflicts in European history originated from such prejudice.

Volkan (1998) has introduced the concepts of chosen traumas and chosen glories to explain how negative stereotypes are maintained and intensified. He observes that ethnonational groups have ethnonarratives that convey the distinctive attributes of their respective identities. Within these, chosen traumas are stories of when the group was victimized. These stories help to justify negative attitudes and even vengeful actions against a group's adversaries, even though the stories may be hundreds of years old. We have previously seen that Milošević used the chosen trauma of the 1389 Battle of Kosovo to stir up nationalist feelings of Serbs 600 years after the event. Chosen glories reflect a time when the group was particularly successful; these narratives become an ideal to which people aspire and may engender resentments over why they cannot be as glorious as they once were.

However, individuals who have been in regular contact with members of other groups tend to be less prejudiced than those who have not. For example, the humanist philosophers and scientists of the Renaissance, such as Erasmus, Montaigne, and Grotius, could express relatively tolerant opinions of other Europeans of different faiths, while their less cosmopolitan contemporaries tended to have very negative views of these other groups, be they "papists" or "heretics." In fact, it has been demonstrated that the people who know the least about others tend to have the most stereotypical perceptions of others and favour a confrontational, if not violent, stand regarding potential opponents. The main explanation for this attitude is that people who know more about other people, either through education or direct contact, tend to see members of other groups as human beings rather than savages or barbarians. We may call this the humanization of unfamiliar people.

Contact Theory

The connection between knowledge and prejudice has led to **contact theory**, an important body of knowledge regarding conflict. In 1954, American psychologist Gordon Allport (1897–1967) wrote *The Nature of Prejudice*, in which he tried to verify a simple hypothesis: the increase of direct contact among people of different groups will reduce animosity between them. However, this premise must be qualified. If people of different origins were forced to interact in less than optimal conditions, they may not develop more positive feelings. Allport suggested four conditions for effective contact: the members of the different groups hold equal status in their relationship (even if their groups are unequal in the wider societal context); the individuals need to co-operate; they have a shared goal; and their interaction is supported by local authorities and norms.

Allport's hypothesis has been thoroughly tested in the United States. For instance, Morton Deutsch and Mary Evans Collins (1951) tested an early version of the contact theory by comparing the attitudes of both black and white residents of segregated and non-segregated housing projects in the New York area. They confirmed that the level of prejudice among the groups was correlated to their exposure to people from the other race. Other researchers have verified the contact hypothesis in such environments as schools, military units, and workplaces. Therefore, the intuitive notion that people who know members of other groups will be less prejudiced toward them seems to be generally valid (Wright, Brody, & Aron, 2004).

These research methods inspired many programs of racial integration in the United States, including in the government, armed forces, schools and colleges, counties and cities, and large corporations. Other nations have also been encouraged by such efforts. Some people have even tried to bring together members of diametrically opposed groups, such as Jews and Arabs, with the hope of improving their relationship.[7] There have, however, been some partial refutations of the contact hypothesis. For example, analysts such as Harold D. Forbes (2004) claim that individuals in contact situations can exhibit decreasing levels of prejudice towards individuals from other groups while still maintaining diffuse prejudices against the group as a whole. In other words, it is possible that residual negative attitudes will not be completely dissolved by contact. This possibility remains to be verified again in the future with different methodologies.

The doctrine of multiculturalism and identity politics has put a strain on contact theory. In effect, the theory is somewhat based on the liberal notion that all people are fundamentally the same and that, if they were free to meet other people in a non-threatening environment, they would not entertain prejudices. However, the cultural relativism and separatism currently espoused by many activists tends to accentuate and glorify the differences between groups of people. In a way, it may become more difficult to fight prejudice when otherness is valued more than sameness. What is needed is an approach that celebrates the richness of different cultures while creating space for new hybrid cultural adaptations.

Nevertheless, people in many parts of the world are now at least occasionally in contact with people of different races, languages, cultures, and/or religions. Higher education levels also contribute to more benign attitudes in younger generations. While the worldwide extirpation of prejudice may be a long-term goal, the current increase in personal contact with diverse groups through business travel, migration, tourism, and social media bodes well for the reduction of prejudice among future generations.

Conformity Approaches

Why do people act alike, follow leaders, and lose their freedom of thought in the process? Many social psychologists have studied issues of conformity and obedience. Some of these research programs have been sponsored by governments interested in fostering deference to authority or destroying opposition mass movements. However, most of the research is of a scientific nature, and some is even biased in favour of affirming the autonomy of the individual towards authorities. In conflict studies, this kind of research is important insofar as it helps identify the mechanisms by which small confrontations can become violent mass protests, quiet and ordinary people can become zealous proponents of radical agendas, and intelligent and well-adjusted decision-makers can be swayed into bellicose behaviour under peer pressure.

Crowds

In the late eighteenth century and throughout the nineteenth, there were significant protest crowds mobilized in England and Continental Europe. Originally, these protests constituted "Flour Wars," in which people demanded reasonable prices for staple foods. There were also protests for social and political rights, such as in the French Revolution and England's Chartist Movement. Within this context, French sociologist Gustave Le Bon (1841–1931) used Freud's work to develop a psychological theory of crowds. For Le Bon (1895/2008), crowds were like hysterical women, under the control of irrational emotions, and were unruly mobs made up of society's riff-raff. He postulated that people lost their sense of individual autonomy and used the anonymity of the crowd to do things that they would never do in other circumstances. Like Freud, he thought that crowds were attracted to strong leaders who could control them. Le Bon's theories dominated the field well into the twentieth century. They also influenced Hitler, who indirectly used them as a framework for manipulating crowds in Germany during the 1930s and 1940s.

The 1960s saw the start of several new social movements that were to continue into the 1970s and 1980s, inspiring a renewal in academic study within the discipline (Epstein, 1993). Klandermans (1997) observed that every issue would feature people who would work passionately to address it and to organize protests. Among the people who would hear about the issue, a subgroup would care enough to support the issue. Among these, a smaller group would actually make the effort to attend a protest, thereby joining a crowd. Sopow (2003) made the distinction among passive protesters who might sign petitions, active protesters who might attend rallies, and volatile protesters who might engage in violence.

In the 1990s, Le Bon's theories were called into question on several grounds. For example, George Rudé (1999) performed a historical analysis of the crowds that were the basis of Le Bon's ideas. Rudé examined prison records of those arrested after nineteenth-century protest crowd activity, revealing that those detained were responsible members of society, such as artisans, and not the riff-raff that Le Bon referenced. In his extensive empirical research on crowd activity, Clark McPhail (1991) found that people joined crowds individually or with small groups of friends. He also observed that they maintained their individuality throughout the event, which he calls a temporary gathering. In a rhetorical analysis, Peter Hayes (1992) noted the difference in connotation between the terms *crowd* and *mob*. His analysis showed an ideological connection: conservative thinkers preferred the disparaging language of Le Bon, while those more open to change and dissent preferred to use words such as *crowd* or even *the people* to refer to temporary gatherings intended to engage people in "extra-parliamentary political action." (Joyce, 2002) Finally, theorists examining angry crowds developed a framework for politicians, demonstrating how important it is for the targets of protest to treat protesters with respect and effectively communicate that they received their message (see Susskind & Field, 1996).

A variety of factors may lead either side to initiate violence, especially if people feel threatened or afraid. For example, the police may use violence if a crowd uses Molotov cocktails or destroys property during a protest. The members of the crowd may become violent if they feel that the police are trying to suppress their message or are using excessive force. There are also some protesters for whom violence is a justifiable tactic, given the issues involved (Redekop & Paré, 2010).

Authority and Obedience

The role of leaders is important in matters of conformity. Leaders can frame the issues, stir up emotions, and, in some cases, speak with authority regarding a course of action. People's response to authority is itself an area of social psychological research. In 1961, for example, American psychologist Stanley Milgram (1933–84) conducted a famous experiment at Yale University, showing that people will go along with cruel acts when encouraged by a credible authority figure. In this experiment, 40 male volunteers were assigned the role of "teacher" and were given questions to ask a "student" who sat on the other side of a glass barrier (Milgram, 1974). For every wrong answer, the teacher would give the student an electric shock. The voltage of the shocks increased incrementally, becoming "severe" at 300 volts and "dangerous" at 400. Unbeknownst to the teacher, however, the shocks were actually simulated and the student was an actor. If a volunteer became reluctant to continue, the authoritative "researcher" instructed him to continue (e.g. "You must go on."). Despite hearing the pleas of the student, 26 of the volunteers administered the highest voltage. The Milgram experiments, validated by subsequent research, indicate a propensity to follow orders, especially when there is no support for resistance. When supported by resisters, however, people have a much lower tendency to follow orders. This resonates with the research of Ervin Staub (1989), who has shown how bystanders play a profound role in influencing the behaviour of actors in a given situation.

A distinguished social psychologist, Staub has made a significant contribution in understanding how societies come to support mass murder and genocide. He spent many years working on the issue of why people do good. His experimental research showed that, when encouraged by a bystander, people do heroic things. When he turned his attention to why people do evil, he used the bystander concept in his framework. Staub views participation in extreme violence—torture and mass murder—as being on a continuum of evil. People are initially reluctant to perpetuate such actions; however, with the right factors present, they move along this continuum until they perform individual and systemic acts of violence. Staub's framework includes difficult life circumstances, a threat to human needs, a rhetoric of "us versus them," a tendency to scapegoat, and the silence or encouragement of bystanders. Staub (1989) used this structure to analyze four instances of extreme violence: the Holocaust, the Armenian genocide, the mass murders in Cambodia under Pol Pot, and the missing persons in Argentina. Recently, he has devoted attention to some of the latest wars and acts of terrorism (Staub, 2011).

In 1971, American psychologist Philip Zimbardo (b. 1933) conducted one of the most famous experiments in the history of psychology, one that reveals a great deal about

BOX 7.3 | PRISONER ABUSE

(AP Photo)

An American soldier and his dog watch a detainee at Abu Ghraib prison, 2003.

In 2004, the release of photos such as this one revealed that, during the Iraq War, several American soldiers had tortured Iraqi prisoners under their care in Abu Ghraib prison. The publication of these photos seriously damaged the reputation of the US government and its armed forces. The responsible individuals were tried and sentenced to various punishments, such as prison terms, reprimands, demotions, and dishonourable discharges. What was the cause of this abusive behaviour? Is it conformity, fear, prejudice, revenge? Why are institutions such as the US Army not immune from such actions?

group dynamics, conflict, and violence. The experiment involved a group of volunteers at Stanford University simulating a prison situation (Zimbardo, 2007). A section of a university building was designated as the prison, and the volunteers were divided into "prisoners" and "guards." After only one day, the situation became unruly, and the guards had to take special measures to tame the prisoners. After one week, the treatment of the prisoners became so brutal that the experiment had to be stopped. Zimbardo found that assigning roles in a systemic and inherently violent environment led to individuals joining together in oppressive actions. As in the Milgram experiments, seemingly normal people became extremely violent and abusive in some contexts. Zimbardo (2007) has drawn comparisons between his own experiment and the behaviour exhibited during the Holocaust, the Rwandan genocide, and even Abu Ghraib. The relationship between authority and violence has become an important field of inquiry in recent years.

Another person examining extreme violence is social psychologist James Waller (2007). Waller's thesis is that any person has a capacity to participate in extraordinary evil under certain circumstances. His framework of analysis includes social factors in relation to the actor, the context, and the target of violence. People who become agents of extreme violence, he argues, have an "ancestral shadow" that prompts ethnonationalism, xenophobia, and a desire for social dominance (Waller, 2007). These perpetrators have cultural belief systems, backed by authorities whom they are oriented to follow, that encourage this violence. They disengage the moral faculties that might stand in the way of their violent actions. Their own self-interest and longing to advance within their group strengthens the tendency to follow their group in violence. Social factors include a group culture of cruelty in which there is a repression of conscience, diffusion of responsibility, and tremendous peer pressure. Finally, the targeted victims experience a social death, going from "us–them thinking" to dehumanization and finally blame.

Social psychology has shown that the instigation of violent conflict is not only a function of cold rational calculation or pathological disposition but a process that is influenced by example, peer pressure, and deference to authority. This kind of research provides a strong connection between the psychological approaches to conflict and the sociological models that we will discuss in the next chapter.

CONCLUSION

All the major schools of psychology have dealt with the question of conflict either directly or indirectly. Psychoanalysis has been historically important, not only as a precursor to other approaches but also as a theory that places conflict at the centre of the study of human beings. Personality theories are important insofar as they can demonstrate that some personalities affect conflict and show how personality adjustment and development can help people deal more peacefully with conflict and be less affected by it. The study of conflict in social psychology has been dominated by the relationship between frustration and aggression, which has culminated with the important school of human needs theory. Social psychology has also studied many contributing factors in the emergence and aggravation of conflict, such as perceptions, group behaviour, and authority.

DISCUSSION QUESTIONS

1. Think of an interpersonal conflict that you feel knowledgeable about. Identify ways in which psychoanalytic theory, behaviourism, and needs theory can help understand the motivations, attitudes, and behaviours of the individuals involved.

2. Identify a conflict between groups of people and compare how the different approaches of social psychology help to understand its dynamics. Consider whether frustration is a central issue in the conflict.

3. Do you think that contact theory's conclusions about proximity and the lessening of prejudice are supported in the early twenty-first century? Why or why not?

4. How do you interpret Milgram's and Zimbardo's experiments in terms of obedience and repression? Do they mean that people will always be manipulated by others in the perpetration of heinous and violent acts? Give reasons to support your answers.

5. What are the connections and the important differences between psychological approaches and biological approaches to understanding conflict?

NOTES

1. Hysteria is a severe anxiety disorder that can result in blindness, paralysis, or fainting. Neuroses are all the mental disorders involving anxiety, depression, phobias, and compulsions.

2. We will return to these theorists and other aspects of their work in the section on Marxism in the next chapter.

3. It was also contested during Freud's lifetime by some of his main disciples, most notably Alfred Adler and Carl Jung.

4. Alfred Adler also questioned Freud's views on women's sexuality, but the first complete feminist critique of Freud was written by Karen Horney (1932/1993).

5. Furthermore, many object to the idea that an impulse of death should be present in all human beings, a conception shared by Konrad Lorenz and some of the other sociobiologists that we mentioned in the previous chapter.

6. In 1924, Watson admitted that he may have been gone too far in his assertion that any child could be reared for any task.

7. One has to be careful about this, however. Small-scale experiments in a short-term framework are usually not very successful, especially if they do not adhere to Allport's four conditions.

8 | CONFLICT AS A SOCIAL OUTCOME

CHAPTER OBJECTIVES

This chapter will help you develop an understanding of the

- relationship between political power and conflict;
- theories of capitalism and social class in terms of conflict;
- connections between social change, modernization, and conflict;
- role of culture, particularly religion, in conflict; and
- influence of gender in conflict.

INTRODUCTION

In this chapter, we introduce perspectives that emphasize the social explanations of conflict. These approaches are mainly found in disciplines such as anthropology, sociology, and political science, as well as the multidisciplinary fields of criminology, demography, international relations, and industrial relations. The perspectives that we survey here differ from those of biology and psychology in that they argue that conflict behaviour is largely, if not completely, determined by social factors at the level of large groups and nations. Social scientists tend to look at the culture, social structures, economy, and politics of a society to explain its evolution. However, people do not agree as to the relative importance of these factors in social behaviour. Sociologists, anthropologists, and political scientists share many of the same preoccupations but emphasize different explanatory factors. We focus on the most important theoretical traditions and base our discussion on specific criteria: the approach must have conflict as one of its crucial themes, must have influenced the history of social studies, and must still be used in the twenty-first century. Our review groups these approaches under the topics of power, class, social change, culture, and gender.

POLITICAL POWER AND CONFLICT

There are many definitions of power, but we favour that of American political scientist Robert Dahl (b. 1915), who stated that power is the ability of A to influence B into doing something that he or she would otherwise not do (1957). Power can be achieved through several means, including the use or threat of force, rewards or the promise of rewards, deception, and persuasion. Power is an extremely important tool for attaining various personal and social objectives. But it is also a goal in and of itself for people who consider the acquirement and retention of power as the supreme aim. In the realm of politics, three approaches can help us understand the importance of power: political realism, the Hobbesian tradition, and political **pluralism**.

Political Realism

Political realism claims that conflicts are essentially caused by rivalries over the acquisition, maintenance, and expansion of political power. In the fifth century BCE, Chinese strategist Sun Tzu (544–496 BCE) concluded that power is the goal of politics and war and suggested ways that a sovereign could expand his power by becoming more adept at foreign policy and war (2002). Kautilya (350–283 BCE), the pen name for Indian court counsellor Chanakya, was also a proponent of this view, which he expressed in lessons and tales (see Boesche, 2002). In Greece, Thucydides (460–395 BCE) explained the Peloponnesian War as a consequence of the expansion of Athenian power and the Spartan reaction (431 BCE/1972). These writers explained violent conflict without reference to magic or religion. Instead, they attributed the outbreak of war to the lust for power.[1]

During the Renaissance, Niccolò Machiavelli (1532/2003) created a theory of politics that contradicted the idealist doctrine articulated by Saint Thomas Aquinas (1225–74) and other Catholic theologians.[2] In short, Machiavelli believed that people are motivated by interests and that politics is a means to attain one's goals. In order to practise politics successfully, one needs to play a ruthless game of strategy, deception, and violence against equally pitiless opponents. Put another way, morals have nothing to do with politics. In the twentieth century, the idea that the never-ending competition for political power is the cause of conflict became known as realism, a concept that opposed the idealism that prevailed in Western thought after World War I.

In a realist (or Machiavellian) analysis of conflict, one has to discard socioeconomic, ideological, and identity factors and look for the power motivations of the main actors. It is assumed that people looking to seize or maintain power will be in conflict and that they may use fraud and violence to neutralize their adversaries. The conflict's participants are usually rational beings intent on attaining their goals by using the most effective and efficient ways. This analysis applies well to the harsh power struggles of monarchs and other nobles during the Middle Ages and the early modern period, where people would kill, imprison, deceive, or exile their rivals, and it corresponds to what one can read in many of Shakespeare's plays.

German-American political scientist Hans Morgenthau (1904–80) became the primary realist theorist of the twentieth century. Morgenthau (2005) and other realists analyzed the Cold War as a contest between two superpowers attempting to dominate the planet. The main constraint to both countries was the danger of a nuclear war. Short of this massive recourse, everything was possible. The United States and the Soviet Union gained allies (sometimes by force), threatened and rewarded these allies in order to create large coalitions, spied on each other, sabotaged each other's political and economic projects, and so on. For realists, the contrasted social systems and ideological world views of these two states were insignificant; the rivalry played out in essentially the same manner as that of ancient empires, feudal Christian kingdoms, or absolutist monarchies.

Realists advocate diverse solutions to the problem of international conflict. Though war may be inevitable in certain circumstances (e.g. when an imperialist state attempts to conquer another state by force), realists do not celebrate war as an end in itself. They generally believe that war is a costly and messy way to resolve conflicts and that keeping a **balance of power** between adversaries is a better way to maintain peace. The balance of power is a situation in which states are dissuaded to go to war with one another because of the significant risks of defeat and conquest. Therefore, realists often promote the growth of power capabilities through military preparedness, economic and technological growth, rationalization of government, and the constitution of diplomatic alliances. The overall goal is to create stable constellations of power among rival states, using diplomacy to prevent and resolve divisive issues. International law and institutions are of a secondary value for realists, but they can prove their worth in helping defuse small conflicts and crises among states.

Realist Analysis at the National Level

The realist perspective also applies to internal conflicts. The most famous classic theorists of this approach to domestic politics are Italian economist Vilfredo Pareto (1848–1923), Italian political scientist Gaetano Mosca (1858–1941), and German sociologist Robert Michels (1876–1936), who all wrote at the beginning of the twentieth century and concentrated on the role of elites in politics. Elites exist in all ages and places. While Mosca (1960) described them as small groups of powerful people who share similar objectives and are cohesive, secretive, and unaccountable, Pareto (1991) considered them to be simply the best and brightest of a given society. Generally, elites try to avoid conflicts that could be detrimental to their rule. However, elites of different organizations are often in conflict over power, money, and prestige. As analyzed by Pareto, there are also conflicts within elites, such as those between "lions" and "foxes" (the young and the old elites, respectively). Michels (1999) is primarily known for his formulation of the "iron law of oligarchy," which states that, sooner or later, political parties (and, by extension, all complex organizations) will be dominated by a small authoritarian elite. One can also find versions of elite theory on the political left, such as in the writings of C. Wright Mills (1916–62) and Noam Chomsky (b. 1928), which contend that capitalist countries are led by an undemocratic group of businesspeople and their allies in the government and the mass media (see Mills, 2000; Chomsky, 2007).

In the 1960s, American historian and political scientist Charles Tilly (b. 1929) began studying the formation of modern nation-states in Europe to shed light on how groups compete for power, enlarge their own power, and limit that of their enemies. In view of modernization, holders of office, contenders, and entrepreneurs in violence are the main players. His analysis is a strategic and political one in which strong governments use force efficiently against their enemies and weak governments are preyed upon by contenders. Though influenced by Marxism and modern social sciences, Tilly (2003) shares the Machiavellian emphasis on power and skepticism about the importance of ideals such as democracy and liberty.

Critiques of Realism

The realist approach is still quite influential in conflict analysis because it highlights the question of what people will do to gain or keep political power. The approach is based on simple and general assumptions from which specific hypotheses can be derived and tested. Realism also adeptly uses the rational analysis of human behaviour for a systematic exploration of decisions. Finally, the Machiavellian view of conflict applies to any level and historical period.

However, there are several problems with the realist approach.[3] One immediate challenge is defining two of its major themes: power and interests. Everybody has an idea about power, but the concept is actually hard to define, particularly in terms of whether it is a means or an end. In other words, is power the ultimate goal of politics or merely an instrument to attain other objectives, such as equality, prosperity, liberty, security, and justice? Some analysts go further by claiming that the type of explanation favoured by realism is too vague and impossible to submit to scientific verification (see Vasquez, 1983). A statement such as "This conflict was created by the parties' desire for power" is a trivial generality at best and, at worst, a tautology that cannot be proved or disproved.

Furthermore, realism cannot explain why the struggle for political power has changed so much over time. In modern industrial democracies, political murders and kidnappings are rare, and violence is absent from most electoral contests. Most international transactions are peaceful and take place within the bounds of international law. The use of force is in decline everywhere and military might does not have the same weight in politics as it once had. Realism cannot explain these changes because it does not have a theory of change. For instance, realists could not predict the end of the Cold War because, while they were knowledgeable about the Soviet–American rivalry, they did not pay enough attention to what was happening within the Soviet Union.

Realism has also been criticized for ignoring other factors, such as economics, in its explanation of human behaviour. For example, the advanced democratic nations' preference for commercial liberalization (the gradual decrease in trade barriers) over protectionist economics (policies such as tariffs and import quotas that limit foreign competition) is not only a function of national security. It is also a behaviour that is influenced by other causes: corporate interests of capitalist firms, consumers' preference for cheap and available goods and services, and liberal ideology claiming that free trade is good for prosperity, individual liberties, and peace. Since the 1980s, realists have taken note of this critique and responded with neo-realism (or structural realism). Realists can now seriously study international trade, investment, and technology transfers as aspects of power struggles (Krasner, 2009). However, their opponents continue to argue that the theory remains preoccupied with relations of power and cannot see economic constraints, social structures, or cultural norms as separate conflict factors. Some theorists have even tried to move realism in the direction of post-positivist research programs (see Bar, 2010; Patomäki, 2001), but the potency of such approaches has yet to be determined.

With regard to national, local, and interpersonal matters, Machiavellian approaches also give a very limited, deterministic, vague, and static view of human interaction. It means reducing labour conflicts, marital differences, and commercial disputes to small battles for power. In so doing, the analyst may illuminate a power aspect of the relation in question, but risk neglecting far more important motivations of the actors.

Finally, a constant point of criticism for realism is its relationship with politics and political ethics (Lebow, 2006). Modern-day realists such as Kenneth Waltz (1979, 2001) often claim that theirs is a scientific theory without ethical tints. However, traditional realists such as Morgenthau (2005) thought that the realist was not so much a scientist but an advocate of prudent and conservative statesmanship. Realism is always spread between a scientific ambition and a policy inclination. As a dominant world view among political classes, realism has acquired a normative dimension. With neo-realism, however, the theory has evolved toward a scientific, value-neutral stance. As a result, realists often have difficulty empathizing with the moral goals and dilemmas of conflict participants and may therefore misunderstand some powerful cultural and psychological influences on conflict behaviour.

Power Deficits and Conflict: The Hobbesian Tradition

British philosopher Thomas Hobbes wrote in the seventeenth century, at the time of the European wars of religion and the English Civil War. He presented his conception of the state in his most famous work, *Leviathan*, first published in 1651. Hobbes postulated that, before the creation of government, people lived in anarchy and were entitled to use force to serve their own interests. In this "state of nature," everybody was constantly under the threat of violent death at the hands of others. Therefore, life was "solitary, poor, nasty, brutish, and short" (Hobbes, 1651/2008). The only way to avoid this gloomy situation was for each individual to renounce his or her freedom to use force in social relations.[4] In this perspective, the state has gradually emerged as the only alternative to private violence. Hobbes wanted the power of the state to be absolute in order to prevent feuds and civil wars. Although he advocated monarchical government, he recognized that democratic and aristocratic states could theoretically perform this task.

Hobbes's contribution to politics and law has been immense. He was one of the first modern thinkers in the sense that he tried to create a justification for state power that was not grounded in religion and tradition but in rational thought. He was an early defender of sovereignty, the doctrine that has become the cornerstone of positive international law. Hobbes was also the first contract theorist, meaning that he inaugurated the current intellectual tradition that the state is a sort of contract among people for the implementation of orderly interactions.[5]

Hobbes did not see an end to the international state of nature; therefore, he thought that the relations among states were bound to remain fraught with violence and war. Modern-day realists are all Hobbesians in their belief that international relations constitute an anarchical system where violence and force reign supreme. However, some Hobbesians are not realists in the sense that they do not share Morgenthau's (2005) contention that all politics is a struggle for power. The best-known non-realist Hobbesian is French philosopher and sociologist Raymond Aron (1905–83). Aron (2003) thought of anarchy as a constraint on political actors whose prime motivation is not necessarily the acquisition of political power but can be, for example, ideology, salvation, profit, or glory.

For our purposes, the contribution of Hobbes can be summarized by the following hypothesis: the more powerful state authority is, the less troublesome the conflicts. In other words, the more anarchical a social system is, the more violent conflicts it will harbour. This relationship allows us to elaborate on an elementary sociology of anarchical and ordered social systems. However, contrary to what realists and Hobbesians generally think, there is no need to radically separate the two types. There are many grey areas between them, which can be viewed as a continuum.

As Figure 8.1 illustrates, war represents a completely anarchical system. In large-scale armed conflict, there is no supreme authority over the participants—violence is the rule of the game. In theory, total nuclear war would be the ultimate form of anarchical relations, as states would be caught in a spiral of senseless annihilation.

The next phase in the continuum is anarchical social systems with incomplete rules of the game, such as international relations. Even at their most tense, international relations are only partially controlled by **diplomatic immunity**, rules of **protocol**, recognized third parties (e.g. the secretary-general of the United Nations), commercial relations, personal contacts, the involvement of IGOs and NGOs, and human rights codes. This is why Australian political scientist Hedley Bull (1932–85) described international relations as the anarchical society (2002). The gradual establishment of norms and institutions to replace the "law of the jungle" among states has been one of the main themes of the so-called British School of international relations. The tenants of **constructivism** (or constructionism), another theoretical model of international affairs that we will discuss later, also claim that humankind is not necessarily doomed to anarchy. In 1992, Alexander Wendt (b. 1958), one of the pre-eminent constructivists, wrote: "Anarchy is what states make of it." In other words, anarchy has been a self-fulfilling prophecy as the interests, ideologies, and perceptions of state leaders have converged to support this notion over the years. However, as ideas change, international anarchy becomes increasingly constrained by laws and norms (Wendt, 1999).

Similar to international relations are instances where a state loses authority over parts of its territory, even though some forms of legal command remain. One form of this anarchy is the phenomenon of failed, or collapsed, states, which (as we saw in Chapter 3) are unable to provide a minimal degree of security or services to their populations. They are usually wrecked by violence and are susceptible to armed conflict. Next to failed states are "weak states," regions of civil unrest in which low-intensity conflict and terrorism are widespread and disruptive but most people still pay their taxes, abide by the law, receive

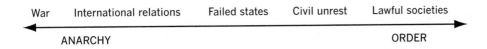

FIGURE 8.1 | THE CONTINUUM BETWEEN ANARCHICAL AND ORDERLY SOCIAL SYSTEMS

minimal services from the government, and keep business ties and personal relations with the outside world. (These troubled regions also include urban areas severely affected by crime and where the state authority is challenged by gangs.) Weak states are quite common in the global South. Most evolve toward an orderly society, but this transition may take decades, as is currently the case with most Latin American and several Asian societies. Some revert to general violence and descend to failed state status (e.g. El Salvador, Nicaragua, and Guatemala in the 1980s; Algeria in the 1990s; and the Ivory Coast in the early 2000s).

Finally, we find lawful societies. Although these societies are the most ordered type on our continuum, the majority are not completely peaceful, even in the developed West. Some rich countries contain weakly ordered pockets, for instance, the violent core of several American cities; some Indigenous reserves in Canada, the United States, and Australia, where there is occasional violence; and some regions of ethnic unrest in Europe (Corsica, Northern Ireland, the Basque region, etc.). The disruptions caused by political unrest or criminality in these countries may limit growth in the particular communities where violence is endemic; however, they are not severe enough to hamper development and growth within the entire society.

The Hobbesian approach is widely used in the study of post-Cold War conflicts, many of which (particularly in the developing world) are attributed to the weakness of the state. Political scientist Mohammed Ayoob (2001) summarizes the typical Hobbesian position: "The problem of order in the Third World cannot be tackled by trying to transcend the Westphalian model (a world made up of sovereign states) but by attempting to strengthen it. The root cause of disorder in the Third World is linked to the inadequacy of state authority and not to the excessive use of state power" (p. 140). Another well-known exponent of this thesis is political scientist Kal J. Holsti (1996), who has defended the idea that the gradual pacification of international relations is basically due to the extension of state power.

This type of analysis is often used to explain the propensity of some countries to develop violent conflicts and is therefore influential in policy-making. For instance, many states and funding agencies emphasize the restructuring and strengthening of the state in their development policies. This is especially the case with **peacebuilding** programs where state reinforcement policies (e.g. reform of security forces, modernization of the legal system, rationalization of the bureaucracy) take a prominent place, at least in the medium term.

While the Hobbesian approach offers a pertinent and useful model of emphasizing the role of power deficits and vacuums in the emergence of violent conflicts, it suffers from major flaws that keep it from being a complete paradigm for the explanation of conflicts. The main problem is that the causes of the weakness and failure of states are not stated in the theory. Even if we agree with the proposition that weak and failed states are more likely to experience significant degrees of violence, we still have to explain why these states are in this predicament. Has the rapid pace of modernization not given them time to adapt to the new reality or develop efficient public governance? Did colonialism decimate cultures and create artificial boundaries? Has foreign economic exploitation left these states too weak financially? Have the local elites made bad public policy choices? Are there cultural elements that block the construction of the modern state? The Hobbesian approach does not provide answers to these questions. Furthermore, it tends to equate violence with conflict. As we saw in Part I, this association is often inaccurate. In fact, there is more violence in some orderly countries than in anarchical systems (see Chapter 3). Most analysts of large-scale violence contend that authoritarian and totalitarian states have killed more people in the twentieth century than all the wars put together (Rummel, 1997; Harff, 2003; Pinker, 2011).

In sum, the Hobbesian approach offers us a model emphasizing the study of the role of power deficits and power vacuums in the emergence of violent conflicts. This is a pertinent and useful model, but it may not constitute a genuine theory of conflict.

Pluralist Approaches

Political pluralism, which has led to political group theory and resource mobilization theory, is another approach to conflict that relies on the concept of political power. This approach does not, however, encompass the philosophical overtones found in realism and the Hobbesian perspective. Political pluralism was developed in the 1950s, when analysts such as David Truman (1951) became dissatisfied with both the legal–institutional approach to politics, which they found too rigid and static, and the elite–realist theory, which they considered inconsistent with the realities of contemporary democracies. These scholars sought to construct an approach that could comprehend the manifestations of peaceful political struggles in the United States and other Western democracies. Their concept is simple: the essence of democracy is a competition among groups for the determination of public policy. The groups will rival each other by using a mixture of co-optation and alliances, intimidation and deception, and persuasion and eloquence. Because there are many groups with varied goals and tactics and a fluid and overlapping membership, pluralism could abandon the controversial conspiracy aspects of elite theory and embrace a more benign understanding of modern politics. The term **polyarchy** is also employed to signify the plurality of important groups that define public policy, collectively or in coalitions (Dahl, 1972).

Pluralism is often a more appropriate means of explaining a number of public policy outcomes than Machiavellianism. For instance, interest groups and public opinion regularly defeat governments and industrialists in large-scale projects. While such an outcome is rather puzzling to elite theorists, pluralists argue that representative coalitions led by competent leaders and assisted by favourable media coverage can often impose their preferences in the political arena. Pluralism is also particularly applicable to the study of electoral politics. In fact, one could say that it is the dominant approach to politics, given that media reporters and pundits usually analyze the outcomes of elections and policy contests in terms of the strength, external support, skills, timing, and resolve of opposing coalitions.

The pluralist approach to politics extends well beyond the confines of democratic political systems. In the 1960s, philosophical liberals seeking an alternative to realist determinism adapted pluralism to international affairs. For example, American political scientist Ernst B. Haas (1924–2003) thought that the progress of integration in the European Economic Community (EEC—the ancestor of the European Union) was a function of both state interests (the variable preferred by realists) and social pressure (from interest groups, political parties, and public opinion) (1964). Later, pluralists began studying economic and social interdependence with the intent to prove that modern-day states are sensitive and vulnerable to foreign influences, including those from smaller states and non-governmental movements (Deutsch, 1988; Keohane, 1989; Rosenau, 1990).

In the comparative study of violent conflict, many authors have used approaches that are reminiscent of the pluralist analysis. For example, Ted Robert Gurr (2000) advocates a comprehensive social understanding of ethnopolitical conflicts that is broadly related to a pluralistic approach to the politics of conflicts. Leader of the Minorities at Risk project, Gurr is particularly interested in the conditions that lead some minorities to choose peaceful protests and others to use violence. In his view, minorities with a very salient identity and incentives, opportunities, and capacities for action will seek their political and social affirmation (Gurr, 2000). However, the direction of that action, peaceful or violent, has a lot to do with context, the main variable being the type of political regime in which the minority lives. Simply put, minorities in authoritarian systems tend to be more prone to violence than those living in democratic contexts. Gurr found strong statistical support for the hypothesis that ethnopolitical violence is largely a function of authoritarian relations. However, the theory does not explain all cases.

Nowadays, many theorists have incorporated political pluralism into their analyses of the age of globalization. For instance, German sociologist Ulrich Beck (2006), a critic of capitalist globalization, goes further than many liberals by claiming that the world of interstate relations is a thing of the past and is being replaced by globalized politics, a system of many international, transnational, and local actors and issues. While most of the anti-globalization supporters consider themselves pluralists, a term that they associate with old-style capitalists, they do analyze the emergence of a global polyarchy of interests in the process of globalization.

Pluralism offers a non-deterministic view of politics, where a number of factors are involved in conflicts and their evolution. As such, the pluralist framework can be used at several levels of analysis. For example, in the study of bureaucratic decisions and actions, an analyst might look at how groups and cliques try to dominate large modern organizations. However, because pluralism is concerned with large political groups in conflict, its value in examining interpersonal and small group conflicts is dubious. The theory has also been harshly criticized in social science literature for its alleged idealization of the democratic process. Many analysts have pointed to democracy's shortcomings in the promotion of the views and interests of many segments of societies, including the poor, women, and minorities. It is also possible that pluralists neglect the cultural and ideological factors behind human action. In particular, it can be asked whether the pluralist framework reflects characteristics of Western democracies rather than universal principles. Though partly superseded by other forms of analysis and weakened by accusations of ethnocentrism, pluralism highlights the non-deterministic and dynamic aspects of conflict in complex political systems.

ECONOMIC AND CLASS CONFLICT

In this section, we review schools of thought that emphasize the role of capitalism in the development of conflict. The basic hypotheses underlying these approaches are as follows: capitalism is an economic system that fosters severe conflicts, especially class conflict; all major conflicts within and among societies are the consequences of the capitalist system; and capitalism will be destroyed by the conflicts that it has generated.

Classical Marxism

The oldest and best-known theory regarding capitalism is Marxism, developed in the mid-nineteenth century by German philosopher Karl Marx (1818–83) and his lifelong collaborator Friedrich Engels (1820–95) to explain the Industrial Revolution, understand the workings of capitalism, and offer a way out of labour exploitation and misery.[6] They used the emerging science of political economy—spearheaded by Adam Smith—as a basis for their analysis.[7] As discussed in Chapter 5, Smith (1776/2003) believed that individual desires for wealth and comfort drove the economy and that governments should give individuals as much freedom as possible in order to generate maximum wealth for all. Smith advocated free enterprise, free trade, and civic liberties as the pillars of capitalist development. Marx and Engels were in complete opposition to this view. They thought that liberal individualism would only enrich a privileged social class and impoverish most people.

However, it is important to remember that Marxism is more than a school of political economy. It is also a complete view of nature and history that has conflict as its central explanatory factor. In effect, Marx and Engels borrowed from German philosopher Georg Hegel (1770–1831) the notion that nature and history work in a dialectical fashion, meaning that any significant change in nature or human affairs is the result of the resolution of a conflict between two opposite forces.[8] According to Marxism, the main principles of human history are that there have always been social classes in opposition and the violent resolution of these oppositions is the main factor of historical change (Marx & Engels, 1848/1988). Each society is built on a dominant **mode of production** (the way the economy is organized), with a certain level of technology and a certain type of ownership of the **means of production** (the land, resources, buildings, machines, and all other items needed to produce goods and services). Capitalism, then, is a mode of production based on industrial technology and private ownership of the means of production.

This approach, called historical materialism, states that the main contradiction in modern capitalist society is the relationship between the owners of the means of production (the bourgeoisie) and the people who sell their labour for a living (the proletariat). According to Marx and Engels, capitalism could develop only by severely exploiting the proletariat because the surplus value from labour was the only source of wealth accumulation in this system. They also believed that this trend could only increase, as history showed that the average profit rate tended to fall and had to be countered by further exploitation (Marx, 1867/1992). Therefore, no amount of social reformism or political advocacy could reverse this situation, as the bourgeoisie would never agree to anything that could jeopardize their business investments. In the very materialistic and deterministic approach of historical materialism, politics, ideologies, religion, science, and the arts have no existence outside the underlying economic system in which they develop. They are only a weak superstructure reflecting the more solid economic infrastructure beneath it. For Marx, parliamentary rivalries were considered insignificant contests between members of the dominant class. The only reality that mattered was that affluent people benefited from the harsh exploitation of the proletariat. Only one scenario was possible: the aggravation of class struggles followed by worker uprisings and capped by a large-scale social revolution toppling capitalism and replacing it with a socialist system.

Marxism reminds us to look at the economic conditions of any conflict. For instance, a conflict between two ethnic groups may be fuelled by their economic rivalry for employment in a modernizing capitalist economy and not by their cultural differences. Conflicts are often about who gets what in a society, and Marxist theory posits that capitalist societies will experience bitter conflicts between social classes. This critical perspective led Marx and Engels to believe that, although the changes brought about by capitalism were sometimes beneficial (e.g. the destruction of the last vestiges of feudalism and the spreading of rationalism), they were mostly negative. This position is at the source of all social science critiques of capitalism, and it inspires modern social movements opposed to globalization. Today, even as Marxism has lost some of its pertinence, its legacy exists in the approaches that blame capitalism and globalization as the root causes of violent conflict and deduce that only a radical change to the world economic system will help in the resolution of differences.

Before Marx and Engels defined the concept of social class, people were thought of as being separated by order or estate (the three fundamental orders of feudalism: nobility, church, and commoners), ethnicity, religion, or trade (peasants, artisans, merchants, etc.). Social class is a crucial notion for the analysis of industrial societies and, while not the only social structure that matters, also an element in the understanding of many conflicts.[9] Class conflicts have been an important factor in all newly industrialized societies, from nineteenth-century Great Britain and France to modern-day Mexico and Brazil.

However, there are many criticisms of classical Marxism. We will concentrate on two. First, capitalism has not been toppled by the proletariat and has evolved in ways that Marx and Engels did not foresee. Contrary to their predictions, communist revolutions did not occur in industrialized countries but in agrarian contexts (e.g. Russia, China, and Cuba). Other communist "revolutions" were imposed or facilitated by the Soviet Union and China, as in North Korea, North Vietnam, and Yugoslavia. Capitalism has also proven much more resilient than Marxists predicted. Starting in the nineteenth century, bourgeois governments have enacted labour reforms. Workers' parties have been created and have participated in reforms since the early twentieth century. The welfare state, a compromise between the liberal state of Smith and the socialist ideals of Marx and Engels, has led to many improvements to the lot of the working classes. Also, industrial production has changed enormously. Marx and Engels thought that capitalism would turn workers into adjuncts to their machines, performing increasingly repetitive and degrading tasks for dwindling wages. In fact, high technology and the development of the service industries have meant that the majority of workers in advanced economies hold white-collar and technical positions, using their brains much more than their muscles to earn a living.

Second, the class struggle is not the only significant fracture in modern societies. In fact, it is often a secondary factor of conflict in several countries. In post-industrial economies, the working class has receded and the middle classes have grown. The unionized and well-remunerated industrial workers of today are not in a life-or-death struggle with their employers but often share the same interest in seeing the company prosper, especially when the workers (individually or collectively) own shares of the company. The educated and mobile technicians and white-collar workers of the post-industrial society do not see themselves as proletarians preparing for revolution. They are often unconcerned with unionization and worker solidarity. Furthermore, the interests of blue-collar and white-collar employees are often at odds. In sum, the class situation has become more complex and less acute than what had been predicted by the founders of Marxism.

Marxism after Marx and Engels

In the late nineteenth century, it became obvious to many socialists that Marx and Engels's predictions of revolution would not materialize in the near future and might never happen. The second generation of Marxists had to explain this situation. It can even be said that the whole history of Marxism since Marx and Engels has been dominated by the puzzling question of why capitalism has not fallen. The communist movement has split into many schools and sects over this matter. Here, we will summarize a few attempts to explain the resilience and growth of capitalism since the Industrial Revolution.[10]

The most important explanation was that capitalism had not yet run its course and had to go through a second stage before being destroyed by the workers. This stage, known as imperialism, has been characterized by two fundamental changes: the concentration and monopolization of capital and the state-backed expansion of capitalism into new regions of the world (Lenin, 1969). For turn-of-the-century Marxists, these two processes improved the return on investments and thereby allowed capitalism to survive (recall that Marx and Engels argued that the law of falling profit rates was the real mechanism behind the doom of capitalism). For German philosopher and economist Rosa Luxemburg

(1871–1919), the exploitation of the world could be profitable only as long as the rates of return were interesting. After a few decades, capitalism would exhaust its overseas reservoirs of surplus value and would face insolvency and overproduction (Luxemburg, 2003). In the meantime, the proletariat would develop and capitalist countries would find themselves waging a global class struggle against the impoverished regions of imperialist exploitation. According to Russian leader Vladimir Oulianov Lenin (1870–1924), the competition among capitalist states would lead to a world war that would be the death knell for capitalism because the workers would rather topple their governments than take arms against their foreign comrades. These hopes evaporated in August 1914, when World War I started without massive labour unrest. Revolutions did occur in Russia in 1917 and in Germany two years later, but only the former succeeded. Communism did not spread like wildfire. Instead, Russia was alone as a revolutionary state.

Marxism became the official ideology of the Soviet Union, but it had to be modified to explain the events of the revolution and to fit in with the new circumstances. Until the 1980s, the Leninist idea was the official credo of the regime. Internationally, the Communist Party of the Soviet Union was presented as the leader of the proletariat. The class struggle was played at the highest level in the confrontation between the Soviet Union and the imperialist powers, including the Cold War.

Several Marxists did not agree with this model. The partisans of Leon Trotsky, the exiled rival of Stalin, rejected the Soviet Union's authoritarian leadership over the international communist movement and thought that the class struggle should be played out everywhere, including in the USSR, until the true proletarian world revolution occurred. Other communists thought that the Soviet analysis of the world class struggle did not take into account the particular conditions of the developing world. Chinese leader Mao Zedong thought that his country should play a more important role than second fiddle to the Russians and gradually distanced himself from Soviet policy. The Chinese doctrine of the class struggle stated that the main chasm in the global class struggle was between the rich countries (the First World) and the underdeveloped (the Third World). The Soviet Union was a bureaucratized and power-hungry former communist state that was cut off from the real class struggles in the developing world and was leading a feeble Second World. China was the leader of the world's have-nots. This approach was adapted in large part by neo-Marxists, although many did not endorse the part about China leading the world revolution. Since the 1970s, several developments have weakened this thesis, notably the economic growth of several Third World countries, the accession of former impoverished countries to the rank of First World powers (e.g. South Korea, Taiwan, and Singapore), and the conversion of China to market economics.

Other Marxists sought to explain the development of capitalism through political and cultural analysis. In the 1920s, the Frankfurt School (more on this group in Chapter 9) posited that capitalists sustain their rule by developing academic and cultural concepts and theories that legitimize their economic interests (Bottomore, 2003). In the same vein, Herbert Marcuse (1991) wrote that capitalism reduced a human being to a "one-dimensional man" devoid of critical thought and imagination, a thesis that was popular on university campuses in the late 1960s.

In the 1920s, Italian Communist Party leader Antonio Gramsci (1891–1937), who was imprisoned by Mussolini, constructed the theory of **hegemony** to explain continued bourgeois power. Gramsci (1971) described hegemony as the power to impose your own interests by disguising them as universal and incontestable ideals. Accordingly, capitalism succeeded because the dominant class convinced everybody that the bourgeois ideas of free enterprise, human rights, and democracy were in their own interests. One important task for communists, especially the intellectuals and artists, was to weaken this hegemony by developing a critical analysis of capitalist thought. In the 1960s and 1970s, the so-called structuralist Marxists elaborated on this approach. French philosopher Louis Althusser (1918–90) thought that capitalist society was stable because of the role played by "state ideological apparatuses," structures such as government, schools, hospitals, churches, the army, and the mass media that propagated bourgeois ideas in society (2001). One problem that other Marxists have with this approach is that it gives a static view of capitalist society, one in which the class struggle was secondary to the power of institutions. A more fundamental criticism (according to non-Marxists) is that the Gramscian approach paints an unrealistic picture of Western societies, which are in fact extremely varied, fragmented, and self-critical.

The Marxist movement has harboured other thinkers who believe that the nineteenth-century version of the class struggle and the ideal of proletarian revolution do not completely apply to the modern world. French sociologist Nicos Poulantzas (1936–79) thought that the bourgeois class is always divided into "class fractions" with different policy interests (1975). For example, unprofitable heavy industries might demand protection against foreign competition, while the fast-growing high-tech sector favours increased liberty of trade. Because capitalists cannot even agree with one another, the state has to intervene to protect them against themselves. The state is also sometimes utilized by actors such as bureaucrats, the military, and political parties to achieve their ends. This approach brought Marxism closer to mainstream social sciences.

The 1980s saw a revival of the Gramscian perspective in the study of world politics, notably through the works of Stephen Gill (1993). He believes that ideas and institutions have, along with the influence of economic and technological forces, a role to play in the creation of the modern world system. This theory is particularly important in understanding the emergence of American hegemony in the international system. Lately, Gill (2008) has been interested in the international class conflict among the globalized elites, semi-integrated working classes, and excluded labourers and peasants.

However, Marxism no longer has the influence on the study of social conflict that it once had. In the last 30 years, most of the modern left has followed the example of British sociologist Anthony Giddens (b. 1938). Giddens (1984) has criticized the excessive determinism of Marxist thought and has developed the theory of **structuration**, which tries to reconcile the role of human agents and social structures in the explanation of social behaviour. In other words, all people (not only the rich and powerful) have some control over their lives, within the bounds of the society in which they live. This means, among other things, that class conflicts have receded because today's citizens have many more options than past generations. However, progressive social action is still possible in many forms, including the "third way" (between liberalism and socialism) that Giddens theorized for the British Labour Party.

Economic Dependency and World System Theory

In the 1950s, economists began studying the less developed parts of the world to identify the factors inhibiting growth and to propose economic development policies. Many of these analysts were struck by the fact that Latin America had been independent from colonial powers for well over a century but was still significantly behind Europe and the United States in terms of economics. Industrialization was also quite feeble in Latin American countries, despite Marxist predictions that capitalism would export capital and develop industries in the non-Western world to increase its general rate of profit. The concept of **dependency** was created to account for this situation. In short, dependency theory argues that these societies were underdeveloped and poor because they relied on the capital, technology, expertise, and markets of the developed Northern nations (Prebisch, 1950). The main historical form of dependency was a commercial mode characterized by the export of raw materials from the Southern countries to the Northern countries, in exchange for the acquisition of much more sophisticated and valuable manufactured goods (Frank, 1974). According to dependency theory, this **unequal exchange** is only going to worsen, as mounting manufacturing and research and development costs for processed goods makes them increasingly expensive (Emmanuel, 1976). This deterioration in the terms of trade is the main explanation for the expansion of developing nations' debt (Köhler & Tausch, 2002).

In the 1960s and 1970s, famous Norwegian peace and conflict researcher Johan Galtung (b. 1930) developed a structuralist view of dependency that agreed with one proposed by the Latin-American *dependantistas*. Galtung (1971) thought that there were structural links of dependency between not only poor and rich nations but also the poor and dominant social classes within nations. Conversely, the dominant classes of both the rich and poor nations are structurally linked by joint interests across borders. For Galtung, these dependency and co-operation connections create a fracture between the powerful and the powerless that leads to potentially violent conflict. Galtung (1969) has even argued that economic exploitation is in itself a form of violence (**structural violence**), a formulation that is close to the Marxist conception of the class war.

The dependency approach has become very influential. Most of the anti-globalization discourse now comes directly or indirectly from dependency theory. The liberation theology espoused by many Catholic clerics in Latin America is largely inspired by the thesis. Most development and human rights NGOs owe their analyses of the world to dependency. The approach is a potent tool in the examination of trade inequities, debt accumulation, and the actions of multinational corporations. However, it has problems explaining why some countries (e.g. South Korea, Taiwan, and Singapore) have shed their dependency status while others are still mired in misery. In the 1970s, some analysts led by Enrique Cardoso (b. 1931)—who later became president of Brazil—studied dependent development, a phenomenon that they mainly attributed to the decentralization strategies of multinational corporations (Cardoso & Faletto, 1979). This approach is still capable of explaining many situations, such as the industrialization of the northern part of Mexico to serve the US market, but it does not account for many cases of indigenous economic development in the Third World.

The initial dependency view has evolved into world systems theory, notably under the influence of American sociologist Immanual Wallerstein (b. 1930), who has studied the post-Renaissance emergence of a global economy. According to Wallerstein (1979), the main global conflict is the one between the dependent nations of the South (the periphery) and the dominant societies of the North (the core). There also exists a semi-periphery of partially industrialized states, including Mexico, Brazil, Malaysia, Thailand, and Turkey, which has been growing rapidly in the last quarter century. Wallerstein's

(AP Photo/Fotosite, Andre Conti)

Strike at a Volkswagen plant near Sao Paulo, Brazil, in 2001. The placard on the right reads "We are men, not machines."
As a sizable part of industrial production moves to Southern countries, so do many manifestations of class struggles.

theory has been enormously influential the world over, inspiring a great deal of current critical research about development.

Despite obvious resemblances to the Maoist theory and the Luxemburg framework, the dependency/world systems approach is not strictly Marxist. In dependency theory, societies, not classes, are the dominant actors. Its proponents believe that the struggle to free societies from foreign dependency must be conducted by wide political movements including nationalist leaders, local elites, and socialist militants, not by communist parties and governments. Nationalist governments in the tradition of Peron in Argentina, Velasco in Peru, and Goulart in Brazil have represented this approach in the past. Recently, leaders of the nationalist and socialist stripes have emerged in several countries, such as Chavez in Venezuela, Lula in Brazil, and Morales in Bolivia. Another difference is in the approach to American hegemony. While world systems theorists and Marxists are sanguine about the imminent demise of the American empire, they disagree about the levels of political repression and war that this process will generate (Wallerstein, 2003). Galtung (2009) has also been hesitant on the issue, but he has stated that the end of the American empire may be relatively peaceful and lead to a more balanced world.

Despite its popularity, dependency/world systems theory has some weaknesses in the analysis of development and conflict. First, it is a rather deterministic framework that, to the detriment of political and cultural causes, emphasizes economic factors in the explanation of conflict. Second, the link between dependency and conflict is not always clear. On one hand, dependency theorists are tempted to conclude, like Marxists, that capitalism chronically generates violence. However, since the facts do not always accord with this model, such theorists are either constantly predicting imminent violence or removing the study of violence from that of underdevelopment, thereby weakening their explanations of several social-political developments in the world economy. Third, dependency theory states that dependency causes underdevelopment. However, in reality, the situation is exactly the opposite. In general, the more foreign investments received by a developing country, the better its economic situation. It is those countries that are neglected by international capital (because of lack of resources, uneducated workforce, political instability, etc.) that are underdeveloped. Finally, this theory uses foreign factors (e.g. colonialism, policies of big powers, actions of MNCs, roles of international financial organizations such as the IMF) to explain everything negative in developing countries. In so doing, dependency theory is often used to absolve Southern leaders of any responsibility for the state of affairs in their country. Obviously, there are analytical and ethical problems related to such a view of development.

SOCIAL CHANGE AND CONFLICT

The Notion of Progress

The philosophers of the Enlightenment left us the notion of progress, a change that leads to previously unseen outcomes and improves society in material and moral well-being. In archaic societies, the notion of change did not really exist. Things were the way they had always been and would stay the same eternally. Ethnographers qualified these societies as change adverse, or misoneist. Their mental universe was that of the "eternal present." In ancient societies, the notion of change existed but was often seen as a cyclical change, as in the Buddhist and Hindu traditions. Societies indeed changed, but along pre-ordained patterns that would repeat themselves in the future.

In the West, change was primarily associated with negative prospects. For instance, in the Middle Ages, the fall of the Roman Empire was seen as a historical calamity from which Europe had not yet recovered. The notion of change was a seditious idea, for it potentially weakened the authority of popes, kings, and nobles and could only lead to misery, violence, and sin. During the Renaissance and the Reformation, dramatic change transformed Europe (confirming the worst fears of the Catholic Church). By the mid-seventeenth century, after 150 years of controversy and violence, the power of the Church was curtailed, barons and small kings were ousted, powerful kings ruled large unified lands, and the merchant class rose in society. Many people, especially in Protestant kingdoms, thought that change was not so bad after all. They started to think that there was a direction to change, one that led from the darkness of superstition and religion to the enlightenment of science and philosophy, from oppression, scarcity, and war to emancipation, affluence, and peace. Forward-looking change, or progress, was born with the first liberals, such as John Locke (1632–1704), Voltaire (1694–1778) , and David Hume (1711–76). It was the inspiration behind many eighteenth-century scientists, artists, explorers, and philosophers. The French philosophers of this time, such as Denis Diderot (1713–84), developed and spread the idea of progress, notably through the famous *Encyclopédie*. German philosophers such as Immanuel Kant and Georg Hegel also believed in progress, which Kant attributed to a master plan of nature in which people were the unsuspecting players.

In this view, the main conflict in human societies is between the forces of tradition and the forces of progress. For the believers in progress, tradition would always lose, sometimes at the cost of furious rearguard battles. To avoid as much bloodshed as possible, it was therefore imperative to convince the masses that change was in their favour and the old elites that change was inevitable. However, large-scale violence often occurred, leading many liberals and socialists to believe that revolutionary change was the only way to bring about real progress.

In the early nineteenth century, Western European societies were changing at a rapid pace, mostly because of industrialization. The emerging discipline of sociology made modernization its central topic, and one can say that most of nineteenth-century sociology and a large part of twentieth-century social sciences were dominated by this theme. Initially, however, the term *modernization* was not applied. Auguste Comte (1798–1857), the first scholar to call himself a sociologist, talked of progress in the eighteenth-century sense of the term. This ardent promoter of positivist thought elaborated the theory of the three ages (magic, religion, and science) and described his own times as the transition between the age of religion and the age of science. A similar classification was later developed by Edward B. Tylor (1832–1917), the "father of anthropology," with its "savage," "barbarian," and "civilized" eras.

Other social thinkers of the era delighted at creating dichotomies representing the old and the new world. French philosopher Maine de Biran (1766–1824) wrote about societies based on status versus societies based on contract. In this view, the rank, role, and responsibility of a person in an ancient society were determined at birth from an immutable cultural tradition. In contrast, modern individualist societies are based on contract, the negotiated terms of co-operation. German sociologist Ferdinand Tönnies (1855–1935) contrasted the communities (*Gemeinschaft*) of old days with the societies (*Gesellschaft*) of the modern world, the former being based on bloodlines and tradition and the latter on individuals co-operating in the context of a complex division of labour. French sociologist Émile Durkheim (1858–1917) also thought that the division of labour was a determining feature of modernity, along with the loss of religious certainties. In the same vein as Tönnies, he opposed the ancient societies of "mechanical solidarity" with the modern societies of "organic solidarity" (Durkheim, 1972). Max Weber (1998) separated political systems whose legitimacy derived from traditional and religious norms, such as monarchies, from regimes based on the rational–legal criteria of legitimacy, such as modern nation-states.

These scholars thought that Europe was in the midst of a fundamental change from tradition to modernity and that this change created troubles and conflicts. However, they were generally confident that the future would be better than the past. Their main topics of concern were class struggles, human alienation, and the possibility of world wars. For Durkheim (1972), though, the republican ethics of a modern nation-state was the best antidote against class wars, the **anomie** (loss of meaning) of modern individuals, and the bellicose tendencies of the aristocracy and army.

Modernization and Development

In the twentieth century, the study of modernization moved to the United States, where social scientists set themselves the task of explaining modern society and deriving ways to foster its successful evolution. In this endeavour, the leadership of sociologist Talcott Parsons (1902–79) must be mentioned. Parsons (1991) was influenced by European sociology, particularly Durkheim and Spencer, and developed the notion of systems (social, political, economic, cultural, etc.) in social analysis. For Parsons, 1950s America was the prototype of modernity because it had achieved stability, secularism, pluralism, efficiency, and humanism with little turmoil. The question was how to make necessary reforms without endangering the solid basis of modernity. Conflict was a secondary subject for Parsons. In fact, in his structural functionalist approach, violent conflict was seen either as an attribute of pre-modern societies or as an anomaly in modern nations.

After Parsons, social scientists extended their studies to non-Western societies, attempting to verify whether the tenets of structural functionalism could be generalized and offer paths for development and modernization in post-colonial countries. In the

1950s and 1960s, many political scientists were interested in what they called political development, an aspect of general modernization equivalent to the better-known issue of economic development (Almond & Powell, 1966). Political development was a function of institutionalization and secularization. The higher the states ranked on these two variables, the more modern (and therefore more developed) they were. State elites had to adapt or leave things to younger, more educated replacements. David Apter (1966) was also interested in this approach but thought that modernization was a complex political and social endeavour requiring difficult choices at every step. Israeli sociologist Shmuel Eisenstadt (1966) was another well-known modernization theorist of the era.

In the mid-1960s, some discordant voices raised doubts about the developmental approach. Political scientist Samuel P. Huntington (1927–2008) made a distinction between modernization, which he believed was an irreversible historical process, and political development, which he saw as a contingent and fluctuating movement. According to Huntington (1968), political development was not an automatic result of modernization, as exemplified by the post-colonial regimes that espoused authoritarian and paternalistic forms of government after independence. Rapid modernization unaccompanied by sufficient institutionalization is a recipe for instability and strife and led to praetorian regimes, where the army is the only source of order. In sum, in the latter part of the decade, many sociologists also lost their optimism regarding the smooth and gradual modernization of the Third World.

Groups in Conflict

Modernization has had very profound effects on societies and continues to do so. In fact, many social scientists, such as Giddens (1991), believe that modernity is our current universe and that the claims that we have entered the postmodern age are premature at best (see Chapter 9). Many of today's conflicts are about the control or avoidance of modernization by diverse groups in society and in government institutions. Consequently, modernization is often a complicated and violent process.

Marxist writers had long insisted that all major change in history was accompanied by a great deal of violence and was usually crowned by a large-scale social revolution. In 1966, British Marxist historian Barrington Moore (1913–2005) wrote *Social Origins of Dictatorship and Democracy*, a vast study of democratization in the West and in some Third World countries. In this book, Moore argues that democracy exists where bourgeois revolution occurred. In other words, "No bourgeois, no democracy." In places without a democratic bourgeois revolution, you find revolution from above. This type leads to different forms of dictatorship until the bourgeoisie is emancipated.

Non-Marxist writers were also interested in the modernization of European societies but rejected the narrow economic determinism of historical materialism. For example, American political scientist Karl Deutsch (1912–92) wrote that communication was a crucial factor in the transition from traditional kingdoms to modern republics and parliamentary systems. The diffusion of common languages, cultural norms, and critical information through ground and sea transport and the mixing of individuals help explain why countries such as Great Britain and France took a lead in the modernization movement (Deutsch, 1966). Norwegian political scientist Stein Rokkan (1921–79) thought that the process of modernization was more complex than what the Marxists proposed. Rokkan, Angus Campbell, Per Torsvik, and Henry Valen (1970) argued that the construction of the modern democratic state involved four major conflicts: class struggle, separation of church and state, the city–country feud, and accommodation of minority regions and groups. They believed that there is no perfect or universal solution to these grave conflicts but that the most successful modernizing countries are those that have found the most efficient and legitimate ways to manage them.

In the contemporary world, several analysts claim that modernization is one of the major factors of social conflict, even though they do not see themselves as modernization theorists. For instance, Donald L. Horowitz's *Ethnic Groups in Conflict* (2000) has been very influential. Although the main source of Horowitz's explanation of ethnic and religious

(AP Photo/Mamdouh Thabet)

The conflict between the forces of tradition and the supporters of modernity takes many forms. In 2007, hundreds of Egyptian women and girls protested female circumcision by carrying photographs of a 10-year-old girl who died from the procedure. The Egyptian government, supported by most religious authorities, agreed to ban the practice.

rivalries is social psychological, his research shows how the rapid transformations caused by colonialism and post-colonialism have affected the world views of groups in conflict, such as when an ethnic group was favoured by the colonizer and rose rapidly in society ahead of other groups.

Another influential author who has been inspired by the modernization framework is American political scientist Benjamin Barber (b. 1939). In *Jihad vs. McWorld* (1996), Barber studies how the globalized liberal economy is unleashing forces of resistance that are often reactionary and violent. He also argues that, with the phenomenon of globalization, people need to belong to some meaningful group closer to home (hence the rise in ethnonationalism). He contends that the movement toward democracy is a highly controversial change that requires the system's adaptation to different cultural and economic contexts. While he contends that democracy will probably prevail, he advocates for a more participatory and dynamic democracy than the one we currently know.

CULTURES, IDENTITY, AND CONFLICT

The question of the role of culture in the prevention, emergence, and abatement of conflict has received a great deal of attention in recent years. Culture is much more than the production of art or the indication of "civilized" behaviour. The concept refers to all the ideas, customs, norms, technologies, symbols, and art created and transmitted by a given society. Each society, even the most rudimentary one, has its own culture. However, this culture is not shared equally by all members of the society. Many societies include cultural and religious minorities that do not share the same values as the dominant group. Furthermore, even the most homogeneous societies include rebels and misfits who have an adversarial or an ambiguous relationship with the dominant norms.

While culture forms the basis of identity, the two are not the same. Identity is a chosen marker of a person's specificity, often selected for social safety and advancement, relationships, intellectual passions, or meaningful activities. Well-defined identity groups form when culture becomes an instrument of social protection and conformity. For example, cultural affiliations were revived in Yugoslavia during the fall of communism in the early 1990s. People who had been encouraged to think of themselves as Yugoslavs under the dictatorship of Tito worked to obtain their national independence as Croats, Slovenes, Serbs, Kosovars, and Macedonians.

Identities can also be multiple and changing. One can be a member of a cultural group without claiming that it is the main component of one's identity. For example, a person can identify as an American, a New Yorker, a dentist, a bicyclist, or a baseball fan along with or before identifying as an Irish Catholic or an Ashkenazi Jew. Amartya Sen (2006) developed the concept of complex identity, meaning that one can be a part of many different groups without being confined by all the characteristics of any single one. According to Sen, overlapping identities may be the secret to moderation and peacefulness in social relations.

Culture- and identity-based explanations of political unrest and violence have enjoyed a general renewal in the last 20 years. This revival is largely due to analysts encountering the limitations of the materialist and political explanations of conflicts. In the wake of globalization, interest in non-Western cultures has also been growing. In this section, we discuss the relationship between culture and conflict in terms of the following questions: Does the contact of cultures always result in conflict? Are there conflict-prone cultures? What are the roles of nationalism and religion in conflicts?

Intercultural Clashes

The conflict studies literature includes three main models for explaining why people of different cultures engage in conflicts: primordialism, instrumentalism, and constructivism.[11] In the primordialist perspective, groups are in conflict because their members harbour negative feelings—often created by ethnocentric disdain for different cultures—toward each other.[12] This approach believes that cultures do not mix but, like oil and water, tend to repel each other. As we saw in Chapter 7, negative stereotypes have led people to believe that their way of life is superior to that of others. When confronted with alien customs, people often try to avoid contact. Sometimes, this behaviour is just a matter of eluding the presence of others, but it can also mean erecting physical barriers between "us and them," threatening reprisals, or mobilizing for war. It is obvious that there is an element of protectiveness to all cultures and societies. After all, ethnic, linguistic, and religious differences create problems even in the most prosperous, stable, and liberal countries of the contemporary world, such as the United States and Canada.

In the primordialist thesis, ethnic identities were set a long time ago and do not vary rapidly. Therefore, their effects can be felt anywhere and anytime when different groups are in contact. In the case of violent conflict, the most important variable to explain the animosity of the parties is their shared traumas.[13] These traumas are usually linked to the memory of painful periods and events in the group's history, such as foreign occupations, wars, massacres, and military defeats. They are transmitted by folk culture, school curricula, formal erudition, and political propaganda to successive generations.

Huntington's "The Clash of Civilizations" (1993) and *The Clash of Civilizations and the Remaking of World Order* (1996) became the manifestos of the primordialist approach to culture and conflict. In these works, Huntington claims that the main cleavage in today's world is not between states and classes but between civilizations, extremely large cultural groups to which people either consciously or unconsciously identify themselves.[14] He distinguishes eight civilizations: Western (Europe, North America, Australia, and New Zealand), South American, Orthodox (Russia and part of Eastern Europe), Japanese, Sinic (China and several parts of East Asia), Hindu, African (south of the Sahara), and Islamic (North Africa, Middle East, Central Asia, and Indonesia). The major conflicts in the world, according to Huntington, are those between "the West and the rest" and those implicating the Sinic and Islamic civilizations.

According to Huntington, the main problem for the West is that, contrary to the Enlightenment myth, its civilization is not truly universal. Despite the spread of Western norms and technology, liberal ideals have not penetrated the substance of other civilizations. Instead, Western civilization and the seven other groups clash over several issues, such as human rights, democracy, the status of women, the place of religion in politics, the use of force, equality rights, and resource distribution. These differences are also variable. They are usually minor with the Latin American and Orthodox worlds; significant with the African, Indian, and Japanese worlds; and very tense with the Sinic and Islamic worlds.

While the general reaction to Huntington's thesis has been mixed, the academic world's has been mostly hostile. One point of criticism is that the definition of civilization is vague and the classification debatable. For example, scholars have questioned the absence of a Jewish civilization, the separation of Latin America from the Western civilization, and the inclusion of black Africa in one civilization. A second charge is that Huntington downplays the political and economic sources of conflict, which are usually more important than the cultural ones. For instance, the conflicts among peoples of the former Yugoslavia might have been more about territory and autonomy than culture, even though they happened over so-called civilizational fault lines. He also overlooks the great differences of views within civilizations (e.g. between the revolutionary fundamentalist movements in Islam versus governments, and the conflict between Shiites and Sunni Muslims). Finally, he minimizes the extent of the universal culture of human rights and democracy, which is growing globally. The Western, Latin American, Hindu, and Japanese cultures are now heavily influenced by liberal ideals. The progress of human rights is slower, but appreciable, in the African, Muslim, and Sinic worlds. Furthermore, the West, as Sen (2006) observes, has incorporated many cultural elements from other parts of the world.

In contrast to the primordialist thesis, instrumentalism claims that cultural identities are simply a tool in the service of people's material and political interests, such as the control of land and resources (Anderson, 2006). Therefore, culture clashes are not so much about culture as they are about groups competing for food, riches, territory, power, and prestige. In order to strengthen itself and to justify its conquests, a society bent on expansion develops a strong cultural identity accompanied by disregard for other cultures. Such was the case with all conquering empires, from the Romans and Chinese of the ancient world to the British, French, Japanese, and German empires of the twentieth century. At the other end of the spectrum, a group that feels victimized by exploitation and injustice will reinforce its identity to ensure loyalty and participation in the resistance against powerful rivals. This practice has been seen in multiple cases, from Irish Catholics to African Americans and to Indigenous populations around the globe.

The instrumentalist approach has certain parallels with Marxism, which claims that identities are "fabricated" in order to serve class interests (Hobsbawn & Ranger, 1983). This idea echoes the Marxist view that culture is merely a reflection of the mode of production and has no unilateral influence on the course of history. Several non-Marxists, while not sharing this kind of narrow materialism, also come to the same conclusion about identities serving political and economic interests. This instrumentalization of culture means that the religious, linguistic, racial, or ethnic characteristics of a particular group are not a factor of conflict per se but become so when people use them to serve their interests. Usually, the fault of this situation is put on manipulating elites, but the phenomenon is not restricted to leaders. People of all social ranks realize that using identity as a political tool can bring them considerable personal rewards.

Several analysts are dissatisfied with both the primordialist and instrumentalist approaches (see Brown, 2001, p. 211). They claim that the former cannot explain how, despite huge social changes, old humiliations can be vividly remembered for centuries and suddenly be reactivated to serve modern aims. The latter may also be wrong in affirming that culture is malleable and fast-evolving to the point that evil leaders can create trauma myths at will to serve their interests. In a hybrid view, cultural identities are indeed manipulated and used by the political leadership, but such an instrumentalization is impossible if there are no shared or vivid memories of past traumas in the first place.

The constructivist approach explains social facts in reference to the perceptions, ideals, and habits of human actors (Searle, 1995). One of the strengths of this theory is that culture is viewed as an evolving structure, not as a set of immutable traditions. In constructivism, the elements that shape social rules and norms and legitimize these changes are what matter. This resolutely idealist approach stresses factors such as science and reason, morals and values, and ideals and projects in transforming reality. For constructivists, ethnic identities and conflicts are created over time in a complex process that is not entirely under the control of the dominant elites.

Nationalism

The role of cultural identities in political conflict can be observed in the phenomenon of nationalism, an ideology that emerged in Europe in the late eighteenth century. While the term has been defined in many ways, we will describe it as the idea that all people sharing a culture and a territory should be in charge of their own destiny. They should unify, build a national government, and consolidate their territorial hold by resisting foreign powers and even by conquering parts of their national territory controlled by another group. This idea has inspired the national unification efforts of European countries, notably France, Germany, Poland, and Italy. The result has been the model of the nation-state, or a government dominated and tailored by an ethnic group.[15] This model has also led to the creation of new countries on all continents, even in regions of Africa where there is no real dominant group that could aspire to create a true nation-state in the European sense.[16]

The nationality principle as it emerged in Europe in the late eighteenth and early nineteenth centuries fuelled the ambitions of hitherto submissive nations to rise against their imperial masters and create their own homelands. Poland, Serbia, Bulgaria, Greece, and

Hungary are only a few nations that periodically rebelled against their controlling empires. With the decline of European empires after World War I, the nationality principle became the dominant model of state-building. In other words, people generally believed that it was better and more natural to base a political system on culture rather than on force or abstract principles.

In practice, nationalism has often been a contributor to peace and has been recognized as such in the World War I treaties and the Covenant of the League of Nations. Beginning in the 1830s, empires such as Austria-Hungary, Russia, and the Ottoman had to use an increasing level of force to govern reckless minority populations. The oppressed groups often turned to foreign governments to protect them, thereby threatening the European order, which was based on the rule of non-interference in internal matters. Several wars of the nineteenth century were caused by separatist rebellions, and World War I was the result of nationalist clashes in the Balkans. Eventually, the national independence of minority populations made ethnic and religious claims a marginal political phenomenon in Europe for most of the twentieth century. For decades, class struggles and ideological battles have been more distracting problems in the West.

Moreover, the nationalist principle has been diluted to a large degree by human rights norms in modern democratic Europe. For example, Italy is not only the country of Italian people, but it is also a republic based on human rights and on a democratic constitution. Thus, the Italian identity is that of a person speaking Italian, following Italian customs, and living in a democratic constitutional republic. Furthermore, the individualistic revolution and the arrival of non-European immigrants have further reduced the salience of nationalism in the political life of Western countries.

Nevertheless, nationalism is often perceived as the cause of all modern wars, including the Napoleonic Wars and the two world wars. This association is legitimate to an extent because the respective nationalism of Napoleonic France and unified Germany clashed with the nationalism of their neighbours. For example, in the nineteenth and early twentieth centuries, both France and Germany claimed to own Alsace, a bilingual and bicultural region in the westernmost part of France. Germany seized it in 1871 and lost it after World War I. The Germans took it again in 1940, but gave it up in 1945. The battle over the region was a very acrimonious nationalist contention.[17]

Nationalism seemed to disappear from Europe after World War II. However, it returned with the end of communism and was blamed for the turmoil in several regions, notably the Balkans and the Caucasus. Ethnic groups under the domination of Yugoslavia or the Soviet Union wanted their independence and refused to federate with other ethnic groups in revamped multinational states. Slovenia, Croatia, Kosovo, Macedonia, and the Croats and Muslims of what is now Bosnia and Herzegovina wanted to leave Yugoslavia. When Serbia tried to keep them in its fold, civil war followed. In the meantime, Romania and Russia disagreed about the borders of the new tiny country of Moldavia, and Ukraine and Russia had several disputes, notably about the custody of the Black Sea Fleet and nuclear weapons. In the Caucasus, Georgia had its own quarrels with Russia, and Armenia and

BOX 8.1 | RECENT STATE CREATION

The process of state creation did not end with African and Asian decolonization. Following the dissolution of the Soviet Union in 1991, 14 new states were established (see Figure A). The dismantling of Yugoslavia resulted in the formation of another seven (Figure B). We have already seen how the nationalism of some of these new nations has led to conflict in the Balkans and the Caucasus. The Central Asian region has seen a number of tensions as well.

FIGURE A | STATES OF THE FORMER SOVIET UNION

Source: Coal Qualitiy of the Former Soviet Union by USGS (U.S. Geological Survery) at http://pubs.usgs.gov/of/2001/ofr-01-104/fsucoal/html/readme.htm#fig1.

FIGURE B | STATES OF THE FORMER YUGOSLAVIA

Note that, while Kosovo declared its independence in 2008, Serbia refuses to recognize it as a separate country.

Source: www.law.ed.ac.uk/citsee/countryprofiles.

BOX 8.2 | CONFLICT-PRONE AND CONFLICT-AVOIDANT CULTURES

The issue of violent conflicts and war often raises the question of why some cultural groups undertake martial actions while others use more peaceful methods. Typically, the cultures of powerful and expansionist nations are seen as intransigent and bellicose and those of weak groups as being associated with accommodation and respect. These descriptions are exemplified in the contrast between aggressive Germany and timid Belgium at the start of both world wars. Similarly, we often juxtapose the violent propensities of Western colonialists with the inherent placidity of indigenous populations. The question of the cultural origins of aggression and violence is an important one because it can shed light on the peaceful and aggressive sides of human nature and on how the two can combine in different cultures. Philosophers have long differed as to the intrinsic goodness or villainy of people. The debate has been continued by anthropologists who are, after all, the specialists in cultures.

In nineteenth-century anthropology, it was generally assumed that there were combative and peaceful "races." This conception supported the period's ideas of the "national character" and racial determinants of behaviour. It was assumed that most "savages" were warlike, while most "civilized" societies were peaceful. In the twentieth century, however, the American school of anthropology—under the powerful influence of Franz Boas and his disciples Ruth Benedict (1887–1948) and Margaret Mead (1901–78)—began to doubt the precept that primitive cultures were mostly aggressive and basically turned the dominant thesis upside down. In his studies of the Baffin Island Inuit and the British Columbian Tsimshian, Kwakiutl, and Kutenai tribes (which he described as peaceful cultures), Boas (1928/1987) found no examples of mass violence. Mead (1961), who studied the Samoans of the Pacific and the Arapesh of New Guinea, reached the same conclusions.

The implications of this thought were clear: human beings are not intrinsically aggressive, and violence is a cultural attribute of some societies at a particular point in time. In fact, the "civilized" are more violent than the primitive. This dogma is still widespread in the anthropological community and informs a great deal of the research on ancient and traditional societies, creating a normative bias favourable to them and a dim view of their encounters with technologically advanced civilizations. Essentially, primitive cultures are used as the primary example of the idea that humanity is naturally good and that war is not inevitable.

However, this dogma has been increasingly criticized since the 1960s. Archaeologists have discovered plenty of new evidence of large-scale massacres and combats to cast doubt on the thesis that mass violence was unknown to primitive people (Keeley, 1996). Another reason for this skepticism is the rise of case studies of extremely violent tribes, conducted in the wake of Napoleon Chagnon (1983)'s famous monographs on the Yanomamö people of Brazil.

Mainstream cultural anthropologists have replied to these attacks by, among other things, preparing case studies on peaceful primitive tribes. Such groups include the Zapotec of Mexico, the Semai of peninsular Malaysia, and the Paliyans of South India (see Fry & Björkqvist, 1997; Kemp & Fry, 2004; and Howell & Willis, 1989). These societies seem to have lived peacefully for an extended period of time and have developed strong communitarian ways of dealing with

continued

BOX 8.2 | *continued*

conflict, as well as a culture of respect, non-violence, and conflict resolution that enables them to eschew the use of force in their relations (Fry, 2007).

However, we must realize that these case studies concern tiny tribes surrounded by other villages and ethnic groups that do not exhibit these peaceful traits. Their current state of peacefulness could be a historical situation caused by the pacification of their region by more powerful tribes, colonizers, or the government. As Steven Pinker (2011, p. 54) states, these societies are historically unrepresentative of what archaic tribes were about. Another problem with this type of evidence is that anthropologists can cite many more examples of bloodthirsty cultures than purely pacifist ones. The fact is that there are variations in the degree of bellicosity of human societies. At one end, are the Zapotec and the modern Semai and at the other the Yanomamö and the Guayaki (Clastres, 2000). The majority of the world's cultures are between these extremes. The difficulty is determining the part that culture, as opposed to nature, resources, power struggles, etc., plays in the explanation of violent behaviour. However, these examples show that culture explains a part of the variance in conflict-prone behaviour across places and time.

Azerbaijan fought to recover the region of Nagorno-Karabakh. For many, nationalism was again showing its ugly head and threatening peace in Europe. For instance, like the Ottomans in the nineteenth century, the Serbs were quick to use force to keep separatists in line, and violence soon spread. Fortunately, the process of national liberation in the Balkans and Eastern Europe was non-violent in many cases. Ukraine, Belarus, the Czech Republic, Slovakia, Moldavia, the Baltic states (Estonia, Lithuania, and Latvia) and the five "stans" of Central Asia (Kazakhstan, Uzbekistan, Kyrgyzstan, Turkmenistan, and Tajikistan) separated peacefully.[18] Furthermore, interventions by the international community have limited the human and material destruction of several of the violent nationalist quarrels.

Religion and Conflict

Religion is one of the main components of culture. It shapes a large part of the norms, customs, and artistic productions of a given society. Throughout history, societies have often clashed over religious beliefs, for instance, in the long episode of the Crusades between Islam and Christianity. Even within religious traditions (such as the ones shown in Figure 8.2), groups of people have fought over the interpretation of sacred scriptures and appropriate rituals and symbols. The schisms in Christianity and Islam testify to such conflicts. In order to keep religion from becoming a topic of discord among citizens, many modern governments have tried to exclude religion from public life (and even to ban it completely, as in the case of communist systems), creating new conflicts with religious groups.

Religion seems an inexhaustible source of conflict and violence and has been criticized as such for centuries. During the Enlightenment, French philosopher Voltaire satirized several aspects of religion, including its role in fostering violence, repression, and war.

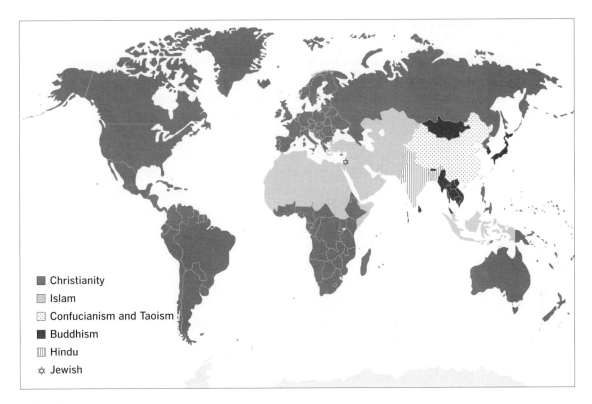

FIGURE 8.2 | PREVAILING RELIGIONS OF THE WORLD

Source: www.education.mapsofworld.com.

This view has served as a basic argument for atheists and free thinkers ever since. During most of the twentieth century and especially during the Cold War, however, religion was a secondary issue in violent conflicts involving the West. As divisive issues, political ideologies seemed to be much more important than faith. The importance of religion was also rapidly decreasing in Western populations, which were becoming more individualistic and rationalistic. Fervent Christians were fewer and fewer and seemed resigned to the marginalization of their faith in society and politics. Religious tensions and feuds in other parts of the world, such as the partition of India and Pakistan, the Israeli–Arab conflict, and the civil wars in Lebanon and Sudan, were often ignored by the Western public. However, the increase in religion-inspired terrorism in the 1990s gradually brought the reality of religious differences to the attention of many Westerners. Such acts have led to a rise in anti-religious sentiment in the West, even in the United States, where religion is a significant part of life (Hitchens, 2007). Despite these instances, religion is also a factor of peace. Some religions are conducive to peaceful behaviour, such as the non-violent strands and sects of Buddhism, Hinduism, Islam, and Christianity. Religion can also restrain political passions and be used in conflict resolution by facilitating **forgiveness** and reconciliation (Appleby, 2000).

Religious Violence

In the study of religion, we find the same sort of division between instrumentalists and primordialists that we saw about culture in general. The instrumentalists believe that religious identity is mostly inflated as a political tool and need not remain a durable divisive marker among people. The primordialists are convinced that religious differences are deeply rooted in history and the human psyche and are not amenable to easy resolution. Religion is an important factor for primordialists such as Huntington. Of the eight civilizations that he identified, five are characterized by a dominant religion: the Hindu and Islam civilizations are named for the religion practised in each, and the Western, Latin American, and Orthodox civilizations are Christian.

Movements of religious fundamentalism and fanaticism exist in all civilizations. For centuries, Christianity has been the inspiration and justification for horrible violence directed toward heretics, dissenters, minority groups, and people of other faiths (such as Jews and Muslims). Wars, massacres, crusades, inquisitions, conquests, and other forms of mass violence have been undertaken on behalf of Christian ideals. Christians have also fought against each other, as seen in the French Wars of Religion and the Thirty Years' War, conflicts between Catholics and Protestants that brought large-scale misery to Europe. Even in recent centuries, Christian extremists have been guilty of violence and intimidation in many parts of the world, including the United States (Southern racists), Spain (the Spanish Civil War and the Franco regime), South America (various authoritarian governments), Northern Ireland (republican Catholic terrorists and Protestant militias), and Uganda (the Lord's Resistance Army). Some Christian clergymen have encouraged their co-religionists to wage war and inflict violence in numerous situations, notably in the Yugoslav Wars and the Rwandan genocide. In all these cases, we must distinguish Church-sponsored war and violence from instances where Christianity was congruent with other historical identity markers and situations where individual leaders identifying themselves as Christian prompted violence through specious arguments grounded in their faith.

Recently, violent actions by Christian, Hindu, Jewish, and Muslim radicals have stimulated research on the potential of organized religions to foster and aggravate conflicts (see Juergensmeyer, 2003; Stern, 2004). Even followers of Buddhism, which is supposed to be a fundamentally peaceful religion, have been guilty of extreme acts of violence. In the bloody civil war in Sri Lanka, for example, the Singhalese majority has supported harsh military and police actions against the Hindu Tamils.

Perhaps the most controversial religion in terms of violent conflict is Islam. One of the starting points of Huntington's (1991) hypotheses on the role of culture and religion in politics was his concern that Islam seems to be refractory to political democracy. In the 1990s, Huntington (1996, p. 257) also observed that Islamic peoples and states were involved in 50 per cent of violent conflicts. Within a number of countries where Islam is the dominant religion, there is persecution of religious minorities, and in several there is outright violent conflict between Sunni and Shiite communities living side by side.[19] In a well-known and very controversial formulation, Huntington (1996, pp. 254–258) posited that the borders of the Islam civilization are bloody, meaning that Islam is at war with other religions both within and beyond the Muslim world.

Following 9/11, the literature about Islam and conflicts has flourished. Some analysts, such as Bernard Lewis (1993, 2010), claim that, while certain historical events, perceptions, and misunderstandings have pitted Islam against the West, it is not too late to alter perceptions and behaviours. Others defend the thesis that Islam is an intrinsically conquering and violent religion, which means that the West must resist Islam, externally and internally, until Islam becomes more tolerant (see Spencer, 2002). This conclusion offends many Muslims around the globe. It also irritates many specialists of religion and violence, who argue that there should be an immutable aggressive essence to a religion. Another perspective is that Islamic violence does not stem from the religion's strength but from its gradual loss of influence in the modern, westernized world (Roy, 1994). In this view, Islamic terrorism is a rearguard battle waged by the remaining nostalgic admirers of the golden age of Islam that alienates ordinary Muslims and is therefore self-defeating (Kepel, 2004). This thesis creates interesting comparisons with other fundamentalist movements resisting modernity, such as the radical Hindu organizations in India.

Muslim scholars often argue that analyses by non-Muslims are often reductionist, boiling the essence of Islam down to stereotypical manifestations. They insist on making a distinction between Islam as a religion and the various cultures in which we find a majority of Muslims. The world of Islam is highly complex and is engaged in debates about change at many different levels. For example, the concept of jihad, which has been used as a rallying cry for militant Muslims engaged in political violence, is like a red flag for many outside the Islamic tradition. However, many contend that, within Islam, the primary sense of jihad is an inner struggle over what is morally right and how to live accordingly. Reformist Muslim thinkers such as Reza Eslami-Somea (2010) argue for a more sophisticated interpretation of Islam in keeping with modern reality. This approach involves a distinction between the earlier Mecca-based teachings of the Koran, which in the early centuries of Islam were overshadowed for historical cultural reasons, and the Medina-based teachings. The Mecca-based teachings emphasized "the basic values of justice as well as the equality and inherent dignity of all human beings, regardless of gender, race, religion, or any innate characteristics" (Eslami-Somea, 2010, p. 136). Reinterpreting Islamic law through the lens of these earlier teachings would more closely align it with human rights, universal justice, and many of the underlying values of democratic society.

The most widespread perspective in the media and among Muslims themselves is that radical political Islam has grown out of the frustration and resentment of the Arab Muslim masses but does not represent the essence of the religion (Esposito, 2003). The ire of the Muslims has been fanned by colonialism, economic underdevelopment, and exploitation; the imposition of the state of Israel on the Middle East (and the many wars that have followed); the tyrannical governments of Arab countries (often supported by Western states); and the persecution of Muslims in some countries. Waleed El-Ansary (2010) argues that many Muslims are open to Western contributions—such as democracy—while being troubled by the policies and actions of Western nations, which "can employ the clash of civilizations thesis as a camouflage to dominate other civilizations on the pretext that those civilizations are its enemies" (p. 113).

In fact, these many analysts contend two things. First, the Islamic backlash was stimulated by the sometimes excessive efforts of modernization and westernization engineered by Middle East despots who were influenced and sponsored by great powers. The example usually mentioned in this regard is that of Iran under the Shah, where the religious elites were marginalized from power and took their revenge by overthrowing the government in 1979. Second, in the tyrannical societies of the Middle East, the mosque is the only institution that cannot be attacked by the state. Opponents therefore tend to congregate around imams and ayatollahs to organize politically and prepare a change of regime. The Muslim clergy and preachers, relatively immune from persecution, take the lead in opposition movements.

As a result of these problems, a culture of violence is present in some segments of the Islamic world, where many people are socialized in violence in their homes and schools; several governments perpetrate and celebrate violence; and some opposition movements promote violence as the means of change. A vicious cycle of people using more violence to escape violence has also occasionally been created. However, there are many movements trying to break this pattern. For example, a Muslim-based peace education program was founded in Indonesia in 2000. Two years later, it was offering an Islamic peace education course in a hundred schools, involving 37,000 young adults (Husin, 2010, p. 154). In 2011, peaceful protest movements have emerged in several Muslim countries, notably Tunisia, Egypt, Yemen, Libya, and Syria, raising possible alternatives to violent Islamic opposition. While the results of the process are unclear, what changed was the large and persistent response of thousands of people engaged in protest and their effectiveness in bringing down some despotic regimes. The incidence of state repression and violent uprisings should not detract from the large peaceful mobilization that took place in these countries.

Religion and the Modern Secular State

Another issue related to religion is the conflict between religious groups and the secular state in democratic societies. As alluded to earlier, most democratic states separated church and state in the nineteenth and twentieth centuries. Consequently, there is no official religion in the country; religions do not have public monopolies (e.g. being in charge of schools and hospitals); and the historical privileges of certain religions (e.g. tax immunities) are being revoked. The secularization of public life is based on liberal and egalitarian principles implemented to avoid discriminating against individuals on the basis of their religious affiliation. The state is rigorously neutral in religious matters. Secularization was also pursued as a way to avoid conflicts between religions and between religious and non-religious people. This strategy has worked relatively well in the West for most of the twentieth century. The main exceptions are regimes that enforced one religion (such as Franco's Spain and Salazar's Portugal) and totalitarian countries that persecuted religions (such as Nazi Germany and the Soviet Union).

Recently, the consensus regarding the secularization of public space has been contested. Religious minority groups have demanded the authorization to wear symbols of their religion on their uniforms. For example, a Sikh constable who wanted to wear a turban with his Royal Canadian Mounted Police uniform won his case at the Supreme Court level. Groups have also requested special rooms and time accommodations to perform their rituals (e.g. prayer rooms and Ramadan exemptions for Muslims working in public institutions). The reaction to such petitions has been mixed. Generally, accommodation has been more rapidly forthcoming in nations favouring multiculturalism as a public policy, where a strong tradition of civil liberties exists and legal challenges are widespread. The Scandinavian countries, Great Britain, the United States, Canada, Australia, New Zealand, and India are in this category. In countries where integration to the dominant culture is the norm and where civil liberties advocacy is less prevalent (e.g. France, Italy, Greece, and most of Eastern Europe), there has been more resistance. However, we should not be too categorical here. There have been many accommodations made in the pro-integration countries, and there is a great deal of resistance to religious demands in multiculturalist countries. For example, Muslim prayer rooms are quite common in French society, even though the state is adamantly secular. On the other hand, Canadian francophones, themselves a minority, are more integrationist than the multiculturalist anglophones and seem more reluctant to accept any compromise with religious minority groups at face value.

The integration of religious minorities is not always easy. Religious demands potentially challenge several precepts of the modern democratic state, such as secularization, equality before the law, and the emancipation of women. Conversely, charters of rights, constitutions, and legal precedents protect the rights of individuals and religious minorities to practise their religion unhindered. Therefore, courts and administrative authorities usually adjudicate in favour of complainants. Most of these judgments are accepted by the public, but settlements that seem to contradict basic social and historical principles are sometimes considered unfair by the majority. Politicians are afraid to intervene in favour of majorities for fear of being negatively labelled by religious minorities, human rights organizations, and the news media. Occasionally, a sentiment of alienation and frustration grows in majority populations, which takes the form of political support for conservative parties and populist movements. As a result, the relations between the religious majorities and minorities become even more difficult. The management and resolution of these religious differences have become two of the main problems of modern democracy.

Religion and Conflict Resolution

In spite of its role in fostering some conflicts, religion can have a positive influence on the management, resolution, and abatement of conflicts, including violent ones.[20] Some religious denominations—including Quakers, Mennonites, and the Church of the Brethren—have elected to renounce the use of violence and to propagate non-violence in the world. Since the eighteenth century, these groups have been at the forefront of many public opinion campaigns against war, slavery, and torture, particularly in Great Britain and the United States. Many peace and conflict studies specialists referenced in this book are from the Christian pacifist tradition. For instance, Mary Parker Follett and Lewis Richardson were Quakers. One can also find pacifist strands in mainstream Christian denominations, such as the contributions of Lanza del Vasto, Jean Vanier, and Dom Helder Camara in the Catholic faith. **Pacifism** is also well represented in other religious traditions, for example, the Baha'i faith, Tibetan Buddhism, and Jainism.[21]

Some of the greatest advocates of non-violence and the peaceful settlement of differences in the twentieth century have been religious leaders, such as Mahatma Gandhi, Martin Luther King, Jr, Desmond Tutu, Pope John XXIII, and the Dalai Lama. Religion-inspired individuals like US presidents Woodrow Wilson (founder of the League of Nations) and Jimmy Carter (seasoned international negotiator), South African President Nelson Mandela (a sought-after international mediator), French diplomat Jean Monnet (founder of European integration), Costa Rican President Oscar Arias (instigator of the Central American peace process), and Polish union leader Lech Walesa (architect of the peaceful break with communism) have also promoted peaceful conflict resolution. Without these individuals, the resolution of world wars, civil wars, and the Cold War would have been far more difficult and violent.

With the rise of peacebuilding in the 1980s, religion has taken on a new importance.[22] In countries where democratic development is weak, civil society is non-existent, and many members of the elite have been eliminated or compromised by warring parties, religious leaders are often key interlocutors for local governments, foreign actors, and international organizations. Their role in fostering reconciliation is crucial. John Paul Lederach (1995, 1997), one of the pioneers of conflict studies, has often insisted on this point. Religious leader engagement in the context of a theatre of armed conflict is an emerging concept, and religion-based peacemaking is becoming a significant field of studies in its own right (Hertog, 2010).

R. Scott Appleby (2001) offers us three case studies of religious individuals who made a major contribution to the peaceful transformation of their respective countries. One is Bishop Tutu, one of the main promoters of the Truth and Reconciliation Commission (TRC) of South Africa, which was a key element in the country's painful but peaceful transition from apartheid to multiracial democracy. Another is Buddhist Primate of Cambodia Maha Ghosananda, who led a month-long march to convince people to vote in the country's 1993 elections. Finally, there are the members of the Sant'Egidio community (a Catholic lay order), who facilitated the dialogue that ended the civil war in Mozambique in 1992. These examples show the significant contributions of religion to peace, and we will revisit them in Chapter 16. For now, let us reiterate the point that religion is a factor of human differences and conflicts but can also be an inevitable part of their resolution.

GENDER AND CONFLICT

The study of the relationship between gender and conflict has expanded since the 1970s. This growth is largely due to the emergence of the feminist perspective, which has made important inroads in the social and human sciences. Gender is also now an inescapable dimension of the study of human societies. In this section, we discuss how conflict can emerge from gender and affect gender relations. We also consider the question of whether gender influences conflict behaviour.

We should acknowledge here that not all studies of the relationship between gender and conflict are related to the social sciences. One can study gender differences using biological, psychological, or philosophical models. This diversity is why there are references to gender and feminist issues in other chapters of this book. However, the bulk of the material on gender is found in this section because of the underlying principle guiding most research, that gender is a social construct. According to this perspective, gender is not to be confused with sex. Although these terms are often used interchangeably (and in some contexts do not create any confusion), they mean different things in the study of human beings and societies. Sex refers to an observable biological difference among individuals regarding their respective roles in procreation. Gender is an identity based on sexual characteristics and imposes a certain number of social norms upon the sexes. Men are supposed to behave in a certain way, women in another. Contrary to sex, which is an anatomical reality, gender is cultural and therefore changeable. The definition of gender has evolved among cultures and has changed even more rapidly since the twentieth century, when Western women began making unprecedented gains.

Conflict between the Genders

A common way to look at the question of gender and conflict is to refer to the "eternal conflict" between men and women. This approach is the stuff of countless plays, novels, and comedy routines. It refers to an unchanging and universal "battle of the sexes," in which men and women fight for dominance in a relationship. In this view, the origins of conflicts between men and women are a sort of metaphysical fatality of the human race. This perspective leads only to vague and spurious hypotheses such as "Men and women will always fight" or platitudes such as "Can't live with them, can't live without them." The battle of the sexes scenario cannot help us to explain or predict the type of relations in different couples and families. It does nothing to understand the various roles, limitations, and possibilities for women in different eras or cultures. It is seen by many, especially feminists, as downplaying the real power discrepancies between men and women and the subordinate role that most women have experienced in marital relationships. Furthermore, this view of men and women has a pessimistic overtone, suggesting that nothing can positively transform the relationships between the sexes.

However, according to feminists such as Susan Faludi (1991), there is a war between men and women because men collectively and consciously resist women's efforts to assert their rights. The unequal relationship between men and women that character-izes most historical human societies is partly maintained by repressing women, which creates conflicts. Although the "war" rhetoric is not shared by all feminists, the idea that the emancipation of women creates conflicts with men is widespread and supported by evidence. Issues such as equal pay for equal work, access to managerial positions, and the sharing of domestic tasks keep flaring up in the political system, private organizations, and households. The progress in liberation is often deemed too slow by a part of the female population, whose expectations of fair treatment have risen faster than social reforms. However, many signs point to a rapid improvement in the condition of women, so much so that a men's movement has even emerged. Various elements of this movement have tried to explore male identity, push for equality (in a pro-feminist manner), protest male violence against women, and, in another mode, contest the favourable treatment that women often receive in divorce cases, criminal justice, affirmative action policies, and popular culture (Farrell, 1993; D. Thomas, 1993).

Although the liberation of women has been relatively peaceful in Europe and North America, this is not the case in most parts of the world where the resistance to women's rights is stronger. In many non-Western societies, schools, health care networks, workplaces, and political institutions usually favour men. The key to women's liberation in these countries is most likely to be found in the improvement of public education, as educated women tend to find more work, be more knowledgeable about their rights, bear fewer children, and take better care of their health (Sen, 2000). In the most conservative societies, however, practices such as the exclusion of girls from education, sexual mutilations, the wearing of restrictive clothing, and domestic violence are vehemently supported. Gender biases are woven into many cultures; to challenge them is to challenge a way of life. Few women dare oppose such constraints, and the few who do (along with the men who support them) risk their liberty, welfare, and even their lives.

Genders, Conflict, and Violence

Aggression is often considered a male characteristic and is attributed to the male in all species. Biologists believe that it is a hereditary trait owing to the needs of food acquisition, protection of females and offspring, and dominance over rivals.[23] The human male tends to be taller and heavier and to display more aggressive behaviour than the female. His body secretes higher levels of the hormone testosterone, which is associated with anger and aggression. The problem for women is that, in most societies and most eras, these characteristics have translated into their submission to men. To feminists, this submission—visible in strict gender roles, violence towards women, and ideologies that value the male gender—is a noxious cultural artefact that must be destroyed.

Whatever the natural propensities of males and females for violence, it remains that the evolution of technology, including armaments, has gradually reduced the importance of size and strength in the survival of individuals. The strong male can no longer use his size to acquire more food and possessions than others. This change obviously favours women in the long run. However, size and strength still play a role in criminality, including domestic intimidation and violence. The predominance of men in this domain is well documented in crime statistics and historical surveys of political violence. Men are responsible for the overwhelming majority of violent crimes, such as murder, assault, rape, and destruction of property. The overwhelming majority of inmates in the United States and Canada are male. Most wars have been initiated and waged by men, and men have been responsible for most of the massacres and mass terror perpetrated by organized groups.

According to radical feminists, men are collectively responsible for all the violence in all the history of the world. Andrea Dworkin (1981) has written: "Men are distinguished from women by their commitment to do violence rather than to be victimised by it" (p. 51). This sweeping generalization makes little case for the fact that most victims of mass violence in history have been male, but it is characteristic of a widespread belief in the innate brutality of men. In this perspective, females are the only victims of violence and are never involved in its initiation or perpetuation. Men, in turn, are perceived

(AP Photo/Vincent Yu)

North Korean women sailors practise marching in Pyongyang, 2010. The presence of women in armed forces around the world is now a common sight. Is it something that is imposed upon them, or do some women naturally share the martial mentality found in many men?

as potentially violent, even when they are peaceful and victimized. However, another perspective has recently been advanced by Robin Morgan (2000), who argues that women play a role in making heroes (or even sexually attractive partners) of violent men. There are even studies about the active and direct participation of women in violence and war (see McKelvey, 2007; Sjoberg & Gentry, 2008).

Furthermore, the theories and evidence discussed in this section do not mean that every man is likely to initiate violence at any time. It means only that, statistically speaking, a larger proportion of men than women may engage in violent behaviour in most circumstances. It should be remembered that aggressiveness is not equally shared by all individual males and that there are aggressive women too. Men and women are not of a different essence; they are human beings who display a variety of character traits. When talking about men versus women, we should always mean "most men" or "a large proportion of men," not "all men." As political scientist Joshua Goldstein (2003) argues in *War and Gender*, we are talking about statistical distributions, not essential differences, between genders. Using indicators such as testosterone levels, size, strength, and brain functions, Goldstein found that more men than women are inclined toward violence. However, he could not conclude that there is a radically different proclivity for violence between the genders (Goldstein, 2003, p. 182). In effect, most men have only a moderate inclination for violence. There is even a minority of men with no violent dispositions whatsoever and a minority of women who are quite violent.

Gendered Victims of Conflict

One of the main themes of the modern literature on conflicts and gender concerns the victimization of women in conflicts, particularly violent conflicts. Analysts in this field present two main arguments. The first is that, although attacks on women are integral to warfare, not enough attention has been devoted to the fate of women in wars (Lorentzen & Turpin, 1998). Second, the victimization of women in times of armed conflict is far from over and may even have risen in recent years (Barstow, 2000; Giles & Hyndman, 2004).

There is no doubt that women have been victims of warfare in all eras. Too often, historical records have dwelled on the sacrifice of men but almost ignored the plight of women. Immense battles and prolonged campaigns may have killed thousands of men, but their wives and daughters have also suffered. Losing the breadwinner of the family meant that women were often left to a miserable existence. Furthermore, women were robbed, raped, tortured, and killed by invading armies. They were also coerced into slavery and forced marriage by the same men who had killed their husbands, brothers, and fathers. Therefore, the historiography of violence and war must take into account the fate of women in its narratives.[24]

For feminists, the victimization of women during wars is an extreme case of the constant repression and violence exerted against women in all eras. However, these attacks have varied over time. For most of history, conquerors were ruthless toward women, as they were against all defenceless people. The Mongolian hordes, for instance, often killed every non-combatant in their paths: women, children, the elderly, and sick and wounded men. In other eras, these groups were often spared. While the ancient Greek, Roman, and Arab armies were brutal in some cases, they did show mercy in particular cases, especially to the people whom they were closer to and those who rapidly submitted to their rule. In the modern West, non-combatants were relatively spared by war for a while. The dynastic conflicts of the eighteenth century, the Napoleonic Wars, and World War I were mostly waged by young men and their professional officers. Women and civilians were undoubtedly affected by these wars, but the direct violence that they experienced was less than in preceding conflicts, such as the Thirty Years' War and other religious conflicts of the sixteenth and seventeenth centuries.

World War II broke that trend, killing far more civilians (a great part of which were women) than men in uniform through mass executions, widespread deportations, prolonged sieges, and intense aerial bombing and artillery fire. The wars that followed— be they ideological civil conflicts, wars of colonial liberation, or ethnic and religious insurrections—displayed the same pattern of massive attacks on women and non-combatants. After the Cold War, the examples of the former Yugoslavia, the Democratic Republic of the Congo, and Sudan show that women are still targeted in contemporary warfare. The mass rapes in Bosnia seemed to indicate that men would stop at nothing in order to dominate and punish women, supporting the feminist perspective that the fate of women has not changed a lot and that much remains to be done.[25]

The issue of rape in armed conflicts has taken on much importance since the 1990s. Because Western countries are more attuned to issues of human rights and because women are more widely represented in the media, the government, and humanitarian organizations, recent cases of mass rapes have received much attention (Stiglmayer, 1994).[26] Rape is understood by feminists as a weapon targeted at women. In some cases, it forces women to endure unwanted pregnancies. It humiliates and terrorizes women in order to demonstrate to them that they are second-class citizens, always at the mercy of men.

Gender and the Initiation and Resolution of Conflict

Another issue regarding gender is whether women and men behave differently in the initiation and resolution of conflict. The dominant view on this subject, based as much on traditional views as on pop culture, is that women are natural conflict resolvers. Instead of delighting in conflict and competition like men, women are supposedly more inclined to seek negotiated solutions to differences among people. Women are more empathetic, less power hungry, and less violent than men. They communicate better and, because they share the status of victims, they are more understanding of the costs and consequences of injustice.

For many people, the reasons for these characteristics are biological. Perhaps women are more conciliatory and sensitive because they give birth and nurture babies. Some sociobiologists and some essentialist feminists may agree with this argument. For others, the fact that women are often facilitators may be related to their general powerlessness.

Historically, their only recourse to conflict was mollification. One could say that this necessity to induce conflict resolution has been integrated into women's psyches. Therefore, even modern Western women equipped with a good education and a position of power should be more apt at conflict resolution than men at the same level. These theories are difficult to prove, and ideology is often a substitute for verification. People often use anecdotal evidence, such as mentioning the role of their mothers in resolving family conflicts. Similarly, historical evidence is not very useful here because most women were not in a position to influence political events until the second half of the twentieth century.

Several studies have been conducted by social psychologists, social scientists, and economists to understand decisional and co-operative behaviour, some of which have focused on gender differences. For instance, game theorists have tried to verify whether women and men play the Prisoners' Dilemma (PD) and other games differently. The conclusions are mixed. While some researchers, such as Robert H. Frank, Thomas Gilovich, and Dennis T. Regan (1993), found that women are more co-operative than men, others such as Anatol Rapoport and Albert M. Chammah (1965) concluded exactly the opposite. Some experimenters influenced by feminist literature have tended to observe slight gender effects in games. One observation was that women play slightly more co-operatively in the first round but display more uncooperative behaviour in subsequent rounds (Ortmann & Tichy, 1999). Another is that women in weak positions play less rationally than men in similar situations (Schwartz-Shea, 2002). These studies can be used to generalize behaviour traits among women, but we should not forget that co-operation generally increases in PD games for both sexes and can increase more rapidly when stakes are higher, when people play face to face, and when the experimenters give more instructions to the subjects. Furthermore, most PD experiments did not show a significant difference between the genders, suggesting that the vast majority of male and female subjects behave in exactly the same way.

Other ways to test differences between the genders in conflict and co-operation are through negotiation role-playing and the scientific observation of actual negotiation, particularly in management styles. In their review of the managerial, psychological, and social science literature, Jennifer L. Holt and Cynthia James DeVore (2005) noticed that, in most empirical studies, females frequently self-report that they use a "compromising" style more than men, who often admit a tendency to use a "forcing" style.[27] In the same vein, other scholars observe that men are more likely to use a competing style than women (see Thomas, Thomas, & Schaubhut, 2008). Some observe small but significant differences in the negotiation style of women and men, the latter acting less competitively (e.g. Calhoun & Smith, 1999). Others such as Linda Babcock and Sara Laschever (2003) allude to research suggesting that women tend to avoid negotiation and, when they do negotiate, have poorer outcomes than men.

However, a large number of sources assess that there are no significant differences between men and women in negotiation and managing styles. Loraleigh Keashley (1994) conducted an exhaustive review of the literature related to **conflict management** in couples, families, and work environments published between the 1970s and the early

1990s. She concluded that "the research provides little evidence of gender differences in abilities and skills related to conflict management" (Keashley, 1994). Likewise, many other studies conclude that, if one controls for variables such as personality type, hierarchical power, socioeconomic status, and reputation, there is no difference between men and women in leadership and conflict management. While women tend to define themselves in stereotypical ways (e.g. more in touch with emotions), they do not display a different leadership style when compared to men (Ross-Smith, Kornberger, Chesterman, & Anandakumar, 2007; Cliff, Langdon, & Aldrich, 2005).

In other words, the behavioural differences, whether actual or perceived, might be primarily caused by social inequality and personality factors. Men at the bottom of the pile and men who are less assertive may not score much differently than low-ranked and traditional women. Powerful and driven women, in turn, compare to authoritarian and ambitious men. In fact, some studies talk of "masculine individuals," "feminine individuals," and "androgynous individuals" without regard to the actual sex of the subject (see Brewer, Mitchell, & Weber, 2002). Such differences are also slight when other factors are considered. The historical evolution toward women's empowerment may mean that they will continue to diminish. The reality for some women is that their increased status and opportunities create conflicts or put them in situations of political or economic conflict in which they were not involved in the past. Women may choose to take part in these conflicts, avoid confrontation, or act as a third party, just as men do.

CONCLUSION

In this chapter, we discussed social science approaches to understanding large-scale conflicts. We traced the emergence of political realism in its Machiavellian and Hobbesian manifestations as well as the role of pluralism and interest groups within society. Marxism and its subsequent theories illustrated the role of class, class distinction, economics, and the emergence of **hegemonic structures**. We also considered other social factors in terms of conflict and conflict resolution, namely modernization, nationalism, and culture. We focused on how religion can act as a basis for the emergence of civilizations, the cause of divisions between groups that use religion as an identity marker, and as both motivator of conflict and peace. Finally, we looked at gender's part in social conflict, noting that gender as a social construct changes through time and within different cultures. Overall, this chapter demonstrates that single-factor explanations for conflict have been supplanted by approaches that are sensitive to the complex interplay of many elements.

DISCUSSION QUESTIONS

1. Consider how the various factors discussed in this chapter apply to a current social conflict.

2. Is the quest for domination and power a cause of conflict in itself or a consequence of other psychological or sociological factors? Give reasons to support your answer.

3. Are class conflicts a major factor in today's society? If so, how and where are they important? Are they likely to persist?

4. Compare the role of religion in conflict in North America and Europe, with the situation in Africa and Asia.

NOTES

1. For example, Thucydides' analysis of the Peloponnesian War is devoid of references to Greek deities, spells, and fate as causes of conflicts (unlike those written by Homer and Herodotus). Instead, Thucydides proposes a more empirical and pragmatic account that focuses on power, interests, force, and alliances—notions that are still used today.

2. As mentioned in Chapter 5, Machiavelli was one of the first to apply a rationalist approach to the study of conflict. However, his ideas also apply to the social view of conflict because he emphasized the role of power, a social determinant of behaviour.

3. For a broad view of the debates about realism, see Dougherty and Pfaltzgraff (2000), Jørgensen (2010), and Viotti and Kauppi (2009).

4. Note that Hobbes and his followers have traditionally ignored the fact that violence against women, children, the weak, and the elderly has only recently been outlawed by the state.

5. Other contract theorists include John Locke, Montesquieu, and Jean-Jacques Rousseau. The Fathers of the American Republic shared their ideas; the US Constitution is the classic legal document inspired by this logic.

6. One of the most popular compendia of original Marxist writings still in print is by Robert C. Tucker (1978).

7. Marx and Engels named their theory scientific socialism to distinguish it from the previous and less structured utopian socialism of Charles Fourier (1772–1837), Pierre-Joseph Proudhon (1809–65), and Robert Owen (1771–1858).

8. Marx and Engels's view of nature, which is called dialectical materialism, basically states that nature exists objectively, has its own rules that science can explain, and evolves in a dialectical fashion. Thus, belief in God is not required to explain anything.

9. The non-Marxist study of social class has been pioneered by German sociologist Ralf Dahrendorf (1959).

10. A comprehensive source on the classic Marxist debates is Giddens and Held (1982).

11. On the initial debate between primordialist and instrumentalist approaches, see Esman (1994) and Brown (1996).

12. See the essays in Stack (1986) and Isaacs (1975).

13. This is similar to the concept of chosen traumas developed by Vamik Volkan and described in Chapter 7.

14. Huntington is not the first to analyze international relations in this perspective. He reminds us that one of the leaders of the peace movement, Johan Galtung (1992), offers a similar analysis.

15. Walker Connor (1994) argues that there have been only a handful of countries that have

come close to the myth of the nation-state. Instead, each state features significant minorities—some traditional, some regional, and some a result of population movements.

16. Nationalism, however, is not the only principle of political unification. Some states were dynasties, meaning that they belonged to a royal family to whom nobles and commoners were personally joined by oaths of fidelity (e.g. Old France and England). Others were empires, created when a dynamic people conquered other societies that, for reasons of survival or expediency, accepted this foreign rule (e.g. Rome and Persia). In religious states (e.g. Byzantium and the Abbasid Caliphate), the government was created for the believers of a certain faith and followed the precepts of that religion. Republics such as the United States and Brazil are based on universalistic principles of liberty, while countries such as Canada and Belgium are built by several nations assembled in a federalist or decentralized political system.

17. One should not forget that the Napoleonic Wars and the two world wars owe more to the imperialistic ambitions and the ideological fantasies of Napoleon Bonaparte, Kaiser Wilhelm, and Adolf Hitler, respectively, than to nationalism. Nationalism is responsible for these wars primarily in the sense that it unified and reinforced the French and German states. However, the impetus for those powers to risk their own national survival by waging large-scale wars against mighty coalitions for debatable, if not foolish ideals, cannot be attributed to nationalism alone.

18. Most of the former countries of the Soviet Union have had several issues with one another, with Russia, and with their own national minorities. Here, we are referring to the relatively peaceful period between 1989 and 1995.

19. There has, however, been a certain toleration of Jewish and Christian minorities within the Islamic world for centuries. In fact, Jews often fared better in Muslim countries than in Christian lands, where they experienced massacres and discrimination.

20. R. Scott Appleby (2000) has been an intellectual leader in this field. He develops both sides of the religion argument but insists on the positive aspects of religion. He also includes the category of "militant peacemaker" for those who are motivated by their faith to work tirelessly for peace, sometimes at great personal sacrifice.

21. Baha'í includes elements of Islam, Christianity, and Buddhism, and is present in Central Asia and India. Jainism is an old religion of India practised by approximately 5 million people.

22. The awareness of the importance of religion in conflict and conflict resolution is exemplified in Appleby and Cizik (2010).

23. Several biologists have since partly revised certain assumptions about aggressiveness. For instance, in his study of primates, Frans de Waal (1989) concluded that the capacity for reconciliation is as hardwired in males as the aggressive instinct. His focus on the gentle, playful, and extremely sexually active Bonobo chimps launched a wave of interest in this species, which could prove that aggression and violence are not the default behavioural mode of higher animals, including human beings.

24. Two examples of this kind of historical research are Grayzel (2002) and Yalom (1995).

25. However, as we saw in Chapter 2, there are now fewer wars with fewer victims, and victims are better protected. Surely women and not only men have benefited from this evolution.

26. It should be noted that numerous forms of violence inflicted on men in wars, such as torture, detainment, beatings, forced labour, rape, and mutilations, do not receive much coverage in the media or the academic literature.

27. These categories are from the five presented by Blake and Mouton (1964).

9 | RECENT PHILOSOPHICAL APPROACHES TO CONFLICT

CHAPTER OBJECTIVES

This chapter will help you develop an understanding of the

- meaning of philosophy and its role in conflict studies;

- complementary roles of empirical sciences and philosophical approaches to conflict; and

- genesis, contributions, and limitations of critical theory, postmodernism, Self–Other relations, and mimetic theory.

INTRODUCTION

This chapter examines philosophy's contribution to the analysis of conflict. We present four current Western philosophical trends that directly speak to issues related to conflict studies. The first two theories, critical theory and postmodernism, have both expanded beyond the fields of philosophy and linguistics and are now widely used in the humanities and social sciences. The third examines the relationship between the Self and Other in an abstract way. Finally, René Girard's mimetic theory has been taught and discussed extensively in the field of conflict studies. With each theory, we examine its origins and its main proponents and concepts. We also consider the contribution to conflict studies and the predominant critiques of each model.

THE PHILOSOPHICAL TRADITION

Philosophy comes from the Greek words *philos* ("love") and *sophia* ("wisdom"); hence, philosophers are lovers of wisdom. The Western philosophical tradition dates back to ancient Greece, where Plato and Aristotle were the most famous philosophers. During the Christian era of the West, theology was greatly influenced by philosophy, and these two disciplines constituted the heart of systematic approaches to knowledge. It was British philosopher Francis Bacon (1561–1626) who first identified a methodology based on observation, the development of hypotheses, and their systematic testing, leading to what became known as the scientific method. With the Enlightenment came a separation of empirical methodologies, including most of the different sciences, and knowledge based on deduction, reflection, conceptual development, logic, interpretation, and reflection on meaning as derived from experience. As Isaac Newton (1643–1727) created mathematical formulas to explain forces between stars and planets, he established a model for scientific inquiry that became an ideal for scientists. Enlightenment philosophers such as Adam Smith, John Locke, David Hume, and Immanuel Kant advanced concepts of market economics, individual rights, and the importance of reason and morality. Georg Hegel set out a grand scheme to explain intellectual development through the constant circle of thesis, antithesis, and new synthesis (an idea later adapted by Marx). With the emergence of specialized disciplines, philosophy lost its central and dominant place in intellectual life; in effect, empirical-based knowledge became more important than insights gained through reflection, self-awareness, and critical thought regarding interpretive systems (Wilber, 2000).

In the twentieth century, there developed in the Anglo-American tradition the analytic and linguistic approach to philosophy. Bertrand Russell (1872–1970), known for both his atheism and pacifism, was also a mathematician. He influenced philosophers such as Ludwig Wittgenstein (1889–1951), who reflected deeply on how language is used to shape reality, and A.J. Ayer (1910–89), who became the foremost exponent of logical positivism and argued that the only knowledge that had any legitimacy was that which could be proved scientifically. During the same time in Europe, existentialism dominated, with French philosophers and writers Jean-Paul Sartre (1905–80) and Albert Camus (1913–60) writing dark novels and plays about the deep contradictions of life and the impossibility of finding transcendent meaning. Martin Heidegger (1889–1976) reflected on what it meant for anything to really exist. Hannah Arendt (1906–75), influenced by Heidegger, examined the phenomenon of totalitarianism, drawing out the key features of the Nazi and communist systems that tried to completely control their subjects. Each of these philosophers developed ideas that raise questions about the nature, meaning, dynamics, and logic of conflict.

Philosophy is important in conflict studies for several reasons. As a discipline, it promotes a rigorous examination of concepts—what they mean, where they come from, what alternatives exist. The branch of philosophy concerned with **ontology**, the study of what it means to be or exist, allows us to explore the nature of what it means to be human in relation to the biosphere and the infinity of the universe. **Epistemology**, the study of what it means to know something, helps us compare the relative truth claims of the different sciences and critically examine the methodologies used to establish these assertions. A significant amount of conflict is the result of a clash of interpretations— parties see different meanings and significance in their experiences. **Hermeneutics** is the branch of philosophy concerned with how we make meaning out of texts, artistic expressions, and experiences. Another source of conflict is differences between ideologies, world views, and cultural backgrounds. Philosophy introduces reflective and reflexive processes whereby we become aware of the presuppositions, values, and biases that shape our own approaches to life while simultaneously recognizing the same factors that shape the perspective of our Other, the one who is different and with whom we may be in conflict. Finally, the field of ethics probes the nature of values, principles, and judgments about what is good or bad—something we explore in more detail in Part IV.

The empirical sciences presented in chapters 5 to 8 have provided significant insights into the nature of conflict. Methodologies that develop clear hypotheses and gather data to verify or disprove these theories do us a tremendous service in helping to separate what is accurate and significant from what is conjectural and specious. Philosophical approaches are also concerned with providing sound knowledge; however, the methodology is different. There is a value on sound reasoning, critical reflection, self-awareness, deductive theorization, deconstruction, and participant analysis, as well as a sensitivity to what lies behind the systems of thought that generate knowledge. Furthermore, knowledge claims are scrutinized in the light of a long history of human thought, sometimes illuminating long-standing underlying values that skew our approach to generating knowledge.[1]

Another fundamental point about philosophical approaches is their rejection of the positivist separation between facts and values. Social scientists tend to believe that their inquiry should be as neutral as possible in order to avoid biases and errors resulting from tainted judgment. In other words, analysts of conflict should not express their personal political and social ideas in their writings or teaching. However, the proponents of the philosophical approaches that we discuss in this chapter believe that facts and values cannot be separated. The term often used to describe their position is **reflexivity**, the disposition to consider everything with a skeptical eye and to criticize all social institutions, including the state, family, gender, religion, and culture. Reflexive approaches contend that theory itself is as problematic as reality. Therefore, it is necessary to constantly question theoretical postulates and methods and to evaluate theory and research for their contribution to productive questioning.

In conflict studies, this perspective means deconstructing the cultural mechanisms of domination, oppression, and violence to reveal that the propensity to participate in conflict and be aggressive is largely a learned behaviour rather than a natural tendency. Many discourses and practices of resistance to the dominant order are legitimized by these philosophical schools of thought. In general, supporters of the approaches under review here emphasize a critical and even subversive reading of social norms and institutions. Furthermore, these approaches do not separate analysis from action. More precisely, as they overtly take the side of the powerless and the marginalized in conflicts, they believe that theory is a tool in the emancipation of human beings from nefarious and outdated ways.

CRITICAL THEORY

Critical theory is an attempt to understand and challenge the cultural, social, and historical structures that dominate society and to liberate human beings from capitalist and authoritarian oppression. The source of critical theory is in the works of the Frankfurt School, whose members set out to merge the considerable visions of Marx and Freud into a truly critical perspective on the norms, habits, and institutions of the twentieth century (see Chapter 7 and the sections on Marxism in Chapter 8). Although they accepted the general diagnosis of Marx on the ill effects and transient nature of capitalism, these theorists opposed historical materialism as a complete explanation of society. Instead, they believed that psychological and cultural variables had more influence on history than communists would acknowledge. Members of the Frankfurt School became cultural critics of capitalism, contending that law, politics, ideologies, and even mass culture such as cinema and popular music were instruments of domination that had to be criticized and replaced by new cultural forms free of the constraints of tradition and ideology.

Furthermore, they were concerned that dogmatic Marxism could become very dangerous for individual liberties.

Jürgen Habermas and His Influence

The best-known contemporary exponent of critical theory is German philosopher Jürgen Habermas (b. 1929), a student of Frankfurt School members Max Horkheimer and Theodor Adorno. In his long career, Habermas (1984) has concentrated on the study of society and politics, with the intent of ameliorating the human condition through liberating political and communicative processes. Although he has not specialized in conflicts per se, his writings on conflict issues and resolution have influenced conflict studies specialists the world over.

For Habermas, the main objective of theory is to help in the emancipation of human-kind. He has adopted the Marxist notion that human institutions should be understood in their historical context. An institution such as the state, for instance, is neither eternal nor fixed. It is a human construction born for certain ends at a certain time, and it will be superseded by other institutions in the future. To think otherwise is to be guilty of reification, a term used by Marx to represent the confusion between an abstraction (here, the immutable state) and historical reality (the evolution of governance in the globalized world).

Although strongly influenced by Marx, Habermas (1990) argues that Marxists have exaggerated the role of economics and class struggles in human history. He believes, in particular, that stressing the role of a single class in social evolution is an analytical mistake and a recipe for violence and authoritarianism. Furthermore, reducing human rights and democracy to bourgeois ideas is a disservice to the masses of people whose possibilities for emancipation have been strengthened by democratization. Habermas (1996) looks to another great German philosopher, Kant, for inspiration. Kant provides an ethical philosophy (the categorical imperative[2]), a commitment to dialogue and tolerance, and an optimistic view of human history (the universal republic) that complements the critical perspective of Marx. In contrast to postmodernists, Habermas is not opposed to rationalism but believes that it is the key to emancipation. People must use reason, communication, and dialogue (communicative rationality) to discover what is good for them and what can be done to conciliate different interests in society.

Habermas and other proponents of critical theory admit that the approach is overtly idealistic, even utopian (a moniker that they proudly use). They favour high ideals that they know might be out of reach because lower ideals could lead them to support less progressive policies. Critical theory is openly cosmopolitan, meaning that it rejects the current division of the world into states and endorses a new form of political organization that assembles people rather than institutions. Habermas's cosmopolitanism is partly an inheritance from Kant. However, Habermas reverses Kant's top-down federation of republics by calling for a universal integration that starts at the bottom and moves upwards (dialogical cosmopolitanism).

Critical Theory and Contemporary Conflict

In critical theory, conflicts are about interests, power, and ideas. Capitalism, authoritarianism, and injustice are crucial causes of conflicts. Critical theorists are especially concerned about globalization, which they equate with the worst excesses of laissez-faire capitalism. Since the state is currently weakening in the battle against the forces of private profit, traditional welfare-state politics is seen as insufficient to change the course of events. Old-style socialist parties and trade unions cannot reverse this trend; therefore, the struggle against globalization has to take other forms. One avenue is to reinforce international organizations, especially the European Union (EU). Habermas and other prominent critical theorists strongly support the EU because it counterbalances US hegemony, promotes democracy and welfare policies, and illustrates that the state model can be superseded by something else. However, the EU is still an organization of states and, as such, cannot be promoted as the ultimate challenge to capitalist globalization.[3]

(AP Photo/Carolyn Kaster)

A demonstrator stands face to face with riot police during the July 2010 G8 and G20 summits. Can one really have a discussion with the state? Are radical protesters truly interested in dialogue? How would Habermas answer these questions?

The opposition to global free trade, led by strong developing states such as China, India, and Brazil, is another important source of modern conflict and promises to impede globalization. However, as it is led by states (some of them tyrannical and/or corrupt), it is neither a true democratic nor empowering movement.

Critical theorists primarily count on popular mobilization to produce social change. Ulrich Beck (2006) has attacked globalization for fostering inequalities around the world. He argues that globalization's ultimate form depends on a fundamental power contest between pro- and anti-globalization forces. He contends that nothing is lost for the proponents of alternative globalization, as they possess sources of power that are far from negligible in the modern world. For example, consumers can boycott certain products, pressure groups can "shame" governments and companies, and large groups can attract sympathetic governments to their cause. In other words, civil society is the main vector of democratic cosmopolitanism.

The same arguments have been developed in a more theoretical way by Andrew Linklater, the foremost critical theorist of international relations. Like Habermas, Linklater (1998) has been trying to revive Kant's ideals for a cosmopolitan world society. However, because sovereign nation-states are a part of the problem, they must be tamed and made more amenable to popular pressures for change. He has also written about how the so-called British school of international relations, by focusing on diplomacy, conflict resolution, democratization, and the humanization of world affairs, has offered some ideas for the transition between the world of states and the emerging world of human beings. Recently, Linklater (2007) has concentrated on the notion of harm in international affairs, analyzing the many ways in which the current world system damages people: directly and indirectly, violently and non-violently, intentionally and incidentally, etc. He advocates a Habermasian democratic dialogue that will allow humankind to move past the state system and into a cosmopolitan democracy.

It is clear that critical theorists believe that globalization increases the level of conflict. Some of the conflicts played out in domestic politics are now transnational and international matters, as is the case with many economic and social issues. The total numbers of issue areas and actors in conflict are also rising, as evidenced by conflicts regarding the environment and high technology. However, as we have seen in chapters 3 and 4, the evidence does not indicate that globalization has led to an increase in violent conflicts. Habermas (1996) has acknowledged the possibility that violent conflict will diminish with the extension of liberal democracy. Contrary to Marxists, critical theorists do not exclusively blame capitalism for violent conflict. Because they believe that ideas have lives of their own and matter in human affairs, critical theorists claim that violent behaviours stem from preconceived notions about what is possible and what should be done in politics. When people think that violence is inevitable, they are more prone to use it. In addition, the lack of communication between people in conflict situations is a factor of violence. For example, Habermas (1984) has long advocated dialogue as the best alternative to strife but realizes that improvement in communication is a long historical process.

Contributions and Criticisms of Critical Theory

In terms of conflict analysis, critical theory has several benefits. One important merit of this approach is its development of a healthy and profitable skepticism regarding social norms and institutions. While some older approaches are also highly critical of the ways of the world, they tend to offer a very selective reading of history. Neo-Marxism, for example, clings to social class as a fundamental category of explanation, despite all evidence to its decline in advanced industrial societies. Critical theory also provides a way of seeing diverse negative influences on human behaviour, not only those related to capitalism. It allows the observer to avoid ideological pitfalls, for instance, Marxism's relative neglect of non-capitalist and pre-capitalist oppression. Furthermore, it rejects the traditional disciplinary boundaries and fosters a more comprehensive analysis of conflict.

Critical theory offers a humanistic perspective on injustice, oppression, and conflict. It forces analysts to look beyond traditional objects of study such as the state, political elites, and social classes. It helps identify and understand many victimized people, including women, cultural groups, and sexual minorities. It is one of the theoretical foundations for the current interest in difference and identity, which influences not only conflict analysis but also public policy regarding multiculturalism, women's rights, and empowerment.

By rejecting the positivist differentiation between facts and value, critical theory promotes an ethics of resistance to the established powers. However, it does not advocate a nihilistic or violent position but one that emphasizes democracy, dialogue, and deliberation in human affairs. No longer the bourgeois ideologue rejected by the Marxists, Kant has become an inspirational figure. Thus, critical theory appeals to the idealism and optimism of many students of society who are disappointed by the conformism of the old approaches, the radicalism of Marxism, and the indecision of postmodernism.

Critical theory is not without its detractors, however. True Marxists have never appreciated the Frankfurt School's departure from economic determinism and class analysis. They contend that, by abandoning historical materialism, the Frankfurt School is similar to the liberal approach to the study of society (Lukács, 1971). Postmodern writers also argue that critical theory does not go far enough. They condemn critical theory mostly for its fidelity to rationalism and therefore consider it a modernist, universalistic, and Western ethnocentric view of the world (Thomassen, 2006).

The more conventional approaches generally claim that critical theory fails as an analysis of conflict for a variety of reasons. For example, it has not created specific or original hypotheses on the origins of conflict. Most of its analysis relies on standard Marxist and anti-globalization fare, completed by ideological, cultural, and political inquiry. From a positivist point of view, critical theory deplores the injustice of the world without explaining it. Finally, critical theory does not provide testable hypotheses and is by definition (much like Marxism) unverifiable.

POSTMODERNISM

The Postmodern Condition

In May 1968, thousands of university students in Paris protested against the government, attempting to bring down the establishment, change the lifestyle of the culture, and restore authentic values. Although the students' revolt also led to worker strikes and nearly toppled Charles de Gaulle's government, it ultimately failed, notably because left-wing parties and trade unions refused to enter into a violent confrontation with the government. Many young academics of the time were quite disappointed with this situation; in the following years, French philosophy would be heavily influenced by the failure of the riots. Doubt, skepticism, and even pessimism began to seep into academia. German philosophers such as Heidegger and Friedrich Nietzsche (1844–1900), who had never had much influence in France, were studied and commented upon. The result would be the development of postmodern thought.[4]

Although the May 1968 riots did not upset the French republic, Jean-François Lyotard (1924–98) and others labelled the time as the start of a new era in human history. In 1979, Lyotard wrote *La condition post-moderne* (*The Postmodern Condition*), often regarded as a manifesto of postmodernism.[5] A major theme of Lyotard's work was the end of metanarratives, the large-scale theories of society prevalent during the Age of Reason— the belief in progress and science, Marxism, liberalism, etc. As these metanarratives failed to improve the human condition, the postmodern age is characterized by profound skepticism of all faiths, ideologies, and ideals. In terms of conflict analysis, Lyotard's theses make three main arguments. First, for postmodernists, conflicts are often caused by the illusions of progress and emancipation offered by metanarratives. Therefore, cynicism vis-à-vis metanarratives could become a powerful antidote to ideological conflicts, religious disputes, and ethnic strife. In other words, if people stopped believing in grandiose world views, they would become more tolerant and peaceful toward each other. The second claim is that social scientists who adhere to a form of the metanarrative are misguided. Not only are they unable to actually explain social reality, but they also risk replicating the tenets of those metanarratives that are at the source of conflict. For instance, realists who insist on the permanence of power politics are complicit in the reproduction of power lust, the cause of so many conflicts. The third consequence is the establishment of a pluralist mentality whereby the narratives, values, and meaning systems of diverse cultures and groups could be accepted and valued on their own terms, even though there might be contradictions between them.

One of the most important postmodernists was philosopher Jacques Derrida (1930–2004), known for his concept of deconstruction. Like Lyotard, Derrida was not a specialist of conflict. He was not even a student of politics or society but was mainly interested in language and literature.[6] Influenced by linguists of the structuralist tradition, Derrida (2001) wanted to persuade his readers that the entire Western tradition was based on the exclusion of "otherness" and that rationalism was nothing more than the domination of the male logocentric world view. He believed that philosophers could expose these beliefs by deconstructing texts to reveal their true structures.

Although he did not call himself a postmodernist, philosopher Michel Foucault (1926–84) greatly influenced the movement. Along with Lyotard and Derrida, he was interested in the origins and uses of Western metanarratives. Foucault (1980, 1984) coined the concept of archaeology of knowledge to express his method of revealing the beginnings and development of ideas.[7] He applied his method to topics such as the treatment of mental illness, imprisonment, and sexuality, attempting to show how order and discipline have been the main goals of regulating these diverse fields. Foucault thought that, despite the superficial differences between eras, repression has always been the order of the day. Even modern democracies are elaborate surveillance systems. One of his main themes is that of the relationship between power and knowledge. For Foucault, the production of knowledge is intimately related to the will to dominate others. Knowledge is created and disseminated to support some claims to power. In his writings, these connections are often expressed by the concept of knowledge-power. Foucault's influence has been so profound that he may be considered responsible for the shift in the humanities and social sciences from the study of change to the study of control in all its manifestations.

Postmodernist philosophy has influenced the post-colonial movement, starting with literary theorist Edward Said (1935–2003). With the publication of *Orientalism* in 1978, Said became famous for proposing that Western intellectuals and scientists have created an imaginary picture of the non-Western world, or the Orient. Over time, the Orient was framed as a place of superstition and cruelty in opposition to the rational and benevolent West. The myth of Orientalism has strongly shaped Westerners' perception of regions such as the Middle East and even non-Westerners' view of themselves. One conclusion of this approach—sometimes also known as post-colonialism—is that the conflicts and violence in the Middle East stem from the Orientalist designs of Westerners and their allies.

The influence of postmodern research is also found in many new academic fields, such as gender and women studies, African-American or black studies, queer studies, and cultural studies. It has generated much interest in the discourses of oppression and resistance articulated by the protagonists of social conflicts. In gender studies, for example, Cynthia Enloe's *Bananas, Beaches and Bases* (2000) represents an application of postmodernism to questions of international security and war. According to Enloe, all narratives of foreign policy and defence are gendered. To be more precise, they are masculine, and their purpose is to strengthen male domination of and female exclusion from politics.

Contributions and Shortfalls of Postmodernism

One of postmodernism's main contributions to conflict studies is that it brought the importance of studying conflict to the attention of researchers worldwide. The theory has stressed the significance of critically decoding the mentalities and ideologies of the parties in conflict, which are major factors in their propensity to use violence. Furthermore, postmodernism has forced us to critically analyze established attitudes and theories, insisting that they are strongly influenced by Western norms and attitudes rooted in the rationalist model and tainted by prejudices against non-Western cultures, non-Christian religions, women, and sexual minorities. Postmodernism has therefore become one of the major intellectual weapons against the white male establishment of affluent countries.

At the same time, postmodernism remains a very controversial group of approaches that has drawn criticism from all sides. Sartre accused Foucault of being a bourgeois writer intent on protecting capitalism by elaborating a seemingly radical theory that would make people abandon Marxism (see Miller, 1994). Habermas has had several arguments with postmodernists, including a famous debate with Lyotard in the 1970s. Habermas's main contention was that postmodernism is a reactionary philosophy that does not endorse a precise revolutionary project. As we have seen before, he believes in the Enlightenment and in universalism, as reflected by his fondness for the contributions of Kant and Marx.[8]

More scientific-minded intellectuals have usually considered postmodernism a confused and incomprehensible doctrine. Despite his own sympathy for critical and radical ideas, American linguist Noam Chomsky (b. 1928) has observed that nobody has ever been able to explain the exact definition of postmodernism to him (Chomsky & Otero, 2003, p. 93). Most natural scientists believe that postmodernism is an intellectual fraud, as was classically illustrated by the Sokal affair.[9]

There are also logical problems with postmodernism. A simple way to express them is the proposition that, if all metanarratives are wrong, we cannot believe the postmodern metanarrative. How can we assess that the postmodern critiques of gender domination, logocentrism, and Orientalism are true and warrant political stances of resistance, empowerment, and affirmation? In other words, what are the moral and political guides of a theory that has rejected moral and political guides? Is postmodernism not just an elaborate ideological contraption imagined for the pursuit of anti-establishment policies?

Finally, another well-known rejection of postmodernism concerns its moral relativism and even nihilism. In its radical pluralism, arguing that every identity group narrative has equal validity, there appears to be no way of arriving at more universal norms. Those with a strong commitment to finding a sound moral basis for action would see postmodernists as encouraging passivity, complacency, and even deviance with their rejection of universal norms of behaviour (see Chapter 14 for a more complete discussion of ethics). Postmodernists would answer that the principle of respect for other perspectives is a significant overarching moral position.

RELATIONS BETWEEN SELF AND OTHER

A number of contemporary philosophers have concentrated on the relationship between Self and Other as a source of conflict.[10] This area of inquiry has involved questions regarding the nature of selfness and otherness, responsibilities for the Other, and the qualities of actions that implicate Self and Other. Precursors to the Self–Other philosophy presented here are Hegel's concept of dialectics and Heidegger's outlook that being finds expression in its diachronic engagement with the world and that authentic being is grounded in relationships (Page, 2008, p. 170).

The Philosophy of Paul Ricoeur

Regarding the nature of selfness and otherness, French philosopher Paul Ricoeur (1913–2005) argues that the Self forms its identity in relation to the Other (1990/1992). The Self can be any self, such as myself, yourself, himself, or herself. Whichever one is understood to be the Self as a philosophical concept, there is always an other-than-self that becomes the Other. The concept of Other can be understood in two senses: as simply the Other with whom the Self is in a relationship or as a relationship of profound antagonism. In the second description, the Self no longer sees the humanity of the Other.

The significance of this argument relates to the famous formulation of seventeenth-century philosopher René Descartes: "I think therefore I am." This unitary notion of the Self has initiated an emphasis on individualism that has permeated Western society since the Enlightenment. For Ricoeur, the Cartesian understanding needs to recognize that we are always in relation with others and that our perceptions of ourselves and the world are formed in relation with our Other. As we stated earlier, Hegel's concept of dialectic was that, for every thesis or world view, there is an antithesis leading to a new synthesis. Ricoeur's understanding of dialectic is that there are two parts to a whole that cannot be dissolved into one another but are both necessary for an entity to be complete. The Self and Other is one such dialectic. What this means for our understanding of conflict is that, rather than thinking of autonomous, self-sufficient Selves conflicting with one another over things, ideas, or interests, we can think of each Self as having been formed in relation to the Other. In other words, the Other is implicated at every stage and level of conflict.

In her study of key political philosophers from the West, philosopher Janine Chanteur (1992) examines the normal state of relationships among human beings. She found overwhelming evidence that, for these philosophers, there is a state of war, or extreme conflict, that is considered the normative relationship between Self and Other. Peace has been thought of as a temporary break in this state—an opportunity to prepare for the next war. In order for this situation to be the case, Chanteur postulates that there must be a profound dehumanization of the Other, such that it is justifiable to kill the Other in war. This dehumanization exemplifies what she calls an ontological rift, a separation from the Other, which she sees rooted in a profound sense of otherness between the genders. Similar to Ricoeur's critique of Descartes' statement, Chanteur criticizes the use of the term *man* to refer to all humanity. Rather, she maintains that it takes a man and a woman to represent humanity, just as Ricoeur argues that it takes Self and Other in a dialectal relationship to show all that is involved in humanity.

An important dimension of conflict, therefore, involves actions performed within the context of the conflict. While not addressing conflict specifically, Ricoeur's philosophy of action is instructive. For every action, there is an actor who is its agent, the person who plans, intends, and then carries out the act. This deed has a particular meaning within the actor's frame of reference (Ricoeur, 1990/1992). There is also the sufferer, the person who is subjected to the action, or acted upon. For example, in a colonial environment, the colonial power is the actor and those dominated are the sufferers. Being acted upon creates dependency and diminishes a capacity for taking action.

Ricoeur, along with philosopher Alasdair MacIntyre (1981), also distinguishes among basic actions, action chains, and action practices. A basic action makes sense on its own (e.g. a move in chess). An action chain is a set of basic actions connected to one another (e.g. a chess game), while an action practice comprises action chains performed regularly (e.g. becoming a chess player). These terms are useful in analyzing conflict because we can see various conflicts as basic clashes that are short-lived, as conflict chains that involve a set of escalating actions and reactions, or as conflict practices, in which a conflict becomes ongoing and is woven into the lives and identities of the parties.

Emmanuel Levinas and Bernard Lonergan

French philosopher Emmanuel Levinas (1906–95) developed a philosophy of the face—specifically the face of the Other.[11] If we start with a sense of the distant, dehumanized Other, we can say that it presents itself to the Self through its face. What happens when the Self is confronted with the face of this Other? Levinas (1961/1969) speaks of first seeing the face as representing vulnerability, which results in a murderous temptation to kill the Other. However, he argues that, when we think about what we are confronted with, we realize that it is the exterior manifestation of something quite phenomenal: a transcendent Other, an infinite universe of being. With this realization comes the overwhelming sense of an infinite and ethical responsibility for the Other (Levinas, 1978).

This primal ethical responsibility is not bound by particular moral principles but is a simple profound sense of care about the Other. It stands in contrast to the Biblical story of Cain and Abel. When Cain is confronted about killing his brother, he replies, "Am I my brother's keeper?" Levinas's philosophy of the face claims that the answer is yes. Like Ricoeur, his philosophy shows how the life of the Self is intertwined with that of the Other. Levinas scholar Sandor Goodhart (2009) maintains that the ethical responsibility precedes the formation of the Self. For him, part of the resolution of conflict is to reconcile oneself with the image of the Other embedded within the Self. Conflict with the Other is not just a conflict between entities, but it is always intrapersonal at the same time.

Canadian theologian Bernard Lonergan (1904–84) also offers concepts that can be useful in the analysis of conflict. The intellectual operations analyzed by Lonergan (1958/1978) are perceiving, understanding, judging, and deciding. Through the act of perceiving, we give meaning to our experiences. We recognize certain things as being within our range of experience, from simple objects and actions to more complex entities, such as a given person's cultural background. Understanding involves reflection on what we perceive. This operation might entail considering what a person deems important to his or

(AP Photo/Rafiq Maqbool)

A US paratrooper crosses paths with Afghan women in 2004. Can the chasm that often separates such individuals be bridged? In some instances, is otherness unsolvable?

her identity. The act of judging relies on what has been perceived and understood. For example, debating whether a request for support is legitimate and ranks above other requests is judging. For Lonergan, judging also entails giving a value to what has been understood. Finally, the operation of deciding leads to taking action. In fact, it can be drawn out until such time as action is taken.

Bias can play a role in each of these operations and can be helpful in understanding various dynamics of conflict. Lonergan (1958/1978) uses the term *scotosis* to elaborate on bias. Scotosis is a blind spot within the mind that leads to unconsciously blocking insights. In other words, it is a mechanism that prevents us from learning or understanding something that might help us reject stereotypes about certain people. Lonergan developed four kinds of bias. Dramatic bias comes from dramatic events in our lives. In personal, or egotistical, bias, we do not wish to have an insight that diminishes our own sense of power, prestige, or relative advantage. Group bias shares attitudes, such as stereotypes, between groups. Finally, general bias is rooted in a love of the practical, short-term way of addressing a challenge. This general bias prohibits us from seeing that another approach might have more long-term benefit or might be of greater benefit to the whole of society.

A key aspect of conversion is coming to terms with our biases. This kind of change could be moral, in which we realize a new principle to guide action; intellectual, in which we understand something in a whole new way; or religious, in which we develop a new capacity to connect with an Other, find a source of inner strength, or transcend an overwhelming obstacle. In each case, it means becoming aware of a bias, thereby opening up our consciousness to become aware of something previously blocked by groupthink, ego, or stereotypes. Conversion, in Lonergan's sense, opens us up to a whole new range of insights. In other words, it expands our horizon of future possibilities.

Theologian Cyril Orji (2008) has used Lonergan's work as the basis for his analysis of ethnic and religious conflict in Africa, demonstrating how it helps to understand intrastate dynamics in that continent. According to Orji, the four types of biases have led to profound barriers between different identity groups in post-colonial Africa. He uses Nigeria as a case study, showing how biases have turned perceptions, understandings, judgments and decisions related to the exchanges between Hausas and Ibos, Fulanis and Hausas, Christians and Muslims, and Christians and practitioners of traditional African religions into negativity and violence, preventing people from understanding one another in mutually sympathetic ways.

Roles and Limitations of the Self–Other Framework

As we explore philosophies of Self and Other, we realize that they provide a vocabulary and set of concepts to describe what others would call deep-rooted, identity-based, and intractable conflicts. They enable us to first step back from particular conflicts and examine their dynamics in the abstract. This examination shows that our lives are connected with one another and that we define ourselves in terms of our Other. There may be a huge dehumanizing rift between us, but we ultimately realize that the Other is a vulnerable yet infinitely valuable human being just like we are. This perspective also offers a broad ethical vision for humanity.

However, much of the language of this philosophy is highly abstract, making it difficult to apply it to real situations. There is also considerable potential for the theory to be misunderstood or incorrectly employed. In each case, the methodology has involved examining texts and reflecting on their meaning in terms of the self-knowledge of the philosophers involved. What is lacking is the translation of these insights into problems that can be subjected to empirical testing and eventual adaptation to applications in the field. One exception is the highly technical work of Lonergan, which has been adapted to mediation through the combined expertise of Lonergan scholarship and mediation practice (see Chapter 11 for an analysis of insight mediation).

MIMETIC THEORY: THE CONTRIBUTION OF RENÉ GIRARD

The practical dynamics of Self and Other are brought to another level of realization through the mimetic theory of French literary critic and philosopher René Girard (b. 1923). In the 1950s, Girard (1976) reached the following conclusion from his careful study of prominent writers: desire is based on what we perceive as the desire of another. In other words, we imitate the desires of others. Girard called this imitation mimetic desire. When two parties desire the same thing, it can lead to rivalry and violence. When there is conflict within a community, it can cause a crisis. As Girard (1977, 1987b, 1989) explored the phenomenon of mimetic desire through a study of the classics, psychology, and anthropology, he discovered that such crises are often resolved through **scapegoating**, which is also a factor in sacrificial systems based on myth and ritual. We will explore these concepts further and show how they can be applied to conflict and **conflict transformation**.

Mimetic Desire

Humans have a strong capacity to imitate intentions and desires. As Girard (1976, 1978) points out, when we notice that someone else has a desire for something, we often start to imagine having the same object ourselves and thereby develop a desire for it. The object of desire may be something concrete or abstract, such as recognition, a promotion, or affection. This desire is not spontaneous but is mediated through the Model, the one whose desire we imitate. When the Model stands in the way of us getting the object, it becomes, in Girard's words, an obstacle. There is a triangular structure in mimetic desire that involves a Self, a Model, and an Object. This relationship is akin to Freud's Oedipus complex, which was also triangular. However, Girard would argue that Freud's structure is correct but too confined in its application. The complex is but one limited example of a broader phenomenon of desire imitation.

There are a few points to be noted about mimetic desire. First, there can be a feedback loop established whereby desire is intensified. In this case, Party A, the initial Model, notices that Party B desires the same object. Party A then imitates the desire of Party B in a role reversal, desiring the object even more. Party B notes this change and likewise desires the object more, resulting in a cycle of increasing desire. Second, the more people identify with one another, the more the mimetic desire intensifies. This is why sibling rivalry is so powerful. Third, mimetic desire is stronger in a closed relational system where two or more parties interact a great deal. Some of the most intense group conflicts are between parties that have a historic relation and many points of commonality.[12] Historically, we can see that, during the colonial period, the colonial powers—France, England, Spain, Portugal, etc.—had mimetic desire for colonies in every part of the world. Finally, if the object of desire is extremely valuable or if the Model is very prestigious, mimetic desire increases.[13]

In a **mimetic rivalry**, two parties consistently desire what the other has or wants. Each time one of the parties shows an interest in something new, the other immediately wants the same thing. As a rivalry intensifies, it can be obsessive. People become mimetic doubles (Girard, 1978). There is a preoccupation with getting ahead of the other, so much so that, if one suffers a minor relative loss, it is blown out of proportion. Conversely, if one gets ahead in the rivalry, it is cause for major celebration. In this state, people define their identities in relation to their doubles, with whom they have a love–hate relationship: love because they want to be the other and hate because they cannot.

When people are frustrated by obstacles, their rival's success, or a perceived injustice that keeps them from acquiring the desired object, there is a temptation to resort to violence. This violence may be an act of theft, murder, or anything else that increases their relative advantage by harming a mimetic model. As soon as violence enters the equation, there is a tendency for it to be reciprocated and "returned with interest" (to use a Girardian phrase), creating a vicious cycle of escalating violence.

Scapegoating

One way that a community can prevent the outbreak of mimetic violence at a point of crisis is through scapegoating. In scapegoating, all the individual frustrations of the community members are projected onto a single person or group, which is expelled from the community or killed. The community is reconciled, as all members are united in the action against the scapegoat. However, this process works only if the scapegoat mechanism is hidden from the community. In other words, people do not consciously decide to scapegoat a person or a group but come to a collective decision that the scapegoat is responsible for all their problems, thereby legitimizing their actions. Girard (1987a) uses the biblical examples of Jesus and Job to show that, in reality, the scapegoat is an innocent victim.

Scapegoats have certain characteristics in common (Girard, 1989). They are different from other members of their communities. This difference makes them stand out, giving the other members of the community a sense of similarity in contrast and the opportunity to unite against the one who is different. Scapegoats are perceived as having done something wrong. This perception is used to justify the scapegoat action, which is always perceived as the right thing by the community. Scapegoats must be powerful enough to have plausibly caused the problems in the community. This power may be positive (the scapegoat is rich or has a good position) or negative (the scapegoat could do a lot of damage). However, they must also have a degree of vulnerability. If a scapegoat is too powerful, he or she could retaliate and the process could fail.

Mimetic Theory and Conflict

Mimetic theory helps to explain some aspects of political life. Where politicians model a desire for power, others mimetically desire the same thing and rivalries develop. Often leaders are hypermimetic, wanting to be better than everyone else, even their predecessors. Alexander the Great was a mimetic model for Julius Caesar, who lamented that he had not accomplished as much as Alexander by the time he was the same age. Richard Nixon had John F. Kennedy as a mimetic model ("Why did the people love him so?"), and it is clear that similar patterns persist in any political system. Countries that identify with one another have ongoing mimetic rivalries that can be quite antagonistic. One example is the rivalry between Turkey and Greece, where the object of desire—Cyprus—continues to be divided between Turkish and Greek Cypriots.

Often the initial phase of a conflict can be traced to mimetic desire. One party has a desired object, and the second party imitates the desire. The conflict begins when the latter

BOX 9.1 | SACRIFICIAL SYSTEMS

As Girard (1977, 1989) studied culture and reflected on its origins in terms of scapegoating, he saw that sacrificial systems resemble scapegoating. For example, a community can use sacrifices to achieve the same kind of reconciliation that occurs through scapegoating. When animals or people are sacrificed, they are drawn from a group that is designated as a proper, legitimate class of potential victims. The sacrificial system includes a myth that gives meaning to the sacrifice and plays a **healing** role in the ritual. Everyone becomes united through the ritual, and the community is cleansed of its frustrations. The myth is also grounded in actual scapegoating that previously helped the community. While myth conceals aspects of the scapegoating, it reveals enough so that the perceptive analyst can see the traces of the initial act.

When a sacrificial system stops working for a community, there is a sacrificial crisis (Girard, 1977). People do not know how to handle the frustrations, projections, desires, or reciprocal violence within their communities. Eventually, they find a new scapegoat and develop a new form of sacrificial system. Girard (2010) argues that, with the unmasking of the scapegoat mechanism and the development of post-Enlightenment critical thought, sacrificial systems no longer control violence. He sees the potential for runaway violence, which could have disastrous consequences for humankind.

attempts to obtain the desired object. Mimetic theory also helps to explain the escalation of conflict, particularly when violence is involved. Parties continue to imitate what was done to them by returning violence "with interest," as Girard notes repeatedly.

Mimetic Theory and Conflict Transformation

Rebecca Adams (2000), a Girardian scholar, has shown how mimetic theory can be used to understand transformative actions. Suppose there is a victim or a Self that is limited in his or her capacity to live well or take action. Such a person has low self-esteem and cannot imagine a way out of his or her predicament. If this Limited Self (LS) has a mimetic Model who desires the well-being of the LS and if the LS imitates this desire, he or she desires his or her own well-being. This process is a first step toward healing and empowerment. There are other aspects of mimetic modelling of positive attitudes that can play a transforming role. For example, a conflict resolution practitioner can model a desire for resolution or transformation. If the parties to a conflict imitate this desire, they begin to imagine resolving their conflict.

Stories of conflict transformation, justice advocacy, and reconciliation can serve as mimetic models for people in conflict. Mahatma Gandhi served as a mimetic model of non-violent action for Martin Luther King, Jr, and both leaders continue to inspire non-violent protest movements around the world. Similarly, stories of reconciliation such as that of South Africa, even though incomplete, continue to stimulate similar transformations in other situations of gross inequity.

Assessment of the Mimetic Theory

Mimetic theory has become a popular theory in the humanities. The reliance on biblical and other ancient sources makes Girard a favourite among religion-minded students. The exploration of Judeo-Christian myths also appeals to literary scholars, philosophers, and anthropologists. Girard offers a simple action–reaction model with an escalation effect that is presented in elegant and evocative language. It is applicable to any conflict, including inner and interpersonal ones. It is accessible to people from many fields and is therefore truly multidisciplinary. For all these reasons, Girard's model is well adapted to the new discipline of conflict studies.

However, there are some limitations of Girardian thought in relation to conflict. First, most of Girard's own work has been in relation to literary, psychological, philosophical, religious, and anthropological texts. While this approach has been useful in developing a certain type of theory, dealing with real people in real conflicts is another challenge. Girard (2001) makes grand claims for the uniqueness and pre-eminence of Christianity in disclosing mimetic phenomena and their implications.

By his own admission, Girard has focused almost exclusively on issues of violence without a full exploration of mimetic theory's creative dimensions. The Girardian theory can therefore sometimes come across as reducing everything to mimetic desire and scapegoating. However, identity-based conflicts are very complex, with many factors involved. While **mimesis** may play a role, there are other dynamics to consider.

Most behaviourally inclined scholars would find that the Girardian model is more metaphysical than scientific and would probably be disinclined to test or adopt it. Girard (2006) would answer that his theory is, in fact, scientific, in that it is a systematic and critical study of a phenomenon that brings together insights from anthropology, classical literature, and contemporary society. Perhaps other scholars will subject the Girardian model to empirical tests and deduce a more specific application of the theory to conflict analysis.

CONCLUSION

The chapter introduced philosophy as a field that probes questions regarding the meaning of existence, morality, knowledge, logic, language, reason, and science. For centuries, it played a central role in the quest for knowledge and understanding; however, the Enlightenment brought a new emphasis on empirical knowledge gained from a systematic methodology involving hypotheses, observation, and experimentation. Philosophy kept alive the probing of what lies behind different approaches to how we know things and how we interpret reality. Four such approaches are critical theory, postmodernism, philosophies of Self and Other, and mimetic theory. Each perspective offers insight into conflict analysis, focusing on why people engage in conflicts, particularly those involving violence. Despite their differences, they underline the importance of looking at the

Other: the stranger, the victim, and the perpetrator. They highlight the need to question even the most basic assumptions about conflict. The answers may not always be at hand and the solutions may sometimes seem nebulous and far away, but the effort to ask the right people meaningful questions about the important matters is a step in the peaceful resolution of conflicts. Furthermore, philosophical schools address the issue of norms and values, contending that analysts cannot separate them from their examination of society, as positivist analysts argue. This view has influenced the social sciences and humanities to the point that positivism, while still very influential, has lost its hegemonic position.

However, we cannot forget the fundamental differences among these philosophical approaches. The main one concerns the role of reason in human affairs. While critical theory, for instance, is mostly rationalist and materialist, postmodernism is mostly anti-rationalist and idealist. The authors in the Christian tradition that we have encountered (for example, Ricoeur and Girard) believe that reason has its place but is not sufficient to bring about peace or conflict resolution and must be supplemented by empathy and spirituality. The philosophical traditions are as diversified as the social sciences and psychological schools of thought that we previously discussed.

DISCUSSION QUESTIONS

1. Why is philosophy an important discipline for conflict studies?

2. Choose a particular conflict and examine how the philosophical theories presented in this chapter shed light on its dynamics.

3. The distinction between the Self and the Other is a powerful analytical tool. Does this mean that this fundamental schism is unavoidable and will always lead to conflicts? Why or why not?

4. Do mimetic theory and scapegoating apply to all conflicts? Do they lead to approaches that may lessen the violence and harm of conflicts? Give reasons to support your answers.

NOTES

1. For example, philosopher Grace Jantzen (1948–2006) wrote a trilogy on the origins of violence in which she traces how Western thought since the ancient Greeks has had an underlying fascination with death—manifested as both necrophilia (love of death) and necrophobia (fear of death)—see Jantzen, 2004, 2009. She suggests an alternate philosophy of natality, offering birth as an alternate root metaphor resulting in a value of creativity and new beginnings.

2. The categorical imperative requires people to act in a way that would be acceptable for all people to follow in a similar situation.

3. Furthermore, Habermas (2009, esp. Chapter 6) has lamented that the organization is in poor shape due to a number of internal and external factors.

4. Besides *postmodernism*, the terms *post-structuralism*, *post-rationalism*, and *deconstructionism* are also used. However, there is some debate about the use of these terms and the differences (or lack thereof) between them. For the purposes of brevity and simplicity, we will use *postmodern* throughout this chapter.

5. Lyotard's book is mainly about postmodernity, the contemporary historical period that Lyotard thought followed modernity (the age of enlightenment and material progress that began in the eighteenth century). Nevertheless, the two terms are often related as postmodernism is seen by its supporters as the first philosophical school of postmodernity.

6. For an introduction to Derrida's works, which often focus on literature, culture, and religion, see Derrida (2001), Caputo (1996), and Cherif (2008).

7. Related to this concept is the genealogy of ideas, a notion that Foucault borrowed from Nietzsche.

8. However, Habermas has collaborated with Lyotard on certain political petitions, including a well-known denunciation of the American-led invasion of Iraq in 2003. See Borradori (2004), a volume of interviews with the two philosophers on terrorism and modern conflicts.

9. In 1996, American physicist Alan Sokal critiqued postmodernism by submitting a hoax article to *Social Text*, a leading cultural studies journal. The journal published the article without peer review, despite the fact that it was actually a non-sensical divagation using advanced scientific vocabulary and fashionable postmodern concepts.

10. This relationship is an important theme in all French post-war philosophy, including that of Derrida and Foucault. Furthermore, Vincent Descombes (1980) named his history of modern French philosophy *Le même et l'autre (The Same and the Other)*.

11. Levinas studied under Heidegger before World War II but, after the war, struggled with Heidegger's support for National Socialism. Levinas's theories can be seen as a rejection of the limitations of Heidegger's thought. Levinas and Derrida influenced one another.

12. This theory helps to explain Freud's narcissism of small differences and the observations of some scholars of ethnic conflict (e.g. Horowitz, 2000) that the most intense conflicts tend to occur between people who are either closely related or who share many of the same characteristics.

13. For a further description of these phenomena, see Redekop (2002), especially chapters 2 and 3.

PART IV | CONFLICT RESOLUTION

This part examines conflict from the perspective of those who are directly involved as parties or interveners. Theorists and practitioners have developed a variety of concepts and frameworks to analyze conflict styles, conflict transformation processes, and the dynamics of establishing and maintaining peace. Although certain concepts apply more directly to particular levels of conflict, they collectively provide a language that can be used to make people conscious of how they participate in conflict.

In Chapter 10, we look at conflict from the perspective of the conflicting parties, examining behavioural styles, levels of consciousness, tactics, communication, and conflict escalation. Chapter 11 shifts the focus to the processes used to address conflict. Some methods, such as negotiation, can be carried out by the parties themselves. Others, such as mediation, require the assistance of a third party.

A significant armed conflict with many victims must be addressed in a multi-faceted way. Chapter 12 covers an array of complex issues that must be faced in these violent situations. It traces the emergence of diplomacy and examines peacekeeping, humanitarian intervention, and peacebuilding. The role of the United Nations in these areas is also discussed.

Chapter 13 addresses the challenge of reconciliation, which involves a profound transformation of people, relationships, and institutions. Reconciliation is understood as both a goal and a process. As a goal, it raises the following question: What is the optimum relationship between conflicting people or groups? As a process, it includes a number of components implemented over time.

10 | HOW PEOPLE BEHAVE IN CONFLICT

CHAPTER OBJECTIVES

This chapter will help you develop an understanding of the

- approaches people use in conflict;
- levels of consciousness of people in conflict and their impact on behaviour and attitudes;
- tactics used in conflict;
- role of communication in conflict behaviour; and
- dynamics of conflict escalation.

INTRODUCTION

This chapter examines factors that influence how people act when confronted with conflict. For more than three decades, a popular analysis has focused on behavioural approaches. We therefore begin by discussing six methods: aggression, avoidance, accommodation, compromise, collaboration, and non-action. While non-action is not part of the categories popular in North America, we include it because it is a distinctive approach to conflict in Hindu/Indian and Confucian/Taoist/Chinese traditions. Another form of analysis emphasizes levels of consciousness—narcissistic, tribal, rational, pluralistic, empathetic openness, interconnectedness, and transcendence. It is also useful to take note of the different tactics people use when in a conflict situation. Finally, communication plays a significant role in conflict; often there is a discrepancy between what people intend to communicate and the message that is received. As we illustrate in this chapter, all these dynamics come into play during cycles of conflict.

BEHAVIOURAL APPROACHES

In 1977, Kenneth Thomas and Ralph Kilmann introduced the **Thomas-Kilmann Conflict Mode Instrument**, which became a classic way of analyzing conflict styles (Schaubhut, 2007). In this device, participants are asked a series of 30 questions designed to measure levels of assertiveness (determination to achieve goals) and co-operativeness (determination to maintain relationships). As Figure 10.1 shows, these levels correspond to five behavioural types.[1] A low level of both assertiveness and co-operativeness yields avoidance, while a high level of both produces collaborative behaviour. High assertiveness and low co-operativeness means a competing style; high co-operativeness and low assertiveness results in an accommodating style. Mid-range levels of both qualities are a compromising style. Since it was first developed, this instrument has been used extensively to assess the conflict styles of tens of thousands of people. Organizations have used it to help promote better teamwork, and the five behavioural styles have been employed by many training programs and analytical approaches to conflict behaviour. Extensive research has also linked the results to those of the Myers-Briggs Type Indicator assessment, as well as to differences in political party affiliation, gender, behavioural patterns, and organizational communication styles (Schaubhut, 2007, p. 8).[2]

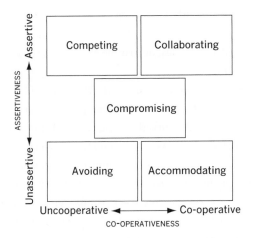

FIGURE 10.1 | THOMAS–KILMANN CONFLICT MODES

Source: Leaetta Hough, The Five Conflict-Handling Modes found in the Thomas-Kilmann Conflict Mode Instrument, CPP.

These behaviours are theoretical constructs that can help people reflect critically on their own behaviour in conflict situations, as well as on how groups, organizations, and states approach conflict. In one interesting study, conflict specialists Brian Polkinghorn and Sean Bryne (2001) examined the styles of 384 university students in areas with a high level of violent conflict—Bosnia and Herzegovina, Israel, Northern Ireland, and South Africa—looking for correlations based on ethnicity, religion, and gender. One result was that males who had been engaged in conflict tended to adopt an avoidance style. In other words, having experienced violent conflict, they wanted to diminish the chances of it recurring. Awareness of our own experience of conflict can therefore help us reflect on our attitudes toward future conflict.

As we discuss the various approaches to conflict behaviour, it is important to note that people demonstrate them in different ways. Developmental psychologists make a helpful distinction between the proximate self and the distal self (Wilber 2000). The proximate self experiences things, including conflict, directly and without reflection. When we are in this mode and are angry, we directly experience all the emotions and symptoms associated with anger. If someone tells us we are angry, we might become even angrier. The situation controls us. In the distal mode, the overall self becomes conscious of what is happening and the distal self views the proximate self like a third-party observer (McGuigan, 2006, p. 45). When we observe from our distal self perspective, we become conscious of what we are experiencing and reflect on it. We may even try to discover the reasons why we experience things in a certain way. When we start becoming angry in the distal self mode, we think to ourselves, "I am becoming angry. I feel the energy rising. I sense that my face is flushed and that my hands are sweaty." As we become aware of our anger, we can re-channel that energy. Others may not even notice the fact that we had an angry impulse. In this mode, people reflect on conflict and, based on an awareness of their own values, emotions, and understandings, determine that this is the best method for them.

To distinguish between these two modes, we use specific vocabulary in our discussion of conflict behaviour. The word *style* indicates Thomas and Kilmann's five types and emphasizes primal behaviour, the natural way that people react when in a conflict, corresponding to the proximate self. Corresponding to the distal self, *orientation* refers to what people consider an appropriate way to respond during a conflict. *Approach* is a combination of style and orientation and can be congruent or incongruent. In cases where people would advocate for the style that they use and there is complete accord between style and orientation, the approach is congruent. For example, a person who believes that both parties in a conflict have to compromise and follows this practice in his or her own conflicts exhibits a congruent approach. However, some people might have a style that is at variance with their orientation. Because of learned patterns of behaviour or emotional memories, they may act in a way that is different from how they think they should act or how they might respond if they had time to reflect. Their approach is incongruent. For example, a person might believe in collaboration but exhibit an aggressive style when confronted with a conflict. Another person might feel that it is good to be assertive but slip into avoidance mode during a conflict.

Behavioural approaches can be associated with issues of justice and identity, third-party intervention, conflict resolution, and reconciliation. In most conflicts, parties appeal to a standard of justice or perceived injustice to rationalize their position (see Chapter 15). The degree of emotional engagement may impact the conflict approach. People may be natural avoiders but, prompted by an extreme injustice, may become aggressive. Justice-related institutions such as courts, human rights tribunals, and truth and reconciliation commissions play an important role in helping individuals and groups to resolve conflicts. At other levels (e.g. organizational grievance processes), there is a concept of justice that regulates the process. A sense of justice is also involved in protests and individual approaches to conflict. When respect for rule of law and procedural justice is present, those who might be inclined to be aggressive will suppress some of their impulses and be more co-operative because they know that it might benefit them. These examples suggest that behaviour might be subject to the dialectic between one's stylistic inclinations and other social factors. One of these elements is alcohol. Intoxication results in a diminished capacity for reflection; hence, the proximate self comes to the fore, sometimes with great intensity. However, a man who physically abuses his wife while under the influence of alcohol might never assault his employer while in the same state, suggesting that he has internalized the idea that this behaviour is unacceptable at a profound enough level that it still regulates his actions.

Another factor that could increase the emotional component of a conflict and alter behavioural approach is a threat to identity needs (see Chapter 7). Also related to identity are the norms and teachings of an identity group, which can lead people to act in a way that conforms to a certain approach. For example, when Charles Carl Roberts IV killed a number of Amish girls in their Pennsylvania school in 2006, the parents' response was to offer forgiveness because that is the norm within their community. Some individuals might even have internal tensions between an approach that is a natural preference and cultural norms that discourage this behaviour. There is also a mimetic effect (see Chapter 9) in that people imitate the approaches of their role models and are influenced by the approaches of those with whom they are in conflict.

Conflict approaches have significant implications for interveners and any processes that might be used to deal with conflict. Those who are collaborative problem-solvers will eagerly participate in processes such as mediation, whereas avoiders will be reluctant to get involved. Those with an aggressive approach could take advantage of those inclined to be accommodating. It is therefore useful for those leading such processes to be aware of the different approaches. Furthermore, conflict approaches should also be taken into account in violent or exceptionally emotional conflict that demands reconciliation. In instances of widespread atrocities, for example, people who are not particularly aggressive are drawn into supporting extremely violent actions. After the fact, they may wish to avoid any confrontation over their past actions or to defend or deny vigorously what they did. In the sections that follow, we examine six approaches to conflict. While there is not one that is always the most effective or desirable, each has its place in certain circumstances. Each approach can also be exercised in a healthy way or used in a manner that is toxic to good relations.

Aggressive Approach

If we understand conflict as a clash of interests, ideas, desires, or any of the other things people fight about, one approach is for people to do everything in their power to get what they want or to have their position prevail. As a result, conflicts can become aggressive. Aggression can be expressed in a variety of ways, including the use of force, intimidation, deception, or psychological games. People may also be passive-aggressive, working in subtle ways to get what they want.

Some people simply have an aggressive style: they are abrupt and directly express what they want. Their orientation, however, may be less aggressive. They may see conflict as healthy competition and not really want to get ahead at another's expense. Conversely, others come across as calm, and their expressions of what they want are subtle and well nuanced. They appear to be accommodating, but their orientation is highly aggressive— they will do everything they can to win and do not care if others are hurt in the process. They deliberately demonstrate a different style because they think that it will help them win and make them look good.

Examples of the aggressive approach exist in both psychological modes and at various levels of society. In the proximate mode and at the interpersonal level, young children who compete over toys and do whatever they can to get what they want exemplify this approach. In the distal mode and at the international level, there are some politicians, bureaucrats, and diplomats who suggest that nation-states should pursue national

(Don Hammond/DesignPics)

This couple is engaged in a proximate mode argument. Both are very emotional, and the man may be using an aggressive approach. What approach is the woman using? Is she also being aggressive and just waiting for her chance to get back at her partner? Is she trying to avoid the conflict?

interests aggressively. In other words, an aggressive approach is explicitly advocated as being desirable and necessary. Other political leaders, however, might support the avoidance or collaborative approaches.

At a variety of levels, there are people who are aggressive in a proximate mode but would reflect negatively on this approach. There are also people who have a Hobbesian view of the world and believe that it is important for people to be aggressive in order to survive and prosper. Such people feel that those who do not believe in aggression are unrealistic and weak. According to conflict analysts Linda M. Johnston and Michelle LeBaron (2007), people using an aggressive approach will seek a win–lose solution, try to control the discourse, and use everything in their power to win.[3] We should note, however, that such an approach may be inappropriate and ineffective in situations of injustice.

Avoidance Approach

Conflict avoidance is an ambiguous term that varies with different aspects of conflict (see Chapter 1) and different levels. At the international level, for example, this approach is understood as preventing a war. There is also the question of what is actually avoided. At an interpersonal level, is it avoiding a clash that might result from a difficult conversation about something controversial? At an organizational or group level, does it mean stifling conversations that might be controversial? Is it a fear of confronting injustices or problems in the group? At an international level, does avoidance mean a commitment to the status quo? What is the relation to saving face?

When discussing conflict avoidance, it is important to be clear on what understanding of conflict is being avoided. As is evident from earlier parts of this book, conflict can play positive and negative roles in people's lives. For those who see conflict as associated with positive change and creativity, conflict avoidance can be perceived as a reluctance to enter fully into the dynamics of life. For those who associate conflict with psychological and physical suffering, avoiding conflict is tantamount to evading pain. A distinction must also be made between not getting into conflict situations and refusing to deal with conflict when it presents itself. Each approach to understanding conflict in Part II also casts the conflict in a different light—if there are emotional memories involved (see Chapter 6), avoidance might mean holding these in abeyance. If the conflict is an issue of political power (see Chapter 8), avoidance might mean reducing the risk of losing power.

People can avoid conflict actively or passively. On the active side, they can go out of their way to avoid people with whom they have a problem. If they do interact, they can vigorously guide the conversation into areas where conflict potential is minimal. If a conflict is about to start, they might actively withdraw from the situation. Another active method is to be pleasant or conform to the needs and interests of the other party (this practice is similar to accommodation, but the motivation is different). Some cultivate a congenial personality as a way of eluding what they regard as unpleasant conflict. On the passive side, people can remain quiet or refrain from getting involved. Avoidance is also a matter of degree. Some people are averse to conflict and consistently steer away from any kind of clash. Others are selective; they will avoid only certain types of conflicts or conflicts with particular people. In some cases, they may simply say that they do not have time to take up certain issues (e.g. "I want to choose my battles.").

The motivations for conflict avoidance are diverse. For some, it is fear rooted in personal hurt, insecurity, or emotional memories of victimization in a previous conflict (Holoway, 2008). In this case, people will go to considerable lengths to avoid conflict. For others, it is a fear of losing the conflict or having to change. Another motivator is a value system that conceptualizes conflict as a bad thing. Avoidance, then, is a strong orientation.

As with aggression, there may be incongruity between style and orientation in the avoidance approach. Some people may exhibit conflict-avoiding behaviour as a matter of style; however, they do not care about whether conflict is good or bad and are not particularly afraid. They just feel that they will get ahead and have a better life if they simply mind their own business. Others may have an open and confrontational style but believe that conflict is terrible and to be avoided; after a conflict, they feel guilty about being drawn in. Another aspect of conflict avoidance is prevention, where a strategic plan identifies potential red flags before there is a conflict. These areas may be addressed either discreetly or openly in a constructive manner so that no conflict occurs.

When it comes to the group level, avoidance works in two ways. First, groups develop a culture of avoidance so that internal conflicts do not occur. This culture could be the result of a lack of competence or confidence in addressing issues. Second, at the inter-group level, conflict avoidance has different connotations depending on the context. If the groups have a history of ethnocultural antagonism and violence, conflict avoidance is similar to violence prevention. Another situation is that of a complex conflict involving group identities. Conflict in one area of life could have implications for another set of social relations; therefore, efforts could be made to avoid conflict in the secondary context. Such was the case of the Hicksite and Orthodox Quakers' conflict in 1827 (Cavey, 2000). The Hicksites wanted to preserve the mystical, non-hierarchical, and inclusive tradition of the Quaker movement while continuing to be vitally involved in social issues. The Orthodox group elevated the scriptural authority of the movement and advocated a more hierarchical and evangelical approach. The conflict affected the levels of Quaker meeting (church organization), kinship groups (families might have members in each group), and socioeconomic groupings. The schism could have potentially divided families. However, Verna Cavey (2000) points out that conflict avoidance prevented this outcome:

> The conflict style of avoidance was effective in preserving family relations, so that many Quakers used the techniques of silence, patience, and tenderness to avoid confrontation with separated kin. Conversations were kept to safe topics of weather, gardening and strawberry preserves, as Quakers struggled to find ways to communicate during an awkward period following separation. As a result, most familial ties were maintained, although it is acknowledged that in some cases Quakers did migrate away from meeting, neighbourhood, and family tensions. (p. 142)

Accommodating Approach

The accommodating approach involves actively trying to reduce the level of conflict by fulfilling the interests and desires of the other party. Why and in what circumstances might this be the chosen approach? To address this question, we will introduce Party A (the one accommodating) and Party B (the one being accommodated). The answers lie in the nature and character of Party A, the nature and character of Party B, and the relationship between the two parties.

In one instance, Party A is in a long-term relationship with Party B. The parties can neither avoid one another nor avoid the conflict. The interest in preserving the relationship is more important than the issues involved in the conflict, so Party A accommodates Party B. In another instance, Party A has been taught to put others' interests before his or her own. Party A accommodates Party B in order to be true to this teaching. Accommodation could also be expressed as love, whereby Party A obliges the interests of Party B out of this emotion. Note that this action does not exhaust caring responses—sometimes the most caring thing is to confront (Augsburger, 1981). In a third instance, Party B is a powerful figure and has a fierce temper. Out of fear of being hurt when Party B is provoked, Party A accommodates Party B's interests. This could be the approach of people whose partners have violent tempers.

Because Party A and Party B could be collective or individual entities, the examples work at different levels. When it comes to groups, accommodating differences to reduce conflict can be controversial, especially when ethnic and religious differences are involved. In Quebec, this approach became a political issue resulting in the government-sponsored Bouchard–Taylor Commission on Reasonable Accommodation (Bouchard & Taylor, 2008). In its report, the commission made 37 recommendations, including the following with regard to government employees wearing religious symbols:

- judges, Crown prosecutors, police officers, prison guards and the president and vice-president of the National Assembly of Québec be prohibited from doing so;
- teachers, public servants, health professionals and all other government employees be authorized to do so. (p. 271)

This policy recommendation promotes a balanced approach to accommodation of differences. However, even attempts at accommodation cannot always resolve differences, and the controversies over the wearing of the hijab continue in Quebec.

American political scientist Gene Sharp (2003) has a distinct view to accommodation in the context of what he calls acute conflicts. Suppose there is a repressive regime that has no interest in accommodating the demands of opposition groups. However, if these groups' non-violent actions render the regime vulnerable, it will be non-violently coerced into accommodating these demands through some form of compromise. This theory is discussed in more detail in Chapter 16.

Compromising Approach

The compromising approach acknowledges that there are real clashes of positions, interests, and desires that cannot be avoided. There is no real attempt to run away from the problem or comply immediately with the demands of the other to avoid conflict. Instead, there is a sense that each position might have validity and that the best approach is for each side to relinquish some aspect of what they want out of the situation. If each side compromises, neither will have won or lost. If anything, the compromiser wants to avoid there being a clear winner or loser.

The compromising approach is moderately low on both the amount of energy put into the conflict and its resolution. There is a willingness to concede something to the other, but it is contingent on the other party conceding something as well. As an approach to conflict behaviour, compromising includes a good deal of variation, such as

- actively working to find a compromise by proposing some concessions contingent on the other reciprocating;
- passively waiting until the other side is willing to make a concession and then reciprocating; and
- proposing a variety of options that include compromises on both sides.

With regard to orientation, there are many people who believe in the importance of compromise. It is a value to them that seems fair. There are others who are oriented toward avoidance and use compromise as a means to get the conflict out of the way. Still others are oriented toward aggression and want desperately to win. When they realize that they cannot get everything they want, they resort to a compromise approach to limit their losses. With regard to mode, there are people who are proximate compromisers; without thinking, they naturally look for a compromise when faced with a conflict. Others are distal compromisers, meaning that, when they reflect on the situation, they make a conscious decision that compromise is the best approach.

Collaborative Approach

Compromise and collaboration depend on an engagement between parties. Both can occur with the parties to the conflict being the only actors; however, they may also involve third parties who work as mediators, facilitators, or leaders of another process to enable

(CP PHOTO/Jonathan Hayward)

Former Canadian prime minister Paul Martin and premiers pose for photographs after signing a new health care deal on 16 September 2004. Canadian federalism is a constant negotiation between the federal government and the provinces. While compromising is the dominant approach, hard bargaining and true collaboration are also practised.

the parties to manage, resolve, or transform the conflict that divides them. While the compromise approach is best qualified as a willingness to compromise, the collaborative approach is a joint enterprise aimed at finding a win–win solution, rebuilding the relationship, or clearing up the misunderstanding.

Collaboration can be expressed as a style and an orientation. Some people immediately start asking questions about the nature of the conflict: What is really going on here? How did it start? What are the roots of the conflict? What can be done about it? They recognize that the best answers come from the parties involved and so take the initiative to establish communication and engage the other in a process that will provide the best possible outcome, which is occasionally a win–win solution. They may exhibit this style for pragmatic reasons because it seems to work for them.

With a collaborative orientation, there is a commitment to work together with the other party. If someone has studied interest-based negotiation, for example, he or she will want to establish the interests of the different parties and try to find a creative solution that will accommodate the different issues. There may be a value dimension to this orientation; people may believe that collaboration is the best way and exhibit the approach out of moral duty.

While these five approaches were developed to describe how people handle conflict, negotiation specialist Raymond Saner (2005) uses them to discuss how people behave in negotiations. He observes that good negotiators can operate effectively with each approach as needed, depending on the circumstances. In this regard, there can be a discrepancy between the approach that a negotiator thinks he or she is using and how it is perceived by others. The more expert the negotiator, the greater congruence between what is thought to be projected and how it is perceived. Saner also uses these styles to map the progression of negotiations, which occasionally begin with collaboration but deteriorate to avoidance and a breakdown in negotiations.

Non-Action/Non-Striving Approach

Non-action is described and advocated within Taoist, Buddhist, and Hindu thought as potentially the wisest course to follow in any particular conflict situation. This approach is not the same as conflict avoidance or accommodation, nor does it mean passivity. On the contrary, it claims that taking no overt action is seen as a form of action.[4] Like the aggressive and avoidance approaches, this approach does not depend on the actions of the other party. Like the compromise and collaborative approaches, non-action may show respect for the position, interests, and attitudes of both parties.

Arriving at a point where non-action is possible demands a high level of self-consciousness combined with a value system that diminishes the importance of acquisition of things, positions, or other items associated with interests. Letting go of desire allows one to detach from many aspects of the conflict—memories, interests, desires, emotions, and impulses that led to the conflict in the first place. Detachment also extends to potential gains. By not pursuing action to achieve any particular result, new realizations, understandings, and insights are possible. This approach requires willpower; various forms of meditation in Eastern traditions are designed to achieve both detachment and self-discipline.[5]

Non-action takes on meaning within a context that recognizes a distinction between receptive- and power-oriented kinds of energy. Receptive (ying) energy shows openness to new possibilities and to an understanding of the other. Power (yang) energy is inclined toward asserting the self and, in the extreme, dominating the other. Non-action can be understood from both these perspectives. As an expression of receptivity, it allows a party to wait for something new to happen or for the other party to change. As power, it shows a capacity to withstand the temptation to use harmful aggression or imitate the conflict-prone actions of the other party.

Non-action may be expressed through different styles and orientations. For some, non-action as a matter of style may represent what comes easy. For others, it represents a discipline arrived at through years of meditation and growth in self-awareness. People might choose a non-action orientation as a result of careful thought. They become committed to this approach as a matter of principle or choose it as the best option in a given situation. In the case of people with a high level of emotional intelligence and awareness, this option may the easiest to appropriate. In other cases, especially where emotions are screaming for an aggressive approach, non-action may be the most difficult approach to adopt. What qualifies for non-action is (non-) acting with a full awareness of interconnectedness among beings, events, and thoughts and a detachment from particular ends. The Chinese concept of *wu-wei*, translated as non-action or non-struggle, is developed within Taoism as flowing with energy or movement inherent in a situation (Kohn, 1992, p. 50).

An example of non-action involves Steve Bell,[6] a Canadian singer-songwriter and son of a Christian minister. As a young adult, Bell started singing in bars, exemplifying many behaviours at variance with his upbringing. His father came to the city where Bell was performing, but he said nothing about his gig. One evening, he arrived at the bar to see his father sitting at one of the tables. There was the potential for a conflict over values. After the evening, Bell's father said nothing—there was no judgment. He had been engaged in the situation but took no overt action in response. His presence was what was important.

Introducing non-action as a concept that is rooted in ancient thought and practices of Southern and Eastern Asia illustrates how attitudes toward and behaviours in conflict are shaped by culture. Having examined key behavioural approaches, manifest as style and orientation, we will now look at how people approach conflict at different levels of consciousness.

LEVELS OF CONSCIOUSNESS

As we discussed earlier in this chapter, the distal self has a capacity to reflect on conflict, on how it affects him or her, and how he or she wishes to respond. With this information, cognition can trump emotion as the primary determinate of behaviour. Self-awareness is also expanded or limited by one's level of consciousness. Each level represents a stage of development with its own capacity to handle complexity. We have already made the case that conflict is a complex clash of values, identity needs, interests, positions, world views, and historical baggage over a host of issues. Many of these aspects can be present at the same time. There is also a context that includes the participation of other parties who could profit from the continuation of the conflict. Non-rational factors, such as chosen traumas, demonization, and mimetic desire, can also enter into the situation. Irrational factors are present in the form of mental illness and delusions caused by mind-altering substances. In other words, many factors in conflict can make for a complex situation.

In the early twentieth century, Swiss developmental psychologist Jean Piaget (1896–1980) showed how children develop cognitively through a number of stages (1932, 1952). Since then, several researchers have focused on the idea of development levels. Applying Piaget's stages of development to morality, American psychologist Lawrence Kohlberg (1981, 1969/1984) did extensive tests on moral issues and identified a number of levels of moral development. American psychologist and feminist Carol Gilligan (1982) contended that Kohlberg's stages had a strong male bias and identified corresponding levels for women. Building on the work of psychologist Clare Graves, Don Edward Beck and Christopher C. Cowan (1996) came up with a model of spiral dynamics, arguing that people develop consciousness through an evolving spiral that adds the capacity for complexity with each turn. Meanwhile, developmental psychologist Robert Kegan (1982, 1993, 2001) spent decades developing a more sophisticated classification of levels of consciousness, along with an elaborate measuring process that allowed for accurate assessment of individual development. Subsequently, conflict resolution specialist Richard McGuigan (2006, 2012) applied Kegan's methodology to conflict. McGuigan demonstrated that people with a more developed level of consciousness could deal constructively with more complex conflicts. He also showed that, when conflicts are too difficult for people to handle, they regress to a less developed level of consciousness.

Developmental stages are a function of the capacity to identify with others and to accept the guidance of law and normative principles without falling into a debilitating legalism. With regard to identification with others, the initial stage is narcissistic. That is, there is a preoccupation with the self, and the interests, feelings, and experiences of others are inconsequential. As consciousness develops, there is an ever-expanding sense of identification with others. This developmental concept is similar to concepts developed by Morton Deutsch, James Jasper, and Vamik Volkan, social psychologists whose work is significant in the field of conflict studies. Deutsch (1973) introduces the concept of scope of justice. When one is concerned with seeking justice, is it for the sake of oneself, one's family, or one's kinship group? Does the scope include one's enemy? Similarly, Jasper (1997) shows how the history of protest crowds has included a development from protesting the suffering of one's family to that of people with whom one identifies and to that of people who have no voice and are unrelated to the protesters. Each level shows growth in consciousness. Volkan (1998) uses the metaphor of the identity tent—how far do the boundaries of this tent go? Who is included in one's sense of identity connectedness? One way of framing consciousness is to say that, the more developed the level of consciousness, the broader the scope of justice and the more inclusive the identity tent.

At a very basic level, the attitude toward law and principles includes a sense of capriciousness. The self initially decides what to do and how to respond on a whim. With development, there is an awareness of consistency, mutual agreement, and principle. At a collective level, there is development to the rule of law, which gains primary importance at a certain stage. One of the factors for Mikhail Gorbachev's refusal to use power capriciously within the Soviet system was his commitment to rule of law. His insistence on this principle played a key role in his loss of power, but it contributed greatly to the collapse of the Soviet Union and the end of the Cold War.

People's approaches to conflict can be seen as a function of their level of consciousness. In the remainder of this section, we consider some of the more prominent levels, showing how the response to conflict varies with each.[7] As previously mentioned, the first stage is the narcissistic one, where "It's all about me and my perspective." This preoccupation is evident in children. Its extension into adulthood may be the result of development being stymied or narcissistic wounding, in which the hurt caused by a traumatic event or violent conflict leaves such severe emotional scars that victims cannot think of anything but their own hurt (Moses, 1990). At this level, people want to get ahead and protect themselves from being hurt by injustice, exploitation, or loss. In a conflict situation, there are immediate reactions, usually very emotional. Arguments are based on one's own perspective; there is little empathy for or consideration of another perspective.

At the tribal level, people primarily look out for their own group.[8] This concern may be for a kinship group, ethnic group, linguistic group, religious group, or a community of people who share the same values and identify with one another. Peg Neuhauser (1988) has developed a concept of tribal warfare within organizations that shows how various divisions in a business, organization, or bureaucracy can work for their own group self-interest to the detriment of the larger entity. Where tribe-based societies still exist, it is possible for members to be at many different levels. Some may put their own tribe or kin above all other values.

At the rational–legal level, people are mainly guided by a set of principles. What flows logically from these principles or laws is what they find acceptable. They are committed to fairness, but this fairness is defined according to their values. Within their frame of reference, they can accept the legitimacy of other perspectives, as long as they logically align with their principles. Arun Gandhi (2003) provides an interesting example in the context of living in an ashram with his grandfather, Mahatma Gandhi. At the time, the elder Gandhi charged five rupees for his signature, which was in high demand. Arun desperately wanted a signature because everyone else was getting one. He tried to trick his grandfather into signing something for him, but the elder Gandhi refused to sign. "But

I am your grandson!" was the argument. Mahatma Gandhi was firm: even his precious protégé had to follow the same rules as everyone else. This lack of special treatment corresponds to a rational level of consciousness that insists that laws and rules apply to everyone.

At the pluralistic level, people accept that there are different value systems and sets of principles. They are committed to tolerate diversity as long as it does not impinge upon them too negatively. Tolerant coexistence is the order of the day. In fact, toleration itself becomes a value and a principle. Scholars such as McGuigan (2006) associate postmodernism with this level, insofar as there is an advocacy for tolerance, even valuing, the narratives and world views of many groups that diverge from a more mainstream Western perspective.

Some people go beyond simply tolerating the existence of other perspectives. They are empathetically understanding, meaning that they have a capacity to enter into the world view of those radically different from themselves. They can identify the other's values and come to see how, within the other's perspective, it makes sense to express certain feelings and reactions.

Finally, according to some people, there are higher levels of consciousness such as interconnectedness and transcendence. In the former, one starts to sense profound associations among many divergent perspectives and approaches. The mutual influences of many factors are appreciated. One can not only enter into other perspectives but can also see how they connect with many other entities. Much of complexity theory expresses this level of consciousness. The transcendent level features a belief that there is a reality that pervades, includes, and goes beyond what can be comprehended of its individual parts. These parts each have a role to play; however, the whole is greater than their sum. There is also a sense of unity with all that exists.

People at every level of consciousness have a capacity to continue to experience and understand all the levels that they have already encountered. However, those at the less developed levels cannot understand or perceive reality as experienced by those at more complex levels. Each approach plays itself out in a different way at each level. With an awareness of these levels, one can better appreciate the diversity of ways that people deal with conflict.

TACTICS

The potential outcomes of a conflict can be quite complex, depending on the objectives of the parties involved. For example, a person might want to obtain the object that is at the heart of the conflict, prevent the other party from obtaining it, or reduce its value so that, if the other party wins it, it is a hollow victory. In order to achieve any of these objectives, each of which will likely diminish the position or interests of the other, there are a variety of tactics that can be used. Of the 13 tactics described below, the first 7 were used in a pilot research study by Johnston and LeBaron (2007).

1.   Ingratiation: The main goal in this tactic is gaining the favour of the other party. Gifts, compliments, and special recognition figure into the specifics. The biblical story of Esther is a good example of ingratiation. Esther was in the harem of King Ahasuerus of the Medo-Persian Empire. Haman, a senior public servant, had devised a plot to kill many Jews and got the king to sign off on the plan. Neither man knew that Esther was Jewish. She hosted dinner parties with the king and Haman, thus ingratiating herself to both of them. During the third party, the king asked if there was anything he could do for her; she asked for help for her people. The truth of the plot was revealed, and Haman was punished.

2.   Sarcasm: Johnston and LeBaron (2007, p. 6) define sarcasm as the offering of a jibe that is intended to mock, sneer, or taunt the Other. Sarcasm is often ironical, satirical, or humorous but usually contemptuous. Its intention is to upset, intimidate, gain power over, or even embitter the Other toward the party. It is most effective when the Other is already sensitive to comments made by the party, is insecure about their relationship to the party, or when the party has power and/or control over the Other. Sarcasm in any form can throw the other party off, thus giving an edge to the person using this tactic. Related to sarcasm is any form of humour that diminishes a person.

3.   Guilt trip: As Johnston and LeBaron (2007) point out, the basic message of the guilt trip is that a person did something wrong. If the guilt trip works, the one using the tactic has a strategic advantage in what follows. The person feeling guilty will think he or she owes something to the other party. This tactic is a key element in many protests.

4.   Shame trip: A shame trip conveys the message that a person is bad. Johnston and LeBaron (2007) write: "Shaming tends to leave the victim not wanting to approach the person who did the shaming because it involved the direct attack to his or her personhood. Shaming involves a sense of worthlessness and powerlessness accompanied by a sense of being exposed" (p. 3). Researchers have found that an initial response to shame-trip tactics is that the person tends to withdraw, giving the shamer a temporary advantage. However, the shame could turn into resentful anger and result in conflict intensification (see Tangney, Wagner, Hill-Barlow, Marschall, & Gramzow, 1996).

5.   Persuasive argumentation: When one party has an advantage because of superior verbal skills, a commanding presence, expertise, or inside knowledge, he or she can present overwhelming arguments for his or her particular case. This strategy can provide great advantage in a conflict, especially if the other party has been caught off-guard and has not had time to reflect on the issues. This may take any of the remaining eight tactics, in which the interested party gets the other to "lower his/her aspirations through a series of logical or seemingly reasonable appeals . . . [or] do things that are in the Party's best [interests]"(Johnston & LeBaron, 2007, p. 8).

6.   Threats: A party to a conflict could also use threats to achieve his or her objectives. These threats could involve direct violence or indirect harm through changing circumstances. A favourite method in organized crime and corporate domination is to threaten to lower prices to the point where a small competitor would be forced out of business. Threats can be clearly expressed or implied (e.g. "If you know what is good for you, you will . . .").

7.   Irrevocable commitments: This tactic involves a party forcing the other's hand by pushing the boundaries of a conflict in a way that has negative consequences for the other. For example, Party A has a piece of property with many trees that he knows Party B would like to buy. He asks a high price, which Party B thinks is unreasonable. Party A claims that, since Party B is not willing to pay the asking price, he will have to clear the land for other purposes and starts cutting down the trees. Because the trees are a central feature of the land for Party B, she is under pressure to come up with the full price or risk never owning the property.

8.   Domination/Intimidation: Domination can take many different forms. It can include a strong physical presence with the implied threat of harm. It can be economic or legal or manifest through a dominating spirit. For example, employees might not disagree with their employer because they lack the courage or self-esteem or because they are afraid of losing their jobs. Where there is rampant sexism or racism within the culture, a particular member of the dominant group could assert him- or herself, knowing that there would be societal support.

9.   Selective use of rules: A variety of principles, norms, or laws could apply to a particular conflict. One party could continuously refer only to those that are in his or her best interests. Some of these rules might pertain to identity legitimization. One example of this tactic occurred during a joint art project of Palestinian and Jewish women in Boston (Metz, 1990). The Palestinians claimed that there was no such thing as a distinctive pan-Jewish culture—there were German-Jewish, Polish-Jewish, American-Jewish, and other ethnospecific Jewish cultures. The Jewish women argued that there was no such thing as a distinct Palestinian culture— there was only Arab culture that subsumed things Palestinian. For each party, admitting the validity of the other's identity would, in effect, offer some validation to the other's claim to the Gaza Strip. Each group tried to formulate rules to determine what constituted a culture, thereby enhancing its particular side and diminishing that of the other.

10. Playing the victim: This tactic focuses on a party's suffering. If the suffering is significant enough, it can silence the rival—for example, "Who could criticize Party A after what he went through?" Within the Middle East, both Israelis and Palestinians draw on their narratives of suffering to enhance their positions. As a result, dialogue between the groups is very difficult.

11. Use of memory: Recalling all the negative words and actions of one's rival is another way of achieving one's objectives. This strategy could have the effect of

guilt-tripping or shame-tripping the other. Use of memory is often a factor in marital conflict. When Party A does something that upsets Party B, Party B recounts similar past instances. In response, Party A dredges up weaknesses and failures of Party B, and the conflict intensifies until every issue from the past is on the table.

12. Use of imagination: Highlighting the dire consequences of the other person's perspective is also a conflict tactic. In this method, any positive consequences would be minimized and the risks maximized. The result would be to diminish the value of the other's position.

13. Lateral violence: Members of an oppressed group may turn on one another, undermining any who might be getting ahead. This strategy is referred to as the crab bucket effect—where crabs in a bucket prevent one another from escaping. Lateral violence may take the form of gossiping, innuendo, insults, public disgrace, or the formation of cluster groups in opposition to another community member.

When we consider the various approaches to conflict, we can see how they might manifest themselves through certain tactics. It is clear that the competitive, aggressively oriented person who is out to win would use any of these strategies. However, the thoughtless use of tactics might work against them. The victim of sarcasm or guilt trips could store up resentment and turn against the aggressive person in a surprise attack. The conflict avoider might use ingratiation as a way of avoiding conflict. When backed into a corner, he or she could retort with sarcasm or a guilt trip as a defensive measure. Playing the victim could work in some cases to avoid further conflict (e.g. "I have suffered enough; leave me alone."). The compromiser might use any of these techniques as a pre-negotiation strategy so that the solution is skewed in his or her favour. The accommodator could use some of these tactics against him- or herself so as to justify the accommodating actions.

COMMUNICATION

Communication plays a significant role in conflict. Perspectives are communicated from one party to another; misunderstandings intensify conflict; emotions are communicated through words, tones, and body language; events and how they are described and remembered are interpreted differently. Communicating can be considered an action, and certain misunderstandings a result of communication style.

Speech Acts

Paul Ricoeur (1981, 1990/1992) approaches communication from the perspective of action. In this case, Party A communicates with Party B through a speech act, which has three dimensions (see Figure 10.2). The **locutionary** dimension includes what is said and how it was said; the **illocutionary** dimension represents the intended consequence of the speech act; and the **perlocutionary** dimension represents the actual impact (i.e. the reaction of the person receiving the communication). Let us consider an example. Party A asks Party B why she was outside his son's bedroom on Wednesday night. The illocutionary dimension depends on whether Party A wishes to score a point through a rhetorical question or push Party B to provide an answer and perhaps give some incriminating information. Suppose that Party B deduces from the question that someone was outside the son's bedroom. This information leads her to figure out that it was a mutual friend, which explains why she could not find this friend on Wednesday night. Party B has an "aha" experience and is relieved. The actual impact is therefore totally different than the intended locution.

Conflict can occur when there is a discrepancy between the illocutionary and the perlocutionary dimensions of a speech act. In other words, people simply misunderstand one another's intentions and/or what was communicated. However, Ricoeur's analysis also applies to other forms of communication, such as texting. It is also important to note that the locutionary dimension includes both verbal and non-verbal aspects, such as actions, tone of voice, and facial expressions (Knapp & Hall, 2002). If Party A stepped forward in a menacing way while asking his question, part of the locution would be "Answer my question or you will be sorry." Our actions communicate emotions, intentions, or implied consequences. Likewise, our tone of voice and facial features communicate other messages. The perlocutionary dimension takes place simultaneously or immediately following the locution. A person's facial expression can indicate how he or she has received a message almost immediately.

Taking this analysis a step further provides other questions regarding communication. From a structuralist perspective, we could ask if the message really got through and, from a functionalist perspective, whether it had the desired effect (Wilson & Sabee, 2003, p. 4). The successful communication act includes accomplishing both. The illocutionary and perlocutionary dimensions partially align if the message was understood. They are

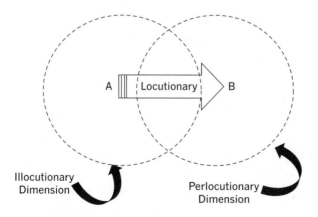

FIGURE 10.2 | SPEECH ACT

in congruence if it is understood and has the desired effect. Whether this balance occurs depends on communication styles, non-verbal communication, the communication and listening skills of each party, and the relationship (including attitudes and intentions) between the parties.

Communication Style

Psycholinguist Deborah Tannen (1986) has identified a number of communication styles that can contribute to conflict. In effect, she explores how the illocutionary and perlocutionary dimensions can become incongruent. For our purposes, we will look at three of Tannen's styles.

> Paragraph versus rapid interruptions: Some people talk in long paragraphs while the other listens respectfully and then responds in kind. Others offer short communication "bytes" that are quickly interrupted by the other party, creating a conversation that rapidly moves from one to the other. If a paragraph speaker tries to talk with an interrupter, he or she might take the interruption as a form of rudeness. The interrupter will take the lack of immediate feedback as a sign that the other is not listening.

> Empathy versus problem-solving: Some people communicate their problems for the sake of establishing relationships and receiving validation and empathy. Others communicate to convey information and get ideas on how to solve their problems. The empathy seeker can be quite annoyed by the problem-solver's advice. The problem-solver can be frustrated by the repetitions and statements of understanding from the empathic communicator.

> Metamessages: Along with the words that are said, there are other messages—metamessages—sent by the tone of voice, the context, or what is not said. For instance, a person receiving a critique of their writing might get the metamessage that the critic did not like the essay, even though that was never said. It could be that the critic thought that engaging in a thoughtful debate with the ideas in the essay was the highest form of praise. The contradiction between a message and the accompanying metamessage results in a double bind.

One example of how communication style plays a role in conflict is the conflict between Israeli Jews and Palestinian Muslims.[9] *Musayara* is an Arab style based on accommodation and involving repetition, indirect communication, and considerable elaboration (Maoz & Ellis, 2003). On the other hand, European Jews in Israel have adopted *dugri*, a style based on directness and characterized by logical assertions emphatically delivered with constant interruptions and rapid exchanges (Zupnik, 2000). It is easy to see how these different styles, which are also embedded with cultural values, could generate misunder-standings, stereotypes, and hurt feelings in encounters between the two groups.

Non-Verbal Communication

Communication is a dynamic process with constant non-verbal feedback. People nod, lift their heads, lean forward, and use a number of other subtle movements to give an indication of how they are responding to the locution of the other. Often there is reciprocity of both friendly and non-friendly communicative gestures. Mark Knapp and Judith Hall (2002, pp. 71, 83, 85) have examined research relating to non-verbal communication in great detail. They have found that those skilled in this area exhibit a high social and emotional intelligence and are warm, well adjusted, and cognitively complex. These skills are learned but are at the tacit level, meaning that we cannot quite put them into words. Generally, women are slightly more skilled than men, but in certain types of situations that pertain to their experience, men are better at reading non-verbal signals.

Non-verbal communication skills are on both the encoding and decoding sides of communication. Encoding means that we can add value to our verbal communication through our facial features, intonation, posture, and gestures. Decoding means that we can perceive non-verbal signals from the other party. For example, non-verbal signals can be used to indicate a sense of superiority or inferiority. Someone with a dominant attitude will have an overbearing posture, speak loudly, and be quick to turn attention to someone else. A person who feels inferior will send a message through a slumped posture, a deferring intonation, or perhaps silence. Human babies have shown a capacity to imitate certain facial and other gestures when they are only a few days old (Bouissac, 2003, p. 20). We continue to learn such expressions by copying what we see among those around us. Some gestures are so common within cultures that using a certain signal can indicate that one is at home in that particular culture.

Communication and Listening Skills

Language is intimately linked to culture. Words take on layers of meaning as they are used within a cultural context. The more a communicator is aware of the language and culture of the receiver, the better he or she is able to communicate effectively, whether in informal conversations or formal intercultural negotiations.

An important aspect of language is metaphor.[10] Many metaphors are embedded in ordinary language and carry with them layers of meaning. For instance, the word *up* designates a physical direction or an increase (e.g. in the stock market), but it is also used to talk about mood—"I am feeling up today" (Lakoff & Johnson, 1981). Many metaphors are directly related to conflict and are consistent with an aggressive style: "Those are *fighting* words"; "How can we *attack* the argument?"; "If you take my portion, I will *kill* you." Others are more similar to other styles: "How can we *patch* things up?"; "Could we agree to *put this behind us*?"; "I think we can *iron things out*." A skilled communicator uses metaphor and other aspects of language effectively. Attention to metaphor is important in understanding conflict. Metaphors can be a source of misunderstanding, such as when they are understood differently by the speaker and the listener or by people of different cultures. Metaphors can also be used to frame a conflict in a particular way. For example, a heated debate could be framed as a fight. Creatively using a new metaphor in a conflict can open up new avenues to explore.

A person sends many messages with one speech act. For instance, Party A says, "It is good to finally meet you in person. We seem to have had some misunderstandings in our correspondence, but I am sure we can work them out." The metamessages of these statements could be "Through face-to-face communication, we can be more effective"; "I value our relationship, so I am willing to put in some effort"; "Misunderstandings can be solved"; "It is better to work things out than to leave them alone"; or "You deserve credit for making the effort to come and talk about this problem." The metaphor "work them out" signifies that the misunderstandings are significant but can be resolved. These metamessages assume a culture in which direct communication is valued. They can also be communicated through tone of voice, welcoming gestures, or eye contact if such behaviour is considered culturally appropriate and understood to convey sincerity.

Listening is also an important part of the communication process. Just as the speaker is communicating many messages with the locution, the listener is picking up on a number of messages. One popular concept in conflict resolution circles is that of active listening, in which the listener indicates that he or she is both listening and understanding the message. Active listening can be accomplished by repeating the message (e.g. "What I hear you saying is . . ."). Another form of listening is empathic listening, which is listening for the speaker's emotions and passions (McLean, 2005, p. 37). In critical listening, one is attentive to the details, assumptions, and logic of the speaker (McLean, 2005, p. 38). A comprehensive approach is evident in the Chinese character for listening, which includes listening with your ears, eyes, heart, and undivided attention (see Figure 10.3).

FIGURE 10.3 | CHINESE SYMBOL FOR LISTENING

The section on the left denotes the ear. There are four sections on the right: the top one represents "you," followed by "eyes," "undivided attention," and "heart."

Source: www.mckenley-simpson.co.uk/inspiration/chinese_symbol_for_listen.php (accessed 12 Mar. 2011).

Listening also takes place within a broader cultural setting and a specific context. Depending on the latter, the literal meaning of the locution might not be the speaker's intention. The communication might be ironic, symbolic, rhetorical, or hyperbolic (Wyer & Adaval, 2003, p. 291). A listener must be able to pick up on the contextual clues to understand the speaker's intended meaning.

Relationship

The nature of the relationship between parties and what is desired in the relationship are important in the understanding of communication. For instance, one member may have excellent communication skills that allow him or her to achieve the goal of misleading, insulting, or betraying the other; however, this type of communication would not help the relationship. On the other hand, someone might mislead another person unintentionally while trying to be helpful. In other words, there is a behavioural and intentional aspect to communication. If one wishes to mislead and is successful, there is congruence between these aspects, but the problem may be relational. If one does not wish to mislead but does so, the problem is miscommunication. For example, Party A might say, with a suggestive inflection, "You might want to check out the stock of Company X." Party B might think that Party A has inside knowledge and is helping him as a friend; however, Party A might want to deflect attention away from Company Y, where there is good money to be made. In this case, Party A is trying to mislead Party B. If Party B loses money on the venture and confronts Party A, her response could be, "I never suggested that you invest; I just wanted you to check it out."

Aggressive communication is that which harms someone (Avtgis & Chory, 2010, p. 285). Social scientists attribute this type of communication to two causes: rational choice (getting back at someone because of an injustice) or a result of frustration. A third explanation is lateral violence brought on by mimetic desire—"Because you have something that I cannot have, I will try to ensure that you do not keep it or enjoy it." Verbal aggressiveness attacks the self-concept of the other and runs counter to the development of healthy relationships (Avtgis & Chory, 2010, p. 291).

Conflict management specialists Stephen Littlejohn and Kathy Domenici (2007, p. 112) have developed the concept of facework in relation to communication. Derived from the phrase "saving face," this theory includes the autonomy face (respect for one's independence), fellowship face (being included and accepted), and competence face (the sense of being able to make a valuable contribution). Many of the dynamics of conflict are explained through facework. Negative or destructive facework attacks the self, resulting in defensive reactions. Positive, respectful facework can help to mend broken relationships.

CONFLICT ESCALATION

The anatomy of a conflict includes a number of escalating stages (see Figure 10.4).[11] Let us consider an example. Suppose that Party A, a country that wishes to use an uninhabited

FIGURE 10.4 | ANATOMY OF A CONFLICT

Note: This figure resembles the representation commonly found in conflict studies literature. Swanström and Weissmann (2005) show a number of variations, including overlays of cycles in complex conflict situations where different conflicts occur simultaneously.

island for a communication tower, offends Party B, immediately triggering a reaction. Party B then takes a position against Party A, which includes all the reasons why the latter has acted unjustly and what changes need to take place, as well as a strategy that is consistent with Party B's behavioural approach. Each position reflects the interests of the party involved.

In the next stage, both parties use tactics to strengthen their positions. In the process, they might offend one another even more, thus intensifying the conflict. If violence is introduced by either party, it is returned with interest, thereby also escalating the conflict. The actions not only contribute to the behavioural side of the conflict, but they also have an influence on attitudes (see Mitchell, 1981). The parties develop stereotypical notions of one another, in which they frame themselves as being superior. Memories of past victimization, desires, and the dire consequences of the other side winning intensify these negative attitudes. If the actions threaten the identity of either side or harm those close to either, it becomes more likely that the affected party will become entrenched in its position.

Eventually, one side will win or the conflict will morph into what international mediator I. William Zartman (1989) calls a hurting stalemate. At this point, a number of things could happen. If the parties learn to live with the conflict, it becomes latent. There could be resentment and hatred beneath the surface, but the parties would coexist despite their hostile feelings. Another possible outcome is an intervention that generates negotiation, mediation, or arbitration. This result could settle some or most of the disputed issues (see chapters 11 and 12). If the attitudes continue, the conflict can be managed until another trigger event occurs and the conflict resumes. An intervention could also include conflict transformation and reconciliation, complete with apologies and gestures of forgiveness. Peace could be achieved, new relationships formed, and structures changed.

CONCLUSION

In this chapter, we examined four main factors that influence people's actions in conflict: behavioural approach, level of consciousness, tactics, and communication. We began by surveying the most popular approaches in the field of conflict studies and added the non-action approach, which is prevalent in Asia.

Along with these approaches, conflict behaviour is influenced by level of consciousness, specifically how people define their identities and the degree to which they can appreciate others' perspectives. Based on their approach and consciousness level, people also choose a variety of tactics to give them an advantage in conflict. Communication also affects conflict. While effective communication can help to resolve conflicts, miscommunication can intensify them. These four factors contribute to the progression of a conflict, particularly in its escalation and possible outcomes. For example, an aggressive approach or a miscommunication can exacerbate and/or extend a conflict. The next chapters continue our discussion of how people deal with conflict, particularly in terms of how conflict can be resolved, managed, and transformed.

DISCUSSION QUESTIONS

1. Choose a conflict in which you know the parties involved and try to determine each party's behavioural approach. How do these approaches affect the dynamics of the conflict?

2. Choose two public figures engaged in conflict. What do their statements regarding the conflict indicate about their levels of consciousness?

3. Which of the tactics listed in this chapter have you used in conflict situations? What tactics have been used on you? Discuss the success of both your and your rivals' tactics.

4. Create a hypothetical conflict scenario and write a short dialogue that illustrates how the conflict escalates through miscommunication.

5. Examine a current conflict from the perspective of Figure 10.4. Where would you place it on the graph? Give reasons to support your placement.

NOTES

1   This method is an adaptation of Robert Blake and Jane Mouton's managerial grid. See Blake and Mouton (1964); Kriesberg (2003, pp. 122–123); and Kraybill (2009).

2. Although they accept the behavioural categories developed by Thomas and Kilmann, some researchers are dissatisfied with the specific instrument. For example, having used the approach for years, Ron Kraybill saw certain weaknesses in the forced choice approach and a degree of cultural bias. Using the same five categories, he created the Kraybill Conflict Style Inventory (see http://peace.mennolink.org/resources/conflictstyle/index.html).

3.   In their study, Johnston and LeBaron defined the styles and had 20 professional mediators review their work. The authors then refined their definitions based on this feedback.

4.   Between 1991 and 1994, Robert Birt, then president of the Canadian Institute for Conflict Resolution, developed an approach to Community-Based Conflict Resolution and Third Party Neutral that was largely based on a Taoist framework. Birt is perhaps the first person to use the concept of non-action as a response to conflict in the West.

5.   We are grateful to Rupa Menon for her helpful comments on this concept from the perspective of the Hindu tradition.

6.   This example is used with Steve Bell's permission.

7.   The categories listed here are designed to relate to conflict in a straightforward manner. For comparative charts of developmental levels, see McGuigan (2006, p. 53) and Wilber (2000, pp. 197–217).

8.   This use of the term tribal is metaphorical and is not meant to suggest that people who identify with real tribes are necessarily functioning at this level of consciousness.

9.   We are grateful to Corey Gil-Shuster for pointing out this example to us.

10. For an effective overview of metaphors, see Lakoff and Johnson (1981).

INTRODUCTION

As we have seen in previous chapters, conflicts can be complex, with many contributing factors and a range of goals for the parties involved. The impulse to address a conflict may be based on a desire to settle issues, limit losses, restore relationships, answer nagging questions, or gain closure. In this chapter, we examine seven processes used to achieve these objectives: negotiation, **conciliation**, group intervention, mediation, arbitration, **adjudication**, and authoritative allocation. We also look at traditional, modern, and unusual methods. With each type, we discuss the various subgroups, characteristics, and applications.

ADDRESSING CONFLICT

Throughout history, every culture has had some means of dealing with conflict through a combination of councils of elders or wise individuals and a form of talking circle. During the Roman Republic, written law, professional courts, and legal institutions evolved, turning Western countries into law-based societies in which many conflicts are dealt with in court. More recently, alternative dispute resolution (ADR) processes—such as facilitation, negotiation, mediation, and arbitration—have been revived to address conflict outside a strict legal framework. Community-based methods may include informal means such as dialogue and talking circles. Each of these processes can reflect a variety of approaches, schools of thought, and emphases—from problem-solving to relationship-building and understanding. Some focus on feelings and others on material realities.

Dealing with conflict can be described in various ways. Dispute settlement focuses on finding agreement on contested issues that are subject to negotiation. Reaching a settlement involves finding common ground, which may start with identifying shared interests. Conflict resolution goes beyond settlement to deal with underlying issues that complicate the situation. The goal of intervention processes is also described as conflict management—keeping the actions associated with conflict within certain bounds such that the destructive elements can be minimized and contained—and conflict transformation, which involves a reorientation of the parties involved such that their relationship to one another and to the issues can proceed in a positive and constructive manner. Recognizing some of the limitations of the term *conflict resolution*, we will continue to use it as a generic term for the goal of peaceful ways to deal with conflict.

11 | PROCESSES FOR DEALING WITH CONFLICT

CHAPTER OBJECTIVES

This chapter will help you develop an understanding of the

- factors that need to be considered in the peaceful resolution of conflict;
- distributive and integrative approaches to negotiation;
- process of conciliation;
- dynamics of group intervention processes, including facilitation and dialogue;
- interest-based, transformative, narrative, and insight approaches to mediation;
- characteristics of and issues faced by third-party interveners/conflict resolution practitioners;
- roles of arbitration, adjudication, and authoritative allocation;
- traditional approaches to conflict resolution in indigenous cultures; and
- creation of modern integrated conflict resolution systems.

The use of resolution processes can be subverted for strategic gains. For those in a dominant position who find the status quo advantageous, there can be a demonstrable willingness to negotiate but never settle, to mediate but never find agreement. The processes can be used to buy time, entrench a situation that benefits one party, or even to flush out information that can later be used to strengthen a position. Similarly, weaker parties may wish to stall the resolution to strengthen their position or avoid an unfavourable settlement.

Resolution processes involve a number of distinctions. Some are conducted by the parties themselves, whereas others are led or assisted by third parties. Some processes occur informally through open conversations. Others, such as those in a court of law or public commission, are extremely formal. Some come about through chance encounter, while others take months of preparation. Some are motivated by pragmatic self-interest, others by necessity or a commitment to peaceful relationships as a value or matter of principle.

Processes have also been adapted for different levels of conflict. At times, the processes themselves might be complex, such as instances where several parties are involved in a conflict and there are numerous issues at different levels. For instance, a hostile encounter between rebels and a government could involve death, abduction, property destruction, and displacement of people. The cessation of hostilities, repatriation of people, reparations, new form of government, power-sharing, boundaries, and a host of other issues need to be the focus of negotiation, mediation, and other processes. In other situations, a particular conflict may be indicative of a larger one. For example, a local community conflict over a corporation's dumping of toxic materials includes larger policy issues at both the national and international levels. Within large organizations, conflict management systems use specific criteria to identify the type of conflict and the processes that should be used to address it. Conflict resolution specialists, such as mediators, are also trained to recognize the type of conflict and the appropriate resolution process.

Selecting and applying a resolution process can be a complex endeavour. In simple terms, a resolution process involves identifying the parties involved and their clashing positions, gathering and analyzing information, reframing the issues, generating resolution options, finding agreement on an option, ratifying the agreement, and implementing its conditions. Note that this process, shown in further detail in Table 11.1, can be guided by the parties themselves or by a third party. Each step might be relatively straightforward; on the other hand, each might be highly complex and time-consuming. Likewise, the process might unfold sequentially or cyclical, as new information might require revisiting what could be at stake or who might be critically involved. For example, in 1987 Prime Minister Brian Mulroney negotiated the Meech Lake Accord with the 10 premiers. During the three years of ratification, various Aboriginal leaders stated their displeasure at being excluded from the process. It was only when Manitoba MLA Elijah Harper held up ratification that the Prime Minister's Office began making overtures to Aboriginal people. By then it was too late, and the accord was never ratified. In this case, a failure to identify all parties had implications for the other steps in the process and changed the outcome.

TABLE 11.1 | THE BASIC STRUCTURE OF RESOLUTION PROCESSES

Step 1: Pre-Conflict Resolution Process: Identify the parties to the conflict.

Step 2: Determine the different positions and demands of the parties.

Step 3: Explore the different positions and their implications for the parties.
- What are the issues and problems to be resolved?
- What are the interests and motivations of the parties?
- What factors need to be considered to understand the presenting issues and propose solutions—historical, personal, contingent, systemic?

Step 4: Gather any necessary additional information.
- What resources can the parties use in the conflict?
- What are the limitations upon the parties?
- Are third parties needed to ratify any solution? What role might these parties play?
- If third parties are involved, do they have an interest in the resolution or intensification of the conflict?

Step 5: Reframe the issues so that the parties can generate solutions.

Step 6: Generate options for a possible resolution.

Step 7: Choose from the options and come to an agreement. This step may involve creating a hybrid solution from aspects of the different options.

Step 8: Consolidate the agreement and determine how best to verify its implementation and to follow up on the resolution.

NEGOTIATION

For centuries, people have been formally and informally negotiating their way through conflicts. Negotiation is a communicative process involving two or more parties with conflicting interests, needs, values, identities, goals, and rights. However, the parties also share a goal of reaching agreement regarding their particular conflict. The process of negotiation includes parties identifying what they want and need and determining together what each party will get. The latter component can be based on better understanding, a conception of justice, the creation of new possibilities, or the exercise of power—through pushing the issue or using force, deception, or tactics that provide a strategic advantage. The image of a negotiating table is frequently used to indicate that negotiations occur through face-to-face encounters at a designated place. However, the table may become a metaphorical way of talking about the negotiation context, as new software programs and online dispute resolution (ODR) allow for negotiation by electronic means (Kritek, 2002).[1]

Negotiations of difficult conflicts often take place in relational systems where parties are critically engaged with one another. In the examples given in Table 11.2, the parties' inability to reach a negotiated settlement can result in a third party assisting or deciding for them. In the case of the couple, decisions could be made by a judge. Labour management conflicts could go to binding arbitration. In an intranational conflict such as the one in Bosnia and Herzegovina, a solution was imposed through the Dayton Accords. However, the relational system does not demand that parties work toward a settlement or

TABLE 11.2 | EXAMPLES OF NEGOTIATION AT DIFFERENT LEVELS

Level	Example
Interpersonal	Married partners in the process of separating who have to decide on the division of their property and the custody of their children
Group	Collective agreement between a union and the management of a corporation
Intranational	Ethnonational groups trying to reach an agreement on constitutional changes that could avoid an insurrection or a secession
International	Countries attempting to develop clear goals for emission reduction in order to limit climate change

reconciliation. Examples include a boyfriend and girlfriend who break up over a conflict and go their separate ways; a customer in conflict with a corporation who simply shops at another store; and conflicts between provincial governments in which one side waits for an election so that they can deal with other leaders.

Over the last century, there has been tremendous growth in the theory and practice of negotiation. Two key approaches in the field are distributive and integrative negotiation. In the following sections, we examine both types, as well as the steps and specific dynamics that they entail.

Distributive Negotiation

In a **distributive negotiation**, there are a number of goods available and each party wants to maximize the number that he or she acquires. To illustrate this approach, let us consider Figure 11.1. Before the negotiation, Party A and Party B will each develop a negotiating strategy to achieve at least half of the goods available (indicated by point "y" on the figure). During the actual negotiation, different tactics can be used to gain advantages and ensure that this goal is met.

As part of the strategy development, both parties will also determine their **best alternative to a negotiated agreement (BATNA)**, the position that they would pursue if negotiations fell apart. Generally, the more favourable the BATNA, the stronger the position of the negotiators. For instance, a union that has the right to form a legal strike if it cannot reach an agreement is in better position vis-à-vis management than a union without this alternative. Therefore, negotiators try to find BATNAs that will give them more leverage and/or present their BATNA to the other party as more attractive than it actually is.

In Figure 11.1, point "x" represents what Party A would get without there being an agreement. By defining the BATNA, he or she can determine throughout the negotiation whether it is worth continuing. Suppose that Party B insists on getting significantly more than half the goods. If it becomes clear that the only possible agreement entitles Party A to a portion less than his or her BATNA, he or she can simply walk away from the negotiation and be better off. If one of Party A's tactics is to threaten to walk in order to get

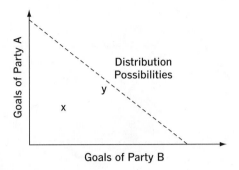

FIGURE 11.1 | DISTRIBUTIVE NEGOTIATION

Source: Adapted from Saner, R. (2005). *The expert negotiator* (2nd ed.). Leiden: Martinus Nijhoff, p. 91.

a better deal, it must be done when the offer is not as good as the BATNA, in which case Party A would be bluffing and would risk having the bluff called.

Integrative Negotiation

The concept of integrative negotiation emerged in the 1920s through the work of management expert Mary Parker Follett (1868–1933). Contrary to many of her contemporaries, Follett (1995) did not see conflict as an organizational pathology but as a normal occurrence of social life. She claimed that conflict can even be constructive because its successful management and resolution require the development of new attitudes and organizational innovations. While she preferred negotiation and compromise to the authoritative settlement of conflict, Follett believed that these methods still failed to address the underlying causes of conflict. She emphasized what she called the mutual gains approach to conflict resolution, encouraging parties in conflict to focus on innovative solutions that could be beneficial to both. Decades after her death, her ideas were revived by management guru Peter Drucker (1909–2005). However, it was the work of a group of outstanding individuals associated with the founding of the Harvard Program on Negotiation (PON) in the 1980s that brought Fowlett's methods to the centre of the emerging field of conflict resolution, particularly the theory and practice of negotiation.

One of the most influential books during this period was Roger Fisher and William Ury's *Getting to Yes*, first published in 1981. Central to their approach was interest-based negotiation, wherein negotiators identify their underlying interests and try to find areas of overlap that accommodate the interests of both parties at the same time (see Figure 11.2). Negotiators then work on expanding this shared interest area to craft an agreement that optimizes the possibilities for each party. Interest-based negotiation is an alternative to what Fisher and Ury (1981) call negotiation over positions, which is the practice of defining demands, trying to impose them through persuasion, deception, or intimidation, and compromising them if there is no way to predominate. *Getting to Yes* identified a number of key factors that would make interest-based negotiation work: separate people from

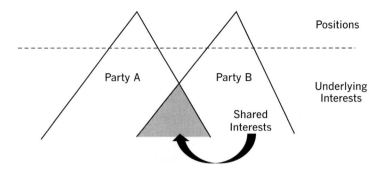

FIGURE 11.2 | SHARED INTERESTS

the problem, identify the interests, and use mutually agreed-upon objective principles or criteria to judge the options. The goal, then, is to find a win–win solution.

Integrative negotiation is based on the principles of fairness—finding a solution that is equitable—creativity, and optimization of benefits. Figure 11.3 retains the line of distributive possibilities but adds one for integrative possibilities. The latter is equidistant from each party, indicating that any point along the line would be equitable. The goal would be to proceed as far up this line as possible so that each party would get as much as possible. The section labelled increased efficiency indicates the added value of integrative bargaining.

Interest-based negotiation and integrative bargaining work from similar premises and toward similar goals. In each case, another level of analysis combined with a collaborative approach opens the possibility for a creative solution that benefits all parties. In order to maximize the potential for such an outcome, there must be an open exploration of

BOX 11.1 | INTEGRATIVE NEGOTIATION: A CLASSIC STORY

There are many parables for illustrating interest-based conflict resolution. One classic story, recounted by Fisher and Ury (1981) and Deborah Kolb and Judith Williams (2003), concerns two sisters who each wanted to make a cake that required an orange. However, there was only one orange available and the stores were closed. The question of who should get the orange led to a conflict, which escalated when past experiences of who got preferred treatment were mentioned. During the conflict, someone asked what cakes the sisters were making. The first sister said she was making fruitcake, which required the rind of a whole orange. The second sister was making a delicate chiffon cake, which needed the juice of an orange. By identifying their interests, the sisters realized that they could both use the same orange. In a distributive negotiation model, the orange is a zero-sum commodity; the solution would be for one sister to get the whole orange or for both sisters to get half. The integrative model, however, considered the orange's components. Through this analysis, a creative solution that met both sisters' interests could be found.

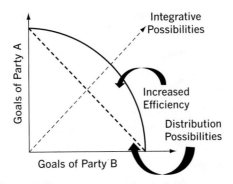

FIGURE 11.3 | INTEGRATIVE NEGOTIATION

Source: Adapted from Saner, R. (2005). *The expert negotiator* (2nd ed.). Leiden: Martinus Nijhoff, p. 91.

interests, desires, and needs. The goods available must be broken down into component parts—both tangible and intangible—so as to make a number of different combinations possible. Intangible parts might include the timing of the agreement, public recognition, guarantees, etc. Increased efficiency can be achieved by finding non-zero-sum components, elements that can be acquired by both parties. Information is an example of this type of component: if one party has the information, it does not mean that the other does not.

It is not always possible to find an optimum solution under an integrative bargaining approach. This reality does not stop parties from using an integrative approach in which they aim for fairness. In modern labour negotiations, for example, it is common for parties to agree to use an integrative approach but to retain the option of reverting to distributive negotiation. However, if either party shifts into a highly competitive distributive approach, the pressure mounts for the other party to reciprocate, sometimes thought of as "playing hardball." Some effort at persuasion may be necessary later if one party wishes to return to the integrative model—the argument being, of course, that both sides could be better off as a result.

Steps of a Negotiation

The following steps can be used in both the distributive and integrative approaches to negotiation. The process may be skewed somewhat, particularly if relations are hostile or some of the relationship-building aspects cannot be pursued.

Pre-Negotiation

Before negotiations start, there are certain things that must be settled—geographic location, venue, time frame, participants, and agenda. Whatever is decided on each of these matters could give an advantage to one party. For example, if the negotiation is between clearly identified groups with their own territory, negotiations held in one group's terrain could give strategic advantage to that group. If the negotiations are controversial, the potential of public protest needs to be considered if the time and place become public knowledge. The venue and how it is arranged are important as well. Do people sit at tables? If so, how are they arranged and who sits where? In some cultures, there is a great deal of significance attached to such things as who faces the door. In one negotiation between North Korea and the United States, the Koreans insisted on shorter chairs for the Americans, who tended to be taller. The Koreans did not want the Americans to have the psychological advantage of looking down on them. It is also important to have agreement on the date and time of the negotiations. Similarly, if there are teams of negotiators representing groups, each side must know in advance who will be part of the negotiations. In cases of hierarchies, it is advisable to make certain that people of similar rank or distinction are on each side. It is also useful to know who will make the final decision on what is negotiated. Finally, each side should agree on the agenda, or what is on the negotiating table.

Saner's Four Phases of Formal Negotiation

Raymond Saner (2005, p. 150–152) developed the following four phases of a formal negotiation: warming up; presenting positions; edging closer; and concluding or breaking down. In the warming-up phase, parties get to know one another, establish a good atmosphere, familiarize themselves with the venue (if it is a new place), and determine the scope, meaning, and intentions for the negotiations. In some cultures, such as those of the Arab world or Asia, this phase is most significant. During this phase, people explore networks of relationships, long-term desires, and background issues. If personal relationships are positive, the negotiations will often go much more smoothly than if they are negative. Generally, there is an open flow of information because it is in everyone's interest to understand what is at stake. The only information not shared might be that which could be used for a surprise tactic during the negotiation.

In distributive negotiations, the initial position and how it is presented is extremely important (Saner, 2005, pp. 56–60). One will demand more than one expects to receive, but how much more? That is the critical question. If one makes a completely unrealistic demand, one loses credibility, an essential quality in negotiations. If the initial demand is close to an anticipated solution and the opponent counters with a relatively higher demand, the resulting give-and-take and relatively equal compromises will favour the opponent. That is why the order of presenting is important. One tactic is to start first and use the opportunity to frame the negotiation in a manner in which your position seems most reasonable, supporting it with background information. Another strategy is to get the other party to speak first, therefore giving you important information that you can use to establish your position. When it comes to the initial exchanges, it is important to use the conditional tense: "If you could consider this, we might be open to that." People also sometimes use the "salami tactic," making only tiny concessions at a time and thus giving them a relative advantage (Saner, 2005, pp. 58–59).

During the edging closer phase, negotiators get creative in developing options. People explore the particular needs, desires, and interests of the other party, deciding how to give relative weight to bargaining options. If Party A learns that something that would cost him or her very little means a lot to Party B, it becomes an attractive concession to make. Different bundles of bargaining options can be put together if there is more than one item on the table.

If the negotiations have been successful and developed options that are acceptable to both parties, the negotiators will either find a way of choosing among the possible solutions or turn the decision-making over to those they represent. When a deal is agreed upon in a formal negotiation, it is documented and signed by the leaders of each side. In some cases, the agreement needs to be ratified through special processes. For example, a labour agreement might need to be approved by union members to take effect.

When there are no acceptable options, the parties may become deadlocked, meaning that there is an extended period of non-agreement and that no action (such as a deadline or special event) can move the negotiations ahead (Narlikar, 2010, pp. 2–3). Deadlocks can result from many factors. For example, negotiators may not be able to convince the group that they represent to endorse the deal. In many situations, there is a two-way negotiation—negotiators bargain with the other side in the formal negotiation and confer informally with the leaders of the groups they represent to persuade them to make the necessary concessions. In this kind of situation, saving face can be very important, especially if the leaders have made public statements in advance that limit negotiating options. A deadlock can lead to a delay, a stalemate, or a decision to break off negotiations (Narlikar, 2010). A stalemate might also become a hurting stalemate, in which the lack of an agreement causes harm, not benefit (Touval & Zartman, 1985).

Specific Dynamics of Negotiation

The dynamics of negotiation processes can be subtle and hard to discern. In this section, we describe shadow negotiations, uneven tables, and multi-party negotiations.

Shadow Negotiation

In *Everyday Negotiation: Navigating the Hidden Agendas in Bargaining*, Deborah Kolb and Judith Williams (2003) refer to shadow negotiation and hidden agendas.[2] Shadow negotiation refers to the fact that there are two parallel sets of dynamics in every negotiation. The first (and visible) set includes the issues presented for negotiation. The second concerns how the parties are doing in relation to the process: Who is controlling the dynamics? How is the process working for each of them? Hidden agendas refer to how the negotiations should be executed. This subject raises three interrelated questions:

- How does one effectively advocate for one's own interests?
- How does one build a collaborative relationship with the other party?
- How does one balance advocacy and connection?

Effective advocacy takes place from a position of strength in terms of negotiating capacity. Central to this strength is having the confidence to advocate with conviction and the ability to deconstruct countermoves by naming, interrupting, and re-directing them. This strength is enhanced by having options, including a well-developed BATNA. The idea of strength comes from a focus on oneself, while connection involves a focus on the other. Because shadow negotiation is all about what is hidden, careful attention to the other will reveal important aspects that might be concealed. Connection is enhanced by carefully listening to the story of the other, keeping in mind how one would feel in his or her place. Appreciating the situation, the feelings, and the face of the other (note the reference to facework in Chapter 10) creates an environment that is more conducive to collaboration.

Negotiating at an Uneven Table

There are times when the two sides in a negotiation are unevenly matched. Phyllis Beck Kritek (2002) has examined this phenomenon in great detail. For example, a negotiation could have experienced negotiators who are accustomed to standard practices on one side and a group with no negotiation experience on the other. Other instances include those used to having authority and a sense of entitlement opposite those who do not attempt to dominate the situation. Kritek uses the hospital setting, where doctors are used to being in charge and may override concerns of other staff members, as an illustration of this relationship. She points out that, while those who are disadvantaged feel the power discrepancy, those with advantages have trouble identifying the problem and doing something about it. If they do recognize it, they must decide whether to address or ignore it. If they choose the latter and use their advantages to the full, they must recognize that they are not trying to resolve the conflict but to win. Addressing the imbalance from the position of power is tricky because many actions could take the form of paternalism, which just reinforces the problem.

After describing some counterproductive ways of dealing with the situation through tactics such as manipulation, Kritek (2002, p. 335) presents ways in which those at a structural disadvantage can prepare themselves for negotiation. She develops what she calls ways of being that enable those in a disadvantaged position to hold their own at an uneven table. These methods include honouring their own integrity, drawing a line in the sand, expanding the context, innovating, and knowing when to leave.

Multi-Party Negotiation

If there are many parties in a negotiation, the complexity of the process increases. Every party has its own interests, needs, and goals. The perceptions of a conflict's nature and solutions might also vary considerably. Furthermore, there are dynamics regarding coalitions. Some coalitions form around particular desired outcomes, while others attempt to balance power dynamics—for instance, weaker parties might come together to oppose a dominant player. Constructive coalitions build bridges between groups or bring groups

BOX 11.2 | THE IMPORTANCE OF CULTURAL INCLUSIVENESS IN NEGOTIATION

From Kritek, P. B. (2002). *Negotiating at an uneven table: Developing moral courage in resolving our conflicts* (pp. 39–40). San Francisco: Jossey-Bass.

I once served on a statewide committee looking at maldistribution of health care services and hoping to alter this with changes in health care professionals' education practices. There were several Native American reservations in the state. Health care needs on these reservations were profound. Historically, these needs had been easily rendered invisible . . . An honest effort was made to change this pattern, to invite representatives from the tribal councils to the table. They attended the first organizational meeting.

The tribal councils, of course, had a well-developed model for deliberating on conflicts: requesting all parties to speak their mind on the issue one by one and uninterrupted, in a deliberative fashion; consulting the elders, seeking guidance from spirits that might help in the conflict; reflection. The approach to conflict offered by the statewide committee was open discussion and political posturing, a tug of war among competing agendas. The tribal representatives sat silently watching, saying nothing. Later one participant commented to me privately that the American Indians were sure not going to get their fair share if they didn't participate better. No one asked them to speak their mind during this time. They would only have had the opportunity to speak if they had chosen to participate in the competition for airtime. At the second meeting, they were absent.

with cross-cutting issues together. (Cross-cutting occurs when a potential solution brings together elements of a number of parties.) As groups are brought together, momentum toward an agreement builds, a process called logrolling. On the other hand, coalitions sometimes form to block a particular agreement (Hampson, 1995, pp. 41–48). Principles and process can play an important role. All the possibilities for either distributive or integrative negotiation apply. It becomes very important to articulate and consolidate small agreements along the way before moving on to the next phase. Finally, negotiations take place formally when all parties are together and informally when there are side meetings between two or more players.

In the international context, multi-party negotiation is a notoriously difficult process, which some authors have likened to herding cats (see Crocker, Hampson, & Aall, 1999). Discussions on trade and the environment are only two examples of multilateral negotiations that have extended for months, even years. Obviously, international negotiations are difficult because of the complexity of the issues and the number of participants. Moreover, any state can refuse an agreement if it is not satisfied, and many states have a formal or informal right of veto over negotiation proceedings.[3]

CONCILIATION

In its most general sense, conciliation is a process whereby a neutral third party works with those in conflict to settle their differences. In old diplomatic practice, the term was synonymous with mediation, but it is currently often used in relation to labour disputes. Parties involved in conciliation processes may meet directly, but it is not necessary. The conciliator may instead meet with the parties separately and convey messages between them. Conciliators can also play a lead-in role to mediation or arbitration, either trying to obtain an agreement early on or helping to negotiate the terms of the process. In this case, their role is similar to good offices, a term used in the international context (see Chapter 12). A conciliator may prepare a recommended compromise or settlement agreement, which becomes a legally binding contract if it is accepted by the parties.

Related to conciliation is the concept of gestures of conciliation, which Christopher Mitchell (2000) defines as the "first moves in major efforts to bring about the peaceful resolution of protracted conflicts in which adversaries have become enmeshed, and for which no generally acceptable solution appears possible" (p. xvi). Mitchell uses former Egyptian president Anwar Sadat's visit to Israel in 1977 as a key example of a conciliatory gesture. After nearly three decades of simmering and, at times, outright violent conflict between the two countries, this visit paved the way to an eventual peace process. In the same manner, parties in less intractable conflict can make gestures of conciliation to indicate a willingness to start a process aimed at resolution or transformation. A conciliator can advance the process by drawing attention to conciliatory gestures.

GROUP INTERVENTION PROCESSES

Conflict can sometimes pervade a group. There may be widespread disaffection with a group's leadership, a host of interpersonal rivalries resulting in lateral violence, or tensions between various groups within the same organization. Such conflicts need to be addressed by group processes, including facilitation and dialogue.

Facilitation

The word *facilitate* is derived from the Latin *facilis*, meaning "easy"; hence, the root concept of this process is to make something easy. In relation to conflict, facilitation processes are meant to assist people with clashing perspectives in working together to achieve common goals or understanding, usually by encouraging creativity. These processes also help to foster trust and build relationships (Jeong, 2010, p. 192). Facilitation as a process has a life of its own unrelated to conflict[4]; however it can play a key role in group intervention. Facilitated processes may take less than an hour or last several days. Those in the latter category include a series of built-in subprocesses.

Rather than making substantive decisions in the negotiation, a facilitator designs the gathering and facilitation processes (Ghais, 2005, p. 2). To prepare for both, it is important to assess the situation. This review could entail a social mapping of the situation to identify the parties, subgroups, affected groups, and people who could make a difference. From this information, the facilitator can determine how large the group should be. For everyone to have input and to have enough different voices present, the optimum number of participants in many facilitated processes is between 8 and 12. If there are larger groups involved, it is often important to have the option of dividing large groups into smaller optimum-sized groups, each with its own facilitator. If the conflict involves factions within a community, all of them should be represented in the facilitation. The gathering process involves both determining who should attend and extending a personal invitation, which can function as a way of framing the intervention for the participants and discovering the private concerns of the individuals involved.

The facilitation process itself begins with a context statement given by the facilitator or by the "client" who has asked the facilitator to intervene. Next, the facilitator presents the steps of the process with their anticipated time periods. He or she then gets a mandate to proceed with the process by asking the group whether it agrees to the agenda. If there is the possibility of highly disruptive behaviour, the facilitator may also establish some ground rules. For instance, if it is anticipated that some people will dominate the air time, the facilitator could stipulate that no one speaks longer than a certain amount of time and that, whenever two people wish to speak at once, preference will be given to the person who has not yet spoken.

A basic facilitation process involves brainstorming. The key to using this activity productively is to have an appropriate question. If there is considerable misunderstanding present among members of the group, they could brainstorm around the meaning of a key concept. The question would take the form of "What is the meaning of X?" In brainstorming, the emphasis is on the quantity of responses. Each idea is accepted without judgment and publicly recorded. Additional processes can include the theming of the brainstorming responses and the prioritizing of the themes. A brainstorming process could also start with a clarification question and continue with action questions. If there is a clear conflict present in the group, the question could take the form of "How did this conflict get started?" Participants could brainstorm various key events, and the facilitator could track them in historical order. In this manner, the group starts working together.

Edward de Bono (1992) has contributed enormously to the study of creativity and how groups can work together to find new solutions to problems. One of his key concepts is lateral thinking, which uses the creative side of the brain to make associations between indirectly related concepts. A facilitator will sometimes start a session with a word association process unrelated to the issue at hand, thereby getting the group to work together, establishing a positive mood, and stimulating the creative side of the brain.

Moving into the substantial portion of the process, the facilitator will use a sequential series of questions, each building on what came before. This method will be based on the assessment of the situation and the comments received during the gathering process.

If at all possible, the group should start accomplishing something early on so that the facilitator can build on the goodwill. Sometimes, it is important that the group handle a serious challenge. If there is an emotional outburst, for instance, the facilitator could get permission from the group to stop the flow of the process and introduce a subprocess addressing the role of emotions. Eventually, the process will lead to the generation of constructive options for the group to consider as a way forward. These possibilities could then be themed and developed as recommendations for decision-makers. If the group has to make a decision, it must decide on the rules for decision-making—is it through a majority rule or consensus? Facilitators have developed a number of creative processes to help groups decide on priorities. For instance, a number of options are described on separate sheets of paper attached to the wall. Participants are given a number of coloured adhesive dots, which they stick on the options that they value. At the end of the exercise, it is clear which option is the most favoured.

Dialogue

Deriving from the Greek words *dia* ("through") and *logos* ("word, meaning, reasoning"), the word *dialogue* refers to the free flow of meaning. As Figure 11.4 shows, dialogue is only one form of discourse. While debate includes an attempt to beat one's opponent, discussion can be used to analyze, oppose, or voice disagreement. Inquiry involves a curiosity about something, what it is or how it works.[5] Dialogue, however, has the potential to create meaning and mutual understanding.

Dialogue as a specific process was developed by scientist David Bohm (1917–92). Frustrated by the ongoing conflict between scientists Albert Einstein and Niels Bohr (each of whom had his own circle of followers who would not talk to the other), Bohm (1996) conceptualized dialogue as a process in which people would learn to think together. At the heart of the dialogue process is a reflective/reflexive process in which people learn to become aware of their own reactions to another person's comments. This awareness extends to mind, emotions, and body. For example, as someone speaks, the listener might have thoughts that contradict what is being said, note tension in his or her stomach, and feel sad or angry. The internal questions would include, Why is this happening to me? What does this reaction tell me about myself? Out of this awareness and consideration, the reflecting self would respond with whatever was deemed to be of most importance to the group.

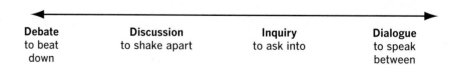

Debate	Discussion	Inquiry	Dialogue
to beat	to shake apart	to ask into	to speak
down			between

FIGURE 11.4 | TYPES OF DISCOURSE

CASE STUDY 11.1 | A GROUP INTERVENTION PROCESS: PROTESTER–POLICE CONFLICT

For a full account of this conflict, see Redekop, V.N., & Paré, S. (2010). *Beyond control: A mutual respect approach to protest crowd–police relations.* London, England: Bloomsbury Academic.

In 2000, I was asked to address a conflict in Ottawa between protesters and police. From the perspective of the former, the issue was one of repressive policing. To the latter, it was one of crowd control or management. I invited Shirley Paré, a retired military officer, to be part of my third-party team in order to create a sense of balance and neutrality. A number of group processes drawing on facilitation and dialogue were used. One was a three-day interactive seminar bringing both sides together. During the seminar, people were given a theoretical perspective and asked to work on it in small groups. One aspect was to present a scenario with a challenge: protesters and police worked together to find a way to manage a difficult situation without resorting to violence.

This facilitated seminar was also offered to police and protest leaders after the 2001 Quebec Summit of the Americas, at which a record amount of tear gas was used. As part of the approach, there was a **circle process** debriefing on the summit with protesters who had been at the receiving end of tear gas and police who had been active at the summit. Participants from both sides spoke openly of their experiences; at the end, their perceptions of each other had shifted.

Soon after, there was a G20 meeting of finance ministers scheduled for Ottawa. The chief of police asked us to use a similar process to prepare for the summit. We had only one evening for the process, which started with a dinner at which participants were assigned to tables of four—each with two protesters and two police—with questions to work on over dinner. We then met together, reviewed some insights from the previous seminar, and allowed all the participants to respond in an open manner. We agreed to reconvene after the G20 meeting to debrief the event.

During the G20, a number of things went wrong. An approved snake march was blocked. A Quaker grandmother was hit in the face by a police officer. A police dog got loose and attacked protesters. As a result, the Police Services Board convened meetings where protesters could present testimony of what had occurred. At the end of the last meeting, the chief of police announced that our debrief would be held the next day. This notice also made the French and English news.

We decided to welcome whoever would come. The result was a facilitated session with a group of over 80 protesters and 14 police officers. After approximately two hours of angry venting from protesters and some responses from police officers, the participants were asked to consider the following question: What recommendations would you make to encourage positive interactions between protesters and police? There were four flipcharts used for the facilitation, each with a scribe prepared to record ideas. In the end, we got 93 positive recommendations.

By drawing out the humanity of the parties, dialogue is useful in situations where there might be a deep philosophical clash of perspectives. The presence and initial instructions of a dialogue leader is key to a successful dialogue. Even if his or her interventions might be limited once the dialogue begins, he or she sets the tone and maintains a positive presence. The leader may also help to resolve the conflict by summarizing key points or using a summary to pose a question, thereby guiding the process.

MEDIATION

When parties are unable to negotiate a settlement on their own, they may turn to mediation. The term *mediation* comes from the Latin *medius*, which means "middle"—the root metaphor of mediate is to be in the middle. Mediation may be thought of as facilitated negotiation in that it involves the use of third parties to guide those in conflict through a process to resolve or transform the situation. More precisely, it is a process, led by a third party, that enables parties in conflict to communicate with each other as they explore the issues, generate options, and negotiate a mutually acceptable decision on how to deal with the conflict. Like negotiation, forms of mediation have been used for centuries. During the twentieth century, mediation processes became formalized and many organizations started to train mediators, resulting in some common practices. Generally, mediations are conducted in private and the proceedings are strictly confidential.

(AP Photo/Karel Prinsloo)

In 2007 and 2008, Kenya was afflicted by wide political violence as the partisans of the president and the opposition battled over the results of a national election. Former UN secretary-general Kofi Annan (centre) was called in to lead a negotiation between Kenyan President Mwai Kibaki (left) and opposition leader Raila Odinga (right). The dialogue process, held in Nairobi, led to an agreement and the lessening of tensions.

Examining the parts of our description will help to identify many of the issues related to mediation. The reference to facilitated negotiation draws attention to the fact that the process is made easier by someone whose focus is on the process itself. Like the various approaches to negotiation, mediation can be based on distributive or integrative negotiation. It also involves a series of steps that do not necessarily follow a linear pattern but can be cyclical.

The phrase "led by a third party" emphasizes that this person is in charge of the process. However, the outcome is very much up to the participants. Notice that this part of the definition did not include the word *neutral*. In many mediations, the mediator attempts or is required to be neutral so as to not have a bias that favours either party. Nevertheless, there are situations in which mediators might have a stake in the conflict's resolution, and in some cases it is important that the mediator be trusted by and perhaps have influence over one of the parties. This latter case is more common when it comes to international mediation. A mediator can also use different approaches. Some are laissez-faire, basically refereeing a negotiation but offering no suggestions. Others make suggestions, offer incentives, or pressure parties to make concessions and thereby move the negotiations ahead. Some mediators have particular expertise (e.g. knowledge of the law) that enables them to advise the parties on whether a proposal will withstand legal challenges.

An essential aspect of mediation is the communication between the parties involved. When parties are in conflict with each other, communication may be impeded by lack of trust, strong emotions, different communication or conflict styles, or a history of misunderstanding. Mediation allows each party to speak directly to the mediator in the presence of the other party, making communication easier. Through communication, parties in a conflict can begin to explore the relevant issues and generate possible solutions. The exploration of issues may include presenting contested subjects as well as letting the parties express their memories, interests, needs, desires, and visions of future consequences. The issues themselves may be analyzed according to the various components—material and intangible—or reframed by different words or sets of values. For example, two adult siblings may be in conflict over how to divide a number of paintings left to them by their artist parents. The mediator could reframe "paintings" as "objects made by the parents." The addition of toys made by the parents makes the division easier. How issues are explored changes with the approach taken by the mediator. Generating options may be conducted in a manner reminiscent of distributive negotiation or a highly creative process akin to integrative negotiation.

Finally, "agreeing on how to deal with the conflict" is deliberately vague so as to encompass many potential outcomes. It is possible that the mediation will allow for the settlement of the presenting disputes and resolve the underlying values. The process may transform the situation, including the relationship, or enable the parties to manage the conflict without resolving it, if they agree to disagree and keep their distance. The parties may be incapable of reaching a negotiated settlement, even with a mediator, and wish to

BOX 11.3 | THE TRANSFORMATIVE IMPACT OF A CREATIVE MEDIATOR

To illustrate how a mediator can make a difference in a conflict, William Ury (2010) likes to tell the story of three siblings whose deceased father left them 17 camels and the following instructions: the oldest should get half, the middle child one-third, and the youngest one-ninth. Frustrated by the impossibility of dividing the camels in this way, the siblings went to a village elder for help. She told them that she would donate a camel to the inheritance. The 18 camels were then divided into groups of 9, 6, and 2. The remaining camel was returned to the elder. By introducing some new information or reframing the situation, a mediator can help parties see their situation in a new light, enabling them to come up with a solution that they might not have discovered otherwise.

use arbitration or the legal system so that they will not have to make a decision. The goals of mediation can vary considerably depending on the relationship between the parties, the approach of the mediator, and the particular context of the conflict.

Along with our definition of mediation, there are others that emphasize a particular style. Kenneth Melchin and Cheryl Picard (2008) offer one that focuses on the strictly supportive and benevolent role of the mediator:

> Mediators hold no stakes in the content of the dispute. Rather they help disputants by managing the process. Their work is to open doors of communication and help parties recognize the legitimacy of the other parties' involvement in the process. They facilitate the process, expand resources, and help explore problems. They can be "agents of reality" to help construct realistic settlement frameworks. They can help educate participants in the skills of communication, and they can take some of the heat off disputants who are charged with the task of negotiating on behalf of others. They can exercise leadership in moving negotiations forward with procedural and, at times, even substantive suggestions. Flexibility and creativity are central features of mediation. (p. 41)

This excerpt suggests that a mediator's leadership role is limited to making suggestions. Note the difference in the following definition, regarding mediation in the context of violent international conflict, presented by Saadia Touval and I. William Zartman (1985):

> Mediation is a form of third-party intervention in conflict for the purpose of abating or resolving that conflict through negotiation . . . it is an intervention that must be acceptable to the adversaries in the conflict, who cooperate diplomatically with the intervener . . . In addition to helping adversaries communicate (providing "good offices") and endeavouring to change their

images of each other (conciliation), mediators often suggest compromises and may negotiate and bargain with adversaries in an attempt to induce them to change their stance. (p. 7)

From Melchin and Picard's notion that a mediator "can even" offer substantive suggestions, we have the notion that they "often suggest compromises" and negotiate with the parties, trying to get them to change. This difference anticipates a spectrum of mediation that ranges from facilitative (process-oriented) to evaluative mediation, in which mediators assess the arguments and positions of disputants (Jeong, 2010, p. 182). An even more power-oriented form of mediation includes the use of "carrots" (rewards for agreement) and "sticks" (threats or implied threats of what might happen if there is no willingness to compromise) to induce changes. This approach is more likely to be used in international mediation (see Chapter 12). Drawing on the work of Jacob Bercovitch, Chung-Chain Teng (2008) states:

> Mediation is a process of conflict management and is related to, but distinct from, the parties' own negotiations. Mediation consists of the following elements: it must have intervention from an outsider (who may be an individual, an organization, a group, or a state); it prevents parties from resorting to physical force or invoking the authority of the law; and it will change parties' perceptions of behaviour. The most important ingredient is that of the mediator or third party. (p. 41)

While Bercovitch (1992, p. 7) places mediation into a system composed of the parties, mediator, process, and context, Teng (2008, pp. 41–42) presents it within the realm of conflict management and as a sustained alternative to formal law-driven approaches, suggesting that it is one form of ADR. He goes on to draw on Wehr and Lederach's distinction between an outsider-neutral model and an insider-partial model. An outsider-neutral mediator is not connected to the parties, has no vested interest in a particular outcome, and draws authority from professional roles and functions. The insider-partial mediator comes from within the conflict, must live with the consequences, and draws authority from relationships of trust with the parties.

What is common throughout the literature is that parties ultimately decide on the outcome; enhanced communication is essential; and some form of reframing, reinterpreting, or creatively generating possibilities is part of the process. Whether the assistance is facilitative, evaluative, manipulative, or mildly coercive is a matter of position, context, and debate.

An important question to examine is why parties choose mediation. Why not just negotiate the issues themselves? In some cases, the parties may have tried and failed to do so. They may be desperate to come to terms with a conflict because the cost of its continuing is too high. They are motivated to settle the dispute or resolve the conflict, but they simply cannot resume a bilateral process. There might be a communications breakdown or a great deal of emotion. For example, some people may be afraid that an interaction will quickly turn into exchanges of sarcasm or shouting, making progress impossible. In a related matter, there may even be issues of personal safety, and mediation could help make the negotiation process more secure. Sometimes, a lack of skills makes parties seek the help of professional mediators. Many parties to conflict have not been trained to negotiate and have never been involved in such a process. They do not know how to analyze the issues and stakes and may not be sophisticated in either representing themselves or listening carefully to the other parties. In truth, there are situations so complex that even a skilled negotiator might have trouble dealing with both the issues involved and the demands of guiding the process. Finally, an important reason for seeking mediation is to avoid a power imbalance that might prevent a fair negotiation. A party with less information, skills, and financial resources may be intimidated by his or her opponent. Mediation is often perceived as a way to reduce the differences in capabilities and strength of the two parties. Mediation processes are designed to address these problems through the use of a skilled mediator who creates a safe space, guides the process, elicits information from both parties, creates a fair playing field, and frames the issues in such a way as to empower the parties to understand the issues, stakes, alternatives, and options.

(AP Photo)

This photo serves as a metaphor for how a third party creates a safe space by putting enough physical and psychological distance between the parties so that they can talk without hurting one another. This environment is achieved through the physical set-up of the mediation room, the presence of a mediator and perhaps an assistant who observes, and the use of ground rules. If the emotions get too high during the process, a mediator can call a time out, have separate caucus meetings, remind parties of the ground rules, or ask them to reflect on their purpose for being there and their long-term objectives. The photo also illustrates how people can be overtaken by emotions in a conflict setting.

Approaches to Mediation

Since the 1970s, there has been tremendous development in the field of mediation, specifically in the number of parties using mediation at all levels, the number of mediators and the skills they bring to their craft, and the theoretical and practical approaches to the field. To show how the field has grown, we will discuss four of these approaches: interest-based, transformative, narrative, and insight (see also Table 11.3).

Interest-Based Mediation

Emerging from interest-based negotiation, this approach is associated with problem-solving, decision-making, and integrative bargaining. In terms of the approaches to conflict in Part II, it particularly resonates with rational choice, cognitive psychology, a mild form of realism, and the individualistic philosophy of the liberal tradition. The underlying premise is that people wish to maximize their interests and will choose integrative approaches (win–win) over distributive ones (win–lose). By framing the

TABLE 11.3 | COMPARISON OF FOUR APPROACHES TO MEDIATION

	Interest-Based	Transformative	Narrative	Insight
Philosophical Orientation	Liberalism, individualism, cognitive psychology, realism	Self–Other relationship, moral vision	Postmodernism	Lonergan's theories
Goals	Settlement of issues, resolution, agreement, win–win outcomes	Empowerment, recognition, new relationships, change of structures, justice	Shared alternate narrative, new relationships, reflexivity	Mutual learning, direct and indirect insights, new relationships
Emphasis	Identifying interests, creating new options, solving problems, achieving impartiality	Transforming relationships and structures	Deconstructing narratives and generating shared alternate narratives	Attending to cares and threats as deeper motivations in conflict, de-linking these from the issues
Key Questions	Why do you take the position you do? Why not try this option?	What do you like about the other party? What kind of relationship would you like to have?	What are the values underlying various elements of your story?	What cares and threats do you have?
Applicability	Workplace, business/commercial, low level of on-going contact	Long-standing relationship between parties, high cultural component, strong emotions involved	Long-standing relationship, significant differences in perspective, power, culture, gender-based conflict	Major misunderstandings, different world views, high emotions
Styles	Task-oriented	Social and emotional, high degree of empathy	Analytic, engaged, reflexive	Curious, engaged, analytical, empathetic, reflexive

approach as interest-based from the beginning, there is an assumption that parties will accept the goal of finding a fair solution that optimizes the gains for each side.

In this way, conflict is framed positively as offering the possibility to create something new. The process becomes a challenge akin to solving a problem or puzzle (hence the emphasis on mediation as a cognitive endeavour). The creativity comes about in the analytic process used to uncover the underlying interests, reframe the challenge, generate options that incorporate the parties' different interests, evaluate these options in the light of the various interests, and refine the options until one is found mutually acceptable. The key to uncovering the interests is to ask why a given party takes a given position. Finding the answer involves an exploration of purpose and goals served by the position. There might be some historical reasons for certain interests. The reframing of the conflict as a positive challenge helps to unleash some creativity. For example, a conflict between neighbours over the construction of a new building could be reframed as a challenge to design the kind of building that would be acceptable to both parties. The more a given position can be understood as serving a number of interests, the more likely it is to create new and acceptable options.

One of the keys to successful interest-based negotiation concerns assessments and decision-making. Decisions need to be made along the way regarding the process, and both parties have to decide together on a final option that either resolves the conflict or enables it to be managed in a tolerable manner. Such decisions are also influenced by the parties' interests. As discussed in Chapter 1, interests can be thought of as those things that directly or indirectly benefit a person. Substantial interests can be tangible (e.g. increasing material possessions or wealth) or intangible (e.g. gaining recognition, promotion, or convenience). Non-substantial interests may be related to principles, history, or saving face. Preserving relationships might even be seen as an interest. In conflict literature, interests sometimes include needs, interests that have a higher level of value attached to them or that are tied to identity and are therefore non-negotiable (see Figure 11.5). Needs are also differentiated on the basis of substantial needs (security and welfare needs) and psychological needs. Interest-based mediation tends to focus on

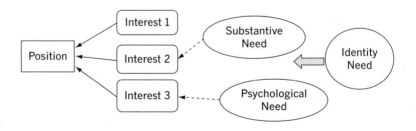

FIGURE 11.5 | POSITIONS AND INTERESTS

BOX 11.4 | EXAMPLE OF INTEREST-BASED MEDIATION

Adapted by the authors from a true story.

Two brothers, John and Adam, owned a business together. When John, the older brother, announced that he wanted to retire and claim his 40 per cent of the business, Adam argued that the company could not survive a sudden withdrawal of capital. They agreed to seek the assistance of a mediator, who helped them identify their interests. John wanted to stop working full-time and wanted resources to enjoy his retirement. Adam wanted his brother to remain with the company because customers were loyal to him. Because Adam wanted to pass the company on to his children (who worked with him), he also had an interest in preserving its financial health.

Taking all interests into account, the brothers found a mutually acceptable solution. They determined a price for John's shares and agreed that the money would be paid over a period of 10 years, thus ensuring the financial solvency of the company. John would be encouraged to work when he felt like it, thereby reassuring the customers that he was still involved. As long as he worked at least one-quarter time, John would be compensated for his work and be entitled to a new car every year. After 10 years or whenever he decided to retire completely, he would keep the last car.

interests rather than needs, particularly psychological needs in which emotions become key substantial factors in the negotiation.

While emotions are not seen as the object of interest-based mediation, they are considered factors to be acknowledged and managed through the process. People often come to mediation with a host of emotions—anger, fear, frustration, anxiety—and the mediator deals with these by establishing a safe space, presenting ground rules that limit negative emotional expressions (such as threats or name-calling) and providing a safe outlet (such as a separate caucus session) to allow for the expression of emotion. When identified in conjunction with a particular interest, emotions can serve as indicators of that interest's relative importance. Emotional expressions can also be suspect, as either diversions from the substantial issues or potential means of manipulation (e.g. getting the mediator to take sides).

Interest-based is by far the most popular model of mediation. It is used in family matters, business disputes, organizational feuds, and international diplomacy. However, in some cases, it does not fulfill the needs of the parties and may not be successful. The other approaches have grown out of and in response to interest-based mediation.

Transformative Mediation

In 1994, Robert A. Baruch Bush and Joseph P. Folger wrote *The Promise of Mediation*, which proved to be a classic in the field of conflict resolution. They took issue with interest-based/problem-solving mediation, arguing that the greatest stake in many conflicts is the relationship between the parties. According to the authors, the transformation of the relationship is a major achievement. Furthermore, such transformation increases the chances of successfully negotiating the conflict's substantive issues.

In their comparative analysis of interest-based and transformative approaches, Bush and Folger (1994) stress that the former is based on a philosophical tradition that values the individual, particularly as it is oriented toward satisfying interests. In contrast, they present a relational world view in which relationships are key to understanding human reality. Drawing on the concept of stages of growth developed by Lawrence Kohlberg (1981) and expanded upon by Carol Gilligan (1982), they see the transformative approach as focusing on the parties' moral development. Though they do not acknowledge it, the philosophical underpinnings are akin to those of Paul Ricoeur (1990/1992) and Emmanuel Levinas (1961/1969), who stress the importance of the Self–Other relationship and the ethical responsibility for the Other (see Chapter 9).

At the heart of the transformative approach is the empowerment of each party and his or her recognition of the other's experience and perspective. Bush and Folger (1994) define empowerment as "the restoration to individuals of a sense of their own value and strength and their own capacity to handle life's problems" and recognition as "the evocation in individuals of acknowledgement and empathy for the situation and problems of others" (p. 2). They argue that both are important goals that will lead to moral transformation of the parties individually and to a new relationship between them. Like interest-based mediation, this approach includes generating options, clarifying the implications for the parties, and making appropriate decisions. However, the difference is the manner in which the mediator uses each step to foster empowerment and recognition. As a result, what is considered pertinent to the process is expanded. In fact, Bush and Folger criticize interest-based mediators for dropping those issues that do not lend themselves to interest-based bargaining.

A somewhat different approach to transformation is offered by John Paul Lederach (2003), a leader in peacebuilding: "Conflict transformation is to *envision and respond to the ebb and flow of social conflict* as life-giving opportunities for creating *constructive change processes* that *reduce violence, increase justice in direct interaction and social structures*, and respond to real-life problems in *human relationships*" (p. 14, emphasis in original). For Lederach, the problem with conflict resolution is that the emphasis on bringing closure to a particular conflict can cause issues of justice, structural change, and relationships to be overlooked. A specific conflict occurs in a broad, complex context and represents an opportunity to examine this wider situation. From this perspective, relationships are subject to change, as are the structures within which the relationships take on meaning. Like Bush and Folger, Lederach works from a moral base; his particular orientation emphasizes the convergence of justice and peace.

Narrative Mediation

Introduced by John Winslade and Gerald Monk (2000), narrative mediation also focuses on the relationship between and perspective of the parties. Like the Lederach approach, it claims that both occur within social and cultural structures. Philosophically, narrative mediation is rooted in postmodern thought, with its emphasis on the affirmation of divergent narratives and a methodology of deconstruction.

Winslade and Monk (2000) concur with Bush and Folger (1994) that interest-based mediation downplays the relational and identity dimensions of conflict by focusing on its substantive issues. They also agree with the transformational emphasis on building trust. What sets them apart is their attention to language and the social constructs that impact the parties' interpretation of the conflict. In particular, they draw on social constructivist theory to support their approach.

Narrative mediation is rooted in the understanding that our conflicts are embedded in narratives. Used to define who we are in relation to others, our stories include assumptions about power relationships, legitimacy, and culture. It is impossible for anyone, including mediators, to be value-free in relation to these issues. Hence, reflexivity, a capacity to reflect critically on one's own place within a given situation, is an important skill for mediators and the parties involved.

The process of narrative mediation starts with the stories of the different parties. During this engagement phase, the mediator is attentive to tone, metaphors, and the language used to describe the problem and the other party. The narratives are then deconstructed. This second phase involves getting the parties to externalize their own narratives—to look at them objectively and to consider what is revealed about power relationships, experiences of oppression on both sides, and how the problem is perceived. In the third phase, the parties and the mediator work together on an alternative story that both parties can agree upon. Throughout, the mediator is always genuinely curious, trying to learn and understand. The mediator also reflects back to the participants what he or she is learning and how it affects him or her. Basically, this process involves empowerment, as each party gains his or her own voice, and recognition, as each party learns to listen to the story of the other. The crafting of a new alternative narrative that both parties can identify with demands creativity and an ability to transcend entrenched views and perspectives. New understandings of the role of the surrounding social situation help the parties to see how they are influenced—often unwittingly—by values, social constructs (such as gender), and language.

Insight Mediation

Insight mediation works from the conceptual framework of Bernard Lonergan (1958/1978) and was developed by Melchin and Picard (2008; see also Picard, 1998). Lonergan's work centres on the mental processes involved in perceiving, understanding, judging, and acting. As we perform these different activities, we generate insights. At the heart of insight mediation is a process of generating direct and inverse comprehension by attending to values, cares, and threats as manifest in feelings. The validation of insights then provides a basis for an exploration of options.

Direct insights are those "aha" moments when we discover something new that answers our questions in a given situation. Melchin and Picard (2008) describe them as follows:

> Direct insights are inner experiences of meaning that require questioning, pursuing clues, examining data, probing feelings, and hitting on answers. They involve an experience of transformation in our world of meaning that is deeply personal, deeply inward, and deeply felt. Yet, in spite of this, it is also true that direct insights transform our sense of the outer world. They shape and reshape the way we see, hear and feel the world. There is something profoundly extroverted about them that restructures our sense of the world around us. Insights are profoundly inner, and they constitute our sense of the outer world. (p. 62)

An example of a direct insight involves a conflict between a husband and wife over meal preparation. The husband thought that he was doing his share because he eagerly helped with the cooking and clean-up. Yet the wife constantly thought that she was doing more than her share. As they talked, the husband had the insight that half the work—including planning the meal and buying the ingredients—occurs before cooking begins. He realized that he was doing only one-quarter of the work. With this direct insight, he started taking the initiative in meal planning, thus restructuring his behaviour.

Indirect insights imply a realization that we are asking the wrong question. In our example, the husband asked, "What can I do to help?" Once he changed his approach to "Have you already planned dinner? If not, I suggest the following meal and will drop by the store to pick up what we need," the question produced more positive results.

Melchin and Picard (2008) argue that we are social beings and that our actions, positions, and responses are always in relation to others. As we interact, our values, cares, and threats are significant motivators. Often these function at a tacit level—we are not conscious of the fact that we value certain things or care about how things are done as profoundly as we do. Evidence of the profundity of cares and values is found in our feelings. Strong passions about an event or pattern in our lives indicate that we value and care about what is happening. Insight mediators encourage narratives about feelings, narratives that provide a historical base and hence insights into values, cares, and threats of the particular parties. These stories are subject to validation as mediators identify the insights and ensure that they ring true to the participants. Identifying the values, cares, and threats can then lead to a process of delinking certain actions from the feelings associated with them. Consider a situation where two roommates have different values related to tidiness. The messy practices of Party A go against some deep values of fastidious Party B, resulting in sarcasm, threats, and provocative actions (e.g. hiding all the things that Party A leaves lying around the apartment). As they talk about their values and cares, Party B can separate some of the messy habits from the (attributed) values of Party A—"He doesn't care about how the place looks." Realizing how important cleanliness is to Party B, Party A can show an openness to change. Validated insights and delinking thus serve as a basis for new ways of dealing with the conflict at hand.

Culture and Mediation

Aside from cultural clashes being the root of a given conflict, there are three other ways in which issues of culture impinge on mediation processes: the culture of the parties in conflict, the cultural context of the conflict, and the philosophical grounding of the mediation process. There are two scenarios regarding the first issue. One is that the parties come from the same culture, but the mediator is from another. There may even be a language difference. In this instance, the mediator may need a cultural coach so as to learn some of the significant nuances of communication within the parties' culture. In the second scenario, each party comes from a different culture. To assist in the mediation, issues of culture and communication could be discussed. If communication styles are different (note, for instance, the cultural differences between Palestinians and Jewish Israelis described in Chapter 10), it may be necessary to bring these differences into the open and agree upon ground rules that will help to minimize misunderstandings.

The second issue may require varying the mediation approach to suit the values of a particular culture. In some Asian cultures, for instance, saving face is extremely important; therefore, it would be better to elicit directly from the participants how they might be responsible for the conflict rather than have one of the parties make bold accusations that take the form of guilt- or shame-tripping. While looking a person in the eye is a sign of trustworthiness in some cultures, it is a show of disrespect in others. In some cultures, such as in India, it is highly insulting to show someone the sole of your shoe. A party who casually stretches his legs out and crosses his feet might cause the other party to react to a perceived insult and inadvertently change the dynamics of the process.

Finally, we have already discussed how the mediator's philosophical orientation has a profound effect on how the mediation process is conducted. As one is attentive to matters of what Johan Galtung refers to as deep culture, it becomes clear that the goals and manner of a mediation process can change. In some cultures, community harmony is of supreme importance—more so than individual satisfaction. In this case, framing the issues would include the community dimension. In other cultures, upholding traditional values and teachings is paramount. Accordingly, the teachings become an important aspect in selecting an acceptable resolution.

Applications of Mediation

Since the 1960s, the use of mediation has grown significantly in North America, Europe, Australia, and New Zealand. This growth has taken place in a number of areas: families, schools, communities, the workplace, the civil and criminal justice systems, and international affairs.

Family mediation has grown significantly as divorce rates have increased. Recognition of adversarial approaches to separation agreements and custody issues has led to the realization that family and divorce conflict lends itself to mediation. For example, where children are involved, divorce does not generally mean that a dysfunctional relationship can be totally severed; there remains the need for ongoing communication with regard to the children. Hence, it is important that family mediators focus on issues of property division, custody, and communication issues. One of the ways they try to move things forward constructively is to remind divorcing parents that their priority is to look out for the interests of the children. Some mediators even display pictures of the children throughout the mediation sessions. Besides having general competence as mediators, they also need to be knowledgeable about family issues and family law. It helps if family mediators can immediately rule out certain options that cannot work legally. They also have to be attentive to issues of abuse, violence, and threats that can undermine mediation processes.

Mediation is also used to resolve conflicts in schools. Starting in the 1980s, students in some high schools in Canada were offered mediation training. They then offered mediation services to their peers when there was a conflict. Subsequently, training programs have been developed for elementary schools and broad-based training programs for youth have been developed.[6]

Like family and peer mediation, community mediation programs have become more common. Since the 1960s, these procedures have been initiated in many cities in the United States, Canada, Europe, Australia, and New Zealand. They are often organized out of existing civil society institutions (e.g. NGOs and churches) or as stand-alone institutions. Their purpose is to assist neighbours in handling disputes and to deal with community issues by using mediation or facilitated group processes.

Another area where mediation is implemented is in labour relations. Beginning in the twentieth century, there has been a trend to recognize the importance of labour to business, the public sector, and the general economy and to grant legal rights to unions. Such recognition and rights came as the result of strikes and demonstrations, some of which turned violent. In 1900, the Government of Canada passed the Conciliation Act, which gave the Department of Labour a mandate to provide resources to help deal with labour issues. The department currently provides mediation, conciliation, and arbitration services.[7] During both world wars, some governments improved conflict resolution in the workplace in order to guarantee high levels of work and industrial peace for the war effort. For instance, a US Conciliation Service was created in 1917.

Presently, most contracts between unions and management are arrived at through negotiation between the two parties. When negotiations bog down, a mediator may be called in. Labour mediation focuses on the terms of a given contract and, in this regard, is about positions and power. One source of negative power for the union is its capacity to strike, which can bring the activities of a given enterprise to a halt. In turn, management can impose a lockout or use non-union workers during a strike. There are strong values and passions (and, in some jurisdictions, laws) against the use of such workers. Deadlines are a key component of the labour mediation process. Critical junctures such as strike votes and strike and contract dates are important to the bargaining process. Sometimes, the parties wait until the last minute to make concessions, causing a marathon mediation session.

Since the 1980s, Western economies have encountered several difficulties, many due to the rise of foreign competitors. This has led to massive layoffs and to a decrease in unionization. There has been increased reference to interests in labour negotiations. Integrative negotiation and mediation have become widespread, contributing to a reduction in the number of strikes and an increase in the number of mediated settlements. For instance, when General Motors and Chrysler were facing bankruptcy in 2008, their workers accepted drastic pay cuts because there was a mutual interest to keep the corporations afloat. Large organizations such as these and government departments also currently have internal conflict resolution systems, complete with departments equipped to handle conflict. Personnel within these programs provide conflict resolution skills training, mediation services, and group interventions. In smaller organizations, human resources personnel take mediation training to handle workplace conflict.

Mediation also appears in both the civil and criminal justice systems. During the 1960s, the dramatic increase in litigation cases in many jurisdictions and the high cost of legal fees provided people with strong motivation to seek forms of ADR. Alternatives to the court system, such as mediation, arbitration, and fact-finding, were developed. Some areas now have mandatory mediation, which requires parties to try mediation before the court will accept their civil case. Many lawyers now offer mediation services, and professional mediators also work in law firms.

Mediation in the criminal justice system is in some ways connected to **restorative justice**, which involves victims meeting with their offenders. This process gives victims a voice, something that is traditionally missing in criminal court (Zehr, 1990/2005). Often these mediations focus on the consequences for the offender. The basic question guiding the mediation is, What can be done to make things right? In the case of theft or property crimes, an offender can repair the damage or replace what was stolen. In cases of break and enter and crimes against the person—including assault, rape, and homicide—there are implications for the victims that cannot be rectified easily.

There are several dimensions to victim–offender mediation. At an initial level, there are actions required of the offender that can be made part of the sentence. At an emotional level, there are a number of aspects that benefit the victim. First, it is important that the offender answer questions such as Why me? What led you to do this? What have you done since? Will it happen again? Second, the offender's verbal or non-verbal expressions of remorse can help in the healing process. Third, the victim must tell the offender directly how the crime has affected him or her. Fourth, a victim may wish to offer words or signs of forgiveness. Victim–offender mediation can occur before trial, after a guilty verdict, or after an offender has gone to jail. Restorative justice literature provides descriptions of available programs and many evaluations of their impact.[8] The meeting of victim and offender can be a very difficult process for both parties. However, this form of mediation can be transformative, as the victim can begin to heal and the offender can realize the effects of his or her actions.

CASE STUDY 11.2 | MEDIATION INTERVENTION IN A WEST COAST FISHERIES CONFLICT

Richard McGuigan, Diamond Management Consulting

Since the early 1980s, one of the biggest drives in managing sustainable fisheries has been catch monitoring, which addresses species conservation in general. In recent years, however, concerns regarding non-directed catch (bycatch, or fish that are accidentally caught and usually go to waste) have steadily grown in recent years. For example, one of the critical concerns on the BC coast is the conservation of rockfish stocks, a common component of non-directed catch. Historically, regulations have often required fishers to discard their non-directed rockfish catch at sea. Environmental groups have steadily pushed for improved conservation and accountability for non-directed catch in the BC fishing industry.

To address at-sea discards and the impact on rockfish species, the Department of Fisheries and Oceans (DFO) established the Inshore Rockfish Conservation Strategy in 2002. The strategy led to the Commercial Groundfish Initiative, a series of meetings held in 2003. In October of that year, DFO, the British Columbia Ministry of Agriculture, Food and Fisheries, and representatives of the groundfish industry responded to the five criteria determined by the initiative by creating the Commercial Groundfish Integrated Advisory Committee (CGIAC). The purpose of the CGIAC was to establish a strategic approach for the future direction of the commercial groundfish industry.

Diamond Management Consulting (Richard McGuigan and Sylvia McMechan, mediators) were selected by the stakeholders to design and mediate/facilitate a consensus-based decision process that would lead to an effective solution to this challenging conflict. The issues were exceedingly complex, and there was a long, deep history of acrimonious conflict between the stakeholders. Complicating our work was a significant power asymmetry and varying commitment to consensus. Most of the negotiators were captains who were not accustomed to collaborating in conflict resolution! We slowly built the foundation for the process: we began with training in collaborative negotiating, developed guiding principles for the process, and maintained a firm hand during the initial agreement phase. Over an 18-month period, meeting monthly for up to a week at a time, an agreement was reached that would radically change groundfish management on the BC coast. The results were a more sustainable groundfish industry and dramatically improved relationships among the stakeholders. The process was an outstanding success and continues to this day. The same stakeholder group still plays a key role in the ongoing management of the fishery and makes decisions by consensus.

Finally, mediation plays a role in resolving international conflicts. Since World War II, the majority of violent conflicts have been subject to mediation attempts. Either the parties involved choose to try mediation or international organizations (e.g. the UN) or states convince both sides to mediate. In other instances, NGOs have made their mediation services available. A mediator is often chosen to mediate an international conflict because he or she has influence with one or both parties. Some mediators become involved because they have a stake in the conflict's resolution. A mediating state may wish to see its own influence and interests protected through the negotiating process. As a result, the issue of neutrality is not as prevalent in international mediation as it is in domestic settings. International mediators also frequently use rewards or threats (carrots or sticks) to encourage parties to reach an agreement. For instance, a mediator could promise massive amounts of aid or threaten economic **sanctions**. The use of mediation to resolve violent international conflicts is discussed further in Chapter 12.

ARBITRATION

Besides negotiation and mediation, arbitration is the third principal process of non-judicial peaceful conflict resolution. Arbitration is the process by which an impartial third party is asked to provide the solution to a dispute. Unlike a mediator, an arbitrator does not merely suggest ways to resolve a conflict but has the final word. Therefore, arbitration is an authoritative conflict resolution process in the sense that the third party, not the protagonists, controls the process and decides the outcome.

The advantages of arbitration over mediation explain why it is widely used in many settings. Arbitration is more rigorous than mediation. Arbiters often decide according to clear legal and technical rules and precedents; therefore, their decisions are less vulnerable to legal challenges than negotiated accords. This is one reason why arbitration is extensively used in labour relations and commercial disputes where the recourse to tribunals is a looming (and very expensive) possibility. Arbitration is also faster than mediation. In effect, the arbiter may give the parties only a minimal amount of time to present their cases and accord him- or herself a short period to prepare a decision. Thus, the arbitration's entire timetable can often be set ahead of time, which is definitively an advantage in the corporate world. Furthermore, the fact that the parties are bound to the decision of the arbiter generally precludes a failure of the process and the convening of another round of talks. Because many small claims and technical issues can be submitted to arbitration, the process can even take place without the parties and the arbiter being in the same location. Arbitration through telephone or Internet conferencing is relatively common in many fields, such as between clients and providers in the telecom industry.

Structurally speaking, a lot of arbitration concerns conflicts that are relatively simple. For instance, many liability claims basically involve determining the amount of compensation to be paid by one firm to another. Much arbitration therefore deals with disputes rather than conflicts, in the sense that the parties agree on the rules of the game and that a straightforward and relatively satisfying compromise can usually be found. In fact, arbitration is rare in cases of deep-rooted conflicts or major political feuds implying a possibility of violence. The fact is that the parties to grave conflicts can always expect to find a tolerable solution in a negotiation, while arbitration implies the risk of being defeated and even humiliated.

The Scope of Arbitration

Most arbitration in modern societies is compulsory, in the sense that the parties commit to the process from the moment they enter into a relationship. For example, many commercial contracts incorporate clauses forcing the signatories to go to arbitration if there is a controversy over the application of the accord. Most collective agreements also follow this practice. The parties agree to bring contests and grievances to ADR mechanisms such as mediation and arbitration.

The range of arbitration varies on a scale between informal and quasi-judicial processes. Informal arbitration is practised in traditional societies, for example, when an elder is asked to find a solution to a family quarrel. In modern societies, this informality is relatively rare given that most arbitration concerns commercial matters.

While in some contexts the arbiter must render his or her decisions strictly according to the law, in other contexts there is some autonomy for the arbiter to use his or her judgment for finding accommodation. For example, he or she could try an integrative approach to find solutions to collective agreement issues. He or she could also use **med-arb**, a process that starts in a mediation mode but goes to arbitration if the parties fail to agree on a settlement.

Various forms of arbitration have been used in most societies for a long time. For instance, the roles of arbiter and *iudex* (judge) were constitutionally recognized in ancient Rome's Law of the Twelve Tables (450 BCE). Therefore, according to the fundamental law of their republic, Roman citizens had the right to use arbitration or adjudication in the resolution of their conflicts. During the Middle Ages, arbitration was a familiar way to deal with conflict. For instance, merchant and artisan guilds used it to settle commercial and labour differences. Many of the features of modern arbitration date from that period, such as the use of retired workers and executives as arbiters, the recourse to panels of three or more arbiters, and the practice whereby the sides in the dispute choose one arbiter each, who then select the third. In Great Britain, many of the craft and specialist corporations had used arbitration for centuries in their labour relations and wanted to keep this favourable practice alive during the Industrial Revolution (Jaffe, 2000). This issue was hotly debated among owners and workers because the capitalists were afraid of losing power to the workers and believed that the old ways of the guilds did not apply to private companies. During the nineteenth century, the British Parliament passed several laws alternatively opening and restricting the right to arbitration.

Eventually, in the twentieth century, the owners understood that arbitration was in their interests of limiting the influence of unions over workers (Treble, 1990). Arbitration has since been used extensively in commercial and labour matters. Along with mediation and conciliation, it is one of the services often offered by governments to settle labour disputes. In their differences with their labour unions, governments are frequent users of arbitration, such as in the settlement of grievances that cannot be resolved informally or through mediation. For many people, the most spectacular use of arbitration is in professional sports, when third parties are asked to settle differences between a team and a player over a contract. In baseball, final-offer arbitration has been offered as a service to the teams and players since 1974 (Schellenberg, 1996). Arbitration has even been used to resolve collective issues between the owners and the players' association.

Table 11.4 presents one example of the range of mediation and arbitration areas in the United States. Each section has its own specialized arbitration program with its own rules. The American Arbitration Association has an extensive infrastructure that includes sets of rules for different jurisdictions and for different types of conflict.

Shortcomings of Arbitration

Compared to using the legal system to sue someone, arbitration is a fast, efficient, and economical form of ADR. It is also often a favourable alternative to mediation and negotiation, especially for commercial disputes and low-stakes conflicts. However, arbitration gives the parties involved less control over the process and outcomes and entails the risk that one or both parties may be dissatisfied with the result and threaten to restart the quarrel.

The main shortcoming of arbitration is that it is rarely applicable to hard issues of identity and politics. There are two fundamental problems in this respect. In some cases, the parties believe that no third party has the clout, neutrality, and/or prestige to resolve their differences. Such is the case in many civil and interstate wars, as we will see in the next chapter. The other problem is that very few adversaries in a grave conflict will take a

TABLE 11.4 | FIELDS OF MEDIATION AND ARBITRATION
IN THE UNITED STATES

Claims Programs
Class Arbitration
Commercial Disputes
Construction Industry
Energy Industry
Financial Services
Health Care Industry
Insurance Industry
International ADR

Source: © 2007 American Arbitration Association. All rights reserved.

chance to be rebuked in their claims by a third party. Nevertheless, arbitration is a crucial conflict resolution mechanism that has proven its worth in countless labour, commercial, and liability matters. In the labour world, for instance, it has avoided the escalation of differences over collective agreements and grievances into full-fledged conflicts. Modern market economies would be in poor shape without widespread arbitration. It remains to be seen, however, if interpersonal, community, and political conflict in the Western world can be resolved by renewed forms of informal arbitration.

ADJUDICATION

Adjudication refers to the legal process where a judge or jury uses the law as the only guide to decide on the outcome of a conflict. This form of conflict resolution is generally framed in a win–lose manner; however, in some cases, a judge may try to conciliate the parties to some extent in his or her decisions and sentencing. Like arbitration, adjudication is an authoritative process in which neutrality is crucial. Any suggestion that a judge or jury may be biased will aggravate one party, increasing the risk of mistrial and pushing the parties to initiate further opposition via protests, publicity, or violence. In fact, the legal option offers some complainants the advantage of potentially winning or dismissing a case through procedural and technical irregularities, a possibility that does not exist in conciliation, mediation, or some arbitration procedures.

Although adjudication and arbitration have some similarities, they also differ in other ways. The main distinction is that the role of an arbiter is to settle a conflict, while a judge has to uphold justice. Arbiters can base their decisions on matters such as fairness, expediency, damage control, innovation, or reconciliation. But judges must ensure that the legal process is served and may not be concerned about the resolution of the conflict. In other words, the main principle of legal adjudication is to serve justice, not to resolve conflict. Legal judgments can stop some conflicts or put them to rest for a while. However, even after trial, many people will still feel that they have been treated unfairly and will continue to fight for their rights. One of the main advantages of court proceedings is the right of appeal, which, to some extent, acts as a guarantee against procedural errors and as a possibility for the losing side to have another trial. The right of appeal is not universal. It is non-existent or seriously limited in many old societies and in authoritarian systems. Even in rule of law countries, the right of appeal is governed by strict rules and is unavailable beyond the Supreme Court level.[9]

While court judgments are legally weightier than arbitral decisions, adjudication has certain drawbacks. It is more expensive than arbitration because the level of proof and procedural standards are higher. This increased complexity means that the adjudication process takes longer than arbitration. The former is also less predictable, as judges who are unfamiliar with the issue might render unusual decisions (Thomas, 1993). While arbitration and mediation can be conducted without the presence of the public or media and the terms of the settlement can remain between the parties, adjudication is less discreet.

In many cases, as with arbitration, parties in a harsh identity or political conflict do not wish their case to be decided by a third party. There are also some conflicts that do not belong in courts of law, for instance, low-level conflicts between individuals or groups where no laws have been broken, there are no major property issues, or where people's rights are not threatened. For these reasons, lawyers and judges try to settle most conflicts through conciliation, mediation, and arbitration before they reach the courthouse.

This textbook is not about law, and we cannot pretend to describe here all the variations in litigation and adjudication across eras, continents, and domains. We will instead focus on the main types of law and how the legal system can inhibit and sometimes fuel conflict.

Types of Law

As there are different traditions and methods of conflict resolution, there are many forms of law. These types are usually grouped under three main legal traditions: religious, civil, and common. **Religious law** includes, for example, the canon law of the Catholic Church, Islamic law, and Jewish law. Religious codes vary in scope and sophistication and are either written or orally transmitted. Their main characteristics are that they are considered by the faithful to have been revealed and are usually transmitted by clergy assisted by competent laypersons. This type of law is very influential the world over, particularly in countries where Islam is well represented. **Civil law**, the most widespread form of law, is written by a legislator and compiled in a code that becomes the main authority on the law. The main forms of modern civil law have their origins in Roman law, which was compiled into the Justinian Code (from Emperor Justinian) by Byzantine jurists in the sixth century. The Napoleonic Code, enacted in nineteenth-century France by the famous emperor, is a well-known version of civil law that has inspired many countries. Finally, **common law**, spread among Anglo-Saxon countries, is validated primarily by tribunals. While the sources of common law are diverse (tradition and legislation, notably), the courts use precedents and reasoning to determine the exact content of the law. The main areas of civil and common law are listed in Table 11.5.

These three legal traditions coexist in several areas (see Figure 11.6). For instance, in Quebec and Louisiana, the French civil code is applied to civil matters, while criminal justice (a federal responsibility) follows the common law tradition. In India, most matters in society are governed by common law, but Islamic law applies to Muslim citizens in domains such as marriage, and many community disputes are resolved through traditional customary practices. Sometimes, a legal case will fall under two concurrent codes, which is itself a cause of conflict.

In regards to adjudication, legal systems specify the process, the kind of evidence that can be entered, and the kinds of questions that can be asked. There are also specially defined rights for the parties involved. Given the complexity of the system, parties in a dispute are generally represented by lawyers, giving them less direct control over the process. Legal systems and legal traditions within these systems determine who can make

TABLE 11.5 | MAIN DOMAINS OF SECULAR LAW IN MODERN SOCIETIES

Administrative law (the management of the state)

Constitutional law (the government of people)

Contract law (agreements passed among people)

Criminal law (the punishment of offences)

Environmental law (defence of the natural world)

Family law (marriage and divorce)

Human rights law (protection of the dignity and liberty of the person)

International humanitarian law (the protection of people against abuse)

International law (relations among states)

Labour law (the conditions of work in unionized settings)

Property law (the ownership and transfer of property)

Tort law (compensations for wrongdoings)

Trust law (property that is in care of another party)

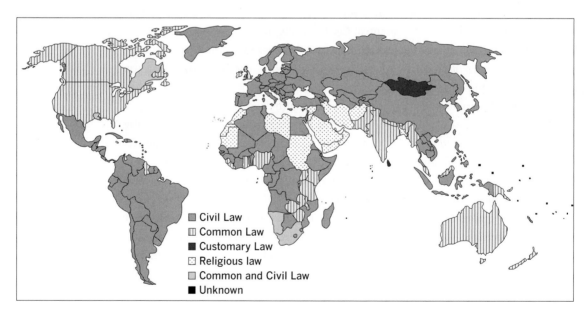

Civil Law
Common Law
Customary Law
Religious law
Common and Civil Law
Unknown

FIGURE 11.6 | LEGAL SYSTEMS OF THE WORLD

Source: University of Ottawa: JuriGlobe World Legal Systems Research Group, www.juriglobe.ca/eng/index.php.

the final decision in a case. For example, panels of judges are fairly common in Western Europe but are not widespread in North America (with the important exception of Supreme Court settings). The use of juries is limited to criminal law cases in Canada but is a feature of many civil proceedings in the United States.

Domains of the Law

In most jurisdictions, legal proceedings take two forms: civil and criminal. This has, however, not always been the case, as many traditional law settings did not make a strict separation between criminal and civil cases. Even in the West, criminal law evolved from civil law during the Renaissance, when the state became dominant over private interests in society and began to prosecute all criminal acts.

In a civil case, one party alleges that the other party has wronged him or her in a way that does not constitute a criminal act. The emphasis is on the effects of the deed. The parties speak only if they are put on the witness stand. Whoever provides testimony can be cross-examined by the lawyer of the other party, a process that can call into question the veracity of what was said. A judge or jury decides if the defendant wronged the other party (through, for example, breach of contract or failure of due diligence) and, if so, how much must be paid in damages. Lawyers frequently negotiate settlements behind the scenes, sometimes with the involvement of the judge.

If a party's actions broke a **criminal law**, the case goes to criminal court for adjudication. In this situation, the crime is considered to be committed against the Crown in monarchies and against the state in republican democracies. The prosecutor does not represent the victim per se but can meet with him or her beforehand. In common law and other jurisdictions, the accused is considered innocent until proven guilty beyond a reasonable doubt. If there is a guilty verdict, the judge must decide on a punishment appropriate to the crime.[10] For some crimes, such as murder, there may be a minimum punishment, thus limiting the discretion of the judge. In the case of conflicts that involve crime, the adjudication is clearly win–lose and does nothing to resolve the conflict. However, a guilty verdict does provide victims with a sense of justice. And, in property crime cases, a judge may require the guilty party to make financial reparations.

The Indispensable Role of the Courts

Because many conflicts start from a sense of injustice shared by at least one side, the use of the legal system seems to be the natural response to conflict. It is largely through litigation that disadvantaged groups such as manual workers, women, minorities, and the poor have fought and won the battles that have improved their lot in liberal democracies. An impartial and efficient justice system with a right of appeal is a basic feature of all modern rule of law societies.

Unfortunately, the recourse to legal adjudication is a costly, time-consuming, and harsh process. It is not equally available to all, and those on the lower rungs of the socioeconomic ladder cannot always muster the resources to fight against governments, large corporations, or wealthy individuals. Even large civil society organizations such as trade unions, NGOs, and professional associations can be a match for any but the most organized and persistent individual litigants. The negative aspects of adjudication have risen to incredible heights in North America, with lawyers' fees increasing dramatically, backlogs lasting for years, and aggressiveness in procedural and extra-procedural contexts reaching a fevered pitch. The judicial means of conflict resolution is definitely not to everyone's taste, which explains why many people and groups would rather drop a case than get into a long and costly legal action. Fortunately, ADR in all its aspects offers alternatives to most people. Gradually, the Western world is rehabilitating the non-judicial ways that had been marginalized with the emergence of the unified state. Nevertheless, adjudication will maintain its rightful place at the top of the conflict resolution pyramid. It is one of the important duties of states and civil societies to see that the judicial system is fair, well funded, and accessible to all people.

AUTHORITATIVE ALLOCATION

Many conflicts are resolved thorough authoritative allocation, meaning that a person or a group of people can legally and legitimately impose a solution upon the parties, with or without deliberation. This last qualification is important because, contrary to arbitration or adjudication, legitimate authority has the privilege to impose settlements of conflicts even without cognizance of the case. For instance, a strong government's demand that conflicting parties simply stop fighting should, theoretically, be enough to convince them to abandon their feud. However, this kind of authoritarian behaviour is not the preferred way in the modern world, particularly in democracies, where it would rapidly delegitimize a government. Furthermore, this approach does nothing to end acrimony and revenge between the disputants and may lead to worse problems.

Authoritative allocation can be made by any person or group with a form of authority in society, including government officials, parents, clan or tribe elders, religious figures, and employers. In politics, legitimate decision-makers are sometimes determined by heredity (e.g. monarchs and aristocrats), elected by other people (politicians), or nominated by rulers (civil servants). Hereditary rulers are quite rare in today's world, and we can safely predict that their number will not rise significantly. In many countries, elected politicians are responsible for making the ultimate decisions about conflicts in society. While the legislature—which passes the laws—theoretically has the upper hand, the actual situation is not that clear. In most stable parliamentary systems where one party or a coalition can have a plurality (e.g. Great Britain and Canada), the executive (those who implement decisions) controls the political process for reasons of expediency and competence. In presidential systems (e.g. the United States and France), the president, who is elected directly by the people, has as much—if not more—influence on major decisions as the legislators.

While authoritative allocation can include force, not all instances include this feature. For example, religious denominations, associational bodies, and most family units do not use force. In these situations, the authority to settle a conflict comes from religion, contract, or tradition. The authority figures usually use a mixture of persuasion, rewards, and sanctions to enforce their decisions.

Direct Democracy

Presidents, prime ministers, and legislators make most decisions of a national scope for the people. This is why we speak of indirect rule in democracies. Direct democracy, however, means that the people, not their representatives, decide on an issue. For example, people can directly affect the results of a conflict by voting in an election or referendum. As previously mentioned, electoral contests are often peaceful expressions of deeper conflicts in society, such as those between the forces of tradition and the forces of progress or between representatives of different social classes. Many elections turn out to be important factors in the prevention, management, and resolution of conflict. They allow the winning side to authoritatively allocate values in society and to determine who will get what, and when. However, when the parties represent only ethnoreligious groupings, are in a win–lose stance, or refuse to make accommodations when in power, elections can also aggravate conflicts. As a result, many elections have led to tense and polarized situations where violence is possible. This outcome explains the paradox observed in the 1990s that new democracies can be quite violent until they develop into a pluralist mode (Snyder, 2000).

Referendums, or plebiscites, are another form of direct democracy used to settle an issue. In Canada, the population of Quebec has voted in two referendums regarding sovereignty, declining to leave Canada both times. In Europe in the 2000s, referendums on further integration have been won and lost in different countries, forcing the pro-Europe forces to modify European Charter projects and to slow down integration in general. Such popular consultations do not usually resolve the long-standing issues, but they defuse violence, allow both sides to express their views, and enable government reforms, compromises, and/or integrative solutions to be introduced in further talks.

Elections and referendums have a crucial importance in other areas. Groups such as trade unions, political parties, and associations use elections to select their executives and consult the membership on certain issues (e.g. a strike vote). These consultations often decide the solution to disputes and conflicts regarding what direction should be taken by the organization. The democratic way is sometimes used in businesses, especially in those that are of the co-operative model (controlled by the individual members) or owned by a multitude of small shareholders. Democratic consultations are also found in countless families, groups of friends, workplace units, and recreation teams and clubs. These examples show that the old models in which notable men, elders, and parents made all decisions unilaterally are definitely out of fashion in established democracies and are unlikely to make a comeback.

There is some controversy about the extension of direct democracy, such as the use of more referendums in public life. Some people believe that this form of consultation is more just to the common person and can bring more legitimacy to the political system than legislative debates. Others are afraid that mass consultations may polarize the system and preclude the elaboration of moderate reforms and constructive discussions among social groups. Mass consultations can also be used against minorities and lead to further discrimination. Contemporary political science literature contains a detailed and complex study of democratic consultations. From the perspective of conflict studies, elections and referendums are two of the most important tools available in conflict resolution. However, if the system is to avoid entrenching animosities, they must be used with caution and the winners must be magnanimous and open to discussion.

The Delegation of Authority

Many people in a position to impose a conflict resolution are not elected but nominated by people in power, who delegate a fraction of their authority to them. In democratic countries, such people are generally chosen on the basis of merit, meaning that they usually have strong decision-making skills and a relevant technical expertise (hence, the word *technocrats* is applied to some of them). The holders of delegated authority can be, for example, civil servants, political advisors, administrators in organizations, or business executives. In many small-scale conflicts with the government, people go directly to civil servants, hoping to get a favourable decision. Consumers unhappy with a good or service usually demand to see the manager in order to override stubborn employees. Executives often intervene in workplace quarrels and often have the last word regarding the solution to a conflict.

However, people with delegated authority often work within a hierarchy of authority. For instance, an executive works for a president, board of directors, and/or owner. Executives who abuse their power not only jeopardize the position of their supervisors but also risk alienating their subordinates, their clients, and their peers. In modern-day large organizations, executives are expected to consult and listen to their employees and, if there is controversy, to use conciliation and mediation among rival parties before making an authoritative decision, which is widely regarded as a last resort. Furthermore, they are required to explain and justify their most controversial decisions.

Affluent societies are composed of an ever-increasing proportion of people with delegated authority. However, this growth does not always translate into more authoritative resolution of conflicts because the responsibility of those numerous officials is limited. They are also often in conflict with other people who share their claim to authoritative decision-making. Nevertheless, the importance of top-level executives and elected officials in conflict management and resolution is still unequalled and is mandated by the necessities of responsibility and legitimacy.

TRADITIONAL PROCESSES

Traditional indigenous societies around the world have developed their own ways of dealing with conflict, ranging from circle processes to tribal councils and open-ended dialogue processes. These methods are usually highly communitarian because any conflict, even an interpersonal one, has implications for the whole community. People in conflict are therefore expected to explain their situation in public and hear the comments and suggestions of people who may not have a direct stake in the feud. In case of failure or wrongdoing, they are expected to make amends and reconcile. Traditional approaches have generally involved some combination of community representatives meeting to discuss the conflict, councils of elders or respected leaders gathering to hear the parties and then making a decision, and the nomination of a wise person to hear the case and make a decision, functioning as a blend of mediator and arbitrator. As a result, components of traditional conflict resolution are in fact multi-purpose. For instance, local assemblies can help defuse a family feud in an African village as well as provide adjudication, commercial arbitration, political decision-making, consultation with the population, and communication to the people from the government.

Circle Process

Refined by the First Nations peoples of North America and by indigenous peoples in other parts of the world, a circle process begins with a prayer or a ritual to put people in a positive frame of mind. The leader provides teachings that orient what will happen during the circle. A talking stick, feather, or rock will often be used, and the teachings will include instructions that the talking object travels in only one direction, that only the person holding the object can speak (for as long as he or she likes), and that the others must listen carefully to the speaker. In the case of deep conflicts, it may be necessary to have several consecutive circle processes over several days. In the event of a full set of circle processes, the first circle identifies the primary issues. The second brings out the painful dimensions of the conflict. The third circle is the healing circle, while the fourth brings a sense of wholeness and closure. Circle processes tend to be indeterminate in that, even though there may be an issue that needs to be addressed, there is not a fixed goal.

A variation on the circle process is the sentencing circle, which has become popular as a restorative justice measure for both young and adult Aboriginal offenders. The sentencing circle is made up of an elder or respected member of the community, victim(s), offender(s), the families of both parties, and members from the criminal justice community. As the participants go around the circle, they explore the implications of the crime and what should be done about it. Their conclusions are given to a judge, who can incorporate them into the sentence.

Palaver

The word **palaver** refers specifically to West African community gatherings, but variations of the practice are widespread in small rural settings in the global South. Palavers are public meetings held to discuss problems and projects, such as farming or hunting issues, the appointment of people to leadership positions, government initiatives, or quarrels between community members. In Africa, the palaver often takes place under the "palaver tree" or in a dedicated "palaver house." The process can be lengthy, sometimes lasting for days.

When dealing with a conflict, the assembly will hear the testimony of all parties to the conflict, even marginal ones such as family members or neighbours. The audience then participates in the debate. In some settings, it is expected that everyone will say something, even if it is only to repeat other people's arguments. In some parts of Africa, the speeches and arguments regarding a conflict between two parties are noted in the soil or on a tablet, with a vertical stroke used for each specific argument and a horizontal line to divide one party's arguments from the other's. In some places, the palaver is almost a collective arbiter that attempts to reach a unanimous decision on the problem at hand. The community assembly can also serve as a consultative body for the local authorities. It is common to see the affairs of the community being decided by a smaller committee made up of notables or elders after holding an extensive public discussion.

Gacaca

The traditional approach in Rwanda is *gacaca* (pronounced "gachacha"), derived from the root word *grass*. Like the palaver, this approach involves the community. A group of "judges" or wise people sits on the grass, and the parties to the conflict present their cases. People from the community can ask questions or offer their perspectives. Afterwards, the judges confer and decide what needs to be done. After the 1994 genocide in Rwanda, this traditional process was revived and modified by the government in order to deal with low-level perpetrators of the atrocity (see Case Study 11.3). The process saved the country a lot of money by precluding hundreds of court trials and, in some cases, yielded reconciliation and closure. However, some Rwandans feel that the authoritarian regime's use of the traditional multi-purpose institution of gacaca as a low-level tribunal has been somewhat truncated and has tainted the approach.

CASE STUDY 11.3 | GACACA IN RWANDA

After the 1994 genocide of Tutsis and moderate Hutus in Rwanda, less than 15 per cent of the estimated 700,000 who participated in the massacre were in prison. Some of the leaders were tried in Arusha, Tanzania, by the International Criminal Tribunal for Rwanda, and some of the mid-level *génocidaires* faced criminal prosecution in Rwanda. However, the government had to do something about the remaining participants. To give them each a court trial would take so long that many would die of old age before the process was finished. To simply free them would send a message that people could commit genocide with impunity. The government's solution was to bring back the traditional gacaca process at the community level and use gacaca courts to try perpetrators who were not responsible for the planning of the genocide and had not killed a large number of people. Initially, there was no mandate for gacaca courts to try cases of torture and rape; however, they were later used to try rape cases in private.

With over 12,000 courts and 150,000 judges (of whom approximately one-quarter were women), the scale of the gacaca courts was enormous. The 2001 legislation provided a framework in which there were three administrative levels: regions, sectors, and cells. At the cell (or local community) level, a gacaca court was constituted with nine judges who were each called an inyangamugayo, the Kinyarwanda word for wise person. Criteria were established for the selection of these nine, along with seven deputies. Decisions could be appealed from the cell to the sector level and from there to the regional court.

Hearings took place outside and in the presence of the entire community (there was strong pressure for people to participate; the usual attendance number was 200). The nine judges would sit behind a table while the accused was brought forward, charges were read, and a plea (usually guilty) was entered. Members of the community would then be allowed to speak to the accused's guilt or innocence, functioning as lawyers, prosecutors, and witnesses. What might have been a matter of suspicion and gossip was brought out into the open. Families could ask perpetrators where the bodies of their loved ones were hidden. They could also ask about the circumstances of the person's death. The judges would decide on guilt or innocence and determine a punishment, which could include a prison term of up to 30 years. It was hoped that the punishment would enable perpetrators to eventually be integrated into the community and play a useful role.

Using the gacaca courts was a creative solution to a colossal challenge. However, the process did encounter some grave problems. In some cases, witnesses were intimidated or even killed. Some judges were disguised perpetrators; they were removed when discovered. Many cases of judges accepting money for dismissing charges were also reported. Culturally, declaring guilt sometimes represented an act of defiance rather than remorse. The number of victims that were confessed did not add up to the number actually killed. The process did not necessarily have the effect of reconciling relationships between the groups involved. Generally, the gacaca courts tried civilians because most military perpetrators were not known locally and the government made no effort to identify them from among those who were reintegrated into the army. The courts also lacked independence: the government was involved in the decision-making process in order to favour certain individuals for political purposes. In most cases, the proceedings were not properly recorded for future use. Furthermore, the courts were not authorized to deal with victim compensation issues.

Bashingantahe

In Burundi, the traditional conflict resolution process involves three or four *bashingantahe* individuals, who are specially and unanimously appointed by the community to lead the process. A bashingantahe is traditionally a man who is respected by everyone and seen as being fair. The conflict resolution process involves disputants bringing their conflict to the bashingantahe group in a public place open to all community members. A special ceremonial stick adds dignity to the proceedings. Those who speak hold the stick and hit the earth with it when they have finished. When all the presentations are over, the bashingantahe council dismisses the public and deliberates. After they have deliberated, they give their verdict and advice on how to proceed to the conflicting parties.

The Future of Traditional Conflict Resolution

In the West, traditional conflict resolution mechanisms have almost disappeared over time in favour of law and politics. The ADR techniques discussed in this chapter are rarely based on a precise tradition but are recent creations destined to relieve the legal system and are gradually finding a place in the culture and mores of the citizenry. However, in the global South, many countries understand the value of traditional community mechanisms in reducing the use of litigation and developing social capital. Traditional mechanisms are increasingly maintained, sometimes in a modified form, in order to complement the modern political and legal mechanisms imported from the West. In sum, the conflict resolution systems of the non-Western world comprise traditional elements, religious components, political and administrative structures, and modern judicial institutions.

Among North American Aboriginal peoples, there are special challenges to conflict resolution in a post-colonial context. In Canada, the Indian Act dismantled traditional institutions and gave Indian agents appointed by the government significant delegated powers over Aboriginal peoples. One traditional method that was abandoned was the election of leaders, which traditionally meant each clan or kinship group would have its own representatives. Under the Indian Act, each person has one vote; hence the largest kinship group usually elected the chief and a majority of council members, and the resources of the reserve were then used in a way that favoured this group. While traditionally there was no court system to hold leaders accountable, there were accountability measures built into the political organization. Among the members of the Iroquois Confederacy, for instance, the Council of Chiefs was appointed by the clan mothers. These women had the power to remove any chief whose performance did not respect the values of the community. The system also made certain that every kinship group was represented and that there was a well-developed process of achieving consensus among the members of the confederacy.

Many of the corruption and institutional challenges facing indigenous societies can be seen as a legacy of colonialism, which established delegated political and conflict resolution processes dominated by people selected by the colonial power. This practice often led to widespread political piracy, in which political office was used for personal gain. Indigenous leaders and researchers are currently working with communities to develop new forms of governance, complete with conflict resolution mechanisms, to provide a structure that will allow for self-government and contribute to economic and personal growth. Canada's Aboriginal peoples are rediscovering their traditions and want to put them to good use. However, they have to make decisions about how to insert their community practices within the framework of human rights, democracy, and accountability. They will have to establish their own hybrid system of conflict resolution.

MODERN CONFLICT RESOLUTION SYSTEMS

Large commercial or administrative organizations, municipalities and other urban organizations, and public services such as school boards and hospitals are under a great deal of stress when conflicts occur between employees, between management and employees, or between the organization and its clients. Lawsuits are very expensive and often aggravate the problem. Therefore, these organizations have developed a number of ADR mechanisms that allow for the resolution of most conflict without litigation and the management of unsettled conflicts. Modern conflict resolution systems reflect the idea that these methods should follow the shape of a pyramid. At the base, the larger number of conflicts should be resolved through informal mechanisms such as one-to-one negotiation and peer mediation. Authorities such as supervisors and managers should be as involved as possible in facilitating and mediating small conflicts. At a higher level of conflict, professional mediation services should be used. Arbitration is a possibility in many grievance issues. Finally, administrative and civil tribunals constitute the last option and the top of the pyramid.

This structure can also be applied to entire countries. In China, for example, mediation boards at the local and regional levels constitute the first line of conflict resolution mechanisms. Mediation is widely used, especially by people who do not have the status or connections to appeal to political authorities (Diamant, 2000). Administrative and Communist Party mechanisms are also used. Tribunals, however, are clearly seen as a last resort in a country where human rights are not a main priority and the use of the legal system is kept to a minimum (Michelson, 2007). It is possible that many Chinese people would like to have better access to tribunals, especially in a rapidly growing industrial economy. However, the system is built to avoid confrontation and perpetuate the myth of national consensus.

UNUSUAL METHODS OF CONFLICT RESOLUTION

Two unusual but theoretically usable strategies to resolve conflict are chance and skills contests. The use of each dates back centuries, with instances of chance being mentioned in the Hebrew Bible as the means of choosing King Saul in 1000 BCE.

Chance

There are instances where chance is used as a way out of certain conflicts. For example, a parent could stop his or her children from fighting over a toy or cookie by setting up a draw where the winner gets the coveted item. In many competitions, chance can be involved in the determination of the winner or at least give one side an advantage, such as when a football team wins the coin toss before the game.

Although ancient Athenians chose some people for high office by drawing names from an urn, the use of chance is less common in matters of great political and social importance. The use of chance in conflict resolution is also rare. While it is theoretically possible that adversaries in a cause may determine the winner in a card game or with the toss of a coin, no major recent examples come to mind. Chance determination is neutral and quick. It leaves no ambiguity as to the result. However, not many decision-makers would risk lives or treasury over a roll of the dice.

Skills Contests

There are many types of contests that could serve as a tool to determine who will predominate in a conflict. A long-standing form of contest for this purpose has been the duel. For centuries, men have used this violent contest to determine guilt or innocence (the judicial duels of Germanic customary law applied in Medieval Europe) or to establish predominance and honour (honour duels). In replacement of duels, sport competitions, games, and other skills contests pit two champions from opposite sides against each other. In modern times, elections and referendums are forms of contests that are applied to the solution of major conflicts. However, they are also types of authoritative allocation.

CONCLUSION

In this chapter, we examined how people consciously deal with conflict by using processes that help with communicating, identifying problems, reframing issues, and generating possible solutions. These processes can be directed by the people in conflict or involve third parties. Some third-party processes (mediation, facilitation, and conciliation) encourage negotiation, while others (e.g. arbitration and adjudication) are authoritative processes. There are traditional processes and new, hybrid ones (med–arb). Each process has its strengths and weaknesses. Therefore, every complex society needs several complementary mechanisms to prevent, manage, and resolve conflicts before they negatively affect social relations. Most of these approaches will be revisited in the next chapter, where we examine ways of resolving violent interstate and international conflict, particularly insurrections, civil wars, and armed conflict.

DISCUSSION QUESTIONS

1. Choose a conflict that you feel knowledgeable about. Show how negotiations would proceed in a distributive manner and what options would be generated by an integrative approach.

2. Think of three current conflicts that could potentially go to mediation. Discuss the approach that you think would be most effective in each case.

3. When is it advisable to use arbitration or adjudication to deal with a conflict? Give reasons to support your answer.

4. Choose an institution. How are conflicts within this establishment currently re-solved? What would be an optimum conflict resolution system for this institution? What kind of skill training would be needed to put it into place?

NOTES

1. See the National Center for Technology and Dispute Resolution (www.odr.info/) for in-formation on international ODR forums and Cyberweek, the organization's annual free online conference.

2. This book was originally published in 2000 as *The Shadow Negotiation: How Women Can Master the Hidden Agendas that Determine Bargaining Success*. The book was hailed as one of the most significant new titles in the field of negotiation, containing lessons that applied to both male and female readers.

3. A formal veto, such as that of the five permanent members of the UN Security Council, is the legal power to block an agreement. An informal veto is not a legal privilege but is nevertheless crucial in some negotiations. For instance, since World War II, major trade agreements have not been implemented if the United States, the world's largest economic power, has not agreed to them.

4. According to Ghais (2005, p. 2), facilitation became popular in the 1970s in the context of managing groups in organizations.

5. There is a distinct process known as appreciative inquiry, in which questions are asked as a "coevolutionary search for the best in people, their organizations, and the relevant world around them" (Cooperrider and Whitney, n.d.).

6. YOUCAN (www.youcan.ca) is one example of an organization that has trained thousands of young people in Canada and internationally.

7. For information on services provided in Canada, see www.hrsdc.gc.ca/eng/labour/labour_relations/mediation/index.shtml. The governments of a number of provinces and other countries also provide mediation services.

8. For further discussion, see Chapter 16.

9. An exception is the European Court of Human Rights, which acts as a last recourse in human rights cases in EU countries.

10. Note that a restorative justice approach emphasizes finding a consequence that makes things right (see Chapter 15).

12 | THE PREVENTION AND RESOLUTION OF VIOLENT CONFLICT

CHAPTER OBJECTIVES

This chapter will help you develop an understanding of the

- use of diplomacy and negotiation to resolve violent conflict;
- role of third parties, including international organizations, in the facilitation, mediation, arbitration, and adjudication of violent conflict;
- implementation of peace agreements;
- adjunct conflict resolution activities of monitoring and peacekeeping;
- elements of coercive peace and security actions;
- concept of peacebuilding; and
- use of confidence-building measures, disarmament, and arms control to prevent violent conflict.

INTRODUCTION

As we saw in Chapter 4, the level of violence in the international system is slowly decreasing. Although there are several fundamental reasons for this decline, this chapter focuses on transformations in the resolution, management, and prevention of violent conflicts. Practices such as diplomacy, negotiation and mediation, peacekeeping and peacebuilding, confidence-building measures, and disarmament and arms control are some of the elements involved in taming violent conflict. We discuss each of these factors in the following pages. We concentrate on large-scale conflicts within and between states because they affect large populations and international society. Major armed conflicts also have characteristics that make their settlements different from those of smaller feuds.

DIPLOMACY

While diplomacy is not the only means of resolving conflicts and is not devoted solely to that goal, it is still the main instrument used to settle conflicts between states. It also plays a crucial role in other forms of peaceful interactions, such as international law, trade, travel, and communications. The term is usually applied to the peaceful relations between states, but it is also used liberally to include all forms of delicate and complex interactions that settle possible disruptions between people. For example, people talk of "office diplomacy" when dealing with difficult co-workers or explosive situations. In such cases, one may ask other people to act "diplomatically."

In a more traditional sense, diplomacy means the art of peacefully managing the relations between states through negotiation. While diplomacy concerns itself with many other things, the settlement and prevention of violent conflict has always been paramount. Before discussing the modern settlement of disputes, let us recall briefly the evolution of diplomacy.[1]

The Emergence of Diplomacy

In the ancient world, the Greek cities were known to entertain constant diplomatic relations. After all, they were in close proximity, and their citizens spoke the same language and practised the same religion. The cities negotiated alliances, neutrality pledges, truces, and peace treaties in their ongoing rivalries. Sometimes, they would also ally against the threat of invaders, such as the Persians. However, diplomatic relations among subsequent kingdoms and empires were usually much less frequent and fruitful. Furthermore, many governments did not grant protection to foreign envoys, who could be held hostage or even executed during severe conflicts.

During the Middle Ages, diplomacy was a personal service to the monarch because he or she owned the kingdom. Rulers could use whomever they wanted to serve as envoys: priests, monks, bishops, friends, family, businessmen, military officers, artists, or intellectuals. Because they were relatively immune from violence, priests and monks were often used for diplomatic roles during this period. Diplomacy, however, was intermittent, non-professionalized, and poorly protected. All that changed during the Renaissance. Like the Greek city states of yore, Italian kingdoms maintained constant diplomatic relations. In the fifteenth century, they began establishing permanent embassies, which enabled negotiations to be conducted continuously and helped create complex and diversified relations between the kingdoms. However, it also made it possible for states to spy on each other and to support seditious groups in the host country. Diplomats could also be taken hostage and forced to influence the policies of their government.

Classic Diplomacy

With the development of diplomatic relations, it became important to verify that foreign diplomats were actual envoys of their government. People who officially represent a government are called **plenipotentiaries**, a title accorded through the exchange of official correspondence, usually to career diplomats. An official delegation may also include advisors, experts, and administrative and support staff. However, only the plenipotentiaries can negotiate and sign a document with a foreign power. Furthermore, diplomatic recognition is a worthy privilege that cannot be accorded to everyone. Countries started to develop diplomatic accreditation for the top diplomats, who had to present their letters of credence to the host chief of state in order to be recognized as true representatives of their sovereign. This sometimes fastidious process is still applied today to guarantee the good and ordered conduct of diplomatic relations.

Over time, it also became clear that, for diplomatic relations to be fruitful, diplomats and their facilities had to be protected against vindictive governments and hostile crowds. The principles of diplomatic immunity and extraterritoriality that we know now emerged in the sixteenth century. These rules basically state that accredited diplomats, their belongings, and their residences belong to their own government and therefore cannot be seized or destroyed by the host country. In other words, every embassy is a small piece of real estate belonging to a foreign government.

Another issue of diplomacy was the question of protocol, particularly rules of precedence. How should diplomats be announced? In what order should they enter or speak at a ceremony? In 1661, a major diplomatic incident occurred in London when the French ambassador's carriage travelled ahead of the Spanish carriage, insulting the Spanish ambassador. A scuffle erupted between their guards, and a Frenchman was killed. Louis XIV suspended diplomatic relations with Spain, and the incident may have resulted in war if the Spanish king had not eventually apologized (Nicolson, 1988, p. 99). An international rule of precedence was eventually agreed upon, and several protocols for introductions, ceremonies, and public appearances were devised.[2] From the seventeenth century on, the French court etiquette became the standard for guiding proper dress and behaviour in diplomatic circles. While protocol and etiquette rules have evolved over time, notably to account for technological and cultural innovation and to accommodate foreign participants, they are often perceived as superficial and outdated. Nevertheless, these formalities avoid incidents that could jeopardize diplomatic processes.[3]

A diplomatic profession started to emerge by the eighteenth century, when young aristocrats were trained to become plenipotentiaries. Usually, they received the classical curriculum of history, dead languages, and literary studies. The study of modern languages became important to conducting diplomacy after Latin lost its status. Italian, then French and (since World War II) English, became the predominant languages of diplomacy.

Pluralist Diplomacy

In the twentieth century, diplomacy evolved rapidly and increased substantially in scope. The classic model was also superseded by a new paradigm that we can label pluralist diplomacy. While diplomats once dealt mostly with consular issues and questions of war and peace, they are currently expected to conduct negotiations in several areas, including trade, money, and investment; foreign assistance; scientific and cultural co-operation; technical standards and norms; and tourism and student exchanges. In fact, no field of public policy now escapes international negotiations. The traditional position of diplomats as plenipotentiaries is threatened as they often have to take a back seat to specialists, administrators, and politicos in several fields, especially when expertise is warranted or when public opinion weighs on the issue. Furthermore, NGOs want to participate in international negotiations. Business associations and labour unions want to be on trade liberalization negotiation teams. Pacifists and academics want to participate in peace and security forums. As a result, many Western governments allow non-state representatives to sit in on delegations as experts and advisors. A good example of this practice is Canada's initiative to ban land mines, which included close co-operation between the Department of Foreign Affairs and International Trade and members of NGOs, who were even invited to be part of international delegations.

Heads of state and government leaders are also more present in current foreign negotiations. With the development of air transportation, no city is more than 24 hours away from another one. Summit diplomacy is also very widespread. Think of the G7/ G8 and G20 meetings, the large environmental summits (Rio 1992, Copenhagen 2009), and the annual UN fall meeting, where heads of state and governments converge to pass their message, get photo ops, and negotiate multilaterally and bilaterally. This presence of political leaders is related to the deepening of democracy in that it reflects leaders' desire to get more support for their policies and gain publicity by hobnobbing with the world's most powerful politicians. Diplomacy has never been completely immune to public opinion, but in the age of mass media, pressure groups, and opinion polls, political leaders and diplomats are now accountable to the public and to the groups of civil society. Consequently, foreign policy has lost some of its aura and autonomy. It is now public policy, just like any other domain of government administration.

Another change in diplomacy lies in treaty negotiation. In the old days, diplomats saw their job as negotiating accords that would be profitable to their government in the short- and medium-term. However, in the wake of the Westphalia treaties in the seventeenth century, pacts among states have resulted in the creation and rapid development of international public law. Accordingly, any accord signed by two or more governments can be seen as a brick in the edifice of world regulations. This dimension of diplomacy has grown even more since World War II, with the creation of an interdependent world society and its trade, economic assistance, human co-operation, and environmental components. Although diplomats still work first and foremost for the advancement of their respective states, their role also includes a wider scope. The accords that they sign may create or strengthen an international norm that will have generally positive or negative repercussions down the road. Diplomats also tend to consider that there are universal goals to their actions and that the national interest is not necessarily opposed to common purposes. Even the national interest has been redefined in multilateral terms. For example, who would have predicted that France and Germany would define their national interests in terms of European integration and institutions in the early twenty-first century?

This growing universalism is also a consequence of a more humanistic outlook on world affairs. Diplomats, like the rest of the population, are more humanistic, empathic, and peaceful than their predecessors. They are people of their age, a period where war is an unwelcome option in international affairs, abuse against vulnerable people raises disapproval, and racist and xenophobic attitudes are frowned upon.

Track II Diplomacy

Since the 1960s, many authors and activists have defended a new negotiation model known as track II diplomacy, informal diplomacy, or citizens' diplomacy.[4] The basic idea is to include non-diplomats in a negotiation, people who are close to the governing parties (and therefore have influence) but far enough removed so that they are free to test out new ideas in the hope of finding an acceptable solution. As one moves from this track to others, more participants are drawn from civil society and eventually from the grass-roots.

For example, in the 1960s, former diplomat John Burton, psychologist Leonard Doob, and others experimented with the formula of the Problem-Solving Workshop, notably in the Middle East, Africa, and Northern Ireland, where they led small groups of political leaders, civil servants, and notables in discussing ways to resolve conflicts.[5] Track II diplomacy is about exchanging points of view, brainstorming solutions, negotiating limited local agreements (left to proper authorities to approve), expressing feelings, or enabling reconciliation initiatives.

In some situations, governments actively encourage unofficial diplomacy in an effort to gain progress on secondary issues, prepare further negotiations, test possible solutions to conflicts, or assure the public that work is being done. In effect, track II diplomacy is not always unofficial but is usually sanctioned by political authorities. Characteristically, in the case of authoritarian governments, participants are drawn from the ranks of the bureaucracy or are closely guided by officials. In fact, this form of diplomacy mostly involves government-endorsed elites, such as local politicians, religious leaders, businesspeople, community leaders, academics, and journalists. It is not difficult to understand why: these notables are chosen because they represent the views of other people and are sufficiently aware of the big picture to be able to work with one another. In certain contexts, the fact that talks must be conducted in the language of the majority or in a second language (i.e. English or French) limits participation to those who meet this criterion, which favours the elites over the masses. Unofficial diplomacy has been criticized for repeatedly including the same type of people—or indeed the same individuals (see Ball, Milner, & Taylor, 2006). Some authors have advocated a sort of track III diplomacy, where people from regions affected by conflict can meet with minimal intervention from government officials or social elites (Kraft, 2002).

Despite these reservations, unofficial diplomacy is here to stay. It can fulfill many tasks of negotiation, especially at the local level, and can help develop and test proposals for the future. It can serve as a good method for evaluating potential negotiators and emerging opinion leaders in peace processes. It is also a good sounding board for current innovative ideas and public opinion.

NEGOTIATED PEACE SETTLEMENTS

In this section, we present the evolution of negotiated peace agreements that have led to new kinds of relationships between states. We also note the development of increasingly magnanimous peace agreements that endeavour to pave the way toward a more lasting peace between the relevant parties.

Vae Victis!

Throughout history, most armed conflicts have been resolved by the military victory of one side. In many civilizations, especially in ancient times, the victor would punish the defeated harshly or even eliminate it altogether. "*Vae victis,*" said the Romans, or "Woe to the fallen."

The first aspect of victory was the plundering of the defeated's possessions. Such assets were seen as the rewards of the victor and, for many armies, one of the main means of paying the soldiers. Enslavement of populations, a lucrative business, was another normal consequence of many wars. From the Greeks and the Romans to the Ottoman Empire and the old African kingdoms, slavery was largely fed by wars. Plunder and enslavement were a punishment for the enemy, a deterrent to future wars, and a way to weaken the defeated society for a long time. In fact, victors often demanded severe compensations (a practice that continued until the twentieth century) and heavy taxes from the conquered party to cover the costs of the war and keep the losers subjugated.

What the victorious armies could not take with them or eat on the spot, they would burn or kill. The physical and symbolic punishment of the vanquished population was another classic consequence of the end of war. Readers of Thucydides' *History of the Peloponnesian War* will remember that, after defeating the mutinous island colony of Melos, the Athenians killed all the men and boys and sent the women into slavery. In the fourteenth century, Mongol hordes killed masses of people for pleasure and intimidation. The legend is that, when Tamerlane entered conquered cities, he was sometimes greeted by the spectacle of high pyramids made from the chopped heads of the local inhabitants. Conquerors often tortured and mutilated their enemies in order to weaken and intimidate them. After his victorious Gaul campaign, Julius Caesar sent back thousands of captured enemy soldiers with their hands cut off at the wrist in order to deter any resistance to Roman rule and to impose on Gaul tribes the economic cost of taking care of "useless" men. As we have seen in earlier chapters, rape has been another form of punishment. Finally, the victor might impose symbolic humiliations. For example, the Romans would make their captives pass under the Claudine Forks, a wooden contraption that forced the walking prisoners to bow their head to the Roman ensigns. Many conquerors also forced their victims to renounce their faith and adopt the victor's creed.

Landmark Peace Agreements

Although they were uncommon, negotiated settlements of wars exist in all eras. These agreements were occasionally signed when the war had reached a stalemate or when the parties decided that ending the war was more profitable than extending it. The use of negotiation to end wars has increased in the West since the seventeenth century.

One seminal peace agreement from this time is the aforementioned 1648 Peace of Westphalia, the importance of which we can still appreciate today. The treaties of Westphalia were signed by the winners and losers of the Thirty Years' War, an extremely violent armed conflict that devastated the Holy Roman Empire after its Catholic emperor used force to try to submit the Protestant princes to his authority. Foreign powers got involved; for example, Spain backed the emperor, while Sweden supported his rebellious Protestant subjects. France, a Catholic power, put its weight with the Protestants in order to weaken Spain, its old rival. Eventually, the Empire and Spain had to admit defeat.

The Westphalia treaties are one of the most important diplomatic documents of all time. They effectively robbed the emperor of his last powers, paving the way for new kingdoms and nations (although it took another two centuries for Germany and Italy to emerge). The temporal power of the Church of Rome was curtailed, and religious wars were stopped. The treaties also crystallized the borders of Europe. While borders were a fuzzy concept before Westphalia, the signatories agreed that clear borders were needed to establish ordered kingdoms, limit territorial contests, and avoid the transnational depredations of mercenaries and brigands. Experts were sent to establish those lines and to put them on maps. Some fortifications were dismantled, while new walls and towers were erected elsewhere to mark the borders and observe local activity.

The main achievement of the Westphalia treaties was to confirm that the choice of religion in a given country belonged to the monarch. Countries could become Protestant or Catholic and offer certain privileges to the minority religion (e.g. France under Henri IV). The modern notion of sovereignty, or the exclusive power of the state over other political actors, was strengthened by this important settlement.[6] Finally, by implying that periodical consultation between great powers could help in the peaceful management of their relations, the treaties of Westphalia can be understood as a distant precursor of modern multilateral summit diplomacy.

Other early peace settlements were based on punitive measures. Not only did the defeated states have to give up what they may have gained before or during the war, but they also had to offer some compensation for the costs of the war. If they were considered instigators, they were especially targeted and had to pay hefty monetary or territorial reparations. For instance, in the 1763 Treaty of Paris—which ended the Seven Years' War and took three years to negotiate—France had to cede most of its empire (including Canada, Louisiana, and its colonies in India) to England and Spain.[7]

Aside from the occasional official apology and promises of non-aggression from the van-quished party, early peace accords did not include many measures enabling a lasting peace. Military occupation of all or parts of the defeated country were, however, a fixture of these agreements. Needless to say, this occupation was often brutal and predatory and did not help in solving the differences between countries. In the ancient world and during the Middle Ages, hostages were sometimes taken to insure that the parties would keep their word. Another form of post-conflict settlement was the arrangement of dynastic marriages that would link two royal or noble families and presumably reduce the chances of future war. Disarmament and confidence-building measures were sometimes arranged—as in the Peace of Westphalia—but these are more a feature of the contemporary world.

Because early peace settlements were generally not constructed to address all the root causes of the conflict, subsequent wars were often waged, particularly when the losing party tried to regain its lost ground and honour. However, there have been exceptions to this rule. The most famous one is the Congress of Vienna, called by Prince Metternich, the prime minister of Austria, to end the Napoleonic wars.[8] Between October 1814 and June 1815 (while Napoleon was a prisoner on the island of Elba), negotiations about the future of France and Europe took place amidst elegant and luxurious festivities in the Austrian capital. Prince Metternich had a brilliant idea: to facilitate the return of France to monarchical rule and the future stability of dynastic Europe, he invited the French to the negotiation table. In his mind, a punishing stand against France could only encourage Napoleon's partisans to revive their imperialistic dreams. The final agreement was very magnanimous. France was exempt from having to pay monetary compensation, allowed to keep its colonies, and considered a permanent member of the Concert of Europe, the informal council of great powers that was to manage European affairs.[9] The Congress of Vienna introduced the generous treatment of vanquished powers, a principle that came to predominate 150 years later.

After Vienna, however, victors returned to their old ways. For example, Prussia imposed very high reparations on the defeated French following the war of 1870–1. After World War I, the Allied powers negotiated the terms of the peace agreement, excluding the Central powers. The 1919 Treaty of Versailles forced large reparation sums and harsh conditions on Germany because it was declared to be the instigator of the Great War.[10] Germany had to abandon its overseas colonies and the parts of Europe that it occupied and keep its armed forces to a minimum. France was especially interested in weakening Germany, and Great Britain and Italy were not far behind. American President Woodrow Wilson wanted a more magnanimous offer but could not restrain his allies. The Treaty of Versailles is often portrayed as a major cause of World War II in that it alienated the German people and planted the seed for a renewal of German imperialism.[11]

The victorious Allied powers of World War II avoided some of the mistakes of 1919.[12] They chose not to impose reparations on Germany, Italy, or Japan. Actually, the Americans did the very opposite: they financed the reconstruction of the Axis powers. Japan was even allowed to keep its emperor at the helm, despite the fact that he could have been tried for war crimes. The Americans believed that such actions would keep these countries from becoming communist; however, the avoidance of future wars was also on their minds.

Since World War II, great powers have generally been magnanimous in their treatment of defeated countries. Today, reconstruction and peacebuilding efforts occur almost everywhere there has been an armed conflict. The United States has devoted significant sums of money to the rehabilitation of some of the countries that they have attacked and invaded, such as the Dominican Republic, Grenada, Panama, Bosnia, Serbia, Afghanistan, and Iraq.[13] It seems that self-interest and humanitarianism have converged in these cases.

The Increase in Negotiated Settlements

The practice of negotiating peace treaties to end foreign wars has increased enormously since 1945.[14] Heavy reparations are a thing of the past, although there can be sanctions. Furthermore, international assistance for monitoring the peace, rebuilding infrastructure, and stimulating development has been forthcoming.

There are several reasons for this change. For one thing, wars are very expensive. The costs of armaments, transportation, and facilities are astronomical. Weapons systems are very complex and need to be upgraded continuously, as exemplified by advanced aircraft.[15] Furthermore, most of today's soldiers are professionals rather than conscripted people or volunteers and therefore need to be well compensated for their efforts and the risks that they incur. The military must also compete with other employers and offer reasonable working conditions in order to attract young people to its ranks. Affluent and even emerging countries now find their armies very costly.

The human costs are also a contributing factor to the rise of negotiated peace agreements. Although contemporary wars are less deadly than past wars, they seem more so for two main reasons: media exposure and the value accorded to human life. In 1993, videos of 18 dead American soldiers dragged through the streets of Mogadishu were enough to convince President Clinton to end the Somalia mission and pull out of potential trouble spots in Africa. With the emergence of 24-hour news coverage in the late 1980s, people have talked of a "CNN effect."[16] The expression "body bag syndrome" has also been coined to describe the reluctance of the American public to engage in foreign wars. Historian Edward Luttwak (1994b) has tried to explain the phenomenon in relation to the dwindling demography of affluent countries.[17] However, what we should remember from Chapter 7 is that the growth of humanism and individualism has meant that the intrinsic value of human life has risen independently of demographics in the Western world, a situation that is unlikely to decrease.

Another reason that peace treaties have become more common is that great powers are generally interested in a rapid and negotiated solution to interstate wars when they sense that the conflict's escalation risks engulfing them in dangerous war preparations. With nuclear weapons at the ready, it is always dangerous to let a regional conflict get out of hand. Of course, there are exceptions to this rule, such as the Israeli–Arab conflicts. Although Israel and Syria's continued rivalry poses a threat to regional and world security, it is unlikely that the two countries will go to war as long as other powers (e.g. Jordan, Iraq, Lebanon, and especially Egypt) are at peace with the Jewish state or are neutralized.

While the financial and human costs and escalation risks partly explain why there are more negotiated settlements today, we should not forget the effect of international institutions and processes. The UN and other international organizations are very active in trying to facilitate peaceful settlements, providing conciliation and mediation services, helping in the monitoring of ceasefires and peace agreements, and mobilizing support for political and economic reforms. Great powers, neutral powers, and neighbouring states regularly offer their services to mediate conflicts and supply troops for peacekeeping duties. More important, perhaps, a cultural change regarding war has occurred. War is no longer seen as inescapable but as a social behaviour that, to a degree, can be mitigated and avoided. It is no longer a necessary evil of human existence but a situation that can be resolved in negotiations, with the help of third parties.

The Case of Intrastate Wars

Historically, intrastate wars have been less amenable to negotiation and resolution than those at the international level. Instead, they have usually been settled by the victory of one side. Most of the religious wars of the fifteenth and sixteenth centuries were extinguished in this way. For example, the domination of Anglicanism in Great Britain came out of successive Catholic defeats, such as the repression of Catholics by Henry VIII (1534), the execution of Mary Stuart (1587), and the Glorious Revolution (1688).

(AP Photo/Bob Daugherty)

The Camp David Agreement, perhaps the most famous interstate peace treaty in recent history, was signed in 1979. Mediated by US President Jimmy Carter (centre) and signed by Egyptian President Anwar Sadat (left) and Israeli Prime Minister Menachem Begin (right), the treaty contributed to the attempts to stabilize Middle Eastern politics. However, it did not settle the Palestinian–Israeli conflict.

There is one exception to this rule that should be noted. In 1589, Protestant Prince Henri de Navarre became king of France under the name of Henri IV. In order to end a religious war of over 30 years and gain the loyalty of his subjects, he agreed to convert to Catholicism. Nine years later, he signed the famed Edict of Nantes, which granted French Protestants freedom of conscience and reserved a few cities where they could worship openly. The end of the religious war in France is one of the rare occurrences of a peaceful resolution of a major internal conflict before the twentieth century. In retrospect, the Edict of Nantes can be seen as an early example of tolerance, although this word was not used at that time.[18] Tolerance was a revolutionary idea in Renaissance Europe, when people usually thought that there was no salvation beyond their faith.[19] The concept became a mainstay of the Enlightenment thinkers. Although tolerance seems a bit outdated nowadays and is criticized by many minority advocates who believe that mere tolerance is paternalistic and inefficient for accommodating difference, we should not forget its lasting effects on the pacification of social relations.

Since World War II, most violent conflicts have occurred at the intrastate level. In the late twentieth century, the peaceful resolution of such conflicts occurred at a growing frequency and included international diplomacy. In the past, these conflicts were ignored by outsiders or fuelled by foreign parties that sought political advantage in backing one of the warring factions. The situation has changed considerably in the last few decades. While it is true that some recent internal wars were neglected or supported by foreign parties (e.g. those in Myanmar and the Democratic Republic of the Congo, respectively), most have featured some kind of international effort to try to achieve a peaceful resolution.

CONTEMPORARY PEACE AGREEMENTS

The Pacific Settlement of Disputes

The Charter of the United Nations (1945) was devised to "save successive generations from the scourge of war" (Preamble). In order to achieve this worthy goal, the UN identifies peaceful and forceful means at the disposal of nations. We will focus on the former means here. (The latter, referred to as collective security, is covered in the section on coercive actions.)

Chapter VI of the UN charter is devoted to the "pacific settlement of disputes." In its opening article (art. 33), it states that "(t)he parties to any dispute, the continuance of which is likely to endanger the maintenance of international peace and security, shall, first of all, seek a solution by negotiation, enquiry, mediation, conciliation, arbitration, judicial settlement, resort to regional agencies or arrangements or other peaceful means of their own choice." Several tools for conflict resolution are listed here. Negotiation, arbitration, and judicial settlements (i.e. adjudication) are true means of ending conflicts, while the others are mostly variations on or aids to negotiation. It is also important to mention here that, of these three types, negotiation and all its manifestations are by far the most widespread means of peaceful settlement.

Arbitration and Adjudication

As we have seen in Chapter 11, arbitration uses a third party to authoritatively decide on the solution to a conflict. Adjudication is settlement by a tribunal using law as its main guide. While these methods can resolve various types of conflict, they are rarely used to settle violent international conflict.

In the nineteenth century, many people in several organizations of civil society asked for the generalization of arbitration and adjudication in international conflicts. At the first Hague Peace Conference in 1899, it was decided to set up the Permanent Court of Arbitration (PCA), an organization that still exists. The PCA, originally financed by famed American financier Andrew Carnegie, has been involved in many small conflicts between states and even non-state actors over the years. However, it was not involved in the most famous case of international arbitration: the settlement of the Russo-Japanese War by American President Theodore Roosevelt in 1905. These two expansionist countries had waged a war over territories in China and Korea, with Japan winning decisively at the naval battle of Tsushima and the siege of Port Arthur. However, in order to facilitate a way out of the contentious issues that led to the war, they asked for an arbiter. Roosevelt acted rapidly and wisely and was awarded the Nobel Peace Prize for his efforts. The only recent example of the arbitration of a potentially violent conflict is Pope John Paul II's involvement in the controversy between Chile and Argentina over some small islands in the Beagle Channel. The outcome was a 1984 treaty between the two neighbours. However, it seems that the issue was not resolved to the satisfaction of Argentina, which has elected to keep its options open in claiming the islands.

In the wake of the Treaty of Versailles, the public push for adjudication in international affairs led to the creation of the Permanent Court of International Justice (PCIJ) in 1922. After World War II, this organization was replaced by the International Court of Justice (ICJ), also based in The Hague.[20] The ICJ has been useful in settling a number of conflicts, often in the fields of maritime borders, extraditions, and aerial incidents.[21] Some complaints have been related to violent conflicts. For example, Serbia tried to have the 1999 NATO intervention in Kosovo declared illegal in a series of cases against individual NATO states. The Serbs, diplomatically isolated, were trying everything they could to regain some kind of respectability. The NATO powers, convinced that they could not lose, agreed to go before the ICJ and won.

Because it cannot force a state to appear in front of the tribunal, the ICJ deals mostly with secondary issues, not major conflicts. For major conflicts, states are often afraid to be declared in the wrong and have to suffer the consequences. Therefore, they generally prefer to resolve violent conflicts through negotiation. Unlike a judicial decision, which can be one-sided and humiliating, negotiation allows the parties to find middle-ground agreements, creative solutions, and face-saving measures.

That said, we should not reject the role of international arbitration and adjudication too quickly. These modes of conflict resolution are actually widespread in the system, notably in trade matters. The World Trade Organization (WTO) and other trade institutions, such as the European Union (EU) and the North American Free Trade Association, use arbitration mechanisms and trade tribunals to settle contentious issues, particularly those regarding trade barriers, dumping, and discrimination. Bilaterally, states have also used informal arbitration by renowned experts over trade issues. States generally comply well with the decisions of trade panels, but they always maintain the option of renegotiating a decision that they deem unfavourable to their interests. In sum, although arbitration and adjudication have not become the main instruments of conflict resolution as was hoped for by nineteenth-century progressives, they have become crucial to the maintenance of an ordered trade system, an important part of sustaining a co-operative world.

Negotiating Peace Agreements

The objective of the negotiations between warring parties is the signing of a peace agreement. These accords include the terms of the basic settlement of the conflict, accompanied by a number of measures designed to safeguard the transition to peace. In this section, we examine the following methods of negotiating a peace agreement: direct negotiation, good offices, inquiry, ceasefire, and mediation.

In direct negotiation, the two parties discuss an issue face to face, without any help from third parties. This approach has been observed in the many negotiations between India and Pakistan since their independence in 1947, as well as in the 1973 peace talks between the United States and Vietnam, which led to the former's withdrawal from Indochina. Unassisted negotiations have also been observed in the case of disarmament agreements between the superpowers during the Cold War. To put things into perspective, there are hundreds of unassisted negotiations between states and over myriad topics of joint interests every year. For instance, two countries sharing a long border and a high level of trade, such as the United States and Canada, are constantly in negotiation over many issues.

For nations in violent conflict, direct negotiations are sometimes preferred by strong states that do not want smaller powers interfering in their business. However, such negotiations are not always possible. When hostilities and stakes are high, the parties often cut all diplomatic links and allow anger and resentment to rule out even the most informal talks. Third parties are therefore required to bring the enemies to the negotiation table.

The old diplomatic expression "good offices" describes the use of third parties to facilitate communication between adversaries. (The word *facilitation* is often used in its place today.) This role is very well suited to the secretary-general of the UN and other major international civil servants. Actually, the function of a "special representative" of the UN's secretary-general providing assistance and support to the parties in conflict has rapidly increased since the end of the Cold War. States have also been known to be good facilitators, such as in the case of Norway easing the way into the American mediation between Israel and the Palestine Liberation Organization in the Oslo talks of 1993. In recent years, the practice of selecting a few states (known as a group of friends) to assist negotiation in international conflict has risen. Non-governmental actors such as humanitarian organizations, religious leaders, and prestigious individuals have also acted as facilitators in transmitting messages between warring parties.

Facilitation is not always enough to ease negotiation. Oftentimes, a third party will be asked to provide information about the contentious situation to the parties. The secretary-general of the UN (often represented by a special envoy) is regularly asked to perform fact-finding missions that can provide a neutral assessment of a particular situation. This process prevents a negotiation from becoming bogged down in arguments about facts and figures.

Sometimes, third parties also informally provide accurate military intelligence to, for instance, reassure rivals that neither is preparing a surprise attack. Because most of this valuable information is gathered through aircraft and satellites, it usually comes from great powers. Although commercial real-time imagery is now available and occasionally consulted by the UN, the organization must still rely on its members for military intelligence.

The pacific settlement of international disputes has also been helped by the development of measures such as ceasefires. A ceasefire, as the name implies, is an agreement to stop hostilities in a certain place for a certain time. During the Middle Ages, there were truces on Sundays and on holy days. With the decline of church authority, those truces were gradually abandoned. However, ceasefires re-emerged in the twentieth century and are now a common and crucial fixture in conflict resolution that allow for diplomacy to take precedence over fighting and offer settlement possibilities.[22] The secretary-general of the UN always calls for (and frequently obtains) a ceasefire when starting a negotiation process. The generalization of ceasefires is one of the essential, if overlooked, aspects of contemporary conflict resolution.

Mediation is another method used to resolve violent conflicts. The use of third parties as mediators in wars has existed for a long time, but this practice has grown considerably in twentieth-century international and domestic relations. When mediation is performed by international organizations or certain international commissions of inquiry, the term *international conciliation* is used in international public law.

Among states, the United States has been responsible for most of the mediation attempts in the post-Cold War period. Why is this so? First, the United States pursues its national interests in every part of the planet. No conflict escapes its scrutiny because any could endanger investments and trade, weaken allies, or force military interventions. Mediation is often the least costly and demanding action that a great power can take in times of war, and the United States is powerful enough to impose its mediations the world over, by threats if necessary. Second, countries plagued by violence often demand American involvement because they think that it will end the conflict sooner and avoid further damages. The capacity of the United States to reward co-operation and punish non-compliance through foreign aid, investments, and trade openings is also taken into consideration by states in conflicts.

For example, the United States has been the main mediator in the Israeli–Arab conflicts since the 1940s because Israel, a state with many enemies, believes that the United States is a reliable ally that will not let it down. US mediations have been crucial for the evacuation of the Suez Canal (1956), the Yom Kippur War ceasefire (1973), the Israel–Egypt peace treaty (1977), the withdrawal from Lebanon (1983), the Oslo accords (1993), and the end of the Lebanon War (2006). It may be surprising that the mediator of these agreements is a close friend of Israel. However, in international affairs, things are sometimes different than in domestic politics. Such a manifestly biased mediator would be unacceptable in a wage dispute, but the United States is sought after as a mediator in the Middle East and elsewhere even when people believe that it is not a neutral third party (Zartman & Touval, 2001).

Nevertheless, states that have fewer power resources but enjoy a good reputation and the support of many other states can perform mediation. Regional powers, neutral states, and neighbouring states are sometimes involved in the process. For example, Tanzania was active in mediation in the 1970s, as was Libya in the 1990s and 2000s. Their roles were helped by the personalities of their respective leaders, Julius Nyerere and Muammar Gaddafi, whose reputations of standing up to former colonial powers gave them good credit in Africa.[23]

CASE STUDY 12.1 | THE ESQUIPULAS PROCESS

During the 1980s, several civil wars raged in Central America. In Guatemala, the government committed scores of human rights abuses against Indigenous rural communities and the guerrillas. The regime of Napoleon Duarte in El Salvador had to fight a communist insurgency while trying to control extreme right-wing militias. In Nicaragua, the Sandinista movement, backed by the Soviet Union, took power, while the United States supported the Contra forces and Indigenous insurrections directed against the communist government. These violent conflicts were killing thousands of people, destroying property and crops, and generally delaying the economic development of the region. Central American wars were largely fed by injustice and repression but were also encouraged by foreign powers (chiefly the United States and the Soviet Union) and by neighbouring states (for example, Nicaragua and Cuba supported communist insurgencies).

In 1983, the Contadora Group of Mexico, Colombia, Venezuela, and Panama started a peace process that led to an agreement, but it was not implemented. Three years later, a new process began under the leadership of Costa Rican President Oscar Arias. Generally respected by conservatives, liberals, and communists, Arias was always interested in building political and economic bridges between Central American countries. He led a country that remained immune from violent clashes for two major reasons: since 1949 it had had a stable democracy and no armed forces. Arias wrote a new proposal that was inspired by the Contadora process and led to the negotiation of the Esquipulas II accords. Signed in 1987, these agreements included measures to favour democracy and human rights, demobilization and disarmament of armed forces, and humanitarian assistance. It also insisted on ending foreign assistance to rebel groups. Arias's work earned him the 1987 Nobel Peace Prize.

Following the Esquipulas process, the Nicaraguan government and opposition agreed on the dismantling of Contra guerrillas and the holding of free elections in 1990. Peace accords were signed in El Salvador in 1992 and Guatemala in 1996. The accords and elections in Central America were monitored by missions of the UN and the Organization of American States (OAS). Although poverty and exploitation are still present in Central America, the region has remained peaceful and democracy is taking root. Economic reforms and political stability have led to significant increases in welfare.

Non-governmental actors have also been involved in mediation. The most famous example is that of the lay Catholic community of Sant'Egidio, which mediated the peace process between the armed factions of Mozambique. The community invited representatives of the two groups to meet at their Rome headquarters, and an accord was signed in 1992. Mozambique came out of civil war relatively easily (if we compare it to cases such as Sudan or Angola) and has been quiet and democratic ever since. Even private citizens have used their influence to try to mediate conflicts. First among them is former US president Jimmy Carter, who has been involved in numerous attempts at good offices and mediations, notably in North Korea, Haiti, and Bosnia. President Carter also created the Carter Center, an organization committed to human rights, and won the 2002 Nobel Peace Prize.

Non-state third-party mediation is a recent phenomenon in contemporary affairs.[24] It is still relatively rare but will probably grow. However, it should be remembered that, in most cases, non-state mediators have been successful only when backed by great powers because they cannot personally offer threats, rewards, or guarantees to help the parties in conflict reach an agreement. In fact, such is the situation in world affairs. As we said before, the main mediators are often those who can entice the disputants to discuss the conflict by using their power to punish and reward.

Experts of mediation such as William Zartman (1989, 1995a) usually contend that mediation works best when the parties have reached a state of **mutually hurting stalemate**. This situation happens when both start to realize that any reasonably negotiated solution would be better for their interests than pursuing their military hostilities. This realization usually occurs when the parties have lost many fighters, their economy is in shambles, their foreign sources of support are drying up, and their leaders are personally exhausted. Then, as Zartman says, the situation is **ripe** for a negotiated solution.

In such a negotiation, the mediator will try to convince the parties that fighting is contrary to their interests and that agreements are within reach and of little cost. The mediator will ask the parties to compromise on some points, give up some demands, and accept the involvement of other third parties (e.g. in peacekeeping). At times, a good mediator will be able to devise imaginative solutions to thorny problems. However, negotiations often fail because the disputants are deeply divided over the questions. To convince parties to return to the negotiation table, it is often necessary to use pressure.

Third-party mediation, even when performed by a neutral agent, is not necessarily an ideal and just process. One party is often clearly weaker than the other and has to give up more. Sometimes, solutions that do not respect the principles of efficiency, fairness, or justice must be sought in order to stop the fighting. Despite all their faults, negotiated agreements reduce the carnage and destruction of war, generally allow the parties to save some of their resources and reputation in the process, and protect the weaker party against further reprisals.

Content of Peace Agreements

In the simplest peace treaties between states, the parties agree to return to the *status quo ante bellum*, meaning that things should just return to what they were before the war. Borders are re-established, and armed forces withdraw to their barracks. In most cases, however, things are more complex. Some states may want to receive territories or financial reparations. Refugees, prisoners of war, and war booty must be returned. Plus, the signatories must agree on some guarantees that the accord will be upheld. Sometimes, measures such as buffer zones, limitations on dangerous weapons, and verification by third parties are established. Such peace treaties can be complicated and detailed (Bell, 2008). However, these agreements pale in comparison with those that end civil wars. Because the parties fight over many things (e.g. government, state institutions, values, social norms, economic organization), complex and comprehensive agreements are necessary for their reconciliation. The parties cannot just go back to their borders and act as if nothing happened.

While the size and complexity of peace agreements have increased over time, there is no universal template. Elements that are included in some accords might be neglected in others. In these cases, the missing pieces can be dealt with in separate documents negotiated concurrently or after the original agreement.[25] Obviously, a peace agreement will address questions such as the return of refugees, disarmament of combatants, relocation and demobilization of armed forces, demining, reconstruction, humanitarian aid, and so on.

More fundamentally, a peace agreement is a political arrangement for ensuring peaceful relations between groups that were at war. It must therefore address crucial issues such as the following: Should the country change its form of government? If so, would a parliamentary, presidential, or mixed system be best? Should the constitution be rewritten? Should powers be decentralized? Which powers? Should the electoral system remain the same? Should the country adopt some kind of proportional representation to assure the presence of minorities in government?[26]

Nowadays, most political arrangements favour democracy. This is a fundamental trend in the international system, as we have seen before. As for the rest, there are differences. For instance, some countries emerging from war do not see the need to rewrite their constitutions. Most Latin American countries did not modify their US-inspired republican constitutions after violent conflicts. For them, ensuring respect for the existing constitution was the paramount objective. In Africa and Asia, however, constitutions were sometimes rewritten or altered to maximize the chances for peace. Mixed systems in the French tradition (with an elected parliament and cabinet led by a prime minister, along with a president elected by the population) seem quite popular in today's developing world. Decentralization also appears to be gaining ground, although true federal systems remain uncommon. Some innovative, albeit idiosyncratic, regimes—such as the three entities system in Bosnia and Herzegovina—have also been devised.[27]

Another set of issues in peace agreements concerns institutional reforms in the public service, security forces, and subsidiary organs of the state. Prior to and during a war, these institutions are often politicized, corrupt, and lawless. They are populated by members of the dominant party, family members, and business partners of the ruling elite. These people often abused their office and paid themselves by diverting money or engaging in the black market or extortion. Reforms of state institutions toward professionalization, transparency, and accountability are often high on the agenda of peace agreements.

Economic issues have also been prominent in several peace accords. When economic disparities and poverty are among the main causes of the conflict, it is normal that the parties discuss and implement ways of resolving these problems. For instance, some agreements have included land reform, rural marketing schemes, or road construction, with the intent of providing better revenues to peasant populations. Fiscal reforms intended to force the wealthy to pay for accrued public services, notably in health, education, and basic infrastructures, have been promoted (albeit not always implemented as intended). Promises for diverse regulatory reforms devoted to facilitate business creation, workforce retraining, union certification, and imports and exports are also part of some peace agreements.

Other questions that a peace agreement must address are related to human rights and law. Should the country adopt a charter of rights? What should be included in this charter? How can human rights be guaranteed? Are human rights commissions necessary? Is the judicial system up to the task? What judicial reforms should be implemented? The idea that there are fundamental human rights that cannot be infringed upon by the executive or the legislature has been gaining ground in the world since the end of the Cold War.[28] Therefore, many charters of rights (and not only those of post-war countries) embody this principle. Consequently, national legislation must be modified to better include and protect human rights. Judicial systems are improved and professionalized in order to provide better access and fairer results to the appellants. Human rights monitoring bodies are also quite widespread: some are general (e.g. human rights commissions), while others are devised to supervise the activities of institutions such as the civil service, the police, or the army.

A classic thorny point in all peace negotiations is the issue of how to deal with the massive number of human rights infractions and incidents of repression that occurred before and during the war. In certain situations, people have been imprisoned, tortured, raped, starved, or massacred by government and insurgent officials at all levels. Should all these people be tried or only the leaders? What about other suspects who were not taken to court?

Countries emerging from civil war and/or large-scale repression have dealt with these issues in a variety of ways (La Haye, 2008). Some have ignored human rights infractions and tried to forget the whole thing. Such was the case in many former communist countries and in Chile after the dictatorship. In other countries (e.g. Peru and Argentina), only a few prominent figures were tried, and the rest went scot-free. Sometimes, the main suspects were tried by UN tribunals because the relevant countries were unable to prosecute the offenders. This approach was used for Bosnia, Sierra Leone, Liberia, and Rwanda. In other cases, the prosecutions extended to a number of high- and medium-level officials but stopped there.

In most countries recovering from heavy political violence, the main instrument used to shed light on atrocities, reveal responsibility, and generate apologies has been truth and reconciliation commissions (TRC). Many peace agreements include a provision to create such an organization. The best-known example of a TRC is that of South Africa in the years after apartheid. This commission, inspired by and presided over by Nobel Peace Prize winner Desmond Tutu, sought to disclose human rights abuses that occurred during the white rule period (Gibson, 2004). It offered perpetrators and witnesses who agreed to testify immunity from prosecution. This TRC has often been portrayed as a success and has inspired the creation of similar bodies in different parts of the world. However, several TRCs had been conducted before, notably in Central America (Hayner, 1994). More than 28 TRCs have been held, some still ongoing (e.g. Canada's commission on residential schools). These commissions have differed on several fronts. Some were quasi-legal entities with a capacity to subpoena witnesses, while others could only invite the participation of witnesses. Some were devised with a large mandate covering an extended period, the entire country, and all levels of abuse. Others were more specialized in outlook.

TRCs offer countries emerging from large-scale political violence a complement or alternative to judicial pursuits, which can be very long and costly and reveal only a certain number of cases. They allow for the discovery of facts (e.g. the whereabouts of the remains of executed people) that may be very difficult to ascertain from other methods. They give victims and their friends and relatives the opportunity to express their emotions, ask questions, and gain a sense of closure (Chapman, 2001). They provide a way to point the finger at bad policies and at human rights abusers without sending the country into a political crisis over guilt, reparations, or power-sharing.

PEACE MISSIONS

The next step in the creation of a lasting peace is to apply the conditions of the peace agreement. In the end, the parties are responsible for applying or ignoring the peace treaty. Most of the actions required will originate from the former warring parties. For instance, if a former combatant group is insincere about its intentions to participate in the democratic process, it may ruin the elections and cause the country to revert to chaos. The ultimate purpose of post-conflict policies is to avoid defection from the peace process. One instrument for this goal that has been prevalent since the 1950s is the use of third parties as guarantors, verifiers, and sometimes enforcers of peace agreements. In this section, we survey some of the peaceful and coercive ways in which third parties are involved in defusing potential disputes and protecting vulnerable populations from armed conflict.

Observation

Traditionally, the main problem with ceasefires and peace treaties is that they can be used by a party to launch a surprise attack. Therefore, third parties are needed to guarantee that such truces are effectively maintained. In fact, ceasefires are so successful nowadays primarily because we can verify them reasonably well through a combination of neutral troops (e.g. UN blue helmets), satellites and aircraft, and even ordinary citizens using modern means of communication. The UN, in particular, has distinguished itself in the monitoring of ceasefires. Ever since its creation, the UN has deployed military observers in some of the most dangerous corners of the world, from Kashmir to the Golan Heights, to prevent the breaching of ceasefires. These efforts have not always been successful, but the presence of neutral military observers has prevented some violence in those parts of the world.

Observers are also routinely employed to monitor the implementation of peace treaties. In some cases, borders must be patrolled and combatants must disarm. Civilians must return to their homes unharmed. When the government and opposition forces agree and where contentious issues are minimal, **observation missions** are enough to guarantee the safe return to peace. Such was the case in most Central American countries after the civil wars of the 1980s and early 1990s. However, in other situations, observation missions were insufficient. For example, the UN contingent in Rwanda was unable to protect the Tutsi minority from genocide after the unravelling of the Arusha Peace Accords in 1994. Observation missions are small, and the soldiers carry light arms only. Therefore, they cannot achieve much when significant violence occurs, and they often have to be pulled out at the first sign of trouble.

Peacekeeping

In October 1956, British and French paratroopers landed in Egypt and seized the Suez Canal, while Israeli troops attacked Egyptian positions in the Sinai desert and made their way to the canal. The two European powers waged this attack to stop Egyptian President Gamal Abdel Nasser from nationalizing the canal, which was a private Anglo-French property at the time. Israel allied with them to create for itself a defensive buffer zone

(AP Photo/Eyob Alemayexu)

A Canadian soldier patrols the demilitarized zone between Ethiopia and Eritrea in 2001, one of the last traditional peace-keeping missions performed by Canadians. Since interstate wars are now relatively rare, most peacekeeping missions occur after civil wars and involve complex deployments, often in the heart of cities and villages.

in the Sinai. The United States and the Soviet Union were furious at this action because it destabilized the dangerous Cold War balance. President Eisenhower, who was running for re-election, did not want to look weak and told the European allies to withdraw. Nevertheless, Western diplomats wanted to avoid another war in the Sinai and were concerned about ending this crisis without humiliating their allies. UN Secretary-General Dag Hammarskjöld and Canadian Foreign Minister Lester B. Pearson devised a solution. They suggested the deployment of a sizeable contingent of foreign troops, the United Nations Emergency Force (UNEF), to protect the canal and separate the Egyptians from the Israelis. Peacekeeping was born and has been an interesting addition to the international instruments devised to stabilize volatile situations.

Peacekeeping missions differ from observation missions in that the former are interposition operations used to create and enforce a buffer zone between adversaries. Peacekeepers are therefore more numerous and better armed than observers. However, they are instructed to use their weapons only in self-defence.[29] Peacekeeping missions were deployed in certain situations during the Cold War, such as Cyprus, the Democratic Republic of the Congo (DRC), India, and Pakistan, and were useful in defusing some tensions that may have threatened the East–West equilibrium.

Preventive Deployments

In some situations, the UN has used peacekeeping in a preventive manner, meaning that the contingent was not part of a resolution to safeguard a ceasefire or a peace agreement but charged to preclude a situation from becoming violent. The best-known example of preventive deployment is that in Macedonia between 1995 and 1999, which was undertaken to keep this neighbour of troubled Bosnia and Serbia from sliding into chaos.

To a certain extent, the various UN and OAS peace missions in Haiti since 1993 could be considered preventive because the country never experienced a full-fledged insurrection. Instead, it faced political repression by the government met by low-level violent resistance from the population. After the ousting of putsch leader Colonel Cedras in 1993, the UN Mission in Haiti (UNMIH) prevented other military personnel from trying to usurp power from the new president, Jean-Bertrand Aristide. This action prompted a violent clash between the two sides. In 2004, the forced withdrawal of Aristide by the leaders of the second UN mission (MINUSTAH) avoided the country's descent into violence.[30]

Preventive deployments have often been advocated by UN officials and academic experts over the years. However, there are some limitations to this method. First is the question of where and when to deploy preventive missions. As we have seen before, peacekeepers who are sent into volatile situations may become hostages to better armed and ruthless factions. Second, the insertion of preventive forces in unresolved situations may become an alternative to genuine peace agreements and actually delay or even derail a peace process if the parties find that a preventive deployment serves their interests. Finally, financing is also an issue. International organizations are financed by their wealthiest members, who are sometimes reluctant to add financial burdens to their international peace and security expenses. Preventive forces will always be seen with suspicion as they may draw money away from more promising interventions.

COERCIVE ACTIONS AND PEACE: CHAPTER VII AND BEYOND

It is crucial to keep in mind that the international society of states has never renounced the use of force to stop aggression and violence in the world. The Charter of the United Nations has also never completely ruled out the possible use of force. Although it has outlawed unilateral aggression against another state, it still permits the use of force in self-defence or in collective attempts to stop an aggression. The latter is called collective security and is dealt with in Chapter VII of the charter.

Sanctions

When persuasion and negotiations are unable to stop an aggression, the United Nations Security Council (UNSC) can impose sanctions against the aggressor state.[31] At the first level are diplomatic sanctions. When these restrictions are imposed, countries are to remove their ambassadors from the targeted country. Diplomats from that country are also to be expelled from host countries. Limitations on travel are another type of sanction that is intended to hurt the aggressor's dominant class and business elite. Arms and high technology embargos can be used to restrict access to sophisticated armaments.

Specific commercial sanctions that can block imports and/or exports are often implemented next. Because of its strategic importance, oil is a traditional sanction instrument. General across-the-board economic sanctions, which constitute a severe form of penalty, are sometimes imposed. Such measures can weaken a country considerably and decrease the well-being of its population. In the case of a tyrannical leader holding onto power, his or her foreign assets, as well as those of his or her country, can be frozen.

Although economic sanctions are the main instrument of collective security and have been used in several instances, their record is mixed. They had some impact on cases such as Rhodesia (now Zimbabwe) in the 1970s and South Africa from the 1970s to 1990s, where they put pressure on those racist regimes to accede to black majority rule. However, their impact has generally been insignificant or even negative since the League of Nations sanctions against Japan and Italy in the 1930s failed to stop the Manchurian and Ethiopian invasions, respectively. In most cases, sanctions were ineffective against authoritarian governments that were impervious to the needs of their populations and that could use their propaganda machines to turn public opinion against foreign powers. The main consequence of economic sanctions is often the aggravation of most of the population's living conditions, including accrued deaths due to malnutrition, starvation, epidemics, or lack of medicine. The initial theory behind the idea of such sanctions is that leaders threatened by popular uprisings and coups d'état would eventually agree to negotiate an end to the war. This hypothesis often fails when autocratic and brutal governments are concerned.

As a last resort, the UNSC may mount a military intervention against a state that is unmoved by all pressures and sanctions. This kind of sanction was authorized against North Korea in 1950 and Iraq in 1990. The fact is that UNSC members are often divided on the pertinence of authorizing military operations against a state. The five permanent members can use their right of veto to block coercive actions that are directed against one of their allies or that will involve them in an unwanted, costly, and unpopular UN operation.

The case of Iraq in 1990–1 is a good example of sanctions at work. When President Saddam Hussein invaded the small kingdom of Kuwait in 1990, a large coalition of states opposed his move and requested that he abandon his conquest. The UNSC imposed diplomatic sanctions, then air travel restrictions and economic sanctions, and finally authorized the coalition (led by the United States) to force the Iraqis out of Kuwait. When, in the following years, it became clear that Iraq was not co-operating with the international inspectors in charge of dismantling the country's weapons of mass destruction (WMDs) programs, the UNSC inflicted new economic sanctions that were very costly for the Iraqi people. They restricted the export of oil—by far the country's main commodity—and the supply of foreign goods, including food and medicine. Still, the regime did not comply with the UNSC but tried to portray the Iraqi people as the innocent victims of an international conspiracy. The UN then decided to organize a "food for oil" program that allowed Iraq to sell some oil on the world market and buy food and medicine for its citizens. The program was partly successful in that it increased the supply of basic commodities to Iraq, but Iraqi government officials and shady international middlemen still managed to limit the inflow of food and line their own pockets with some of the money generated by the program. Without enough medical supplies, the health of the Iraqi people deteriorated. In the end, Hussein never complied with UNSC demands for full inspections of his weapons facilities. He was deposed during the US-led invasion in 2004.

In recent years, the international community has been more interested in so-called smart sanctions, which target the elites of a society rather than the masses. These sanctions include restrictions on travel; freezes on money transfers, investments, and assets; targeted trade restrictions (e.g. weapons, high technology); and sporting and cultural boycotts. They are limited to some extent by banking secrecy, the black market, and the support of allied states. Even under the stricter UN sanctions, the Iraqi leadership enjoyed a very comfortable lifestyle, although it could not travel outside of the country. The same is true of the North Korean leadership. It remains to be seen whether smarter trade sanctions will convince future rogue regimes to negotiate in good faith.

Peace Enforcement

The collective security aspects of the UN Charter were devised to stop wars between states, which are on the wane. After the Cold War, however, there was a surge of civil wars created by the power vacuum that followed American and Soviet withdrawals from unstable zones. Fortunately, the newfound entente between the superpowers enabled the UN to intervene in internal wars. However, peacekeeping rapidly showed its limits, especially in Bosnia and Herzegovina. Some Chapter VI peacekeeping operations had to resort to force for reasons of self-defence, civilian protection, and government constraint. These actions are sometimes called Chapter VI and a half operations and have been found in Bosnia, Somalia, the DRC, and Chad.

More muscular interventions were sometimes warranted, and the UNSC members had no choice but to invoke Chapter VII stipulations on domestic situations. As in many texts of law, the language of the charter is general enough to allow for some interpretation. For instance, the expressions "international peace and security," "threats to the peace," "breach of the peace," and "international aggression" (see, especially, art. 39) have been reinterpreted to include instances of domestic organized violence that could have repercussions on foreign third parties, thereby justifying a collective intervention.

Article 47 of the charter requires that military interventions be directed by a UN multilateral command, the Military Staff Committee. However, great powers have always been reluctant to put their forces under foreign command, and this institution has never been effectively activated. Starting in the 1990s, the UN has instead authorized groups of states (such as the US-led coalition of the Gulf War) and regional organizations (such as NATO in Bosnia and Herzegovina) to undertake military interventions on its behalf.[32] Since that time, the term **peace enforcement** has been used to represent the changes from the original practice of collective security. Such operations by groups of states operating with a Chapter VII UN mandate are numerous and include Bosnia, Haiti, Somalia, Sierra Leone, Liberia, East Timor, and Afghanistan.

The military operations assumed under Chapter VII have strongly influenced the course of major internal conflicts. For example, the NATO campaign in Bosnia and Yugoslavia in 1994 brought the Serbian government back to the negotiation table and led to the signing of the Dayton Accords. Military interventions also ended the awful massacres in East Timor, Sierra Leone, and Liberia and prevented conflicts in countries such as the Central African Republic, Ivory Coast, and Afghanistan from expanding or reigniting.

Nevertheless, peace enforcement is criticized. Many in the peace movement would prefer that the UN never authorize the use of force. In the global South, peace enforcement is often viewed as a tool used by great powers to reassert their authority over weaker states. Still, a number of people in the developing world criticize such missions for exactly the opposite reason. In other words, they believe that, in poor countries that are strategically or economically unimportant, peace enforcement is not used enough. Another criticism of peace enforcement missions is that they are very expensive and distract resources from pursuits such as development aid, democratization, and peacebuilding, which could bring more long-term benefits.[33]

Peace enforcement in domestic settings by various coalitions of states is now a well-established practice. Its role in conflict resolution has proven invaluable in certain cases, but it is not a substitute for peaceful conflict resolution and prevention. It is, therefore, still a last-resort measure.

Humanitarian Intervention

Another question has confronted decision-makers, experts, and the general public in the 1990s and 2000s: Should foreign states be allowed to intervene forcefully against a government that is mistreating its population? Proponents of **humanitarian intervention** claim that the international community is morally entitled to use coercion against any government committing massive human rights violations that lead to a large number of casualties in unarmed populations.[34]

During the nineteenth century, many decision-makers among Europe's great powers thought that they were the guardians of Christian ethnic groups oppressed by the Ottoman Empire and reserved the right to use force to protect their foreign brethren. For example, the French used the humanitarian argument to justify an intervention in Lebanon on the side of the Christian minority in 1864. The problem with humanitarian intervention today is that, unless called for in accordance with Chapter VII of the UN Charter, or in self-defence, war is forbidden in the international system. The sovereign equality of nations remains the cornerstone of the UN Charter; therefore, it contains no references to armed humanitarian interference.

However, in the early 1990s, the increased sensitivity for human rights and the decreased tolerance for violence stimulated calls for intervention in several cases, such as Bosnia and Herzegovina, Rwanda, Liberia, and Sierra Leone.[35] There were decisive forceful interventions by NATO in the first case, by Nigeria in the second, and by Great Britain in the last.[36] These interventions were partly motivated by humanitarian concerns but were made possible by political interests. Unfortunately, many other interventions that may have saved lives in other countries were not undertaken. International society did not have a policy regarding massacres and abuses that could not be dealt with under the international peace and security clause of Chapter VII. The case of Rwanda was especially appalling because the Canadian commander of the small UN peacekeeping forces, General Roméo Dallaire (2003), had requested an 800-men contingent with a stronger mandate to help him protect the victims in the capital city, to be followed by 5,000 well-armed professional soldiers to stop the killings across the country. Alas, the permanent members of the UNSC did not understand or care about the grave humanitarian situation developing in Rwanda and did not authorize a larger intervention.

When NATO bombed Serbia to protect the people of Kosovo in 1999, some Western politicians, including Canadian Foreign Minister Lloyd Axworthy, defended the operation as a humanitarian intervention. In the wake of this event, the Canadian government established the International Commission on Intervention and State Sovereignty. Under the chairmanship of former Australian foreign minister Gareth Evans, this group published *The Responsibility to Protect* (2001), a document containing guidelines about the use of force to protect lives. The authors proposed the notion that states have the responsibility to protect their own population against large-scale abuses. In some circumstances and as a last resort, foreign states can undertake violent interventions to protect the populations of a state. The set of criteria used by the commission resembles the traditional just war criteria for determining whether a war is worthy of pursuit (see Chapter 14). For the commission, armed humanitarian interventions should be used only as a final option and when it will reduce human suffering, is authorized by a legitimate authority (i.e. the UN), and has a reasonable chance of success. In the course of such interventions, the protagonists should act from a clear mandate and chain of command, scrupulously follow the laws of war, and provide humanitarian relief.

The principle of humanitarian intervention received official recognition in 2005 in a resolution put forward by Secretary-General Kofi Annan at the UN General Assembly. However, the resolution is vague and only mildly constraining. Many states and citizens harbour reservations about humanitarian interventions because they conceive of them as a new form of imperialistic interventionism. Others doubt that humanitarian interventions can be undertaken often and significantly. For example, the cases of the DRC and Sudan have often been mentioned as potential applications of the responsibility to protect. The massacres of civilians in Darfur were even briefly alluded to as a genocide by President George W. Bush and Secretary of State Colin Powell in 2004. However, the United States and other Western powers balked at organizing costly, murderous, and politically unpopular operations in those distant lands. For some critics, the American invasion of Iraq gave intervention a bad name and precluded intervention in Darfur, consequently killing the idea of humanitarian intervention (see Weiss, 2004; Williams & Bellamy, 2005). This argument might be exaggerated, however. Darfur was the theatre of horrible abuses,

---

BOX 12.1 | CRITERIA FOR ARMED HUMANITARIAN INTERVENTION

From International Commission on Intervention and State Sovereignty. (2001). *The responsibility to protect*. Ottawa: International Development Research Center, p. xiii.

1) Just Cause (large actual or impending loss of life)
2) Precautionary Principles
   a) Right intention (reduce human suffering)
   b) Last recourse
   c) Proportionality
   d) Reasonable chances of success
3) Appropriate Authority (UN endorsement)
4) Operational Principles
   a) Clear mandate
   b) Clear chain of command
   c) Gradualism and limits to the use of force
   d) Rules of engagement are proportional and humane
   e) The use of force should not become the goal
   f) Coordination with humanitarian organizations

but it was not obvious to most states that it was genocide. The international response—as in the DRC—was to send a peacekeeping force instead. The situation has improved somewhat in both countries, but the conflicts are not completely resolved.

It is probable that humanitarian interventions will not be widely practised. Against big countries with significant armed forces, this method would amount to large-scale wars and is therefore unlikely to be supported by the international community. However, despite this limitation, the UNSC has authorized the use of sanctions and armed force for humanitarian reasons when a moderate use of force could be successful. Furthermore, the humanitarian concern has entered the decision process regarding Chapter VII interventions. In other words, grave abuses of human rights may sometimes tip the balance in favour of peace enforcement operations. The intervention in Afghanistan, for example, was initially justified by the war on terrorism, then by the principle of international peace and security, and later by humanitarian concerns for the country's people.

Humanitarian interventions are not a means to resolve conflicts peacefully. To the contrary, they are an act of war destined to force states into doing what is wanted of them. They are also not concerned with conflict resolution but with justice and humanity. Nevertheless, their links with conflicts and conflict resolution—if only because they are usually undertaken under a Chapter VII mandate—are numerous enough that they can be considered a part of conflict studies.

PEACEBUILDING

Ceasefires and peace treaties in and of themselves do not ensure orderly and thriving societies. Over the last two decades, peacebuilding has emerged as a concept to describe the deliberate steps taken to transform post-conflict societies. This section examines the roots and stages of the concept, as well as its record.

The Emergence of a Concept

In 1995, UN Secretary-General Boutros Boutros-Ghali published *An Agenda for Peace*, a document devoted to identifying the priorities of the organization in the post-Cold War world. The most intriguing and innovative concept of the document was that of peacebuilding. Originally labelled as post-conflict peacebuilding, it was defined as any initiative that could "identify and support structures which will tend to strengthen and solidify peace in order to avoid a relapse into conflict" (Boutros-Ghali, 1995, p. 21). While Boutros-Ghali initially argued that peacebuilding was supposed to take place after hostilities had ceased, he later conceded that it could occur during or even before an armed conflict. For instance, agreeing to a humanitarian ceasefire during a conflict in order to protect endangered populations is a form of co-operation that can be useful for future peace negotiations.

Peacebuilding is not to be confused with reconstruction, although there are some commonalities between the two. Reconstruction, as the word easily suggests, is concerned with rebuilding infrastructures and houses destroyed or damaged by war, returning cultivable land to use, recivilianizing the state and industry, and restarting services offered by government agencies. Peacebuilding is more than reconstruction. It is about creating the conditions for a lasting peace, which implies not simply rebuilding what already existed but forming new attitudes, behaviours, and institutions (Doyle & Sambanis, 2006; Berdal, 2009).

Peacebuilding often takes place alongside peacekeeping deployments in post-conflict areas, and non-specialists often confuse the two terms. However, peacekeeping is first and foremost about monitoring and patrolling a ceasefire zone. It may or may not include peacebuilding-oriented activities. Early peacekeeping missions, such as UNEF I and II in the Middle East, were not mandated for anything other than maintaining a ceasefire. It should be mentioned, though, that, since the 1990s, UN blue helmets have been increasingly involved in the provision of humanitarian aid, the maintenance of public order, and the performance of some development assistance services that fall under the peacebuilding mantle. Such tasks have been referred to as second generation peace operations (see Mackinlay & Chopra, 1992; Warner, 1995; Arbuckle, 2006).

Two other misconceptions about peacebuilding should be refuted here. First, many people tend to associate peacebuilding—as well as peacekeeping—exclusively to UN operations. This is not true; peacebuilding efforts are now incorporated into all major post-war missions endorsed by regional organizations such as the EU, NATO, the OAS, and the African Union and are a part of all efforts sustained by individual states and informal coalitions. Second, peacebuilding is often thought of as a form of development aid. While it is true that most peacebuilding is funded by overseas development assistance (ODA) budgets, host governments must implement and partly finance their own peacebuilding policies. For example, while foreign donors can help the post-conflict democratization process in a given state, it is the responsibility of the national government, civil society groups, and the citizenry to develop and sustain their own democratic attitudes and behaviours if democratization is to succeed.

Peacebuilding is often thought of as a means of inserting the concept of **positive peace** into the mainstream discourse. Coined by Johan Galtung (1964, 1969, 1981), positive peace connects true peace to a process of emancipation and development, not simply to the absence of war (**negative peace**). Another concept that is associated with peacebuilding is that of **human security**, a term popularized by Axworthy in the 1990s (McRae & Hubert, 2001). Human security means that the real objective of security is not to protect the state or society but to attend to the needs of individual human beings (Tadjbakhsh, 2007; Goucha & Crowley, 2008). It calls for a conception of security that is more in touch with the demands and perceptions of ordinary people, including dealing with matters such as economic insecurity, environmental degradation, health concerns, criminal activity, and gender and ethnic inequalities. When peacebuilding is seen as an application of positive peace and/or human security, it assumes a more ambitious dimension and fuels the hopes of those who are working for a world that is more just and peaceful.

However, the philosophy of peacebuilding remains unclear (Paris, 2001). Many people feel that the term does not need such an idealistic connotation but that it should be taken at face value, as a set of interesting policies to perform in post-war situations. Nevertheless, critics such as Kenneth Bush (2004) have argued that such a perspective is vulnerable to the "commodification" of peacebuilding, or the transformation of an emancipating ideal into a technocratic practice that becomes its own industry with its own interests.

The Four Transitions

For the sake of clarity, peacebuilding can be analyzed as a series of four mostly simultaneous and somewhat overlapping transitions between a state of war and a stable peace: the security transition, political transition, economic transition, and social-cultural transition. The security transition is the first and the most spectacular phase. Some people will even confuse it with the whole of peacebuilding, even though it is only one aspect and is closely associated with peacekeeping and peace enforcement. Peacebuilding activities pursuant to the security transition comprise, among other things, the promotion of the following:

- demobilization, disarmament, and rehabilitation of combatants (often labelled together as DDR)
- lawful and non-threatening policing
- professionalization of security forces
- elimination of unexploded ordnance
- effective surveillance of borders

The political transition refers to a regime's passage from being unaccountable and repressive to democratic and liberal. In effect, liberal democracy is now a fundamental objective of all peacebuilding efforts. Political transition includes the following activities:

- establishment of a viable and representative interim government
- organization of fair elections
- creation and consolidation of representative parties and interest groups
- protection of women and minorities
- accountability and effectiveness of public administrations
- fair and accessible legal system

The economic transition attempts to facilitate a state's shift from a war economy to a peaceful economy and to create the conditions for long-term economic development. It includes the following measures:

- instilling confidence in the accounting and management of public institutions
- favouring open bidding and hiring on merit instead of favoritism
- rebuilding and repairing infrastructure and housing destroyed by war

- training and educating the workforce
- increasing fiscal revenues and fighting tax evasion and corruption

Finally, the social-cultural transition can be defined as the passage from a culture of violent conflict and intolerance to the general attitudes of peaceful conflict resolution and dialogue. In this pursuit, the following peacebuilding policies can be noted:

- enabling contacts among people from different communities (often through cultural, artistic, and sporting activities)
- favouring reconciliation, truth, and dialogue
- training people in the peaceful resolution of conflicts
- eliminating structural and ingrained prejudice through the transformation of school curricula
- encouraging professional, neutral, and positive media reporting

The Peacebuilding Record

Genuine peacebuilding has been around only since the late years of the Cold War. The UN Namibia operation in 1988–9 is often recognized as the first peace mission with a

(AP Photo/Jerome Delay)

The holding of free and fair elections is one of the most important aspects of the transition from war to peace and generates high hopes in the population. One of the most spectacular post-war elections saw the victory of the first female head of state in Africa, Liberian President Ellen Johnson Sirleaf, shown here at her inauguration on 16 January 2006.

real peacebuilding component. This mission was highly successful—refugees were brought home; public order was maintained; and free elections were held. In 1991, the UN embarked on a massive peacebuilding effort in Cambodia, which had been ravaged by colonialism, invasions, civil wars, and genocide. Over 40,000 foreign personnel were mobilized for a vast two-year assistance effort that was the showcase for demonstrating that the UN could do marvels for countries emerging from the worst catastrophes. The Cambodia operation was a qualified success (Doyle, 1995). Intense humanitarian efforts were undertaken; demining was started on a grand scale; people were relocated in their towns and villages; and a lawful state was created. Although Cambodian democracy has encountered several difficulties, the system has held and the country's economy has taken off. Another success story is the UN mission to Mozambique in 1992–4, which helped the country smoothly transition from civil war to competitive democracy.

However, other peacebuilding endeavours have not been so successful. The expensive electoral and humanitarian assistance to Angola went up in smoke when the UNITA movement restarted the civil war after its electoral defeat in 1992. The mission in Somalia ended in shameful withdrawal in 1994. Hostilities in Bosnia and Herzegovina kept escalating despite conciliatory UN attempts until NATO decided to go to war against Serbia in 1995. The small mission in Rwanda could not stop the worst genocide since World War II. For a while, the peacebuilding record started to look quite negative. Roland Paris (1997) wrote that it was primarily unsuccessful, attributing most of the blame to attempts to create liberal and democratic states before consolidating them. However, these worst cases were not repeated later on and the peacebuilding record started to improve.[37]

While some missions have been dismal failures, it can be argued that peacebuilding has been a qualified success overall. Operations in Central America (Guatemala, El Salvador, Nicaragua), Namibia, Cambodia, Mozambique, East Timor, Croatia, and Bosnia and Herzegovina are generally considered to have been instrumental in bringing these countries to a lasting peace. Another group of missions can be said to have been half successful, such as Sierra Leone, Liberia, and Haiti. Finally, there are recent or current missions that have not yet yielded unmitigated results: Kosovo, Afghanistan, the DRC, Sudan, and the Ivory Coast.

In recent years, peacebuilding has looked more and more like a new form of nation-building. This term was used in the 1950s and 1960s to describe large-scale interventions designed to turn former European colonies into successful states on the Western model. These efforts have been largely discredited, given that only a small proportion of the new states developed rapidly as stable free-market democracies enjoying economic growth. Nevertheless, some contemporary peace missions—notably the ambitious effort in Afghanistan—are often compared to nation-building. For example, Canadian government documents and websites use the terms *comprehensive approach, 3D approach* (for diplomacy, defence, and development aid), and the *whole of government approach* to describe the integrated attempts at turning this remote, violent, and destitute country into a unified and responsible member of the twenty-first-century international community. Depending on their political leanings, modern-day critics of peacebuilding attack these efforts as an imperialistic enterprise, a waste of lives and money, or as a dangerous pipe dream. Time will tell if such apprehensions are founded.

However, one should not conflate peacebuilding and nation-building. Peacebuilding can be modulated for different circumstances. In some cases, it can be relatively cheap and light and cannot be confused with nation-building. Only in some societies marked by extreme poverty and violence, and where the international community has decided to invest heavily, do peacebuilding activities become very ambitious.

Peacebuilding is one of the major innovations in peace operations since World War II. It has failed at times, but most of these disappointments cannot be attributed only to the incompetence or unwillingness of foreign and local partners to implement adequate policies for the four transitions. Most failures originated from the imperfections of the peace process itself and the work of rogue actors trying to keep their claims to power alive. In this sense, the so-called failures of peacebuilding are simply collapses of peace processes, the likes of which are always going to happen. Overall, peacebuilding policies have smoothed the peace process and enticed actors to try collaboration instead of confrontation. They have also allowed actors to think about wide, practical, and long-term measures to bring about the necessary conditions of peace.

CONFIDENCE-BUILDING MEASURES

Confidence-building measures (CBMs)—also known as confidence- and security-building measures (CSBMs)—are the policies and processes established to lessen the possibility of crises and wars between states and/or armed factions. CBMs are devised to reassure actual or potential adversaries and to entice reciprocal co-operation (Hoffmann, 2006). For example, a UN peace force can be considered a CBM, as its purpose is to guarantee that the parties to a peace agreement do not attempt a surprise attack, provocation, or some other kind of violent mischief.

While third parties such as powerful states or international organizations are sought after to protect peace accords, CBMs can be put in place without a third party. They can instead be negotiated privately by the two parties. For instance, many of the CBMs in the nuclear field during the Cold War were negotiated by the United States and the Soviet Union alone. CBMs can also be decided unilaterally. For instance, a state may announce that it is withdrawing its border troops to reassure its neighbours about its intentions.

There are many types of CBMs, and there is constant innovation in this domain. Some CBMs are aimed at improving transparency about the size and disposition of armed forces. For example, from the 1970s to the end of the Cold War, NATO and the Warsaw Pact traded information about troop numbers and locations. The parties also notified each other as to their military manoeuvres and naval exercises so as to avoid misunderstandings about the functions of those deployments.

In order to increase transparency, rival states may consent to have their agreements verified by each other or a third party, such as a UN force. In 1955, President Eisenhower proposed that the United States and Soviet Union allow periodic surveillance flights over each other's territories to ensure that neither side was preparing an attack. The Soviets refused, and it was not until 1992 that President George H.W. Bush could finally put together the Treaty on Open Skies, which has been signed by both superpowers and 32 other countries. Even as satellites now permit countries to monitor the situation at a safe distance, such agreements are still implemented as symbolic measures, especially in the case of adversaries that do not enjoy a full satellite capability (e.g. India and Pakistan).

The placement of military units far from borders, coasts, shared bodies of waters, and other sensitive places is a classic CBM. During the Cold War, for instance, NATO and the Warsaw Pacts entered such agreements, notably through the MBFR (Mutual and Balanced Force Reductions) in the 1970s. Another standard CBM is the improvement in communications between adversaries in order to exchange messages rapidly, clearly, and safely. After the Cuban Missile Crisis, the Soviet Union and the United States established the "red telephone" line, allowing their leaders to communicate directly in case of a crisis.[38] Eventually, more advanced means of communication were installed between Moscow and Washington. In recent years, New Delhi and Islamabad have set up such means of communications to manage their periodic crises more safely.

Better means of armed forces and weapons control are another significant type of CBM. For example, among nuclear powers of the 1960s, the creation of instruments such as double key systems, secret access codes, and protected lines of communications was an effective way of reassuring rivals and the general public that weapons could not be fired inadvertently or be subject to unauthorized seizure. This control added an element of moderation in the tense encounters between nuclear powers. Partial disarmament measures also acted as a powerful CBM in fragile peace situations. For example, the partial disarmament treaties of the Cold War era were symbolically and politically significant in the reduction of tensions.

Finally, a large number of goodwill gestures involving ordinary citizens have served as CBMs in many cases. For instance, the Indians and Pakistanis agreed to resume bus service between New Delhi and Lahore after their confrontation of 1999. Family reunification initiatives have also been put forward between these two countries, as well as China and Taiwan and (during the Cold War) East and West Germany.

DISARMAMENT AND ARMS CONTROL

The reduction of armaments has often been understood as a valuable complement to peace and humanitarian efforts. Disarmament has assumed a much more dramatic importance with the invention of nuclear weapons and other WMDs in the twentieth century.

General and Complete Disarmament

Traditionally, the purpose of disarmament has been to forbid weapons, the logic being that people will not fight wars without armaments. The language of many UN resolutions and international treaties still resounds from this moral call for "general and complete disarmament," or the elimination of all categories of weapons. A strand of literature on the peace dividend argues that the conversion of military know-how and expenditures into valuable civilian pursuits is one of the keys to economic development (see Chan 1995; Gleditsch, Lindgren, Mouhleb, Smit, & de Soysa, 2000). In the Bible, one can find the famous injunction to "turn swords into ploughshares" (Isaiah 2:4; Micah 4:3), an ideal that has been symbolized by a large statue located at the UN's headquarters in New York City.

Unfortunately, governments have rarely disarmed. There are some exceptions, but most of them are tiny countries—Vanuatu, Andorra, and Monaco—that cannot afford to maintain a standing army. The most significant case of a country with more than a million inhabitants and no standing army is Costa Rica, which freely disarmed in 1949 (as of 2010, it has a national security force of 8,000). The other cases of demilitarization and disarmament have been imposed by the international community or foreign conquerors. For instance, after World War I, Germany could maintain only a small army devoid of the heavy and significant weapons of the day. This restriction led to a great deal of resentment, and the Nazi government started rearming the moment it took power in 1933. After World War II, Germany's and Japan's armaments were limited. Japan was not allowed to keep a standing army but sustained a self-defence force (which is now an army, if not by name). Both countries could have become nuclear powers, but the American and other Western governments were adamant that they not acquire an atomic capability. A more recent example of forced disarmament is Haiti. In 1995, the country was disarmed and its army abolished when foreign donors decided that it could impede democracy and growth.

While the ideals of general and complete disarmament are far from being realized, disarmament has taken other routes (Burns, 2009). One has been the banning of exceedingly dangerous weapons. In 1139, the Second Lateran Council banned the crossbow, which was seen as a mortal threat to the aristocratic class fighting in armour.[39] Most similar interdictions over the centuries did not work. For instance, the Hague Convention of 1904 banned maritime mines, but they became prevalent in both world wars. Another well-known disarmament treaty is the Ottawa Convention (1999), which bans antipersonnel land mines but has not yet been ratified by many of the foremost military powers.

The most significant case of disarmament concerns chemical weapons (e.g. poisonous gas). Banned by the first Hague Convention (1899), these weapons were still used extensively during World War I, generating much public outrage and a second ban by the 1925 Geneva Protocol. Chemical weapons were not deployed during World War II, and only a handful of countries have used them since. In 1997, the Chemical Weapons Convention (CWC), which completely prohibits the use, deployment, storage, and experimentation of such weapons, entered into force. A verification body, the Organisation for the Prohibition of Chemical Weapons (OPCW), has even been created to supervise the ban. The OPCW is allowed to inspect the industrial and military sites of its 188 signatories.

Other notable efforts to eliminate dangerous weapons have been less successful. In 1972, a protocol was signed that forbade the use of biological weapons (e.g. poisons such as anthrax or diseases such as smallpox). However, the protocol does not specifically forbid the research and development or storage of these weapons. Over the years, attempts to sign a genuine treaty akin to the CWC have failed, but the issue will likely surface again. Chemical, biological, radiological (the spread of radioactive materials in the air or water), and nuclear weapons are known as WMDs because they can kill a large number of people in one stroke. Important disarmament efforts are devoted to all four types, but nuclear weapons draw the most attention.[40]

The Case of Nuclear Weapons

After the bombings of Hiroshima and Nagasaki in 1945, the world realized that the absolute weapon had been created. Many calls for its abolition were heard in the months following the end of the war, and the US government even entertained the revolutionary Acheson–Lilienthal Plan, which called for the United States giving up its weapons to the UN. A future Atomic Energy Authority would operate all civilian nuclear facilities around the globe in order to avoid the dissemination of nuclear know-how and materials usable for weapons. Discussions of this plan were held in late 1946 at the UN; however, the talks were unsuccessful because the United States and the Soviet Union distrusted each other.

After the failure of the Acheson–Lilienthal Plan, the Soviet Union, Great Britain, France, and China acquired the atomic bomb. In the 1960s, attention became focused on the dangers of a widespread acquisition of nuclear armaments. To stop the dissemination of nuclear capabilities, states negotiated the Nuclear Non-Proliferation Treaty (NPT) in 1968. Signatories of this agreement were offered full co-operation in the scientific and industrial uses of the atom in exchange for their renunciation of nuclear weapons. Furthermore, in the NPT's well-known Article VI, the five nuclear powers of the day promised to eliminate their nuclear weapons at an unspecified date. The NPT has become one of the most important nuclear treaties and is complemented by a number of agreements and institutions ensuring the peaceful use of nuclear energy.[41]

Nevertheless, four non-signatories have acquired nuclear armaments: Israel, South Africa (those armaments were dismantled after apartheid), India, and Pakistan. Furthermore, at least three members of the NPT (Libya, Iraq, and North Korea) pursued the illegal development of nuclear weapons. Libya and Iraq have since given up this endeavour, but North Korea has become a nuclear state and has used this position to extort money from foreign powers. There are also strong suspicions that Iran has contravened its obligations under the NPT.

Theoretically, the NPT should ban all nuclear weapons in the international system by denying them to non-nuclear states and imposing disarmament on the five nuclear powers. However, the situation has not evolved towards that ideal, and the periodic review conferences of the NPT have been raucous affairs where the mass of developing states blame the "big five" for not eliminating their nuclear weapons. The nuclear-weapons states have replied that, although they have considerably reduced their arsenals since the end of the Cold War, they cannot unilaterally disarm when there are at least four nuclear powers outside the NPT.

Because of the difficulties with the elimination of nuclear weapons, the superpowers of the Cold War prefer arms reductions and the elimination of certain weapons to a complete ban (Quinlan, 2009). They have also implemented CBMs such as transparency agreements, secure channels of communication, and fail-safe procedures designed to prevent the unauthorized or reckless use of nuclear weapons. These policies are usually subsumed under the term **arms control**. While arms control includes a set of measures intended to decrease the possibility of the use of weapons, it is not disarmament. As such, it remains a controversial subject among those who would prefer an outright ban on nuclear weapons.

Nevertheless, arms control has proven useful as a tool to manage rivalries and crises and prevent escalation. Between the early 1960s and the late 1980s and despite the Cold War, the United States and the Soviet Union signed several important treaties that forbade open-air nuclear testing (Test Ban Treaty, 1963), the deployment of nuclear weapons in space and on the moon (Outer Space Treaty, 1967) and on the ocean floor (Seabed Treaty, 1972), and the deployment of nuclear defensive systems (ABM Treaty, 1974); limited the number of weapons and their vectors (SALT I and II, 1974 and 1976, and START, 1991); and eliminated medium-range weapons (INF Treaty, 1988). In 2010, in the perspective of another debated renewal conference of the NPT, US President Obama and Russian President Medvedev agreed to further cuts in strategic weapons.

Although the nuclear threat has receded dramatically since the end of the Cold War, it has resurfaced in two regions of the world. In South Asia, the relationship between Pakistan and India is extremely tense. The partition of the two states in 1947 resulted in casualties on both sides, and the countries have since fought two wars (in 1965 and 1971). Tensions regarding Kashmir and terrorism are especially high. New Delhi acquired its nuclear capacity in 1974, after it tested a nuclear device, but officially denied possessing nuclear weapons. In 1998, both regional rivals tested nuclear weapons on consecutive days and weeks. One year later, grave border incidents in the very remote Siachen Glacier in the Himalayas almost precipitated another war.

Because it is unlikely that the political differences between India and Pakistan will be resolved soon, their disarmament is out of the question. The most that can be done is to institute a degree of confidence and some arms control measures in order to avoid an intemperate use of nuclear weapons or their leaking into the hands of terrorist organizations or irresponsible government officials. Fortunately, several bilateral confidence-building agreements have been negotiated between India and Pakistan over the years, and more are on the horizon.[42]

The other region of concern is, of course, the Middle East. Israel began building nuclear weapons in the 1960s. While the exact size and composition of its nuclear arsenal is unknown, it has had the result of irritating neighbouring states and pushing some into illegal nuclear research of their own. As we saw earlier, Libya, Iraq, and probably Syria have entertained nuclear ambitions before renouncing them, either freely or under foreign pressure. The case of Iran is most preoccupying nowadays. The country has built a large nuclear infrastructure, officially for civilian purposes, but the type of installations, Iran's secrecy, and its unwillingness to submit to full inspections have created concern. Add to the mix the militant Islamic nature of the government and the radicalism of President Ahmadinejad and you have a recipe for widespread fears not only in Israel but also Saudi Arabia and the Western great powers. For the moment, the compromise positions offered by Moscow have not been followed through by Tehran, and sanctions have been put in place. The spectre of an aerial strike on Iran looms over a very tricky situation. The hopes for a more manageable Iranian government were shattered after the elections and subsequent protests of 2008.

The prospects for complete nuclear disarmament appear dim. An effective defence against them is not in the cards yet. Partial disarmament and arms control measures contribute to lessening the nuclear threat. However, the illicit trade in nuclear weapons sustained by North Korea and Pakistan in the 1990s and 2000s, as well as the possibility of the use of nuclear weapons by terrorists, has increased the potential for the use of nuclear arms.[43] For the moment, only significant progress in the settlement of international conflicts can decrease the risk. Of course, in the long-term, democratization, trade, and economic well-being will probably have deeper effects on peace between nuclear weapons states.

Disarmament in the Field

The question of disarmament is fundamental in peace agreements and peacebuilding. It is necessary to disarm rebel groups, militias, vigilante organizations, political parties, crime lords, and other actors that could upset the peace. However, other conditions must be put in place for disarmament and tension reduction to occur. These stipulations come under the encompassing label of demobilization, disarmament, and reinsertion (DDR), meaning that efforts will be made to dismantle armed factions, seize and destroy their weapons, and provide combatants with opportunities to reintegrate into civilian life (Porto, Alden, & Parsons, 2007).

Fundamentally, DDR requires a sound peace accord with solid security guarantees and financial incentives for the ex-rebels. Usually, former rebels will be convinced to renounce their organizations and their weapons if they get something interesting in return. In many cases, some can be integrated into a security institution such as the national army or the police, while the more educated ones can be given administrative jobs. Otherwise, the main solution is to provide money, land, and agricultural tools to former combatants in order to entice them to work the land. These incentive-based schemes have been relatively successful, recovering thousands of weapons in some cases. The public destruction of large amounts of weapons has even become a standard symbol of peace, such as the burning of light arms in Bamako, Mali, in 1996 after the Touareg Rebellion. However, it is not a universal panacea, as militias and individual soldiers often make more money by selling their weapons abroad than to peacebuilding agencies. Former rebel groups might also hide caches of weapons in case of trouble. The weapons that end up in storage and for destruction are often old and broken. Functioning used weapons are often sold, exchanged, or hidden rather than destroyed.

For many people, the ultimate solution to the problem of political violence lies in the prohibition, or at least the severe regulation, of the arms trade.[44] This answer is an old demand of the pacifist movement, dating from the nineteenth century. During the 1920s, many activists blamed the onset of World War I on the "merchants of death," the private companies that stood to gain the most from the war. Many social movements demanded the nationalization of armament industries and more stringent regulations on arms transfers. As a result, many European firms were nationalized and export regulations were strengthened in some countries. But, as we know, these measures did not prevent World War II or subsequent wars.

Schemes for the international regulation of the arms trade reappeared intermittently afterwards, but it was not until the end of the Cold War that they gained wide attention (Rogers, 2009). The time seemed ripe for a plan to collectively strengthen export permit regulations that would limit the amount of weapons being sold to countries at war or those abusing human rights. Many countries (such as Canada) strengthened their arms sales policy, but the major arms exporters remained unfavourable to such tight regulations. Furthermore, second-tier arms exporters (e.g. Ukraine) profited from the situation by selling large quantities of small arms to developing countries, including some with the worst human rights records. A significant private black market also supplied a major portion of the light weapons used in civil insurgencies. Part of the problem is that most of today's armed conflicts occur in impoverished regions of the world where light, unsophisticated, and inexpensive weapons are used. Some of those weapons come from great powers, but many are provided by second-tier producers, black market dealers, and small countries (Stohl & Grillot, 2009). The regulation of small arms is not an easy task, as it affects the power and trade interests of several countries. However, it can be expected that, over time, democratic governments will issue more restrictions on arms exports, especially as a means of blocking supplies to states and opposition movements with aggressive tendencies and disregard for human rights.

CONCLUSION

The pacific settlement of disputes has increased gradually among states and in civil wars since the nineteenth century and has been especially rapid since the end of the Cold War. Although instruments of international peace such as arbitration and adjudication are not as effective as originally thought, they are sometimes useful and therefore have their legitimate place in conflict resolution.

Negotiation remains the main instrument of peaceful conflict resolution, and many developments have made this method more successful over time. For instance, the involvement of third parties (other states, international organizations, or private citizens) has become a prevalent and basic feature of peaceful conflict resolution. Negotiated settlements are also helped by facilitation and fact-finding missions conducted by third parties, and ceasefire and peace accord oversight. Another important development for parties in conflict is in the content and implementation of peace agreements. Not only do these accords tend to be less punitive than in the past, but they also usually include reconstruction and peacebuilding policies, address important political, economic, and social points of contention, and are followed by reforms towards democratization and social-economic development.

Despite the successes of peaceful conflict resolution, the coercive actions of sanctions, peace enforcement, and humanitarian intervention are still used in the international system. They have been used more or less successfully in several internal conflicts of the post-Cold War world. While the use of force will always be controversial in international peace settlements, it cannot be excluded. However violent conflicts are resolved, the four main transitions of peacebuilding are significant parts of transforming post-conflict states. Although not always successful, peacebuilding has led to the creation of many stable and peaceful areas in the world. Finally, another aspect to violent conflicts is conflict prevention. Confidence-building measures and disarmament are two processes that can help to lower the possibility of such conflicts.

DISCUSSION QUESTIONS

1. Are coercive actions useful for the prevention and settlement of armed conflicts? Why or why not?

2. Where do you see the greatest potential for diminishing violent armed conflict in the future—negotiations, mediations, international agreements, humanitarian interventions, or arms control? Give reasons to support your answer.

3. What factors enhance the capacity for successful peacebuilding after a violent conflict?

4. Discuss the importance of the UN in the development of peaceful relations and enhanced human security.

5. What alternatives to the UN exist in terms of international peace and security?

NOTES

1. For inclusive studies of diplomacy, see Anderson (1993), Berridge (2005), Rana (2006), and Satow (1979). A short, classic introduction to diplomacy is Nicolson (1988).

2. The rules take into account the status of the person and the length of his or her posting. For large international meetings of the UN, orders of appearance often follow the alphabetization of the country's English name. Hence, Albania will speak before Algeria, Finland before France, and so on.

3. Remember that some rules of protocol and etiquette are also used in business negotiations, trade fairs, academic meetings, and other non-governmental settings.

4. See McDonald (1991, 2008), Diamond and McDonald (1996), Chataway (1998), and Fisher (2006).

5. See Burton (2010), Burton and Dukes (1990), and Doob (1970).

6. See Croxton (1999). It must be noted that the term *sovereignty* was not used in the treaties, although it had been theorized earlier, notably by French jurist Jean Bodin (1529–96).

7. Instead, 15 years later, France took its revenge by financially and militarily supporting the United States in the American Revolution.

8. On the Congress of Vienna, see Kissinger (1973), Nicolson (2000), Langhorne (1986), and Dupont (2003).

9. Alas, the treaty was not implemented because Napoleon regained power and the war resumed. After the French defeat at Waterloo in 1815, a subsequent treaty imposed a more classic settlement. France had to pay reparations and return the Saarland region and its booty from previous campaigns. It was also partly occupied by foreign troops for five years.

10. On the Treaty of Versailles, see Macmillan (2002), Adelman (2007), and Marks (2003).

11. The treaty became a propaganda theme of German nationalists and fascists, based on the myths that Germany had not wanted the war and that it had never been defeated by the Allied powers (the armistice being a simple ceasefire in their mind).

12. See Hogan (1987), Milward (2006), Farquharson (1997), and Morsink (1999).

13. However, the countries that did not change their form of government as a result of American attacks (e.g. Cuba, North Korea, Vietnam, Libya) were not offered any assistance.

14. For more information on the early development of peace treaties, see Lesaffer (2004). For an overview of all peace agreements since 1945, see the United States Institute of Peace (www.usip.org) and Conciliation Resources' *Accord: an International Review of Peace Initiatives* (www.c-r.org/accord).

15. For example, in the last 30 years, the United States has introduced only two fighter-bombers: the Nighthawk F-117 in the late 1980s and the Raptor F-22 in 1991. The Nighthawk was retired in 2008 to pay for the Raptor, the estimated unit cost of which reached US$339 million. The US Senate decided to end the program in 2009. Currently, the country's main military aircraft project is the Lightning II F-35, a polyvalent aircraft built in co-operation with the British and other allies. It is remarkable that even the pre-eminent military power can no longer develop state-of-the-art aircraft projects but has to rely on its partners to complete less ambitious programs.

16. On the relationship between media exposure and war attitudes, see Stahl (2010), Baum and Groeling (2010), and Kull, Ramsay, and Lewis (2004).

17. Keegan's theory claims that the value of each descendant increases as the overall number of children decreases, making people reluctant to send young people to be killed in foreign wars. This relationship could explain why the United States, for instance, would be reluctant to get involved in a bloody war in populous countries such as Sudan or the DRC.

18. Unfortunately, the edict was revoked in 1685 by Louis XIV (a descendent of Henri IV), launching the Huguenots' exodus to Protestant lands.

19. Despite their different religious affiliations, some humanist intellectuals of the Renaissance, such as Montaigne, Erasmus, and Grotius, practised tolerance in their relations with each other.

20. The ICJ should not be confused with the International Criminal Court (ICC), created in 2002 to try individuals accused of crimes against humanity. The ICJ is a tribunal for states, not individuals.

21. The first case decided by the Court was Corfu Channel (*United Kingdom v. Albania*) in 1947. As of January 2012, the court has heard 152 cases (for the full list, see www.icj-cij.org/docket/index.php?p1=3&p2=2).

22. To those diplomatic ceasefires, we should add the more recent development of humanitarian ceasefires, designed to relieve the suffering of populations affected by war. Humanitarian ceasefires can be used to evacuate civilians from a battle zone, protect relief convoys, care for the sick and injured, or immunize children. They have been used in many locations, from Sri Lanka to Sudan, but their application is not universal. They are also usually short-lived and fragile.

23. However, it is also well known that Gaddafi was involved in fuelling many of the conflicts that he tried to mediate.

24. The method was more common in the Middle Ages, when Catholic Church officials often acted as third parties in numerous conflicts in Europe.

25. On the evolution of peace agreements, see Wallensteen and Sollenberg (1997) and Stedman, Rothchild, and Cousens (2002).

26. The International Institute for Democracy and Electoral Assistance (IDEA) continues to develop resources on the strengths and weaknesses of different political arrangements. One notable example is *Democracy and Deep-Rooted Conflict: Options for Negotiators* (1998). For a list of publications, see www.idea.int/publications/catalogue.cfm.

27. On democratic transitions and recent trends in constitutional matters the world over, see Diamond and Morlino (2005), Collier (2009), and Cheema (2005).

28. On the generalization of human rights, see Donnelly (2002), Robertson and Merrills (1996), Brems (2001), and Ishay (2004).

29. In UN documentation, observer and interposition missions are often both referred to as peacekeeping missions, obfuscating significant differences between them.

30. That said, many Haitians have criticized the removal of Aristide as an anti-democratic act that defied the wishes of the majority of Haitian voters.

31. On sanctions, see Taylor (2010), Cortright (2002), and Matam Farrall (2007).

32. Some parts of the UN Charter, such as articles 48 and 49 (joint actions for the peace), Article 51 (self-defence), and Chapter VIII (regional arrangements) have been interpreted to show the charter's latitude and even inconsistency regarding the direction of coercive endeavours.

33. On the debates about peace enforcement, see Osman (2002) and Coleman (2007).

34. Humanitarian intervention was eloquently defended in the late 1980s, notably by Italian jurist Mario Bettati and the founder of Médecins sans Frontières, Frenchman Bernard Kouchner (Bettati & Kouchner, 1987) and by Argentine jurist Fernando Tesón (1988).

35. An imposing academic literature on humanitarian intervention has also developed. See Holzgreff and Keohane (2003), Lang (2003), and Bellamy (2009).

36. In Rwanda, a non-lethal French intervention occurred after the genocide to protect Hutu refugee populations.

37. Paris (2004) also provides a tamer evaluation of peacebuilding.

38. The first "red telephone" was actually a teletype machine.

39. This ban was not followed, and it was actually the longbow that decimated chivalry in the Middle Ages.

40. On the arms control and disarmament efforts devoted to WMDs, see Busch and Joyner (2009) and Burns (2009).

41. On nuclear proliferation debates, see Sagan and Waltz (2002) and Brown, Coté Jr, Lynn-Jones, and Miller (2010).

42. On the India–Pakistan situation, see Ganguly and Kapur (2010), as well as the articles in Sagan (2009).

43. See Kroenig (2010), Corera (2006), and Allison (2005).

44. One such NGO is Project Ploughshares (http://ploughshares.ca), which does extensive research on armaments.

13 | RECONCILIATION

CHAPTER OBJECTIVES

This chapter will help you develop an understanding of the

- definitions of reconciliation, along with root concepts from different cultural-linguistic traditions;

- approaches to reconciliation based on various disciplines;

- complexity of reconciliation and its links to emergent creativity;

- goals and processes of reconciliation; and

- distinctions and similarities between reconciliation processes at different levels of conflict.

INTRODUCTION

The violence of deep-rooted conflict causes a profound rift between individuals and groups, one that is marked by depersonalization and demonization. It may leave lasting scars that are both visible and invisible, such as in cases of **post-traumatic stress disorder (PTSD)**. The resulting enmity can last for generations, even centuries. Apart from these worst-case scenarios, subtle forms of violence inflict significant wounds that diminish one or more of the parties involved. For instance, there may be structural inequalities that permanently hold groups in inferior positions. When there are reciprocal manifestations of violence, the hurt can be mutual. In other instances, one party is clearly the perpetrator and the other the victim. The violence of deep-rooted conflict can occur at any level, from the interpersonal to international. It can become entrenched as a malicious structure that overwhelms relational systems, taking on a life of its own. Usually, the harms, motivations, interpretations, and challenges of this type of conflict are complex.

As we have seen in the previous chapters, some serious conflicts persist while others are managed or resolved. This chapter focuses on another possibility: reconciliation. Reconciliation means to stop imitating the entrenched patterns of past violence and to imagine and create patterns of well-being that meet the needs of all parties. In other words, it is the transformative and constructive set of approaches used to enable people to cope with the profound negative emotions, attitudes, orientations, and behaviours associated with violent deep-rooted conflict. These methods include coming to terms with the legacy of past violence and creating a new life together (Bloomfield, Barnes, & Huyse, 2003, p. 14). This endeavour is a multi-faceted one that is generally seen as both a goal and a process applicable to all levels of conflict. The following pages examine these dual aspects, focusing on the many intertwined concepts that contribute to reconciliation. We also include three case studies that show how reconciliation has been achieved in various types of conflict. While reconciliation is not always complete or even possible, this chapter describes in theoretical and practical terms what can be accomplished in some of the most challenging circumstances.

ETYMOLOGIES

We can add to our understanding of reconciliation by examining the root concepts used in different languages (Redekop, 2002). The word *reconciliation* derives from three Latin words: *re* ("again"), *con* ("together"), and *ciliere* ("call"). These words suggest that people are apart and need to be brought together again. In Kinyarwanda (the language of Rwanda), the root concept conveys straightening sticks so that there can be a free flow of energy between them. This metaphor means that reconciliation not only opens up communication but also involves a profound opening of the spirit and a change in the situation—a transformation. The Greek word *katallasso* signifies a change so that the parties have a positive disposition toward each other. The Somali phrase, *heshiis, nabad raadin* means "Let us talk." In China, the emphasis is on making concessions to live in harmony. Similarly, the Inuit word *inuuquatigiikkannilirniq* means to restore a way of living in harmonious interdependence with one another and with nature. The Hebrew term *peshera*, however, stresses making an agreement. Together, these different linguistic traditions form a gestalt that suggests that reconciliation calls people together to communicate openly and changes their mutual orientation so that they can agree on what it means to live in harmony.

APPROACHES TO RECONCILIATION

Some approaches to reconciliation emphasize the political dimension (Bloomfield et al., 2003). As Erin Daly and Jeremy Sarkin (2007) point out:

> Reconciliation initiatives are appealing because they can respond to the multifarious needs of each nation as it transitions from one dispensation to another. They can simultaneously be legal and political; they can be national and international; they can respond to both public and private needs; they can be moral and pragmatic; they can be transformative, while maintaining connection to the past. The appeal of reconciliation is broad because its promise is virtually infinite. (p.12)

This broad description is enhanced through the empirical study of William Long and Peter Brecke (2003), who examine reconciliation by comparing the dynamics between states after violent conflict and in the context of civil wars. Their study points to two models: forgiveness and signalling. Effective in civil conflicts, the forgiveness process is "characterized by truth telling, redefinition of the identity of the former belligerents, partial justice, and a call for [a] new relationship" (Long & Brecke, 2003, p. 3). Within the international context, the signalling model claims that "when a reconciliation event was part of a costly, novel, voluntary, and irrevocable concession in a negotiated bargain, it contributed meaningfully to a reduction in future conflict" (p. 3). These two models are grounded in different assumptions about rationality. While the forgiveness model assumes that "humans possess numerous, patterned, specific, problem-solving capabilities as a result of interaction with past environments and that those capabilities work in synch with our emotional repertoire," signalling stresses rational choice (p. 4).

Long and Brecke (2003) focused on reconciliation events characterized by public gatherings in which high-ranking officials indicated, through their statements and symbolic gestures, a readiness and willingness to work together. Their study examined reconciliation events in the cases of 10 intranational and 8 international conflicts. At the intranational level, seven of the countries studied experienced peaceful relations. Reconciliation efforts in these states included "recognition of harm and public truth-telling," "redefinition of self and other," "justice short of revenge," and "commitment to a renewed but different relationship" (Long & Brecke, 2003, pp. 65–72). Where peace did not ensue, the reconciliation events were of a signalling nature only. In the international domain, five out of the eight situations studied showed that, whenever the conditions associated with signalling were in place, peaceful relations ensued. These factors were costliness/vulnerability, novelty, and making concessions that were voluntary and irrevocable/non-contingent (p. 117). One example of the signalling model is in the relationship between Germany and the Soviet Union. In 1990, the Treaty on the Final Settlement with Respect to Germany was signed, allowing for the reunification of the country. Designed to alleviate some fears of the Soviets, who had suffered bitterly during World War II and feared a strong Germany within NATO, the treaty limited the size of Germany's armed forces (voluntary vulnerability) and created a nuclear-free zone in the eastern part of the country. The Germans also agreed to pay 55 billion Deutschmarks (costly and irrevocable) in reparations (pp. 77–80).

Recognizing that social scientists have traditionally attributed conflicts to "disagreements on the division of scarce and coveted resources" and their ending to being "predicated on the parties' ability to agree on a formula for their division," Arie Nadler, Thomas E. Malloy, and Jeffrey Fisher (2008, p. 4) point to the realization among social psychologists that more is needed. They define intergroup reconciliation as

> a *process* that leads to a *stable end* to conflict and is predicated *on changes in the nature of adversarial relations* between the adversaries *and each of the parties' conflict-related needs, emotions, and cognitions.* This emphasis on the reconciliation processes is consistent with broad socio-political changes and emerging trends in social-psychological research and theory on intergroup relations. (Nadler, Malloy, & Fisher, 2008, p. 4, emphasis in original)

Wayne Booth (2005) and Melissa Nobles (2008) both stress the role of communication in reconciliation but in different ways. While Booth believes that learning to listen is the process and goal, Nobles claims that communicative acts such as apologies are important for changing structures (political, economic, and legal arrangements) and policies. Jacqueline Ismael (2007) uses a multiplicity of factors to describe reconciliation in terms of a complex system and argues that, in keeping with how humans have learned to deal with conflict for their own survival, reconciliation should emerge spontaneously in vio-

TABLE 13.1 | TRAITS OF RECONCILIATION

Issue	Applied to Reconciliation
Goal	historic reconciliation
Parties	societies (could also apply to individuals and groups)
Nature of peace	genuine, no further claims
Future relations desired	good relations
Importance of mutual acceptance	essential
Terms of reference	justice
Truth about wrongdoing	should be commonly acknowledged
Historic responsibility	should be acknowledged and faced
Social and political restructuring	major restructuring

Source: Rouhana 2004, p. 34 in Ismael, Jacqueline S. (2007) "Introduction," in Jacqueline S. Ismael and William W. Haddad (eds.), *Barriers to Reconciliation: Case Studies on Iraq and the Palestine-Israel Conflict.* Lanham: University Press of America. (parenthetical material added)

lent communities. Where it does not, she argues that there are barriers to reconciliation that often come from outside the community. Table 13.1 is based on Ismael's quotes of Nadim Rouhana.

Another approach to reconciliation emphasizes the role of religion (see McFaul, 2006; Axworthy, 2008; Baum & Wells, 1997; Kim, Kollontai, & Hoyland, 2008). South African theologians John de Gruchy (2002) and Michael Battle (1997) show how the Christian theology of Archbishop Desmond Tutu drew on the concept of *ubuntu*— "our humanity is realized in the humanity of the other"—to develop a framework for the South African Truth and Reconciliation Commission. In *Conflict and Reconciliation: The Contribution of Religions*, John Bowker (2008) examines the Hindu, Buddhist, Confucian, Jewish, Christian, and Muslim approaches to reconciliation. Each of these religions contributes its own basic concepts and root metaphors to the subject. Regarding Hinduism, Gavin Flood (2008) remarks that Gandhi believed that social justice and reconciliation could be achieved "only through the implementation of truth through non-violence" (p. 80). Joseph Montville (as cited in Johnston, 1994, p. 332) makes the connection between reconciliation and religion through the capacity of third-party religious leaders to inspire the trust needed to proceed. Among Native Americans, there are traditions of peace leaders who played a special role in making and sustaining peace through their conciliatory efforts (Pesantubee, 2004, pp. 34–5).

THE COMPLEXITY OF RECONCILIATION

We have pointed out that reconciliation is highly relational yet addresses issues of past injustices and fears for the future. Although it can also be extremely rational, its motivation and results have a profound emotional dimension (Long & Brecke, 2003; Kelman, 2008). It involves locutionary actions that could have layers of symbolic meaning. Reconciliation demands justice yet invokes mercy (Lederach, 1997, p. 28). It calls for truth yet wants certain truths to be "remembered rightly" so that they cease to have a hold on how we define ourselves (Volf, 2006). It requires work, but the timing and results of what has an impact are matters of synchronicity and surprise. In short, reconciliation has all the hallmarks of a complex adaptive system (see Chapter 6). Within such systems, new developments transpire through emergent creativity (Kauffman, 2008). New combinations of ideas and possibilities create something that is unpredictable and cannot be reduced to its individual components.

Reconciliation starts with a Self and an Other who are profoundly separated by hurt, resentment, distrust, or hatred. Change must occur at the intrapsychic level of each party (where these feelings are experienced) and include outward change with a noticeable reduction in antagonism. The alteration also takes place in the relationship, where it is exhibited in joint actions and changes in structures and understood as the ongoing patterns of orientation, attitudes, and behaviours. Intra- and interpsychic changes can be very complex. They involve changes in identity, in how the Other is perceived and understood, and in what is desired by each party and by the relationship between them (Kelman, 2008).

One documented example of what is entailed in these changes is a long-term dialogue between Jewish children of Holocaust survivors and children of high-ranking Nazi officers (see Hammerich, Pfafflin, Pogany-Wnendt, Siebert, & Sonntag, 2009). Both groups came to the situation with considerable trauma inherited from their respective parents. The participants had to wrestle with the degree to which they represented their parents' experiences and actions and had to construct new and separate identities. There were many emotions experienced through the process. As they continued the dialogue, people from both sides were able to empathize with the experiences of the other. For those children who had been taught to keep their Jewish identity secret, speaking openly about it was a major step. For the Germans who had happy memories of their parents, it was a struggle to connect these experiences with their parents' actions. Because the children did not directly experience the violence as perpetrators or victims, they did not have to express remorse for their actions or offer forgiveness. However, the transformation that occurred in both groups highlights the depths of human experience implicated in reconciliation, including the twists and turns, the reaching out and retreating, the agonizing over inner contradictions, and the eventual move toward well-being.

These aspects of reconciliation are presented in Figure 13.1. For both the Self and the Other, there are intrapsychic processes that are private and hidden, though they can be discussed. As the parties encounter one another, they present themselves in a particular way (e.g. detached, cold, hostile, warm, or open). This way of being is conveyed through facial features, gestures, posture, and highly nuanced non-verbal communication. There is also verbal communication that occurs in the context of discussion, debate, negotiation,

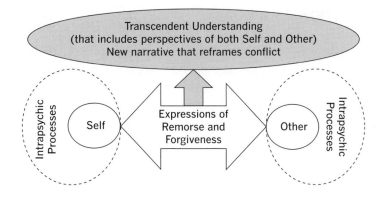

FIGURE 13.1 | RECONCILIATION AS EMERGENT CREATIVITY

mediation, or dialogue. Reconciliation actions or gestures of conciliation can have layers of meaning associated with them. If they are personally costly and risky, their potential impact increases enormously.

As a result of interaction and intrapsychic struggles, parties begin to see themselves and others differently. For example, they have a new appreciation for the impact of past actions (they no longer tend to minimize the hurt they have caused or maximize the wrongs they have suffered). Through this perspective, a series of new possibilities of orientation and attitude can emerge, beginning with a new capacity for remorse that is expressed in an apology. A willingness to embrace the Other and an openness to forgive him or her also becomes possible. The likelihood of these actions increases as the process continues. The changes in attitude lead to desiring new things for each other and for the relationship. There is a shift from wishing that the Other would suffer, die, or disappear to hoping, at a minimum, that he or she could live. The first step is to imagine coexistence, which does not necessarily imply closeness, trust, or liking one another but is an acceptance of the reality that the Other will not go away. In time, the process of reconciliation can lead to new relationships.

The changes in orientation and attitude make new actions—including basic actions, action chains, and action practices—possible. Practices can also lead to the development of new institutions that concretely manifest the changes in relationships. This progress can occur at the individual and collective levels. For example, the French-German reconciliation involved the creation of a new trade agreement, which became the basis for European economic union (see Case Study 13.1, page 344). Eventually, a transcendent position that includes the perspectives of both parties and leads to a new narrative that both can validate emerges. With mutual understanding and a new narrative comes a more complex identity that is inclusive of the Other.

RECONCILIATION AS A GOAL

The desire to transform a conflict situation can occur when there is still overt violence or when the main conflict has subsided and the post-conflict phase is marked by latent resentment and hatred. In the latter situation, people live with the negative effects of the conflict and are affected by them in a profound way. For example, many survivors of the Bosnian War had no interest in returning to their farms or homes years after they were forced to leave. Another example is Rwandan Tutsis who are unable to be in the presence of a Hutu person.

The goals of reconciliation are closely related to the violence of conflict and its causes, which lead to what Janine Chanteur (1992) describes as ontological rifts (see Chapter 9). Reconciliation objectives can be broken down into five areas: sense of justice; personal healing and empowerment; new (or renewed) relationships marked by mutual trust; structural change; and transcendence.[1] These components are intertwined. For instance, a sense of justice can be a catalyst to personal healing. Personal healing makes one capable of building new relationships. New relationships and mutual understanding can provide the impetus for structural change, which can aid in transcending the conflict. There is a continuum of reconciliation that can be analyzed through each element. However, results in the five areas may be mixed. It is also possible that complete reconciliation will not be achieved.

Sense of Justice

As we will see in Chapter 15, a serious injustice affects the balance of a relationship. That victims are deliberately harmed through violence means that perpetrators "owe" them something. If the violence is illegal and/or immoral, the wider community also feels that the perpetrators should be punished. The passions of resentment, hatred, and indignation do not justify punishment in and of themselves, but they do speak to the need to rebalance the situation with something that looks and feels like justice (Moore 1987, pp. 179–219). Without a sense of justice, it becomes harder for personal and group healing to occur.

A key question in achieving justice is who has to take what action. Perpetrators of violence frequently either deny or justify their actions. What would happen if they were oriented toward remorse and doing everything in their power to "make amends" (Radzik, 2009)? Victims are often portrayed as seeking their "pound of flesh" and ensuring that their perpetrators do not go unpunished. There is a need to probe what justice might mean in any given situation. Martha Minow (1998), dean of Harvard Law School, argues for a careful balance between vengeance, which on its own can make matters worse, and forgiveness, which can negate a sense of justice if it comes too quickly and without any accountability.

One approach to justice for large-scale atrocities is **retributive justice**, which seeks to punish the perpetrators. After World War II, the Nuremberg Trials prosecuted the most prominent leaders of Nazi Germany. Most of those tried were executed, while the others received life sentences or lengthy prison terms or were acquitted. In 2002, the International Criminal Court was established in The Hague to try people accused of crimes against humanity. Whether applied in a local or international court, the impact of the retributive approach is the same: people are made to suffer for the horrible things they have done. However, mercy can also be extended. For example, prison terms can be reduced.

Another approach is restorative justice, in which perpetrators can be held directly accountable to their victims and can make things right (see Chapter 15). There is a growing trend to explore ways to make reparations for both recent and historical victimization (see Aertsen, Arsovska, Rohne, Valiñas, & Vanspauwen, 2008; Berg & Schaefer, 2009). Justice issues can also be addressed by examining "systemic political and economic justices, both of which are pre-requisites for the evolution of a more just society" (du Bois & du Bois-Pedain, 2008, p. 292). These methods raise a bigger question: Are there other ways to achieve a sense of justice associated with reconciliation processes?

Personal Healing and Empowerment

A violent conflict includes several harms that require healing. There are physical harms, such as the injuries, diseases, and unwanted pregnancies that can be caused by rape. There are psychological damages, such as PTSD, which can make it impossible for people to do certain required tasks. There are also emotional challenges based on sadness over losses, shame from indignities experienced, and depression over loss of the ability to function. Debilitating anger, resentment, and hatred also diminish one's capacity to live fully.

In what has become a classic text, psychiatrist Judith Herman's *Trauma and Recovery* (1997) describes how trauma can disempower people. Historically, the realization of the reality of PTSD resulted from both the experience of soldiers who had been shell-shocked and women who had been victims of sexual violence. Significant trauma can result in uncontrolled flashbacks where traumatic events are replayed, anxiety about security, and a dissociation that makes it impossible to develop authentic, trusting relationships with anyone.

For Emmanuel Levinas (1961/1969), the worst form of violence is that which deprives people of a capacity to take action: "[It] does not consist so much in injuring and annihilating persons as in interrupting their continuity, making them play roles in which they no longer recognize themselves, making them betray not only commitments but their own substance, making them carry out actions that will destroy every possibility for action" (p. 21). Certainly, this is one of the effects of violent deep-rooted conflict. People lose a sense of agency and become dependent on others to make decisions for them. They can retreat into a shell of despondency or they can become part of a "herd"—unthinkingly going along with the crowd and doing what they are told.

Other oppressive psychological factors are guilt, which is associated with bad actions, and shame, which frames one as inherently bad. Both victims and perpetrators are prone to these feelings—victims because they can easily blame themselves for what happened and perpetrators because they might realize that what they did was wrong and unjustified. For example, some Hutus who killed their neighbours in response to radio broadcasts encouraging such action have expressed profound remorse. For victims, the correlates, directed at the Other, are resentment for hurtful action and hatred toward the one who did the hurting (Murphy & Hampton, 1988).

Added to these emotional and psychological effects are the cognitive challenges of making sense of the hurt and spiritual emptiness that comes with the despair of thinking that there is no way out of the conflict. These negative maladies can lead to alcohol or drug abuse as a way of masking the inner pain and, in turn, produce secondary problems.

For Austrian psychiatrist Victor Frankl (1946/1984), healing came through his discovery of meaning within the concentration camp. Realizing that his Nazi captors could not control what he thought about, he found a sense of agency through his own thoughts. In his case, Frankl chose to make meaning out of his love for his wife, whose location he did not know. Out of his own experience, he developed logo therapy, which is based on the development of a capacity to find meaning in one's situation. There are many psychotherapy approaches that can help with healing, including cognitive therapy (how we think about trauma), narrative therapy (dealing with the story), somatic therapy (dealing with the effects on the body), and behaviour therapy.

Another way to heal is through forgiveness. Forgiveness itself is a very delicate and complex term. For Jeffrie Murphy and Jean Hampton (1988), forgiveness means to no longer define the Other in terms of the violent act directed against the Self. It can also be thought of as a release of the right, desire (even passion), or inclination to make the Other suffer.

Healing can also come from the development of agency, or building on achievements. The recognition for success can then contribute to self-esteem and added capacity for action. For some people, this method can be taken to the extreme. Hammerich and colleagues (2009) point to the trend among some children of Holocaust survivors to become compulsive overachievers. Finally, healing can be enabled through rituals. These practices may be symbolic value-laden actions designed specifically for post-conflict situations or be taken from historical cultural or religious traditions (Schirch, 2005). In a comparative study of three communities, Jarem Sawatsky (2009) synthesized a shared concept of healing justice that he defined as

> a collective paradigm or imagination, usually drawing on an ancient wisdom tradition that seeks to find ways of surviving together:
>
> - by structuring life so that the means reflect the end of respect for life and
> - by treating harms as opportunities to transform suffering and root causes of harm and, at the same time, to cultivate conditions of respectful living within the interrelated aspects of self, other, community/ies, social structures, environment and Spirit. (pp. 242–243)

Healing takes time and is generally aided by a supportive environment, professional help, friends, and participation in constructive changes. While Sawatsky's study is based on communities with a particular emphasis on these themes, the lessons learned could be instructive to groups in need of healing justice. His study shows that the same emphases can be derived from very different historical traditions.

New Relationships

When atrocities occur, relationships are severed. These ruptures often include a multitude of feelings. On the one hand, there are recollections of a time when relationships were positive; on the other are feelings of betrayal and loss. New relationships are needed not only because they are good in and of themselves but also because they can avoid further violence between the parties. For example, during the *gacaca* courts in Rwanda, some Tutsis were murdered because their testimony on what they had witnessed could convict *génocidaires*.

Through the process of reconciliation, people will establish new and hopefully positive relationships with former antagonists. There is a full spectrum of relationship types. At one end is a simple commitment to no longer harm one another through violent practices. Former antagonists may not like each other but agree to live together in a community. Where trust is minimal, they may need legal and other safeguards, such as physical separation or third-party intervention, to ensure their security. Another step is coexistence and tolerance based on trust that the parties will not harm one another. Further on the continuum is collaboration, where people work together on joint initiatives. Finally, there may be friendship, mutual care, and bonding. In some instances, however, this type of relationship will not be forged by the participants in the conflict but by future generations.

Relationships may be thought of as both individual and collective. Collective relationships range from kinship groups to larger identity groups and nations. Building new relationships at each level entails different processes and results. At the international level, relationships are defined by formal relations, treaties, and agreements. Formal apologies also play a role at this and other levels. At the intergroup level, reparations, symbolic acts, and encounters between group members can play an important role.

Structural Change

Within the context of deep-rooted conflict, there are several types of structures that both affect and are affected by the conflict. These structures may be political (one group gets shut out of political power), economic (people are exploited and there is a huge differential between rich and poor), or physical (people may be physically separated, hurt, or deprived of basic sustenance needs). There are also language-related structures of inequality—designations of people may insult or condescend to another, or one language may be more dominant (Redekop, 2002, Chapter 5).

If reconciliation does not result in a change of oppressive structures, victimization will continue and any gains will soon dissipate. Therefore, one of the goals of reconciliation must be structural change. The formation of the European Union can be seen as a structural manifestation of post-World War II reconciliation. Civil rights legislation in the United States, giving political rights to African Americans, is another example. On the linguistic side, the use of gender inclusive language is a discursive structural change in response to the dismantling of patriarchy. As part of the post-apartheid reconciliation between black and white South Africans, discriminatory laws were changed. Civil and political rights became equal, and everyone could vote. Beaches, hospitals, and neighbourhoods were desegregated, allowing black people to go to any public place. Taking the idea of structural change a step further, François du Bois and Antje du Bois-Pedain (2008) state:

> Reconciliation is fundamentally about citizenship, belonging; it comes into view only once political community is successfully imagined (though, of course, not yet successfully realised). Through a politics of reconciliation, people reconstitute themselves as citizens of a different society, one in which others matter, and are owed life chances, too. It is on this lived commitment to a just and inclusive society that, ultimately, both political stability and the pursuit of justice crucially depend. (p. 292)

From these observations, it becomes apparent that structural change involves action at the political, social, and personal levels. Although such modifications can occur without deliberate reconciliation processes, many instances of full reconciliation demand structural change.

One way of looking at structural change is through the lens of human rights. These rights can be articulated through bills, charters, or declarations. While these statements provide a set of standards, they need to be incorporated into the lives of those that are affected by them. To do so takes political will, mechanisms of accountability, and vigilance on the part of citizens and bystanders.

Transcendence

The earlier discussion on reconciliation as emergent creativity demonstrated the theory that intrapsychic and interactive processes combined with reconciliation actions can lead to some profound changes in identity, relationship, and structure. These changes can be framed with the concept of transcendence, which means to go beyond the limits of the previous situation. One aspect of transcendence is to develop a perspective that includes those of both victim and perpetrator. This process requires a good deal of maturity and inner development. It comes from learning to name one's own perspectives, to develop the distal self so as to be able to look at the proximate self objectively (see Chapter 10), and to do the same with those of the Other—that is, to look objectively at how the Other experienced a hurtful event and how he or she interpreted the experience.

Transcendence can also mean to rise above the difficulties and challenges and move ahead in a positive way. This interpretation was exemplified by Nelson Mandela when, after becoming president of South Africa, he decided to support the country's rugby team. During his 27.5 years in prison, Mandela got to know his Afrikaner captors. He learned their language, read their literature, and learned what was important to them. He discovered that rugby was a great source of pride to them and was important for their identity. His own African National Congress (ANC) wanted to disband the team as a way of getting even with white South Africans. However, Mandela was committed to a South Africa that was open to all. His symbolic gesture of support for the rugby team showed that he could transcend the differences and envisage a creative and inclusive new identity.

A possible component of transcendence is spirituality. There is a growing body of literature on spirituality looking at it from many different disciplines (see Flanagan & Jupp, 2007; Harper, 2005; Ferrer, 2002; Beauregard & O'Leary, 2007). It is now considered distinct from religion, though it may draw on different religions to understand particular phenomena (King, 2008). Spirituality may be seen as providing a capacity for inner strength in the face of personal challenges, a profound bond between people, and a connection to transcendent realities and an ethical orientation of care for others (Lederach, 1999, pp. 152–153; Redekop, 2011). In another perspective, John Paul Lederach (2005) associates transcendence with the unleashing of the moral imagination, which for him is the paradoxical imagining of a new, positive future while being rooted in present realities.

RECONCILIATION AS A PROCESS

Reconciliation can be an iterative process involving progress, regress, and reassessment of certain aspects. In a large-scale conflict, there may be a large number of subprocesses involved, drawing on the methods described in chapters 11 and 12. While some processes are formal and deliberate, others are informal and happen through a synchronous coming together of people and events. For example, an unexpected death might bring antagonistic parties together. Someone working toward reconciliation can make use of these spontaneous events to build positive momentum.

The reconciliation process must be able to handle the complex goals and conflicts involved. While there is no formula or sure-fire way to ensure reconciliation, a number of elements make it more likely. As Figure 13.2 shows, these factors are represented in three groups: pre-requisites, discursive and symbolic processes, and **meta-requisites**. To proceed with reconciliation, certain pre-requisites are needed. They are not absolute in the sense that they all need to be present for progress to be made, but their presence goes a long way to expedite subsequent steps. Discursive and symbolic processes lie at the heart of reconciliation, while meta-requisites are components that need to be present throughout the reconciliation or introduced at particular times during the various subprocesses. The result of the process should relate to the five goals discussed in the previous section.

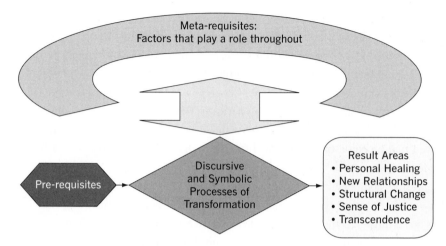

FIGURE 13.2 | RECONCILIATION

Pre-Requisites

Reconciliation starts with an impulse grounded in a conviction that such an outcome is desirable and attainable. This belief translates into an ethical vision for reconciliation in that it maintains that reconciliation is worth the effort. Let us be clear: reconciliation is work, but (paradoxically) some of the greatest breakthroughs come surprisingly and unwittingly.

The vision needs to be turned into a mandate that can be given to individuals or institutions. To obtain this pre-requisite, someone has to take the initiative to prepare for reconciliation processes. For instance, Mandela had a vision for reconciliation. He established the Truth and Reconciliation Commission (TRC) to further the goal of reconciliation and gave a particular mandate to Archbishop Tutu to manage the institution. In Case Study 13.2 (see page 345), we discuss how the New Sudan Council of Churches set up a peace commission with a particular mandate for Telar Deng to address the conflict between Nuers and Dinkas.

Along with a vision and mandate, the population involved must also believe in the process enough to give it a try. Daly and Sarkin (2007) observe that people must believe that governmental efforts promoting reconciliation are legitimate and not simply excuses for offering impunity. They point out that the success of a reconciliation program depends on the general public's support of the process.

Another pre-requisite is resources. If there is to be a sustained effort at reconciliation, resources need to be in place to make it happen. Such resources include the right people, training to provide adequate skills for the various processes, finances, and appropriate locations.

The final pre-requisite that we will mention is the freedom from threat. Reconciliation processes become impossible if there is immediate danger of violence. Occasionally, the

(AP Photo/Adil Bradlow)

The TRC of South Africa is renowned for the quality of its work, its innovations, and its profound effect on the country. This photo was taken on 29 October 1998, when Archbishop Desmond Tutu, chairperson of the TRC, gave President Mandela the commission's final report.

establishment of proper conditions becomes a separate process. Secret meetings in safe locations away from the fighting are sometimes the initial steps leading to negotiations for ceasefires. If the overt fighting is over, attention needs to be paid to what might intimidate participants from becoming fully involved in the processes. In the case of intranational reconciliation, it is of utmost importance to establish fair and effective governance structures that provide a secure environment (Daly & Sarkin, 2007, p. 240).

Discursive and Symbolic Processes

Egyptian President Anwar Sadat's conciliatory gesture of visiting Jerusalem in 1977 was an act with many layers of meaning. It was bold, costly, and led to a number of subsequent processes, such as the Camp David Agreement. The mediated sessions at Camp David were supplemented by informal conversations in a relaxed setting. This instance illustrates how symbolic action and discursive processes complement one another within a larger process of political reconciliation.

Group and interpersonal reconciliation can likewise involve symbolic and ritual elements along with formal processes (Schirch, 2005). The latter can include negotiations, mediations, facilitations, conferences, dialogue sessions, circle processes, or legal or quasi-legal formalized sessions (see Chapter 11). Any of these processes can be used independently or in a sequence.

Rituals and symbolic processes affect many aspects of a person, including emotions. According to Lisa Schirch (2005), "[R]itual uses symbolic actions to communicate a forming or transforming message in a unique social space," and symbolic actions use "symbols, senses, and emotions rather than words of rational thought" (p. 17). Examples include eating together, shaking hands, honouring identity markers such as flags, and enjoying cultural or sporting events. Schirch recounts stories of participants of the Mozambique Civil War being reunited with their communities through rituals of purification, some of which involved animal sacrifice. These rituals "communicated the complex message of recovery and rebirth, cleansing and forgiveness. They transformed individuals, communities, and the nation" (Schirch, 2005, pp. 10–11). Symbolic acts and rituals have additional impact if they take place in an extraordinary location. Schirch adds that "[S]ome rituals reinforce the status quo by forming people's worldviews, identities, and relationships. Other rituals mark and assist in the process of change. People's worldviews, identities, and relationships may be transformed in a ritual process" (pp. 10–11).

Within social psychology, there is a distinction between instrumental and socio-emotional approaches to reconciliation (see Nadler et al., 2008). Instrumental approaches find common superordinate goals that divided people can work on together. Socio-emotional approaches confront the needs, emotions, history, and future imagination of the people directly involved. Both, however, need discursive processes to consult with and mobilize people. In the remainder of this section, we focus on eight practices that fit more intuitively within the latter approach: truth-telling; dialogue; expression and acknowledgement; transformation of attitudes; remorse, apology, and amends; mercy and forgiveness; reframing; and opening horizons.

Lederach (2005, p. 143) sees truth as a key component in reconciliation, an observation that is corroborated by the cries of victims and victim groups around the world. Truth validates the experience of victims and provides a way forward. Those who lost loved ones under mysterious circumstances during South African apartheid were tremendously relieved when, in the course of the TRC hearings, they discovered what had happened to their relatives and where the remains could be found. The same commission established the collective and undeniable truth of what happened under apartheid. In fact, the truth about missing people is a crucial but sometimes neglected aspect of peacebuilding and reconciliation. In some cases, testimonies help to confirm events, but the search for physical traces of death and disappearance is a necessary, although expensive, activity in all post-conflict and post-repression countries. When victimization is either unacknowledged or denied, however, it creates havoc for victims.

There are two main types of truth, both of which must be brought into the open for people to be satisfied. Empirical truth is the truth as observed, while hermeneutical truth is that which is experienced and interpreted. Because the latter influences what people see in a situation, there can be various accounts of the same event. Not only is establishing truth an important goal in reconciliation, but the reconciliation of different truths is also a challenge.

The truth of what happened needs to emerge through the various processes. Truth includes documentation of events, the actual effects of conflict on the relevant individuals and groups, and the real and perceived intentions of those involved. For example, rape is wrong and hurtful in any circumstance, but there is an added dimension of indignity when it is used as a weapon to humiliate a people.

In Chapter 11, dialogue was described as the full and free exchange of information among people. It includes mutual listening for the cognitive aspects of the locutionary actions (the meaning of the words) and the intentions and emotions being conveyed (illocutionary dimension), as well as a consciousness of the impact of what is said (perlocutionary dimension). Dialogue can take place through structured dialogue sessions or develop in a variety of processes.

Related to dialogue is expression of loss and woundedness and acknowledgement by the other party. In the course of the process, people will express what they lost, what was damaged, what injuries were sustained, what costs were incurred, and who was killed. All these things are observable and verifiable. They will also talk about their own suffering, possibly through the language of woundedness. The loss of children and friends can result in trauma, emotional wounds of profound inner pain, and hermeneutical wounds that question one's world view. These aspects can be understood through empathetic listening and validated by appropriate expressions of acknowledgement.

With exchanges and insights, attitudes are transformed—a person can see his or her actions in a new light and become open to the perspectives of the other party. This transformation represents a turning point in the reconciliation process. In other words, it creates the possibility of altering the situation through a change of attitude, orientation, or behaviour. This change can occur gradually or be caused by a particular event or expression that allows parties to see each other in a new light.

The next process is remorse, apology, and amends. Those who have perpetrated violence may come to realize the harm that they have done. To aid in the reconciliation, offenders must go from denying or justifying their actions to fully acknowledging and deeply regretting the hurt that they have caused. This change leads to expressions of remorse and apology and a willingness to make amends. Apologies should include the following elements: acknowledgement of the hurt of the other, responsibility for causing the hurt, a statement that the action was wrong (along with expressions of remorse), and assurances that it will not happen again. Making amends includes restoring to the victim those things that were taken or destroyed but can be replaced and committing to ameliorate the harmful effects of the action wherever possible (Radzik, 2009). These effects include not only the actual hurt but also the diminishment of the victim's dignity and status and the offender's lack of respect for laws and morality.

Victims may respond to expressions of remorse by indicating that forgiveness and mercy are possible. The word *possible* is important here because it suggests tentativeness, conditionality, and an exploratory position. Actual forgiveness and mercy must be suitably framed so that it does not come about as "cheap grace," meaning that it should not be a matter of course, a right, or something trivial (Minow, 1998). Forgiveness is a matter of degree and may transpire through various stages, ranging from giving up an urge for vengeance to being willing to tolerate the presence of the other to the building of a new relationship. However, not all stages can be attained in every situation. Forgiveness can be thought of as occurring within a process that includes truth-telling, remorse, apology, and reparation. Forgiveness as letting go of resentment, hatred, and passion for revenge can be an important step in the healing of victims.

Another part of reconciliation is reframing. This process is described by Daly and Sarkin (2007) as creating "a metastructure that reframes the issues by encompassing the range of experience, rather than forcing people to choose between *us* and *them*" (p. 255). This metastructure could involve a new narrative that provides an inclusive identity such that the perspectives of the different parties are represented in a common history that they can all embrace. It could also involve new inclusive legal and economic structures.[2]

Finally, the processes of reconciliation should open up new horizons for future associations. Prospects could include trust-building initiatives, agreement on superordinate goals, or steps to move from tolerant coexistence to mutually satisfying and upbuilding relationships. Along the way, safe distances (psychological and/or physical) may need to be created to address fears of further violence. There may also have to be agreement to monitor reconciliation goals. For example, a mandate could be to review assessment processes annually and then biannually for a specific period of time. Included in these new horizons are the results of processes directed toward achieving particular reconciliation goals.

Meta-Requisites

Certain elements of reconciliation must be accessed throughout the process. These meta-requisites are **gradual reciprocated initiatives in tension-reduction (GRIT)**, institution-building, process skills, support of the third side, and teachings of blessings (Redekop, 2008).

Charles E. Osgood (1916–91), former head of the American Psychological Association, developed the concept of GRIT in the 1960s. According to Osgood (1962), this theory entails one party taking a small step in acknowledging the interests of the other. This action may prompt the other party to take a small step, which is again reciprocated. By taking steps that involve minimum risk, it is possible to reduce tensions and build trust. This process could be used as a precursor to formal reconciliation processes. It could also play a role when negotiations are at an impasse or a misunderstanding impedes the entire process.

On a grand scale, the reconciliation process sometimes involves the evolution of new institutions of government. In many cases, conflicting parties agree to such reforms by signing peace accords or some other type of political agreement. Reforms in the direction of democracy, rule of law, decentralization, or federalism can go a long way in reconciling aggrieved linguistic groups, ethnic minorities, religious communities, or neglected regions with the majority of the population. In less far-reaching ways, the process of reconciliation may call for the creation of intervening institutions. TRCs are such institutions.

Another meta-requisite in reconciliation is process skills. Good process leaders can make all the difference when it comes to reconciliation. They need to have a spirit of inclusion and a respectful manner that makes all parties feel completely included. They must be able to pick up on underlying messages, elicit clarification, and synthesize information in a manner such that participants get the message. Leaders must express empathy in a way that makes participants feel that their woundedness is understood at a profound level. However, they must also be tough regarding the enforcement of ground rules so that neither side hijacks the process. Other process skills include honesty, transparency, great integrity, and mastery of the processes and subprocesses.

The third side, a concept developed by William Ury (2000), is also an important element in reconciliation. The third side is not just an individual third party neutral but a whole community that has a role to play even though it is not implicated in the specific conflict. For example, the New Sudan Council of Churches (2002) played a significant role in the reconciliation between the Nuers and the Dinkas. By not staging any attacks during the Wunlit Conference (in 1999), the Sudan's People's Liberation Army and the Government of Sudan were also supportive. Ury identifies a number of roles for the third side to play, including bridge-building.

The emergence of human civilization has depended on finding ways for humans to live together without destroying one another. Every culture has collections of stories, moral injunctions, and wisdom that help find a way in the face of difficult conflict. These collections inspire the ethical imagination, which provides the impetus to reconcile in the first place. In addition to religious and cultural insights, other revelations have been generated by participants in reconciliation processes, social scientists, artists, and philosophers. Teachings of blessing refer to the normative and descriptive literature that assists in the motivation to reconcile, the clarification of particular reconciliation goals, and the refinement of rituals and processes.[3] The use of the word *teaching* suggests that these insights need to be disseminated, explored, and understood. To find such teachings, one has to interpret texts from the perspective of reconciliation. In other words, one should always ask how a teaching could help the reconciliation process.

CASE STUDIES OF RECONCILIATION

The three case studies described in this section include a reconciliation between nations, one between tribes, and another between individuals. In each case, we provide a narrative of the reconciliation process and demonstrate how the elements of reconciliation were applied.

CASE STUDY 13.1 | FRENCH–GERMAN RECONCILIATION

From the Franco-Prussian War (1870–1) through both world wars, France and Germany were bitter enemies. Hatred, suspicion, fear, and resentment were high after three wars in 75 years. At the end of World War II, Germany was devastated and was divided into four administrative zones administered by the United States, France, Great Britain, and the Soviet Union, respectively. Germans could not travel between zones without a permit, and passports were virtually non-existent.

Moral Re-Armament (MRA), a movement founded by American minister Frank Buchman in the 1920s and committed to working on reconciliation, made an immense contribution to the relatively swift rapprochement between France and Germany—a reconciliation that formed the backbone of the European Union. MRA organized the first substantial reconciliation processes between the two countries. Its basic concept was that, if conflict transformation was to occur, people from both sides had to begin by listening to one another in a favourable environment. The Swiss group acquired the large and ornate Caux Palace Hotel for large-scale meetings. It also used its network of contacts in the Swiss foreign ministry and occupied Germany to acquire travel permits for German representatives. Starting in 1946, French and German participants came to Switzerland, occasionally for weeks at a time. Budgetary constraints meant that people had to work together to do kitchen work and housekeeping between gatherings. Given food shortages back in Germany, the healthy food and dinner conversations were appreciated by the participants. The Alpine view also made everyone feel privileged to be there, establishing an esprit de corps (Luttwak, 1994a).

Between 1946 and 1950, 1,938 French and 3,113 German people were involved in the meetings at Caux (Luttwak, 1994a). The participants included politicians (such as German Chancellor Konrad Adenauer and future president of France François Mitterand), trade unionists, industrialists, education leaders, media representatives, and clergy. A key figure on the French side was Robert Schuman, who served as his country's foreign minister and (separately) prime minister. Born in Germany to a French-German family, Schuman became a French politician after WWI when Alsace and Lorraine went back to France. He is regarded as the architect of the Franco-German reconciliation. In 1950, he announced that France would support the integration of the French and German mining and steel industries through a common market that would be called the European Coal and Steel Community (ECSC). The idea was to make war impossible by integrating major strategic German and French industries. The ECSC was followed by the European Economic Community and later by the current European Union.

The archival collections of correspondence and notes of the Caux sessions make it clear that there was a considerable transformation of attitudes. Germans who arrived feeling sorry for themselves changed their perspective dramatically, "combining expressions of intense gratitude for being received as equals and even as friends of the other participants, avowals of guilt and repentance, repudiations of past belief in Hitler and his ideology, and promises that Germans would never again be guilty of aggression" (Luttwak, 1994a, p. 54).

In this case, a third-party group had the initial vision for bringing the German and French people together. As significant leaders from both sides participated, the vision and mandate developed. Some of the processes were formal, but many were informal and behind the scenes.

A major part of the reconciliation was truth-telling, which occurred in a welcoming space in neutral territory. Regarding the results, structural change was evident in the formation of the ECSC. At the individual level, there were signs of personal healing. Transcendence was also apparent as parties started to define themselves as European and not just members of their respective nations.[1]

(AP Photo/Herve Merliac)

French President François Mitterand (right) and German Chancellor Helmut Kohl join hands during a French–German reconciliation ceremony on 22 September 1984. The ceremony was held near Verdun, the site of the epic and bloody battle between the French and German armies of World War I.

---

1. It must be mentioned here that many people and groups in France were opposed to this type of reconciliation. They felt that they did not have to atone for anything because France had been invaded and occupied by Germany.

CASE STUDY 13.2 | THE NUERS AND DINKAS OF SOUTHERN SUDAN

Based on New Sudan Council of Churches. (2002). *Inside Sudan: The story of people-to-people peacemaking in southern Sudan.* Nairobi, Kenya: NSCC; Redekop, V. N. (2007a). Reconciling Nuers with Dinkas: A Girardian approach to conflict resolution. *Religion—An International Journal,* 37, 64–84; and Telar Deng and Vern Neufeld Redekop, personal communication, 2003.

During the civil war between northern and southern Sudan in the 1990s, the two largest tribes of the south—the Nuers and the Dinkas—became embroiled in a deadly conflict that left houses destroyed, children abducted, and people killed. A contributing factor to the conflict was the fact that the Sudan People's Liberation Army/Movement (SPLA/M) was dominated by Dinkas and was fighting the north, while many Nuers were part of the Sudan Independence Movement/Army (SIM/A) in the south. The conflict also involved access to water and other resources.

Both tribes were primarily Christian but retained much of their traditional, indigenous culture. In 1992–3, the New Sudan Council of Churches (based in Tanzania because of the war) set up a peace commission with a mandate to address violent conflicts in the south. The commission was headed by Telar Deng, a Christian with a law degree. Over a period of four years, subprocesses set the stage for the Wunlit Conference, which ended the conflict in 1999.

The first subprocess was the Yei Dialogue, which brought together top leaders of SPLA/M and religious leaders. The result was that John Garang, head of SPLA/M, offered his support to peace efforts within southern Sudan. What followed was the 1997 dialogue, in which approximately 30 Nuer and Dinka religious leaders and elders met to examine the possibilities for peace. After not speaking to each other for seven years, parties from both sides lived together in huts for several days. At one of their meetings, Bishop Nathaniel Garang (a Dinka) held up a chair with his arthritic hand as a symbolic gesture. "Who will help me with the burden of leadership?" he called out. A Nuer bishop responded that he would. The move had a catalytic effect: all those present committed to help end the conflict. They agreed to stop abductions and other violent actions and work on peace.

The third subprocess began with five Nuer chiefs and one woman leader visiting the Dinkas. They undertook this task with much fear, realizing that negative passions were high. The visit included a constructive exchange of views and led to a reciprocal exchange, as a similar delegation of Dinkas visited the Nuers. This was in preparation for the Wunlit Conference.

Deng and his team planned the Wunlit Conference carefully. They selected Wunlit as a venue because it was so small that it was not on the map; therefore, there was no way that it would be bombed by planes from the north (eventually the Government of Sudan committed to stop attacking the south during the time of the conference). Thatched huts had to be built to accommodate 1,500 people. Delegates also had to be selected. It was determined that 160 official delegates would come from each side. Loudspeakers were installed so that people outside the conference building could hear the proceedings. SPLA/M would provide a security ring around Wunlit to preclude any attacks. Not fully trusting the officers, the organizers arranged for the SPLA/M members' wives to be part of the conference, thus ensuring that this faction would not disrupt the conference. People with facilitation skills also became part of the team leading the proceedings.

At the opening of the conference, over 1,000 people gathered in a circle around Mabior, the white bull. They sang and chanted, raising the emotional level of the group. Some young men with spears killed the bull as a sacrifice for peace and reconciliation. That evening, everyone ate portions of the same animal. Achol Jok Ajuong cried through the ceremony and prayed for peace as he remembered his six daughters who had been raped and killed. The next morning, the conference started with teachings that framed the goals and orientation of the conference. These admonitions made it clear that the goal was reconciliation undertaken in good faith and with a positive spirit. The first three days were devoted to people from both sides telling their experiences of the conflict. The next three were for rebuttal and clarification. At one point, a Dinka chief was talking sorrowfully about the impact of his children being abducted. A Nuer chief gave the nod to an aide and, while the man was still talking, his children appeared at the door.

After the six days of storytelling and response, the reconciliation team, which had been listening carefully, devised six areas that needed attention. The conference delegates were divided into six working groups and given a mandate to think of recommendations to guide future actions. At the end of the conference, there was another ritual sacrifice of a white bull. A covenant articulating a shared commitment to live together in peace was prepared, with the recommendations of the six working groups attached. Everyone added their thumbprint to indicate their support. As the bull was sacrificed, one of the leaders pronounced, "May the same thing happen to anyone who does not live up to the terms of the covenant." One of the conditions that was immediately acted upon was public education, thereby ensuring that all members of both tribes would know what had happened and would be oriented toward peace. The conference was so successful that, despite some initial incidents, peace has been maintained between the groups.

CASE STUDY 13.3 | IMAM MUHAMMAD ASHAFA AND PASTOR JAMES WUYE

Based on Little, D. (2007). Warriors and brothers: Imam Muhammad Ashafa and pastor James Wuye. In D. Little (Ed.), *Peacemakers in action: Profiles of religion in conflict resolution* (pp. 247–277). Cambridge, United Kingdom: Cambridge University Press; and Channer, A. (Producer/Director). (2006). *The imam and the pastor* [Motion picture]. United Kingdom: FLTfilms. For a 10-minute excerpt of the film, see www.youtube.com/watch?v=oapAA0XUaH4. For more information, see www.iofcafrica.org/.

In the 1990s, violence between Muslim and Christian militia groups in the Kaduna state of Nigeria left hundreds dead. Muhammad Ashafa and James Wuye were opposing leaders of these groups. During the conflict, close friends of Ashafa were killed and Wuye lost a hand.

After a chilly encounter at a conference (where they were introduced to each other by a mutual acquaintance), each man had experiences in the context of his particular religion that opened him to change. Ashafa was approached by an imam whom he admired. This imam told him that the Islamic tradition emphasizes forgiveness and peace and discourages hatred. The words touched Ashafa in a profound way. For his part, Wuye attended a Pentecostal church (primarily to wink at the young women in the choir). One particular Sunday, he had the feeling that the pastor was speaking just to him. The words questioned the malicious thoughts that he had toward Ashafa.

After these independent events, Wuye's mother became seriously ill. Ashafa and some of his friends visited Wuye to show his concern. Ashafa also attended the funeral when she died. Wuye was initially suspicious but gradually opened himself up to these friendly gestures and agreed to meet with Ashafa. Together, they determined to work together on reconciliation. They visited each other's houses of worship and continued to share with one another how they had become involved in the conflict.

As they established personal links, the two men developed a vision for reconciliation between their respective communities. They founded the Interfaith Mediation Centre and, using the organization as an institutional base, travelled together throughout their state, leading workshops designed to enhance mutual understanding between Christians and Muslims and contribute to reconciliation. Ashafa became an imam and Wuye a Pentecostal pastor. During the first three years of their collaboration, Pastor James had a sustained impulse to smother Imam Ashafa with a pillow while he slept. Eventually, this urge was replaced by a profound mutual love and respect.

One of Ashafa and Wuye's significant accomplishments was mobilizing a whole community to hold a public ceremony of reconciliation. A commemorative plaque was prepared, and state political leaders came to speak at the event. Religious leaders expressed their willingness to offer forgiveness for the killing of many within their respective groups. At the end of the ceremony, hundreds of participants from the different groups celebrated and danced together.

The reconciliation of Ashafa and Wuye was not directed by an outside party, but third parties did play a role in introducing them and presenting them with teachings of blessing that influenced their attitudes and gave them a vision for reconciliation. In the early stages, Wuye responded to Ashafa's gestures of goodwill (GRIT), creating positive reciprocity. In the end, their personal reconciliation led to the establishment of an institution that promotes reconciliation.

CONCLUSION

Reconciliation is not a mechanical process. What works in one situation may not work in another (Daly & Sarkin, 2007, pp. 239–40). Reconciliation is not a matter of technique, and its outcomes cannot be dictated. But there is evidence that processes associated with reconciliation actually work. This chapter discussed the various approaches and goals to reconciliation. It also examined the pre-requisites, discursive and symbolic processes, and meta-requisites that are involved. Three specific cases demonstrated how these elements have been used to achieve reconciliation.

There are many examples of profound transformation in the wake of deep hurt. Often it takes the leadership of people who have a vision that goes beyond what seems reasonably possible. Before Mandela's release, for example, popular wisdom was that a civil war in South Africa was inevitable. Mandela's overpowering vision and passion for reconciliation led to a country that has equal political rights for everyone. Therefore, reconciliation as a complex adaptive system deserves much additional research to discover the features of its success in many of the most unlikely situations.

DISCUSSION QUESTIONS

1. Choose a current conflict. Based on the case studies in this chapter, suggest a possible scenario for reconciliation.

2. Reflect on the different elements of reconciliation. Choose five that emerge as particularly significant and rank them in order of priority.

3. What are the relationships between a signalling model of reconciliation at the international level and the socio-emotional and instrumental models developed in social psychology? How does each play a necessary role?

4. Recall a time when you were deeply hurt by someone and resented, perhaps even hated, him or her as a result. What factors would you consider to be important if you were to reconcile with this person?

NOTES

1. Hamber and Kelly (2009) provide a comparable list of five strands:

   • developing a shared vision of an interdependent and fair society
   • acknowledging and dealing with the past
   • building positive relationships
   • significant cultural and attitudinal change
   • substantial social, economic, and political change (pp. 291–292)

2. Note also the work of Charles Ingrao, who initiated the Scholars Initiative, a project that engaged over 200 scholars to work on 10 controversial issues regarding the Balkan conflicts of the 1990s. Each working group included scholars from both sides of the issues. For the research reports, see www.cla.purdue.edu/history/facstaff/Ingrao/si/scholars.htm.

3. For a complete discussion of this term and its use in the context of conflict studies and reconciliation, see Redekop (2007b).

PART V | ETHICAL ISSUES

In the previous four parts of this text, we have defined conflict and examined how it manifests itself at different levels. We have analyzed the causes of conflict from a wide range of disciplines. Using these perspectives, we have also looked at how people engage in conflict and the processes they use to manage, resolve, and transform conflict. Reconciliation of deep-rooted conflict and practical challenges in dealing with violent conflict have also been subjects of interest. This final section focuses on the role of ethics in conflict, particularly in terms of values, fairness, justice, and normative practices.

It is hard to think about conflict without considering the actions associated with engaging in it. The resolution, management, transformation, reconciliation, and other ways of dealing with conflict also include a strong action component. Likewise, ethics is concerned with action.

To address ethical questions and concerns, Chapter 14 presents the various definitions of ethics and explores the normative frameworks within which people engage in conflict. Justice, discussed in Chapter 15, pertains both to conflict and resolution. People in conflict usually defend their positions in terms of fighting injustices or aspiring to a sense of justice. Similarly, those who intervene in conflict situations frame their involvement in terms of justice. The goal of many interventions is peace; in fact, peace studies as a field is often coupled with conflict studies. Peace, then, is the focus of Chapter 16. Finally, Chapter 17 discusses the concept of an ethical vision for conflict specialists and the moral dilemmas that they must often face.

14 | CONFLICT, VIOLENCE, AND ETHICS

CHAPTER OBJECTIVES

This chapter will help you develop an understanding of the

- role of values, principles, and goals in shaping ethical thought;
- interplay between deontology and teleology;
- importance of intended and unintended consequences;
- function of ethics in generating and restraining conflict; and
- history and elements of just war theory.

INTRODUCTION

This chapter examines the relationship between ethics and conflict. We begin by discussing how our values, principles, and goals influence our actions and decisions, as well as how they can lead to or avoid conflicts. In order to understand how ethical thinking affects the study and the practice of conflict, the majority of the chapter focuses on ethical considerations regarding war, particularly those represented by **just war theory**. After tracing the evolution of this theory and its contribution to international law, we discuss the various conditions that are required for such a conflict to be deemed just.

VALUES, PRINCIPLES, AND GOALS

Ethics is concerned with how values, principles, and goals shape our behaviour and enable us to judge the appropriateness of certain actions and their consequences. Ethics links with conflict because people's motivations and actions, along with their impacts, can all be subject to ethical analysis and reflection. Most conflicts are simultaneously prompted and constrained by different values, principles, and goals. People fight for certain values and restrain themselves based on others. At another level, the question of what ethical position is appropriate in a certain situation creates a good deal of conflict. That is, values, principles, and goals can also cause conflict.

In the field of ethics, a distinction is made between **deontology** (the study of moral duty) and **teleology** (the study of the intended goals of an action). Together, these approaches balance intentions with moral principles. Another important school of thought is **consequentialist ethics**, which is concerned with consequences, particularly when the outcome of any action in a given situation is negative. The ethical dilemma in such a circumstance is having to choose "the lesser of two evils." **Virtue ethics** looks at the ethical actor's character from the perspective of well-developed practices that exemplify virtues. Keeping in mind the need to balance different approaches, we will examine values, principles, and goals in turn.

Moral Values

There are many ways in which we use the word *value*. It is used commercially when we talk about getting good *value* for our money. We use it to talk about *valuables* in a material sense. We also *value* friendships, relationships, and family. When it is used with the adjective *moral*, it refers to a value that has individual and collective meaning. For instance, we might accept certain values because they have been taught to us by our families, acquired from our culture, or reinforced by our own experiences. In this section, we focus on three examples of moral values that can play a role in conflicts: personal freedom, human dignity, and the common good.

When we think of personal freedom as a value, we include such things as freedom of movement, expression, religion, and assembly. In many parts of the world, these freedoms are associated with basic human rights. They are listed in constitutions and guaranteed by many formal structures. Throughout history, wars have been fought "for the sake of freedom," indicating a high individual and collective value within society. Possible threats to this freedom include the state, capricious rulers, foreign domination, criminals, and incarceration (if we are found guilty of a crime, in which case the loss of freedom is justified by society). Personal freedom as a value has many objective indicators. In an instance where freedom is present, it is taken for granted. People freely do whatever they want unless their exercise of freedom constrains that of someone else or violates some law. When it is lacking, for example, in a case where it is against the law to criticize the government, people take special care to not be detected if they do speak freely. They may also try to leave the country or participate in resistance movements to change the government.

Personal freedom as a value can clearly be invoked at the individual level—people react when someone limits their freedom. It can also play a major role among collective identity groups that want the freedom to do or not do certain things within society. Furthermore, it can be important at the national and international levels. Conflict ensues when one party exercises personal freedom in a manner that limits the freedom of others. The same value then becomes a driving force for conflict if the arguments regarding the behaviour centre on freedom. Religious freedom is particularly vulnerable to conflict when religious practices are in the public domain and/or have an impact on others.

Human dignity refers to the worth of each individual. As history shows, this value has not been applied universally. During the era of slavery in the Americas, for instance, people of African origin were not included in this value by the dominant society. A conflict that results in dehumanization puts pressure on human dignity, while instances of genocide negate it completely. Like personal freedom, human dignity has been associated with human rights. There are laws in many countries that protect the dignity of society's most vulnerable people. Many conflicts arise out of actions that are framed as encroaching on human dignity. One of the most controversial examples of this situation is the abortion debate. On one side are people who use the value of human dignity to argue against abortion. On the other are those who argue for the dignity of women and freedom of choice.

Our third example of a moral value is the common good. This value has less consensus than the previous two. Those that are strictly individualistic tend to think that the highest social good is to allow people the opportunity to do anything to improve their own situations. However, there are others who think in terms of what might be best for their community and country, or even the globe. This value recognizes that some aspects of life can be attended to in only a collective manner and that there are some goods that benefit everyone. When it comes to matters of lifestyle in relation to the environment, there may be instances in which a value for the common good limits personal freedoms, causing conflicts between those who feel that personal freedom is primary and those who consider the common good the highest priority. For instance, some business owners might feel that they have a right to dump toxic waste into holes on their property and would resist policies restricting their actions on the grounds that toxins would leach into the water supply.

Values may function at the tacit level without us ever clearly articulating them. We may not even recognize them as values until they are threatened. Moral psychologist Marc Hauser (2006) points out that humans seem to be programmed with certain moral categories that can be organized into three questions: What is obligatory? What is forbidden? What is permitted? According to Hauser, we appropriate particular normative answers to these questions from the social environments in which we are raised. The process is akin to learning a language. We have a capacity and a set of internal categories that enable us to learn the language that we are exposed to in our social environment. Similarly, argues Hauser, we have an ability to learn whatever moral values exist in that setting. Each moral framework has its own specific answers to the three questions. For any particular individual or group, there could be a unique set of answers that combines elements from different frameworks.

Principles

In early societies, values were expressed as taboos. Eventually, however, they became informal teachings and well-articulated principles. Associated with the deontological side of ethics, principles can be formulated as teachings to guide behaviour, moral codes of conduct, or laws to be enforced. Each represents a different degree of formality.

Most cultures and religions feature teachings that have evolved to help people live well. Included in many of these teachings are guiding principles to assist in dealing with conflict. In some cultures, elders pass on the teachings orally. In others, they are written down. The first five books of the Hebrew Bible, the Torah, constitute one example of such teachings. These books contain stories to impart moral values; apodictic law, understood as general overarching commandments; and casuistic law, which is conditional (i.e. "If this happens, then do this"). Within the Roman Catholic Church, social teachings function as a moral authority. The pope also periodically releases an encyclical that is meant to provide moral guidance. Vatican II, a council of the Catholic Church held between 1962 and 1965, generated a number of moral principles that significantly reset the moral teachings of the religion.

Without necessarily referring to them as such, most organizations also have teachings that explain their respective principles. Even organized crime syndicates have their own moral codes, which happen to be at odds with the rest of society. This difference suggests that moral principles are subject to debate and evaluation. Various professional organizations and other groups distill moral values and principles into tightly written codes of conduct. These codes are the basis for making decisions about practices and for disciplining members of the association.[1]

When moral principles are formalized, they become law. Law and ethics, then, have an ambiguous relationship. On the one hand, many laws reflect moral values and principles. On the other, a law has a life of its own. Legality does not always equal morality. While moral values may change, laws do not. Instead, they are amended or nullified by new laws. By finding loopholes in the law, people ensure that even actions that might be immoral are considered legal. The circumstances in which laws are applied could also differ from the lawmakers' intentions. Consequently, actions that would seem wrong in one context would seem appropriate in another. For example, a doctor speeding to the hospital to save someone's life is breaking the law. However, she is also attending to her own professional code of conduct and personal values.

Ethical Goals and Intended Consequences

Considering goals and intentions involves the teleological dimension of ethical reflection and analysis. An ethical goal entails an intention to achieve positive consequences through certain actions. In the example of the speeding doctor, her intended goal of saving a life puts the principle of obeying the speed limit in a different light.

Examining intention raises some interesting ethical issues. If the intention is clearly unrealistic and the goal therefore unattainable, is action still justified? What about unintended consequences? Attaining a certain goal can yield some negative effects. This outcome is particularly the case in military operations that result in collateral damage. In assessing the ethical implications of an action, the intended goals must be subject to ethical evaluation (such as by comparing them to other potential goals) and the unintended consequences considered.

In any situation, there is always the question of whether the ends justify the means. In technical language, does the teleological override the deontological? Overemphasizing the importance of moral principle or law could result in hurting people. One such case involved Christian missionaries who were active in places where polygamy was the custom. Their insistence that the male converts follow the moral principle of monogamy meant that some wives were put aside. Within their culture, these women had no rights and suffered terribly. If there are good intentions but negative consequences to an action, the principle of proportionality becomes important. In other words, are the good intentions important enough to justify the negative consequences?

ETHICAL DRIVERS OF CONFLICT

People are driven to conflict on account of their moral values, principles, and ethical goals. They often clash over what they consider to be right in a given situation. This type of conflict may occur because people have different moral values and therefore see things differently. Another possibility is that they both have the same values but disagree over which ones are implicated in a certain circumstance. If the sense of rightness involves the parties themselves, each might exaggerate an aspect of the situation so that, even if they are operating on the same principle, they may see the situation differently.

Other conflicts arise because one party believes that the other is breaking the law, transgressing human rights, or otherwise acting contrary to moral principles. Such conflicts occur at all levels, from the interpersonal to the international. Similarly, some people may feel that moral distinctions are black and white and that they are on the side of the right. They might even think that they have the authority of God on their side. This sense of moral rightness makes them believe that they must do everything in their power to stop others from transgressing a moral principle. The result could be, for instance, a bombing in the name of a moral cause, an act that is considered terrorism by others (Juergensmeyer, 2003).

Finally, people have significant conflicts over what moral principles should guide their group. Homosexuality, for example, has created bitter conflicts and serious divisions in many Christian churches. Some insist on a deontology that designates homosexual practice as morally wrong in all cases; others claim that it is morally wrong to exclude and judge one group of people on the basis of sexual orientation.

THE JUST WAR TRADITION

Throughout this text, we have shown that conflict may involve the use of violence. In a primary sense, violence involves the use of force to inflict harm on an individual or group.[2] The force may be real or threatened and the harm physical or psychological. In extreme situations, it results in death. At the next level, we find emotional or psychological violence resulting in fear, trauma, and some form of incapacitation. Another type is passive violence, understood as harmful action that does not involve the use of physical force but includes "discrimination, oppression (economic, political, social, cultural, religious, racial, gender), name-calling, [and] gossiping" (Gandhi, 2003, p. 110). Oppression is also considered a separate form, referred to as structural violence by theorists such as Galtung. Slavery and apartheid are clear examples of this type of violence. Less clear for some but unambiguously attacked by others are the political, legal, social, and economic factors that lead to extreme poverty and high levels of maternal mortality in many countries (Jones, 2007). Symbolic violence further harms victims by imposing narratives and categories regarding the violence. For instance, torture victims can be made to feel shame for their ordeals and survivors of rape, especially in the context of war, may be shunned by relatives, communities, or former lovers (Scheper-Hughes & Bourgois, 2004, p. 1). Finally, as was pointed out in Chapter 13, Emmanuel Levinas (1961/1969) claimed that the worst form of violence is to deprive someone of a capacity to take any meaningful action. A graphic example is the violence of Nazi concentration camps, which transformed people into what Primo Levi (1988) describes as the living dead—people who walked around in a trance and had no motivation, their feelings deadened and their motions mere mechanical repetitions.

Making sense of the various forms of violence often involves ethics. Can we simply say that all violence is bad and hope it will go away? What if violent atrocities, such as the torture of innocent people or genocide, are being committed? Should violence be used to stop the atrocities?[3] Are there not other instances in which violence is called for, such as in self-defence, in response to a grave injustice, or in an attempt to stop an aggressive tyrant? If we admit to the violence of war being used in some instances, are there moral limits to this manner of engaging in conflict? If so, on what might they be based?

In cases of war, for example, we use moral language in our arguments over whether a war is justified or being conducted properly (Walzer, 1977/2006, p. xxi). Historically, the dominant tradition that seeks to identify moral limits of warfare is just war theory. In the remainder of this section, we provide an overview of the evolution of this theory and its contribution to international law. We also examine its main components: *jus ad bellum* (the justice of going to war), *jus in bello* (the moral restraints on how wars should be fought), *jus post bellum* (the principles that guide parties following a war; see Reichberg, Syse, & Begby, 2006, p. 634; Orend, 2000), and *jus potentia ad bellum* (preparing for war).

Finally, we consider some of the debates regarding the theory. While reading the following pages, keep in mind that the moral framework of just war also has links to domestic issues, particularly in policies regarding the use of force in policing and maintaining public order. It is generally accepted in both the domestic and international arenas that the use of force is a last resort to be used in proportion to the wrong being addressed and that the decision to use force must be made by legitimate authorities.

The Evolution of Just War Theory

Many ancient cultures limit violence in the context of war. Aztecs fought with a fixed number of warriors; Chinese thinker Lao Tse advised good generals to achieve their purpose without loving violence; and Chinese philosopher Sun Tzu urged that captives be treated well (Christopher, 1994, pp. 8–9). The Hindu Book of Manu (fourth century BCE) restricted the types of weapons that could be used in war (e.g. none with poison, barbs, or fire) and listed many groups that could not be attacked (e.g. no one sleeping, naked, disarmed, wounded, or in flight).

Aristotle was the first to use the term *just war* (Christopher, 1994, p. 10). He presented the following reasons for going to war: to take vengeance on those who have wronged us; to protect ourselves from being wronged through acts of aggression; to defend our kin or allies when they are attacked; and to gain some advantage for the city, such as glory or resources. Aristotle was clear that war was never to be an end in itself but a means to peace (see Barnes, 1984, pp. 2102–2103).

Roman jurist and philosopher Marcus Cicero (106–43 BCE) also played a significant role in the development of the just war tradition. In particular, he advanced a number of principles related to *jus ad bellum* that have continued to the present-day. For instance, war must be officially declared by a proper authority but only as a last resort and after reparations have been demanded. When war is declared, antagonists must be notified. Before there are any hostilities, the antagonist must be given an opportunity to settle peacefully (Christopher, 1994, pp. 12–13). Roman law, which was applicable throughout the Roman Empire, incorporated similar principles such that a war could be considered only if it met these conditions. Regarding *jus in bello*, the Romans made it clear that only soldiers and officers could engage in fighting. Those who were formally discharged but continued fighting could be charged with murder. There was also a duty to protect those who surrendered. Those who contravened these and other laws regarding war could be convicted of war crimes (Christopher, 1994, p. 14).

Saint Augustine of Hippo (354–430), a Christian theologian and bishop living at the time that Christianity became the official religion of the Roman Empire, drew on the philosophy of Cicero and others to develop a new synthesis that combined just war principles with Christian theology. Augustine's frame of reference included two kingdoms, or cities, that coexisted in the same time and place. The city of God was infused with *caritas*, a love for the well-being of the other. The earthly city was dominated by *cupiditas*, or self-love, manifest in desires for things of a temporal nature. Political authorities were established in the latter city to maintain order, justice, and peace. This peace was different from the concord and harmony that characterized peace in the city of God. Given the realities of the earthly city, Augustine reluctantly concluded that the violence of war would have to be used to obtain justice (avenge injuries)[4] and to achieve the kind of peace that would be tolerable for all.

Like Cicero, Augustine affirmed the need for war to be declared by the right authority. Included in this idea was the possibility of God directing that war be waged to achieve a good end, notably peace. Augustine also highlighted the importance of intentionality—war must be undertaken with good intentions, preferably by virtuous leaders. However, good laws are not dependent on the intentions of those behind them but can be judged on their own merit. In other words, good laws can be passed by bad people.[5] For Augustine, this relationship was significant in relation to war because it was of supreme importance that soldiers followed orders for the sake of upholding the law but could never be held accountable for a decision to go to war, which was that of the ruler. Regarding the fighting of wars, Augustine argued that wars should never be fought for the sake of glory. Instead, he emphasized compassion toward the enemy and a post-victory peace that would afford dignity to the other side. He also developed the principle of sanctuary, that people seeking refuge in churches were not to be harmed. His work influenced later thinkers, notably Saint Thomas Aquinas and Hugo Grotius.

In the twelfth century, a monk named Gratian assembled *Decretum Gratiani*, a book that organized teachings pertaining to values and human behaviour, including ones on how to conduct just wars. Augustine's ideas on the subject, which had been scattered in documents written over a period of years, were also catalogued and commented on by

Gratian. This book became the basis for canon law, the legal framework of the Roman Catholic Church. Such status was a major development, considering that the Church dominated Western Europe until the Reformation. Gratian's work also became the foundation on which arguments for the ethics of political decisions were made. Hence, just war principles were the standard for political life in Europe. Whether they were followed, however, is another question.

Aquinas, immersed as he was in both Aristotle and Augustine and having the work of Gratian available, provided a new level of coherency to the just war tradition. One of his main contributions, the concept of natural law, is methodological. Based on the observation of and reflection on human tendencies, the principles of natural law form the grounds of moral argument. For instance, people tend to live in societies, creating the need for some form of government with laws to establish justice and order (Christopher, 1994, p. 50). Just war theory became grounded in secular premises thanks largely to the influence of Aquinas. Aquinas was the first to articulate clearly that *jus ad bellum* demands that all three conditions need to be in place: "It must be declared by the authority of a head of a state (proper authority), for a proportionally good reason (**just cause**), and with a morally good aim (right intention)" (Christopher, 1994, p. 51). The first condition also involves appealing to a higher authority—in many cases a head of state—if one exists. (This element anticipates the situation in which the United Nations Security Council [UNSC] becomes a higher authority that can legitimately call for the use of armed forces against a belligerent state.) Regarding the second and third, he makes it clear that a war with a just cause can be unjust if there is a wrong intention, such as a "cruel thirst for vengeance, an unpacific and relentless spirit, the fever of revolt, the lust of power, and such like things."[6]

Aquinas also contributed the important ethical concept of the double effect. This principle states that, in the course of attempting to accomplish a just goal, there may be secondary effects that go beyond the intended objectives. Consider the example of acting in self-defence when attacked: the intended effect is to save one's life, but an unintended consequence is that the attacker is killed. The judgment of an action is based on the intended effects (Reichberg et al., 2006, p. 189). Reading Aquinas leaves one with the general impression that he sees a just war as one that either helps the victimized poor or contributes to the common good by protecting a jurisdiction from oppressive actions. Hence, the soldier, acting on directives from a superior, is capable of virtuous action by assisting the vulnerable.

In the centuries immediately following Aquinas, two events raised new issues concerning the development of just war theory: the colonial era and the Reformation. After studying Aquinas and French humanism in Paris, Francisco de Vitoria (1492–1546) returned to Spain and became the chair of theology at the University of Salamanca. He grew deeply concerned about reports that Spaniards were committing massacres and pillaging in the new world of the Americas. In 1539, he delivered a lecture, later published as *De Indis*, in which he addressed the ethical issues involved. He argued that the people of these lands were neither subjects of Spain nor members of the Church; therefore, they were not under the jurisdiction of the king or pope. Furthermore, they had a capacity to govern themselves, meaning that the colonizers had no right to attack them. Self-defence was allowed; however, all other actions were to be for the well-being of the indigenous peoples. Vitoria's arguments influenced what eventually became the principle of state sovereignty. In another lecture, published as "On the Law of War," he argued for the ethical principle of respecting the common good of all nations and addressed the question of who should be involved in the decision to go to war. According to Vitoria, monarchs should consult a council of wise people who would critically examine any reasons for going to war with a view to averting it, if possible (Christopher, 1994, p. 55). The standard was that any decision to go to war would be made by a group of advisors and be based on the war's merits. In other words, war for the sake of a ruler's personal benefit was to be avoided.

Just as Vitoria's theories were developed in a particular context, Dutch jurist Hugo Grotius (1583–1645) was compelled to write his *Law of Nations* by a specific event. During the Thirty Years' War, Grotius (as cited in Reichberg et al., 2006) observed

> a lack of restraint in relation to war, such as even barbarous races should be ashamed of. Men rush to arms for slight causes . . . and when arms have once been taken up there is no longer any respect for law, divine or human; it is as if, in accordance with a general decree, frenzy had openly been let loose for the committing of all crimes. (pp. 390–91)

His goal was to introduce a system of law that would regulate the waging of wars, people's behaviour during wars, and their attempts to keep the peace. He drew on the works of all the key thinkers of the Western tradition to create a framework that represented a shift from a moral tradition centred in the Church to what he hoped would be an international law.

Grotius argued that there are two types of law: natural and volitional. Natural law, as developed by Aquinas, is based on patterns of human interactions that can be expressed in universal laws (similar to the laws of physics), which "are the first principles from which human reason deduces moral truths" (Christopher, 1994, p. 68). Although based on natural law, volitional laws depend on context and can be set aside in particular circumstances. Grotius distinguished among volitional laws for domestic relationships, municipal laws, and national laws. As we stated earlier, the tendency of humans to live in society is a natural law. To expedite our life together, it is important to enter into and abide by volitional laws, such as pacts. These laws "obligate, prohibit, or, by forfeit, permit" (Christopher, 1994, p. 70). When it comes to war, Grotius consistently argued that, even when violence might be permitted, it is better to desist. Although he was not a pacifist, his underlying interest was always to eliminate war.

BOX 14.1 | A RESOUNDING CONFRONTATION ABOUT THE USE OF FORCE

Decisions regarding just wars are now usually made at the international level. In one of the most dramatic confrontations of recent years, the American and British governments tried to secure a UN resolution authorizing an intervention in Iraq. In this photo, taken on 5 March 2003, foreign ministers Igor Ivanov of Russia (left), Dominique de Villepin of France (centre), and Joschka Fischer of Germany (right) announced that their governments would "not allow" such a resolution. That same month, the United States and their allies proceeded without UN authorization, initiating what was seen by most other countries as an illegitimate and illegal war.

(AP Photo/Laurent Rebours)

Jus ad bellum

The decision to go to war involves a consideration of the following: just cause, responsibility to protect, proportionality, reasonable chance of success, legitimate authority, last resort, right intention, and just fight. Note that Grotius affirmed all but the last two items on this list. Except in acute emergency cases of self-defence or threats to international peace and security, it is generally agreed that *all* conditions of *jus ad bellum* need to be met for a war to be justified.

As was previously discussed, just cause was traditionally considered to be a gross injustice on the part of the enemy, such as the seizing of land or the harming of one's citizens. However, the current literature regarding just cause includes some new considerations. For example, the term could also relate to the oppression of a vulnerable group. In 2002, the UN adopted the policy of responsibility to protect (R2P; see Chapter 12). This policy, developed by a multicultural and multi-religious panel, states that governments have the responsibility to protect their citizens from grave human rights abuses. Where they cannot or will not do so, the international community has an obligation to intervene. The conditions of R2P can be framed as defining a just cause for military action.

The next criterion for a just war is proportionality. In other words, the benefits of winning a war must be proportional to the damage inflicted or the costs incurred. Furthermore, there must be a reasonable chance of success. Since just war must be fought as a lesser evil in cases of grave injustice, there is no point in undertaking a war that may fail, create large-scale massacres, or drag on forever. The resulting miseries would be worse than what the war is supposed to cure. Such a war could eventually become an unjust war. A consequence of reasonable chance of success is that militarily powerful states are less likely to be forced to face a just war than small countries because it is unlikely that the latter would succeed. In the context of R2P, there is also little probability that great powers and regional powers committing human rights abuses would be attacked.

Failure to succeed is often used by opponents of recent military interventions. They point to the fact that the United States, even with its huge military capability, has had serious trouble in Iraq and does not seem to predominate in Afghanistan. These examples suggest that even wars fought for good causes can turn into pointless and potentially disastrous expeditions because quick victory cannot be found on the battlefield. This lack of success is especially the case when Western powers are confronted with terrorism, which combines moral idealism with violence (Eagleton, 2005, p. 76). The "just cause" of those engaged in terrorism is derived from their ideology and belief that they are on the right side of the moral equation. For them, success is measured through the lens of terror itself—they are out to terrorize a population and do not discriminate between combatants and non-combatants.

The condition of legitimate authority has been referred to throughout this chapter, so we will provide only a brief recap here. Traditionally, this authority has been a head of state (in pre-democratic times) or a duly elected government. In more recent years, the UNSC has emerged as another legitimate authority that can decide on military interventions.

For a decision to wage war to be just, it must be made as a last resort, after every other option for resolving the conflict has been tried. These options include negotiation, mediation, arbitration, good offices of a third party, multi-track diplomacy, and any of the other options described in chapters 11 and 12.

Another condition for *jus ad bellum* is right intention. Fighting with the right intention is difficult to discern at first glance because intentionality can be considered an internal attitude. However, intentionality in something as public as deciding to go to war is easier to see, as there are stated goals, outcomes, and rationale. There may, however, still be hidden reasons. For instance, a politician might know that fighting and winning a war will help him or her win the next election.

Anthony Coates (2006) reveals a darker side of the question of intentionality, even going so far as to suggest that a right attitude toward the enemy should be a separate condition. He points out that a decision to go to war can be based on "fierce and implacable" hatred:

Such hatred is not simply a matter of spontaneous feelings aroused by the experience of war itself, and in particular, by the extreme threat to self-preservation which the enemy may pose. It is systematic and anterior to war itself. What is at issue here is a culture of hatred that predisposes belligerents both to resort to war and conduct war mercilessly. This hatred is a "public" hatred. It is the response of those who feel themselves (collectively) to be "by nature enemies." The enemy is dehumanised or, worse still, demonised. The enemy is the Other, the complete antithesis of the collective self, the embodiment of absolute evil . . . Perversely, what [belligerents] have learnt is an *ethic* of harshness. The destruction of the enemy has become a moral duty. (Coates, 2006, p. 217, emphasis in original)

Coates illustrates this argument by comparing the Germans' moral orientation toward the peoples of the Western and Eastern fronts during World War II. Despite their intense rivalry with France, the Germans could identify with Western Europeans. By and large, they treated Western prisoners of war with some dignity, and most survived the war. The Slavic peoples of the Eastern front, particularly the Russians, were hated by the Germans. Added to this animosity was a war of ideology—the Third Reich was passionately anti-communist. The tendency to kill the local population and execute prisoners of war was much higher on the Eastern Front, as a matter of policy. Likewise, the Americans were more brutal to the Japanese than they were to the Germans, even though they were at war with both. Racism contributed to this behaviour, as well as the fact that the Germans were prepared to surrender but the Japanese usually fought to the end. Coates insists that hatred has no place within just war theory. He calls for charity understood as "the sustained recognition of the moral equality and worth of the enemy" (Coates, 2006, p. 218). This moral equality transcends divisions and limits the tendency to go to war.

The final condition concerns the ability to fight the war justly. In other words, will the *jus in bello* criteria be met? Mark Woods (2007, p. 28) argues that a major consideration in fighting justly is the effect on the environment. Military initiatives are notorious for sacrificing environmental considerations for strategic gain. Hence, if it is clear that the only way to fight a potential war would harm the environment, this consequence would serve as a reason for avoiding war. However, most just war theorists do not go that far when considering a just fight.

Jus in bello

This aspect of the just war tradition refers to how wars should be fought once they are started. These decisions are made by military commanders and include the principles of proportionality and discrimination. Many of the provisions of *jus in bello* were formally introduced as international law in the Geneva Conventions.[7]

Just as proportionality is a factor in the decision to go to war, it is also involved in every step of fighting a war. For each manoeuvre, the following question must be asked: Is the potential gain commensurate to the damage that will be caused? Decisions regarding proportionality are frequently made with short-term goals in mind. For instance, the use of Agent Orange to destroy vegetation in large areas of Vietnam meant that the Viet Cong could not hide in the jungle and could easily be killed with helicopter gunships. However, it also had long-term effects on the land and the health of its people.

In the course of fighting a war, there must also be discrimination between combatants and non-combatants. Officially, combatants are members of the armed forces, excluding religious and medical personnel; however, other people who are significantly engaged in the war effort could also be included in this category (ICRC, 2012). Non-combatants are those who are uninvolved in the fighting. The number of non-combatant victims of armed conflict increased throughout the twentieth century. It is not always easy to distinguish between combatants and non-combatants in many violent situations, particularly when combatants engaged in guerrilla tactics make it a point to blend in with the civilian population.

Scholars such as Woods (2007, p. 21) argue that the principle of discrimination should apply to the environment as well. There are now international treaties that regulate war and its effects on the environment. One such agreement is the United Nations Convention on the Prohibition of Military or Any Other Hostile Use of Environmental Modification Techniques (1976). ENMOD, as it is called, came in the wake of the aforementioned use of Agent Orange and other chemicals.

Jus post bellum

Elements of justice after a war include the kind of settlement that is signed, the accountability of those who have committed crimes against humanity, and the reparations to victims. A new element of *jus post bellum* is the consideration of what should happen after humanitarian intervention. For instance, should the intervening bodies make reparations to those victimized through the interventions? In other words, can interveners be held responsible for collateral damage?

Jus potentia ad bellum

While the previous three categories refer to justice in cases of pending or actual war, *jus potentia ad bellum* is concerned with the justice of preparing for war in the general sense (Coates, 2006). This type includes a consideration of the massive budgets for arms procurement, the environmental effects of military exercises, and the consequences of arms cascading (the sale of obsolete weapons on the international market, providing insurgent groups, criminal syndicates, and individuals with cheap armaments). There are many advances in the preparedness for war. One is the development of large-scale mercenary companies that conduct war for a fee and generally operate outside the normal limitations placed on national armies. Another is information-gathering technology, which can be highly intrusive and can interfere with privacy rights.

Reflections on Just War Theory

The overall framework of just war theory has helped create international law by contributing to a host of treaties and conventions. It also continues to play a role in debates about any type of armed struggle. Within the narrative of just war theory, the interplay between deontology and teleology becomes evident. It is also clear that the concept works heuristically in that each of the principles forms a basis for asking questions about the legitimacy of any violent action.

One downside of just war thinking is that parties might disagree on whether a war meets the various criteria. For example, if people determine that their cause and hence their war is just, they will fight passionately for a moral principle that they believe in but may not be accepted by others. In this case, they frame the war as a "Holy War." One tragic example occurred in 1095, when Pope Urban II launched just such a war to reclaim the Holy Land for Christianity—a war that marked the beginning of the Crusades.

An alternative to just war thinking is the realist position that states are out to defend their interests and will use whatever means necessary to advance them. Reluctance to go to war is thus conceived in terms of how such a decision would adversely affect national interests. Just war analyst Nicholas Fotion (2007) frames each just war principle according to interests, showing how they illuminate aspects of what might be included in the interests of a particular party. Michael Walzer (1977/2006, p. 24), one of the most significant exponents of just war theory, argues for a normative approach. This method claims that, as human beings, we owe it to ourselves to establish values and express principles that limit our violent tendencies. Decisions to engage in wars are human decisions, as are the decisions on how to fight.

Walzer's arguments are set in the context of Clausewitzian theory. Carl von Clausewitz, a nineteenth-century German thinker, conceptualized total, or absolute, war as violence reciprocated between parties in a limitless escalation of destruction. This vision has also been taken up by René Girard (2010) as an apocalyptic reality that humans have a very real capacity for our mutual destruction. For the student of conflict studies, the challenge is to find ways of strengthening all the values, processes, institutions, ideas, and motivating visions that can prevent the runaway violence that Clausewitz envisioned in the abstract. Just war theory includes principles that can be modified and used in the service of such an endeavour.

CONCLUSION

In this chapter, we defined ethics as a type of human discourse and intellectual inquiry that is concerned with normative aspects of action as expressed in values, principles, and goals. We noted that values as expressed in principles (deontology), which can range from informal taboos to formal codes of conduct and law, should be balanced by values expressed in goals (teleology). Attention to teleology reveals the importance of considering intended and unintended consequences of actions. People are often driven into conflict by their respective values; however, they also restrain themselves based on other personal values or those of their society.

The chapter also focused on just war theory as a sustained historical inquiry into the inherent values of war and the ways that violence can be restrained and regulated, including within states. The various components of just war theory illustrate how ethical discourse has played a role in the development of human civilization, international law, and contemporary arguments regarding the use of lethal force.

DISCUSSION QUESTIONS

1. Discuss the importance of ethics in the understanding of the genesis and dynamics of conflict.

2. Choose a current conflict and identify some of the values that are important to each party. What are the deontological and teleological considerations of the parties?

3. Which just war principle is most important in today's world? Give reasons to support your answer.

NOTES

1. Urbanist Jane Jacobs (2005) argued that the failure of professional bodies to hold their members accountable to their codes of conduct and ethical values can be a key factor in societal decline.

2. The Violence Prevention Alliance defines violence as "the intentional use of physical force or power, threatened or actual, against oneself, another person, or against a group or community, that either results in or has a high likelihood of resulting in injury, death, psychological harm, maldevelopment, or deprivation." See www.who.int/violenceprevention/approach/definition/en/index.html.

3. For a graphic example of torturers being killed during a peacekeeping mission, see Grossman (1995, pp. 217–221).

4. See Swift (Ed. and Trans.), *The Earthly Fathers*, as cited in Reichberg, Syse, and Begby (2006, p. 82).

5. See Fortin and Kries (Eds.), Augustine: Political Writings, as cited in Reichberg, et al. (2006, p. 76).

6. Aquinas borrowed this quote from Augustine. See Christopher (1994, p. 52).

7. For texts of the Geneva Conventions, see www.icrc.org/ihl.nsf/CONVPRES.

15 | WHAT ROLE DOES JUSTICE PLAY?

CHAPTER OBJECTIVES

This chapter will help you develop an understanding of the

- links between justice, injustice, and conflict;
- historical development of the concept of justice;
- passions associated with injustice;
- relationship between justice and law;
- various paradigms of justice, ranging from primitive justice to retributive and restorative justice; and
- concepts of mercy, pardon, and forgiveness.

INTRODUCTION

The language of justice is woven into conflict discourse. People in conflict tend to support their positions by referring to justice or injustice, either explicitly (e.g. "We want justice" or "It is a travesty of justice") or implicitly in their discussion of a conflict's particular issues. People often speak of justice without reflecting on its meaning. They are usually clear about what they consider unjust and how the situation should be corrected, but these convictions do not necessarily mean that they understand the concept.

In this chapter, we examine the relationship between justice and conflict. We outline the evolution of justice, theories regarding just institutions, and the aspects of an unjust action. We also discuss various paradigms of social and criminal justice and how they attempt to restore balance in a conflict. Finally, we look at the role of mercy, pardon, and forgiveness in justice.

JUSTICE AND CONFLICT

The concept of justice relates to conflict in several ways. Many of the issues and motivations operative in conflicts are inspired by a desire for justice. For instance, people usually use the notion of rights—as in "I have a right to do such and such" or "You have no right to do that to me"—to frame their positions in a conflict. As we have mentioned throughout this book, many conflicts are played out in formal legal settings. When a conflict leads to injury, death, or another form of victimization, justice frameworks are used to determine the proper response. There are also conflicts about the basic principles of justice, what the laws should be and how they should be interpreted. These conflicts are based on clashing interests and values, which are influenced by historical cultures, education, and experience. The different concepts of justice and their meaning in concrete situations can lead to conflicts regarding the interpretation of events (i.e. whether an action constituted an injustice).[1] Some conflicts arise over the nature and intensity of punishments, while others revert to basic notions of balance and fairness to define grievances that cause conflict. We tend to make judgments based on "a sense of justice," a complex internal construction based on experience, interpretations, and moral teachings (Rawls, 1971/1999, pp. 496–505). When a conflict appears to be resolved but one or more parties feel that an injustice has not been addressed, it is only a matter of time before the conflict is reignited.

Justice is involved in all levels of conflict and reflects issues from the past, present, and future. For example, people are upset by past injustices. At an individual level, this hurt concerns emotional memories that may go back for decades. Such memories might also include the harm inflicted upon family members (Volkan, 1998). At a collective level, there is a regard for justice as it relates to ancestors. Reparations may be sought for particular injustices, such as the effects of slavery, residential schools, or social dislocation.[2] People also seek justice for their present experiences and insist on an imagined future where injustices are addressed and rectified. Included in this future is a vision of justice for children and subsequent generations (Tremmel, 2006).

People's ideas of justice also influence how they react to certain situations. In their discussion of Morton Deutsch's theories, Tom R. Tyler and Maura A. Belliveau (1995) describe how the psychologist came to recognize the significance of justice through his work on the question of conflict and co-operation in social housing projects (see Chapter 7):

> [He] found that the social conflict he was examining was expressed by those involved in social justice terms. People invoked principles of justice and injustice to explain their satisfaction or dissatisfaction with their state, and those feelings of social justice and injustice shaped people's behavioral reactions to their experiences. In other words, issues of justice were the medium through which people framed, discussed, and reacted to issues of social conflict. Hence, social justice became the inevitable focus of a social scientist interested in the realities of intergroup conflict and cooperation. (p. 291)

ORIGINS OF JUSTICE

The origins of justice can be explored through various methodologies. One approach is to examine how the concept evolved historically, which is where we will begin. Other ways to proceed include combinations of game theory (to see if we naturally think ethically), neuroscience (to see whether thoughts about justice involve particular parts of the brain), and behavioural psychology (to see what happens when we experience justice or injustice). We will touch on recent developments in these areas, particularly those that offer insights into how justice emerged with human development.

Historical Concepts of Justice

The roots of the concept of justice can be traced to ancient Greek, Roman, and Judaic traditions.

Greek and Roman conceptions of justice are based on the relationships between certain goddesses. In Greek mythology, Themis represents divine order. Married to Zeus, Themis had several daughters, including Dike (goddess of justice), Eunomis (goddess of good law), and Eirene (goddess of peace). This family points to the conceptual connections between justice, governance, and peace. For example, Themis and Dike are both depicted with balance scales in their hands, demonstrating a link between maintaining justice, making judgments, and being fair.[3] In one famous image, Dike is shown strangling and hitting Adikia, the goddess of injustice.

The Greek concepts of justice, law, and peace inspired the Roman idea of *jus*, from which we get the words *justice* and *judge*, and *lex*, from which the term *law* was derived (Kolbert, 1979). In the Roman tradition, the goddess Dike became Justicia. In Western civilization, the composite goddess of Justice (including Themis, Dike, and Justicia) evolved through the centuries and came to be represented as a blindfolded woman holding balance scales and carrying a sword, thereby indicating the importance of impartiality and, in a later development, the use of coercion to enforce justice.

Along with the contributions of the Greeks and Romans, some of the most sophisticated conceptual developments regarding justice come from the ancient Israelites, who were influenced by Mesopotamian and Egyptian civilizations. One of the oldest law codes was the Code of Hammurabi, a Babylonian king who is depicted as receiving the laws from the sun-god Šamaš, the god of law and father of Justice and Right (Cook, 1903, pp. 4–5). The code deals with a number of matters, including theft, kidnapping, land laws, family, professionals (e.g. fees for doctors), and slaves (e.g. ferocious penalties for those going against their masters), and stipulates how to respond to behaviours that go against the rules of the community (Cook, 1903, pp. 8–10). Living consistently with the code ensured that a king would govern long and "lead his subjects in righteousness"; anyone disobeying the code would cause many awful outcomes, including the ruin of the city and the "disappearance of his name and memory"(Cook, 1903, p. 13).

The Hebrew Bible also contains a number of codes—Covenant Code (Exodus), Holiness Code (Leviticus), Deuteronomic Code (Deuteronomy), etc. The idea of a covenant treaty among the Hittites was that it established a formal bond between parties such that their interests became enmeshed. It could be a covenant of solidarity—your friends are my friends, your enemies my enemies, and vice versa—or an asymmetrical covenant between victor and vanquished. In the latter case, the covenant could include an annual tribute. The Hebrews adapted the concept of covenant to frame their relationship with God. Legal codes thus became the definition of how to live properly within this agreement. Justice was expressed by religious devotion and treating one's fellow human being with dignity, respect, and love. For the Hebrews, justice was about both fairness and "honorable relations" as divinely prescribed (Martens, 2009).

The Hebrew prophets stand out historically as a group that established high standards that continue to affect how we frame injustices. They pointed out the many ways that the people of Israel departed from the way of life indicated by the Torah. They also moved the discussion of justice from a strictly legal framework to a more complex formulation that includes intentionality,[4] consequences, and structural injustices.[5] For them, the key words were *tsedaqah* (righteousness) and *mishpat* (justice). Tsedaqah inspired concepts of justice and law that put more emphasis on relationships. Hebrew Bible scholar Elmer Martens (2009) describes mishpat as follows:

The Hebrew word *mishpat* "justice" is a noun that derives from the verb *sha-phat*, which means "to decide," "to govern." The word mishpat has a legal, court-room setting (Deut. 1: 16–18). However decisions are part of everyday behaviour, certainly within the family . . . Decisions are not only made in court but at the level of relationships. How do ethnic groups relate to one another? How do those who govern relate to the governed? How do members within a society which includes aliens and orphans relate to each other? How do the rich relate to the poor? How is one to relate to parents, to children, to employers and to employees? (p. 125)

Martens (2009) further illustrates how the ancient Israelites believed that justice had both a retributive and a compassionate side. The former is seen in God "returning your deeds upon your head" (Ezek. 16: 38–43; Jer. 12: 1, 14–17). The latter is evident in the links between justice and words such as *hesed* ("caring, loyal love"), *emet* ("truth") and *rahamim* ("compassion"; the root metaphor being "womb"). With these connections in mind, Enrique Nardoni (2004) synthesizes justice as "compassionate, generous, reliable and faithful goodness, always ready to serve the needs of others and to foster their well-being" (p. 102). Ted Grimsrud (1999) concludes that justice in the Hebrew Bible is primarily about "healing, about bringing wholeness and restoring beauty and harmony" (p. 85).

Behavioural Aspects of Justice

A recent study by Katarina Gospic and colleagues (2011) used the game of Ultimatum to examine the role of the amygdala in feelings about justice and injustice (for information regarding game theory and the amygdala, see chapters 5 and 6, respectively). Ultimatum involves two players. Player A is given a sum of money and told to offer to share it with Player B. If Player B rejects the offer, the money is taken back and neither player gets anything. If he or she accepts the offer, the players get to keep the money. The idea of the game is to determine the point where players tend to reject the offer based on the injustice of the situation. Player A's offer was usually accepted if he or she offered to share the money equally. When the offer was substantially less than half of the total, Player B tended to think that it was not worth the injustice of receiving a small amount and rejected it. He or she would, in effect, punish Player A for making such a small offer.

While the control group in this study played the game with no interference, the experimental group was given a pharmacological treatment that suppressed the function of the amygdala without inhibiting the feeling of unfairness as determined by the cortex. The tendency to immediately punish Party A for a grossly unfair offer was considerably higher in the control group, where the amygdala of the participants prompted punitive action. The heavy involvement of the amygdala indicates that there is a strong emotional involvement in issues of justice and that the emotional part of the brain influences thought processes. Therefore, this study suggests that a sense of justice/injustice brings together both our brain's cognitive capacities and emotional aspects and that emotion plays a strong role in determining our immediate reactions to perceived injustices.

Another study regarding our sense of injustice was conducted by Ernst Fehr, Helen Bernhard, and Bettina Rockenbach (2008). It showed that children aged 3 to 4 tend to behave selfishly but most develop an aversion to inequality by the age of 8. However, this propensity to be fair is accompanied by parochialism, a tendency to favour those belonging to one's group. Given our needs for connectedness and the importance of stable groups for survival, it would seem that a sense of justice is an early and important aspect of human development.

JUST INSTITUTIONS

Institutions provide the framework for how we live and work together. As such, they establish a locus for justice that includes the workings of the institution and the relational systems within it. There can also be institutions within institutions. Some justice-related conflicts address the question of who can be included in a given institution, such as government. American philosopher John Rawls (1921–2002) begins his classic, *A Theory of Justice* (1971/1999), with the following:

> Justice is the first virtue of social institutions, as truth is of systems of thought. A theory however elegant and economical must be rejected or revised if it is untrue; likewise laws and institutions no matter how efficient and well-arranged must be reformed or abolished if they are unjust. Each person possesses an inviolability founded on justice that even the welfare of society as a whole cannot override . . . The only thing that permits us to acquiesce in an erroneous theory is the lack of a better one; analogously, an injustice is tolerable only when it is necessary to avoid an even greater injustice. Being first virtues of human activities, truth and justice are uncompromising. (p. 3)

Human interaction within communities or societies (i.e. any context that involves groups of people that have to get along over a period of time) needs to be ordered by norms, rules, or laws that give definition to the respective institution. It is essential that these norms, rules, or laws be just and justly observed. They can be formalized, as they are in large institutions such as states or formal organizations, or they can function at an informal, tacit level in institutions such as neighborhoods and families. Given its identification as a virtue, justice is closely tied to ethics; however, Rawls puts the individual's rights at the heart of the concept. Significantly, this arrangement leaves out the common good, which may ultimately benefit individuals and sub-institutions, such as minority groups, within larger institutions.

Rawls (1971/1999) also offers a definition of institutions:

By major institutions I understand the political constitution and the principal economic and social arrangements. Thus the legal protection of freedom of thought and liberty of conscience, competitive markets, private property in the means of production, and the monogamous family are examples of major institutions. Taken together as one scheme, the major institutions define men's rights and duties and influence their life prospects, what they can expect to do. The basic structure is the primary subject of justice because its effects are so profound and present from the start. (pp. 6–7)

Philosopher Paul Ricoeur (1990/1992) offers another perspective. He describes an ethical intention as "aiming at the good life, with and for others, in just institutions" (p. 172). For Ricoeur, an institution is

the structure of living together as this belongs to a historical community— people, nation, region and so forth—a structure irreducible to interpersonal relations and yet bound up with these in a remarkable sense . . . What fundamentally characterizes the idea of institution is the bond of common mores and not that of constraining rules. In this we are carried back to *ēthos* from *power in common* from which ethics takes its name. A felicitous manner of emphasizing the ethical primacy of living together over constraints related to judicial systems and to political organization is to mark, following Hannah Arendt, the gap separating *power in common* and *domination*. (p. 194, emphasis in original)

These two definitions illustrate some important distinctions regarding the meaning of just institutions. Both concepts refer to groups of people being bound together and interacting in ways that shape who they are. In essence, an institution provides its members with an identity marker that allows them to relate to one another and share a common set of values. However, Rawls's approach is synchronic: there is a political constitution and a set of arrangements that determine the exchange of goods and social standing within the institution. For Ricoeur, the diachronic, temporal dimension of an institution is of primary importance. Institutions have a history (a defining narrative, if you like) and a collective vista toward a future horizon. While Rawls's definition states that institutions are seen through the eyes of an individual, Ricoeur's emphasizes the collective dimension—our capacity to do more if we work together. Rawls claims that institutions provide freedoms and opportunities within the confines of their defining laws and principles. Ricoeur distinguishes between institutions that mobilize the power of collective action and those that have a coercive side to them.

For Rawls (1971/1999), justice may be ascribed to laws, institutions, systems, and "particular actions of many kinds," including "decisions, judgments and imputations," "attitudes and dispositions and people." However, "the primary subject of justice is the basic structure of society, or more exactly, the way in which the major institutions distribute fundamental rights and duties and determine the division of advantages from social cooperation" (Rawls, 1971/1999, p. 6). Justice as fairness is to govern this distribution within institutions. This objective is expressed in the following two principles, the first of which is especially significant:

> First: each person is to have an equal right to the most extensive scheme of equal basic liberties compatible with a similar scheme of liberties for others.

> Second: social and economic inequalities are to be arranged so that they are both (a) reasonably expected to be to everyone's advantage, and (b) attached to positions and offices open to all. (Rawls, 1971/1999, p. 53)

Just institutions, then, have rules and laws that are consistent with these principles, as well as an administration that adheres to the doctrines. However, the administration of justice is a complex matter:

> The inevitable vagueness of laws in general and the wide scope allowed for their interpretation encourages an arbitrariness in reaching decisions which only an allegiance to justice can allay. Thus it is maintained that where we find formal justice, the rule of law and the honoring of legitimate expectations, we are likely to find substantive justice as well. The desire to follow rules impartially and consistently, to treat similar cases similarly, and to accept the consequences of the application of public norms is intimately connected with the desire, or at least the willingness, to recognize the rights and liberties of others and to share fairly in the benefits and burdens of social cooperation. (Rawls, 1971/1999, p. 52)

The goods that are distributed as benefits are not only tangibles such as income and wealth but also abstract values such as recognition and self-respect (Rawls, 1971/1999, p. 54). The burdens include the work and sense of responsibility needed to maintain the institution and produce the benefits. Once the rules have been set and an administration of justice established, there is still the question of how one plays within the rules. At this level, maxims and strategies for effectively using the rules to one's advantage are developed and the concept of justice comes into practical play (Rawls, 1971/1999, p. 49).

To summarize Rawls's position, people commit (explicitly or tacitly) to belong to institutions that are governed by rules. For these institutions to be just, fairness as defined by the principles of liberty and equal distribution must be evident; the formal administration of justice must be impartial (procedural justice); and the manner in which people live within the confines of the laws and rules should lead to "socially desirable ends" (Rawls, 1971/1999, p. 49). Overall, there is a need to balance competing claims, laws, and principles. This equilibrium is achieved through a complex exercise of a sense of justice and an understanding of the priority of key principles.[6]

JUSTICE IN CONTEXT

In interpersonal social relations, conflict often starts with judgments about who got what and how they got it, as well as how decisions affecting the lives of people were made. These two sets of questions are concerned with distributive justice and procedural justice.

Distributive Justice

Over the years, concerns about the equitable distribution of resources have led to the concept of **distributive justice**—that principles of rightness and fairness are important in the allocation of economic goods. Distributive justice is an important issue at the political level, where there are debates about who gets what (see Chapter 8), and within organizations and communities. Social conflict is derived from judgments—based on principles that define the values of those making the decisions—about who gets what and how they get it.

A number of theorists, such as Folger, Sheppard, and Buttram (1995), follow Morton Deutsch by taking a functional approach to justice principles. That is, they attempt to find the key functions of an organization or social group. These functions are then expressed as goals, which are conveyed in a value-laden principle identified by Deutsch (as cited in Folger et al., 1995, p. 262) in relation to distributive justice. In distributive justice, the principles of **equity**, equality, and needs are particularly significant. Equity is important for those oriented toward economic issues. Those interested in solidarity stress equality, and need takes precedence among those for whom care is a value/goal.

Equity is the principle that people should receive an amount proportional to their contribution, which is a function of ability and effort. As such, equity emphasizes merit. When this principle is practised, the output and efficiency of the social unit increases. At the individual level, equity increases motivation to work or contribute to the group. However, people often perceive their own contribution to be greater than others might consider it to be and minimize the relative contribution of others. This behaviour can be the basis for conflict. Conflict can also erupt when people disagree over whose contribution deserves recognition.

Equality is the principle that everyone should be treated equally. It is a social expression of rights that are guaranteed in charters and constitutions. When everyone perceives that they are treated equally, there is a sense of solidarity and connectedness. However, people sometimes play different roles and are in different situations, which makes it difficult to evaluate whether they are really treated equally. Such is the case, for example, between salaried employees and consultants in some organizations. Employees may balk at what they perceive to be the high per diems for the consultants. In turn, the consultants point out that they have to prepare on their own time and generate contacts but have less job security and no health benefits.

Attentiveness to needs recognizes that different people have different needs or have different needs at different times. For example, someone who suffers a physical injury and cannot work for a month has particular needs at that particular time. Some people have chronic mental or physical ailments that preclude them from working. Many parents are caught between needing to attend to their children and needing to earn an income. Social policy regarding needs varies from country to country. In some countries, there is a strong emphasis on ensuring that everyone has a right to medical care and enough food to survive. It is considered an injustice if someone is deprived of these basic needs. In countries that emphasize equity, it is considered unjust for people to be given "handouts" without working. These examples show how ideas of justice depend on which principles are given priority.

From a social justice perspective, it is important for the common good that all members of society achieve a basic level of well-being and that a social safety net is established. Social justice also attends to structural forms of injustice (e.g. discrimination against minority groups, the failure of governments to fulfill treaties with indigenous people). For example, social justice is a factor in policies that assist linguistic groups in preserving their language and obtaining services in their mother tongue.

(AP Photo/Jerry Lampen, Pool)

After the Cold War, an unprecedented level of co-operation against human rights abuses led to the creation of international tribunals as a means of judging people accused of war crimes, crimes against humanity, or genocides. This photo shows former Bosnian Serb leader Radovan Karadžić appearing before the International Criminal Tribunal for the former Yugoslavia (ICTY) in The Hague, Netherlands, in 2008. Karadžić is accused of committing several crimes against humanity and violating the laws of war during the Bosnian War.

Procedural Justice

As cultures have evolved, institutions for making justice and dealing with conflict have grown. Within traditional societies, where people belong to clearly established kinship groups and everybody knows one another, justice-making institutions are part of the culture. Religion is also totally integrated into people's lives. Generally, there is an esteemed elder, shaman, or respected leader who convenes the conflicting parties and, based on a customary response for how things can be rectified, makes a final decision regarding the problem. Other possible institutions in this environment are a village council, a council of elders, or a council of clan mothers or other esteemed group that makes a decision on the situation.

In authoritarian situations, a monarch or dictator rules by decree. This ruler has the power to make and enforce laws and to control justice-making institutions. What he or she decides in a situation determines what is just. In reaction to the abuses of authority-based institutions, a number of institutions that separate the different components of justice-making have evolved. Some are designated to establish laws that define injustices, while others interpret and adjudicate these laws and carry out the punishment. For example, new international institutions, such as truth and reconciliation commissions and the International Criminal Court, were formed in the final decades of the twentieth century to address grave acts of injustice.

ASPECTS OF AN UNJUST ACTION

Few things stir people's passions as much as gross injustices that severely harm an individual or group. While these events are often referred to as crimes, criminologist Louk Hulsman (1986) observes: "If we compare 'criminal events' with other events, there is—on the level of those directly involved—nothing which distinguishes those 'criminal' events intrinsically from other difficult or unpleasant situations . . . All this means that there is an 'ontological reality' of crime" (pp. 65–66).

We can understand these dynamics better if we identify exactly what occurs during an unjust action involving a victim and a perpetrator. Philosopher Jean Hampton (Murphy & Hampton, 1988) shows that there are three significant aspects to an unjust action: the hurt caused by the action, the diminishment of the victim (i.e. the victim is, in effect, told that the perpetrator has a right to act upon him or her in a way that lowers his or her worth relative to the perpetrator and other community members), and the action's violation of the moral norms or legal code of the community. We can add a fourth aspect, namely the long-term effects of the wrongdoing. Each of these elements arouses a different passion, leading to impulses that undergird retributive justice.

Hampton (Murphy & Hampton, 1988) points to a philosophical tradition that regards passions and sentiments as having both an emotional and a cognitive dimension. This approach is very important when it comes to injustices because the emotional component

TABLE 15.1 | ASPECTS OF VIOLENT ACTIONS AND THEIR CONSEQUENCES

Aspect of Action	Passion in Relation to Action	Hatred Directed against Perpetrator	Actions (Imagined and Real)
Injury, pain, and loss	Hurt, anger, and woundedness	Simple hatred	Simple revenge causing at least as much pain; withdrawal—building walls, creating distance
Diminishment	Resentment	Spiteful, retributive hatred	Demean and diminish; punishment—defeat offender, value victim
Breaking moral code	Moral resentment and indignation	Moral hatred	Punishment—re-enforce values, rule of law, deter similar behaviour
Residual and ongoing consequences; permanent loss	Trauma, fear of recurrence, long-term grief	Latent, long-lasting hatred	Continuous recounting of story; victims' rights advocacy; eventual retaliation

is primarily aroused by the interpretation of an action, itself a cognitive function. Corresponding to the four aspects of the action are passions directed toward the action and hatreds directed toward the agent (see Table 15.1). The latter enters the situation when the perpetrator's identity and character are linked to the action. Actions that respond to the wrongdoing are generally performed in the name of justice, which is not considered complete until these four aspects have been addressed.

As Table 15.1 shows, an unjust action can cause resentment and/or indignation. Hampton (Murphy & Hampton, 1988) provides the following distinction between these two terms: "indignation is the emotional protest against immoral treatment whose object is the defense of the value which this action violated, whereas resentment is an emotion whose object is the defiant reaffirmation of one's rank and value in the face of treatment calling them into question in one's own mind" (pp. 59–60). From this distinction, we get the sense of two sets of emotional responses, one based on the contravening of a law or moral code and another on diminishment. In the words of moral psychology, one party has done something that the other considers to be forbidden. Further to this distinction is Hampton's connection between indignation and moral hatred:

> But indignant people often experience a con-attitude towards those who committed the immoral actions, so just as resentment can be linked with one kind of hatred towards the insulter, indignation can be linked with another kind of hatred towards the insulter, which I call moral hatred. The indignant person who opposes the message in the insulter's action is expressing aversion for the immoral cause her action promotes, and feels

aversion to the insulter herself—her character, her habits, her disposition, or the whole of her—if he takes her, or at least certain components of her, to be thoroughly identified with that cause. Such aversion for her cause and to *her* is motivated by morality; for this reason I have named it "moral hatred." It involves believing, by virtue of the insulter's association with the evil cause, that she has "rotted" or "gone bad" so that she now lacks some measure of goodness or moral health. (Murphy & Hampton, 1988, p. 80)

These arguments show that, where there are injustices, there are passions that are not to be taken lightly. Awareness of the passions involved in a justice-related conflict is important for the parties concerned and anyone involved in intervention. Society often finds the passions of victims or witnesses difficult to bear—to the point that victims who show their emotions are ostracized. Susan Jacoby (1983) puts it this way:

It is not the survivor per se who is rejected and labeled "unbalanced" but the survivor who insistently raises the issues of accountability and retribution. The anger that proceeds from unredressed suffering can be more terrifying than the original facts of suffering; moreover, the outraged, as distinct from the ostensibly detached, witness not only expects us to listen but also to *do something* about the wrongs that have been enumerated. (p. 355)

BOX 15.1 | THE EXPERIENCE OF INJUSTICE

From Lederach, J. P. (1999). *The journey toward reconciliation.* Scottdale, PA: Herald Press, p. 38.

John Paul Lederach, who has distinguished himself in the area of peacebuilding and reconciliation, was himself a victim in Nicaragua. In this excerpt, he reflects on his own experience and passions.

In less than a year, I had faced a variety of dangers. I had been accused of being a Communist Sandinista spy. My daughter's life had been threatened. I had received multiple assassination threats. I had been called a dog of the CIA. I had been stoned.

No longer do I question the suspicious, paranoid attitudes of those in war. Now I know the craziness of a fearful mind that looks behind and thinks every person is a possible threat.

No longer do I wonder how one group could see another as a real threat to their existence. I know how it feels to be falsely accused, arrested, and interrogated.

No longer do I doubt the reality of an anger that flows into hate. I have experienced such anger from my own heart, and I have been the object of such hatred.

. . . I am drawn to the cry that flows from the angry heart. I have come to believe much more deeply in the proper place of righteous indignation.

Hence, passions implicate broader communities in a variety of ways. Some are repulsed; some feel numb and are immobilized; some suffer secondary trauma as they identify with victims; and some develop a mimetic contagion as they get hooked into the emotions of the victim or witness and insist on doing something about the situation.

PARADIGMS OF JUSTICE

The words that we use to designate harmful actions are value laden and have legal consequences. If something is framed as a crime, our attitude toward the action changes and particular actions and procedures to achieve justice are immediately imagined. This position translates into a political will to put significant resources into seeking justice. The result is a criminal justice system. Within this system are various paradigms of justice, including primitive, strict, retributive, and restorative.

Primitive Justice

The primitive justice paradigm functions as revenge and represents the basic impulse to retaliate when hurt. This form of justice is evident at every level. One child hits another, who immediately hits back. One government evicts diplomats from another country, and a similar number are immediately returned from that country. Of course, much of vengeful violence is lethal.

Primitive justice can be understood in terms of René Girard's mimetic theory (see Chapter 9). Girard (1976, 1977, 1978, 1987b, 1989) points out that human beings are highly mimetic: they can imitate attitudes, gestures, and actions. When these are violent, they are reciprocated. In Girard's terms, they are "returned with interest" because people who are victimized tend to exaggerate both the extent of the victimization and the negative intentions lying behind it. For their part, perpetrators minimize the extent of the violence and exaggerate the degree to which the violence was "justified."

Victims seeking revenge want to ensure that their perpetrators suffer as much as they have. This desire goes back to the idea of justice as balance. However, "an eye for an eye and a tooth for a tooth" can be seen as limiting the revenge instinct. Usually, the new victims (the former perpetrators) feel that they are suffering more. The violence is again reciprocated with interest and the violence continues to escalate.

Primitive justice may take the form of scapegoating. Those in solidarity with a victim may take the law into their own hands and unite in violent, vengeful action against the perpetrator, who has proved his or her illegitimacy through the initial act of violence. By projecting negative emotions (accumulated from both the current crime and past offences) onto the perpetrator, scapegoating provides the community with catharsis.

Humankind is generally attuned to primitive justice, which is often framed as "good guys versus bad guys." Someone is hurt in what we interpret as a gratuitous or oppressive action, and we want the perpetrator to suffer. Many movies and television shows enact this simple theme. As viewers, we cheer inwardly as the rescuer exacts justice for the victim by making the bad guy suffer.[7]

Strict justice is a variation on the theme of primitive justice. In its pure form, it holds that the perpetrator of violence should suffer exactly as much as his or her victim. The idea is to balance the suffering (Walgrave, 2004). Strict justice differs from revenge in that the justice-making action is not performed by or on behalf of the victim. Unlike justice paradigms that have systems attached (e.g. retributive justice), strict justice is more an ideological grounding for a particular approach to justice. Miroslav Volf (1996), a Croatian-American theologian who was severely victimized during months of interrogation, has argued that strict justice increases the total amount of suffering/violence, that it is practically unachievable, and that it assumes a simple approach to guilt. He calls for something that could still involve a measure of punishment but that is less severe than strict justice.

Retributive Justice

The retributive justice paradigm contains the same impulse as primitive justice. It differs, however, on a number of points. The process is done by a third party, thus reducing the degree of passion behind the justice-making action. The perpetrator's suffering—defined as punishment—becomes standardized and usually differs in kind from the initial violence. (However, capital punishment for murder is, of course, similar to the initial violent act). The unjust action of the perpetrator gets reframed as a crime committed against the community at large or as a non-criminal injury. In the latter case, a civil court proceeding may rule that the person at fault must compensate the victim. In retributive justice, the conflict over who did what, whether it was a crime, whether one is guilty, and the degree of punishment is argued by lawyers who are one step removed from the parties directly involved. Finally, there are broad limits to the type of punishment. For example, it cannot be cruel or unusual.

One way of framing the step from primitive to retributive justice is that the latter puts the brakes on the process.[8] In other words, it limits the intensification of the conflict. It also introduces a process of truth-seeking and conscious decision-making to ensure that the call for justice is based on a true wrong. For instance, an accident could be incorrectly construed as intentional wrongdoing.

Retributive justice has its own stable of metaphors related to punishment. Punishment is thought of as one getting one's "just deserts" and paying one's "debt to society." Prison sentences, often referred to as doing time, are often the means of paying this debt. If prison sentences are made more severe by law, an administration frames itself as being "tough on crime." While toughness is presented as a positive quality, the phrase "soft on crime" is always used pejoratively, even though less punitive approaches might be more demanding of offenders.

Jacoby (1983) argues that revenge and retribution have a purpose and should be taken seriously. Her point is reinforced by the general abhorrence that someone could "get away

(AP Photo/Harry Cabluck)

Attendees of an Amnesty International rally in Austin, TX, in 2005 protest the death penalty. Capital punishment is the ultimate form of retributive justice and remains a source of social conflict, especially in the United States.

with doing X." "Get away with" implies that justice demands that one be held accountable for their actions.

Procedural justice, discussed earlier in this chapter, is generally considered to be part of retributive justice systems. However, it also adds two significant aspects. First is the insistence that the very process of achieving justice does not commit injustices. The rights of all involved must be defined and respected. The process must also be shown to be transparent and fair as opposed to ones conducted in secret where the outcomes are determined in advance. Second, the principles of rightness and balance operative in one case should apply to other similar cases.

Procedural justice is at the heart of the rule of law in contemporary democracies, and it has been developed and generalized after centuries of epic struggles between the rulers and the population. A well-developed justice system has a number of important advantages in dealing with conflicts. Procedural justice relies on detailed rules of evidence that are applied consistently, eliminating some undue influences on the process. The system can address instances where people lie or conceal events. If there is to be accountability in society, it is important to have institutions that can make a reasoned decision about guilt or innocence. When other approaches falter or do not apply, the justice system is always accessible as a last resort. Furthermore, there are crimes so horrible that most people feel that justice must include some form of punishment.

However, there are several problems inherent in retributive justice. First, little is done for victims. Second, as Martha Minow (1998) points out, it does not constructively change the situation that led to the violence. Third, as Paul Ricoeur (2000) maintains, it assumes that the action can be assigned to a well-defined perpetrator who can be clearly held accountable for the hurtful action. In reality, the situation is often ambiguous. Fourth, retributive justice does not address the systemic or structural factors involved. Finally, in pursuing retribution through the state, the victim is modelling him- or herself after the perpetrator, becoming like the one who is hated.

Restorative Justice

Restorative justice as a paradigm emerged from the interaction between action and theory. In 1974, a group of young men in Elmira, ON, vandalized several properties. Dave Worth and Mark Jantzi, their probation officers, suggested to the judge that the perpetrators should meet with their victims. The judge agreed and these youth, with the support of Worth and Jantzi, visited homeowners in order to make things right. Out of this initial action, programs that bring victims and offenders together to find a way to make reparations and, in certain situations, repair the relationship, were developed—hence the term *restorative justice*.

As restorative justice evolved, legal historian Howard Zehr and former British Columbia deputy minister of corrections Edgar Epp realized that it entailed a fundamental change in how harmful actions were perceived and dealt with—this change was profound enough that it involved a whole new paradigm. Eventually, Zehr (1990/2005) wrote *Changing Lenses*, his seminal work on restorative justice. In this book, he points out that crimes are really actions taken against people (victims) and their communities. Frequently, retributive justice does nothing for these victims and the punishment becomes a school for crime that leaves perpetrators worse off and more inclined to re-offend. Furthermore, the impact of crime on the community is often overlooked. Epp (1982) also critiqued punishment-oriented justice that used long prison terms as a way of achieving justice, pointing out the permanent injuries caused by long years of incarceration.

Restorative justice as a paradigm focuses on the harm done to victims and communities and how perpetrators can undo the damage. Unlike retributive justice, which finds a punishment to fit the crime, restorative justice emphasizes finding consequences to fit the context. Rather than making a perpetrator suffer for an injustice or hurtful action, he or she goes out of his or her way to do positive things for the victim and/or the community. The goal is to restore balance.

In the 1980s, Sheriff Doug Call of Batavia County, NY, brought restorative justice to serious personal crimes such as rape and homicide. His campaign slogan of "We have to get tough on criminals by holding them accountable to their victims" helped him to win an election. As he supported victims, Call found that 9 out of 10 wanted to meet the perpetrator because they had unanswered questions that only he or she could answer. He provided a structure for the two sides to meet, and out of these meetings came some creative sentences that were oriented toward doing something positive for the community. In one instance, a drunk driver had killed a man. In the meeting with the victim's widow, it was agreed that the perpetrator would buy a Jaws of Life machine for rescuing people from crashed cars.

As theoretical work continued to be done on restorative justice, it became clear that the paradigm resonated with teachings in the Hebrew Bible, such as if someone steals X, they are to give back Y. This realization led to further work on apology and forgiveness. Resonance was also found with indigenous approaches to justice. Village courts in Africa and hearings before elders in Aboriginal communities in the Americas, Australia, and New Zealand were seen to be based partly on restorative justice principles (however, harsh punishments are not unknown to primitive societies). As described in Chapter 11, new programs, such as sentencing circles based on Aboriginal circle processes were developed.

Just as the retributive justice paradigm figures into how we address crimes and other injustices, so too are restorative justice principles invoked at different levels. In personal relationships, people try to work things out through dialogue rather than retaliation. In large organizations, conflict resolution systems empower those caught up in conflict or injustice to find a solution. Restorative justice principles were used by Desmond Tutu (1999) in structuring the South African Truth and Reconciliation Commission. International IDEA applies these ideas to peacebuilding efforts in post-armed conflict situations (Bloomfield, et al. 2003).

There are, however, some difficulties with the restorative justice paradigm. It is difficult to accommodate within significant power differentials. Trying to bring victim and perpetrator together in family violence situations can be catastrophic if there are threats or intimidation; therefore, the process has to be adapted to handle such a situation. Perpetrators who are intellectually challenged or mentally ill are sometimes not up to the demands of confrontations and questions. Because the paradigm is context specific, and hence more complex, it is also hard to establish norms for responses to particular crimes. Not all victims and offenders are open to restorative justice processes, which demand a certain amount of good faith. These and other situations suggest that some cases demand the procedural rigour of a court system to establish the truth of what happened and what might be an appropriate way of holding offenders accountable. Gerry Johnstone (2002) raises some significant questions and challenges regarding this matter: "We need to ask whether a shift to restorative justice would result in a whole range of deleterious consequences such as a trivialization of evil, a loss of security, a less fair system, an undesirable extension of police power, an erosion of important procedural safeguards, unwelcome net-widening, or a weakening of already weak parties" (pp. 7–8). These are important challenges that have to be kept in mind as restorative justice programs develop.

MERCY, PARDON, AND FORGIVENESS

Mercy is a concept that has cogency within the paradigms of primitive and retributive justice. While it comes from the realization that a perpetrator deserves punishment or revenge, it means that this justice-making violence is diminished or renounced. It is like the cancelling of a debt, an action of the person within the justice framework who has a mandate to decide the punishment. Mercy can result in reducing a prison sentence or issuing a pardon. As the formal action of extending mercy, a pardon formally releases a person with a prison sentence or criminal record from the negative actions associated with such a punishment.

Forgiveness involves a victim of injustice surrendering the right to demand punishment or revenge. It is a letting go of the impulse to harm the perpetrator and a release from demands that could be made in response. It does not, however, necessarily mean forgetting the injustice or trusting a former perpetrator. Forgiveness can be a matter of degree, from a reluctant letting go of a right to seek violent punishment to being open to a new relationship and to the wholehearted embrace of the other party. A key element is that the offender will no longer be defined by their wrongful action (Murphy & Hampton, 1988). Forgiveness is like a gift: it cannot be demanded or even expected of a person. There are times in victim–offender mediation sessions when victims will forgive offenders after an apology or after hearing the latter's circumstances. Forgiveness might figure into restorative justice, but it does not come about as a matter of course. On another level, corporate forgiveness means that a group or nation will demand nothing further from a perpetrator and will reorient their relationship.

CONCLUSION

At the heart of many conflicts are severe injustices. These actions can be defined formally as the breaking of laws, be they at the interpersonal, intergroup, or international levels. They are also based on the perceptions of victims, who believe that their experience is unjust. Root metaphors for justice include balance and rightness, leading to an association between justice and fairness. A sense of rightness extends to relationships; hence, justice is understood as that which contributes to good relationships. There is a strong normative dimension to justice. That is, justice lines up with historical values and normative practices within society. Justice and injustice can be a matter of ambiguity, judgment, and debate. Distributive justice, for instance, can be thought of as embodying the principles of equity, equality, and need. The degree to which each of these ideas is emphasized is a matter of judgment. If there is a grave injustice, it can be framed as a crime, which is defined in law. In the face of injustice, there is a strong propensity to seek revenge. Justice-oriented institutions have been put in place to transform this impulse into justice-seeking actions based on retribution, such that a criminal justice system will punish those found guilty of seriously harming others. Over the last three decades of the twentieth century, the restorative justice movement emphasized holding offenders accountable to victims and communities by their meeting and agreeing on ways to re-establish balance. People achieve a sense of justice through positive actions on the part of the offender (e.g. apology and reparations), through seeing an offender suffer through punishment, or through extending mercy and forgiveness.

DISCUSSION QUESTIONS

1. Think of a conflict in which you were involved. Did you frame your position in terms of being a victim of injustice and your actions as being just? On what basis did you justify your actions?

2. At the political level, there are many conflicts over who gets what. How do principles of equity, equality, and need help determine the issues in these conflicts?

3. Is punishment always a requirement in obtaining justice? Why or why not? To what degree is punishment a function of how people have been taught to respond to wrongdoing? Think, for example, about how punishment figures into the treatment of children at home and at school.

NOTES

1. For a thorough discussion of the connection between interpretation and how we understand justice and the different approaches to it, see Warnke (1992).

2. See Berg and Schaefer (2009) for a compendium of studies of historical injustices.

3. For further information, see http://ancienthistory.about.com/od/greekgoddessesoly/p/ Themis.htm and www.theoi.com/Ouranios/HoraDike.html.

4. For example, Jeremiah 6: 13 states: "For from the least to the greatest of them everyone is greedy for unjust gain; and from prophet to priest, everyone deals falsely." In this excerpt, the motivation of greed is parallel to dealing falsely, the action. See Jeremiah 31: 31ff for a description of a new covenant in which the Torah will be written on people's hearts, meaning that they will be motivated to live it spontaneously.

5. Jeremiah 22: 15–17 contrasts King Josiah, who consistently judged honestly and looked out for the poor and needy, with his son Shallum, who was out for dishonest gain, shed innocent blood, and practised oppression and violence. Amos 6: 4–7 decries an upper class that is out of touch with the decline of the country.

6. Even though Rawls has been highly influential, his work has been subject to criticism. For an analysis of the many critiques and a framework that builds on his work, see Päivänsalo (2007).

7. For a full analysis of this phenomenon, see Wink (1992).

8. This constraint on revenge was already present in ancient Israel, where there were cities and places of refuge where a murderer could be safe from revenge until a justice procedure could be followed.

INTRODUCTION

This chapter focuses on the concept of peace and its connection to conflict. We begin by tracing the various forms of peace and discussing how the peace movement, pacifism, and non-violence have influenced how people approach conflict. We also examine how an interest in peace led to the development of peace research and peace education as fields of study. Finally, we look at the challenges of adopting peace as an orientation and the difficulties faced by the peace movement.

DEFINITIONS OF PEACE

Ancient languages and established religious traditions, as well as contemporary authors, provide different definitions of peace. The relationship between justice and peace is particularly significant, notably in the distinction between positive and negative peace.

Ancient Meanings of Peace

The English word *peace* is derived through the Old French *pais*, from the Latin *pax* or *pacis*. However, our idea of peace is also influenced by the ancient Greeks and Romans. The Greek word *eirene* initially stood for a "state of peace," or an interlude between wars, and then as a state of mind. Philosopher Epictetus (as cited in Foerster, 1964/1980) thought of it more as "the absence of hostile feelings than of the presence of kindly feelings to others" (p. 401). In ancient Rome, the Augustan period was known as a golden age (Pax Romana) in which peace came about through a strong hand and legal security was achieved. From the Greeks and Romans, we also get the concept of a peace treaty that concludes a war. Both civilizations associated peace with the gods. Eirene, the Greek goddess of peace, is associated with abundance, while the Roman goddess Pax is crowned with a laurel that represents success in a competition, the peace of the winner in battle.

In the Judaic tradition, the ancient Hebrew word *shalom* conveyed the idea of well-being, wholeness, and prosperity. Although more concerned with good relationships than a state of being, the term is also used to speak of a time without war. There is a strong association with justice in that injustice detracts from peace. An example of this connection applies the connotation of wholeness to stones used as weights for trade. People could cheat by having weight shaved off the stone; therefore, a complete stone meant that trading practices were honest and fair. In the ancient Hebrew corpus, shalom functions as the focus for a utopian

CHAPTER OBJECTIVES

This chapter will help you develop an understanding of the

- meanings of peace;
- meaning and challenges of a just peace;
- philosophy and historical development of pacifism;
- theory and practice of non-violence;
- emergence and growth of peace research and peace education; and
- challenges and problems of the peace movement in relation to armed conflict.

vision of society and cultivates the expectation of a harmonious time when "swords will be beaten into ploughshares" (Isaiah 2: 4; Micah 4: 3) and "the wolf will dwell with the lamb" (Isaiah 11: 6). A word used in parallel with shalom is *berikah* ("blessing"), which connotes sustained well-being and abundance.

In the Hindu and Buddhist traditions, peace is associated with the positive transformation of karma. Karma may be thought of as life energy that has continuity and is affected by that of others. Japanese Buddhist teacher Daisaku Ikeda (Galtung & Ikeda, 1995) puts it this way: "In a sense, human life and, in particular work for peace represent struggles between positive and negative energy. Some minus aspects are violence, destruction, schism and hostility; among the positive aspects are nonviolence, creativity, union and harmony" (p. 74). This understanding of peace both resonates with and complements Greek, Roman, and Hebrew ideas of eirene, pax, and shalom.

Positive and Negative Peace

Contemporary peace theorists such as Kenneth Boulding (1978), Elise Boulding (2000), and Johan Galtung (1996) refer to two types of peace: positive and negative. Positive peace refers to human flourishing and corresponds to John W. Burton's (1990a) concept of conflict provention, which he defines as "taking steps to remove sources of conflict, and more positively to promote conditions in which collaborative and valued relationships control behavior" (p. vi). Negative peace frames peace as the absence of war. Negative peace does not necessarily lead to positive peace; however, it is a necessary condition for this type.

While the link between peace and justice is important to peace scholars, the popular usage of the term *peace* is often limited to the negative form. For instance, when people talk of "industrial peace," "peace in the family," or "peace in the classroom," they strictly refer to an absence of disruption and violence. Despite the efforts of peace researchers, the idea of negative peace is still endorsed by many academics who prefer its clarity regarding the absence of overt violence and its independence from normative conceptions of justice and happiness. Nevertheless, the idea of positive peace is spreading, particularly in the domain of peacebuilding, where peace is associated with the diminishment of structures of oppression and violence and the building of structures that contribute to well-being. One example is *Indigenous Peoples and Peacebuilding: A Compilation of Best Practices*, which sees peacebuilding as addressing "*physical* violence, *structural* violence and *cultural* violence (beliefs and value systems that can be subject to prejudice and become part of a discourse prompting violence), as well as the relational aspects that are guiding these kinds of violence patterns" (UNSSC, 2010, p. 8). Frameworks for peacebuilding are also based on positive peace.

Just Peace

In recent years, it has become clear to many in the peace field that peace without justice is incomplete. If injustices prevail after hostilities cease and people agree to coexist without violence, peace has not really been achieved. Peace also does not include people committing human rights abuses or crimes against humanity with impunity. There must, therefore, be

TABLE 16.1 | CONTINUUM OF MORAL POSSIBILITIES

Genocide

War

Hobbesian Non-War (see Chapter 8)

Just War (see Chapter 14)

Stable Peace (fighting has stopped)

Just Peace (peace with a sense of justice)

Positive Peace (minimizing structural violence)

Global Care (see Ethics of Care section in Chapter 17)

Source: Compiled from Allan, P. (2006). Measuring international ethics: A moral scale of war, peace, justice and global care. In Pierre Allan & Alexis Keller (Eds.), *What is a just peace?* New York, NY: Oxford University Press, p. 104.

a sense of justice within any peaceful situation. While this idea is important and represents a movement on the part of peace advocates to include justice within their ethical vision, it overlooks the issue of how to deal with grave injustices committed or allowed by powerful and uncompromising leaders. This problem is explored in depth in *What Is A Just Peace?*, edited by Pierre Allan and Alexis Keller (2006a).The articles in this text ask whether there is a just peace that corresponds to the theory of a just war (see Chapter 14). For example, Allan (2006) proposes a continuum of moral possibilities that move from least to most desirable (see Table 16.1). The first four are oriented toward conflict, the last four toward peace.

Allan and Keller (2006b) suggest a process-based approach to achieving a just peace that includes the following steps:

- thin recognition: acknowledging the other entity
- thick recognition: mutual recognition of core identity features of Self and Other from each perspective
- renouncement: significant and costly concessions made by each party
- rule: a text, complete with appropriate symbolic elements, that expresses what has been achieved in the first three steps and sets out rules that both sides accept.

Throughout the process, the principle of recognizing entities, perspectives, and the deeper context within which a perspective is formed becomes crucial. Its absence also helps to explain some basic weaknesses in the initial, Eurocentric development of the law of nations (Keller, 2006). The work of Allan and Keller resonates with Aquinas's emphasis on peace as the indirect work of justice and the direct work of charity.

The various traditions and approaches to peace reveal that it is a complex, multi-faceted phenomenon. While it is difficult to define peace precisely, there is a discursive and conceptual field regarding the term, one that includes the absence of open violence and war and the presence of justice, peaceful dispositions, emancipation, empowerment, and development.

PEACE AS AN ORIENTATION

Although most people value peace at some level, it might not be their primary value (Frank, 1962). It may be in conflict with other values, such as the national interest, political ideals, or conceptions of justice. On the other hand, some people consider peace a central orientation, a value that influences how they live their lives and their approaches to interpreting events and searching for truth. Among those who position themselves within the broader peace movement are pacifists.

Pacifism takes a strong position against the use of force generally and lethal force in particular. The term can also be described as espousing a deontological position that sees the use of deadly force as morally wrong. Teleologically, pacifists would suggest that the introduction of violence leads to increased violence and produces a categorical change within a conflict. Preparing for and engaging in war are therefore wrong. This belief raises some difficult questions regarding pacifism, including how and on what basis one can take such a position. The following sections consider such questions.

The Peace Movement

The primary expression of pacifism is the peace movement, which encompasses diverse activities such as political pressure, non-violent action, peace research, and peace education. Even people who are not philosophically pacifists adhere, at least to some degree, to the peace movement. The modern political peace movement developed within the European and Anglo-Saxon world of the late nineteenth and early twentieth centuries. It was influential in the processes that led to the two Hague conventions (1899 and 1907), the creation of the League of Nations (1919), and the Briand–Kellogg General Treaty for the Renunciation of War (1928). However, with World War II, peace advocacy was pushed to the fringe, both politically and academically. Political realism, with its value system that espoused looking out for the interests of the nation-state (see Chapter 8), became dominant as a political philosophy. Furthermore, having a value-free social science became a dominant part of academic life, making it difficult to legitimize anything with a normative orientation. Added to this problem was a growing secularization that suspected any truth claim coming out of religion, particularly Christianity. Even within this religion, the dominant position from the late 1930s on was marked by realism.

At the individual level, many discounted peace-oriented rhetoric because of its hortatory nature; people accustomed to a mindset of choice, individual freedom, and self-interest did not take well to being told that they should be working for peace (Page, 2008). Furthermore, the rhetorical tone of those advocating for peace as a normative position often seemed self-righteous and judgmental, as though they were "pulling moral rank." Given the post-World War II cultural context, many simply thought of the "peaceniks" as idealists who had some noble beliefs but were somewhat detached from the real world.

The peace movement was also methodologically doubted because of its normative orientation. Furthermore, because there was a widespread implicit assumption that humanity was basically aggressive, a great deal of research within the biological and social sciences focused on exploring the nature of aggression and violence. This investigation then fed into examining ways to manage or control aggressiveness. To even imagine a human inclination toward peace and a truly peaceful world contradicted the dominant methodology.

Philosophically, there was a problem with the normative aspects of peace advocacy. Part of this drawback concerned a more general difficulty with moral norms in the wake of secularization, which was highlighted by moral relativism and personal philosophies of liberation from moral constraint. English and American philosophy of the period was dominated by analytical philosophy, which included logical positivism (a philosophical equivalent to the methodology of social sciences). Continental philosophy included existentialism, which offered little hope for an ethical vision to gain meaning or relevance.

During the Cold War, the peace movement faced a number of difficulties. Given the intense anti-Soviet sentiments, especially in the United States, those advocating for peace and disarmament were framed as being "soft on communism" or Soviet sympathizers. What was designated as the peace movement also included people with different motivations and methodologies. Some were philosophical pacifists, some were religious pacifists, and others were sympathetic to Marxist ideas and joined communist parties in the West. Some of these groups received support from the Soviet Union. Combining these two factors meant that more radical expressions of peace advocacy had a strong impact on public perceptions, making identification with the peace movement highly unpopular.

These problems add up to the following question: On what grounds can a normative value of peace be sustained? In *Peace Education: Exploring Ethical and Philosophical Foundations*, James Page (2008) uses philosophical ethics to addresses this query. He looks at five historical ethical streams that have the potential to support such a position: virtue ethics, consequentialist ethics, philosophical conservatism, aesthetic ethics, and ethics of care. As mentioned in Chapter 14, virtue ethics emphasizes the qualities of the person who would contribute to peace, while consequentialism examines the results of actions (e.g. a peace-oriented consequentialism would emphasize whether a given action would contribute to peace-oriented outcomes). Political conservatism stresses the achievement of peaceful ends in a way that draws on the best traditions of society and emphasizes gradual change within an established political system. Aesthetic ethics locates peace within what is good, desirable, and conducive to well-being. Finally, an ethics of care draws on the work of Ricoeur and Levinas (see Chapter 9) to emphasize responsibility for and inclusion of the Other when considering an action's moral value.

Forms of Pacifism

There are a number of different forms of pacifism. At the extreme is condemnation of all armed engagements. Some pacifists limit their ethical stance to their own personal involvement; they might support certain cases of state-sponsored violence but could not bring themselves to participate. Others might be pacifist by inclination, using their orientation to question the preparation for and use of violence, but would be open to

BOX 16.1 | THE CRUCIBLE OF WAR: WOODROW WILSON

(The Granger Collection, New York)

Before he became president of the United States in 1913, Woodrow Wilson was an academic sympathetic to the peace movement. During the first four years of his presidency, Wilson had to face an increasing German belligerence. His principles led him to prefer peace, but his country was increasingly driven toward war, especially because of the submarine war in the Atlantic and Germany's machinations to bring Mexico into a war with the United States. Wilson tried to negotiate with imperial Germany and delayed his country's entry into World War I as long as he could. Finally, he reluctantly agreed to join the war under the conditions expressed in his Fourteen Points, one of which was to create a permanent League of Nations to prevent future wars. These agonizing decisions regarding war and peace were very hard on Wilson, both psychologically and physically. The negotiation of the Versailles Treaty took such a toll that he was unable to defend the treaty against his opponents in the US Congress, who rejected it and American participation in the League of Nations. Wilson lost this fight, but he had stayed true to his humanistic principles by fighting a war for peace and democracy.

some grey areas that allow for the use of force in extreme circumstances. The two main foundations for pacifism are religion and philosophy.

Religious-Based Pacifism

Many pacifists have come to their convictions based on historical religious traditions. Within Jainism and Buddhism, there have been strong pacifist streams going back 2,500 years. These religions' concept of *ahimsa* (non-injury) taught their members to "Cherish compassion even to your enemy," which precluded any military service (Brock, 1998, p. 1). Some of these religions extended pacifism to the point of forbidding the killing of animals. Hinduism and Confucianism include many traditions that have significantly limited the use of force and violence. A number of leaders in peace research, peace education, and peace activism have been affected by these traditions. Johan Galtung, who was a conscientious objector before becoming a leader in peace research, was strongly influenced by Buddhism. Thich Nhat Hanh (b. 1926) is an outstanding Buddhist teacher of peace (see Hanh, 1987, 2003).

In Christianity, many of the New Testament teachings of Jesus Christ and Saint Paul are of a pacifist nature. Examples from Jesus include "If someone strikes you on the cheek, turn the other also" (Matthew 5: 39); "Love your enemies" (Matthew 5: 44; Luke 6: 27; Romans 12: 20); and "Do not repay evil with evil but overcome evil with good" (Romans 12: 21). Conversely, some of their other teachings imply that there is a place for armed force on the part of the state. The most significant text is in Romans 13: 4, where Paul warns that state authorities "bear the sword" to punish wrongdoers. At one point, Jesus urges his followers to buy swords (Luke 22: 36). This contradiction has been a point of constant debate within Christian denominations.

There is evidence that the early Christian Church was mostly pacifist in its orientation. For instance, in some cases soldiers had to give up their careers in order to become Christians (Brock, 1998, pp. 5–7; Hornus, 1980). All that changed in the post-Constantine era, when Christians went from being a persecuted minority to being accepted and eventually forming the official religion of the Roman Empire. With this change of status, maintaining a pacifist position was untenable; the Empire relied on force for its survival. The peace teachings of Jesus were reframed as an ideal that was either meant for another age or not meant to be followed literally. It was in this new context that Augustine developed the just war tradition that was presented in Chapter 14. Remnants of pacifism remained throughout the Church's history, some of which found their place within religious orders and monasteries (notably under the influence of Saint Francis of Assisi). Several pacifist groups emerged in the late Medieval period, including the Waldenses in southern France (late twelfth century), the English Lollards and John Wyclif (mid-fourteenth century), and the Bohemian Taborites (fifteenth century) (Brock, 1998, pp. 8–10).

During the Reformation, churches that held pacifism as an important conviction emerged—these have come to be known as historic peace churches. It was at this time that the Scriptures were translated into the languages of the people and the German Bible was published. The leaders of this new movement, which began in Zurich in 1525, had studied the peace teachings of Jesus and, taking them literally, decided to live by them regardless of the consequences. In 1527, the Schleitheim Confession made a clear commitment to non-resistance—a refusal to use military force against anyone (Brock, 1998, p. 14). Though this edict was the standard for church members, it was acknowledged that states could use the sword. In continental Europe, the peace churches included the Anabaptists (Mennonites, Hutterites, and Amish). For centuries, these small groups lived their pacifist lives unobtrusively as the "quiet in the land." Persecuted at various times, they migrated through Europe and many eventually settled in North America. Since the sixteenth century, however, virtually all of Christendom—Roman Catholic, Orthodox, Anglican/Episcopalian,

BOX 16.2 | PACIFISM COMPARED: TWO STORIES FROM THE MENNONITE TRADITION

A story from the Mennonites shows how pacifist beliefs generate altruistic behaviour even in the face of death. In sixteenth-century Netherlands, Mennonites were persecuted and killed in large numbers on account of their faith, including their refusal to bear arms. One day in 1569, a Mennonite named Dirk Willems was running away from a thief-catcher. As he ran across the ice, his pursuer fell through the surface and was about to drown. Willems turned back and rescued the thief-catcher, saving his life. In doing so, Willems was captured; he was subsequently tried and burned alive in a slow fire (van Braght, 1660/1950, pp. 741–742).

Another episode of Mennonite history demonstrates different effects of mortal threat on the group's peaceful community. Since immigrating to Russia in 1789, the Mennonites in South Russia (now Ukraine) had a special arrangement whereby they could be conscientious objectors. They could be medics or serve in other ways, but they did not have to fight in the Russian armies. During World War I, the Russian Revolution, and the Russian Civil War, there was significant fighting and violence in their region. The German army, who had an affinity for the Mennonites because they spoke German, occupied their territory from time to time during World War I and even gave them guns. From 1918 to 1921, however, followers of anarchist Nestor Machno (a former sheep-herder for a Mennonite farmer) killed Mennonites by the thousands. Faced with the Machnovite threat, some Mennonites organized the Selbstschutz (self-defence)—literally a Mennonite army to protect themselves—while other Mennonites objected that it was contrary to their principles. The Selbstschutz did not endear them with the Russian people, who observed that the Mennonites would not fight to protect the Fatherland but would use violent means to protect themselves when threatened (Toews, 1967, pp. 26–36).

mainline Protestant, and evangelical Christian—has not been pacifist; churches have tended to patriotically support the armed forces of their respective countries.

The Mennonites became more involved in peace issues centuries later, when peace volunteers helped with post-war reconstruction in 1950s Europe. Institutionally, their participation was manifest through the Mennonite Central Committee (MCC), which progressed from a humanitarian assistance movement to a development agency with increasing involvement in peace and justice issues. It provided a vehicle for many young people to gain international experience in over 40 countries. Out of this practical experience came a vision for research, education, and programming in peace and justice (Sampson & Lederach, 2000). The research took the form of more sophisticated theological reflection on the nature of pacifism, with John Howard Yoder (himself a 1950s MCC pax worker in Europe) becoming a world-class ethicist on peace issues. His most influential book, *The Politics of Jesus* (1972), offered a sustained argument to counter the perspective of theological realist Niebuhr. He also identified 20 forms of pacifism (Yoder, 1992).

In terms of education and programming, Eastern Mennonite University established a graduate program in conflict transformation in the 1980s. Some of the professors who were part of the program from the beginning have also been world leaders in various aspects of conflict resolution. Notably, John Paul Lederach and Barry Hart have been important theorists in peacebuilding, and Howard Zehr is often referred to as the grandfather of restorative justice. Lisa Schirch did early work on the role of symbols and rituals in peacebuilding before concentrating on a 3D approach (defence, diplomacy, and development) to addressing violent conflict. Other Mennonite educational institutions have been centres for peace research and education.

Within the Mennonite tradition, there has been an ongoing debate between those who see pacifist teachings applying to individual Christians but not to states and governments and those who want to explore its meaning as a normative principle for society. World War II was a significant challenge to the perspectives of many Mennonites in Canada and the United States. Some were conscientious objectors to the draft and served in other ways. Others thought the threat of National Socialism to be so great that they felt compelled to join the Allied Forces. Some Mennonite churches shunned those who became soldiers, while others tolerated their decisions. The Mennonite experience demonstrates the profound ongoing challenges of severe threats and the question of whether self-defence is warranted. There is also the issue of whether force is needed to counteract human atrocities or other severe injustices.

Another religious group associated with pacifism is the Society of Friends, or Quakers. Originating in England during the Reformation, the Quakers were strong pacifists from the beginning. Unlike the Anabaptists, they established a tradition of activism for peace and justice issues early on—"speaking truth to power." In the eighteenth and nineteenth centuries, they were important leaders in the campaigns against the slave trade and slavery. It is significant that a number of academics who led the way in the emergence of peace research, such as Kenneth Boulding and Elsie Boulding, happened to be Quakers.

In the twentieth century, peace and justice teachings took hold in the Roman Catholic Church. In 1983, the National Conference of Catholic Bishops in the United States released *The Challenge of Peace: God's Promise and Our Response, A Pastoral Letter on War and Peace*, a document that allowed for the right of self-defence but came closer to a pacifist position than had been previously seen. Bishop Dom Elder Camara in Brazil was also a strong proponent of peace, while Dorothy Day and the Catholic Worker movement did much to address social inequalities in the United States. Roman Catholic institutions such as Caritas and Pax Christi are devoted to working for peace. However, the Church and the majority of its followers are still committed to just war theory.

As indicated in this section, pacifists have tended to be conscientious objectors, meaning that their conscience forbids them from being a combatant soldier in any circumstance. Peter Brock (2006) has researched instances of this phenomenon from the 1500s to the end of World War II. While he covers the experiences of Mennonites and Quakers, he also brings to light lesser known groups who often suffered for their position. For instance, Jehovah's Witnesses were executed by the Nazis for refusing to join the army. Nazarenes resisted conscription in Hungary from the 1840s on. Followers of Leo Tolstoy were imprisoned in

BOX 16.3 | CONSCIENTIOUS OBJECTOR: MUHAMMAD ALI

(AP Photo/Ed Kolenovsky)

The most famous conscientious objector is boxer Muhammad Ali, who refused to be drafted for the Vietnam War in 1966, at the peak of his career. The following year, he was sentenced to five years in jail and a heavy fine. Ali did not go to jail but fought the US government all the way to the Supreme Court; he was finally exonerated in 1971.

Russia for refusing to join the army. The Polish Brethren and the Brethren in Christ were historically opposed to the draft, and Seventh Day Adventists have also been conscientious objectors.

Philosophical Pacifism

Philosophical pacifism does not have the long tradition of religious pacifism. In the West, it began during the Enlightenment, when secular philosophers started to reflect on the possibilities of building a better world on earth. For instance, German philosopher Immanuel Kant thought that war was a receding human activity because republics were less bellicose than monarchies and dictatorships. He advocated a world federation of republics that would enable countries to resolve their differences without resorting to war. A world federalist movement emerged in the nineteenth century, advocating the writing of a world constitution and the establishment of a world government. Although this movement has waned somewhat, it has been influential in the emergence of international organizations.

Besides the federalist movement, one can notice pacifists in other areas. For example, many anarchists in the tradition of Henry David Thoreau in the United States, Pierre-Joseph Proudhon in France, and Leo Tolstoy in Russia chose non-violence. Many members of socialist organizations also espoused pacifism, notably H.G. Wells in Great Britain and Jean Jaurès in France. Other philosophical pacifists include philosopher Bertrand Russell and scientist Albert Einstein. Einstein (as cited in Cetto & de la Peña, 2005) declared, "I would unconditionally refuse all war service, direct or indirect, and would seek to persuade my friends to take up the same stance, regardless of how I felt about the causes of any particular war" (pp. 72–73). This strong position guided him throughout his life. He was in torment over the threat of National Socialism in his native Germany. Fearing that Germany might build an atomic bomb in time to be used during the war, he sent two letters to President Franklin D. Roosevelt warning of this possibility and suggesting that the United States begin its own research on nuclear chain reactions. Later, Einstein would deeply regret having sent these letters. Just before his death, he signed the Russell–Einstein Manifesto (we will return to this document later in the chapter).

After World War II, scientific and professional groups with a strong emphasis on peace were formed. In 1947, the *Bulletin of the Atomic Scientists* was created by some members of the American wartime nuclear project who were alarmed at the prospect of nuclear war against the Soviet Union. This publication is still one of the most important sources in the field of nuclear arms control and disarmament. Russell, the co-signer of the Russell–Einstein Manifesto, was also very active in the Ban the Bomb movement during the early years of the Cold War. Another active group is Physicians for the Prevention of Nuclear War, which received the Nobel Peace Prize in 1985. In the social sciences and humanities, many people influenced by pacifism spread their message through their research. Several specialized programs regarding peace and conflict studies attracted many secular pacifists. Some of their publications have influenced public opinion and political decision-making.

Over the years, many other well-known personalities, especially from the arts, letters, and entertainment fields, have endorsed pacifism and non-violence. The opposition to the Vietnam War, which coincided with the countercultural "hippie" movement and European anarchism, saw the emergence of a mass pacifist culture. A popular icon of this movement was ex-Beatle John Lennon, who was very active in the anti-war movement and whose song "Imagine" has become a sort of pacifist anthem. In their productions as well as their personal lives, many popular artists of the twenty-first century, such as U2 singer Bono, actor Sean Penn, and writer Margaret Atwood, display a peace orientation that is influential among their admirers.

Today, non-religious pacifism, humanism, and non-violence are growing in Western societies. Several interest groups and political parties on the political left and in the Green Movement are now officially pacifist, mostly for secular humanistic reasons. In 2003, the opposition to the US-led invasion of Iraq drew millions of people to massive demonstrations around the globe, and most called themselves pacifists.

A word of caution is in order, however. It is unclear whether self-declared pacifists always understand the profound meaning of this position. After all, pacifism tends to rise around the world when the United States enters a foreign war, but many so-called pacifists say nothing about other wars and tend to excuse violence when it is committed by underdogs. Furthermore, in other polls, majorities have approved of humanitarian interventions (which are acts of war) on behalf of oppressed people.[1] Many people subscribe to a sort of "progressive just war theory," where war is justified when it is waged by victims fighting their oppressors or is perpetrated on behalf of those victims. The distinction between modern-day versions of just war theory and pacifism have thus far escaped journalists and pollsters but should be studied by social scientists (Rioux & Prémont, 2007).

Nevertheless, it is to be expected that pacifism will continue to spread as individualistic, humanistic, and democratic attitudes become more entrenched. The greater sentiment of international security experienced by people in developed countries also contributes to the emergence of a sizeable secular pacifist segment.

NON-VIOLENCE

Non-violent protests have been numerous in history, especially since the rise of democracy. The anti-slavery movement, beginning in the late eighteenth century, was led by Quakers and members of other minority denominations. The English Chartists protested for democratic change throughout most of the nineteenth century. Over time, most of their demands (which we now take for granted) came about non-violently. A number of the worker protests and campaigns in the nineteenth and early twentieth centuries, which were fought on the same lines as the anti-slavery moment and often led by the same people, were also peaceful.

Mahatma Gandhi brought non-violent approaches to conflict to a global scale. The concepts behind his approach to non-violence were *satyagraha*, which literally means "truth force," and the aforementioned *ahimsa*. Gandhi strongly believed in working for justice, empowering the weak, and overcoming dominant oppressive forces. For him, recognizing the truth of oppression provided a moral standpoint that placed an oppressive force in an indefensible position. This recognition is the beginning of truth force. He also maintained that one should not submit to an oppressive force but act vigorously to undermine it. However, no action should involve the use of arms or violence because resorting to violence always creates more problems than it solves. Gandhi did not believe in appeasement but felt that populations should be mobilized to act together for the sake of peace and justice. His approach demanded vulnerability—he called on people to be prepared to die rather than succumb to the siren call of violence. However, were he to choose between passively submitting and taking up armed resistance, he would have likely chosen the latter as the lesser of two evils. Even so, the options were never limited to these two because he could creatively imagine many actions consistent with both satyagraha and ahimsa.

Gandhi's approach subsequently inspired Martin Luther King, Jr to espouse non-violent action in the context of the civil rights movement. Since then, millions of people have engaged in non-violent protest for peace and against wars, repressive regimes, and injustices (see Box 16.4). Non-violent protests are now the norm thanks to these examples. Major democratization, labour, and ethnic-religious protests now occur without the hint of violence when the state does not repress harshly, as in most democracies. In 2011, non-violent protests prompted major changes in Tunisia and Egypt. In recent years, the nature of non-violent action has included symbolic acts, such as activists living in or chaining themselves to trees about to be cut down. Some protest groups have used "diversity of tactics" (e.g. breaking windows), methods that are not the same as lethal violence but push the edges of what could be considered non-violent action.

BOX 16.4 | EXAMPLES OF NON-VIOLENT PROTESTS

From Alternatives Non-Violentes. (2002). 100 dates de la non-violence au XXe siècle. Verseilles, France: Author.

Throughout the twentieth century, there was considerable growth in the conceptualization of non-violent action and the number and type of actions exemplifying its principles:

- 1905: A general strike in Finland to protest Russification led to a constitutional Finnish government.
- 1906: Gandhi launched the first civil disobedience campaign against laws that discriminated against people of Indian descent in South Africa.
- 1917: The movement for women's right to vote was initiated in the United States, and Dorothy Day went on a hunger strike.
- 1914–8: Sixteen thousand conscientious objectors went before the courts in Great Britain; most were imprisoned but 30 were condemned to death (not executed).
- 1930: Gandhi organized the Salt March for Indian independence from Great Britain.
- 1942: Norwegian teachers successfully resisted the Nazification of the education system through civil disobedience.
- 1955: Martin Luther King, Jr organized a 382-day boycott of buses in Montgomery, AL, to protest racial discrimination.
- 1967–8: Thousands of protesters engaged in a sit-in around the Pentagon to protest the war in Vietnam.
- 1968: Bishop Dom Elder Camara launched a non-violent campaign for peace and justice and against poverty and dictatorship in Brazil.
- 1974: Twenty non-violent groups in France founded *le Mouvement pour une Alternative Non-Violente* (MAN), the movement for a non-violent alternative.
- 1981–3: Three hundred thousand people demonstrated against the installation of Pershing nuclear missiles.
- 1988: Aung San Suu Kyi started her non-violent struggle for democracy in Burma with an address before 5,000 people.
- 1989: The "Velvet Revolution" in Czechoslovakia brought an end to the Communist regime; the Berlin Wall was dismantled.
- 1992: In Kinshasa, Zaire, a million people marched against the dictatorship of President Mobutu.
- 1999: Non-violent action in Seattle brought the talks of the World Trade Organization to a standstill and started an ongoing movement against the negative effects of globalization.

BOX 16.5 | NON-VIOLENT ACTION

One example of non-violent behaviour is provided by Edgar Epp (1982; supplemented by conversations with Redekop), a Mennonite who was a warden of several institutions before becoming British Columbia's deputy minister of corrections. Epp was committed to peace not only as a way of life but also as a matter of public policy. As warden of Haney Correctional Centre in the 1970s, Epp responded to a riot by disarming the guards, claiming that a violent threat would only increase the level of violence. Unarmed, he personally went into the riot area and successfully negotiated an end to the uprising.

One of the foremost theorists and strategists in the field of non-violent action is Gene Sharp of the Albert Einstein Institution, whose mission is "to advance the worldwide study and strategic use of nonviolence in conflict."[2] To this end, Sharp (2005) has documented and published analyses of effective non-violent campaigns to combat genocide, dictatorship, and repressive policies. His case studies include the 1905 strikes that were part of the first Russian Revolution, resistance to the Nazis during World War II, the ousting of President Marcos from the Philippines in 1986, the Solidarity Movement of Poland and the subsequent demise of the communist regime in 1989, and the resistance to Serbian President Milošević, which culminated in his leaving power in 2000. Central to Sharp's approach are a comprehensive analysis of the situation, a clear set of goals, a broad strategy that can be implemented by the planning group, and carefully chosen tactics (of which he has produced a list of 198). His work has been translated into 30 languages and has provided significant help to non-violent movements working against repressive regimes. It is argued that the Arab Spring of 2011 was based on his book *From Dictatorship to Democracy* (1993), which is available on the Internet in Arabic (see Yi & Zheng, 2011).

PEACE RESEARCH AND EDUCATION

The last half of the twentieth century saw the birth of the fields of peace research and education, as well as the phenomenal growth in their depth and scope. In this section, we trace the history and leading figures of each field and examine some of the key issues each addresses.

History of Peace Research

Peace research is considered a pillar of the study of conflict and conflict resolution (Kriesberg, 1997). It emerged as a distinct field during the mid-1950s, a decade after World War II and the use of the first atomic bombs. David Dunn (2005, pp. 46ff) identifies three significant events in the development of peace research.[3] First was the publication of *Towards a Science of Peace*, written by social psychologist Theodore F. Lenz (1955). This influential work set out core impediments to peace, including skewed values, misuses of science, and ideological impediments. Lenz proposed a rigorous scientific approach to advancing peace, one based on human betterment as a goal rather than personal or partisan objectives. For Lenz, peace research was to be broadly based intellectually, drawing on many disciplines.

The second event was the establishment of a peace research organization at Stanford University's Center for the Advanced Study of the Behavioral Sciences. Key leaders at the time were Kenneth Boulding, who was to play a long-term role in peace research, and Herbert Kelman, a social psychologist who led problem-solving workshops at Harvard. Other members were mathematical biologist Anatol Rapoport, political scientist Harold Lasswell, and anthropologist Clyde Kluckhohm. This group created the *Journal of Conflict Resolution*, which was first published in March 1957. Biologist Mary Clark (1990) also played a leading role throughout by continuing to argue for the importance of connections with the evolution of human culture.

The final event on Dunn's list is the previously mentioned Russell–Einstein Manifesto. Bertrand Russell had been calling on thinkers and military leaders from both sides of the Iron Curtain to discuss the perils of atomic weapons. In 1954, he wrote to Albert Einstein, who had been raising concerns from the perspective of science. In July of the following year, they published their manifesto, calling on governments "to find peaceful means for the settlement of all matters of dispute between them" (Dunn, 2005, p. 50). Signed by a number of Nobel Prize–winning scientists, this document was created in the context of the Pugwash Movement, which brought together physical and social scientists to discuss issues of disarmament and world security.

Developments in peace research continued throughout the late twentieth century. In 1959, Johan Galtung, a significant figure in peace research, started the Peace Research Institute Oslo (PRIO). This organization, which publishes the *Journal of Peace Research*, has made a significant contribution to peace generally and peace research in particular. In the 1960s, peace research organizations grew both in numbers and in significance. The International Peace Research Association (IPRA) was founded in 1964 through the leadership of John Burton. Burton also established the Centre for the Analysis of Conflict with Michael Nicholson, Michael Banks, John Groom, Christopher Mitchell, and Bram Oppenheim, who were to become key authors in the peace field. Norman Alcock established the Canadian Peace Research Institute. In 1966, an act of the Swedish Parliament influenced by the Pugwash Movement established the Stockholm International Peace Research Institute (SIPRI), which became a global leader in peace research and a major contributor to disarmament and arms control issues.

In 1970, after kneeling at a memorial in Poland as a conciliatory gesture, German Chancellor Willy Brandt articulated the need for a public debate on peace research as a science and its importance for peace policy. That year saw the founding of the German Society for Peace and Conflict Research, which soon hosted Galtung as a visiting professor (Dunn, 2005, p. 61). The 1970s also saw the evolution of graduate programs in peace studies at Lancaster University and the opening of London's Richardson Institute for Conflict and Peace

Research, which included Andrew Mack as one of its research scholars (he would go on to head the Peace Research Centre in Australia and become the editor of the *Human Security Report*). One of the institute's visitors was Cynthia Enloe (2000), who did pioneering work in bringing emerging feminist approaches to bear on international relations. Great Britain's first Department of Peace Studies was initiated at the University of Bradford in 1974.

Ten years later, the United States Institute of Peace was founded. This organization has played a key role in funding peace research and peace publications. In 1984, Prime Minister Pierre Trudeau established the Canadian International Institute for Peace and Security, initially headed by Ambassador Geoffrey Pearson. Until it was shut down by Prime Minister Brian Mulroney in 1992, it funded research and hosted conferences on themes of peace.

What is evident from this history is that a few individuals who came together out of a shared interest in peace developed a significant intellectual field replete with institutions, methodologies, and journals (see Table 16.2). In many cases, relationships between key people helped to create new institutions in various parts of the world. Some of these organizations had a significant impact on international institutions such as the United Nations and UNESCO.

Trends in Peace Research

Since its beginnings, peace research has stressed a rigorous scientific basis. This emphasis has included empirical research and even a positivist approach, as well as critical thinking and logical coherence (Dunn, 2005). Alongside scientific rigour, creativity and the search for new solutions have been threads throughout.

Over the last five decades, much peace research has concerned armaments. In this focus, there is a parallel with strategic studies but with a different emphasis. Peace studies has been concerned with the negative effects of increased armament and the potential for arms reduction. Strategic studies has been occupied with issues of balance of power.

TABLE 16.2 | NOTABLE PEACE AND CONFLICT RESOLUTION JOURNALS

Name	Date	Base
Journal of Conflict Resolution	1957	Yale University
Journal of Peace Research	1964	Peace Research Institute Oslo
Bulletin of Peace Proposals	1970	International Peace Research Association and International Peace Research Institute
Current Research on Peace and Violence	1971	Tampere Peace Research Institute
Peace and Change	1975	Peace and Justice Studies Association
International Journal of Peace Studies	1996	Institute for Conflict Analysis and Resolution
The Journal of Peace Education	1996	Peace Education Commission

Source: Based on Dunn, D. (2005). *The first fifty years of peace research: A survey and interpretation.* Aldershot: Ashgate.

New concepts have also emerged from peace research. For instance, as has been previously noted, Galtung (1996) introduced the notion of structural violence, meaning that systematically holding people back from their own development is a form of violence, and Burton (1990a) made the link between human needs and conflict. At a fundamental level, peace research has questioned an exclusive state-centred view of international and even national dynamics. It has introduced categories of analysis that have revealed many human relational dynamics and their significance in a fuller understanding of global conflict. In this pursuit, peace researchers have come from and worked with others from many of the disciplines described in Part II. For example, Rapoport (1992) challenged humanity to abolish war as an institution. He argued that war could be abolished just as slavery as a global institution (notwithstanding some new localized instances) had been. Just as the biosphere signifies the global summation and interconnectedness of all life forms on earth, the noosphere refers to what is happening in the world of ideas. Therefore, as new life forms emerge at key times within the biosphere, there is a similar emergence of new thoughts, paradigms, and patterns of thought within the noosphere. Rapoport presented the idea that peace will find its time and will be accepted as normal by political leaders and thinkers, most of whom believe that war and violent conflict are inevitable.

For John Paul Lederach (2005), the key challenge to building peace is expressed in the question, "How do we transcend the cycles of violence that bewitch our human community while still living in them?" (p. 5). He argues that we start by building a moral imagination that

> requires the capacity to imagine ourselves in a web of relationships that includes our enemies; the ability to sustain a paradoxical curiosity that embraces complexity without reliance on dualistic polarity; the fundamental belief in and pursuit of the creative act; and the acceptance of the inherent risk of stepping into the mystery of the unknown that lies beyond the far too familiar landscape of violence. (Lederach, 2005, p. 5)

Some of these themes point to new and ongoing work by such people as biologist Stuart Kauffman (2008), who is applying complexity theory and new insights about emergent creativity to the generation of positive relationships within the global community.

Reportedly, there may be as many as 800 peace research institutes with 15,000 peace researchers around the world today (Wien, 2009, p. 1). Furthermore, according to Dunn (2005), peace research is now on the cusp of significant growth as it concerns itself with a wide range of interconnected issues, including "AIDS, water, the availability of drugs, the nature and nurture of the global environment, the interconnectedness of the ecosphere, the threat of pollution and allied issues" (Dunn, 2005, p. 78). That these matters are seen as being connected to peace and security is derived from the space derived cosmology in which we see ourselves as "a collectivity on a small ball spinning in space" (p. 78).

Peace Education

A number of initiatives that could be classified as peace education emerged from the peace movements of the nineteenth century and the decades between the world wars. However, peace education as a defined critical field has evolved since the mid-1950s in a manner that parallels peace research. It should be noted that there are varying degrees of peace education in the world because many cultures and religions have inculcated principles and processes to enable their communities to live in peace. Peace educators have drawn upon these doctrines, adding the dimensions of critical assessment, strategic thinking, peace philosophy, and reflexivity. An important actor in this respect is UNESCO, which offers a network for peace educators and devotes a great deal of effort to worldwide peace campaigns, notably through the promotion of the "culture of peace" idea.

Peace education concerns itself with relaying an awareness of the concepts, structures, approaches, values, and processes that people need to thrive. This process occurs informally,

(Toronto Star/GetStock.com)

Schoolchildren check out ornaments placed by other students on a Peace Tree in Toronto. The tree was inaugurated through the city's Mayor's Office to mark the world premiere of Peace Tree Day, a unique festival where children and families from every culture, faith, and race unite to celebrate peace and diversity.

through community-based programs and educational institutions.[4] The content of training stresses respect for all people, human rights, an awareness of oppressive structures and practices, and competence in conflict resolution processes such as those covered in Chapter 11.

BOX 16.6 | A HUMAN RIGHT TO PEACE

From Roche, D. (2003). *The human right to peace*. Ottawa: Novalis, p. 128.

In 1997, former UNESCO director-general Federico Mayor Zaragoza advocated for the recognition of a human right to peace, an initiative celebrated by the peace movement (Roche, 2003, 2007). The resulting Oslo Draft Declaration on the Human Right to Peace sets out the following articles.

Article 1: Peace as a human right

- Every human being has the right to peace, which is inherent in the dignity of the human person. War and all other armed conflicts, violence in all its forms and whatever its origin, and insecurity also, are intrinsically incompatible with the human right to peace;
- The human right to peace must be guaranteed, respected and implemented without any discrimination in either internal or international contexts by all states and other members of the international community;

Article 2: Peace as a duty

- Every human being, all states and other members of the international community and all peoples have the duty to contribute to the maintenance and construction of peace, and to the prevention of armed conflicts and of violence in all its forms. It is incumbent upon them notably to favour disarmament and to oppose by all legitimate means acts of aggression and systematic, massive and flagrant violations of human rights which constitute a threat to peace;
- As inequalities, exclusion and poverty can result in the disruption of peace both at the international level and internally, it is the duty of states to promote and encourage social justice both on their own territory and at the international level, in particular through an appropriate policy aimed at sustainable human development;

Article 3: Peace through the culture of peace

- The culture of peace, whose aim is to build the defences of peace in the minds of human beings every day through education, science and communication, must constitute the means of achieving the global implementation of the human right to peace;
- The culture of peace requires recognition and respect for—and the daily practice of—a set of ethical values and democratic ideals which are based on the intellectual and moral solidarity of humanity.

PEACE CHALLENGES

In the peace movement perspective, it is important that states (the mimetic model for proto-nations and other sub- or transstate groups) take steps toward a world that is truly peace oriented. This process involves a number of challenges. The first is reducing the reliance on weapons and armed forces. High human and financial resources are spent on preparations for war.[5] The procurement patterns of major industrialized nations cascade down to small states that cannot afford to buy weapons. These military expenditures translate into huge opportunity cost: less food, less water development, and fewer resources for education and health. The peace movement stresses the favourable effects of converting military resources to peaceful uses, the "peace dividend" hypothesis.

Second is the need for an ethical vision to guide human relations. If the only ethical vision is one that sees humans as essentially competing to maximize their interests with few moral constraints, policies, programs, and practices will flow naturally from this idea. Covert operations that destabilize governments, secret deals that disempower certain peoples, and distortions of the facts that humiliate groups all seem legitimate to self-interested political and bureaucratic leaders caught in a realist paradigm.

The third challenge is the development of a new guiding mythology to replace the glorification of the good warrior rescuing potential victims from the bad guys. Too often, the same basic myth (with a reversal of good guy and bad guy roles) is used on both sides of the conflict. Humans are capable of a more nuanced approach that includes sympathetically entering the world of the Other and using discursive processes to solve problems. However, this process is not as exciting as the high stimulus, high-risk drama of violent competitive conflict. Populations need to be weaned off their addiction to violent stimuli, an addiction that could even be framed in terms of the brain's neurotransmitters that provide the rush of excitement associated with conflicts (see Chapter 6).

Giving voice to the world of the victims is another challenge. Physicist and mathematician Freeman Dyson (1984) observes that the world of the warriors includes military personnel, politicians, scientists, arms dealers, and strategic security think tanks. The world of the victims includes all those who suffer directly or indirectly from the latent violence of an arms build-up and the use of weapons. Governments, therefore, must be more concerned with victims of militarism and armed conflict.[6]

Finally, building bridges between peace researchers and activists and those in the military and government who have an interest in peace also presents a challenge. The shared interest between these groups is much greater than is generally acknowledged. It is important that strategies for developing a global culture of peace be developed at every level, from local to international.

CRITICAL REFLECTIONS

While peace research and peace education have fuelled peace activism, there are certain difficulties facing the peace movement. For example, many within the movement take a judgmental stance toward people who do not share their orientation. This opinion can even go so far as to dehumanize or demonize those associated with the military. The peace movement often fails to recognize that people who do not share their deontological principles against war are also acting in the interests of peace. Accordingly, there has been a failure to acknowledge the degree to which those in the military risk their lives for the sake of noble principles, which include the freedoms that peace activists enjoy when they protest.

One of the historical weaknesses of the peace movement is that it is intent on weakening Western societies. When criticizing preparation for war and actual military interventions, pacifists are often seen as having a double standard, focusing solely on Western countries while displaying ignorance and even complacency about other offenders. These criticisms may be exaggerated, given that many other states have been the target of peace researchers and activists—for example, the roles of China and India in financing oppressive regimes in Africa is of current concern. The concentration of effort against Western (especially American) actions may owe a lot to the fact that public opinion and the mass media stress issues that are of greater concern to them. However, the perception of bias remains, and the peace movement has to work hard to convince public opinion that it is working to increase (not undermine) security, liberty, and welfare.

The most haunting problem of the peace movement is the issue of addressing grave human rights abuses without using force. For example, could it be rightly argued that using force by the international community to stop the Rwandan genocide would have been wrong? The peace movement correctly claims that peaceful protests have successfully ended human rights abuses in many countries. Nevertheless, there remains the question of dealing with regimes that harshly repress any dissent and are immune to foreign pressures. The doctrine of the responsibility to protect, inspired by just war theory, proposes that the UN take the lead in fighting these groups, using force in some cases. Pacifists, on the other hand, are spared the difficult choices about using force. In Max Weber's terms, they follow an ethics of conviction rather than an ethics of responsibility. Is this position tenable for decision-makers who must decide on the use of police or military force in times of great danger?

There are many grave issues and challenges facing humankind in relation to justice and violence. The peace movement offers a unique perspective on these matters, raising questions that others might not ask. However, in the interest of peace and security, it is important to keep the peace movement open to a respectful dialogue with other perspectives.

CONCLUSION

In this chapter, we presented an overview of those who have questioned the legitimacy of a world view that sees the preparation for and engagement of war as a necessary part of human existence. We examined the concepts of positive and negative peace and traced pacifism as a historic development of religious and philosophical doctrines that have strengthened individual and group convictions against violence, militarism, and war. We also showed that, over the last 50 years, peace research has emerged as a field of scholarly activity that uses empirical, theoretical, and normative methodologies to critically assess concepts related to peace as well as actions that might lead to its realization. Within the same time frame, peace education has come into its own as a field of research and action. While these developments have fuelled peace activism, the concept of peace continues to confront many challenges when addressing both armed conflict and issues of justice.

DISCUSSION QUESTIONS

1. Should we use the positive or negative notion of peace in conflict studies? Give reasons to support your answer.

2. What are the most challenging issues of creating a just peace?

3. What kind of research can encourage the goal of peace?

4. Some within the peace movement advocate for governmental departments of peace. What role might such a department play within government? What are its pros and cons?

NOTES

1. For example, in November 2008, Innovative Research Group polled Canadians for the University of Toronto's Munk Centre and found that 72 per cent approved of the principle of humanitarian intervention. See www.munkdebates.com/MediaStorage/Documents/MunkDebatesPollPressRelease01Dec08.pdf?ext=.pdf.

2. For further information on the institution and Sharp's work, see http://aeinstein.org/.

3. Dunn (2005, pp. 44–46) also sees Quincy Wright's *A Study of War* (1964) and Lewis Richardson's *The Mathematical Psychology of War* (1919) as contributing factors in the emergence of peace research. This historical sketch is largely based on Dunn's work.

4. For an index of peace education institutions in Canada, see www.peace.ca/canpeace education.htm.

5. For a thorough annual review of military expenditures and arms transfers, see the SIPRI Yearbook (www.sipri.org/yearbook). Full text and summaries of SIPRI findings can also be consulted at the organization's main website (www.sipri.org), and similar information is available from Project Ploughshares (http://ploughshares.ca/).

6. This argument has been the inspiration for the doctrine of human security sponsored by Canada and other states since the 1990s.

INTRODUCTION

In Chapter 14, we introduced the concepts of teleology (goals) and deontology (duty, moral principles), showing that both play essential and complementary roles in conflict. This chapter applies these concepts to conflict specialists, who work at many different levels. We start with the idea of an ethical vision that can guide the work of these specialists. We also introduce the concept of reflective practice, emphasizing the need to constantly consider one's actions in terms of the overall ethical vision, and explore the deontological dimension of ethical thinking as it pertains to particular roles for conflict specialists. Finally, we raise some challenging ethical dilemmas within the field.

ETHICAL VISION

Conflict deeply touches people's lives. At its extreme, violent conflict is devastating. Even conflict that is not overtly violent has the potential to disrupt the parties' lives. However, as we have pointed out in this text, conflict can be channelled into creativity and lead to enormous personal growth. The stakes are high for anyone who wishes to intervene in conflict. How one gets involved could intensify a conflict or contribute to its resolution. A conflict's resolution (whether just or unjust) has grave consequences. Hence, it is important that one regard a calling to get involved with great respect and that one reflect on the values that guide engagement.

Conflict specialists can play different roles. Third parties guide processes and sometimes make decisions about a particular conflict. They work as mediators, arbitrators, or adjudicators. How they frame the issues, elicit information, and bring the process to a conclusion have tremendous implications for the parties involved, sometimes lasting years or even generations. Advocates for those in conflict make a big difference in how a situation plays out. Some advocates represent the parties directly; others work as advisors. Like third parties, their influence on people's lives is very significant. Analysts of conflicts also make a difference in people's lives. How they identify the issues, the kinds of information they include, their approach to analyzing conflict, and the implied and direct judgments they make can affect the actions taken in a conflict and its outcome.

Professionals working in the field as mediators, lawyers, judges, arbitrators, consultants, advisors, or analysts are paid to do the work they do. To what degree is their work influenced by the people who pay

CHAPTER OBJECTIVES

This chapter will help you develop an understanding of the

- importance of ethics for conflict specialists;
- role of an ethical vision in determining values and an orientation for practice in the field;
- nature of an ethics of responsibility and an ethics of care;
- significance of having a reflective and reflexive practice;
- deontological principles that are important for practice in the field; and
- moral dilemmas facing practitioners.

them? How do their own biases affect the way they work? How important is it that they reflect on their own motivations in terms of ethical principles? What codes of conduct govern professional associations? How are conflict specialists to be held accountable? These questions show how a study of ethics and attention to values have ramifications for conflict specialists.

Along with conflict specialists, other people work actively to address conflicts. Some are volunteers who get involved on their own, while others become involved in a secondary way. For instance, people who work for the government, NGOs, or business firms may not focus on conflict per se, but their professional lives may implicate them in conflict situations. These people must also consider how their actions affect the lives of people in conflict.

It is also important that people addressing conflict identify the intentions of their actions. An ethical vision is a broad statement of one's core values and goals. One of the first questions in determining an ethical vision is, What is one's orientation regarding the conflict? The attitude may be ego-oriented, in which the primary goal is to make as much money as possible, show off one's expertise and thereby build a more successful career, or demonstrate how one's approach is better than anyone else's. The orientation may be realistically pragmatic: one considers the parties in conflict as simply trying to advance their own self-interests. The overall role is to assist them with a process that gives each party as much as possible while preserving some sense of fairness. A third orientation is concern for the well-being of the parties in conflict. Each of these orientations incorporates certain values and affects one's approach to conflict. However, they are not mutually exclusive.

An ethical vision also includes a desired outcome for the conflict, such as short-term accomplishments, broader impacts, and long-term results. The vision answers the following questions: What do you want to accomplish? What are the basic values guiding your actions and motivations? Another set of questions relates to strategy: How do you conduct yourself in relation to the parties? How do you make decisions and on what basis? Are there certain things you will simply not do? What is the relationship between ends and means? Are there certain principles that guide your actions? These questions are also answered by the ethical vision and the deontological principles that guide particular actions.

There are many sources of ethical teaching that can be drawn upon to form an ethical vision. We present two that can help with the overall orientation of the conflict specialist: an ethics of responsibility and an ethics of care.

Ethics of Responsibility

Ethics of responsibility can be defined in two ways. The more accepted definition comes from Max Weber (1998), who understood it as an ethics that is grounded in reality and that serves tangible and immediate social goals. He contrasted it to an ethics of conviction, which is based on guidelines defined by values and ideology that commit the practitioner to high ideals that may sacrifice many lives and resources or even be unattainable. Arguably, the ethics of responsibility described by Weber guides most decision-makers, but it can be seen as emphasizing conservative stewardship over innovative leadership.

Some modern versions of the concept stress that such a responsibility is for the future, common good, the field of conflict intervention, and the process. Hans Jonas (1984) emphasizes how an ethics of responsibility is for the long term. This perspective is in keeping with Aboriginal teachings that we must constantly think of the well-being of our descendants, including those in the next seven generations. Many conflicts and the situations arising from them have long-term consequences. It is incumbent on those involved in the process of dealing with conflict to be attentive to these possibilities, such as an unwise or unjust resolution. Conflict specialists also have a responsibility to consider the wider communities affected by a given conflict. In some cases, this community can include the natural environment or another non-human factor (Held, 2006, p. 166).

Each conflict is one of a vast number of conflicts that are studied and dealt with in the field of conflict studies. In terms of this discipline, responsibility has two directions. One is to learn from the field so as to apply the best understandings possible to the conflict. At the same time, how each conflict is handled has an impact, however slight, on the field itself. There is, then, a responsibility toward excellence, a duty to move the field forward in a way that has broad positive implications for its future.

Finally, dealing with a conflict frequently entails a process, which can be flexible or follow a clear timetable with well-defined steps. The conflict specialist can be regarded as the custodian of the process. As such, he or she works with the parties on what the process is to be, modifying it with their approval at times and asserting that they get back on track at others. Responsibility for the process means being attentive to what it is and how it is working.

Ethics of Care

An ethics of responsibility can supplement an ethics of care. Since the early 1980s, there has been an emerging body of literature around the latter, with many internal debates about its role in an ethics of justice or virtue ethics (see Clement, 1996; Held, 2006). Some link ethics of care with centuries-old ethical positions emphasizing such concepts as *ren* in the Confucian tradition and love or *caritas* in the Christian tradition (Page, 2008, p. 166). Even Aesara of Lucania, an ancient Greek philosopher, linked care and love to justice (Page, 2008, p. 165). Other congruencies exist with Heidegger's emphasis on what it means to be in the world in relation to others and Levinas's and Ricoeur's further development of the Self–Other relationship (Page, 2008, pp. 170–172; see Chapter 9). The 1980s saw an ethics of care develop out of Carol Gilligan (1982)'s feminist approach to moral development. In the ensuing decades, it matured as an ethical framework (see Held, 2006; Noddings, 2008; Clement, 1996). Here, we will apply a few key themes to the conflict specialist.

Philosopher Virginia Held (2006, p. 10) develops the notion of care as both a practice and a value. The practice of care can be inducted from the fact that everyone has at least received care as a child. Caring as practice means to attend to the needs of the one cared for. As Held (2006) points out,

> it shows us how to respond to needs and why we should. It builds trust and mutual concern and connectedness between persons. It is not a series of individual actions, but a practice that develops, along with its appropriate attitudes. It has attributes and standards that can be described, but more important that can be recommended and that should be continually improved as adequate care becomes closer to being good care. Practices of care should express the caring relations that bring persons together, and they should do so in ways that are progressively more morally satisfactory. (p. 42)

Caring as a value is both an individual and a collective component of moral agency. It integrates emotions of sympathy, empathy, sensitivity, and responsiveness, as well as moral indignation (Held, 2006, pp. 29ff). Care involves a passionate commitment to take action when someone or something needs attention. As an orientation affixed to a vision, it includes a sense of hope that something can be done to fulfill a pressing need.

Care takes place in the context of a dyadic relationship between the carer and the cared for (Noddings, 2008). For a conflict specialist to care about the parties means that, at the time of intervention, attending to the needs and interests of the parties is of paramount importance. Accordingly, the ego and ego needs of the specialist are superseded by a focus on the well-being of the others. To care for both parties, the conflict specialist must become aware of his or her potential biases toward either party and the possible barriers to caring. If the biases and barriers are sufficient, the conflict specialist's role could be limited. For instance, it would be impossible for him or her to be an unbiased (sufficiently neutral) mediator.

Desiring the well-being of the parties puts a conflict specialist in a delicate position. There is always the temptation of projecting one's own interpretation of well-being onto the parties. Likewise, there is the urge to try to be too helpful in the name of care. If autonomy and empowerment figure into well-being, space must be provided to maximize the parties' agency, allowing them to take the initiative, act, create, and find their own solutions. To achieve this outcome, open communication, transparency, and dialogue are required. Sometimes, non-action is the best form of action. At other times, a specialist might act quite aggressively to turn the tide of escalating violent discourse or action.

Caring about relationships is central to an ethics of care. Conflicts often occur within a complex web of relational systems and affect many people. A primary relationship is that between the parties in the conflict. Attending to this relationship requires a conscious focus on its structure. What is the nature of the relationship historically and what is its future potential? Do the parties have to coexist in some kind of a relationship—are they bound by geography or mutual ties that require some contact—or can they go their separate ways? An ethics of care suggests working toward a relationship that will allow the parties to flourish individually and within the relational system.

An ethics of care can also be directed toward the conflict itself. This method means that transforming the conflict dynamics from that which is violent and destructive to that which allows for creativity is an important value. Power can be a key factor in the conflict and its progression. It can be used to dominate or empower or be drawn upon as a resource (Held, 2006, p. 150). The management, resolution, or transformation of a conflict could well involve power dynamics; therefore, an ethics of care demands attentiveness to power and how it is used.

Finally, an ethics of care is concerned with justice. The rights of the parties, relative power, and issues of equality, equity, and need all come into play. A sense of justice occurs

BOX 17.1 | BISHOP SAMUEL RUIZ

(AP Photo/Pascual Gorriz)

Samuel Ruiz (1924–2011), bishop for San Cristóbal de las Casas in the Chiapas region of Mexico, was a crucial mediator in the violent conflict between the Mexican government and the Zapatista resistance movement in the 1990s. He was motivated by an ethics of care for the indigenous population, but he opposed the violent ways of the guerilla movement, led by Subcomandante Marcos. Ruiz was often accused of partiality towards the indigenous people, and this photograph shows him entering an anti-Zapatista town with his supporters after avoiding an attempt against his life. He was nevertheless hailed as an indispensable mediator by all parties because of his ethics of care for the population and his responsible behaviour.

within a context that includes the normative values of the conflicting parties' cultures. While an ethics of care implies a capacity to empathize with the parties, feelings are not enough. There has to be a clear-headed analysis of issues and of what would be fair in a given situation. Because what happens in the course of a conflict affects other people (even indirectly by creating precedent), caring about justice needs to exist throughout.

REFLECTIVE/REFLEXIVE PRACTICE

A reflexive approach to conflict involves self-awareness; lessons learned; and practices, habitus, and character. Specialists must be attentive to who and where they are in relation to a conflict, the parties, and the process. The conflict may relate to others that they person-ally experienced, or parties may provoke painful memories. Specialists may empathize in a particular way with one of the parties. Diversion from the planned process might be a source of frustration, which could be projected onto the parties. Self-awareness is the first step; deciding what to do with that awareness is the second. For example, a perceived internal bias can sometimes be offset by consciously paying attention to the interests and experiences of the less-favoured party (note the types of biases analyzed by Lonergan and presented in Chapter 9).

Reflecting on a particular conflict becomes occasion for identifying lessons learned. These lessons may be about the particular kind of conflict, the process used to address it, or the features that made it unique. An ethical vision for dealing with conflict as well as the principles involved in the process can function as a grid for reflection. A key issue in this process is the role of other parties in the identification of lessons learned. This role is particularly acute when it comes to issues of confidentiality in mediation, conciliation, or other private processes. For this reason, it is often advisable to have a partner who can observe and help debrief the process.

Individual actions lead to action chains, which lead to practices. A conflict specialist who continues in the field develops a way of being and a way of acting that character-izes his or her practice. In the terms of Pierre Bourdieu (2005), this behaviour becomes a habitus that is both reflective of and contributes to the broader field of conflict and the processes for dealing with it. Practice and habitus reflect the character—values, morals, and internalized principles—of the conflict specialist. Pursuing excellence means to take stock of the patterns that have developed through time and consciously decide whether to continue or change the trajectory of how practice, habitus, and character are evolving. For an eloquent example of how these characteristics developed in a particular case, see Box 17.2.

DEONTOLOGICAL MOMENTS

The broad goals expressed in an ethical vision and the self-development of conflict specialists can also be subject to some particular principles: do no harm, attend to power

From Benjamin, R. (2004). The mediator prepares: The practice of theory. In J. Haynes, G. Haynes, & L. Fong (Eds.), *Mediation: Positive conflict management* (pp. ix–xi). Albany, NY: State University of New York Press.

Few who had the opportunity to observe John Haynes mediate disputes would deny his artistry. . . . For many people in the throes of conflict, his reassuring demeanor elicited a calming effect. There was a well-developed sense of theater about John Haynes as he drew from the lead actors—the parties—their best performances. He knew how to reach behind a person's defensive posturing and constructively release the closeted fears that held them in check. He would be the first to admit that he was playing a role, yet there was nothing disingenuous; the compassion he displayed for people mired in disputes was authentic. . . .

John Haynes was not a theorist. While he did describe techniques and suggested strategies in his many books, his work did not delve into abstract theory. He was, however, the epitome of an intuitive practitioner; he did what he did by "tacit knowing," sensing how and when to intervene as opposed to acting by rote prescription. . . . He combined a highly developed intuitive sense with a clear analytical structure, wrapped in a passionate commitment to the belief that people in conflict must be respected and given every opportunity to make their own decisions. With the strong moral groundings of his Quaker background, he lived his beliefs through his work by resisting the ever-present temptations to pass judgment or render opinion. He maintained an unwavering focus on the process of managing disputes and the process was the expression of his values. How he practiced facilitating other peoples' negotiations as a mediator was pure enough that it required no extraneous adornment. His style did not require preambles about the value of collaboration, inquiries into peoples' motivations, or the presumption of setting rules for communication. His empathy for people trying to make sense of difficult situations was self evident in his demeanor and bearing.

. . . His most powerful technique was the use of his own vulnerability. He never assumed he could or should attempt to persuade, cajole, or otherwise convince anyone of anything; therein was the source of his power and effectiveness.

discrepancies, be careful about who pays you, and know your limits. Holding a conflict specialist accountable to these important principles is known as the deontological moment of the practice of ethics.

The first principle is to be certain that the work of the conflict specialist does not make the situation worse. Avoiding harm involves being clear about intentions; however, good intentions alone ensure neither competence nor effectiveness. In complex conflicts, assessment tools might be needed at different stages to determine the impact of the process. Checking in with the parties, identifying criteria for progress, and establishing a non-threatening environment where people are free to voice their criticisms will help prevent doing harm. Specialists might be most prone to causing inadvertent damage when dealing with cultures other than their own. They might miss certain signals, fail to pick up on body language, or transgress local taboos.

Power discrepancies, whether subtle or obvious, are a sensitive issue. One mediator describes a situation in which he was mediating a dispute between a Canadian govern-

BOX 17.3 | OKA CRISIS

(CP Photo/Ryan Remiorz)

In 1990, the mayor of Oka, QC, a town near Montreal, was determined to expand a golf course by cutting down a pine forest that the Mohawk people of Kanesatake claimed was their sacred land. To protest the expansion, a group of Mohawks erected a barricade around the area, which they maintained despite an injunction. On 11 July, the provincial police attempted to remove the blockade by force; there was an exchange of gunfire, and one police officer was killed. The situation immediately intensified as Mohawks near Montreal blockaded the Mercier Bridge, creating a commuting nightmare for thousands of workers. By August, the Canadian forces were called in to deal with the escalating crisis. Aboriginal people from across Canada showed their solidarity by coming to a peace camp, blocking roads, and making plans to retaliate should there be bloodshed.

Quebec Native Affairs Minister John Ciaccia, who was against the enforcement of the injunction, negotiated with the Mohawks while the Quebec public was angry, his own government was skeptical, and the federal government was unsupportive. Most people thought that only the army could resolve the crisis through methodical neutralization work and limited shows of force. Ciaccia was criticized in Quebec for negotiating with masked Warriors, but his intervention was crucial in convincing the Quebec government to seek a peaceful way out of the confrontation. Despite the unpopularity of his task and the power disparity between the parties, Ciaccia was determined to act as a peacemaker. On 26 September, the crisis came to an end when the last group of Mohawks trapped in a treatment centre surrounded by the army decided to simply walk away from the situation.

ment department and Aboriginal communities with leaders who were barely literate.[1] The government had a team of experts who were to determine what could and could not be done. The power discrepancy was enormous. The mediator brought in technical experts from other countries who knew the science related to the issues at hand and were aware of procedures that were not discussed by government experts but could benefit the Aboriginal groups. This process addressed the power imbalances and created new options that made it possible to accommodate the interests of those with less power.

The next principle concerns neutrality. Because professional conflict specialists are paid for their work, it is in their interests to please those who pay the bill. This situation raises questions about how their work might be skewed. Specialists who pose as neutral mediators but scheme with their clients about how to achieve an outcome beneficial to one particular party misrepresent themselves in the process. It becomes important to be transparent about one's intentions and interests in each process. If one cannot play an impartial role based on economic interests, the role could be reframed as one of advocacy or advising. If one is paid to play a role that demands a high level of impartiality, it could be important to establish institutional arms-length relationships so that impartiality can be maintained. Just as an independent judiciary is highly valued in a democracy, professional independence is also vital when it comes to conflict specialists playing different roles.

The last principle is knowing one's limits. One way that a conflict specialist can harm a situation is by getting in over his or her head. If one is dealing with a conflict that is too complex to handle or suddenly demands another type of expertise, it is important to know one's limits and either call in other people to help or refer the conflict to others who have the requisite knowledge. For example, what seems like a legal issue might really demand the intervention of a psychologist. At other times, what presents itself as a psychological issue has legal implications. It takes wisdom to know one's limits and when another professional should get involved.

MORAL DILEMMAS

There are times when different aspects of ethical reasoning come in contact with one another. For instance, in a situation where there is an emotional flare-up by an armed person, all consideration of neutrality, responsibility for process, and other important values might have to be overlooked to prevent the immediate outbreak of violence. Sometimes, every imaginable course of action—including doing nothing—has dire consequences. One then has to choose between greater and lesser evils; in the process, one is challenged to act contrary to deeply held moral values. **Moral dilemmas** occur in all types of conflict, from large-scale and very violent situations to those involving practitioners at the interpersonal level.

For instance, a gripping challenge presented by Lieutenant-General Romeo Dallaire is a hypothetical situation in which peacekeepers are guarding a school filled with 300 civilians.[2]

They see child soldiers armed with automatic weapons on the horizon, approaching to massacre those in the school. What is a "neutral" armed peacekeeper to do?

Another example of a moral dilemma was that faced by Albert Einstein. A pacifist, he had to decide whether to use his scientific knowledge to help the United States build an atomic bomb. Convinced that the Nazis were well on their way to building an A-bomb, he helped the Americans in order to forestall what he perceived as the greater harm. After Hiroshima, Einstein had to live with the results of his decision (Neuenschwander, 2006).

These large high-stakes dilemmas have their parallels in the day-to-day work of mediators and conflict resolution consultants at the personal and group levels. Many predicaments of this type have their roots in the principle of professional confidentiality. Here are some examples:

- In a separate caucus meeting during a divorce mediation, the husband divulges that he has hidden a substantial amount of money in a secret account. This information could significantly affect the final settlement. Should you tell his wife?
- In the course of a major dispute between the government and an oppressed group within society, you find out that members of the latter will engage in civil disobedience to protest their treatment. Do you alert the government? What if the government is paying you?
- In a land dispute involving Aboriginal people, mining companies, and the government, you find out that the mining companies have discovered a significant amount of gold in land that is being claimed by Aboriginal people. The companies are hiding this information and offering a pittance for mineral rights. Do you alert the other parties of the potential injustice?
- You are hired by the government to work on a public dispute involving issues of distributive justice. You are told to give the appearance of doing something but not to work seriously on the project. Do you accept the contract? Do you work with the parties according to this directive or do you work wholeheartedly on a resolution, even though it might cost the government?

In all these instances, there is a conflict between a deontological principle to which one is firmly committed and a teleological ethical vision guiding the action. In the Dallaire case, the deontological principle is to not kill the children; however, this idea conflicts with the goal of protecting unarmed civilian populations. In the Einstein case, the principle of refusing to contribute to the development of armaments was offset by the potential consequences of the Nazis getting an A-bomb first. In the other examples, the principle of confidentiality was in conflict with an ethics of care for oppressed people and a sense of social/distributive justice.

The complexity of people and situations makes moral dilemmas challenging to practitioners. Decisions often need to be made on incomplete information. It is also sometimes difficult to read the intentions of parties who might have a significant impact on the outcome of a given decision. There is a sophisticated practice of scenario development that makes it possible to work through hypothetical situations. Students and practitioners benefit from such simulations, which prepare them for real-world dilemmas. However, it is never quite the same as being in an actual situation where some small surprising change can have an amazing impact.[3] Nevertheless, the study and simulation of ethical dilemmas is important not only in the answers that it provides but also in preparing the mind to react quickly and thoroughly in unforeseen circumstances.

CONCLUSION

Whatever role conflict specialists play in a given conflict, their actions significantly affect the parties involved. It is therefore important that such specialists be guided by an ethical vision that articulates their values and orientation as they take action. Eventually, this vision will shape their ongoing practice. Two sources of this vision are an ethics of responsibility (which takes responsibility for the process, the common good, and the implications for the field of conflict studies) and an ethics of care (which focuses on the well-being of the parties, the relationships, and a sense of justice). Conflict specialists must also continue to be conscious of who they are in relation to the conflict and the process and take steps to reduce the negative impact of their biases. Such reflection is important in identifying lessons learned and patterns related to practice. Deontological principles can form a basis for this reflection and self-assessment. These factors interact in the face of moral dilemmas.

DISCUSSION QUESTIONS

1. Examine how various conflict specialists have dealt with different conflicts. What evidence is there of their ethical vision?

2. Imagine that you are in a challenging and disturbing conflict. Think about the kind of conflict specialist that you would like to have as an intervener. Identify the orientation, qualities, and character of such a person.

3. Would you supplement an ethics of care and an ethics of responsibility with additional values to guide the work of conflict specialists? If so, which values do you think are important? Give reasons to support your answers.

4. Think of your own examples of moral dilemmas that have been or could be faced by specialists in the field.

NOTES

1. Personal communication with Vern Neufeld Redekop.

2. Personal communication with Vern Neufeld Redekop.

3. For accounts of such changes, see Yoder (1983).

CONCLUSION

This book is about how conflict is described, analyzed, understood, and handled. It was written to introduce readers to the wide array of methods that theoreticians and analysts use to deal with these questions. We have cast our glances back in time, looking at historic conceptualizations and tracing the emergence of new ways of approaching conflict. To deal with conflict, humans have applied implicit cultural norms that limit what can be done in the course of a conflict and created institutions, laws, and processes.

We have defined the field of conflict studies in broad terms and extended the field to the social sciences, psychology, the humanities, and even the biological sciences. As expected, there are huge overlaps between conflict studies and other established disciplines. However, we hope that the existence of conflict studies and the contribution of this textbook will inspire specialists to expand their horizons and gather notions and facts from other disciplines.

We have tried not to impose a one-dimensional version of conflict studies. Instead, we have demonstrated that people from varied backgrounds and persuasions do research in this field. While warmongers, terrorists, and mass murderers may not be at home in conflict studies, the field should be open to those who believe that conflicts can generate beneficial changes in human societies and can often be managed and resolved peacefully. Therefore, we have presented approaches based on very different assumptions and methods. Methodological individualism, historical materialism, structuralism, constructivism, and reflexive approaches have all been considered. We understand that there are enormous gaps between these traditions. We simply hope that the more scientific-minded of you have been introduced to the philosophical ways of thinking about conflict and have gained a better appreciation for its ethical aspects. For the students of philosophy and religion, we have provided many examples of empirical and materialist thinking that can also influence the rigour and validation of your research.

It is our impression that, in order to counter the centrifugal claims of the different theories, proponents of conflict studies have tried to diminish the theoretical content of their field by focusing on conflict resolution processes and using general frameworks deemed to be non-ideological and non-controversial. While this practice might be useful for alternative dispute resolution (ADR) training, it does not resolve the problem for conflict analysts and researchers. One way to limit theoretical differences among people from very diverse backgrounds is to promote the theoretical approaches that can be easily merged or that are naturally complementary. However, in this perspective, some theories and methodologies would be excluded from the research program because many of the approaches prevalent in the field are incompatible.

Is there a future for conflict studies? As long as a dialogue exists and mutual enrichment can be observed in the field, our answer is yes. But if it were to separate into rigid categories of reflexive theorists, rationalists, and structuralists, conflict studies may fail to deliver the promises of multidisciplinarity. In other words, the field will succeed if it practises what it preaches. Tolerance, dialogue, listening, negotiation, compromise, creative solutions, and reconciliation must not be mere concepts but actual practices that define the work of conflict studies.

Three major factors also support the idea that conflict studies has a future. First, the number of conflicts at all levels rises as societies become more complex and free. Second, there are many schools of thought regarding the explanation of conflicts, and the exchange between specialists from several disciplines is growing. As a general trend, interdisciplinarity is increasingly sought after and promoted in higher education. Third, the methods of conflict management and resolution are evolving and spreading rapidly in all societies. However, it is unknown whether future students will study human differences in the emerging conflict studies schools and programs. Traditional fields still have the upper hand because of their well-defined scope and methods. While intersciplinarity has proven itself in contexts such as journals of peace and conflict studies, it remains to be seen if students will choose to study in this mixed field. Conflict studies has to prove that it can offer more than a traditional social science or humanities field can. Our field owes a great deal to conventional philosophers, psychologists, and sociologists, but it is also indebted to several truly multidisciplinary individuals such as Mary Parker Follett, Morton Deutsch, Thomas Schelling, Johan Galtung, Ted Gurr, and John W. Burton. Such scholars must be put forward as role models and intellectual references for our students.

However conflict studies develops, conflict resolution is destined to remain a central component of the field. This practice is growing in the Western world, especially in the workplace. Although there are increasing needs on this front, traditional professions are working hard to maintain and expand their predominance in quasi-legal and paralegal domains. It is often logical to directly involve jurists in conflict resolution, but non-jurists who are well trained and aware of the legal environment in which they operate can work in many ADR settings. We contend that conflict resolution specialists can provide a better understanding of the reasons for conflict, the mental processes of the parties, the options for resolution, and the consequences of conflict. Conflict studies graduates could help large institutions, the public service, and community organizations develop better systems for addressing disputes and conflicts in their ranks and with their clients, partners, rivals, and beneficiaries. But this strengthening of non-legal conflict resolution can happen only if people are willing to consider the opportunities and networks needed for the creation of multidisciplinary ADR.

Another important factor is that most ADR in the West is now mandatory. People must see a mediator if they want a divorce or an arbitrator if they want to settle a dispute with a service provider. However, mediation still has to grow in neighbourhoods, families, and commercial environments to improve the public acceptance of ADR. This development would relieve the heavy dependency on legal procedures and avoid authoritative settlements by the political authority. Many non-Western governments have made this connection and are careful not to jettison their traditional modes of conflict resolution, even as they encounter rapid modernization. Although it is unlikely that these institutions will be able to function as they did when societies were highly communitarian, they can be refurbished in order to conserve some social capital at the grassroots level. To create efficient ADR procedures and systems in the developed or developing world, models of analysis and intervention must be created, tested, and compared. A systematic effort in this direction must be started, using theoretical and ethical elaboration, comparative and historical analysis, experimental and quasi-experimental data, and a solid peer review process.

Furthermore, organizations that educate and train conflict resolvers must not only continue to emphasize helping people deal with their differences, but they must also contribute to the professionalization of the field. Conflict resolution is a field where trainers still guide other trainers. To compete with the ADR professions, it may be necessary to educate conflict resolution trainers so that they do not merely transmit the knowledge inherited from past practice but innovate in many directions and submit their methods to experimentation and evaluation.

Amidst all this discussion, it is crucial to never lose sight of the moral and ethical aspects of conflict intervention. Conflict and how we deal with it raises basic questions about our humanity—who we are, how we organize ourselves, what motivates us, and how we know things.

GLOSSARY

Adjudication The settlement of a case by a judge, a panel of judges, an arbitrator, or an arbitration panel. The term is generally used in conflict studies to refer to a legal process led by a judge.

Aggression A type of behaviour that is hostile and even violent and can be directed inward or outward.

Alternative dispute resolution (ADR) A general term for dispute resolution methods, such as mediation and arbitration, used as an alternative to court-based processes.

Altruism Concern for the well-being of others.

Anarchy Situation in which the use of legitimate force is not monopolized by a central political institution.

Anomie A lack of widespread and legitimate cultural norms that guide the behaviour of people.

Arbitration A non-judicial method of handling conflict in which a third party authoritatively decides on the solution.

Arms control Measures designed to lessen the possibility of the proliferation and use of weapons.

Authority The legitimate and superior power of a party that can impose its solution to a problem.

Balance of power A situation of relative force equilibrium in which states or political organizations are dissuaded from going to war with one another because of the significant risks of defeat and conquest that a war would entail.

Bargaining A negotiation emphasizing the give-and-take process needed to reach a compromise.

Best alternative to a negotiated agreement (BATNA) The position that a party in a conflict would pursue if negotiations fell apart and an agreement was not reached.

Circle process A traditional indigenous process of dealing with conflict (and other situations) that involves an opportunity for each participant to express his or her views uninterrupted in a sequence determined by the culture.

Civil law 1) The laws that govern the private rights of people, notably in contracts, responsibility, tort, etc. This type of law is distinguished from criminal law. 2) The legal system in which the source of law is a human-created written code (as opposed to religious, customary, and common law).

Collective agreement A work contract usually negotiated by labour and management but sometimes imposed by an authoritative third party.

Common law The legal system in which the law originates from and evolves through court precedents.

Competition A non-antagonistic rivalry that is played out peacefully.

Compromise A situation where parties make concessions and/or drop some demands in order to find a solution to their dispute.

Conciliation 1) Diplomatic mediation by an intergovernmental third party. 2) Mediation in labour relations, oriented toward the creation of a compromise between parties. 3) A process of interaction with each party to prepare them for face-to-face mediation.

Confidence-building measures (CBMs) Policies and processes established to lessen the possibility of crises and wars between states and/or armed factions.

Conflict An antagonistic relationship between two or more parties caused by intractable divergences over what is mutually significant to each party.

Conflict management The methods and processes used to minimize and contain the negative aspects of a conflict.

Conflict resolution 1) The process of peacefully addressing the divergent positions, interests, and needs of parties in conflict such that all are satisfied with the resulting agreement. 2) A general term for processes that limit the ill-effects of conflict and achieve positive outcomes for parties, including conflict transformation, conflict management, dispute settlement, and mediation.

Conflict studies The multidisciplinary field of study devoted to the analysis and understanding of the causes, contributing factors, and dynamics of conflict; the methods and institutions that steer and manage conflict; the approaches and processes that resolve and transform conflict; and related concepts such as violence, non-violence, peace, genocide, reconciliation, and healing.

Conflict transformation The significant modification of the conditions that led to a conflict and the creation of a new, more peaceful, state of affairs.

Consequentialist ethics The aspect of ethics that examines the moral implications of an action's intended and unintended consequences.

Constructivism (constructionism) An approach that proposes to explain social facts in reference to the perceptions, ideals, habits, and language of human actors.

Contact theory The study of how the increase of direct contact between people of different groups reduces animosity between them.

Contest A formalized way to determine a winner among rivals. Some contests (e.g. duels, draws, elections, and games) can be used to settle conflicts.

Coordination problem The difficulty in reaching the high degree of participant co-operation necessary to achieve an outcome that is favourable to all.

Criminal law The set of laws that deal with harms severe enough to be designated as crimes. Criminal law defines crimes and the punishments associated with them. A related system is correctional law, which governs the administration of prisons and penitentiaries.

Culture All the ideas, customs, norms, technologies, symbols, habits, and arts created and transmitted by a given society.

Democide Any large-scale deliberate elimination of an entire human category.

Democracy In the general sense, any system in which the people are ultimately sovereign and the decision-makers are the people themselves or are accountable to the people. See also *Liberal democracy*.

Democratic transition The evolution of a country from authoritarianism, anarchy, or civil war to liberal democracy.

Demographic transition The passage from the demographic pattern of high fertility/high mortality to low fertility/low mortality, typical of the modern age.

Deontology A study of moral/ethical principles that determine correct action.

Dependency 1) A situation where one party's development is controlled by other parties, for instance, less developed societies that rely on the trade, capital, and technology of industrialized nations. 2) A psychological state in which a party internalizes a sense of inferiority and depends on an outside "superior" party for approval of any initiative before moving ahead.

Desire The impulse or longing to obtain or achieve something.

Deterrence A situation in which one decides not to pursue a conflict or an aggression because of high risks of failure and harm.

Dialogue The process of establishing and developing open communication to create meaning and mutual understanding.

Diplomacy 1) Originally, the art of peacefully managing state relations through negotiation. 2) By extension, any application of negotiations between conflicting parties.

Diplomatic immunity The protection accorded to diplomats against searches and seizures by foreign governments.

Dispute Any notable difference of view or position between people or groups of people.

Distributive justice The distribution of goods in society in a manner that balances equity, equality, and needs.

Distributive negotiation Negotiation based on each party trying to maximize his or her portion of available goods.

Empowerment The process of gaining a capacity to take independent action and accruing control over one's destiny.

Epistemology The study of knowledge and of the means to attain it.

Equality The principle that everyone should be treated equally.

Equity The principle that what people receive should be proportional to their contribution.

Ethnocentrism Belief in the superiority of one's culture over all others; hence, judging other cultures on the basis of one's own values.

Evolutionary stable strategies (ESS) In biology, patterns of behaviour that maximize the chances of survival and procreation.

Facilitation The action of a third party to enable and ease communication and the generation of constructive ideas and potential solutions in a conflict.

Fact-finding mission An impartial inquiry into a conflict with the intention of verifying and transmitting empirical information to the parties.

Failed state A state that cannot maintain public order, extract sufficient fiscal resources, or provide adequate public services.

Forgiveness An action taken by a victim of injustice that gives up a right to demand punishment or revenge.

Free rider One who benefits from the rewards of collective action without contributing to its provision.

Frustration The sentiment experienced by people who are unjustly blocked in the attainment of their needs and desires.

Game theory A generic term used to describe the formalized study of rational decision-making.

Genocide The deliberate elimination of an ethnic, racial, religious, or national group.

Globalization The increased interdependence, communication, and cultural exchange among societies and the gradual creation of a world society. The term is also used to describe the pervasive influence of Western culture, technology, and economic interests on societies around the world.

Good offices A diplomatic expression meaning facilitation by a trusted and esteemed third party.

Gradual reciprocated initiatives in tension-reduction (GRIT) Process in which parties take small steps in acknowledging the interests of the antagonistic party. This action may prompt other small steps from that party, which will be reciprocated in turn.

Healing The restoration of well-being in the face of physical, emotional, and/or psychological wounds.

Hegemon The uncontested dominant power in a given international system.

Hegemonic structure A situation in which a dominant group makes the rules, determines the values, and controls the action and destiny of a subjected group.

Hegemony 1) In classical meaning, the uncontested dominance of a group or state over a social system. 2) In Marxism and critical analysis, the power to impose class interests by disguising them as universal and incontestable ideals.

Hermeneutics The branch of philosophy that concerns itself with how we interpret texts, artistic expression, and experience.

High-intensity armed conflict A series of violent political acts resulting in at least 1,000 deaths per year.

Humanitarian intervention The use of coercion to protect a population from grave human rights abuses committed by a government or militant group.

Human security A conception of security that stresses the protection of ordinary people over that of elites and institutions.

Identity A chosen marker of a person's or group's specificity, usually for reasons of social safety, belonging, recognition, or advancement.

Identity needs Categories for aspects of life that are deemed essential for the preservation and development of the values, connections, and aspirations that define an individual or group.

Ideology A set of social and political ideas developed to provide people with a view of the world and their roles in it.

Illocutionary The intended results of a speech act.

Integrative negotiation An approach to negotiation where the benefits to both parties extend beyond what is possible in a simple division of goods.

Interest-based negotiation A negotiation process in which the parties try to identify their individual and shared interests in a given conflict and find solutions that maximize benefits to both sides.

Interests The goals that people set for themselves to ameliorate their lives and the lives of others.

Intergovernmental organization (IGO) A permanent association of states based on a treaty.

International non-governmental organization (INGO) An international association of individuals.

Interstate war War between states.

Intrastate war War within a state; a civil war.

Jus ad bellum The conditions under which a decision to go to war can be considered just.

Jus post bellum The conditions under which actions taken after a war can be considered just.

Jus in bello The moral restraints regarding how wars should be fought.

Jus potentia ad bellum Principles related to the development of the means to go to war, such as arms procurement.

Just cause In just war theory, a serious infringement to justice that can warrant armed action.

Justice 1) Moral rightness and fairness. 2) The administration of law (i.e. the court system and peripheral organs).

Just war theory The doctrine, initially proposed in ancient Greece and Rome and subsequently elaborated on by the Catholic Church, used to determine when wars are just.

Liberal democracy Democracy based on the rule of law and the election of government leaders.

Liberalism The philosophy that stresses the importance of individual freedoms in the attainment of justice, happiness, and prosperity.

Locutionary What is said in a speech action.

Low-intensity armed conflict A series of violent political acts causing less than 100 direct deaths per year.

Marxism (historical materialism) Theory positing that social classes are in conflict and that the violent resolution of their opposition is the main factor of change in human history.

Means of production In Marxism, the land, resources, buildings, machines, and all other things necessary for producing goods and services.

Med-arb A conflict resolution process where the third party initially acts as a mediator but may also act as an arbitrator if a mediated solution is not possible.

Mediation A negotiation process that is guided or assisted by a third party.

Medium-intensity armed conflict A series of violent political acts causing at least 1,000 deaths between two and ten years.

Meme A unit of cultural knowledge, as conceptualized by biologists.

Meta-requisite Something needed at each stage of a complex process, such as reconciliation.

Methodology A system of methods concerned with the kinds of questions we ask and the manner in which we get answers.

Mimesis Imitation.

Mimetic desire A desire that is based on what other people possess or want to possess.

Mimetic rivalry A situation where two parties each continue to want any good acquired or desired by the other.

Mode of production In Marxism, the way an economy is organized, with a certain level of technology and type of ownership. Capitalism is the contemporary dominant mode of production.

Modernization Passage from a traditional social organization to a modern one, characterized by secularization, urbanization, and specialization, among other things.

Moral dilemma A situation in which one has to decide between two evils, only one of which can be avoided.

Mutually hurting stalemate In Zartman's terminology, the realization of two parties in conflict that the costs of their conflict have become unbearable and more detrimental to their interests than peace.

Nationalism The idea that all people sharing a culture and a territory should be in charge of their own destiny.

Natural law The notion that human beings possess inalienable rights that, along with a sense of justice, go beyond particular legal systems. Natural law is at the source of many ethical, political, and legal systems.

Need Something that is necessary for people's survival and well-being.

Negative peace The conception of peace as the absence of large-scale violence.

Non-governmental organization (NGO) An organization that is independent from any government.

Non-violence The ethical position of people who eschew any use of physical violence for attaining political goals. The term also refers to strategies and tactics that address injustice and instigate change without resorting to the use of violence.

Non-zero-sum game A situation in which the gains of one

party do not necessarily result in losses by other parties. Information is non-zero-sum because it can be shared without anyone losing something. A non-zero-sum game results in variable payoff combinations: joint gains, joint losses, or mixed outcomes.

Observation mission A peace mission where a third party is responsible for the verification of a ceasefire or peace agreement.

Ontology The study of what it means to be or exist.

Pacifism The deontological position that sees the use of deadly force as being wrong in any circumstance.

Palaver A mode of consultation and conflict resolution favoured by traditional communities in Africa and elsewhere that encourages wide participation and ongoing discussion until some compromise can be found.

Paradigm A broad way of perceiving reality and determining what is true.

Payoff In game theory, the results of the decisions made by players. The payoff may be a positive or a negative sum.

Peacebuilding The creation and strengthening of peaceful processes and institutions to avoid a relapse into armed conflict.

Peace dividend The gains from the conversion of military know-how and expenditures into civilian projects.

Peace enforcement Term used to qualify peace missions that are deployed under Chapter VII of the UN Charter.

Peacekeeping A peace mission in which the third party physically separates the combatants and verifies the ceasefire or peace agreement between them.

Perlocutionary The impact and effects of a speech act on the hearer.

Plenipotentiary A person who officially represents a government and has signing authority on behalf of that government.

Pluralism 1) A perspective that the views and values of a variety of cultures are equally respected. 2) The approach that stresses rivalries among groups and institutions in the explanation of conflict in modern liberal democracies.

Politicide The deliberate massive elimination of people based on their class position and/or political affiliation.

Polyarchy The plurality of important groups that influence public policy in liberal democracies, collectively or in coalitions.

Positive law The conception that all law originates with human beings.

Positive peace The view of peace as a process of human emancipation and flourishing.

Post-traumatic stress disorder (PTSD) The long-term debilitating emotional and psychological effects suffered by those involved in severe or violent conflict.

Power According to Dahl, the ability of Party A to persuade Party B to do something that he or she would not otherwise do.

Prisoners' Dilemma (PD) The most famous decision game, in which players must determine whether it is more profitable to co-operate or to defect in their blind interaction with each other.

Protocol The rules of precedence and proper behaviour that govern diplomacy and, by extension, any negotiation.

Public goods Things that are of value to everyone but that do not need everyone's co-operation to be produced.

Rational choice theory A general term for approaches that stress the study of conscious decisions in attaining some objectives.

Realism The theory that the main cause of conflict is people's rivalry for power.

Reconciliation The transformative and constructive approaches enabling people to cope with the profound negative emotions associated with deep-rooted conflict and to form the basis for a lasting peace.

Reflexivity The disposition to study the impact of social forces and theoretical insights on oneself and to consider personal change in order to adapt to and influence the social situation.

Relative deprivation The disappointing comparison of one's situation with a more desirable state of affairs, particularly as perceived to be the position enjoyed by others.

Religious law Law derived from a religious tradition. Some religious laws apply only to religious matters, while others apply to all social relations.

Rent-seekers People who try to live and prosper out of revenues emanating from an activity in which they are monopolistic.

Resource curse hypothesis A phenomenon studied by economists whereby countries well endowed with natural resources tend to have less growth, democracy, and peace.

Restorative justice A paradigm of justice that emphasizes addressing the harm done to victims and communities and what offenders can do to repair the damage, become better people, and restore (if positive before the conflict) or develop better relationships with victims and communities.

Retributive justice A type of justice aimed at restoring balance to an unjust situation by having perpetrators suffer in proportion to the harm that they have caused.

Rights In the natural law tradition, entitlements that come with being born human; in the legal positivist tradition they are acquired through decisions of governments.

Ripe A term used to describe a situation where a conflict resolution process can be implemented and has a fair chance to succeed.

Rule of law The situation where the law is applied justly and equally to all citizens.

Sanctions Punitive measures, such as economic restrictions, decided by a state or group of states against other states. Under Chapter VII of the UN Charter, sanctions can be authorized by the Security Council to protect international peace and security.

Scapegoating The collective action of a community against a person or group deemed responsible for the community's problems, resulting in the banishment or death of the scapegoat and the restoration of harmony and unity within the community.

Secularization The abandonment of religious norms and institutions as dominant guides to social behaviour.

Security The sentiment of freedom from threats of violence and scarcity.

Security dilemma The tension between the temptation to arm oneself against potential adversaries and the prospect that this arming will result in an aggravation of conflict.

Sense of justice The feeling that fairness, rightness, and balance have been attained in the wake of conflict and that the resolution process has been fair.

Social class Group of people sharing the same relationship to the means of production. For instance, the working class does not own the means of production but works for a salary paid by those who do.

Social justice A conception of justice that stresses economic and human rights equality.

Sovereignty The capacity of the state to manage its own affairs without foreign interference.

Spoilers Persons or groups that calculate that they have no interest in a peace process and therefore try to sabotage it.

State The political institution that monopolizes the use of legitimate force over a population living in a territory and has sovereignty in relation to other states or institutions.

Structural violence A situation in which a party is harmed by injustice, even without the open use of force.

Structuration theory An approach elaborated by Giddens that reconciles the role of human agents and social structures in the explanation of social behaviour.

Structure Any large-scale social pattern or institution that influences the behaviour of individuals.

Teleology The aspect of ethics that stresses the moral side of an action's intentions.

Thomas–Kilmann Conflict Mode Instrument A psychological questionnaire used to plot a person's style of engaging in conflict based on the degree to which they try to achieve certain goals or maintain relationships.

Transnational conflicts Conflicts involving organized groups located in different countries.

Trauma A physically and/or psychologically painful and lasting wound or shock.

Unequal exchange A situation in which some countries export low-value items in return for high-value goods, losing money in the process.

Values What one believes should be upheld in society so that people can have happier and more meaningful lives. Justice, equality, liberty, order, religious belief, honour, and tradition are values.

Violence The imposition of harm onto oneself or others. Violence can be verbal, behavioural, physical, structural, or symbolic.

Virtue ethics An approach that stresses the character of the ethical person based on virtues (such as kindness, courage, honour, etc.), which are seen as positive qualities.

Welfare state A state that offers a wide social safety net to the population.

Win–win solution A solution to a dispute or conflict that fulfills the interests of both parties.

Zero-sum game A game in which the sum total of the payoffs for all players is zero. In other words, the gains of some players are always matched by the losses of the others.

REFERENCES

Adams, R. (2000). Loving mimesis and Girard's scapegoat of the text: A creative reassessment of mimetic desire. In W. Swartley (Ed.), *Violence renounced: René Girard, biblical studies, and peacemaking* (pp. 277–307). Telford, PA: Pandora.

Adelman, D.A. (2007). *A shattered peace: Versailles 1919 and the price we pay today.* New York, NY: Wiley.

Adorno, T.W., Frenkel-Brunswik, E., Levinson, D.J., & Nevitt Sanford, R. (1950). *The authoritarian personality: Studies in prejudice series* (Vol. 1). New York, NY: Harper & Row.

Aertsen, I., Arsovska, J., Rohne, H.-C., Valiñas, M., & Vanspauwen, K. (Eds.). (2008). *Restoring justice after large-scale violent conflicts: Kosovo, DR Congo, and the Israeli–Palestinian case.* Cullompton, England: Willan.

Allan, P. (2006). Measuring international ethics: A moral scale of war, peace, justice, and global care. In P. Allan & A. Keller (Eds.), *What is a just peace?* (pp. 90–129). New York, NY: Oxford University Press.

Allan, P., & Keller, A. (Eds.). (2006a). *What is a just peace?* New York, NY: Oxford University Press.

Allan, P., & Keller, A. (Eds.). (2006b). The concept of a just peace, or achieving peace through recognition, renouncement, and rule. In P. Allan & A. Keller (Eds.), *What is a just peace?* New York, NY: Oxford University Press.

Allison, G. (2005). *Nuclear terrorism: The ultimate preventable catastrophe.* New York, NY: Holt.

Allison, G.T. (1969). Conceptual models and the Cuban missile crisis. *American Political Science Review, 63*(3), 689–718.

Allison, G.T. (1971). *Essence of decision: Explaining the Cuban missile crisis.* Boston, MA: Little, Brown.

Allport, G. (1954/1979). *The nature of prejudice* (25th ed.). Cambridge, MA: Perseus.

Almond, G.A., & Powell, G. B. (1966). *Comparative politics: A developmental approach.* Boston, MA: Little, Brown.

Alternatives Non-Violentes. (2002). 100 dates de la non-violence au XXe siècle. Verseilles, France: Alternatives Non-Violentes.

Althusser, L. (2001). *Lenin and philosophy and other essays.* New York, NY: Monthly Review Press.

Anderson, B. (2006). *Imagined communities: Reflections on the origins and spread of nationalism* (2nd ed.). London, England: Verso.

Anderson, M.S. (1993). *The rise of modern diplomacy 1450–1919.* London, England: Longman.

Appleby, R.S. (2000). *The ambivalence of the sacred: Religion, violence, and reconciliation.* Lanham, MD: Rowan & Littlefield.

Appleby, R.S. (2001). Religion as an agent of conflict resolution and peacebuilding. In C. Crocker, F. Hampson, & P. Aall (Eds.), *Turbulent peace: The challenges of managing international conflict* (pp. 821–840). Washington, DC: United States Institute of Peace.

Appleby, R.S., & Cizik, R. (Eds.). (2010). *Engaging religious communities abroad: A new imperative for US foreign policy: Report of the task force on religion and the making of US foreign policy.* Chicago, IL: The Chicago Council on Global Affairs.

Apter, D.E. (1966). *The politics of modernization.* Chicago, IL: Chicago University Press.

Arbuckle, J. (2006). *Military forces in the twenty-first century peace operation: No job for a soldier?* New York, NY: Routledge.

Arnson, C., & Zartman, I. W. (Eds.). (2005). *Rethinking the economics of war: The intersection of need, creed, and greed.* Baltimore, MD: Johns Hopkins University Press.

Aron, R. (2003). *Peace and war: A theory of international relations.* New York, NY: Transaction Books.

Arrow, K.J. (1951). *Social choice and individual values.* New York, NY: Wiley.

Augsburger, D. (1981). *Caring enough to confront.* Scottdale, PA: Herald Press.

Avtgis, T.A., & Chory, R.M. (2010). The dark side of organizational life: Aggressive expression in the workplace. In T.A. Avtgis & A.S. Rancer (Eds.), *Arguments, aggression, and conflict: New directions in theory and research* (pp. 285–304). New York, NY: Routledge.

Axelrod, R.M. (1997). *The complexity of co-operation: Agent-based models of competition and collaboration.* Princeton, NJ: Princeton University Press.

Axelrod, R.M. (1984). *The evolution of co-operation.* New York, NY: Basic Books.

Axworthy, T.S. (Ed.). (2008). *Bridging the divide: Religious dialogue and universal ethics.* Montreal, Quebec: McGill-Queen's University Press.

Ayoob, M. (2001). State making, state breaking, and state failure. In H. Croker & P. Aall (Eds.), *Turbulent peace: The challenges of managing international conflict* (pp. 127–142). Washington, DC: United States Institute of Peace Press.

Babcock, L., & Laschever, S. (2003). *Women don't ask: Negotiations and the gender divide.* Princeton, NJ: Princeton University Press.

Ball, D., Milner, A., & Taylor, B. (2006). Track two security dialogue in the Asia-Pacific: Reflections and future directions. *Asian Security, 2*(3), 174–188.

Bandura, A. (1973). *Aggression: A social learning analysis.* New York, NY: Prentice-Hall.

Bandura, A. (1976). *Social learning theory.* New York, NY: Prentice-Hall.

Bannon, I., & Collier, P. (Eds.). (2003). *Natural resources and violent conflict: Options and actions.* Washington, DC: World Bank.

Bar, J. S. (2010). *Realist constructivism: Rethinking international relations theory.* New York, NY: Cambridge University Press.

Barber, B. R. (1996). *Jihad vs. McWorld.* New York, NY: Ballantine Books.

Barnes, J. (Ed.). (1984). *The complete works of Aristotle* (Vol. 2). Princeton, NJ: Princeton University Press.

Barrett, J.T. (2004). *A history of alternative dispute resolution*. San Francisco, CA: Jossey-Bass.

Bar-Siman-Tov, Y. (Ed.). (2004). *From conflict resolution to reconciliation*. Cary, NC: Oxford University Press.

Barstow, A.L. (Ed.). (2000). *War's dirty secret: Rape, prostitution, and other crimes against women*. Cleveland, OH: The Pilgrim Press.

Battle, M. (1997). *Reconciliation: The ubuntu theology of Desmond Tutu*. Cleveland, OH: The Pilgrim Press.

Baum, G., & Wells, H. (Eds.). (1997). *The reconciliation of peoples: Challenge to the churches.* Maryknoll, NY: WCC Publications.

Baum, M., & Groeling, T.J. (2010). *War stories: The causes and consequences of public views of war*. Princeton, NJ: Princeton University Press.

Beauregard, M., & O'Leary, D. (2007). *The spiritual brain*. New York, NY: HarperCollins.

Beck, D., & Cowan, C. (1996). *Spiral dynamics: Mastering values, leadership, and change*. Cambridge, MA: Blackwell.

Beck, U. (2006). *Power in the global age: A new global political economy*. Malden, MA: Polity Press.

Bell, C. (2008). *On the law of peace: Peace agreements and the lex pacificatoria*. Oxford, England: Oxford University Press.

Bellamy, A.J. (2009). *Responsibility to protect: The global effort to end global atrocities*. Cambridge, England: Polity Press.

Benjamin, R. (2004). The mediator prepares: The practice of theory. In J. Haynes, G. Haynes, & L. Fong (Eds.), *Mediation: Positive conflict management*. Albany, NY: State University of New York Press.

Bercovitch, J. (1992). The structure and diversity of mediation in international relations. In J. Bercovitch & J. Rubin (Eds.), *Mediation in international relations: Multiple approaches to conflict management*. New York, NY: St. Martin's Press.

Berdal, M. (2009). *Building peace after war*. London, England: Routledge/IISS.

Berg, J., Dickhaut, J., & McCabe, K. (1995). Trust, reciprocity, and social history. *Games and Economic Behaviour, 10,*122–142.

Berg, M., & Schaefer, B. (Eds.). (2009). *Historical justice in international perspective: How societies are trying to right the wrongs of the past*. Cambridge, England: Cambridge University Press.

Berridge, G.R. (2005). *Diplomacy: Theory and practice* (3rd ed.). New York, NY: Palgrave Macmillan.

Bettati, M., & Kouchner, B. (1987). *Le devoir d'ingérence*. Paris, France: Denoël.

Blake, R.R., & Mouton, J.S. (1964). *The managerial grid: The key to leadership excellence*. Houston, TX: Gulf.

Bloom, H. (1997). *The Lucifer principle: A scientific expedition into the forces of history*. London, England: Atlantic Books.

Bloomfield, D., Barnes, T., & Huyse, L. (Eds.). (2003). *Reconciliation after violent conflict: A handbook*. Stockholm, Sweden: International IDEA.

Boas, F. (1928/1987). *Anthropology and modern life*. New York, NY: Dover.

Boesche, R. (2002). *The first great political realist: Kautilya and his Arthashastra*. Lanham, MD: Lexington Books.

Bohm, D. (1996). *On dialogue*. London, England: Routledge.

Booth, W. (2002). Introduction: The rhetoric of war and reconciliation. In A. Benson & K.M. Poremski (Eds.), *Roads to reconciliation* (pp. 3–13). Armonk, NY: M. E. Sharpe.

Borofsky, R. (with Albert, B., Hames, R., Hill, K., Martins, L.L., Peters, J., & Turner, T.) (Eds.). (2005). *Yanomami: The fierce controversy and what we can learn from it*. Berkeley, CA: University of California Press.

Borradori, G. (Ed.). (2004). *Philosophy in a time of terror: Dialogues with Jürgen Habermas and Jacques Derrida*. Chicago, IL: Chicago University Press.

Bottomore, T. (2003). *The Frankfurt School and its critics*. London, England: Routledge.

Bouchard, G., & Taylor, C. (2008). *Building the future: A time for reconciliation*. Quebec City, Quebec: Government of Quebec.

Boudon, R. (1981). *The logic of social action*. London, England: Routledge & Kegan Paul.

Boudon, R. (2001). *The origin of values: Essays in the sociology and philosophy of belief*. New Brunswick, NJ: Transaction Books.

Bouissac, P. (2003). Information, imitation, communication: An evolutionary perspective on the semiotics of gestures. In M. Rector, I. Poggi, & N. Trig (Eds.), *Gestures, meaning, and use*. Porto, Portugal: Universidade Fernando Pessoa.

Boulding, E. (2000). *Cultures of peace: The hidden side of history*. Syracuse, NY: Syracuse University Press.

Boulding, K. (1978). *Stable peace*. Austin, TX: University of Texas Press.

Bourdieu, P. (2005). *The social structures of the economy*. Cambridge, England: Polity Press.

Boutros-Ghali, B. (1995). *An agenda for peace: Preventive diplomacy, peacemaking, and peacekeeping* (2nd ed.). New York, NY: United Nations.

Bowker, J. (Ed.). (2008). *Conflict and reconciliation: The contribution of religions*. Toronto, Ontario: The Key.

Box, S. (1983). *Power, crime, and mystification*. New York, NY: Tavistock.

Brems, E. (2001). *Human rights: Universality and diversity*. Boston, MA: Martinus Nijhoff.

Brewer, N., Mitchell, P., & Weber, N. (2002). Gender roles, organizational status, and conflict management styles. *The International Journal of Conflict Management, 13*(1), 78–94.

Brock, P. (1998). *Varieties of pacifism: A survey from antiquity to the outset of the twentieth century*. Toronto, Ontario: University of Toronto Press.

Brock, P. (2006). *Against the draft: Essays on conscientious objection from the radical Reformation to the Second World War*. Toronto, Ontario: University of Toronto Press.

Brodie, B. (Ed.). (1946). *The absolute weapon: Atomic power and world order*. New York, NY: Harcourt.

Brown, M.E. (Ed.). (1996). *The international dimensions of internal conflict*. Cambridge, MA: MIT Press.

Brown, M.E. (2001). Ethnic and internal conflicts. In C. Crocker, F. Hampson, & P. Aall (Eds.), *Turbulent peace: The challenges of managing international conflict* (pp. 209–226). Washington, DC: United States Institute of Peace.

Brown, M.E., Coté, O.R., Jr, Lynn-Jones, S. M., & Miller, S.E. (Eds.). (2010). *Going nuclear: Nuclear proliferation and international security in the twenty-first century*. Cambridge, MA: MIT Press.

Bull, H. (2002). *The anarchical society*. New York, NY: Columbia University Press.

Burns, R.D. (2009). *The evolution of arms control: From antiquity to the nuclear age*. New York, NY: Praeger.

Burton, J.W. (1987). *Resolving deep-rooted conflict: A handbook*. Lanham, MD: University Press of America.

Burton, J.W. (1990a). *Conflict resolution and provention*. New York, NY: St. Martin's Press.

Burton, J.W. (Ed.). (1990b). *Conflict: Human needs theory*. New York, NY: St. Martin's Press.

Burton, J.W. (1993). *Conflict: Human needs theory*. London, England: Palgrave Macmillan.

Burton, J.W. (1996). *Conflict resolution: Its language and process*. London, England: Scarecrow Press.

Burton, J.W. (2010). *Systems, states, diplomacy, and rules*. New York, NY: Cambridge University Press.

Burton, J.W., & Dukes, F. (1990). *Conflict: Readings in management and resolution*. London, England: Macmillan.

Busch, N.E., & Joyner, D.H. (2009). *Combating weapons of mass destruction: The future of international non-proliferation policy*. Atlanta, GA: University of Georgia Press.

Bush, K. (2004). The commodification, compartmentalization, and militarization of peacebuilding. In T. Keating & W.A. Knight (Eds.), *Building sustainable peace* (pp. 23–46). Edmonton, Alberta: University of Alberta Press & UN University Press.

Bush, R.A.B., & Folger, J.P. (1994). *The promise of mediation: Responding to conflict through empowerment and recognition*. San Francisco, CA: Jossey-Bass.

Calhoun, P.S., & Smith, W.P. (1999). Integrative bargaining: Does gender make a difference? *International Journal of Conflict Management, 10*(3), 203–224.

Caputo, J. (Ed.). (1996). *Deconstruction in a nutshell: A conversation with Jacques Derrida*. New York, NY: Fordham University Press.

Cardoso, E., & Faletto, E. (1979). *Dependency and development in Latin America*. Berkeley, CA: University of California Press.

Cavey, V. (2000). Fighting among friends: The Quaker separation of 1827. In P. Coy & L. Woehrle (Eds.), *Social conflicts and collective identities* (pp. 133–147). Lanham, MD: Rowman & Littlefield.

Cetto, A.M., & de la Peña, L. (2005). Einstein, peace, and non-proliferation: A Latin American perspective. In R. Braun & D. Krieger (Eds.), *Einstein—peace now!: Visions and ideas*. Weinheim, Germany: Wiley-VCH.

Chagnon, N. (1983). *Yanomamö: The fierce people* (3rd ed.). New York, NY: Holt, Rinehart, & Winston.

Chan, S. (1995). Grasping the peace dividend: Some propositions on the conversion of swords into plowshares. *Mershon International Studies, 39* (1), 53–95.

Channer, A. (Producer/Director). (2006). *The imam and the pastor* [Motion picture]. United Kingdom: FLTfilms.

Chanteur, J. (1992). *From war to peace* (S.A. Weizs, Trans.). Boulder, CO: Westview.

Chapman, A.R. (2001). Truth commissions as instruments of forgiveness and reconciliation. In R.L. Petersen & R.G. Helmick (Eds.), *Forgiveness and reconciliation: Religion, public policy, and conflict transformation*. Philadelphia, PA: Templeton Foundation Press.

Chataway, C.J. (1998). Track two diplomacy: From a track one perspective. *Negotiation Journal, 14*(3), 269–287.

Cheema, S.G. (2005). *Building democratic institutions: Governance reform in developing countries*. Bloomfield, CT: Kumarian Press.

Cherif, M. (2008). *Islam and the West: A conversation with Jacques Derrida*. Chicago, IL: Chicago University Press.

Chomsky, N. (2003). *Hegemony or survival: America's quest for global dominance*. New York, NY: Metropolitan Books.

Chomsky, N. (2007). *Failed states: The abuse of power and the assault on democracy*. New York, NY: Holt.

Chomsky, N., & Otero, C. Peregrín. (2003). *Chomsky on democracy & education*. New York, NY: Routledge Falmer.

Christopher, P. (1994). *The ethics of war and peace: An introduction to the legal and moral issues*. Upper Saddle River, NJ: Prentice-Hall.

Church, R. (1959). Emotional reactions of rats to the pain of others. *Journal of Comparative & Physiological Psychology, 53*, 132–134.

Clark, M. (1990). Meaningful social bonding as a universal human need. In J. Burton (Ed.), *Conflict: human needs theory* (pp. 34–59). New York, NY: St. Martin's Press.

Clastres, P. (2000). *Chronicle of the Guayaki Indians* (P. Auster, Trans.). New York, NY: Zone Books.

Clement, G. (1996). *Care, autonomy, and justice: Feminism and the ethics of care*. Boulder, CO: Westview.

Cliff, J., Langdon, C., & Aldrich, H. (2005). Walking the talk? Gender rhetoric versus action in small firms. *Organization Studies, 26*(1), 63–91.

Club of Rome. (1972). *The limits to growth*. New York, NY: Universe Books.

Coates, A. (2006). Culture, the enemy, and the moral restraint of war. In R. Sorabji & D. Rodin (Eds.), *The ethics of war: Shared problems in different traditions*. Aldershot, England: Ashgate.

Coleman, K.P. (2007). *International organizations and peace enforcement: The politics of international legitimacy*. New York, NY: Cambridge University Press.

Collier, P. (2000). Doing well out of war: An economic perspective. In M. Berdal & D. Malone (Eds.), *Greed and grievance: Economic agendas in civil wars*. Boulder, CO: Lynne Rienner.

Collier, P. (2009). *Wars, guns, and votes: Democracy in dangerous places*. New York, NY: Harper.

Collier, P., Elliott, V.L., Hegre, H., Hoeffler, A., Reynal-Querol,

M., & Sambanis, N. (2003). *Breaking the conflict trap: Civil war and development policy.* New York, NY: Oxford University Press.

Collier, P., & Hoeffler, A. (2005). Resources, rents, governance, and conflict. *Journal of Conflict Resolution, 49*(4), 625–633.

Connor, W. (1994). *Ethnonationalism: The quest for understanding.* Princeton, NJ: Princeton University Press.

Cook, S. (1903). *The laws of Moses and the code of Hammurabi.* London, England: Adam & Charles Black.

Cooperrider, D.L., & Whitney, D. (n.d.). *A positive revolution in change: Appreciative inquiry.* Retrieved from http://appreciativeinquiry.case.edu/intro/whatisai.cfm

Corera, G. (2006). *Shopping for bombs: Nuclear proliferation, global insecurity, and the rise and fall of the A.Q. Khan network.* New York, NY: Oxford University Press.

Cortright, D. (2002). *Sanctions and the search for security: Challenges to UN action.* Boulder, CO: Lynne Rienner.

Coser, L. (1964). *The functions of social conflict.* New York, NY: The Free Press.

Cramer, C. (2002). Homo economicus goes to war: Methodological individualism, rational choice, and the political economy of war. *World Development, 30*(11), 1845–1864.

Crocker, C.A., Hampson, F.O., & Aall, P. (Eds.). (1999). *Herding cats: Multi-party mediation in a complex world.* Washington, DC: United States Institute of Peace Press.

Croxton, D. (1999). The peace of Westphalia of 1648 and the origins of sovereignty. *The International History Review, 21*(3), 596–591.

Dahl, R. (1957). The concept of power. *Behavioral Science, 2,* 201–215.

Dahl, R. (1972). *Polyarchy: Participation and opposition.* New Haven, CT: Yale University Press.

Dahrendorf, R. (1959). *Class and class conflict in an industrial society.* London, England: Routledge & Kegan Paul.

Dallaire, R. (2003). *Shake hands with the devil: The failure of humanity in Rwanda.* New York, NY: Random House.

Daly, E., & Sarkin, J. (2007). *Reconciliation in divided societies: Finding common ground.* Philadelphia, PA: University of Pennsylvania Press.

Daly, M., & Wilson, M. (1988). *Homicide.* Hawthorne, NY: Aldine de Gruyter.

Daly, M., & Wilson, M. (1998). *The truth about Cinderella.* New Haven, CT: Yale University Press.

Darwin, C. (1859/2008). *The Origin of Species.* New York, NY: Simon & Schuster.

Davies, J.C. (1962). Toward a theory of revolution. *American Sociological Review, 27,* 5–19.

Davis, M.D. (1997). *Game theory: A non-technical introduction.* New York, NY: Dover.

Dawkins, R. (1976). *The selfish gene.* Oxford, England: Oxford University Press.

De Bono, E. (1992). *Serious creativity: Using the power of lateral thinking to create new ideas.* New York, NY: HarperCollins.

De Gruchy, J. (2002). *Reconciliation: Restoring justice.* Minneapolis, MN: Fortress Press.

De Waal, F. (1989). *Peacemaking among primates.* Cambridge, MA: Harvard University Press.

De Waal, F. (2009). *The age of empathy: Nature's lessons for a kinder society.* New York, NY: Three Rivers.

Derrida, J. (2001). *On cosmopolitanism and forgiveness: Thinking in action.* London, England: Routledge.

Descombes, V. (1980). *Modern French philosophy.* Cambridge, England: Cambridge University Press.

Deutsch, K. (1966). *Nationalism and social communication: An inquiry into the foundations of nationality.* Cambridge, MA: MIT Press.

Deutsch, K. (1988). *The analysis of international relations* (3rd ed.). New York, NY: Prentice-Hall.

Deutsch, M. (1960). The effect of motivational orientation upon trust and suspicion. *Human Relations, 13,* 123–139.

Deutsch, M. (1973). *The resolution of conflict.* New Haven, CT: Yale University Press.

Deutsch, M., & Evans Collins, M. (1951). *Interracial housing: A psychological evaluation of a social experiment.* Minneapolis, MN: University of Minnesota.

Diamant, N. (2000). Conflict and conflict resolution in China: Beyond mediation-centered approaches. *Journal of Conflict Resolution, 44*(4), 523–546.

Diamond, J. (1997). *Guns, germs, and steel.* New York, NY: W.W. Norton.

Diamond, J. (2005). *Collapse: How societies choose to fail or succeed.* New York, NY: Viking Books.

Diamond, L. (2009). *The spirit of democracy: The struggle to build free societies throughout the world.* New York, NY: Holt.

Diamond, L., & McDonald, J.W. (1996). *Multi-track diplomacy: A systems approach to peace.* Sterling, VA: Kumarian Press.

Diamond, L., & Morlino, L. (2005). *Assessing the quality of democracy.* Baltimore, MD: Johns Hopkins University Press.

Dollard, J., Miller, N.E., Doob, L.W., Mowrer, O.H., & Sears, R.R. (with Ford, C.S., Hovland, C.I., & Sollenberger, R.T.). (1939). *Frustration and aggression.* London, England: H. Milford, Oxford University Press.

Donnelly, J. (2002). *Universal human rights in theory and practice* (2nd ed.). New York, NY: Cornell University Press.

Doob, L.W. (1970). *Conflict resolution in Africa: Fermeda workshop.* New Haven, CT: Yale University Press.

Dougherty, J.E., & Pfaltzgraff, R.L. (2000). *Contending theories of international relations: A comprehensive survey* (5th ed.). New York, NY: Longman.

Downs, A. (1957). *An economic theory of democracy.* New York, NY: Harper.

Doyle, M.W. (1983a). Kant, liberal legacies, and foreign affairs (Pt. 1). *Philosophy and Public Affairs, 12*(3), 205–235.

Doyle, M.W. (1983b). Kant, liberal legacies, and foreign affairs (Pt. 2). *Philosophy and Public Affairs, 12* (4), 323–353.

Doyle, M.W. (1995). UN peacekeeping in Cambodia: UNTAC's civil mandate. Boulder, CO: Lynne Rienner.

Doyle, M.W., & Sambanis, N. (2006). *Making war and building peace.* Princeton, NJ: Princeton University Press.

Du Bois, F., & Du Bois-Pedain, A. (2008). Post-conflict justice and the reconciliation paradigm. In F. Du Bois & A. Du Bois-Pedain (Eds.), *Justice and reconciliation in post-apartheid South Africa* (pp. 289–311). Cambridge, NY: Cambridge University Press.

Dunbar, R., Barrett, L., & Lycett, J. (2007). *Evolutionary psychology: A beginner's guide*. Oxford, England: Oneworld.

Dunn, D. (2005). *The first fifty years of peace research: A survey and interpretation*. Aldershot, England: Ashgate.

Dupont, C. (2003). History and coalitions: The Vienna congress (1814–1815). *International Negotiation, 8,* 169–178.

Durkheim, É. (1972). *Selected writings*. Cambridge, England: Cambridge University Press.

Dworkin, A. (1981). *Pornography: Men possessing women*. London, England: The Women's Press.

Dyson, F. (1984). *Weapons and hope*. New York, NY: Harper & Row.

Eagleton, T. (2005). *Holy terror*. New York, NY: Oxford University Press.

Easton, D. (1965). *A framework for political analysis*. Englewood Cliffs, NJ: Prentice-Hall.

Eisenstadt, S. N. (1966). *Modernization, protest, and change*. Englewood Cliffs, NJ: Prentice-Hall.

El-Ansary, W. (2010). Economics and the clash of civilizations: Re-examining religion and violence. In Q.-U. Huda (Ed.), *Crescent and dove: Peace and conflict resolution in Islam* (pp. 107–126). Washington, DC: United States Institute of Peace.

Elias, N. (1940/2000). *The civilizing process*. Oxford, England: Blackwell.

Emmanuel, A. (1976). *Unequal exchange: Study of the imperialism of trade*. New York, NY: New Left Books.

Enloe, C. (2000). *Bananas, beaches, and bases*. Berkeley, CA: University of California Press.

Epp, E. (1982). Law breaking and peacemaking. *Canadian Quaker Pamphlet, 15,* 1–32.

Epstein, B. (1993). *Political protest and cultural revolution: Nonviolent direct action in the 1970s and 1980s*. Berkeley, CA: University of California Press.

Erlich, P. (1968). *The population bomb*. New York, NY: Ballantine.

Eslami-Somea, R. (2010). Human rights and Islamic reform. In Q.-U. Huda (Ed.), *Crescent and dove: Peace and conflict resolution in Islam* (pp. 127–150). Washington, DC: United States Institute of Peace.

Esman, M.J. (1994). *Ethnic politics*. Ithaca, NY: Cornell University Press.

Esposito, J.L. (2003). *Unholy war: Terror in the name of Islam*. New York, NY: Oxford University Press.

Eysenk, H.J. (1997). *Dimensions of personality*. Piscataway, NJ: Transaction Books.

Faludi, S. (1991). *Backlash! The undeclared war against American women*. New York, NY: Crown.

Farquharson, J.E. (1997). Anglo-American policy on German reparations from Yalta to Potsdam. *English Historical Review, 112*(448), 904–926.

Farrell, W. (1993). *The myth of male power*. New York, NY: Simon & Schuster.

Fehr, E., Bernhard, H., and Rockenbach, B. (2008 August 28). Egalitarianism in young children. *Nature, 454,* 1079–1083.

Feierabend, I.K., & Feierabend, R.L. (1966). Aggressive behaviour within polities 1948–1962. *Journal of Conflict Resolution, 10*(2), 249–271.

Ferrer, J.N. (2002). *Revisioning transpersonal theory: A participatory vision of human spirituality*. Albany, NY: State University of New York Press.

Fisher, R. (1990). Needs theory, social identity and an eclectic model of conflict. In J. Burton (Ed.), *Conflict: Human needs theory* (pp. 89–112). New York, NY: St. Martin's Press.

Fisher, R., & Ury, W. (1981). *Getting to yes: Negotiating agreement without giving in*. Boston, MA: Houghton Mifflin.

Fisher, R.J. (2006). Coordination between track two and track one diplomacy in successful cases of prenegotiation. *International Negotiation, 11*(1), 65–89.

Flanagan, K., & Jupp, P.C. (Eds.). (2007). *A sociology of spirituality*. Aldershot, England: Ashgate.

Flood, G. (2008). Reconciliation, peace and justice in Hinduism. In J. Bowker, *Conflict and religion: The contribution of religions*. Toronto, Ontario: The Key Publishing House.

Foerster, W. (1964/1980). The Greek concept of *eirene*. In G. Kittel (Ed.), *Theological dictionary of the New Testament* (Vol. 2) (p. 401). Grand Rapids, MI: Eerdmans.

Folger, R., Sheppard, B., and Buttram, R. (1995). Equity, equality, and need: Three faces of social justice. In B. Bunker and J. Rubin (Eds.), *Conflict, cooperation and justice: Essays inspired by the work of Morton Deutsch*. Hoboken, NJ: Wiley.

Follett, M.P. (1995). Constructive conflict. In P. Graham (Ed.), *Mary Parker Follett: Prophet of management* (pp. 67–87). Boston, MA: Harvard Business School Press.

Forbes, H.D. (2004). Ethnic conflict and the contact hypothesis. In Y.-T. Lee, C. McCauley, F. Moghaddam, & S. Worchel (Eds.), *The psychology of ethnic and cultural conflict*. Westport, CT: Praeger.

Fotion, N. (2007). *War and ethics: A new just war theory*. London, England: Continuum.

Foucault, M. (1980). *Power/knowledge: Selected interviews and other writings, 1972–1977* (C. Gordon, Ed.). New York: Vintage.

Foucault, M. (1984).*The Foucault reader* (P. Rabinow, Ed.). New York: Vintage.

Frank, A.G. (1974). *Dependent accumulation and underdevelopment*. London, England: Palgrave Macmillan.

Frank, J. (1962). Psychological problems in the elimination of war. In Q. Wright, W.M. Evan, & M. Deutsch (Eds.), *Preventing World War III: Some proposals*. New York, NY: Simon & Shuster.

Frank, R.H., Gilovich, T., & Regan, D.T. (1993). Does studying economics inhibit co-operation? *Journal of Economic Perspectives, 7,* 159–171.

Frankl, V. (1946/1984). *Man's search for meaning*. New York, NY: Simon & Shuster.

Freund, J. (1983). *Sociologie du conflit.* Paris, France: Presses universitaires de France.

Fromm, E. (1994). *Escape from freedom.* New York, NY: Holt.

Fry, D.P. (2007). *The human potential for peace.* New York, NY: Oxford University Press.

Fry, D.P., & Björkqvist, K. (Eds.). (1997). *Cultural variation in conflict resolution: Alternatives to violence.* Mahwah, NJ: Lawrence Erlbaum.

Fukuyama, F. (1992). *The end of history and the last man.* New York, NY: Avon.

Galtung, J. (1964). An editorial. *Journal of Peace Research, 1*(1), 1–4.

Galtung, J. (1969). Violence, peace, and peace research. *Journal of Peace Research, 6*(3), 167–191.

Galtung, J. (1971). A structural theory of imperialism. *Journal of Peace Research, 8*(2), 81–117.

Galtung, J. (1981). Social cosmology and the concept of peace. *Journal of Peace Research, 17*(2), 183–199.

Galtung, J. (1992). The emerging conflict formations. In K. Tehranian & M. Tehranian (Eds.), *Restructuring for world peace: On the threshold of the twenty-first century* (pp. 23–24). Cresskill: NJ, Hampton Press.

Galtung, J. (1996). *Peace by peaceful means: Peace and conflict, development and civilization.* Thousand Oaks, CA: Sage.

Galtung, J. (2009). *The fall of the US empire: And then what?* Basel, Switzerland: Transcend University Press.

Galtung, J., & Ikeda, D. (1995). *Choose peace: A dialogue between Johan Galtung and Daisaku Ikeda.* London, England: Pluto Press

Gandhi, A. (2003). *Legacy of love: My education in the path of nonviolence.* El Sobrante, CA: North Bay Books.

Ganguly, S., & Kapur, S.P. (2010). *India, Pakistan, and the bomb: Debating nuclear stability in South Asia.* New York, NY: Columbia University Press.

Ghais, S. (2005). *Extreme facilitation: Guiding groups through controversy and complexity.* San Francisco, CA: Jossey-Bass.

Gibson, J. (2004). *Overcoming apartheid: Can truth reconcile a divided nation?* New York, NY: Russell Sage Foundation.

Giddens, A. (1984). *The constitution of society: Outline of the theory of structuration.* Cambridge, England: Polity Press.

Giddens, A. (1991). *The consequences of modernity.* Stanford, CA: Stanford University Press.

Giddens, A., & Held, D. (Eds.). (1982). *Class, power, and conflict: Classical and contemporary debates.* Berkeley, CA: University of California Press.

Giles, W., & Hyndman, J. (Eds.). (2004). *Sites of violence: Gender and conflict zones.* Berkeley, CA: University of California Press.

Gill, S. (1993). *Gramsci, historical materialism, and international relations.* Cambridge, England: Cambridge University Press.

Gill, S. (2008). *Power and resistance in the New World order* (2nd ed.). London, England: Palgrave Macmillan.

Gilligan, C. (1982). *In a different voice: Psychological theory and women's development.* Cambridge, MA: Harvard University Press.

Gillwald, K. (1990). Conflict and needs research. In J. Burton (Ed.), *Conflict: Human needs theory* (pp. 115–124). New York, NY: St. Martin's Press.

Gintis, H. (2009). *Game theory evolving.* Princeton, NJ: Princeton University Press.

Girard, R. (1976). *Deceit, desire, and the novel: Self and other in literary structure* (Y. Freccero, Trans.). Baltimore, MD: Johns Hopkins University Press.

Girard, R. (1977). *Violence and the sacred* (P. Gregory, Trans.). Baltimore, MD: Johns Hopkins University Press.

Girard, R. (1978). *To double business bound: Essays on literature, mimesis, and anthropology.* Baltimore, MD: Johns Hopkins University Press.

Girard, R. (1987a). *Job: The Victim of His People.* Translated by Yvonne Freccero. Stanford: Stanford University Press.

Girard, R. (1987b). *Things hidden since the foundation of the world* (S. Bann, Trans.). Stanford, CA: Stanford University Press.

Girard, R. (1989). *The scapegoat* (Y. Freccero, Trans.). Baltimore, MD: Johns Hopkins University Press.

Girard, R. (2001). *I see Satan fall like lightning.* Maryknoll, NY/Ottawa, Ontario: Orbis/Novalis.

Girard, R. (2010). *Battling to the end: Conversations with Benoît Chantre* (M. Baker, Trans.). East Lansing, MI: Michigan University Press.

Girard, R. (2011). *Sacrifice* (Matthew Pattillo and David Dawson, Trans.). East Lansing, MI: Michigan University Press.

Girard, R. (with Wink, W. & Morrow, D.). (2006). *Dialogue on creative mimesis and peace: Colloquium on violence and religion* [DVD]. Ottawa, Ontario: Saint Paul University.

Gleditsch, N.P. (1998). Armed conflict and the environment: A critique of the literature. *Journal of Peace Research, 35*(3), 381–400.

Gleditsch, N.P., Lindgren, G., Mouhleb, N., Smit, S., & de Soysa, I. (2000). *Making peace pay: A bibliography on disarmament and conversion.* Claremont: Regina Press.

Gobineau, Arthur de (1853-55). *Essai sur l'inégalité des races humaines* (4 vols.). Paris: Didot.

Goldstein, J. (2003). *War and gender: How gender shapes the war system and vice versa.* Cambridge, England: Cambridge University Press.

Goldstein, J., & Pevehouse, J.C. (2010). *International relations* (9th ed.). New York, NY: Longman.

Goleman, D. (1997). *Emotional intelligence.* New York, NY: Bantam Books.

Goleman, D. (2003). *Destructive emotions: A scientific dialogue with the Dalai Lama.* New York, NY: Bantam Books.

González, L., & Viitanen, T.K. (2009). The effect of divorce laws on divorce rates in Europe. *European Economic Review, 53*(2), 127–138.

Goodhart, S. (2009). "A land that devours its inhabitants": Midrashic reading, Levinas, and literary medieval exegesis. In A. Astell & J.A. Jackson (Eds.), *Levinas and medieval literature: The "difficult reading" of English and Rabbinic texts* (pp. 227–253). Pittsburgh, PA: Duquesne University Press.

Gospic, K., Mohlin, E., Fransson, P., Petrovic, P., Johannesson, M., & Ingvar, M. (2011 May 3). Limbic justice—amygdala involvement in immediate rejection in the Ultimatum Game. *PLoS Biol, 9*(5).

Goucha, M., & Crowley, J. (2008). *Rethinking human security.* Paris, France: Wiley-Blackwell & UNESCO.

Gould, S. J. (1978). Sociobiology: The art of storytelling. *New Scientist, 80,* 530–533.

Gramsci, A. (1971). *Selections from the prison notebooks.* New York, NY: International.

Grayzel, S. (2002). *Women and the First World War.* New York, NY: Longman.

Grimsrud, T. (1999). Healing justice: The prophet Amos and a "new" theology of justice. In T. Grimsrud & L. Johns (Eds.), *Peace and justice shall embrace: Power and theopolitics in the Bible.* Telford, PA: Pandora Press.

Grossman, D. (1995). *On killing: The psychological cost of learning to kill in war and society.* New York, NY: Little, Brown.

Gurr, T.R. (1971). *Why men rebel.* Princeton, NJ: Princeton University Press.

Gurr, T.R. (2000). *Peoples versus states: Minorities at risk in the new century.* Washington, DC: United States Institute of Peace.

Haas, E.B. (1964). *Beyond the nation state.* Stanford, CA: Stanford University Press.

Habermas, J. (1984). *The theory of communicative action* (Vols. 1–2) (T. McCarthy, Trans.). Cambridge, England: Polity Press.

Habermas, J. (1990). *The philosophical discourse of modernity.* Cambridge, MA: MIT Press.

Habermas, J. (1996). *Between facts and norms: Contributions to a discourse theory of law and democracy* (W. Rehg, Trans.). Cambridge, MA: MIT Press.

Habermas, J. (2009). *Europe: The faltering project.* Cambridge, England: Polity Press.

Hamber, B. (2007). Forgiveness and reconciliation: Paradise lost or pragmatism? *Peace and Conflict: Journal of Peace Psychology, 13*(1), 115–125.

Hamber, B., & Kelly, G. (2009). Beyond coexistence. In J. Quinn (Ed.), *Reconciliation(s): Transitional justice in post-conflict societies.* Montreal, Quebec: McGill-Queen's University Press.

Hammerich, B., Pfäfflin, J., Pogany-Wnend, P., Siebert, E., & Sonntag, B. (2009). Handing down the Holocaust in Germany: A reflection on the dialogue between second-generation descendants of perpetrators and survivors. In P. Gobod-Madikizela & C. van der Merwe (Eds.), *Memory, narrative, and forgiveness: Perspectives on the unfinished journeys of the past* (pp. 27–46). Newcastle upon Tyne, England: Cambridge Scholars.

Hampson, F. (1995). *Multilateral negotiations: Lessons from arms control, trade, and the environment.* Baltimore, MD: Johns Hopkins University Press.

Hanh, T.N. (1987). *Being peace.* Berkeley, CA: Parallax Press.

Hanh, T.N. (2003). *Joyfully together: The art of building a harmonious community.* Berkeley, CA: Parallax Press.

Hardin, G. (1968). The tragedy of the commons. *Science, 162,* 1243–1248.

Harff, B. (2003). No lessons learned from the Holocaust? Assessing the risks of genocide and political mass murder since 1955. *American Political Science Review, 97,* 57–73.

Harper, C. (2005). *Spiritual information: One hundred perspectives on science and religion.* Philadelphia, PA: Templeton.

Hauser, M.D. (2006). *Moral minds: How nature designed our universal sense of right and wrong.* San Francisco, CA: Ecco/Harper-Collins.

Hayes, P. (1992). *The people and the mob: The ideology of civil conflict in modern Europe.* Westport, CT: Praeger.

Hayner, P. B. (1994). Fifteen truth commissions—1974 to 1994: A comparative study. *Human Rights Quarterly, 16*(4), 597–655.

Held, V. (2006). *The ethics of care: Personal, political, global.* New York, NY: Oxford University Press.

Herman, J. L. (1997). *Trauma and recovery* (Rev. ed.). New York, NY: Basic Books.

Hertog, K. (2010). *The complex reality of religious peacebuilding: Conceptual contributions and critical analysis.* Lanham, MD: Lexington.

Herz, J.H. (1951). *Political realism and political idealism.* Chicago, IL: Chicago University Press.

Hinsley, F.H. (1963). *Power and the pursuit of peace: Theory and practice in the history of relations between states.* Cambridge, England: Cambridge University Press.

Hitchens, C. (2007). *God is not great: How religion poisons everything.* New York, NY: Hachette.

Hobbes, T. (1651/2008). *Leviathan.* Oxford, England: Oxford University Press.

Hobsbawn, E.J., & Ranger, T. (Eds.). (1983). *The invention of tradition.* Cambridge, England: Cambridge University Press.

Hoffman, A. (2006). *Building trust: Overcoming suspicion in international conflicts.* Albany, NY: State University of New York Press.

Hogan, M.J. (1987). *The Marshall Plan: America, Britain, and the reconstruction of Western Europe, 1947–1952.* New York, NY: Cambridge University Press.

Holoway, A. (2008, April). Overcoming conflict avoidance: Keys to improving your relationships. *Suite101.* Retrieved from http://www.suite101.com/content/overcoming-conflict-avoidance a52146

Holsti, K.J. (1991). *Peace and war: Armed conflict and international order, 1648–1989.* Cambridge, England: Cambridge University Press.

Holsti, K.J. (1996). *The state, war, and the state of war.* Cambridge, England: Cambridge University Press.

Holt, J.L., & De Vore, C. J. (2005). Culture, gender, organizational role, and style of conflict resolution: A meta-analysis. *International Journal of Intercultural Relations, 29,* 165–196.

Holzgreff, J.L., & Keohane, R.O. (Eds.). (2003). *Humanitarian intervention: Ethical, legal, and political dilemmas.* Cambridge, England: Cambridge University Press.

Homer-Dixon, T. (1991). On the threshold: Environmental change as causes of acute conflict. *International Security, 16*(2), 76–116.

Homer-Dixon, T. (1993). Environmental scarcity and intergroup conflict. In M.T. Klare & D.T. Thomas (Eds.), *World security: Challenges for a new century* (pp. 290–313). New York, NY: St. Martin's Press.

Homer-Dixon, T. (1994). Environmental scarcities and violent conflict: Evidence from cases. *International Security, 19*(1), 5–40.

Horney, K. (1993). *Feminine psychology.* New York, NY: W.W. Norton.

Hornus, J.-M. (1980). *It is not lawful for me to fight: Early Christian attitudes toward war, violence, and the state* (A. Krider & O. Coburn, Trans.). Scottdale, PA: Herald Press.

Horowitz, D.L. (2000). *Ethnic groups in conflict* (2nd ed.). Berkeley, CA: UCLA Press.

Hovland, C.I., & Sears, R.R. (1940). Minor studies of aggression: VI. Correlation of lynchings with economic indices. *The Journal of Psychology, 9,* 301–310.

Howell, S., & Willis, R. (Eds.). (1989). *Societies at peace: Anthropological perspectives.* London, England: Routledge.

Hulsman, L. (1986). Critical criminology and the concept of crime. *Contemporary Crises: Law, Crime, and Social Policy, 10,* 63–80.

Human Security Centre. (2005). *Human security report 2005: War and peace in the twenty-first century.* New York, NY: Oxford University Press.

Human Security Centre. (2006). *Human Security Brief 2006.* Vancouver, British Columbia: Liu Institute for Global Issues, University of British Columbia.

Human Security Report Project. (2011). *Human security report 2009/2010: The causes of peace and the shrinking costs of war.* New York, NY: Oxford University Press. Retrieved from www.hsrgroup.org/human-security-reports/human-security-report.aspx

Hunt, M. (2007). *The story of psychology.* New York, NY: Anchor Books.

Huntington, S.P. (1968). *Political order in changing societies.* New Haven, CT: Yale University Press.

Huntington, S.P. (1991). *The third wave: Democratization in the late twentieth century.* Norman, OK: University of Oklahoma Press.

Huntington, S.P. (1993). The clash of civilizations. *Foreign Affairs, 72*(3), 112–149.

Huntington, S.P. (1996). *The clash of civilizations and the remaking of world order.* New York, NY: Simon & Schuster.

Husin, A. (2010). Islamic peace education: Changing hearts and minds. In Q.-U. Huda (Ed.), *Crescent and dove: Peace and conflict resolution in Islam* (pp.151–178). Washington, DC: United States Institute of Peace.

Ignatieff, M. (1995). *Blood and belonging: Journeys into the new nationalism.* New York, NY: Farrar, Straus, & Giroux.

Inglehart, R. (1990). *Culture shift in advanced industrial society.* Princeton, NJ: Princeton University Press.

Inglehart, R. (with Abramson, P. R.). (1995). *Value change in global perspective.* Ann Harbor, MI: University of Michigan Press.

Institute for Economics and Peace. (2011). Global peace index 2011: Methodology, results, and findings. Sydney, Australia: Institute for Economics and Peace. Retrieved from www.scribd.com/doc/56503708/2011-GPI-Results-Report

International Commission on Intervention and State Sovereignty. (2001). *The responsibility to protect.* Ottawa, Ontario: International Development Research Center.

International Committee of the Red Cross (ICRC). (2012). Definition of combatants. Retrieved from http://www.icrc.org/customary-ihl/eng/docs/v1_rul_rule3

Isaacs, H.R. (1975). *Idols of the tribe: Group identity and political change.* Cambridge, MA: Harvard University Press.

Ishay, M.R. (2004). *The history of human rights: From ancient times to the globalization era.* Berkeley, CA: University of California Press.

Ismael, J.S. (2007). Introduction. In J.S. Ismael & W.W. Haddad (Eds.), *Barriers to reconciliation: Case studies on Iraq and the Palestine–Israel conflict.* Lanham, MD: University Press of America.

Jacobs, J. (2005). *Dark age ahead.* Toronto, Ontario: Vintage Canada.

Jacoby, S. (1983). *Wild justice: The evolution of revenge.* New York, NY: Harper & Row.

Jaffe, J. (2000). Industrial arbitration, equity, and authority in England, 1800–1850. *Law and History Review, 18*(3), 525–558.

Janis, I.L. (1982). *Groupthink: Psychological studies of policy decisions and fiascos.* Boston, MA: Houghton Mifflin.

Jantzen, G. (2004). *Foundations of violence.* London, England: Routledge.

Jantzen, G. (2009). *Violence to eternity.* London, England: Routledge.

Jasper, J.M. (1997). *The art of moral protest: Culture, biography, and creativity in social movements.* Chicago, IL: University of Chicago Press.

Jeong, H.-W. (2010). *Conflict management and resolution: An introduction.* London, England: Routledge.

Jervis, R. (1976). *Perception and misperception in international politics.* Princeton, NJ: Princeton University Press.

Johnston, D. (1994). Looking ahead: Toward a new paradigm. In D. Johnston & C. Sampson (Eds.), *Religion: The missing dimension of statecraft.* New York, NY: Oxford University Press.

Johnston, L.M., & LeBaron, M. (2007). Conflict tactics in a mediation setting. *Peace and Conflict Review, 2*(2),1–15. Retrieved from http://www.review.upeace.org/pdf.cfm?articulo=78&ejemplar=15

Johnstone, G. (2002). *Restorative justice: Ideas, values, debates.* Cullompton, England: Willan.

Jonas, H. (1984). *The imperative of responsibility: In search of an ethics for the technological age.* Chicago, IL: University of Chicago Press.

Jones, E.K. (2007). Birthing justice: Towards a feminist liberation theo-ethical analysis of economic justice and maternal mortality (Unpublished doctoral dissertation). University of Ottawa, Ottawa, Ontario.

Jørgensen, K.E. (2010). *International relations theory: A new introduction.* London, England: Palgrave Macmillan.

Joyce, P. (2002). *The Politics of Protest: Extra-Parliamentary Politics in Britain since 1970*. Houndmills: Palgrave-Macmillan.

Juergensmeyer, M. (2003). *Terror in the mind of God: The global rise of religious violence* (3rd ed.). Irvine, CA: University of California Press.

Kagan, R. (2008). *The return of history and the end of dreams*. New York, NY: Knopf.

Kahl, C.H. (2006). *States, scarcity, and civil strife in the developing world*. Princeton, NJ: Princeton University Press.

Kahn, H. (1960). *On thermonuclear war*. Princeton, NJ: Princeton University Press.

Kaplan, M.A. (1958). The calculus of nuclear deterrence. *World Politics, 11*, 20–43.

Kauffman, S.A. (1995). *At home in the universe: The search for laws of self-organization and complexity*. New York, NY: Oxford University Press.

Kauffman, S.A. (2008). *Reinventing the sacred: A new view of science, reason, and religion*. New York, NY: Basic Books.

Keashley, L. (1994). Gender and conflict: What does psychological research tell us? In A. Taylor & J. Beinstein Miller (Eds.), *Conflict and gender* (pp. 167–190). Cresskill, NJ: Hampton Press.

Keeley, L. (1996). *War before civilization: The myth of the peaceful savage*. New York, NY: Oxford University Press.

Kegan, R.G. (1982). *The evolving self: Problem and process in human development*. Cambridge, MA: Harvard University Press.

Kegan, R.G. (1993). The evolution of moral meaning-making. In A. Dobrin (Ed.), *Being good and doing right: Readings in moral development*. Lanham, MD: University Press of America.

Kegan, R.G. (2001). Competencies as working epistemologies: Ways we want adults to know. In D.S. Rychen & L.H. Salganik (Eds.), *Defining and selecting key competencies*. Kirkland, WA: Hogrefe & Huber.

Kegley, C.W., Jr. (2009). *World politics: Trend and transformation*. Belmont, CA: Cengage.

Keller, A. (2006). Justice, peace, and history: A reappraisal. In P. Allan & A. Keller (Eds.), *What is a just peace?* New York, NY: Oxford University Press.

Kelman, H.C. (2008). Reconciliation from a social-psychological perspective. In A. Nadler, T. Malloy, & J.D. Fisher (Eds.), *The social psychology of intergroup reconciliation* (pp. 15–32). New York, NY: Oxford University Press.

Kemp, G., & Fry, D.P. (Eds.). (2004). *Keeping the peace: Conflict resolution and peaceful societies around the world*. New York, NY: Routledge.

Kennedy, P. (1987). *The rise and fall of great powers: Economic change and military conflict from 1800 to 2000*. New York, NY: Random House.

Keohane, R.O. (1984). *After hegemony: Co-operation and discord in the world political economy*. Princeton, NJ: Princeton University Press.

Keohane, R.O. (1989). *International institutions and state power: Essays in international relations theory*. Boulder, CO: Westview.

Kepel, G. (2004). *The war for Muslim minds: Islam and the West*. Cambridge, MA: Belknap Press.

Kim, S., Kollontai, P., & Hoyland, G. (2008). *Peace and reconciliation: In search of a shared identity*. Aldershot, England: Ashgate.

King, U. (2008). *The search for spirituality: Our global quest for a spiritual life*. New York, NY: Bluebridge.

Kissinger, H. (1973). *A world restored: Metternich, Castlereagh, and the problems of peace 1812–1822*. Orlando, FL: Mariner Books.

Klandermans, B. (1997). *The social psychology of protest*. Cambridge, MA: Blackwell Publishers.

Knapp, M., & Hall, J. (2002). *Non-verbal communication in human interaction* (5th ed.). Toronto, Ontario: Thompson Learning.

Kohlberg, L. (1981). *The philosophy of moral development* (Vol. 1). New York, NY: Harper & Row.

Kohlberg, L. (1969/1984). Stage and sequence: The cognitive-developmental approach to socialization. In D. Goslin (Ed.), *The psychology of moral development*. New York, NY: Harper & Row.

Köhler, G., & Tausch, A. (2002). *Global Keynesianism: Unequal exchange and global exploitation*. Huntington, NY: Nova Science.

Kohn, L. (1992). *Early Chinese mysticism: Philosophy and soteriology in the Taoist tradition*. Princeton, NJ: Princeton University Press.

Kolb, D., & Williams, J. (2003). *Everyday negotiation: Navigating the hidden agendas in bargaining*. San Francisco, CA: Jossey-Bass.

Kolbert, C.F. (1979). The legal background. In C.F. Kolbert (Ed.), *Justinian: The digest of Roman law: Theft, rapine, damage, and insult*. New York, NY: Penguin.

Kraft, H.J.S. (2002). Track three diplomacy and human rights in Southeast Asia: The Asia Pacific coalition for East Timor. In *Global Networks: A Journal of Transnational Affairs, 2*(1), 49–64.

Krasner, S. (2009). *Power, the state, and sovereignty: Essays on international relations*. London, England: Routledge.

Kraybill, R. (2009). *The Thomas Kilmann conflict mode inventory: Strengths and limitations. Alternatives.* Retrieved from http://peace.mennolink.org/resources/conflictstyle/Thomas_Kilmann_users.html

Kriesberg, L. (1997). The development of the conflict resolution field. In I.W. Zartman & J.L. Rasmussen (Eds.), *Peacemaking in international conflict: Methods and techniques* (pp. 51–72). Washington, DC: United States Institute of Peace Press.

Kriesberg, L. (2003). *Constructive conflicts: From escalation to resolution* (2nd ed.). Lanham, MD: Rowman & Littlefield.

Kritek, P.B. (2002). *Negotiating at an uneven table: Developing moral courage in resolving our conflicts*. San Francisco, CA: Jossey-Bass. Reprinted with permission of John Wiley & Sons, Inc.

Kroenig, M. (2010). *Exporting the bomb: Technology transfer and the spread of nuclear weapons*. Ithaca, NY: Cornell University Press.

Kuhn, T.S. (1962). *The structure of scientific revolutions*. Chicago, IL: University of Chicago Press.

Kull, S., Ramsay, C., & Lewis, E. (2004). Misperceptions, the media, and the Iraq war. In *Political Science Quarterly, 118*(4), 569–598.

La Haye, E. (2008). *War crimes in internal armed conflicts*. New York, NY: Cambridge University Press.

Lakoff, G., & Johnson, M. (1981). *Metaphors we live by*. Chicago, IL: University of Chicago Press.

Lang, A.F., Jr. (Ed.). (2003). *Just intervention*. Washington, DC: Georgetown University Press.

Langhorne, R. (1986). Reflections on the significance of the Congress of Vienna. *Review of International Studies, 12*(4), 313–324.

Lasswell, H.D. (1950). *Politics: Who gets what, when, and how*. New York, NY: Peter Smith.

Le Bon, G. (1895/2008). *The crowd: A study of the popular mind*. New York, NY: Quill Pen Classics.

Lebow, R.N. (2006). *Coercion, co-operation, and ethics in international relations*. London, England: Routledge.

Lederach, J.P. (1995). *Preparing for peace: Conflict transformation across cultures*. Syracuse, NY: Syracuse University Press.

Lederach, J.P. (1997). *Building peace: Sustainable reconciliation in divided societies*. Washington, DC: United States Institute of Peace.

Lederach, J.P. (1999). *The journey toward reconciliation*. Scottdale, PA: Herald Press.

Lederach, J.P. (2003). *The little book of conflict transformation*. Intercourse, PA: Good Books.

Lederach, J.P. (2005). *The moral imagination: The art and soul of building peace*. New York, NY: Oxford University Press.

Lenin, V.I. (1969). *Imperialism: The highest stage of capitalism*. New York, NY: International.

Lenz, T.F. (1955). *Towards a science of peace: Turning point in human destiny*. New York, NY: Bookman.

Lesaffer, R. (2004). *Peace treaties and international law in European history: From the late Middle Ages to World War One*. New York, NY: Cambridge University Press.

Levi, P. (1988). *The drowned and the saved*. New York, NY: Summit Books.

Levinas, E. (1961/1969). *Totality and infinity: An essay on exteriority* (A. Lingis, Trans.). Pittsburgh, PA: Duquesne University Press.

Levinas, E. (1978). *Otherwise than being or beyond essence* (A. Lingis, Trans.). Dordrecht, Netherlands: Kluwer Academic.

Lewis, B. (1993). *Islam and the West*. New York, NY: Oxford University Press.

Lewis, B. (2010). *Faith and power: Religion and politics in the Middle East*. New York, NY: Oxford University Press.

Lewis, T., Amini, F., & Lannon, R. (2000). *A general theory of love*. New York, NY: Random House.

Lewontin, R.C., Rose, S., & Kamin, L.J. (1984). *Not in our genes*. New York, NY: Random House.

Linklater, A. (1998). *The transformation of political community: Ethical foundations of the post-Westphalian era*. Cambridge, England: Polity Press.

Linklater, A. (2007). *Critical theory and world politics: Citizenship, sovereignty, and humanity*. London, England: Routledge.

Little, D. (2007). Warriors and brothers: Imam Muhammad Ashafa and pastor James Wuye. In D. Little (Ed.), *Peacemakers in action: Profiles of religion in conflict resolution* (pp. 247–277). Cambridge, England: Cambridge University Press.

Littlejohn, S., & Domenici, K. (2007). *Communication, conflict, and the management of difference*. Long Grove, IL: Waveland.

Lonergan, B. (1958/1978). *Insight: A study of human understanding*. San Francisco, CA: Harper & Row.

Long, W.J., & Brecke, P. (2003). *War and reconciliation: Reason and emotion in conflict resolution*. Cambridge, MA: MIT Press.

Lopreato, J., & Green, P. (1990). The evolutionary foundations of revolution. In J. van der Dennen & V. Falger (Eds.), *Sociobiology and conflict* (pp. 107–122). New York, NY: Springer.

Lorentzen, L., & Turpin, J. (Eds.). (1998). *The women and war reader*. New York, NY: NYU Press.

Lorenz, K. (1982). *The foundations of ethology: The principle ideas and discoveries in animal behavior*. New York, NY: Simon & Schuster.

Lorenz, K. (2002). *On aggression*. New York, NY: Routledge.

Lukács, G. (1971). *The theory of the novel*. Boston, MA: MIT Press.

Luttwak, E.N. (1994a). Franco–German reconciliation: The overlooked role of the moral re-armament movement. In D. Johnston & C. Sampson (Eds.), *Religion: The missing dimension of statecraft* (pp. 37–63). New York, NY: Oxford University Press.

Luttwak, E.N. (1994b, July/August). Where are the great powers? At home with the kids. *Foreign Affairs, 73*(4), 23–28.

Luxemburg, R. (2003). *The accumulation of capital*. London, England: Routledge.

Lyotard, J.-F. (1979/1984). *The postmodern condition: A report on knowledge*. Minneapolis, MN: University of Minnesota Press.

Machiavelli, N. (1532/2003). *The prince* (G. Bull, Trans.). London, England: Penguin Classics.

MacIntyre, A. (1981). *After virtue: A study in moral theory*. Notre Dame, IN: University of Notre Dame Press.

Mackinlay, J., & Chopra, J. (1992). Second generation multinational operations. *The Washington Quarterly, 15*(3), 113–131.

Macmillan, M. (2002). *Paris 1919*. New York, NY: Random House.

Malthus, R.T. (1798/2008). *An essay on the principle of population*. Oxford, England: Oxford University Press.

Maoz, I., & Ellis, D. (2003). Dialogue and cultural communication codes between Israeli-Jews and Palestinians. *The International Journal of Conflict Management, 14*(3), 255–272.

Marcuse, H. (1991). *One-dimensional man: Studies in the ideology of advanced industrial society*. Boston, MA: Beacon Press.

Marks, S. (2003). *The illusion of peace: International relations in Europe, 1918–1933* (2nd ed.). New York, NY: Palgrave Macmillan.

Martens, E. (2009). Yahweh, justice, and religious pluralism in the Old Testament. In J. Isaac (Ed.), *The Old Testament in the life of God's people*. Winona Lake, IN: Eisenbrauns.

Martin, R. (2007). *The opposable mind*. Boston, MA: Harvard Business School Press.

Marx, K. (1867/1992). *Capital* (Vol.1). London, England: Penguin Classics.

Marx, K., & Engels, F. (1848/1988). *Communist manifesto*. New York, NY: W. W. Norton.

Maslow, A. (1943). A theory of human motivation. *Psychological Review, 50*, 370–96.

Maslow, A. (1948). "Higher" and "lower" needs. *Journal of Psychology, 25*, 433–36.

Maslow, A. (1999). *Toward a psychology of being.* New York, NY: Wiley.

Matam Farrall, J. (2007). *United Nations sanctions and the rule of law.* New York, NY: Cambridge University Press.

McDonald, J.W. (1991). Further exploration of track two diplomacy. In S.J. Thorson & L. Kriesberg (Eds.), *Timing the de-escalation of international conflicts* (pp. 201–220). Syracuse, NY: Syracuse University Press.

McDonald, J.W. (2008). *The shifting grounds of conflict and peace-building: Stories and lessons.* Lanham, MD: Lexington.

McFaul, T.R. (2006).*The future of peace and justice in the global village: The role of the world religions in the twenty-first century.* Westport, CT: Praeger.

McGuigan, R. (2006). *How do evolving deep structures of consciousness impact the disputant's creation of meaning in a conflict?* (Unpublished doctoral dissertation). Union Institute & University, Cincinnati, OH.

McGuigan, R. (2012). Consciousness and conflict (explained better?). *Conflict Resolution Quarterly,* Spring 2012, 29–33.

McKelvey, T. (2007). *One of the guys: Women as aggressors and torturers.* Berkeley, CA: Seal Press.

McLean, S. (2005). *The basics of interpersonal communication.* Boston, MA: Pearson Educational.

McPhail, C. (1991). *The myth of the madding crowd.* New York, NY: Aldine de Gruyter.

McRae, R., & Hubert, D. (Eds.). (2001). *Human security and the new diplomacy: Protecting people, promoting peace.* Montreal, Quebec: McGill-Queen's University Press.

Mead, M. (Ed.). (1961). *Co-operation and competition among primitive people.* Boston, MA: Beacon Press.

Melchin, K., & Picard, C. (2008). *Transforming conflict through insight.* Toronto, Ontario: University of Toronto Press.

Metz, K. (1990). Passionate differences: A working model for cross-cultural communication. *Journal of Feminist Studies in Religion, 6*(1), 131–151.

Michels, R. (1999). *Political parties: A sociological study of the oligarchical tendencies of modern democracy.* New York, NY: Transaction Books.

Michelson, E. (2007). Climbing the conflict pagoda: Grievances and appeals to the official justice system in rural China. *American Sociological Review, 72,* 459–485.

Milgram, S. (1974). *Obedience to authority: An experimental view.* New York, NY: Harper & Row.

Miller, J. (1994). *The passion of Michel Foucault.* New York, NY: Anchor Books.

Mills, C. W. (2000). *The power elite.* New York, NY: Oxford University Press.

Milward, A.S. (2006). *The reconstruction of Western Europe 1945–51.* Berkeley, CA: University of California Press.

Minow, M. (1998). *Between vengeance and forgiveness: Facing history after genocide and mass violence.* Boston, MA: Beacon Press.

Mitchell, C.R. (1981). *The structure of international conflict.* London, England: MacMillan.

Mitchell, C.R. (2000). *Gestures of conciliation: Factors contributing to successful olive branches.* New York, NY: St. Martin's Press.

Montagu, A. (1976). *The nature of human aggression.* New York, NY: Oxford University Press.

Moore, B. (1966). *Social origins of dictatorship and democracy.* Boston, MA: Beacon Press.

Moore, M.S. (1987). The moral worth of retribution. In F. Schoeman (Ed.), *Responsibility, character, and the emotions: New essays in moral psychology.* Cambridge, England: Cambridge University Press.

Morgan, R. (2000). *Demon lover: The roots of terrorism.* New York, NY: Washington Square Press.

Morgenthau, H.J. (2005). *Politics among nations: The struggle for power and peace* (Rev. ed.). New York, NY: McGraw-Hill.

Morsink, J. (1999). *The universal declaration of human rights: Origins, drafting, and intent.* Philadelphia, PA: University of Philadelphia Press.

Mosca, G. (1960). *The ruling class.* New York, NY: McGraw-Hill.

Moses, R. (1990). Self, self-view, and identity. In D. Julius, J. Montville, & V. Volkan (Eds.), *The psychodynamics of international relationships.* Toronto, Ontario: Lexington Books.

Muchembled, R. (2008). *Une histoire de la violence.* Paris, France: Seuil.

Mueller, J. (1989). *Retreat from doomsday: The obsolescence of major war.* New York, NY: Basic Books.

Murphy, J., & Hampton, J. (1988). *Forgiveness and mercy.* Cambridge, England: Cambridge University Press.

Myerson, R.B. (1997). *Game theory: Analysis of conflict.* Cambridge, MA: Harvard University Press.

Nadler, A., Malloy, T., & Fisher, J. D. (2008). Introduction: Intergroup reconciliation: Dimensions and themes. In A. Nadler, T. Malloy, & J.D. Fisher (Eds.), *The social psychology of intergroup reconciliation* (pp. 3–12). New York, NY: Oxford University Press.

Nardoni, E. (2004). *Rise up, o judge: A study of justice in the Biblical world* (S.C. Martin, Trans.). Peabody, MA: Hendrickson.

Narlikar, A. (2010). *Deadlocks in multilateral negotiations: Causes and solutions.* Cambridge, England: Cambridge University Press.

National Conference of Catholic Bishops. (1983). *The challenge of peace: God's promise and our response, a pastoral letter on war and peace.* Washington, DC: United States Catholic Conference.

Neuenschwander, D. (2006). Taking Einstein's ethics into the 21st century: "Remember your humanity." Retrieved from www.spsobserver.org/2006/observer_einstein.pdf

Neuhauser, P. (1988). *Tribal warfare in organizations: Turning tribal conflict into negotiated peace.* San Francisco, CA: HarperCollins.

New Sudan Council of Churches. (2002). *Inside Sudan: The story of people-to-people peacemaking in Southern Sudan.* Nairobi, Kenya: NSCC.

Nicolson, H., Sir. (1988). *Diplomacy.* Washington, DC: Institute for the Study of Diplomacy.

Nicolson, H., Sir. (2000). *The Congress of Vienna: A study in allied unity: 1812–1822* (2nd ed.). New York, NY: Grove Press.

Niehoff, D. (1999). *The biology of violence.* New York, NY: The Free Press.

Nobles, M. (2008). *The politics of official apologies.* Cambridge, England: Cambridge University Press.

Noddings, N. (2008). Caring and peace education. In M. Bajaj (Ed.), *Encyclopedia of peace education.* Charlotte, NC: Information Age.

Noll, D. (2003). *Peacemaking: Practicing at the intersection of law and human conflict.* Telford, PA/Scottdale/PA: Cascadia/Herald Press.

Nudler, O. (1990). On conflicts and metaphors: Toward an extended rationality. In J. Burton (Ed.), *Conflict: Human needs theory* (pp. 177–201). New York, NY: St. Martin's Press.

Nye, J.S. (1991). *Bound to lead: The changing nature of American power.* New York, NY: Basic Books.

Olson, M. (1971). *The logic of collective action.* Cambridge, MA: Harvard University Press.

Orend, B. (2000). *Michael Walzer on war and justice.* Cardiff, Wales: University of Wales Press.

Orji, C. (2008). *Ethnic and religious bias in Africa: An analysis of bias decline and conversion based on the works of Bernard Lonergan.* Milwaukee, WI: Marquette University Press.

Ortmann, A., & Tichy, L.K. (1999). Gender differences in the laboratory: Evidence from prisoner's dilemma games. *Journal of Economic Behavior and Organization, 39,* 327–339.

Osgood, C.E. (1962). *An alternative to war or surrender.* Urbana, IL: University of Illinois Press.

Osman, M.A. (2002). *The United Nations and peace enforcement: Wars, terrorism, and democracy.* Aldershot, England: Ashgate.

Page, J. (2008). *Peace education: Exploring ethical and philosophical foundations.* Charlotte, NC: Information Age.

Päivänsalo, V. (2007). *Balancing reasonable justice: John Rawls and crucial steps beyond.* Aldershot, England: Ashgate.

Pareto, V. (1991). *The rise and fall of elites: An application of theoretical sociology.* New York, NY: Transaction Books.

Paris, R. (1997). Peacebuilding and the limits of liberal internationalism. *International Security, 22*(2), 54–89.

Paris, R. (2001). Human security: Paradigm shift or hot air? *International Security, 26*(2), 87–102.

Paris, R. (2004). *At war's end: Building peace after armed conflict.* Cambridge, England: Cambridge University Press.

Parsons, T. (1991). *The social system.* London, England: Routledge.

Patomäki, H. (2001). *After international relations: Critical realism and the (re)construction of world politics.* London, England: Routledge.

Pearsall, P. (1998). *The heart's code: Tapping the wisdom and power of our heart energy.* New York, NY: Broadway Books.

Peirce, C. S. (1998). *The essential Peirce, Volume 2: Selected Philosophical Writings, 1893–1913.* Bloomington, IN: Indiana University Press.

Pert, C. (1997). *Molecules of emotion: The science behind mind-body medicine.* New York, NY: Touchstone.

Pesantubee, M. (2004). In search of the white path: American Indian peacebuilding. In H. Coward & G. Smith (Eds.), *Religion and peacebuilding.* Albany, NY: State University of New York Press.

Piaget, J. (1932). *The moral judgment of the child.* New York, NY: The Free Press.

Piaget, J. (1952). *The language and thought of a child.* London, England: Routledge.

Picard, C. (1998). *Mediating interpersonal and small group conflict.* Ottawa, Ontario: The Golden Dog Press.

Pinker, S. (2002). *The blank state: The modern denial of human nature.* New York, NY: Penguin.

Pinker, S. (2011). *The better angels of our nature: Why violence has declined.* New York, NY: Viking.

Polkinghorn, B., & Byrne, S. (2001). Between war and peace: An examination of conflict management styles in four ethnic conflict zones. *International Journal of Conflict Management, 12*(1). Retrieved from www.sfu.ca/cfrj/fulltext/byrne.pdf

Porto, J.G., Alden, C., & Parsons, I. (2007). *From soldiers to citizens.* Aldershot, England: Ashgate.

Poulantzas, N. (1975). *Political power and social classes.* London, England: Verso.

Prebisch, R. (1950). *The economic development of Latin America and its principal problems.* New York, NY: United Nations.

Puddington, A. (2011). *Freedom in the world 2011: The authoritarian challenge to democracy.* Retrieved from www.freedomhouse.org/report/freedom-world-2011/essay-freedom-world-2011-authoritarian-challenge-democracy

Putnam, R.D. (2000). *Bowling alone: The collapse and revival of American community.* New York, NY: Simon & Schuster.

Quinlan, M. (2009). *Thinking about nuclear weapons: Principles, problems, prospects.* Oxford, England: Oxford University Press.

Radzik, L. (2009). *Making amends: Atonement in morality, law, and politics.* New York, NY: Oxford University Press.

Rana, K.S. (2006). *The twenty-first century ambassador: Plenipotentiary to chief executive.* New Delhi, India: Oxford University Press.

Rapoport, A. (1992). *Peace: An idea whose time has come.* Ann Arbor, MI: The University of Michigan Press.

Rapoport, A., & Chammah, A.M. (1965). Sex differences in factors contributing to the level of co-operation in the prisoner's dilemma game. *Journal of Personality and Social Psychology, 2,* 231–238.

Rawls, J. (1971/1999). *A theory of justice* (Rev. ed.). Cambridge, MA: Harvard University Press.

Redekop, V.N. (2002). *From violence to blessing: How an understanding of deep-rooted conflict opens paths to reconciliation.* Ottawa, Ontario: Novalis.

Redekop, V.N. (2007a). Reconciling Nuers with Dinkas: A Girardian approach to conflict resolution. *Religion—An International Journal, 37,* 64–84.

Redekop, V.N. (2007b). Teachings of blessing as elements of reconciliation: Intra- and inter-religious hermeneutical challenges and opportunities in the face of violent deep-rooted conflict. In M.E. Courville (Ed.), *The next step in studying religion: A graduate's guide* (pp. 129–146). London, England: Continuum.

Redekop, V.N. (2008). A post-genocidal justice of blessing as an alternative to a justice of violence: The case of Rwanda. In B. Hart (Ed.), *Peacebuilding in Traumatized Societies* (pp. 205–238). Lanham, MD: University Press of America.

Redekop, V.N. (2011). Spirituality, emergent creativity, and reconciliation. In A. Bartoli & S. Allen Nan (Eds.), *Peacemaking: A comprehensive theory and practice reference* (Vol. 2). Westport, CT: Praeger.

Redekop, V.N., & Paré, S. (2010). *Beyond control: A mutual respect approach to protest crowd–police relations.* London, England: Bloomsbury Academic.

Reich, W. (1933/1980). *The mass psychology of fascism* (3rd ed.). New York, NY: Farrar, Straus, & Giroux.

Reichberg, G., Syse, H., & Begby, E. (2006). *The ethics of war: Classic and contemporary readings.* Malden, MA: Blackwell.

Ricoeur, P. (1981). *Hermeneutics and the human sciences: Essays on language, action, and interpretation* (J. Thompson, Ed. & Trans.). Cambridge, England: Cambridge University Press.

Ricoeur, P. (1990/1992). *Oneself as another* (K. Blamey, Trans.). Chicago, IL: University of Chicago Press.

Ricoeur, P. (2000). *The just.* (D. Pellauer, Trans.). Chicago, IL: University of Chicago Press.

Rilling, J., Gutman, D., Zeh, T., Pagnoni, G., Berns, G., & Kilts, C. (2002). A neural basis for social co-operation. *Neuron, 35*(2), 395–405.

Rioux, J.-F. (Ed.). (2007). *L'intervention armée peut-elle être juste? Aspects moraux et éthiques des petites guerres contre le terrorisme et les génocides.* Montreal, Quebec: Fides.

Rioux, J.-F., & Prémont, K. (2007). Diversité des positions éthiques sur les conflits armés. In J.-F. Rioux, (Ed.). (2007). *L'intervention armée peut-elle être juste? Aspects moraux et éthiques des petites guerres contre le terrorisme et les génocides* (pp. 37–70). Montreal, Quebec: Fides.

Robertson, A.H., & Merrills, J.G. (1996). *Human rights in the world: An introduction to the study of the international protection of human rights.* Manchester, England: Manchester University Press.

Roche, D. (2003). *The human right to peace.* Ottawa, Ontario: Novalis.

Roche, D. (2007). *Global conscience.* Ottawa, Ontario: Novalis.

Rogers, C. (1961). *On becoming a person: A therapist's view of psychotherapy.* Boston, MA: Houghton Mifflin.

Rogers, D. (2009). *Post-internationalism and small arms control.* London, England: Ashgate.

Rokkan, S. (with Campbell, A., Torsvik, P., & Valen, H.). (1970). *Citizens, elections, parties: Approaches to the comparative study of the processes of development.* Oslo, Norway: Universitetsforlaget.

Rosenau, J. (1990). *Turbulence in world politics: A theory of change and continuity.* Princeton, NJ: Princeton University Press.

Ross-Smith, A., Kornberger, M., Chesterman, C., & Anandakumar, A. (2007). Women executives: Managing emotions at the top. In P. Lewis & R. Simpson (Eds.), *Gendering emotions in organizations* (pp. 35–56). Houndmills, England: Palgrave Macmillan.

Rotberg, R. I. (Ed.). (2003). *When states fail: Causes and consequences.* Princeton, NJ: Princeton University Press.

Rouhana, N.N. (2004). Group identity and power asymmetry in reconciliation processes: The Israeli–Palestinian case. *Peace and Conflict: Journal of Peace Psychology, 10*(1), 33–52.

Rousseau, J.-J. (1755/2003). *Discourse on the origin of inequality.* London, England: Dover.

Roy, O. (1994). *The failure of political Islam* (C. Volk, Trans.). London, England: I.B. Tauris.

Rudé, G. (1999). *The crowd in history: A study of popular disturbances in France and England, 1730–1848.* London, England: Serif.

Rummel, R. (1997). *Death by government.* New York, NY: Transaction Books.

Russett, B. (1993). *Grasping the democratic peace.* Princeton, NJ: Princeton University Press.

Russett, B., & Maoz, Z. (1992). Alliances, contiguity, wealth, and political stability: Is the lack of conflict among democracies a political artifact? *International Interactions, 17*(4), 245–267.

Sagan, S.D. (Ed.). (2009). *Inside nuclear South Asia.* Stanford, CA: Stanford University Press.

Sagan, S.D., & Waltz, K.N. (Eds.). (2002). *The spread of nuclear weapons: A debate renewed* (2nd ed.). New York, NY: W.W. Norton.

Said, E. (1978). *Orientalism.* New York, NY: Pantheon.

Sally, D. (1995). Conversation and co-operation in social dilemmas: a meta-analysis of experiments from 1958 to 1992. *Rationality and Society, 7*, 58–92.

Sampson, C., & Lederach, J.P. (2000). *From the ground up: Mennonite contributions to international peacebuilding.* New York, NY: Oxford University Press.

Saner, R. (2005). *The expert negotiator* (2nd ed.). Leiden, Netherlands: Martinus Nijhoff.

Satow, E.M. (1979). *A guide to diplomatic practice* (5th ed.). London, England: Longman.

Sawatsky, J. (2009). *The ethic of traditional communities and the spirit of healing justice: Studies from Hollow Water, the Iona Community, and Plum Village.* London, England: Jessica Kingsley.

Schaubhut, N.A. (2007). *Technical brief for the Thomas-Kilmann conflict mode instrument: Description of the updated normative sample and implications for use.* Retrieved from CPP website: www.psychometrics.com/docs/tki%20technical%20brief.pdf

Schellenberg, J.A. (1996). *Conflict resolution: Theory, research, and practice.* Albany, NY: State University of New York Press.

Schelling, T. (1960). *The strategy of conflict.* Cambridge, MA: Harvard University Press.

Schelling, T. (1966). *Arms and influence.* New Haven, CT: Yale University Press.

Scheper-Hughes, N., & Bourgois, P. (2004). Introduction: making sense of violence. In N. Scheper-Hughes & P. Bourgois

(Eds.), *Violence in war and peace: An anthology*. Malden, MA: Blackwell.

Schirch, L. (2005). *Ritual and symbol in peacebuilding*. Bloomfield, CT: Kumarian Press.

Schwartz-Shea, P. (2002). Theorizing gender for experimental game theory: Experiments with "sex status" and "merit status" in an asymmetric game. *Sex Roles, 47*(7/8), 301–319.

Searle, J. (1995). *The construction of social reality*. New York, NY: The Free Press.

Sears, D.O., & McConahay, J.B. (1973). *The politics of violence: The new urban blacks and the Watts Riot*. Boston, MA: Houghton Mifflin.

Sen, A. (2000). *Development as freedom*. New York, NY: Anchor Books.

Sen, A. (2006). *Identity and violence: The illusion of destiny*. New York, NY: W.W. Norton.

Servan-Schreiber, D. (2005). *Guérir*. Paris, France: Robert Laffont.

Sharp, G. (2003). *There are realistic alternatives* [Adobe Acrobat Distiller version]. Retrieved from the Albert Einstein Institution website: www.aeinstein.org/organizations/org/TARA.pdf

Sharp, G. (2005). *Waging non-violent struggle: Twentieth-century practice and twenty-first century potential*. Manchester, NH: Porter Sargent.

Sheldrake, R. (2003). *The sense of being stared at: And other aspects of the extended mind*. New York, NY: Crown.

Simmel, G. (1972). *On individuality and social forms*. Chicago, IL: University of Chicago Press.

Sites, P. (1973). *Control: The basis of social order*. New York, NY: Dunellen.

Sites, P. (1990). Needs as analogues of emotions. In J. W. Burton (Ed.), *Conflict: Human needs theory*. New York, NY: St. Martin's Press.

Sjoberg, L., & Gentry, C.E. (2008). *Mothers, monsters, whores: Women's violence in global politics*. London, England: Zed Books.

Skinner, B. F. (1971). *Beyond freedom and dignity*. New York, NY: Vintage.

Skinner, B.F. (1948/2005). *Walden two*. Indianapolis, IN: Hackett.

Smith, A. (1776/2003). *The wealth of nations*. New York, NY: Bantam.

Snyder, J.L. (1978). Rationality at the brink: The role of cognitive processes in failures of deterrence. *World Politics, 30*(3), 345–366.

Snyder, J.L. (2000). *From voting to violence: Democratization and nationalist conflict*. New York, NY: W.W. Norton.

Sokal, A. (1996). Transgressing the boundaries: Towards a transformative hermeneutics of quantum gravity. *Social Text, 46/47*, 217–252.

Sopow, E.L. (2003). The age of outrage: The role of emotional and organizational factors on protest policing and political opportunity frames. Unpublished doctoral dissertation. Fielding Graduate Institute.

Spencer, H. (1884/1969). *The man versus the state*. Baltimore, MD: Penguin Books.

Spencer, H. (1873/2006). *The study of sociology*. Ann Arbor, MI: University of Michigan Library.

Spencer, R. (2002). *Islam unveiled: Disturbing questions about the world's fastest growing faith*. San Francisco, CA: Encounters Books.

Stack, J.F., Jr. (Ed.). (1986). *The primordial challenge: Ethnicity in the modern world*. New York, NY: Greenwood Press.

Stahl, R. (2010). *Militainment, Inc.: War, media, and popular culture*. New York, NY: Routledge.

State Failure Task Force. (1999). *State Failure Task Force Report: Phase II Findings*. Retrieved from www.wilsoncenter.org/events/docs/Phase2.pdf

Statistics Canada. (2003). *Perspectives on labour and income: The online edition, 4*(8). Retrieved from www.statcan.gc.ca/pub/75-001-x/00803/6606-eng.html

Staub, E. (1989). *The roots of evil: The origins of genocide and other group violence*. Cambridge, England: Cambridge University Press.

Staub, E. (2011). *Overcoming evil: Genocide, violent conflict, and terrorism*. New York, NY: Oxford University Press.

Stedman, S.J., Rothchild, D., & Cousens, E.M. (2002). *Ending civil wars: The implementation of peace agreements* (2nd ed.). Boulder, CO: Lynne Rienner.

Stern, J. (2004). *Terror in the name of God: Why religious militants kill*. New York, NY: Harper Perennial.

Stiglmayer, A. (Ed.). (1994). *Mass rape: The war against women in Bosnia-Herzegovina*. Lincoln, NE: University of Nebraska Press.

Stohl, R., & Grillot, S. (2009). *The international arms trade*. Cambridge, England: Polity Press.

Sun, T. (2002). *The art of war* (J. Minford, Trans.), New York, NY: Viking.

Susskind, L., & Field, P. (1996). *Dealing with an angry public: The mutual gains approach*. New York, NY: The Free Press.

Swanström, N., & Weissmann, M. (2005). *Conflict, conflict prevention, and conflict management and beyond: A conceptual exploration*. Retrieved from www.silkroadstudies.org/new/docs/Concept Papers/2005/concept_paper_ConfPrev.pdf

Sword, D. (2003). *Complex conflict analysis of public protest* (Doctoral thesis). York University, Toronto, Ontario.

Tadjbakhsh, S. (2007). *Human security: Concepts and implications*. New York, NY: Routledge.

Tangney, J.P., Wagner, P.E., Hill-Barlow, D., Marschall, D.E., & Gramzow, R. (1996). Relation of shame and guilt to constructive versus destructive responses to anger across the lifespan. *Journal of Personality and Social Psychology, 70*(4), 797–809.

Tannen, D. (1986). *That's not what I meant!: How conversational style makes or breaks relationships*. New York, NY: Ballantine.

Taylor, B. (2010). *Sanctions as grand strategy*. London, England: International Institute for Strategic Studies.

Teng, C.-C. (2008). Conflict management in East Asia: The China–Taiwan–North Korea conundrum. In J. Bercovitch,

K.-B. Huang, & C.-C. Teng (Eds.), *Conflict management, security, and intervention in East Asia: Third-party mediation in regional conflict*. London, England: Routledge.

Tesón, F.R. (1988). *Humanitarian intervention: An inquiry into law and morality*. Irvington-on-Hudson, NY: Transnational.

Thayer, B.A. (2004). *Darwin and international relations*. Lexington, KY: The University Press of Kentucky.

Thomas, D. (1993). *Not guilty: In defence of the modern man*. London, England: Weidenfeld & Nicolson.

Thomas, K.W., Thomas, G.F., & Schaubhut, N. (2008). Conflict style of men and women at six organizations levels. *International Journal of Conflict Management, 14*(2), 148–166.

Thomas, T.H. (1993). Using arbitration to avoid litigation. *Labor Law Journal, 44*(1), 3–17.

Thomassen, L. (Ed.) (2006). *The Derrida-Habermas Reader*. Chicago, IL.: The University of Chicago Press.

Thornhill, R., & Palmer, C.T. (2000). *A natural history of rape: The biological bases of sexual coercion*. Cambridge, MA: MIT Press.

Thucydides. (431 BCE/1972). *History of the Peloponnesian war* (R. Warner, Trans.). London, England: Penguin Classics.

Thuderoz, C. (2000). *Négociations: essai de sociologie du lien social*. Paris, France: PUF.

Tidwell, A.C. (1998). *Conflict resolved? A critical assessment of conflict resolution*. London, England: Continuum.

Tilly, C. (1975). *The formation of national states in Western Europe*. Princeton, NJ: Princeton University Press.

Tilly, C. (1978). *From mobilization to revolution*. Reading, MA: Addison-Wesley.

Tilly, C. (2003). *The politics of collective violence*. Cambridge, England: Cambridge University Press.

Toews, J.B. (1967). *Lost fatherland: The story of the Mennonite emigration from Soviet Russia, 1921–1927*. Scottdale, PA: Herald Press.

Touraine, A. (1971). *The post-industrial society: Tomorrow's social history: Classes, conflicts, and culture in the programmed society*. New York, NY: Random House.

Touraine, A. (1981). *The voice and the eye: An analysis of social movements*. Cambridge, England: Cambridge University Press.

Touval, S., & Zartman, I.W. (1985). Introduction: Mediation in theory. In S. Touval & I.W. Zartman (Eds.), *International mediation in theory and practice*. Boulder, CO: Westview.

Treble, J.G. (1990). The pit and the pendulum: Arbitration in the British coal industry, 1893–1914. *Economic Journal, 100*(403), 1095–1108.

Tremmel, J.C. (Ed.). (2006). *Handbook of intergenerational justice*. Cheltenham, England: Edward Elgar.

Truman, D. (1951). *The governmental process: Political interests and public opinion*. New York, NY: Knopf.

Tucker, R.C. (Ed.). (1978). *The Marx–Engels reader* (2nd ed.). New York, NY: W. W. Norton.

Tutu, D. (1999). *No future without forgiveness*. Toronto, Ontario: Doubleday.

Tyler, T.R., & Belliveau, M.A. (1995). Tradeoffs in justice principles: Definitions of fairness. In B.B. Bunker & J.Z. Rubin (Eds.), *Conflict, co-operation, and justice: Essays inspired by the work of Morton Deutsch*. San Francisco, CA: Jossey-Bass.

United Nations. (1945). Charter of the United Nations. Retrieved from www.un.org/en/documents/charter/

United Nations. (2007). *Demographic yearbook 2004*. New York, NY: United Nations. Retrieved from http://unstats.un.org/unsd/demographic/products/dyb/DYB2004/Table25.pdf

United Nations Systems Staff College (UNSSC). (2010). *Indigenous peoples and peacebuilding: A compilation of best practices*. Turin, Italy: UNSSC. Retrieved from www.unssc.org/home/sites/unssc.org/files/ind_people.pdf

Ury, W. (2000). *The third side: Why we fight and how we can stop*. New York, NY: Penguin.

Ury, W. (2010). The walk from "no" to "yes." [TED Talk]. Retrieved from www.ted.com/talks/william_ury.html

US Census Bureau. (2004). *Most people make only one trip down the aisle, but first marriages shorter*. Retrieved from www.census.gov/newsroom/releases/archives/marital_status_living_arrangements/cb07-131.html

Van Braght, T. (1660/1950). *Martyrs mirror*. Scottdale, PA: Herald Press.

Vasquez, J. (1983). *The power of power politics: A critique*. New Brunswick, NJ: Rutgers University Press.

Viotti, P.R., & Kauppi, M.V. (2009). *International relations theory* (4th ed.). New York, NY: Longman.

Volf, M. (1996). *Exclusion and embrace: A theological exploration of identity, otherness, and reconciliation*. Nashville, TN: Abingdon Press.

Volf, M. (2006). *The end of memory: Remembering rightly in a violent world*. Grand Rapids, MI: Eerdmans.

Volkan, V.D. (1990). Psychoanalytic aspects of ethnic conflict. In J. Montville (Ed.), *Conflict and peacemaking in multi-ethnic societies* (pp. 81–92). Lexington, MA: Lexington Books.

Volkan, V.D. (1998). *Bloodlines: From ethnic pride to ethnic terror*. Boulder, CO: Westview.

Von Neumann, J., & Morgenstern, O. (1946). *The theory of games and economic behavior*. Princeton, NJ: Princeton University Press.

Walgrave, L. (2004). Has restorative justice appropriately responded to retribution theory and impulses? In H. Zehr & B. Toews (Eds.), *Critical issues in restorative justice* (pp. 47–60). Monsey, NY: Criminal Justice Press.

Wallensteen, P., & Sollenberg, M. (1997). Armed conflict, conflict termination, and peace agreement. In *Journal of Peace Research, 34*(3), 339–358.

Waller, J. (2007). *Becoming evil: How ordinary people commit genocide and mass killing*. New York, NY: Oxford University Press.

Wallerstein, I. (1979). *The capitalist world-economy*. Cambridge, England: Cambridge University Press.

Wallerstein, I. (2003). *The decline of American power: The US in a chaotic world*. New York, NY: New Press.

Waltz, K.N. (1979). *Theory of international politics*. New York, NY: McGraw-Hill.

Waltz, K.N. (2001). *The tragedy of great powers politics.* New York, NY: W.W. Norton.

Walzer, M. (1977/2006). *Just and unjust wars: A moral argument with historical illustrations* (4th ed.). New York, NY: Basic Books.

Warner, D. (1995). *New dimensions of peacekeeping.* Boston, MA: Martinus Nijhoff.

Warnke, G. (1992). *Justice and interpretation.* Cambridge, England: Polity Press.

Watson, J.B. (1930). *Behaviorism* (rev. ed.). Chicago, IL: University of Chicago Press.

Weber, M. (1997). *The theory of social and economic organization.* New York, NY: The Free Press.

Weber, M. (1998). *From Max Weber: Essays in sociology.* New York, NY: Routledge.

Weiss, T.G. (2004). The sunset of humanitarian intervention? The responsibility to protect in a unipolar era. *Security Dialogue, 35*(2), 135–153.

Wendt, A. (1992). Anarchy is what states make of it: The social construction of power politics. *International Organization, 46*(2), 391–425.

Wendt, A. (1999). *Social theory of international politics.* Cambridge, England: Cambridge University Press.

Wien, B. (2009). Introduction. In T. McElwee, B. Welling Hall, J. Liechty, & J. Garber (Eds.), *Peace, justice, and security studies: A curriculum guide* (7th ed.). Boulder, CO: Lynne Rienner.

Wilber, K. (2000). *A brief history of everything.* Boston, MA: Shambhala.

Williams, P.D., & Bellamy, A. J. (2005). The responsibility to protect and the crisis in Darfur. *Security Dialogue, 36*(1), 27–47.

Wilson, E.O. (1975). *Sociobiology: The new synthesis.* Boston, MA: Harvard University Press.

Wilson, S., & Sabee, C. (2003). Explicating communicative competence as a theoretical term. In J. Greene & B. Burleson (Eds.), *Handbook of communication and social interaction skills* (pp. 3–50). Mahway, NJ: Lawrence Erlbaum.

Wink, W. (1992). *Engaging the powers.* Minneapolis, MN: Fortress Press.

Winslade, J., & Monk, G.D. (2000). *Narrative mediation: A new approach to conflict resolution.* San Francisco, CA: Jossey-Bass.

Wolf, A.T., Stahl, K., & Macomber, M.F. (2003). Conflict and cooperation within international river basins: The importance of institutional capability. *Water Resources Update, 125,* 31–40.

Woods, M. (2007). The nature of war and peace: Just war thinking, environmental ethics, and environmental justice. In M. Brough, J. Lango, & H. van der Linden (Eds.), *Rethinking the just war tradition.* Albany, NY: State University of New York Press.

Wright, Q. (1964). *A study of war* (Abridged ed.). Chicago, IL: University of Chicago Press.

Wright, S.C., Brody, S.M., & Aron, A. (2004). Intergroup contact: Still our best hope for improving intergroup relations. In C.S. Crandall & M. Schaller (Eds.), *Social psychology of prejudice: Historical and contemporary issues* (pp. 119–146). Lawrence, KS: Lewinian Press.

Wyer, R., & Adaval, R. (2003). Message reception skills in social communication. In J. Greene & B. Burleson (Eds.), *Handbook of communication and social interaction skills* (pp. 291–355). Mahway, NJ: Lawrence Erlbaum.

Yalom, M. (1995). *Blood sisters: The French revolution in women's memory.* London, England: Pandora Press.

Yi, S., & Zheng, F. (2011, June 6). "Arab Spring" revolutions follow game plan from 1993 book. *Voice of America.* Retrieved from www.voanews.com/english/news/middle-east/Arab-Spring-Revolutions-Follow-Game-Plan-from-1993-Book-123273468.html

Yoder, J.H. (1972). *The politics of Jesus.* Grand Rapids, MI: Eerdmans.

Yoder, J.H. (1983). *What would you do?* Scottdale, PA: Herald Press.

Yoder, J.H. (1992). *Nevertheless: The varieties and shortcomings of religious pacifism.* Scottdale, PA: Herald Press.

Zartman, I.W. (1989). *Ripe for resolution: Conflict and intervention in Africa.* New York, NY: Oxford University Press.

Zartman, I.W. (1995a). *Collapsed states: The disintegration and restoration of legitimate authority.* Boulder, CO: Lynne Rienner.

Zartman, I.W. (1995b). *Elusive peace: Negotiating an end to civil wars.* Washington, DC: Brookings Institution Press.

Zartman, I.W., & Touval, S. (2001). International mediation in the post-cold war era. In C.A. Crocker, F.O. Hampson, & P.R. Aall, (Eds.), *Turbulent peace: The challenges of managing international conflict* (pp. 427–444). Washington, DC: United States Institute of Peace Press.

Zehr, H. (1990/2005). *Changing lenses: A new focus for crime and justice.* Scottdale, PA: Herald Press.

Zimbardo, P. (2007). *The Lucifer effect: Understanding how good people turn evil.* New York, NY: Random House.

Zupnik, Y. (2000). Conversation interruptions in Israeli-Palestinian "dialogue" events. *Discourse Studies, 2*(1), 85–110.

INDEX